A Sampling of UnixWa

MW01274682

From the Folder: Admin_Tools window you can access:

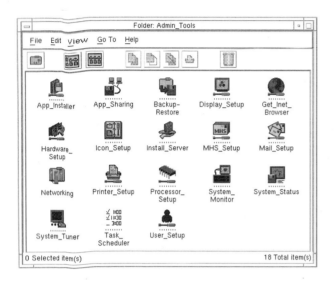

- ▸ App_Installer for installing applications
- ▸ App_Sharing for sharing your applications over the network
- ▸ Backup-Restore for backing up and restoring files
- ▸ Display_Setup for changing your video card setup
- ▸ Get_Inet_Browser for downloading Mosaic from a Novell ftp server
- ▸ Hardware_Setup for changing your hardware configuration
- ▸ Icon_Setup for managing icons
- ▸ Install_Server for performing network installations
- ▸ MHS_Setup for setting up MHS mail
- ▸ Mail_Setup for setting up your e-mail system
- ▸ Networking folder for network administration
- ▸ Printer_Setup for setting up printers
- ▸ Processor_Setup for putting processors on- and offline
- ▸ System_Monitor for monitoring system performance
- ▸ System_Status for checking system information
- ▸ System_Tuner for fine-tuning UnixWare
- ▸ Task_Scheduler for scheduling tasks to run
- ▸ User_Setup for managing user accounts

FOR EVERY COMPUTER QUESTION,
THERE IS A SYBEX BOOK THAT HAS THE ANSWER

Each computer user learns in a different way. Some need thorough, methodical explanations, while others are too busy for details. At Sybex we bring nearly 20 years of experience to developing the book that's right for you. Whatever your needs, we can help you get the most from your software and hardware, at a pace that's comfortable for you.

We start beginners out right. You will learn by seeing and doing with our **Quick & Easy** series: friendly, colorful guidebooks with screen-by-screen illustrations. For hardware novices, the **Your First** series offers valuable purchasing advice and installation support.

Often recognized for excellence in national book reviews, our **Mastering** and **Understanding** titles are designed for the intermediate to advanced user, without leaving the beginner behind. A **Mastering** or **Understanding** book provides the most detailed reference available. Add one of our pocket-sized **Instant Reference** titles for a complete guidance system. Programmers will find that the new **Developer's Handbook** series provides a higher-end user's perspective on developing innovative and original code.

With the breathtaking advances common in computing today comes an ever increasing demand to remain technologically up-to-date. In many of our books, we provide the added value of software, on disks or CDs. Sybex remains your source for information on software development, operating systems, networking, and every kind of desktop application. We even have books for kids. Sybex can help smooth your travels on the **Internet** and provide **Strategies and Secrets** to your favorite computer games.

As you read this book, take note of its quality. Sybex publishes books written by experts—authors chosen for their extensive topical knowledge. In fact, many are professionals working in the computer software field. In addition, each manuscript is thoroughly reviewed by our technical, editorial, and production personnel for accuracy and ease-of-use before you ever see it—our guarantee that you'll buy a quality Sybex book every time.

To manage your hardware headaches and optimize your software potential, ask for a Sybex book.

FOR MORE INFORMATION, PLEASE CONTACT:

Sybex Inc.
2021 Challenger Drive
Alameda, CA 94501
Tel: (510) 523-8233 • (800) 227-2346
Fax: (510) 523-2373

SYBEX

Sybex is committed to using natural resources wisely to preserve and improve our environment. As a leader in the computer books publishing industry, we are aware that over 40% of America's solid waste is paper. This is why we have been printing our books on recycled paper since 1982.

This year our use of recycled paper will result in the saving of more than 153,000 trees. We will lower air pollution effluents by 54,000 pounds, save 6,300,000 gallons of water, and reduce landfill by 27,000 cubic yards.

In choosing a Sybex book you are not only making a choice for the best in skills and information, you are also choosing to enhance the quality of life for all of us.

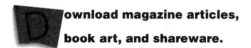
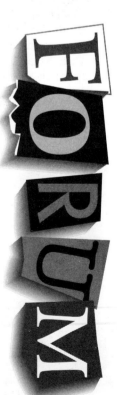

NOVELL'S GUIDE TO
Unix Ware™ 2

SECOND EDITION

CHRIS NEGUS

LARRY SCHUMER

Novell Press, San Jose

Publisher: Rosalie Kearsley
Editor-in-Chief: Dr. R.S. Langer
Acquisitions Manager: Kristine Plachy
Developmental Editor: Guy Hart-Davis
Editor: Valerie Potter
Technical Editor: Peter Fernandez
Novell Technical Advisor: Kelley Lindberg
Book Designer: Helen Bruno
Technical Artist: Cuong Le
Desktop Publisher: Stephanie Hollier
Production Assistant: Dave Nash
Indexer: Nancy Guenther
Cover Designer: Archer Design
Logo Design: Jennifer Gill
Cover Photographer: Mert Carpenter

Library of Congress Card Number: 95-67386
ISBN: 0-7821-1720-1

Manufactured in the United States of America

10 9 8 7 6 5 4 3 2 1

We dedicate this book to Chris' uncle Bob, who loved Chris dearly, knew nothing about computers, had the money to get us started in business, and didn't.

Acknowledgments

Larry and Chris would like to thank the following individuals for their help in making this book a reality (twice!):

Rose Kearsley of Novell Press, for her continuing trust and faith in both us and UnixWare.

Special thanks to the great folks at SYBEX—Guy Hart-Davis, David Kolodney, and Val Potter—for their continued support and encouragement, and to technical editor Peter Fernandez for a job well done. Thanks also to the SYBEX production staff—desktop publisher Stephanie Hollier, production assistant Dave Nash, and technical artist Cuong Le—for their help in putting this book together.

Jonathan Saks, UNIX guru, for sharing his great insights into system monitoring and tuning the UNIX kernel.

Michael Sabrio, Master Script Writer, for his invaluable help with the utilities and scripts.

The UnixWare development teams in Summit, NJ, and Sandy, UT, for their dedication and continuing efforts in improving UnixWare.

The Wasatch Mountain Club, for providing hiking, snowshoeing, and skiing opportunities that kept us sane while trying to meet an insane schedule.

Larry's friend, Gretchen, for being there in mind, body, and spirit.

Yvette Payne, for waiting for Chris at the bus stop.

Patrice Paoletti for helping Chris retrieve the introduction to this book from somewhere in the hyperspace between Utah and California.

And special thanks to Joanna, Larry's 6-year-old daughter, for keeping up the love from so far, far away.

CONTENTS AT A *Glance*

TABLE OF *Contents*

· ·

*I*ntroduction

You bought this book because you wanted to learn about the latest UNIX technology available today. You want to put your hands on it, run real applications, connect to the Internet, access your NetWare servers, open your system to multiple users, and share information with remote computers.

What you get in most other UNIX books is hundreds of pages of old technology. You don't need a chapter on the old **ed** command line editor when there are graphical editors and full-blown word processors, such as Word-Perfect, running on UNIX. If you're not a programmer, you don't need to know how to write **awk** and **sed** scripts. In this book, we've described the old technology only where it's relevant and expounds on the new technology.

What you do need to know about the UNIX system today is how multitasking (the ability to run several programs at a time) can help you do your work. You need to find out how to run applications from anywhere on the network. You need to know how to install a real UNIX system and tune it so it works best for you.

The UNIX system is reaching a point where you no longer have to be an egghead to use it. UNIX is moving from the geek to the chic. With this book, you can learn how to take advantage of the world's most popular advanced operating system in a way that serves you in your work and play.

The UnixWare 2 version of UNIX System V is showcased in this book. UnixWare 2 provides the latest UNIX technology in a form that you can buy for a few hundred dollars and install on your PC. This is the same operating system that runs on supercomputers, powers the telephone system, and keeps Wall Street running. We'll tell you how to use it on your own desktop PC.

Why UNIX System V?

In 1990, AT&T delivered UNIX System V Release 4.0 to the computer industry, unifying all the major variants of UNIX in one product for the first time. Essential features from Berkeley UNIX (BSD), SunOS, Santa Cruz Operation (SCO) UNIX, and Xenix became part of UNIX System V.

Because UNIX System V put all the major UNIX components in one place (and because UNIX technology was becoming more complex and expensive to develop), most computer companies who wanted to provide the UNIX system to their customers licensed UNIX System V from AT&T. Instead of creating their own UNIX systems, companies scaled back on their own UNIX development efforts. More and more UNIX customers were handed AT&T's UNIX System V.

Despite all these improvements, UNIX was still being sold by AT&T as a source code product, rather than a binary product. This meant that those companies that resold UNIX System V for the PC, or with their own hardware, would repackage it and make enough changes to introduce incompatibilities with other UNIX systems. Unfortunately, this was an inevitable result because AT&T left the development of key usability features and hardware support unfinished.

What the industry needed was a real, ready-to-run out of the box version of UNIX from the people who were creating the technology. That reality came about in several stages, resulting in the product called UnixWare.

Soon after UNIX System V Release 4.0 appeared, AT&T split off the organization developing UNIX to a separate subsidiary: UNIX System Laboratories (USL). During its few years of existence, USL added several major enhancements to UNIX that helped position it for wider appeal:

> ▶ **Graphical User Interface**: In Release 4.2, a graphical user interface was added to UNIX that allows you to run graphical, X Window System applications. Because the X Window System is a networked windowing system, applications can be run from any computer on the network and displayed on any X-terminal. The Release 4.2 graphical interface also contains simplified procedures for adding users, configuring networks, and accessing

peripheral devices. These procedures were often quite complex without a graphical interface.

▶ **Application and Hardware Support**: To make UNIX more available to people who are not programmers, USL needed to adapt UNIX System V to run applications written for the different versions of UNIX. It also had to support all kinds of different hardware. Drivers for PC hardware were built into UNIX System V so that the most popular hard disks, CD-ROM drives, video cards, and SCSI devices all work with UNIX without users having to be hackers.

▶ **Multiprocessing**: Instead of buying a whole new computer, new multiprocessing enhancements let users add extra CPU chips to increase the processing that can be done on a single UNIX system. With multiprocessing features, the UNIX system can use two or more processors simultaneously.

With the technology going in the right direction, UNIX was ready to make its push toward delivering an economical, ready-to-run, PC-based UNIX system. That's where UnixWare comes in.

Why UnixWare?

In 1993, Novell purchased UNIX System Laboratories from AT&T, along with the UNIX System V product. The same system engineers, developers, testers, and managers who were once part of USL continued their work on UNIX in Summit, New Jersey, as part of Novell.

Though Novell still licenses the UNIX System V source code technology to other computer vendors, the porting base is the Intel x86 architecture. In other words, PC compatibles using Intel 386, 486, and Pentium processors are used to develop, run, and test the operating system. Hardware-specific code is tailored to the Intel processors, though the framework is built so that hardware-specific pieces can be changed later when UNIX is ported to (i.e., modified to run on) non-Intel processors.

UnixWare is the brand name for Novell's UNIX System V product. It represents the UNIX System V porting base, including all of the latest UNIX technology as it comes hot off the press from Novell. Other UNIX products may take months, or even years, to incorporate the new technology found in UnixWare 2. Plus, UnixWare is tuned and tested for Intel processors. The latest UNIX applications and PC hardware will work with UnixWare.

Because it is produced by Novell, UnixWare's strongest features center on networking support. With UnixWare, you can use NetWare protocols to connect to NetWare servers in a nearly seamless manner. UnixWare also takes advantage of Novell's well-established education, training, and support organizations.

UnixWare is packaged and sold in two basic configurations: the Personal Edition (PE) and the Application Server (AS). The Personal Edition is intended as a single-user, networked platform for running applications. The Application Server is intended to be used as a multiuser system, which may offer services to other systems.

The major features of UnixWare are described in the following sections.

NETWARE CONNECTIVITY

Using a UnixWare system to access a NetWare server is often as easy as double-clicking on an icon that represents the server. UnixWare automatically finds the servers on your network. As long as you can supply a valid login name and password, you can access NetWare volumes, directories, and files on the server as though they were on your UnixWare system.

If your organization uses NetWare, UnixWare can be an excellent choice as the application server. The UnixWare systems can access file and print services on the NetWare servers through your local area network.

In a NetWare network, you can run UnixWare instead of DOS on the personal computers, possibly without changing any hardware (or by just increasing the RAM or hard disk space). You can maintain your NetWare connectivity, run your DOS and Windows applications in a UnixWare window, and begin to integrate powerful networked applications to run from UnixWare.

LOWER COMPUTING COSTS

Before UnixWare, the UNIX system tended to carry a high price tag. The operating system itself could cost a few thousand dollars. Typical workstations, which were needed to run powerful, graphical UNIX systems, used to cost $10,000 or more.

UnixWare drastically reduces the price of running the UNIX system. Because UnixWare was created and tuned for personal computers based on Intel 80386 and newer chips, a system that can run UnixWare (for example, an 80486 with 16MB of RAM and a 200MB hard disk) can be purchased for thousands of dollars less than a RISC-based workstation. Also, the cost of purchasing UnixWare itself is in the low hundreds instead of thousands of dollars.

THE COMPETITION

There are other PC-based UNIX systems available today. Santa Cruz Operation (SCO) offers a PC-based UNIX system with a graphical interface called the SCO Open Desktop (ODT). Sun Microsystems has its own UNIX system for Intel platforms called Solaris. Next Computer has abandoned its own hardware platform to offer the NextStep graphical UNIX system on PCs. Solaris is based on UNIX System V Release 4; the other UNIX systems are based on older versions of the UNIX operating system.

There are two other operating systems competing for the high-end, PC desktop market. IBM's OS/2 operating system is now in its second version. Also, Microsoft offers its Windows NT operating system.

UnixWare is currently the only one of these systems based on the latest version of the UNIX system—UNIX System V Release 4.2 (SVR4.2).

UnixWare Features

When you compare price and features of UnixWare to other high-powered, 32-bit operating systems on the market today, UnixWare is a formidable product. Here are some of the things you can do with UnixWare:

- ▸ Run application programs created for DOS, Windows, or any of several different types of UNIX systems

- Run several graphical applications (X Window, with Motif interface) and character-based applications simultaneously

- Increase your processing power by adding extra CPU chips (if your hardware supports it)

- Run applications stored on a remote system on your computer

- Run X Window applications from a remote system (using the other system's processor) and have them appear on your system's display so you can work with them from there

- Connect dumb terminals or X-terminals to your UnixWare system to allow several users to access your system simultaneously

- Connect to other UNIX systems (such as Sun workstations and SCO UNIX systems) using TCP/IP to provide standard login, file transfer, and remote execution services

- Connect to non-UNIX systems, such as IBM mainframes, using TCP/IP

- Install UnixWare applications over the network from an AS system to other UnixWare systems

- Connect to thousands of users and systems over the Internet (using the TCP/IP package)

- Connect to online database services, such as CompuServe and Dow Jones, using a modem

- Connect on a peer-to-peer basis to other UnixWare systems to share files, processing power, and printers without any additional software

- Connect transparently to NetWare file servers

- Run networking applications from systems over telephone lines

- ▶ Send electronic mail using MHS mail to NetWare servers, UNIX mail, or across the Internet using Domain Name Service

- ▶ Allow DOS workstations to connect to your system using NVT software

What Other UNIX Versions Are Covered in This Book?

Many of the descriptions in this book apply not only to UnixWare, but also to most other versions of UNIX. In particular, if you are running a different UNIX system on a personal computer, especially if it uses the X Window System, many of the descriptions in this book will apply to you.

All of the most popular UNIX products are based on UNIX System V. SCO UNIX, available from the Santa Cruz Operation, is based on an older version of UNIX System V: Release 3.2. Over the years, SCO has patched in features from later versions of UNIX. SCO UNIX has its own graphical interface called Open Desktop. That interface is not described in this book, but because Open Desktop is based on the Motif GUI and the X Window System, many of the descriptions in this book relating to running applications and using the mouse still apply. Also, many of the descriptions of commands and ways of using the file system apply to SCO UNIX.

Solaris, Sun Microsystem's PC-based UNIX product sold through a business unit called SunSoft, is compatible with UNIX System V Release 4. It also relies on the X Window System for working with graphical applications. Because it is based on Release 4, Solaris matches even more of the descriptions in this book than does SCO UNIX.

To a lesser extent, public domain UNIX clones will work as described in this book. Most notable of the "free" UNIX look-alikes is the Linux operating system. Thousands of hackers around the world use and contribute to this UNIX clone. Its main attraction is that it suits hackers who prefer to have more control of the operating system's source code. And if you can hack things together, the price—somewhere between free and cheap—is attractive. Again, the command line environment and the X Window System descriptions in this book will help you when it comes to using Linux.

Amazingly, there are only minor differences between commands for standard operations such as moving, copying, deleting, and editing files among all the different UNIX versions. The layout of the file system is basically the same. And, because most standard shell command line interpreters are available on each UNIX system, working with the Korn Shell (ksh), C Shell (csh), or Bourne Shell (sh) is almost identical among the different UNIX systems.

The most significant differences between UNIX System V as described in this book and those in other UNIX products comes in the area of system administration. You may need to check the documentation that comes with your version of UNIX for specifics on adding hardware or installing applications. Although many administrative commands are the same, some graphical administration tools differ significantly.

THE DESKTOP GRAPHICAL USER INTERFACE

Once UNIX System V Release 4.2 is installed on your PC, you can use the system through the Desktop graphical user interface. The Desktop is made up of windows (areas on the screen where you do your work), icons (small graphics that represent files, directories, and windows), and menus (lists of options from which to choose). You accomplish tasks by pointing and clicking with your mouse.

The Desktop makes it easy to manage the multitasking environment. For example, you might have several applications running simultaneously. One window on your Desktop might contain a FrameMaker session, where you are writing a letter. You might also be running a CD-ROM player application to play music on the PC's CD-ROM drive. Yet another window could be open for reading your electronic mail. Other running applications and open folder windows may be iconized along the bottom of the screen.

NOTE **Using and customizing the Desktop are covered in Chapter 2.**

THE FILE SYSTEM

The data files, application programs, and devices you use with UNIX are organized in a hierarchy in the UNIX file system. Over the years, the file system has become rather large, with separate areas designated for storing different types of files. For example, general user utilities are stored in /usr/bin. Special administrative utilities are stored in the directories /sbin, /usr/sbin, and /etc. The /usr/X/bin directory contains graphical applications. The /home directory contains the directories in which users keep their own data files. All devices for communicating with computer hardware are in the /dev directory.

The UnixWare file system and how to work with it are covered in Chapter 2.

 NOTE

THE SHELL

Before the UNIX Desktop graphical interface, there was the *shell*. The shell, or command line, is where you can type in commands. Though the shell is less intuitive than the Desktop interface, it is much more flexible. There are also many advanced features that are not yet supported on the Desktop. To use these features, you must enter commands from the shell.

To access the shell from the Desktop, you open a Terminal window (accessed from the Applications folder window). From the command line in a Terminal window, you can move around the file system, open files, and run applications.

Accessing the shell and the commands you can use from it are described in Chapter 8.

 NOTE

UNDERSTANDING OPERATING SYSTEMS

An operating system is the software that controls the operation of your computer. It sets up the environment that lets you run applications, store and manage files, and communicate with the computer's hardware.

As a user, your view of the operating system is usually through a command line or graphical interface. When you start an application, the operating system handles the running and management of that application automatically. The operating system directs requests for processing to the computer's processor and manages how the application is held in memory as it runs. If the application needs to save information permanently, the operating system handles how the information is written to hard disk.

In an operating system such as UNIX, the processing that goes on behind the scenes can be very complex. Instead of managing one process, UNIX handles many processes, which may be requested by many users, at the same time. UNIX must also incorporate and manage the interfaces to different storage devices, networks, and specialty devices across the many running processes.

Besides managing processing in the heart of UNIX, which is called the *kernel*, UNIX also includes services that are visible to you, in what is called the *user level*. For example, UnixWare has a print service that allows you to connect and define printers so that many different applications can use those printers. Because UNIX supplies the print service, every application doesn't need to include its own print drivers.

As more computer services are standardized, more services are included in the operating system. For example, UnixWare has a mechanism for storing and sharing Type 1 type fonts and a Service Access Facility that applications can use to plug their services into standard networking interfaces.

More features have also been added into base operating systems to accommodate the need to work with different types of systems. For example, UNIX now includes features to allow SCO UNIX applications to run in UNIX. Networking protocols have been built into the operating system to talk to different systems and networks. UNIX supports IPX/SPX so that it can communicate with NetWare systems.

CLIENT-SERVER COMPUTING WITH UNIXWARE

UNIX is for users who want to expand beyond the bounds of a single-user, stand-alone operating system. In environments where you need to work with several computers, especially with different types of systems and networks, UNIX may be what you need. With UNIX, you can share computing power among a few users in a small office or among thousands of systems and users across the world.

Although you can use UNIX to run one application at a time on a stand-alone system, its strength lies in its ability to network with other systems. In particular, UNIX is well suited for what is called *client-server computing*, which is an economical way to share computing services among a group of computers.

Using UnixWare as an example, a simple UnixWare client-server scenario can include one UnixWare Application Server system and one NetWare server, with a UnixWare Personal Edition system or DOS/Windows client on everyone's desk, all connected by a single LAN. The NetWare server can have a huge disk capacity, so everyone in the office can store and share files from this central location. Users can also share one or more printers connected to the NetWare server. The UnixWare Application Server system can be used to run the application programs that are critical to the office. For example, a large database program stored on the Application Server system might be accessed by several Personal Edition users at the same time or from a DOS client running an X Window System emulation.

By distributing computing services, your whole office environment can become much more cost efficient. You don't need to purchase high-priced computers, printers, or CD-ROM drives for every person who has a computer, but each user can work as though you did.

A "mini" client-server configuration, with two UnixWare systems and a NetWare file server, was used to produce this book. See Appendix A for more information about system configuration and hardware.

NOTE

In a wider view of client-server computing, UNIX can be a major component in what is called *enterprise computing*. Large, multilocation organizations that incorporate many different types of computing systems and networks can use UNIX at almost every level of computing. You can downsize mission-critical applications from mainframes to UNIX. You can use UNIX as a gateway to the Internet. And you can put UNIX on the desktops of users who need to run the networked, mission-critical applications.

UNIX APPLICATION DEVELOPMENT

Many personal productivity applications are available for UNIX, and you can expect the number of packaged applications to grow in the coming years. But if you want to create custom applications for your UnixWare system, a set of sophisticated programming tools for developing your own UnixWare applications is available in the UnixWare Software Development Kit (SDK).

The SDK software is offered as an add-on product you can purchase separately for UnixWare. Because the UNIX system has been used primarily in scientific and corporate computing environments, many application development tools are also available from third-party vendors.

NOTE   **UnixWare applications are covered in Chapter 3.**

About This Book

This book is aimed at helping people who have used NetWare, DOS, or other UNIX systems to become power UNIX users. Although we cover basic operations of the Desktop graphical interface, such as how to use your mouse, open icons, and use standard windows, our focus is on showing you how to stretch the limits of your UNIX system.

Throughout the book, we present our real experiences working with UNIX. We tell you what we went through installing and configuring our systems and try to steer you through some of the trickier aspects of UNIX.

Anyone who needs to administer a UNIX system or group of systems will find this book useful. In particular, we've tried to help you understand what is going on behind the graphical interface, so you have the knowledge you need to help track down and solve any problems.

HOW TO USE THIS BOOK

The way you use this book depends on how you intend to use your UNIX system. Novice users can start at the beginning to get an overview of working in a multiuser, multitasking environment (Chapter 1), then learn how to use the graphical interface and file system (Chapter 2), then move on to working with applications (Chapter 3). Network users can read the networking chapters (Chapters 4 and 5) for information about connecting to NetWare and other UNIX systems. If you are working with DOS or Windows within UnixWare, Chapter 6 will help you maximize your DOS and Windows usage.

If you have never worked with a UNIX system before, read Chapter 8 for information about using the traditional UNIX shell interface. Appendix D contains a quick reference to UNIX commands, along with each command's description and syntax (i.e., the form of the command and the options available with it).

Those of you who are responsible for setting up and maintaining a UNIX system can start with the appendices. Turn to Appendix A for tips on choosing the hardware for your system and installing the software. Turn to Chapter 7 for details on setting up your backup routines to protect your data. When you need to fix problems, see Chapter 10, which offers suggestions for troubleshooting problems.

Anyone who needs to know how to perform a specific task in UNIX can look up that task in Chapter 11. There, you will find step-by-step instructions arranged alphabetically by task for quick reference.

WHAT THIS BOOK CONTAINS

The eleven chapters in this book cover the many aspects of using UNIX. Here is a brief description of their contents:

- ▶ Chapter 1 explains how to use UNIX multitasking, multiuser, and multiprocessor features and what that means to you, the user. It also describes how to set up other users if you are working in a multiuser environment.

- ▶ Chapter 2 provides the basics for working with UNIX. It describes the operations of the Desktop graphical user interface and the structure of the UNIX file system.

▶ Chapter 3 describes how to run applications in UNIX. It covers applications designed for UnixWare as well as those developed for other UNIX platforms.

▶ Chapter 4 is about using UNIX with NetWare. It describes NetWare connectivity in UnixWare and how to access NetWare services over the network.

▶ Chapter 5 covers using UnixWare on a network with other UNIX systems. It describes how to set up networking, such as BNU, TCP/IP, and NFS, to communicate with remote systems.

▶ Chapter 6 explains how to run DOS and Windows within UNIX. Merge lets you use DOS and Windows applications from a Desktop window.

▶ Chapter 7 is about UNIX's Backup and Restore facilities. It describes how to back up your files and later restore them to your system, as necessary.

▶ Chapter 8 explains how to access and work from the UNIX shell. It also contains descriptions of useful commands you can use from the shell command line.

▶ Chapter 9 describes how to monitor your UNIX system's performance, then how to tune your system to improve performance.

▶ Chapter 10 is about troubleshooting. It describes how to track down and correct problems throughout the UNIX system.

▶ Chapter 11 provides a quick reference by task. It includes step-by-step instructions for performing common UNIX tasks.

The appendices contain reference information, as listed here:

▶ Appendix A provides information about installing and setting up UnixWare.

▶ Appendix B tells how to use the software on the CD-ROM included with this book.

▶ Appendix C describes the games that come with UNIX.

▶ Appendix D contains a list of UNIX commands, along with their syntax.

Throughout the chapters and appendices, you will see notes set off from the regular text. (You've already seen several in this introduction.) Three different types of notes are included. A regular note provides supplemental information about the topic being discussed. A tech note is aimed at more advanced users who might want to know what is going on behind the scenes or how to use a more complex function. A warning note alerts you to a potential problem and usually points out how to avoid or solve that problem.

This book contains many examples of commands and configuration files. Sometimes an example won't fit on one line. If that is the case, text wraps to the second line and is indented.

About Service and Support

Behind UnixWare are Novell's service and support organizations, a large network of UnixWare resellers, and Certified NetWare Engineers (CNEs). Because UnixWare is constantly changing, you will probably need to supplement this book and the documentation that comes with the product with up-to-date information from the UnixWare channels.

The UnixWare reseller is the first place to contact for information and support. Resellers are supplied with the latest updates and hardware drivers. They are also alerted about problems and workarounds.

THE UNIXWARE HOTLINE

To contact Novell directly for information about UnixWare, call the toll-free UnixWare hotline. The phone number is (800) 486-4835.

When you call the hotline, you have access to the Novell FAXBACK service. With your touch-tone telephone, you can request to receive information on products, technical questions, and hardware compatibility. You can have this information faxed to you directly. The toll-free number is also how you can get in touch with UnixWare specialists at Novell.

UNIXWARE BULLETIN BOARDS

Through online forums or bulletin boards, you can exchange information about UnixWare. Most of these forums are available on CompuServe and on the Internet.

UnixWare on CompuServe

You can access the UnixWare forum on CompuServe by connecting to CompuServe and typing the following at any CompuServe prompt:

```
GO UNIXWARE
```

Here are some of the UnixWare topics available on CompuServe:

- Sysop Library
- Core OS
- Mail System
- Developer Support
- DOS Merge
- Installation
- X Window
- Networking
- Device Drivers
- Printing
- Applications

To obtain a CompuServe ID, call CompuServe customer service at (800) 848-8990 or (614) 457-8650.

UnixWare on the Internet

If you have a connection to the Internet (using the TCP/IP software included with UnixWare), you can obtain UnixWare support in several ways. A service called Netnews allows people to exchange information about a wide range of topics. The Netnews group called `comp.unix.unixware` has a huge amount of information that applies to UnixWare. Besides including discussions on fixing tricky problems, the newsgroup often has late-breaking news about UnixWare.

## CHAPTER 1

The Multitasking, Multiuser, Multiprocessor System

You can use your UNIX system in a way that is as simple or as powerful as you choose. The traditional DOS paradigm is one person using one machine to run one application at a time. With UNIX, you can still use your computer that way, but you have more choices. The UnixWare Desktop puts an easy-to-use interface over a complex system that is working constantly.

Instead of having one application running at a time, UNIX lets you run many applications at once. You can set up UNIX so that many users can access your system. And you can extend beyond the bounds of your computer to take advantage of the processing power and files from other UNIX and non-UNIX systems. Using the UnixWare system in examples, this chapter describes the concepts of multitasking in a multiuser environment. It also describes how UNIX can incorporate multiple processors to further extend the power of your computer. Understanding these concepts will help you understand the potential of your UNIX system.

 NOTE **The examples in this section are based on the UnixWare version of Unix System V Release 4.2 (SVR4.2). If it is not already set up for you to begin working, turn to Appendix A before continuing. That appendix describes how to install your software and configure your system.**

Logging In and Giving Commands

Before you can access your UnixWare system to do any of the procedures described in this book, you must log in to the system. When you start your computer, you will see a login window, as shown in Figure 1.1.

 NOTE **The screen shown in Figure 1.1 is a representative example of the login window. The actual login screen will have a logo from Novell or whichever company ports the product you are using.**

Type the user name of the owner, whose user account was set up during UnixWare installation. Then type the password for the owner. Click on Login, and the UnixWare Desktop window, shown in Figure 1.2, appears.

In UnixWare, you click with the left mouse button to select an item. To open an icon, you double-click (click twice quickly) with the left button. For more information about using your mouse with Unix-Ware windows, see Chapter 2. That chapter covers the basics of working with the UnixWare Desktop and file system.

NOTE

FIGURE   1.1

The login window

Welcome to snowbird. Please enter your Login ID and Password.

Login ID:

Password:

| Login | Reset | Exit | Help |

Copyright 1984–1994 Novell, Inc. All Rights Reserved.

The Desktop window consists of windows and icons that you can manipulate with your mouse and keyboard to give commands and perform actions. In traditional UNIX systems, you issue commands by typing them from a *shell command line*. To allow both interfaces, the Desktop lets you open a *Terminal* window, which essentially gives you a shell command line from which to type commands.

FIGURE 1.2

*The UnixWare Desktop
window*

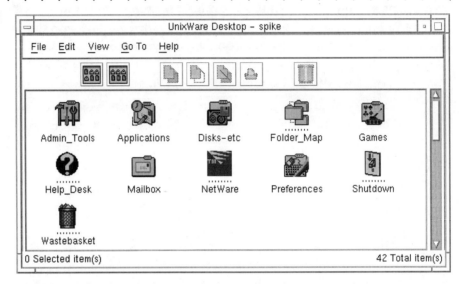

NOTE

Shell command line is a tricky term. Technically, the *shell* is the program that allows you to access the *command line*, from which you enter commands. But the terms are used pretty much interchangeably. In this book, for instance, we will tell you to go to the shell, or to the command line, or to the shell command line, and they all mean the same thing.

Because the Desktop is designed to be easy to use, it is the preferred method when there is a choice between the graphical user or command line (Terminal window) interface. However, certain actions must be performed by typing a command at the command line.

To open a Terminal window for access to a command line, double-click on the Applications icon in your Desktop window. Then, from the Applications folder window, double-click on the Terminal icon to open a Terminal window. In the Terminal window, you see a command line prompt. By default, the dollar sign prompt ($) appears when you have a regular user's permissions, and a number sign prompt (#) appears when you have root permissions. As explained later in this chapter, the *root* is the user who has special permissions to run certain administrative commands or open restricted files.

If you changed your prompt (which you can do during installation, as described in Appendix A), the easiest way to tell your current permissions is to type **id** from the Terminal window. It will show you your user and group permissions.

Understanding Multitasking

Multitasking is the ability to have several tasks running on your computer at the same time. Because of multitasking, you can run more than one application, and several users can be logged in on your computer while the operating system is processing information in the background.

Here are some examples of the kinds of things that can happen at once on a UnixWare system that couldn't happen on a single-tasking system:

➤ A request to print a document arrives on your system and remains in your print queue until it can be handled by your printer. Figure 1.3 shows an example of a document waiting to be printed.

➤ You are formatting some floppy disks while you are doing your other work. Figure 1.4 shows an example of formatting a floppy disk.

➤ Mail comes in from a remote system and appears in your mailbox. Figure 1.5 shows a mail message received from a remote system.

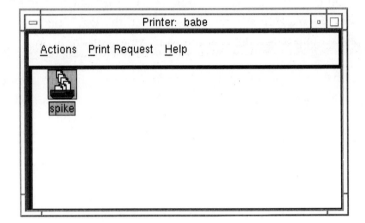

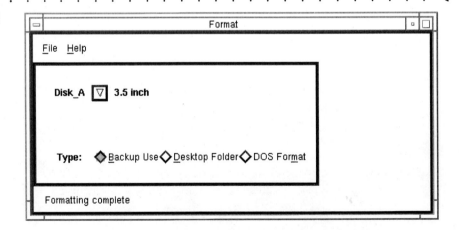

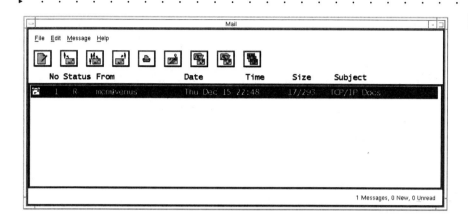

▶ A window appears to alert you of an appointment at a scheduled
time. Figure 1.6 shows an alarm message that was set up
previously.

▶ You have multiple Terminal windows open and logged into different computers. Figure 1.7 shows an example of several Terminal
windows logged into different systems.

FIGURE I.7

Logging into multiple
remote systems

```
                                    Terminal
mars:mcn> rlogin venus
Password:
UnixWare 2.0
venus
Copyright 1984–1994 Novell, Inc.  All Rights Reserved.
Copyright 1987, 1988 Microsoft Corp.  All Rights Reserved.
U.S. Pat. No. 5,349,642
Last login: Thu Apr  5 23:25:15 1995 on pts000

Display Desktop (y/n)? n
venus:mcn>
```

```
                                    Terminal
mars:mcn> rlogin jupiter
Last login: Wed Mar 15 22:45:15 from mars.planet.com
SunOS Release 4.1.3 (GENERIC) #3: Mon Jul27 16:43:54 PDT 1992
You have new mail.
jupiter%
```

```
                                    Terminal
mars:mcn> rlogin venus
UNIX System V/386 Release 4.2 Version 1.1
venus
Copyright (c) 1992 UNIX System Laboratories, Inc.
Copyright (c) 1987, 1988 Microsoft Corp. All rights reserved.
Last login: Thu Dec 15 22:45:15 on pts004

Display Desktop (y/n)? n

venus:mcn>
```

UNDERSTANDING PROCESSES AND DAEMONS

When you start a program, by typing its name on a command line or double-clicking on its icon, the running instance of that program is called a *process*. The UnixWare system can manage hundreds of these processes at once. It makes sure each process has a crack at the computer's processor.

Although the processor is generally shared on a rotating basis, this sharing often happens so quickly that all applications appear to be running at once.

One of the most powerful features of a multitasking system is that many of the processes are running in the background. The fact that processes are already running doesn't prevent you from running your own processes. You may see the light on your system's hard disk or Ethernet board start flashing when you aren't touching the mouse or keyboard. Your system is letting you continue working while it handles a request.

At least a handful of processes are running on your system at all times. Some of these processes are daemon processes that are part of the UnixWare system. A *daemon* process is a process that runs in the background and waits for requests. For example, a print daemon handles print requests and a terminal daemon listens for login requests. Other background processes may be added by a particular application, such as a mail daemon to handle delivery of email messages as they come in.

There is a limit to the total number of processes you can have running, but you won't reach that limit in normal use. The NPROC tunable parameter lets you change the number of processes that can run simultaneously per user on your system. See Chapter 9 for information about changing NPROC and other tunable parameters.

NOTE

The UnixWare system assigns a *process ID* to each process running on the system. UnixWare keeps track of all running processes in its *process table* and shares the computer's processor with each of them.

Listing Runnning Processes

You can display a list of all the processes currently running on your system (the ones in the process table), by using the ps command. You issue this command from a command line, which is available when you open a Terminal window.

From your Desktop, open a Terminal window by double-clicking on the Applications icon in your Desktop window and then double-clicking on the Terminal icon in the Applications folder window. From the Terminal window, at the command line prompt, type the following command:

```
ps -aef
```

You will see a list of the processes that are currently running on your system. Figure 1.8 shows an example of the display, although your list will contain many more lines than are shown here.

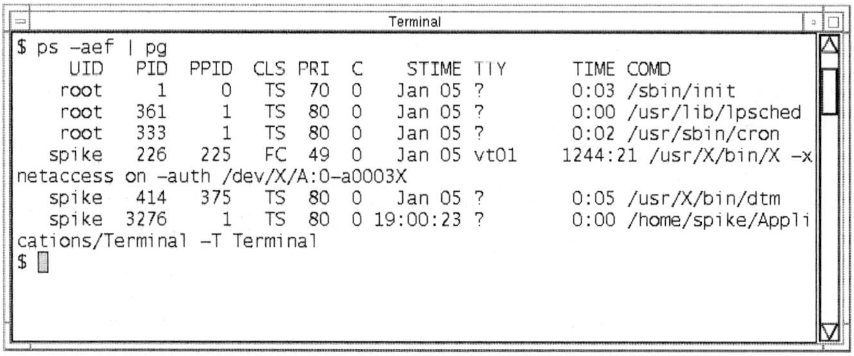

FIGURE 1.8

Viewing a list of running processes

```
Terminal
$ ps -aef | pg
   UID    PID  PPID  CLS PRI  C    STIME TTY       TIME COMD
  root      1     0   TS  70  0   Jan 05 ?         0:03 /sbin/init
  root    361     1   TS  80  0   Jan 05 ?         0:00 /usr/lib/lpsched
  root    333     1   TS  80  0   Jan 05 ?         0:02 /usr/sbin/cron
 spike    226   225   FC  49  0   Jan 05 vt01   1244:21 /usr/X/bin/X -x
netaccess on -auth /dev/X/A:0-a0003X
 spike    414   375   TS  80  0   Jan 05 ?         0:05 /usr/X/bin/dtm
 spike   3276     1   TS  80  0 19:00:23 ?         0:00 /home/spike/Appli
cations/Terminal -T Terminal
$ []
```

The display lists the information in eight columns:

- The UID column shows the user ID for the owner of the process.

- The PID column shows the process ID.

- The PPID column lists the parent process ID. The parent process is the one that initiated this process.

- The CLS column shows the scheduling class for the process. Most processes are time sharing processes (TS). Processes noted as fixed class (FC) or system (SYS) have higher priority than time sharing classes.

- The PRI column shows the priority of the process. Within each scheduling class, the priority defines the level of priority the process has to getting CPU time in relation to other processes in the class.

- The C column shows processor utilization for scheduling.

- The STIME column shows the time the process started. The month and day are shown instead if the process started more than 24 hours ago.

- The TTY column lists the terminal that controls the process. Some processes, run during system startup or by a daemon process, will not have a controlling terminal. Those processes will have question marks instead of a terminal device name.

- The TIME column shows how much of the computer's processor time the process consumed.

- The COMD column shows the command run by the process.

The first three processes listed in Figure 1.8 are *system processes*, which are run by the system when you turn it on and continue to run until you turn the computer off. The next three are *user processes*, which are started when you log in and start up the UnixWare Desktop.

The system processes are owned by the root user (also called the *super-user*). The first one listed is

```
/sbin/init
```

which is the first process run on your system. It starts up all the other system processes. The process ID (PID) of this process is 1, and it has no parent process ID (PPID). The TIME shows that it has consumed only three seconds of processor time.

The next two processes are

```
/usr/lib/lpsched
/usr/sbin/cron
```

These are are two *daemon* (background) processes. Both were started by the
init process, as indicated by the 1 in the PPID column. lpsched is the
print scheduler waiting to handle requests to the printer. cron is the process that checks the system for any processes you scheduled to run at a later
time, such as a backup or file-transfer program, and starts them when
appropriate.

In the example, the user named spike logged in, and the user processes
started to provide spike with the Desktop environment he needs for his
work. The following process:

```
/usr/X/bin/X -xnetaccess on -auth
 /dev/X/A:0-a0003X
```

is the X server process (/usr/X/bin/X), which provides the X Window
System environment. The /dev/X/A:0-a0003X option to the X process
shows that the server is running on local display while -xnetaccess on
indicates that access to the display is open for remote applications to appear
on the X screen. The option -auth says that applications from remote systems are authorized to write to the local display. Because the X process runs
in fixed class mode (FC), it gets greater access to the CPU than regular time
sharing (TS) processes.

The next process:

```
/usr/X/bin/dtm
```

starts the Desktop manager (dtm). The Desktop manager runs in Motif
mode. Motif is now the standard window manager delivered with Unix-
Ware and most other X Window servers with UNIX. The other major con-
tender, OPEN LOOK, is no longer supported by the developers of UNIX.

The last process in the example

```
/home/spike/Applications/Terminal -T Terminal
```

started when spike opened a Terminal window. This just shows that a Terminal window is still active on the Desktop.

UNDERSTANDING SYSTEM STATES

UnixWare makes use of a concept called *system states*. A system state determines the level of activity on your UnixWare system.

When you start up your UnixWare system, the `/etc/inittab` file identifies the system state in which UnixWare comes up, then lists the processes that are run in the identified state. An example of an `/etc/inittab` file is shown in Figure 1.9.

```
Terminal
$ cat /etc/inittab
#
# WARNING: THIS FILE IS AUTOMATICALLY GENERATED.
# Any changes made directly to this file may be overwritten
# at the next system reboot.
# Permanent changes should also be made to files in the
# /etc/conf/init.d directory.
# See Init(4) and idmkinit(1M) for more information.
#
cr::sysinit:/sbin/ckroot >/dev/sysmsg 2>&1
ck::sysinit:/sbin/setclk  >/dev/sysmsg 2>&1
mm::sysinit:/etc/conf/bin/idmodreg >/dev/sysmsg 2>&1
ldmd::sysinit:/etc/conf/bin/idmodload >/dev/sysmsg 2>&1
ap::sysinit:/sbin/autopush -f /etc/ap/chan.ap
ak::sysinit:/sbin/wsinit 1>/etc/wsinit.err 2>&1
bchk::sysinit:/sbin/bcheckrc </dev/console >/dev/sysmsg 2>&1
bu::sysinit:/etc/conf/bin/idrebuild reboot </dev/console >/dev/sysmsg 2>&1
me::sysinit:/etc/conf/bin/idmkenv >/dev/sysmsg 2>&1
ia::sysinit:/sbin/creatiadb </dev/console >/dev/sysmsg 2>&1
is:3:initdefault:
bd:56:wait:/etc/conf/bin/idrebuild </dev/console >/dev/sysmsg 2>&1
r0:0:wait:/sbin/rc0 off 1> /dev/sysmsg 2>&1 </dev/console
r1:1:wait:/sbin/rc1  1> /dev/sysmsg 2>&1 </dev/console
r2:23:wait:/sbin/rc2 1> /dev/sysmsg 2>&1 </dev/console
r3:3:wait:/sbin/rc3 1> /dev/sysmsg 2>&1 </dev/console
r5:5:wait:/sbin/rc0 firm 1> /dev/sysmsg 2>&1 </dev/console
r6:6:wait:/sbin/rc0 reboot 1> /dev/sysmsg 2>&1 </dev/console
li:23:wait:/usr/bin/ln /dev/systty /dev/syscon >/dev/null 2>&1
sc:234:respawn:/usr/lib/saf/sac -t 300
co:12345:respawn:/usr/lib/saf/ttymon -g -v -p "Console Login: " -d /dev/console -l console
d2:23:wait:/sbin/dinit 1> /dev/sysmsg 2>&1 </dev/console
co:12345:once:/usr/bin/mapchan -f /usr/lib/mapchan/88591.dk console
$ 
```

FIGURE 1.9

Sample /etc/inittab *file*

Each `inittab` entry has four fields, which are separated by colons. The first field is a unique tag identifying the entry, the second identifies the system state in which this entry is activated, the third identifies how the entry is started, and the fourth shows exactly which command to run.

For example, the third to last entry in the `inittab` file in Figure 1.9 is

```
co:12345:respawn:/usr/lib/saf/ttymon -g -v
    -p "Console Login: " -d /dev/console -l
    console
```

This shows how the process that lets you log in to your system console (the monitor and keyboard on your PC) is started. The first field identifies this as the `co`, for *console*, entry. The second field, `12345`, shows the system states for this entry. The entry includes all active system states:

- ▶ 1, for single-user state

- ▶ 2, for multiuser state

- ▶ 3, for file-sharing state

- ▶ 4, for undefined state (as administrator, you may define this as you choose)

- ▶ 5, for firmware state (an outdated administrative state that simply reboots if you are running UNIX on a PC)

- ▶ 6, for reboot state

NOTE   *Multiuser* is a bit of a misnomer. Historically, a **UNIX** system administrator would bring the system down from multiuser state to single-user state to do system maintenance. In single-user state, all outside connections to the computer, including connections to each user's terminal, printers, or networks, are stopped. Even if you are the only one using a system, you need to run in a multiuser state to get the graphical user interface (**GUI**) and networking services.

The third field is `respawn`, which says that if this process should terminate for some reason, start up another one. The last field is the command that is actually run. The `ttymon` process displays the "Console Login:" prompt on your display (`/dev/console`) so you can log in. You won't see this process listed when you run the `ps` command to display the list of currently running pro-cesses (as described in the previous section), because it stops once you have logged in. (You could see the process if you logged in to the computer from the network when nobody is logged into the console.)

The `initdefault` line in the `/etc/inittab` file identifies the state in which your system first comes up. In the sample `inittab` file shown in Figure 1.9, the line looks like this:

```
is:3:initdefault:
```

This means that the system will start in the file-sharing state (3). Even though you may be using UNIX as a single-user system, your system starts in file-sharing state. This is because many services, such as printing and networking, come up in this state.

The `inittab` entries that start many of the other processes are tagged `r0`, `r1`, `r2`, `r3`, `r4`, `r5`, and `r6`. If you look at the column to the right of each tag, you'll see which state(s) each of the entries start in. For example, r0 starts in state 0, r1 in state 1, and r2 in states 2 and 3. As you change to a new init state, the r? entry that corresponds to the new `init` state is run. That entry will then start any processes slated to run in its `/etc/rc?.d` directory, where *?* is replaced by the number of the system state. (See "Checking and Changing the System States" later in this chapter for information on how to move from one system state to another.)

For example, when you start your computer and your system starts up in `init` state 3, because there is a 3 in the second field of the `r2` entry, the `/etc/rc2` command is run. The `/etc/rc2` command checks the `/etc/rc2.d` directory and starts any command it finds there that has *S* (for *Startup*) as its first letter.

The commands in the `/etc/rc2.d` directory that begin with *S* are typically shell scripts. A *shell script* is a series of commands put together in a file. When you run the script, the commands in that file are executed. You can actually read these scripts to see what they do. You will learn how to use and create shell scripts in Chapter 8.

 **WARNING** **If you display any of the shell scripts in the** /etc/rc2.d **directory, be careful not to make any changes to them. If you change a startup script, whole features may no longer work. For example, if you change the startup script that begins the print service, you may not be able to print files.**

Here are some of the startup commands in the /etc/rc2.d directory:

- S01MOUNTFSYS makes the different parts of your file system available (*mounts* them).

- S02mse starts up the mouse manager, so your mouse can operate.

- S27nuc starts up the NetWare UNIX Client, so you can access NetWare file servers.

- S55merge does the startup and cleanup needed to run DOS or Windows Merge on your system.

If you look in other /etc/rc?.d directories, you will notice that many of the commands begin with the letter *K*. These represent processes that run when you go from a higher state to a lower state. Usually, they are processes that stop (*kill*) other processes.

For example, when you leave the multiuser state (2) and go to the single-user state (1), the following commands from the /etc/rc1.d directory are run to stop processes related to each command:

- K00ANNOUNCE announces that services are being stopped.

- K20lp stops the print service.

- K50rpc stops remote procedure call services.

- K72nuc shuts down your NetWare connectivity.

Checking and Changing the System State

You can check the current system state using the who command. From your Desktop, open a Terminal window (double-click on the Applications icon, then double-click on the Terminal icon). From the Terminal window, type the following command at the command line prompt:

```
who -r
```

You will see something like

```
.run-level 3 Feb 27 09:49 2 0 S
```

which shows the system state (run-level) as 3 (file-sharing state).

You can change the system state by using the `init` command. (Before you can use `init`, you must log in as the root user. A non-root user cannot change init states.) For example, you might want to change the system state to single-user when you are doing some maintenance on your system and want to prevent anyone from using your file systems remotely or logging into your computer over the network. In this case, you would use the command

```
init 1
```

TECHNOTE

When we opened the Terminal window and changed the UnixWare system state from 3 to 1, the Desktop disappeared. When we restarted it using the `desktop` command, the Desktop came up but we couldn't run Windows Merge. In other words, in system state 1, you won't have access to all of the Desktop's functions.

Another reason you might change the system state is if you need to reboot your system because you just added a new application. Then you would change to system state 6 (reboot state) with this command

```
init 6
```

The following command shuts down your system:

```
init 0
```

UnixWare System Users

This book covers both the UnixWare Personal Edition and Application Server systems. The UnixWare Personal Edition (PE) package is intended to be a single-user system, with or without networking connections to the outside world. Although the Personal Edition system is configured to be used by one user at a time, two users can be logged in simultaneously. For example, one user could work from the console terminal while a second user is conducting a command-line session from a dumb terminal.

The UnixWare Application Server (AS) package is intended for multi-user use, allowing many users to access the system at the same time. The Application Server includes everything in the Personal Edition, plus new features that allow it to serve many users, including a full set of online documentation (the PE has manual pages online, but no system administration or network administration guides) and many extra system utilities.

To allow multiple users to use your UnixWare system, you must set up a separate user account for each person. The users store their files in the separate home folders they have been assigned. Each user can tailor the environment for how he or she uses the system.

During installation, two active user accounts are defined in the Personal Edition system, and three are defined in the Application Server system. Both systems have accounts for the owner and the root. With the Application Server, the *sysadm* (system administrator) user is also added. Other user accounts are available for special administrative tasks. The following sections describe the tasks that these users can perform. The description of the sysadm user is included in the section about reserved users.

THE UNIX OWNER

UNIX SVR4.2 introduces the concept of a system *owner*. This user has the rights to change the system in ways that are not available to all users. For example, the owner can add other users, change the networking configuration, and install software packages.

The Desktop uses the `tfadmin` command to allow the owner special permissions previously available only to the root user.

 TECHNOTE

You can open the User Permissions window from the User Setup window to see the permissions available to the owner. To view ownership permissions, follow these steps:

1 · From the Desktop, double-click on the Admin Tools icon to display the Admin Tools folder window.

2 · Double-click on the User Setup icon. The User Setup: User Accounts window appears. Figure 1.10 shows an example of this window. In this example, the owner of the system is spike.

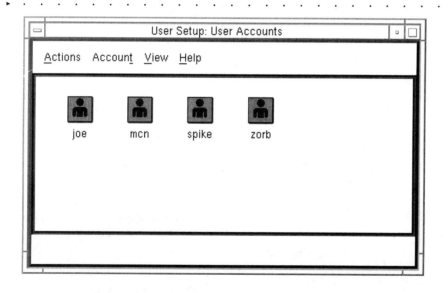

F I G U R E 1.10

*The User Setup: User
Accounts window*

3 · Click on the icon for the owner (spike).

4 · Click on Account to display the Account menu, and then click on Permissions. The User Setup: User Permissions window appears, as shown in the example in Figure 1.11.

FIGURE 1.11

The User Setup: User
Permissions window

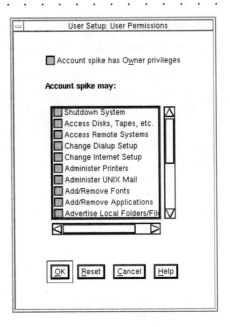

5 · When you are finished viewing the permissions, click on Cancel to exit this window.

The first box at the top of the window is shaded, showing that the selected user is the system owner. When this box is checked, the user can perform any of the functions listed in the window:

▶ **Shutdown System:** Allows you to shut down the system completely (by double-clicking on the Shutdown icon). Other users can simply log out. (Of course, any user can just turn off the power switch, but the Shutdown icon is the preferred method for shutting down your system, since all users logged in at the time are warned that the system is being shut down and all open files are gracefully closed.)

NOTE **The Shutdown icon also gives you the opportunity to save the current state of your Desktop (i.e., the position of open windows and icons).**

▶ **Access Disks, Tapes, etc.:** Lets you read and write files from floppy disks, cartridge tapes, CD-ROMs, or other media in the Disks-etc folder. Most users, not just the owner, have this permission.

▶ **Access Remote Systems:** Lets you log in to remote systems (by double-clicking on a remote system icon, installed from the Internet window or Dialup Setup window). You can also transfer a file to a remote system (by dropping a file icon on a remote system icon). This permission is also given to most users.

▶ **Change Dialup Setup:** Lets you add, delete, or modify remote systems from the Dialup Setup window. These are systems you communicate with over a modem or through a direct line.

▶ **Change Internet Setup:** Lets you add, delete, or modify remote systems from the Internet Setup window. These are systems you communicate with through an Internet connection (usually an Ethernet or Token Ring network).

You do not need Change Internet Setup permission to communicate with any of the systems once they have been configured.

NOTE

▶ **Administer Printers:** Lets you configure local or remote printers for use with your system.

▶ **Administer UNIX Mail:** Lets you perform tasks related to administering UNIX mail.

▶ **Add/Remove Fonts:** Lets you add Type 1 fonts to or delete them from your system, using the Font Setup window. These are the fonts displayed in window headers and Terminal windows. They can also be used by any application that uses Adobe Type 1 fonts.

▶ **Add/Remove Applications:** Lets you use the Application Setup window to install applications on UnixWare. It also lets you remove applications.

▶ **Advertise Local Folders/Files:** Lets you use the File Sharing window to share your folders and files with other systems. *Folder* is the UnixWare term for *directory*.

▶ **Connect to Remote Folders/Files:** Lets you use the File Sharing window to connect to folders and files on other systems so you can use them on your system.

▶ **Access System Monitor:** Lets you open the System Monitor window to monitor the performance of your system and set alarms when selected parameter values are exceeded.

▶ **Change System Tunables:** Lets you change kernel tunable parameters with the System Tuning window.

▶ **Start and Stop Processors:** Lets you use the Processor Setup window to activate licensed processors if you have a multiprocessor computer.

 NOTE   **You can only license additional processors if your computer was designed to support multiple processors.**

▶ **Change Display Setup:** Lets you use the Display Setup window to change video board type, colors, and screen resolution for your screen display.

▶ **Setup Network Installation:** Lets you set up your UnixWare system to install the UnixWare Personal Edition or Application Server on another computer on the network.

▶ **Access NetWare Setup:** Lets you turn on NetWare connectivity on startup and enable peer-to-peer communications through the Netware Setup window.

▶ **Administer MHS Mail:** Lets you configure the MHS (Message Handling System) mail gateway through the MHS Setup window.

▶ **Share Applications:** Lets you share applications with remote systems through the Application Sharing window.

The owner can open the User Permissions windows for other users and assign them permissions to use any of these system features. The owner can even assign another user full ownership permissions.

Ownership permissions apply to the UnixWare system as it is used from the Desktop. Once the owner opens a Terminal window or a virtual terminal to work from a command line, he or she has only the permissions associated with any normal user. The root user is the one who has special permissions for working from the command line.

THE ROOT USER

Before the concept of owner in UNIX, there was the root user. The root user had, and still has, complete control over the operating system. Although the owner can perform the basic tasks necessary for administering the system, you still need to have root user permissions to access certain functions.

In the UnixWare version of UNIX SVR4.2, the root user is not set up as a Desktop user. When you log in as root (using the password assigned during installation), you see a command line prompt instead of the Desktop. The default command line prompt for the root user is a number sign (#).

NOTE

You can make root into a Desktop user by changing the properties in the User Setup window. However, we don't recommend making this change. If your graphical interface (the Desktop window) should become corrupted, you should be able to log in as root to fix the problem from the command line. By keeping root a non-Desktop user, you avoid the potential of trying to fix a garbled interface from a garbled interface.

In order to install an application or work with any system files from a Terminal window, you will usually need to have root permissions. Here are some features that are not available through the Desktop that you must be the root user to perform:

▸ Add a hard disk. You must use the `diskadd` command as root to add a second hard disk to your system.

▶ Add a mouse. To change your mouse, say from a serial mouse to a bus mouse, you must use the /usr/bin/mouseadmin command as the root user.

Other tasks that can only be performed by the root user are described in Chapter 10.

If you are logged in as the owner or some other Desktop user and you know the root password, you can temporarily assign yourself root permissions without leaving the Desktop and logging in again. Open a Terminal window and type the following at the command line prompt:

su

You are prompted for the root password. After you type the password and press Enter, you see the root prompt (#). At this point, you have full permissions to run or change anything on the system.

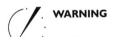 **WARNING**

It is extremely important that you protect your root user password. If others have your root password, they can do anything they want with your system. Don't keep the password on or near your computer. But don't lose your password, or you will need to call the support line for information about how to restore it.

RESERVED USERS

Several user names are reserved by the UNIX system. These users are typically assigned special permissions to do a subset of functions available to the root user. Like the root user, the reserved users go directly to a command line when they log in; they are not Desktop users. To use most reserved user accounts, you must assign passwords for them.

Some examples of reserved users are *uucp*, *sysadm*, and *lp*. In traditional UNIX systems, the uucp user can administer the set of configuration files used to support the uucp command and related basic networking utilities. This user can configure the files in the /etc/uucp directory for defining the remote systems your system can communicate with, the networking devices on your system, and the dialers connected to the computer. In Unix-Ware, you can use the Dialup Setup window to configure the uucp files if you are the owner, and you can also edit these files as the root user, so you don't need to use the uucp user account.

The sysadm account was created to allow a user other than root to access the OA&M administrative interface. OA&M (short for Operations, Administration, and Maintenance) provides a menu- and form-driven administrative interface. OA&M comes with the Application Server and the Personal Edition. There are very few things you can do through OA&M that you can't do more easily through either the Desktop or the command line.

The lp user can administer the printing services on your UnixWare system. This user owns the printing files in /var/spool/lp and has the permissions to start and stop printing services from the command line. Again, the Desktop allows you to do most of the necessary printer setup, so the lp user account is not really necessary with UnixWare.

> **You may wonder why the old reserved user accounts still exist in UNIX SVR4.2. The answer is history. UNIX never throws anything out; in some respects it's beginning to look like our parents' attics.**

NOTE

Everything that lp, uucp, sysadm, and the other reserved users can do can also be done by the root user or by the owner from the GUI. The advantage of using the individual accounts is that you can assign limited administrative responsibilities to a user. For example, you can assign one person as the uucp administrator for all computers in your location without letting that person change printing or other system configuration files.

There are quite a few other reserved user accounts. To see which ones are available on your system, follow these steps:

1 · From the Desktop window, double-click on the Admin Tools icon.

2 · In the Admin Tools folder window, double-click on the User Setup icon.

3 · In the User Setup: User Accounts window, click on View to display the View menu, then click on Reserved. The User Setup: Reserved Accounts window appears, as shown in the example in Figure 1.12. (If OA&M were installed, you would also see a sysadm reserved user account.)

FIGURE 1.12

The User Setup: Reserved Accounts window

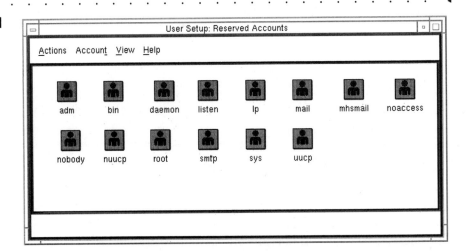

4 · After you are finished viewing the reserved accounts, click on Actions to display the Actions menu, then click on Exit to close the window.

Adding Users and Groups

Each person who will work on your UnixWare system should have his or her own separate user account for two main reasons: so users can tailor their Desktop environment in a way that suits them and so users can keep their work separate and protected from other users. You can also set up

groups and assign users to those groups. The following sections describe
how to add users and groups.

SETTING UP NEW USER ACCOUNTS

Through the User Setup window, you can add new users to your system.
To set up a new user, follow these steps:

1 · From the UnixWare Desktop, double-click on the Admin Tools icon.

2 · Double-click on the User Setup icon.

3 · In the User Setup: User Accounts window, click on Account to
display the Account menu, then click on New. The User Setup:
Add New User Account window appears.

4 · Click on Show Other Options. The full User Setup: Add New
User Account window appears, as shown in Figure 1.13.

F I G U R E 1.13

*The User Setup: Add New
User Account window*

5 · Fill in the fields on this screen. Each of these fields is described
below.

   ► **Login ID:** The name to type in order to log in as that user.
   Typically, this name is fairly short. Often, a person's initials or
   first initial and last name are used.

 NOTE **Though not required, it's a good practice to use all lowercase letters
for the Login ID.**

   ► **Type:** Defines whether this user is set up to use the Unix-
   Ware Desktop graphical user interface. If you click on the
   box next to Desktop, the user's home directory is populated
   with folders designed to be used with the Desktop, such as
   Accessories, Applications, and NetWare. The Desktop will
   start automatically when this user logs in. If you click on
   Nondesktop instead, a command line prompt, not the Desktop, appears after the user logs in.

   ► **Manage User Info via NIS:** If you are centrally managing
   user accounts for a group of computers using a Network Information Service (NIS) server, you can click on this box to
   manage this account using NIS. (NIS is a distributed naming
   service used to locate resources that are distributed across a
   network.) If you do select this item, the Home Folder, Shell,
   User ID, Group, and Comments fields are grayed out and that
   information is taken from the NIS server for the new user.

   ► **Comment:** Typically used to add the user's full name. However, you can put other information here, such as the person's title. For example, you could enter *Spike Jones, President*
   in the Comment field.

   ► **Home Folder:** By default, this is the Login ID name of the
   user in the /home folder. So, for example, if the Login ID were
   spike, the home folder /home/spike would appear in this
   field. In some cases, you may want to assign the user to another

folder. For example, if you have a second hard disk attached to a /home2 folder with lots of space on it, you might want to make /home2/spike the home folder.

▶ **User ID:** Your first new user is typically assigned user ID 101, unless you are matching an ID number on a remote system. You can set the user ID to any number you like above 100 and below 60000 (user ID 0 is assigned to the root user; reserved users are assigned user ID numbers between 0 and 100). However, if you are connected to other computers, give the user the same user ID number on this computer that he or she has on other computers on the network. Some networking applications, such as Remote File Sharing, allow you to pass user permissions from one computer to the next based on the user ID.

▶ **Shell:** Defines the shell command line interpreter that is used when you open a Terminal window. The default is the standard sh shell (/usr/bin/sh). A popular shell among UNIX System V users is the Korn Shell (ksh), which is available with the Application Server. To use ksh as your shell, type /usr/bin/ksh in the Shell field. The Personal Edition includes the Windowing Korn Shell (wksh), which does everything the regular ksh does, plus it lets you create windowing shell scripts. To use wksh as your shell, type /usr/bin/-wksh in the Shell field.

For those who are used to working in BSD UNIX systems, you can use the C shell by typing /user/bin/csh into this field.

NOTE

▶ **X-terminal Name:** Defines the remote X-terminal this user may log in from. Enter the name of the remote X-terminal if you expect this user to occasionally log in from that terminal. Later, from the Internet Setup window, you must add the name and network address of the X-terminal. When the user logs in to your system from the X-terminal, UnixWare will ask if he or she is logging in from the X-terminal name you defined in this field. If the user says yes, the Desktop is started, and the output is directed to the X-terminal.

▸ **Groups:** Gives the user permissions associated with a group of users. See the description of groups later in this chapter for further information on the reasons for assigning groups.

▸ **Locales:** Different locales (countries or areas) have different ways of representing dates and times, as well as having different keyboard layouts. Even if you don't have a different language version installed, you can select a different locale and have the date/time stamps used by the system appear in the format that is appropriate for a particular locale.

6 · If you want to assign the new user to a group, select one of the existing groups on the system. If you want to add this user to a group that doesn't currently exist, click on Cancel, then add the new group before adding this user. (See the section entitled "Setting Up UnixWare Groups" later in the chapter.)

7 · Click on Apply to add the new user to the system.

8 · When prompted, add a new password for the user.

NOTE You should ask the user to replace the password you assigned to the user account with one that he or she will remember. Tell the user to protect the password, because it is the only way that others are prevented from accessing that user's files.

WARNING If you are ever going to have your users assigned to several different UnixWare systems, be sure to match their user IDs across those systems when you add their accounts to each system. It is difficult to change user IDs later, after the user has already created files using old user IDs.

If you don't know what the user's ID number is on a remote system, log in to the remote system and find a file owned by that user. Then use the `ls` command to discover the user's ID number. For example, if you logged in to a remote system and typed

```
ls -l datafile
```

The result might be

```
-rw-r--r-- 1 spike docgroup  0 Feb 28 10:54
    datafile
```

This shows that `datafile` is owned by spike, and his group is `docgroup`. To find the user ID number associated with spike, type

```
ls -n datafile
```

and you might see

```
-rw-r--r-- 1 809  15   0 Feb 28 10:54
    datafile
```

This shows that spike's user ID is 809, and the group ID for `docgroup` is 15.

Another method of checking the user's user ID and group ID is to list the `/etc/passwd` file with the command

```
pg /etc/passwd
```

Figure 1.14 shows an example of the information you might see. The last line

```
joe:x:102:1:Joe:/home/joe:/usr/bin/ksh
```

shows joe's user ID (102) and group ID (1).

VIEWING AND CHANGING USER PERMISSIONS

After you create a user, that user's icon appears in the User Setup window. By default, that user is assigned two special permissions for using the Desktop: Access Remote Systems and Access Disks, Tapes, etc. As the owner, you can assign other permissions to the new user.

FIGURE I.14

Example of the

/etc/passwd *file*

```
                                    Terminal
$ cat /etc/passwd
root:x:0:3:0000-Admin(0000):/:/sbin/sh
daemon:x:1:12:0000-Admin(0000):/:
bin:x:2:2:0000-Admin(0000):/usr/bin:
sys:x:3:3:0000-Admin(0000):/:
adm:x:4:4:0000-Admin(0000):/var/adm:
uucp:x:5:5:0000-uucp(0000):/usr/lib/uucp:
mail:x:6:6:Mail Processes:/etc/mail:
nuucp:x:10:10:0000-uucp(0000):/var/spool/uucppublic:/usr/lib/uucp/uucico
nobody:x:60001:60001:uid no body:/:
noaccess:x:60002:60002:uid no access:/:
lp:x:7:9:0000-LP(0000):/var/spool/lp:/usr/bin/sh
smtp:x:55:6:SMTP Processes:/var/spool/mailq:/usr/bin/sh
listen:x:37:4:Network Admin:/usr/net/nls:/usr/bin/sh
mhsmail:x:61:6:MHS Admin Processes:/var/spool/smf:/usr/bin/sh
spike:x:101:1:Spike Jones:/home/spike:/usr/bin/ksh
zorb:x:808:200:Larry:/home/zorb:/usr/bin/ksh
mcn:x:809:200:Chris:/home/mcn:/usr/bin/ksh
joe:x:102:1:Joe:/home/joe:/usr/bin/ksh
$ []
```

To view or change a user's permissions, from the User Setup: User Accounts window, click on the user's icon, click on Actions, and then click on Permissions. You can view the permissions and then click on Cancel to exit the window. If you change any permissions, click on Apply to apply those changes.

SETTING UP UNIXWARE GROUPS

Setting up user groups makes it easier to control access to files and folders (directories). You probably have files or folders that you want to be accessible to more than one person, but not to everyone. You can create groups and assign users to them, then specify which groups have permissions to which files or folders.

When the system is installed, 19 groups are defined. These groups are primarily for internal and administrative purposes. To see a list of groups currently defined on your system, from the Desktop, double-click on the

```
┌─────────────────────────────────────────────────────────────┐
│ ▭              User Setup: Groups                    ▫ ▢     │
├─────────────────────────────────────────────────────────────┤
│  Actions  Group  View  Help                                  │
│ ┌───────────────────────────────────────────────────────────┐│
│ │  [icon]  [icon]  [icon]  [icon]  [icon]  [icon]  [icon]  [icon] ││
│ │  adm    audit    bin     cron   daemon   doc     dos   dtadmin ││
│ │                                                           ││
│ │  [icon]  [icon]  [icon]  [icon]  [icon]  [icon]  [icon]  [icon] ││
│ │   lp     mail   noaccess nobody  nuucp   other   priv    root  ││
│ │                                                           ││
│ │  [icon]  [icon]  [icon]                                   ││
│ │   sys     tty    uucp                                     ││
│ │                                                           ││
│ └───────────────────────────────────────────────────────────┘│
│ ┌───────────────────────────────────────────────────────────┐│
│ └───────────────────────────────────────────────────────────┘│
└─────────────────────────────────────────────────────────────┘
```

FIGURE 1.15

The User Setup: Groups
window

Admin Tools icon, then double-click on the User Setup icon. In the User
Setup: User Accounts window, click on View, then click on Groups. You see
the User Setup: Groups window, with icons representing the groups on your
system, as shown in Figure 1.15.

> **UnixWare group permissions do not just apply to a particular area of
> the file system. With UnixWare, any file or folder throughout the file sys-
> tem can be assigned to a group. Assigning permissions to files and fold-
> ers is covered in Chapter 2.**

NOTE

To add a new group, follow these steps:

1 • From the UnixWare Desktop, double-click on the Admin Tools icon.

2 • In the Admin Tools window, double-click on the User Setup icon.

3 · In the User Setup: User Accounts window, click on View to display the View menu.

4 · Click on Group, then click on New. The User Setup: Add New Group window appears, as shown in Figure 1.16.

FIGURE 1.16

The User Setup: Add New Group window

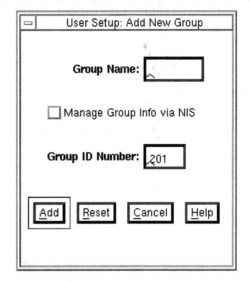

5 · Type the group name you want to use. Typically, these names are eight characters or less. As when you set up a user, you may want to match the group name and ID number with those on other computers to make permissions consistent across a network.

6 · Click on the box next to Manage Group Info via NIS if you want information for this group to be managed on an NIS server. If you do, the group ID field is not available and that information is accessed from the NIS server.

7 · The next available group ID number appears in the Group ID Number field. You can use this number or type over it to assign another number. Group numbers 0 through 99 are reserved for special UNIX groups.

8 · Click on Add to add the group.

Allowing Multiple Simultaneous Users

As mentioned earlier, the Application Server allows multiple users to log in to the system. The Personal Edition only allows two users to log in at the same time.

The ways you can log in to a multiuser system depend on the kind of hardware connected to the system. If you have TCP/IP set up to work over Ethernet or Token Ring, you can log in over the network using a command-line or Desktop session. You can also connect dumb terminals directly to your computer and work from the command line.

With an Ethernet or Token Ring connection set up and TCP/IP configured so that another computer knows about your computer, the other computer can log in to yours using several different methods: from a remote UnixWare system, from an X-terminal, or from a dumb terminal.

LOGGING IN FROM A REMOTE UNIXWARE SYSTEM

One way to log in is from a remote UnixWare system. From another UnixWare system, open the Internet Setup window and add your system's name and network address to the list of known systems. Next, install a remote system icon into a convenient folder.

Once an icon representing your system is installed in a folder, the remote user can simply double-click on the icon and then log in to your system. An example of a remote login session is shown in Figure 1.17.

FIGURE 1.17

Logging in from a remote

system

```
$ rlogin snowbird
Password:
UnixWare 2.0
snowbird
Copyright 1984–1994 Novell, Inc.  All Rights Reserved.
Copyright 1987, 1988 Microsoft Corp.  All Rights Reserved.
U.S. Pat. No. 5,349,642
Last login: Sun Jan  8 18:44:43 1995 on pts005

You have mail
Display Desktop (y/n)? n
snowbird-spike /home/spike> 
```

The user can log in from a remote system and start the Desktop, or just send the output of a single application to the remote system. The steps for using the Internet Setup window, installing a remote system icon, and starting the Desktop from a remote UnixWare system are described in detail in Chapter 5.

LOGGING IN FROM A REMOTE X-TERMINAL

If you have an X-terminal connected to your network, a user can log in from there and start the Desktop. An X-terminal contains just enough processing power to run an X Window System server and to log in to a remote computer. The rest of the work—running applications and working with files—is done by the remote computer's processor.

 NOTE   **See Chapter 5 for details on setting up an X-terminal to run with UnixWare.**

LOGGING IN FROM A DUMB TERMINAL

Most personal computers have two serial ports, labeled COM1 and COM2. You can connect dumb, character-based terminals to these ports so several users can use your system at once. If you need more terminals, you can use a multiport serial board. You do not need any special networking hardware to do this.

The procedure consists of connecting the dumb terminal, running the Dialup Setup window and configuring an incoming-only device, and logging in. Because UNIX was used primarily from dumb character-based terminals for many years, UnixWare supports hundreds of different character-based terminals.

For example, you could use an AT&T 5425 terminal and connect it to the COM2 port on your computer. The cable can be standard RS232C, with a 9-pin female connector for the COM port and a 25-pin male connector for the modem port on the back of the terminal. Then you could access the Setup screen on the terminal and set the speed to 9600 and duplex to full. (Higher speeds are supported, but 9600 is used for this example.)

On your UnixWare system, you must define the port (COM1, COM2, or other) as directly connected to a terminal. You do this through the Dialup Setup window, using the following procedure:

1 · From the UnixWare Desktop, double-click on the Admin Tools icon.

2 · In the Admin Tools window, double-click on the Networking icon.

3 · Double-click on the Dialup Setup icon.

4 · Click on Actions to see the Actions menu, then click on Setup Devices. The Dialup Setup: Devices window appears, as shown in Figure 1.18.

5 · Click on Device, then click on New. The Dialup Setup: Device Properties window appears.

6 · Click on COM1, COM2, or Other, then click on the arrow next to Connects to:. A list of devices appears.

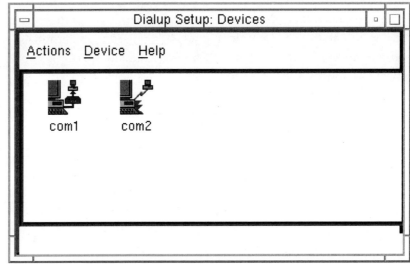

FIGURE 1.18

*The Dialup Setup: Devices
window*

7 · Select Direct. Your screen will look similar to Figure 1.19. Click
on Incoming only.

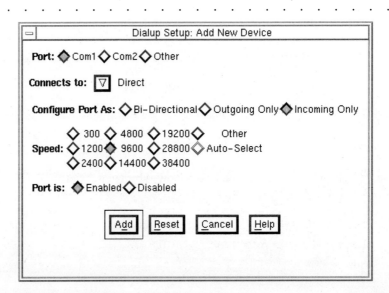

FIGURE 1.19

*The Dialup Setup: Add New
Device window set for a
direct-connect port*

8 · Click on 9600 for the speed (or use a higher speed if your terminal supports it). Click on Enabled to make the port active.

9 · Click on Add. The port is now defined as a direct-connect, incoming port.

10 · Turn on the dumb terminal and press Enter. You should see a login prompt.

11 · Log in as a non-Desktop user.

12 · Set the TERM variable so screen-oriented applications, such as `vi` or spreadsheets, will work properly. For example, if you are using an AT&T 5425 terminal, add the following line to the `.profile` file in your home folder (e.g., `/home/spike/.profile`):

```
TERM=5425;export TERM
```

13 · Log off and then log back in. The new TERM variable is set, and you can use the new login.

Using Multiple Processors

In UNIX System V Release 4.2MP, features were added to allow UNIX to take advantage of more than one processor on a single computer. This multiprocessor feature is in UnixWare 2.

The ability to use multiple processors is built into the UNIX kernel, as well as into several important operating system features. UNIX features that can place particular demands on the CPU, such as the Streams subsystem (which is the framework for handling networking devices) and NetWare UNIX Client features have been multithreaded to allow those functions to direct their work to multiple processors simultaneously.

Not every computer supports multiple processors. In fact, a multiprocessor computer may cost several thousand dollars more than an otherwise comparable single processor computer. The advantage is that if you need the processing power, a computer with three or four processors on it will be less expensive than three or four computers.

Check the documentation that comes with UnixWare for how many processors can be used with UnixWare by default. Novell changed its policy several times. The latest decision, if implemented, would allow either a UnixWare Personal Edition or Application Server to take advantage of up to two processors. You could purchase licenses for up to a total of 32 processors on the Application Server. You could not have more than two processors on the Personal Edition, however.

Once you install the additional processor chips on your computer, per the instructions that come with your computer, all you need to do to have UnixWare take advantage of them is to bring each processor online. You bring processors online and offline with the Processor Setup window.

To bring up the Processor Setup window and bring a processor either offline or online, do the following:

1 · From the UnixWare Desktop, double-click on the Admin Tools icon.

2 · In the Admin Tools window, double-click on the Processor Setup icon. The Processor Administration window appears, as shown in Figure 1.20.

3 · Click on the icon representing the processor you want to activate or deactivate.

4 · Click on either On-line or Off-line to activate or deactivate the processor.

If you want to view properties associated with a particular processor, click on that processor's icon. Then click on Actions and Properties. The Processor Setup: Properties window appears, as shown in Figure 1.21.

The Processor ID shows the number of the processor (the first one is 0). The State shows whether the processor is online or offline. The Processor Type is the type of Intel processor, such as 486 or Pentium. The Floating

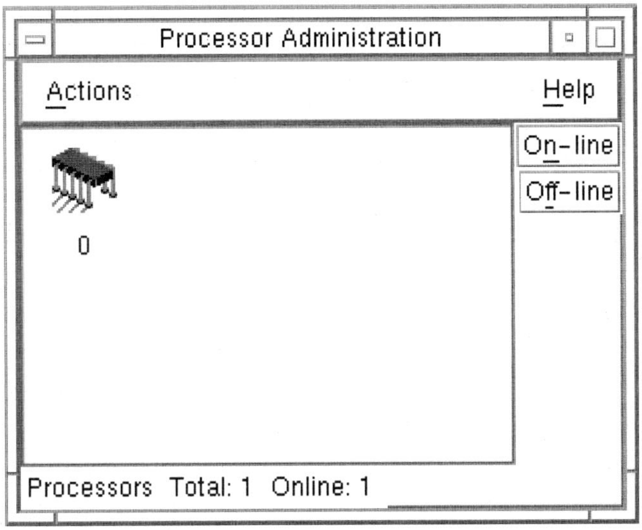

FIGURE 1.20
*The Processor
Administration window*

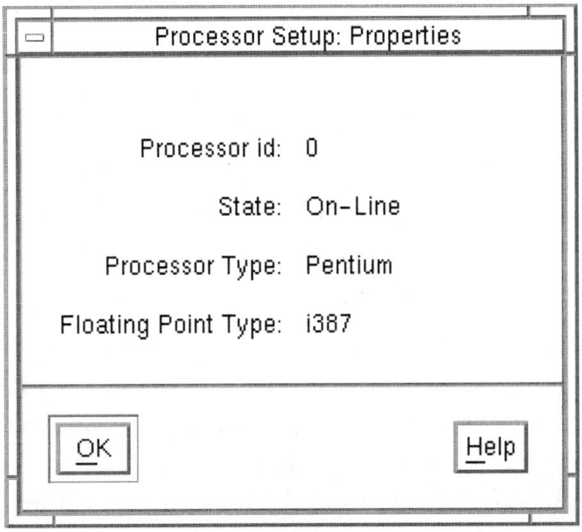

FIGURE 1.21
*The Processor Setup:
Properties window*

Point Type is 387, even if it is built into the CPU chip, as is the case with 486 and Pentium chips. With 386 computers a separate 387 chip is required to run UnixWare.

As you have learned in this chapter, UnixWare allows multiple tasks to be performed at the same time by multiple users. The objective of this chapter is to help you understand what it means to operate a multiuser, multitasking operating system. It also helps you understand why you might want to use multiple processors and how you would turn those processors on and off.

Most of the work that UnixWare does to allow multiple users and processes to operate simultaneously is transparent to you. However, understanding these concepts will help you work with your system.

Through the UnixWare graphical user interface—the Desktop—you can perform your everyday work. Using the Desktop is the subject of the next chapter.

## CHAPTER 2

The UNIX
Graphical
User Interface

Graphical user interfaces (usually referred to as GUIs, pronounced *gooeys*) are not new to UNIX. Sun, for example, has had a GUI on its workstations for some time. SCO has also been providing users with point-and-click convenience with its Open Desktop.

The newest UNIX to be dressed up with a GUI is UNIX System V Release 4.2. Release 4.2 of UNIX is sold by several vendors. For example, Convergent Technology sells this new UNIX product with the GUI as UNIX System V Release 4.2. Novell sells its UNIX product as UnixWare and calls the GUI the UnixWare Desktop, which is described in this chapter.

Novell's UnixWare Desktop lets you easily perform tasks that once could only be performed at the command line by experienced UNIX administrators. Through the Desktop, you use icons, windows, menus, tool bars, and buttons to start applications, manage your files and folders, and maintain your system.

This chapter describes how to work from the UnixWare Desktop and within the UnixWare file system. It summarizes the functions of the Desktop windows, explains how to customize the Desktop to suit your own tastes and work habits, and describes how to work with your files and folders.

Getting Acquainted with UnixWare Windows

In your work with UnixWare, you will move from the Desktop window to the other windows for the various functions you want to use. The following sections describe the windows you can access and how to use your mouse within these windows. For those of you who prefer to work from the keyboard, there is also a description of using the keyboard with UnixWare (a mouse, though, is highly recommended).

THE DESKTOP WINDOW

When you start UnixWare, you see the Desktop window, as shown in Figure 2.1. From here, you can access the other UnixWare windows.

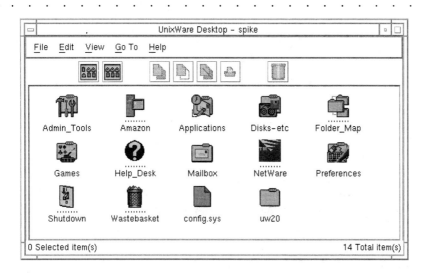

FIGURE 2.1

The UnixWare Desktop
window

The Menu Bar

The UnixWare Desktop window and folder windows have a menu bar just under the title section of the window. The menu bar contains File, Edit, View, Go To, and Help menus. To use one of the menus, click on it to see the menu options, and then click on an option to select it.

Here is a summary of the menus and their options:

▸ The **File** menu contains options for working with your files and exiting the Desktop.

  ▸ **New:** Creates a new file or folder in the currently open folder. Selecting New displays the File: New window.

  ▸ **Open:** Opens the selected icon. A folder icon opens a folder window, an application icon starts an application, and a data file icon starts the associated application with the data file loaded. When you open a folder, the new folder replaces the current folder window. Applications are always opened in their own window.

- **Open - New:** Opens the selected folder, but in a separate window.

- **Print:** Sends the file represented by the selected icon to the default printer. If a default printer is not defined (through Printer Setup), you cannot print the file with this option. Selecting Print displays the Printer: Request Properties window.

- **Find:** Searches for files by name, contents, type, or last modification date. Selecting Find displays the File: Find window.

- **Exit:** Closes the current folder, except for the UnixWare Desktop window.

- **Exit Desktop:** Closes the UnixWare Desktop window and returns you to the graphical login window.

▸ The **Edit** menu contains options for selecting items and "undoing" (reversing) commands.

- **Undo:** Undoes the last copy, rename, move, link, or delete operation.

- **Copy:** Copies selected icons to another folder. Selecting Copy displays the Edit: Copy window.

- **Move:** Moves selected icons to another folder. Selecting Move displays the Edit: Move window.

- **Link:** Links the selected icon to another folder. The icon then becomes available from more than one folder without a new copy being made. Linking an icon takes up less hard disk space than copying the icon. Selecting Link displays the Edit: Link window.

- **Rename:** Gives the selected file or folder a new name, but keeps the file or folder in the current folder. Selecting Rename displays the Edit: Rename window.

▶ **Convert:** Converts the file type from either DOS to UNIX or UNIX to DOS. Selecting Convert displays a pop-up menu with two items: DOS to UNIX and UNIX to DOS. Selecting one of the menu items displays either the Edit: Convert DOS to UNIX or Edit: Convert UNIX to DOS window.

▶ **Delete:** Deletes selected icons. The deleted icons are sent to the Wastebasket from where they can be restored. If they are not restored within a certain amount of time (by default, seven days), they are permanently deleted.

▶ **Select All:** Selects all the icons in the current folder. You can then perform operations, such as moving or copying files, on the entire set of icons.

▶ **Unselect All:** Unselects any icons selected in the current folder.

▶ **Properties:** Changes or displays the icon's owner, group, and permissions. Selecting Properties displays the Edit: Properties window.

▶ The **View** menu contains options for arranging the display on your screen.

▶ **Align:** Aligns the icons in the current folder in straight rows and columns.

▶ **Sort:** Displays a pop-up menu that allows you to sort the icons in the current folder by type, name, size, or time last modified (the icon most recently changed is shown first).

▶ **Format:** Displays a pop-up menu that allows you to change how the icons in the current folder are presented. You can choose Icons (the default view), Short (a small icon and the file's name), or Long (a small icon, file name, size, date created, owner, permissions, and other information).

▶ **Filter:** Defines which icons in the current folder are shown. For example, you can specify that only data files be displayed. Selecting Filter displays the View: Filter window.

▸ The **Go To** menu contains options for navigating through your folders. In addition to the options listed below, as you open folders, they are added to this menu.

  ▸ **Desktop Window:** Moves to the UnixWare Desktop window.

  ▸ **Parent Folder:** Moves you up one folder. For example, if you're in the `home/spike/doc/proj` folder, selecting Parent Folder moves you to the `/home/spike/doc` folder.

  ▸ **Folder List…:** Folders added to the menu (as you open additional folders) are listed here. Selecting one moves you to the specified folder.

  ▸ **Other Folder:** Moves to the folder you specify. Selecting Other Folder displays the Go To: Other Folder window.

  ▸ **Folder Map:** Displays the Folder Map window, which shows a graphical representation of the file system. You can click on the icons shown to move to a new folder.

▸ The **Help** menu contains options for getting help with UnixWare. Here the Desktop window and the folder windows differ slightly: the first option in the Desktop window's Help menu is UnixWare Desktop, while the first option in a folder window's Help menu is Folder.

  ▸ **UnixWare Desktop:** Displays general help on the UnixWare Desktop.

  ▸ **Folder:** Displays online help on folders. All menu options and windows accessible from a folder are covered.

  ▸ **Mouse and Keyboard:** Displays online help for mouse and keyboard shortcuts. The first window displayed shows mouse shortcuts. Click on Keyboard Shortcuts to display a window showing keyboard shortcuts.

  ▸ **Table of Contents:** Lists the help topics available for folders.

> ▶ **Help Desk:** Displays the Help Desk window. From the Help
> Desk window, you can select from all the online help that is
> available for UnixWare. Double-click on an icon in the Help
> Desk window for help on the icon.

The Tool Bar

Directly under the UnixWare Desktop and folder windows' title section
is the tool bar. The tool bar contains shortcut buttons for some commonly
used operations. To use one of the shortcuts, simply click the button to initiate the action or display the appropriate window.

The tool bar, shown in Figure 2.2, contains buttons for Go to Parent
Folder, Align Items, Sort Items by Type, Copy, Move, Link, Print, and Delete. These operations perform exactly the same as if you selected them
from their menus, as described earlier in this chapter.

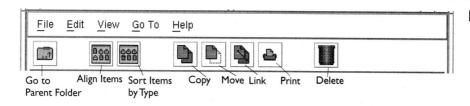

FIGURE 2.2

The Desktop tool bar

**The Go to Parent Folder button is located on all folder windows ex-
cept the UnixWare Desktop window.**

NOTE

The Admin Tools Folder Window

The Admin Tools folder window, shown in Figure 2.3, contains the following administration tools to help you maintain and modify your UNIX
system. It also contains the Networking folder, which contains administration tools related to your system's networking capabilities.

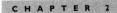

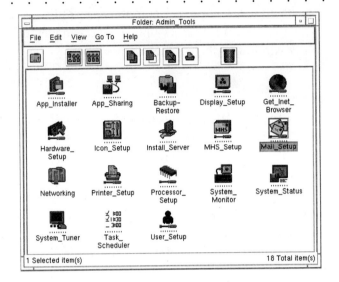

> ▸ **Networking:** This folder contains icons for setting up and using the networking features of UnixWare. The icons available are Dialup Setup, File Sharing, Internet Setup, NetWare Access, and NetWare Setup. These programs are covered in the networking chapters of this book. Figure 2.4 shows the Folder: Networking window.

> ▸ **App Installer:** Installs and removes applications.

> ▸ **App Sharing:** Shares your applications with remote systems.

> ▸ **Backup-Restore:** Backs up from and restores files to your systems.

> ▸ **Display Setup:** Lets you set and change your video display characteristics, such as resolution and number of colors.

> ▸ **Extra Admin:** Invokes the Operations, Administration and Maintenance menu window for system administration tasks. (Only present if you selected *oam* during the installation.)

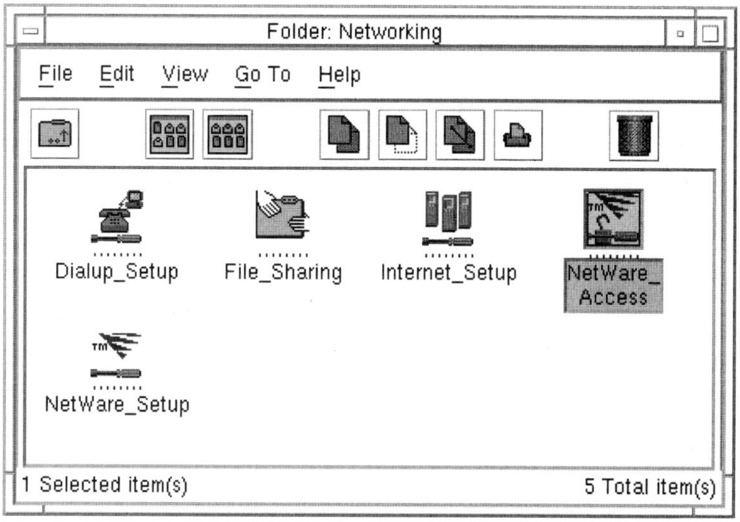

FIGURE 2.4

*The Folder: Networking
window*

▸ **Get Inet Browser:** Supplies instructions for retrieving MOSAIC (a public domain Internet Browser) from a Novell FTP server.

▸ **Hardware Setup:** Lets you set and maintain your hardware IRQs and memory addresses.

▸ **Icon Setup:** Allows you to assign icons to files and applications as well as specify what happens when you manipulate icons.

▸ **Install Server:** Configures an Application Server so that Unix-Ware can be loaded from this server by other systems over the network.

▸ **MHS Setup:** Sets up an MHS (Message Handling System) mail gateway between your UnixWare system and a NetWare system.

▸ **Mail Setup:** Configures a Smarter Host, which is a mail system that maintains alias and routing information. Also sets your system to accept mail sent to the local domain when a system name is not specified and activates mail logging.

▶ **Printer Setup:** Configures printers on your system.

▶ **Processor Setup:** Activates (puts online) or deactivates (takes off-line) your computer's processors when you have a multiprocessor computer. You can also view the properties of your processors.

▶ **System Monitor:** Graphically monitors your system's performance.

▶ **System Status:** Lets you check system information, such as system memory and hard disk usage, and set your system's clock, date, and time zone.

▶ **System Tuner:** Lets you fine tune your system's performance by changing its tunable parameters.

▶ **Task Scheduler:** Runs applications at set times or at regularly scheduled intervals.

▶ **User Setup:** Allows you to add and manage user accounts.

The Applications Folder Window

The Applications folder window, shown in Figure 2.5, contains icons for applications you install from other vendors as well as the applications that come with UnixWare:

▶ **Calculator:** Opens a full-function calculator.

▶ **Clock:** Provides a clock, either digital or analog, with an alarm.

▶ **DOS:** Starts a DOS session.

▶ **Icon Editor:** Lets you modify existing icons or create new ones.

▶ **Mail:** Allows you to read, send, and manage electronic mail from and to users on your system and remote systems.

▶ **Message Monitor:** Opens a window that receives system messages normally sent to the console.

▶ **Online Docs:** Opens the *DynaText* document browser for reading UnixWare online documentation.

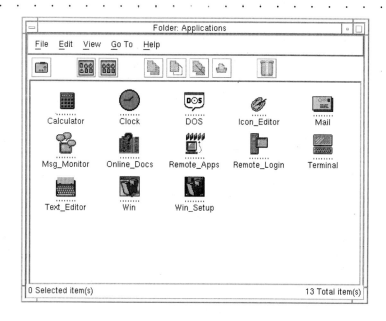

FIGURE 2.5

The Folder: Applications
window

▸ **Remote Applications:** Lets you access applications available to you from remote systems.

▸ **Remote Login:** Lets you log in to a remote system.

▸ **Terminal:** Opens a terminal window for access to the UNIX shell.

▸ **Text Editor:** Opens an editor for editing ASCII text files.

▸ **Win:** Starts a Microsoft Windows session.

▸ **Win Setup:** Allows you to install Microsoft Windows.

The Disks-etc Folder Window

The Disks-etc folder window contains icons representing the removable media drives installed on your system, which may include the following:

▸ **CD-ROM 1:** Provides access to the CD-ROM drive on your system (only present if a CD-ROM player has been installed).

▸ **Cartridge Tape:** Provides access to the cartridge tape drive on your system (only present if a cartridge tape drive has been installed).

▸ **Disk A:** Provides access to the first floppy disk drive on your system.

▸ **Disk B:** Provides access to the second floppy disk drive on your system (only present if you have a second floppy disk drive installed).

Figure 2.6 shows the Folder: Disks-etc window.

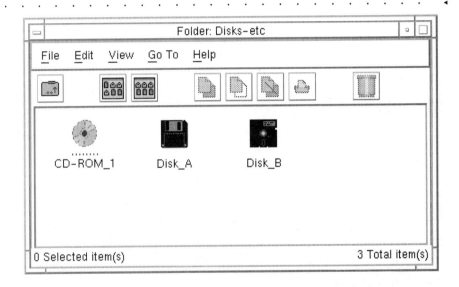

The Folder Map Window

The Folder Map window contains a graphical representation of the file system. It allows you to navigate around the file system by using your mouse to point and click. (More on this later in the chapter.)

The Games Folder Window

The Games folder window contains games you install, as well as the games provided with UnixWare:

- ▸ **Puzzle**: Opens a game in which you arrange the 15 game pieces.

- ▸ **Xtetris**: Opens the UnixWare version of the popular Tetris game.

Figure 2.7 shows the Folder: Games window.

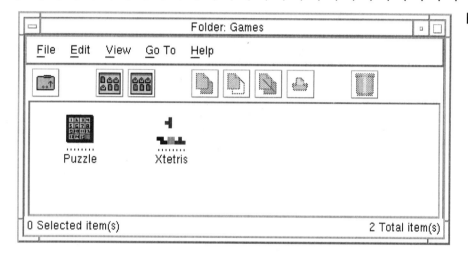

FIGURE 2.7

The Folder: Games window

The Help Desk Window

The Help Desk window, shown in Figure 2.8, contains online information about the UnixWare icons, including those on the Desktop and in other windows.

The Mailbox Folder Window

The Mailbox folder is where your incoming and outgoing mail messages are saved. Until you save or send mail messages, the Mailbox folder window only contains the UUCP Inbox and Mail icons.

FIGURE 2.8

The Help Desk window

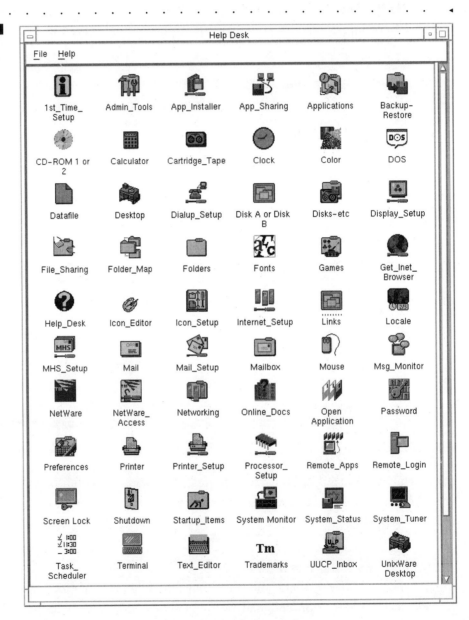

▶ **UUCP Inbox:** The default folder for receiving remote file transfers.

▶ **Mail:** Allows you to read, send, and manage electronic mail from and to users on your system and remote systems.

Figure 2.9 shows the Folder: Mailbox window.

Folder: Mailbox
File   Edit   View   Go To   Help
UUCP_Inbox   Mail
0 Selected item(s)   2 Total item(s)

FIGURE 2.9

The Folder: Mailbox

window

The Preferences Folder Window

The Preferences folder window, shown in Figure 2.10, provides icons that enable you to customize the Desktop:

▶ **Color:** Allows you to change the colors of the Desktop and windows.

▶ **Desktop:** Lets you customize the appearance of the Desktop, such as the spacing between icons and the default folder window size.

▶ **Fonts:** Lets you install and change the fonts used on the Desktop.

▶ **Locale:** Lets you set formats for language, numbers, and dates.

▶ **Mouse:** Lets you define the number of buttons on your mouse.

▶ **Password:** Lets you change your login password.

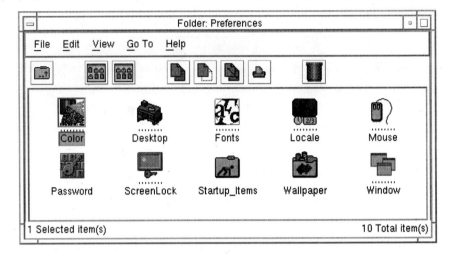

> ▶ **ScreenLock:** Lets you lock the screen after a specified amount of time of inactivity.

> ▶ **Startup Items:** Lets you specify which applications start when the Desktop starts.

> ▶ **Wallpaper:** Lets you select a pattern for the workspace background.

> ▶ **Window:** Lets you set window characteristics for the Desktop.

The windows you can access from the Preferences folder window are shown later in this chapter, in the section about customizing the Desktop.

The Wastebasket Window

The Wastebasket window contains files and folders that you have deleted from your system. Initially, the Wastebasket is empty. Figure 2.11 shows an example of the window with some deleted files.

```
┌─────────────────────────────────────────────────┐
│ [─]              Wastebasket               [□][□] │
├─────────────────────────────────────────────────┤
│  Actions   Edit   View   Help                     │
├─────────────────────────────────────────────────┤
│                                                   │
│      📄          📄          📄                    │
│                                                   │
│    file1:1      file1:2      file2:1               │
│                                                   │
│      📄          📄          📄                    │
│                                                   │
│    file3:1      file4:1      file2:2               │
│                                                   │
├─────────────────────────────────────────────────┤
│  0 Selected item(s)          6 Total item(s)      │
└─────────────────────────────────────────────────┘
```

FIGURE 2.11

The Wastebasket window showing deleted files

USING YOUR MOUSE WITH UNIXWARE

If you learn only one thing about the mouse, learn to press the left mouse button. In UnixWare, this is the Select button. To select an icon or activate a window, point to it with the mouse cursor and press the left mouse button one time. This is called *clicking*. When you select an icon, that icon is highlighted. When you activate a window, its border changes color. You select other items, such as menu options and fields in windows, by clicking on them.

To start an application (open an icon), you also use the left mouse button, but you *double-click* with it, that is, you press the left button twice quickly.

You can move and resize windows and icons by pressing and holding down the left mouse button while you move the mouse. This is called *dragging*.

Another mouse technique you can use on the UnixWare Desktop is called *dragging-and-dropping*. This technique allows you to perform a variety of file operations, such as copying, moving, printing, and deleting files. To drag-and-drop an item, move the mouse cursor to that item, press and hold down the left mouse button, move the mouse (and hence the item) to a new location, and then release the mouse button. Performing specific operations by dragging-and-dropping is described later in this chapter, in the section about working with files.

For both a two- and three-button mouse, the right mouse button is the Menu button. When you click the right mouse button on an icon, the icon's menu is displayed. The Menu button also displays a menu when clicked inside a DOS session.

MANIPULATING WINDOWS AND ICONS

To use the Desktop efficiently, you should know how to work with windows and icons. Two types of icons are associated with the Desktop. The first icon type is found inside windows and represents files, folders, and other windows. The second icon type is displayed when you minimize a window. The window then becomes an icon at the bottom of the Desktop. The iconized window is actually still active (the program is still running) and is referred to as an *active* icon.

Opening and Closing Folders

To open a folder, double-click on its icon. If there are additional folder icons in the folder that are displayed, double-click on those icons to replace the displayed folders with the new folder. For example, when you double-click on the Admin Tools icon in the UnixWare Desktop window, the Admin Tools folder window appears. You can then double-click on the Networking icon in this window to replace the Admin Tools folder window with the Networking folder window.

To close a window, click on File at the top of the window to display the File menu, then click on Exit. Alternatively, you can use the keyboard shortcut, Alt-F4, for closing the active window.

TECHNOTE

We configure the F4 function key along the top of our Gateway 2000programmable keyboards to send Alt-F4 instead of just F4. For us, just pressing F4 closes the active window on the Desktop, which is very handy. And because the Gateway 2000 keyboards have two sets of function keys, we still have a "normal" F4 key on the left side of the keyboard. Programming Gateway 2000 keyboards is discussed later in this chapter.

Moving and Resizing Windows

When you work in a graphical environment (which is a fancy way of saying "with a GUI"), windows can easily clutter the Desktop. Consequently, you will often find yourself moving them out of the way and resizing them so you can get to the window you want.

To move a window, position the mouse cursor in the window's title bar (the bar at the top of the window that contains the window's name), and drag it in the direction you want the window to go. As you drag, the outline of the window moves. When the outline is where you want the window, release the mouse button. The entire window is now displayed in the new location.

Some of your windows may be too large and take up too much of the Desktop. Others may be too small to show enough of what they contain. You can solve either of these problems by resizing windows. You can stretch or shrink a window to any size.

NOTE

Certain windows, such as the Preferences - Color window, cannot be resized. These windows do not have resize corners and borders.

To resize a window by adjusting one of its sides, move the mouse cursor over any part of the window's border, along one of the four sides. The mouse cursor turns into a straight line with an arrow over the sides, top, and bottom. Press and hold down the left mouse button and drag the side inward to shrink the window or outward to enlarge it. Release the mouse button when the window is the size you want. To change a window's size by adjusting two of its sides simultaneously, move the mouse cursor to one of the window's corners. When the cursor changes to a 90-degree angle with an arrow, press and hold down the left mouse button, drag the window to its new size, and then release the button.

Maximizing and Minimizing Windows

Each window on the Desktop has two buttons in the upper-right corner. The one closest to the right edge, which contains a large box, is the Maximize button. The other button, which contains a small box, is the Minimize button.

Use the Maximize button when you want to concentrate on one window. When you click on the Maximize button, the window expands to fill the entire Desktop. Once clicked on, the Maximize button appears pushed in. Clicking on it again returns the window to its original size and location on the Desktop.

Use the Minimize button when you no longer want the window on the Desktop, but don't want to close it completely. Clicking on the Minimize button reduces the window to an active icon. The active icon will appear at the bottom of the Desktop window (unless you change this location through the Window Preferences window, as described later in this chapter). To restore the window to its original size, double-click on its icon.

Working with Active Icons

To open an active icon so that it reappears as a window, double-click on it. Another way to restore an active icon is to single-click on it to display its menu, and then click on Restore.

When you close an active icon, you actually end a running program. Click on the icon to display its menu, and then click on Close.

You can move an active icon to another position on the screen by positioning the mouse cursor over it and dragging (holding down the left mouse button as you move the mouse). As you move the mouse, the outline of the icon moves. Drag the outline to a new location and release the mouse button.

USING THE KEYBOARD WITH THE DESKTOP

The UnixWare Desktop all but requires the use of a mouse. Strictly speaking, you can use the keyboard to select windows, open files, and so on. However, remembering the array of keystroke combinations to accomplish these tasks may be more of a challenge than you are willing to take on.

Even so, there are some useful keystrokes you may want to use. For example, Alt-F3 is a quick way to move the current window to the back (put it behind the other open windows). Table 2.1 lists the keystroke equivalents for various Desktop functions.

FUNCTION	KEY SEQUENCE
General Functions	
Cancel action in progress; close menu or pop-up window	Escape (Esc)
Display Help window	F1
Stop text from scrolling in Terminal window	Ctrl-S
Continue scrolling in Terminal window	Ctrl-P
Undo last action completed	Alt-Backspace
Move to menu bar	F10 ($\rightarrow, \leftarrow, \downarrow, \uparrow$ to move across menu bar)
Display window menu	Shift-Esc
Move current window to back	Alt-F3
Begin window/icon move operation	Alt-F7 ($\rightarrow, \leftarrow, \downarrow, \uparrow$ to drag)
Begin window resize operation	Alt-F8 ($\rightarrow, \leftarrow, \downarrow, \uparrow$ to drag)
Complete window/icon move or resize operation	↵
Select highlighted item	Spacebar or Ctrl-Spacebar
Select/deselect item for item group	Ctrl-&
Close application window or icon	Alt-F4
Display icon menu	Ctrl-M or F4

UnixWare Desktop keyboard functions

T A B L E   2.1

FUNCTION	KEY SEQUENCE
Cursor Movement Functions in Text Editor	
Move cursor up	Up Arrow ($\uparrow$)
Move cursor down	Down Arrow ($\downarrow$)
Move cursor left	Left Arrow ($\leftarrow$)
Move cursor right	Right Arrow ($\rightarrow$)
Move to next field	Tab
Move to previous field	Shift-Tab
Move cursor forward one word in text field	Ctrl-$\rightarrow$
Move cursor backward one word in text field	Ctrl-$\leftarrow$
Move cursor to start of text field or line containing cursor	Home
Move cursor to end of text field or line containing cursor	End
Move cursor to beginning of text window pane	Shift-Ctrl-Home
Move cursor to end of text window pane	Shift-Ctrl-End
Move cursor to beginning of document	Ctrl-Home
Move cursor to end of document	Ctrl-End
Window Navigation Functions	
Move to next window in application	Alt-F6
Move to previous window in application	Shift-Alt-F6
Move to next application	Alt-Esc
Move to previous application	Shift-Alt-Esc
Scrolling Functions	
Scroll up one line	Ctrl-]
Scroll down one line	Ctrl-[

FUNCTION	KEY SEQUENCE
Scroll left one character	Alt-[
Scroll right one character	Alt-]
Move one page up	Page Up
Move one page down	Page Down
Go directly to left edge	Alt-{
Go directly to right edge	Alt-}
Text Editing Functions	
Select character to right of cursor	Shift-→
Select character to left of cursor	Shift-←
Select word to right of cursor	Shift-Ctrl-→
Select word to left of cursor	Shift-Ctrl-←
Select line from cursor to end of line	Shift-End
Select line from cursor to beginning of line	Shift-Home
Select line containing cursor	Ctrl-Alt-←
Move cursor to opposite end of selected text	Alt-Insert
Select all text in document	Ctrl-/
Deselect all text in document	Ctrl-\
Cut selected text to Clipboard	Shift-Delete
Copy selected text to Clipboard	Ctrl-Insert
Paste from Clipboard	Shift-Insert
Delete character to right of cursor	Delete
Delete character to left of cursor	Backspace
Delete word to right of cursor	Shift-Ctrl-Delete

T A B L E   2.1

UnixWare Desktop keyboard functions (continued)

TABLE 2.1
UnixWare Desktop key-
board functions (continued)

FUNCTION	KEY SEQUENCE
Delete word to left of cursor	Shift-Ctrl-Backspace
Delete line from cursor to end of line	Ctrl-Delete
Delete line from cursor to beginning of line	Ctrl-Backspace

As an example of using the keyboard to navigate around the Desktop, follow these steps:

1 · If more than just the Desktop window is open on your screen, press Alt-Esc until the Desktop window is highlighted.

2 · Press F10 to move to the menu bar at the top of the window.

3 · Press → twice to move to the View menu.

4 · Press the spacebar to display the View menu.

5 · Press ↓ until the Format option is highlighted.

6 · Press the spacebar to select Format and display the Format submenu.

7 · Press ↓ to highlight the Short option.

8 · Press the spacebar to select Short. The display in the Desktop window changes, as shown in Figure 2.12.

9 · The first item on the Desktop should be highlighted. Use the arrow keys (←, →, ↑, ↓) to move the highlighting to Admin Tools.

10 · Press Ctrl-M to display the icon menu.

11 · Press the O key to select Open. The Admin Tools folder window opens.

12 · Use the arrow keys to highlight System Status.

13 · Press Ctrl-M to display the icon menu.

14 · Press Esc to close the icon menu.

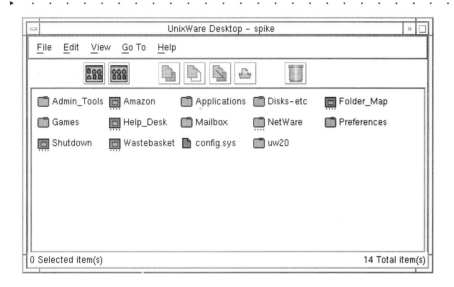

The Desktop in Short format (selected from the View menu)

15 • Press Shift-Esc to display the window menu for the Admin Tools folder window.

16 • Press ↓ to highlight Close.

17 • Press the spacebar to select Close. The Admin Tools folder window closes.

18 • To switch back from the short listing display, repeat steps 1 through 7, but select Icons instead of Short in step 7. If you prefer, you can use the mouse to make the change.

Tailoring the Desktop

All UnixWare users can change their own Desktop characteristics. This allows, for example, your friend to have his offensive purple background for his Desktop, while you maintain a calming green background for yours.

The tailoring you can do to your environment as a user ranges from the way your Desktop looks to the functions of your mouse buttons. Here are just some of the ways you can customize your Desktop:

- ▸ You can change the colors of the background, as well as colors for all basic window elements on the Desktop.

- ▸ You can choose whether active icons line up along the bottom, top, left, or right sides of the Desktop.

- ▸ You can change the spacing between icons in folder windows.

- ▸ You can display the full path of folders at the top of each folder window.

- ▸ You can define the applications working directory to be either your home folder or the Applications folder.

- ▸ You can set up a structure of folders to organize your work in a way that suits you.

You can do most of your customizing from the Preferences windows; however, some changes must be made by editing the .Xdefaults file. Most preferences changes take effect immediately. Changes to the Start Desktop at Login option in the Desktop Preferences window take effect when you restart the Desktop.

 NOTE **The Startup Items icon in the Preferences folder window allows you to define which applications start up automatically when you log in. See Chapter 3 for details.**

COPYING THE ORIGINAL SETTINGS

Most of the Desktop attributes described in the following sections are saved in the .Xdefaults file in your home folder. Before you change any attributes, make a copy of the .Xdefaults file. If the file becomes corrupted for some reason, you will be able to return to the original version.

To make a copy of your `.Xdefaults` file, from the Desktop window, double-click on the Applications icon in the Desktop window, then double-click on Terminal to open a Terminal window. Then type

```
cp $HOME/.Xdefaults $HOME/.Xdefaults.old
```

If you ever need to restore your `.Xdefaults` file later, just copy the old file back to the original name by using the command

```
cp $HOME/.Xdefaults.old $HOME/.Xdefaults
```

Because the `.Xdefaults` file begins with a dot (.), it doesn't appear in your UnixWare Desktop window. However, you can open it by double-clicking on the Text Editor icon in the Applications folder, clicking on File, then Open, and typing `.Xdefaults` in the text box.

NOTE

CHANGING THE VIDEO RESOLUTION AND NUMBER OF COLORS

To take full advantage of the quality of your monitor and video board, you can change the resolution and the number of colors available to Unix-Ware. The resolution is the number of dots on the screen (vertically and horizontally). With higher resolutions, the dots are smaller, so edges of windows and icons look less jagged, and more windows fit on your screen.

The standard VGA mode, which is set when UnixWare is installed, works with any VGA-compatible video board. Standard VGA resolution is 640×480 (640 dots across the screen and 480 dots from top to bottom). Also, the system is set to display 16 colors on your monitor. You can increase the number of colors from 16 to 256 if your video board supports this mode.

You can check and modify your video settings through Display Setup. From the Desktop window, double-click on Admin Tools. In the Admin Tools window, click on the Display Setup icon. The Display Setup window is shown in Figure 2.13.

To change your display to 1280 × 1024 resolution with 256 colors on a 21-inch monitor with a refresh rate of 60Hz (like an old NEC 5D, which

FIGURE 2.13

The Display Setup window showing Standard VGA settings

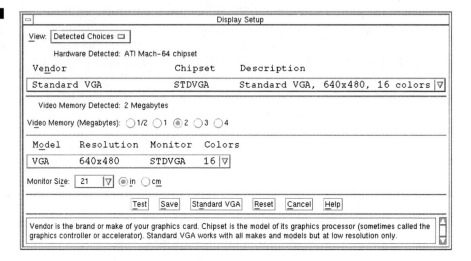

happens to be what we have) for an ATI Graphics Pro Turbo (Mach64) video card, do the following:

1 · Under Vendor, click on the arrow at the far right of the line indicating Standard VGA.

2 · A menu appears displaying a list of possible video controllers, as detected by Display Setup. From the list, click on ATI Technologies, MACH64, ATI GRAPHICS PRO TURBO (MACH64), VLB, PCI.

3 · In the bottom half of the window, click on the arrow on the right side of the line saying ATI_PRO_TURBO, 640 × 480, MULTI-SYNC, 60Hz, 256.

4 · Use the scroll bar at the right of the window that pops up to scroll near the end of the list. Click on ATI_PRO_TURBO, 1280 × 1024, MULTISYNC, 60Hz, 256.

5 · Click on the arrow in the Monitor Size line. In the window that pops up, click on 21.

6 · To make sure that all your selections are valid, click on Test at the bottom of the window. You should see the test pattern at the selected resolution. After a few seconds, the test pattern goes away.

7 · If you don't see the test pattern correctly, change your selections until you successfully see the test pattern.

8 · If all is well, click on Save to save your selections. The next time you log in to the Desktop, the new settings are used. Figure 2.14 shows the Display Setup window set for the ATI video card.

CHANGING SCREEN COLORS

Various colors are assigned to different areas of the Desktop. You can select the colors assigned to each area on the Desktop individually or choose from predefined sets of colors.

To change colors on your Desktop, from the Desktop window double-click on the Preferences icon to display the Preferences window (see Figure 2.10). Next, double-click on the Color icon in the Preferences window. The Preferences - Color window appears, as shown in Figure 2.15.

FIGURE 2.15

The Preferences - Color
window

How you change the colors of your Desktop depends on the number of colors for which your video board is set. If your video board is set to display 16 colors, you can select from several predefined color palettes. However, if your video board is set to display 256 colors, not only do you have more color palettes to choose from, you can also create your own custom palette.

To select a predefined color palette, follow these steps:

I ·   From the list of palettes shown, click on the desired palette. As you select different palettes, the colors of the names for the various Desktop parts change in the bottom part of the window (Active Title Bar, Inactive Title Bar, Main Window, Pop-up Window, Text, Help Link, and Workspace).

2 ·   Click OK when you find a palette you like.

To create a custom palette (256-color or higher systems only), follow these steps:

1 · Copy an existing palette by clicking on a palette and then clicking on Add. In the Add Palettes window, enter a name for your palette in the text box. Click on OK.

2 · Modify your new palette by clicking on the element (Active Title Bar, Inactive Title Bar, Main Window, Pop-up Window, Text, Help Link, or Workspace) that you want to change.

3 · Click on Modify Foreground. The Modify Color window is displayed (see Figure 2.16).

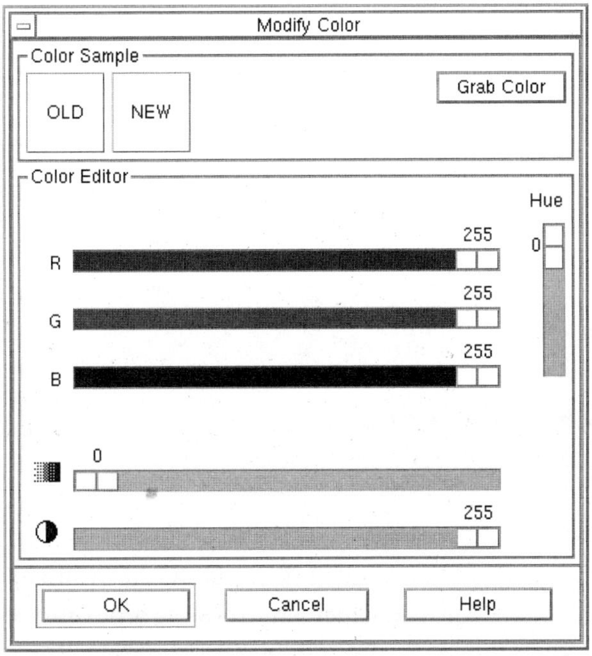

FIGURE 2.16
The Modify Color window for video boards that support 256 colors

4 · In the Modify Color window, use the controls to change the color.

► **Old:** This square shows you the color you're starting with.

> ▸ **New:** This square shows you the new color as you change the controls.

> ▸ **Grab Color:** Use this button to change the cursor to a crosshair. Move the crosshair over any color on the screen to use that color.

> ▸ **R, G, and B:** Use these sliders to change the amount of Red, Green, and Blue, respectively.

> ▸ **Hue:** Use this slider to change the relative amounts of red, green, and blue.

> ▸ **Saturation:** Use this slider (located just above the unlabeled bottom slider) to change the overall intensity of the color.

> ▸ **Value:** Use this slider (the unlabeled bottom slider) to change the overall brightness of the color.

5 · Click on OK when you create a color you like.

6 · Click on Modify Background. Again, the Modify Color window is displayed. Repeat steps 4 and 5 for the background color.

7 · Select another element if desired and repeat steps 3 through 5.

8 · Click on OK in the Preferences - Color window when you're finished making changes.

CHANGING THE WALLPAPER

Instead of using a solid color as the backdrop (wallpaper) of your screen, you can fill the workspace of the screen with a graphic image. The images that come with UnixWare are in xpm format (you can see the .xpm extension on the file names when you double-click on the Wallpaper icon). You can also use GIF files for wallpaper. GIF files are a popular format that is widely available, for example, from public bulletin boards.

Using a graphic image for a backdrop slows down how quickly the Desktop is redrawn when you move or open windows. For faster video performance, we recommend that you leave your background plain.

NOTE

To change the Desktop's backdrop, follow these steps:

1 · From the Desktop window, double-click on the Preferences icon, then double-click on the Wallpaper icon. The Wallpaper folder window appears, as shown in Figure 2.17.

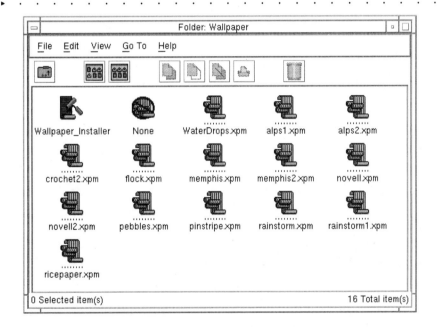

FIGURE 2.17

The Folder: Wallpaper window

The Wallpaper window contains the Wallpaper Installer and wallpaper icons for several graphics.

2 · If you want to display the same wallpaper each time you log in, double-click on the wallpaper icon you want. The workspace fills with copies of the graphic file you selected. Figure 2.18 shows an example of the screen after the `memphis.xpm` file was selected. If you want to remove a selected wallpaper, double-click on the None icon.

The `memphis.xpm` *file as the Desktop wallpaper*

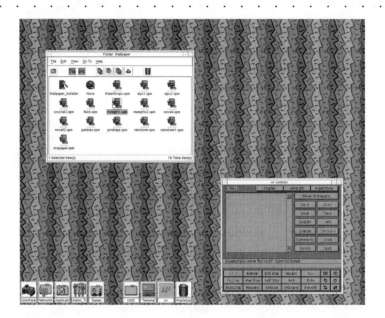

3 · If you want a random wallpaper to be displayed each time you log in, drag-and-drop several of the wallpaper icons onto the Wallpaper Installer. You can view which wallpapers are in the Wallpaper Installer by double-clicking on the Wallpaper Installer.

NOTE **If you want to use GIF files for your wallpaper, open the folder containing the GIF files and drag-and-drop them onto the Wallpaper Installer, as explained in step 3 above, even if you only want one image as your wallpaper. You won't be able to double-click on the GIF icon to see it.**

SETTING UP A SCREEN LOCK

You can set your screen to automatically blank (or display a pattern) and lock when your mouse and keyboard haven't been used for a while. If you use the lock feature, you must type your password before you can resume working.

The screen-saving feature of screen lock is more important for monochrome monitors than it is for color monitors, which don't tend to suffer from burn-in. However, locking the screen and requiring a password can help you maintain the security of your system.

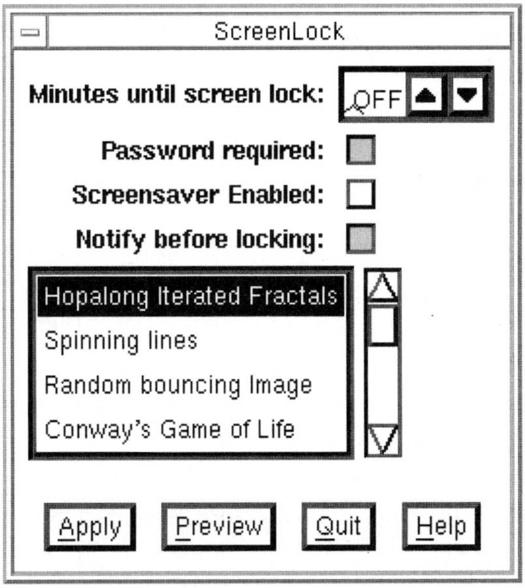
ScreenLock
Minutes until screen lock:
OFF
Password required:
Screensaver Enabled:
Notify before locking:
Hopalong Iterated Fractals
Spinning lines
Random bouncing Image
Conway's Game of Life
Apply
Preview
Quit
Help

FIGURE 2.19
The ScreenLock window

To set up screen locking, double-click on the Preferences icon in the Desktop window and then double-click on the ScreenLock icon. The ScreenLock window appears, as shown in Figure 2.19.

The first field, Minutes until screen lock, shows that the screen lock is off. To turn the screen lock on, click on the up and down arrows next to the word OFF to select an amount of time before the lock goes into effect. You can set the screen to lock after a period of inactivity of 2 to 60 minutes.

The other selections in this window let you specify other screen-locking features:

▶ **Password required:** Click on this box if you want the computer to require you to type your user password before you can resume work after the screen is locked. This feature prevents others from using your idle system. If you don't activate Password required, just press a key or move your mouse to restore your screen.

▶ **Screensaver Enabled:** Click on this box to have the screen blank out completely when the screen locks.

▶ **Notify before locking:** Click on this box if you want to be notified by a chime 30 seconds before your screen blanks (or displays a pattern) and the screen lock takes effect. You can press the Shift key after you hear the chime if you don't want the screen locked.

The scroll box beneath these options contains a list of screensaver patterns. The patterns are moving designs that prevent any part of the monitor from being burned in. Scroll to see the choices and then click on the one you want to try. Next click on the Preview button at the bottom of the window to see what the pattern looks like before you actually set it. Press Enter to return to the ScreenLock window.

After you have made your selections, click on Apply to implement them. The new screen lock settings are active immediately. Click on Quit to close the ScreenLock window.

CHANGING MOUSE PREFERENCES

The Mouse Preferences window lets you change the settings for the number of buttons on your mouse and the time interval for multiple clicks (that is, how long the system will wait between clicks when you double-click on something).

To change mouse settings, double-click on the Preferences icon in the Desktop window, and then double-click on the Mouse icon. The Mouse Preferences window appears, as shown in Figure 2.20.

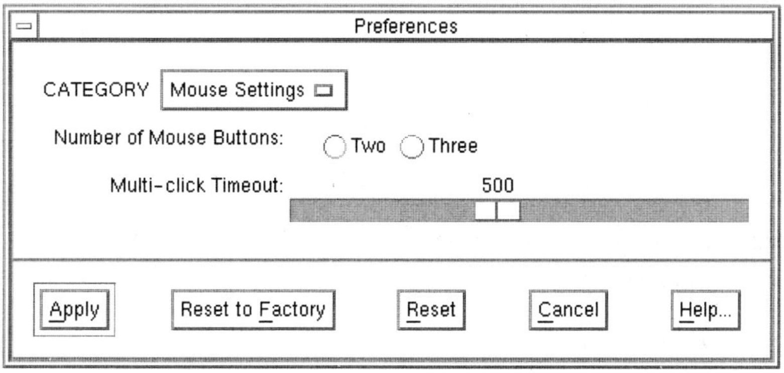

```
┌──────────────────────────────────────────────────────┐
│ ☐                    Preferences                       │
│ ┌────────────────────────────────────────────────────┐│
│ │                                                      ││
│ │  CATEGORY │ Mouse Settings ☐ │                       ││
│ │  Number of Mouse Buttons:    ○ Two  ○ Three          ││
│ │      Multi-click Timeout:          500               ││
│ │                          ▓▓▓▓▓▓▓▓□▓▓▓▓▓▓▓▓▓▓▓▓▓       ││
│ └────────────────────────────────────────────────────┘│
│ ┌────────────────────────────────────────────────────┐│
│ │ │Apply│  │Reset to Factory│  │Reset│  │Cancel│  │Help...│ ││
│ └────────────────────────────────────────────────────┘│
└──────────────────────────────────────────────────────┘
```

FIGURE 2.20

The Mouse Preferences window

You can change the mouse settings as follows:

▶ **Number of Mouse Buttons**: If you change the mouse connected to your system to one with a different number of buttons, you must use Mouse Preferences to let the system know how many buttons your mouse has. Click on Two for a two-button mouse or click on Three for a three-button mouse.

▶ **Multi-click Timeout:** This setting lets you adjust the amount of time the system allows between mouse clicks to accept them as a double-click. For example, if you're a slow clicker and have trouble doing double-clicks, you may want to increase this setting to allow more time between clicks.

After making your selections in the Mouse Preferences window, click on Apply to put them into effect the next time you log in. The Reset to Factory and Reset buttons at the bottom of the Mouse Preferences window set the mouse preferences to those used when you first installed UnixWare and back to those last applied to your Desktop, respectively.

PROGRAMMING YOUR GATEWAY 2000 KEYBOARD

Some keyboards let you program the keys to output several characters with a single keystroke. For example, the Gateway 2000 keyboard has a Progrm Macro key for programming the individual keys on the keyboard. To program a key on a Gateway 2000 keyboard, follow these steps:

1 · Press Ctrl-Progrm Macro. The Program light starts blinking.

 NOTE   **Older Gateway keyboards do not require you to press Ctrl with the Progrm Macro key.**

2 · Press the character key, function key, or key combination (such as Shift-F2) you want to program.

3 · Press the key or keys you want to program into the key or key combination you just pressed.

4 · Press the Progrm Macro key again. The Program light stops blinking.

The Gateway 2000 keyboard has two sets of function keys. You should only program one set of function keys so you always have access to a "clean" set of function keys that can be used as they are defined within a particular application.

By programming the keys on your keyboard, you can customize your system to suit the commands and applications you use most often. For example, you can program the arrow keys to work with your word processor application. If you use WordPerfect, you might want to redefine the keys as follows:

▸ Map the upper-right diagonal arrow to highlight one word forward at a time (first, replace the upper-right diagonal arrow keypress with the Ctrl-Shift-→ keypress).

▸ Map the upper-left diagonal arrow to highlight one word backward (first, replace the upper-left diagonal arrow keypress with the Ctrl-Shift-← keypress).

▸ Map the lower-left diagonal arrow to move one word forward (replace the lower-left diagonal keypress with the Ctrl-→ keypress).

▸ Map the lower-left diagonal arrow to move one word backward (replace the lower-left diagonal keypress with the Ctrl-← keypress).

We also programmed the F12 function key to output `/etc/dfspace`, so we can easily check the space on our disk by pressing the F12 key within a Terminal window.

TECHNOTE

CHANGING THE DESKTOP APPEARANCE

UnixWare allows you to change the overall appearance of the Desktop. Double-click on the Preferences icon in the Desktop window, then double-click on the Desktop icon to display the Desktop Preferences window, as shown in Figure 2.21.

This window offers the following selections:

▸ **Start Desktop at login:** By default, the Desktop starts up when you log in. If you change this setting to No, you see a shell command line prompt when you begin. If you have `/usr/X/bin` in your path, you start the Desktop by typing `desktop` (see Appendix A for details on adding directories to your path). Otherwise, start the Desktop by typing `sh.olsetup`.

▸ **Show Path in Window Titles:** The title bar at the top of a window indicates its name, but not its location in the UnixWare file system. If you change this setting to Yes, the title bar will display the full path name of the window. If you are opening a lot of folders from different parts of the file system, this feature can help you get your bearings.

The Desktop Preferences window

▶ **Folder Window Grid Spacing:** This setting's width and height boxes show the number of pixels occupied by each icon in your folder windows. If the icons in your folders appear too close together, you can increase the values in these boxes to increase the spacing between the icons—just click on the up arrow buttons. Likewise, you can move the icons closer together by decreasing the values (click on the down arrow buttons). Though these settings take effect immediately after you apply them, you won't see the icons change position until you align them by clicking on the Align button on the tool bar.

▶ **Default Folder Window Size:** The first time you open a folder window, two rows and three columns of icons are displayed. The window is sized accordingly. To show more or fewer icons when a folder is opened, change the number of rows or columns that will appear by clicking on the arrow buttons.

▶ **Application's Working Directory:** This option lets you select an application's folder (where it was installed) or your home directory as the working directory for your applications. As a practical matter, you'll probably want neither of these options. We find it much more convenient to have a `work` directory off of our home directory which contains a subdirectory for each project we're working on, for example, `work/utilsref`, `work/uw20`, and `work/nuc`. Though we use many different word processors (after all, we are writers), any particular project usually only uses one, so our files don't get confused between word processors.

▶ **Open Folders in:** Normally, when you open a folder window, it replaces the current folder window. If you prefer to have a completely new window opened instead, select New Window.

▶ **Keep Remote Folders Current:** By default, remote windows (either NetWare windows or windows from another system mounted via NFS) are not automatically updated when files are added or deleted. If you prefer that your remote windows be updated every few seconds, change this setting to Yes. Note that the general performance of your system may be affected if you set this option to Yes.

After you are finished making selections in the Desktop Preferences window, click on Apply. Except for Start Desktop at login, all settings take effect immediately.

CHANGING WINDOW PROPERTIES

The Window Preferences window allows you to change window characteristics, such as input focus, where you click to bring a window from behind to the top of other windows on the Desktop, whether pop-up windows always stay on top of other windows, and where active icons are located on the Desktop.

To make window changes, from the Desktop window, double-click on Preferences, then double-click on the Window icon. The Window Preferences window appears, as shown in Figure 2.22. After making your changes, click on Apply to put your changes into effect.

▶ **To Set Input Area:** Normally, to change the input focus to a different window, you must click somewhere in the window. The clicked-in window now accepts your keyboard input. If you prefer, you can change this setting so that just moving your mouse over a window changes the input focus. Click on Click SELECT (the default) if you want to change input focus by clicking in a window. Click on Move Pointer to simply move the mouse pointer over a window to change input focus.

▶ **To Bring Window to Top:** When you change the input focus to a new window (either by clicking on the window or by moving the mouse pointer over the window—depending on how you have To Set Input Area set), the window doesn't automatically move to the front of the Desktop. By default, you must click on the window's border for it to move to the front. However, by changing this option to Click Anywhere, you can click anywhere in a window to bring it to the front.

▶ **Always Keep Pop-ups in Front:** If you would like to have pop-up windows always stay in front of your other windows, change this option to Yes. By default, this option is set to No and pop-up windows can be covered by other windows. We recommend that you set this to Yes so that a window awaiting input from you is not hidden behind other windows.

▶ **Minimize Windows To:** By default, active icons (icons for minimized windows) appear in a row at the bottom of the window. You can change the location of the icons to the top of the window or have them appear in a column along the left or right edge of the Desktop. For example, if you are using word processing applications, you might want to align icons along the right or left side so that you can see more lines of your documents. To change where active icons are located, click on Top, Bottom, Left, or Right.

▶ **Show Icons:** Normally, active icons are displayed on the Desktop. You may prefer to have them appear in a special window called an Icon box. For example, if you use many different applications, you may want to display the active icons in the Icon box so you can easily move all the active icons around the screen when they get in your way. Click on either In Icon Box or On Workspace (the default).

CHANGING FONTS

You can change the typeface, style, and size of the text that appears in your window headers and in Terminal windows. For example, if you are working on a small screen or at a high resolution, you will probably want to change to a larger size font. In addition, you can install Type I fonts from DOS compatible floppies and use these fonts in any application that makes use of the X Window font mechanism.

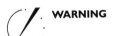 **WARNING**

Not all fonts can be used in window headers and Terminal windows. Also, if you select a font that is too large, the headers may become too big, and very little text will fit in a Terminal window. Therefore, you should select a larger font for a Terminal window only if your screen resolution is 1024 × 769 or higher.

Fonts are set through the Fonts window, in the Preferences folder. To select a different font, follow these steps:

1 · From the Desktop window, double-click on the Preferences folder and then double-click on the Fonts icon. The Fonts window appears, as shown in Figure 2.23.

2 · In the Typeface Family scroll box, click on the name of the font you want to use.

3 · Click on one of the choices for Style. Bold means boldfaced, Oblique is like italics, and Medium is the font in normal style.

4 · Select the type size. If the selected font is a scaleable font, click on the up or down arrow next to the Point Size setting to increase or decrease the point size. If the selected font is a bitmapped font, select the point size from the list shown. The text box at the bottom of the window shows an example of how the text will look with the settings you have selected.

5 · To apply the font, click on Font to display the Font menu. Then click on Apply to Windows to change to this font in window

FIGURE 2.23

The Fonts window

```
┌─────────────────────────────────────────────────────────┐
│ ─    │                  Fonts                    │ □ │ □ │
├─────────────────────────────────────────────────────────┤
│ Actions  Font  View  Help                                 │
├─────────────────────────────────────────────────────────┤
│ Typeface Family              Style           Point Size   │
│ ┌──────────────────┐ ┌──┐ ┌──────────────┐  ┌──┐┌─┐┌─┐  │
│ │ Clean            │ │△ │ │ Bold         │  │12││▲││▼│  │
│ │ Courier          │ │□ │ │ Bold Oblique │  └──┘└─┘└─┘  │
│ │ Fixed            │ │  │ │ Medium       │              │
│ │ Helvetica        │ │▽ │ │ Medium Oblique│              │
│ └──────────────────┘ └──┘ └──────────────┘              │
│ ┌───────────────────────────────────────────────────┐   │
│ │ Type in here                                       │   │
│ │                                                    │   │
│ │                                                    │   │
│ │                                                    │   │
│ │                                                    │   │
│ │                                                    │   │
│ └───────────────────────────────────────────────────┘   │
│ Helvetica  Medium 12 (outline)                            │
└─────────────────────────────────────────────────────────┘
```

headers. Click on Change to "Terminal" Font to apply the font to the text area of a Terminal window.

Only monospaced fonts can be applied to the Terminal window.

NOTE

CHANGING THE LOCALE

You can use the Locale Preferences window to display and change the settings for the display language, input language, numeric format, and date and time formats for the language version of UnixWare you installed. Double-click on the Locale icon in the Preferences folder window to view and change these settings.

Working with Files and Folders

At the heart of the UnixWare system are the files and folders that represent the applications you run, the data you create, and the organization of system information. *Directory* is the traditional UNIX term to refer to a container in the file system. In UnixWare, the term *folder* is used to refer to this container.

When you log in to UnixWare, you are placed into a particular spot in the file system. Unlike DOS, where you begin in the root directory, UnixWare typically drops you into /home/*user* where *user* is replaced by your user name. Figure 2.24 shows an example of the UnixWare file system structure from the perspective of where a user named spike would enter the system.

FIGURE 2.24

The UnixWare file system from spike's home folder

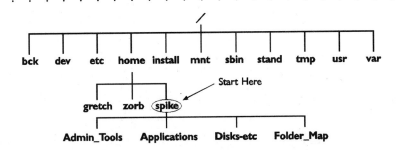

The folders in a UnixWare system form a hierarchy. A folder can contain other folders, which, in turn, can contain more folders. Beginning from your home folder (represented by the UnixWare Desktop), you can move up or down the hierarchy to find the files and applications you need.

OPENING FOLDERS

As you have learned, you can open folders from the Desktop simply by double-clicking on their icons. If that folder contains other folders, you can move down the hierarchy again by double-clicking on one of those folders.

To open a folder that is immediately above the current folder (known as the *parent* folder), from any folder window except the Desktop window, click on the left-most button on the tool bar. The parent folder replaces the current folder in the window.

To open any folder from the Desktop or any other folder window, click on Go To to display the Go To menu, then click on Other Folder. The Go To: Other Folder window is displayed, as shown in Figure 2.25.

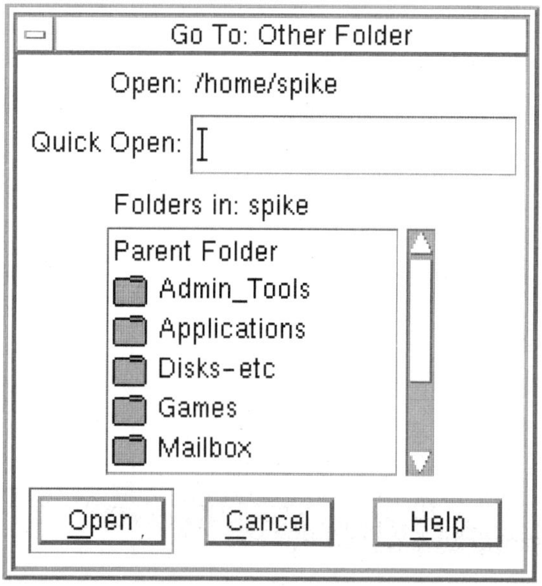

FIGURE 2.25

The Go To: Other Folder
window

You can move up the file system hierarchy by clicking on Parent Folder to move up one level at a time. You can also click on a folder name to move down one level at a time. Alternatively, you can type the full path of the folder you want to open in the Quick Open text box.

The full path consists of the names, beginning at the root folder (/), that lead to the folder you want. For example, `/usr/wp/wpbin` is a full path name. You can also use a relative path name, which is a path in relationship to the current folder. For example, if you want to go to the folder

/home/spike/work/data, and the current folder is /home/spike, you can type work/data to go to that folder. Notice that, unlike in DOS path names, you use a forward slash (/) rather than a backslash (\) to separate the names.

After you locate the folder you want, click on Open to open a window in that folder.

MOVING AMONG FOLDERS

UnixWare provides an easy way to navigate through your file system. From any open folder, click on Go To to display the Go To menu, then click on Folder Map. A folder map, from the current folder to two levels down in the hierarchy, appears. Figure 2.26 shows an example of this display.

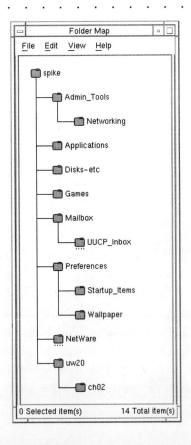

From the Folder Map window, you can move around the file system as follows:

> To open a window in any folder, double-click on that folder's icon.

> To open a folder map beginning at another point in the file system, click on View to display the View menu, then click on Start at Other. When prompted, type another folder name and click on Open.

> To see all the folders below the current point in the file system, click on View, then click on Show all levels.

CREATING A NEW FILE

The simplest representation of a file is a data file containing text. To explore how UnixWare handles files, begin by creating a sample data file. Follow these steps to create the file:

1 · From the Desktop window, click on File to display the File menu, then click on New. The File: New window appears, as shown in Figure 2.27.

2 · Click on the Datafile icon to create a new data file rather than a new folder.

3 · Type `mydata` in the File Name box.

4 · Click on Create. The `mydata` icon appears on your Desktop. (You may have to scroll to see it.)

SETTING FILE ATTRIBUTES AND ACCESS

By default, each new file is given certain attributes, which you can view and change. Among these attributes are the access permissions for users. To see the attributes assigned to your sample data file, click on the `mydata` icon, click on Edit to display the Edit menu, then click on Properties. The Edit: Properties window appears, as shown in Figure 2.28.

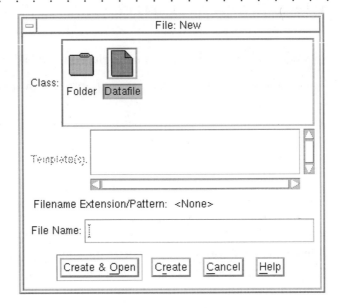

FIGURE 2.27

The File: New window

FIGURE 2.28

The Edit: Properties window

File Names

The file name, `mydata`, appears in the first field. Unlike DOS file names, UNIX file names are case sensitive. This means that you can name one file `mydata` and another `Mydata` without any conflict.

You can make the name as long as you want (the limit is actually several hundred characters), but you should keep it fairly short, because you won't want to type long file names. If you ever expect to use the file with a DOS application, you should try to stick with the eight-character file name, three-character extension DOS file-naming convention.

One restriction on file names is that they cannot contain characters that are special to the UnixWare shell. These are the special characters you shouldn't use in file names:

```
` ' " * & @ # ! ( ) [ ] { } | \ / ? < > ^ % ~
```

File Owner and Group

The owner listed for a file is the user who created it, and the group listed is his or her primary group. After you have created a file, you can assign someone else as its owner or assign it to another group.

Be careful about changing a file's owner. Once you give away owner-ship of a file, you can't get it back unless the other user gives it to you.

 WARNING

Access Permissions

Three types of permissions are associated with a file:

- ▶ **Read:** Lets the user view the contents of a file and copy it to another file.

- ▶ **Write:** Lets the user change the contents of a file or delete the file.

- ▶ **Execute:** Lets the user run the file as an application.

You can assign these permissions to three sets of users: the user who owns the file, the group of users assigned to the file, and all the other users on the system.

Typically, the user who owns the file has Read and Write permissions, while group and other users have just Read permissions, so they can only view or copy the file. To change the default permissions, the owner must click on the Read, Write, and Execute boxes in the Edit: Properties window to turn the permission off or on.

Assigning an Icon Class

When you add a file, an icon class is automatically assigned to the file. The icon class is assigned based on the file's name and, perhaps, the folder in which it is contained. In our example, a Datafile icon class was assigned to `mydata` because the file doesn't have Execute permissions, and its name doesn't match any other criteria. When a file's name ends in `.wp`, the file is represented by a WordPerfectData icon class, indicating that the file was created by WordPerfect. If it ends in `.bat`, the file is assigned to the Merge bat icon class, indicating that it is a merge batch file.

When an icon class is assigned to a file, additional attributes are associated with that file. These attributes relate to how the file is used and represented on the Desktop, but they do not affect how the file is used from a Terminal window.

Here are some attributes assigned to the `mydata` file because it matched the Datafile icon class:

- The Datafile icon is used to represent the file. This icon looks like a dog-eared piece of paper.
- Opening the file starts up the Text Editor with the file loaded into it.
- Printing the file sends the file to the system's default printer.
- Deleting the file removes it from the current folder and places a copy of it temporarily in the Wastebasket.

The icon classes available on your system are defined in the Icon Setup window. By double-clicking on the Icon Setup icon in the Admin Tools window, you can see the icon classes on your system and even add your own classes. See the section on icon setup in Chapter 3 for more information about viewing and adding icon classes.

Other File Attributes

Other attributes associated with a file are not listed in the Edit: Properties window. You can see some of these attributes by using the `ls` command from a Terminal window.

For example, to see the size of the file (in characters), click on the Applications icon in the Desktop window, and then click on the Terminal icon. In the Terminal window, type

```
ls -l mydata
```

You might see something like

```
-rwxr--r-- 1 spike other  257 Feb 28 16:39
  mydata
```

which shows the number of characters in the file is 257.

To see the user and group ID number associated with a file, open a Terminal window and type

```
ls -n mydata
```

The display may show

```
-rwxr--r-- 1 809  1   257 Feb 28 16:39
  mydata
```

which indicates the user ID associated with the file is 809, and the group ID is 1.

FILE TYPES

Along with data files, a UnixWare file system can include other types of files:

- A *link file*, which is one that points to another file. For example, there may be a calendar program on your system called `calendar` that is stored in the `/usr/bin` directory. To make it more convenient to use `calendar`, you can create a link to it in your Applications folder. The application's icon will have dots under it to signify that the file is a link. Because the file is a link, not a copy of calendar, both files point to the same physical copy of the file.

 **TECHNOTE** **There is a difference between hard links and soft links. When you do a drag-and-drop link on the Desktop, or use the Link menu item or Link button on the tool bar, you create a *soft link*. The new file simply points to the name of the original file. A *hard link*, on the other hand, can only be done to a file on the same physical disk partition. For a hard link, both files have the same inode (index) number or file descriptor number, so both files point to the same physical file on the disk.**

- An *executable file*, which is one with Execute permissions. This type of file can be run as a program. It is represented by a generic executable icon, or by the icon for a specific application if its name matches a name defined in the icon class database. For example, an executable file named `xwp` would be represented by a WordPerfect icon, and one named `maker` would be represented by a FrameMaker icon.

- A *device file*, which is actually a device. Devices, such as floppy disks and tapes, are also represented as files in the UnixWare file system. Do not try to access device files directly. The Desktop puts an interface over floppy disk, tape, and CD-ROM devices, so you can read from and write to those media.

MANIPULATING FILES

By using the drag-and-drop method described earlier in this chapter—move the mouse cursor to the file icon, press the left mouse button, drag the icon into an open folder window or on top of a folder icon, and release the mouse button—you can manipulate files in a variety of ways:

▶ To move a file, drag-and-drop it from one folder to another. You will see the message `Move completed`.

▶ To copy a file, drag-and-drop it from one folder to another while pressing the Ctrl key. Drop it on a remote system icon to copy it to another system. You will see the message `Copy completed`.

▶ To print a file, drag-and-drop it on top of a printer icon. The Printer: Request Properties window appears, as shown in Figure 2.29. Make the appropriate selections (such as the type of file you are printing) and click on Apply.

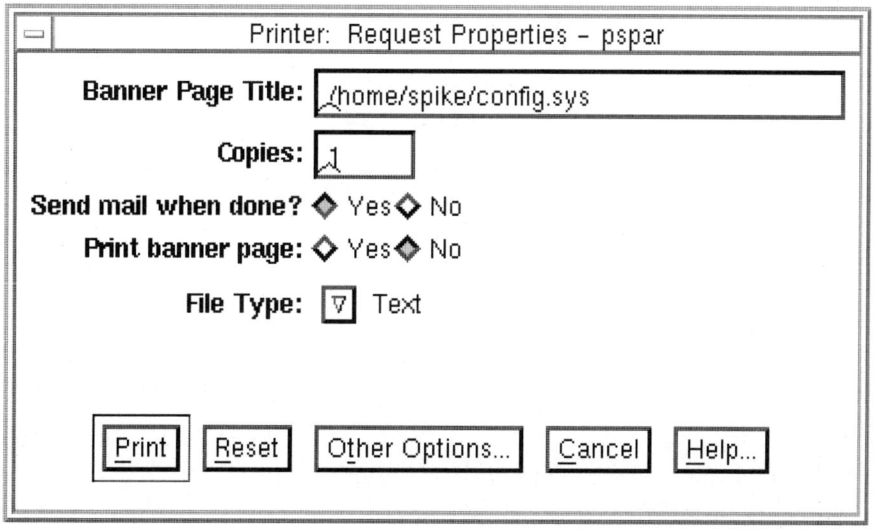

FIGURE 2.29

Printing a file

▶ To delete a file, drag-and-drop it on top of the Wastebasket icon on the Desktop. You will see the message `Delete completed`.

▶ To restore a deleted file, open the Wastebasket (double-click on its icon) and drag-and-drop it to the original folder.

▶ To link a file, drag-and-drop it from one folder to another while pressing the Ctrl and Shift keys. The file icon will have dots beneath it to show the link.

▶ To insert a file into a mail message, drag-and-drop it into an open Mail Sender window.

▶ To insert a file into a file that is being edited, drag-and-drop it into an open Text Editor window.

HOW THE UNIXWARE FILE SYSTEM DIFFERS FROM DOS

The most obvious difference between the UnixWare file system and the DOS file system is that with UnixWare, you are typically less concerned about where files physically reside. In UnixWare, the file system can stretch seamlessly across several hard disks, floppy disks, or even networks.

When you want to use files from a different location in DOS, you must type C:, D:, or another drive letter to get there. UnixWare lets you *mount* another hard disk and connect it to a point in the file system. For example, you could mount a second hard disk on the /usr2 folder (/usr2 is called the *mount point*). To access files on that hard disk, you simply change to the /usr2 folder in the same way you would open a folder on your first hard disk.

Once you understand the concept of expanding the file system by mounting devices, as opposed to requesting a specific device like D:, you can extend that concept to your other work with UnixWare. For example, with NetWare file servers, instead of requesting O: to get to the available servers, simply double-click on the NetWare icon on your Desktop. The NetWare file system is automatically mounted. A folder is displayed showing all NetWare file servers accessible to your system. Then double-click on the NetWare file server you want to access.

Using the File Sharing window, you can advertise and connect folders from remote systems to points in your UnixWare file system. Again, you can simply double-click on the mount point connecting your file system to the remote folder to view the contents of the remote folder. The file system is automatically mounted for you.

 **TECHNOTE**

UnixWare supports the concept of different file system types. For example, by default, UnixWare uses the Veritas file system type (vxfs). Unix-Ware also supports s5 and ufs file system types. Each of these types has different characteristics, such as writing data to disk in different block sizes or supporting different file name lengths. You can access other file system types in UnixWare in the same way that you access the default type.

Other than the way you access folders, files, and devices, the differences between the DOS and UnixWare file systems are minor. UnixWare gives you more flexibility in naming folders and files. Rather than being limited to eight characters for the file name and three characters for its extension, as in DOS, your names can be as long as you want. However, as mentioned previously, if you expect to use a UnixWare folder or file with DOS applications, you should follow the DOS naming convention. DOS Merge deals with longer UnixWare file names by truncating them in strange ways.

Two other differences are path name specification and case sensitivity. UnixWare folder names are separated by slashes (/) rather than backslashes (\) as they are in DOS. And, unlike DOS, UnixWare distinguishes between upper- and lowercase letters. For example, in UnixWare, `myfile` and `MYFILE` represent two different files. In DOS, these file names represent the same file.

In this chapter, you've learned how to use the UnixWare Desktop graphical interface. The interface consists of windows, icons, and menus. By pointing and clicking with a mouse, you select windows, icons, and menu items on the Desktop and initiate actions. You can also use the keyboard to navigate around the Desktop.

Through the various Preferences windows, you can change Desktop characteristics, such as grid spacing and default folder size, Desktop colors, and the Desktop wallpaper. You can also lock your screen while you're away from your computer.

You've also learned that the information you put into UnixWare is stored in a file system consisting of files and folders. By using the Desktop menus and drag-and-drop techniques, you can perform functions such as moving and copying your files and folders.

## CHAPTER 3

Running UnixWare
and UNIX Applications

UNIX by itself is not very useful. UNIX is like a stereo system, which is useless if you have no music to play on it. Think of software applications as the music of UNIX.

In the past several decades, thousands of UNIX applications have been developed. Those applications range from personal productivity tools you might use at home to financial applications that are the lifeblood of major corporations.

If you are coming from a DOS or Windows environment, chances are that many of the applications you are using are not yet available in UNIX versions. The UnixWare version of UNIX System V Release 4.2 deals with this by allowing you to run most DOS applications in a special DOS window. By installing Windows Merge, you can even run most Microsoft Windows applications. (Chapter 6 describes how to run your favorite DOS and Windows applications in UnixWare.) This chapter is about finding, installing, and running UnixWare applications, as well as applications designed for other versions of the UNIX system.

The *Yes UnixWare Resource Guide* is a large listing (over one thousand pages) of applications and hardware that have been tested with UnixWare. The hardware sections include complete systems as well as accessories, adapters, backup devices, and storage devices.

NOTE   **As of this writing, Novell has not completed updating the *Yes Unix-Ware Resource Guide* for Release 2 of UnixWare. However, by the time you purchase this book, the Resource Guide will be available.**

Novell also provides a Fax Back system to provide you with the latest information on applications and hardware. You can access this system by calling (800) 414-LABS (in the United States or Canada) or (801) 429-2776 (from other countries).

When shopping for products, look for vendors that participate in the Novell Yes Partners' Program (see Figure 3.1 for sample logo).

FIGURE 3.1
Yes, It Runs with
UnixWare logo

Novell describes the two levels of this program as follows:

Yes, It Runs with UnixWare logo tells you that the product has been verified by the vendor to work with UnixWare. While Novell will try and assist customers in using products that bear this logo, Novell makes no warranties in regards to these products.

Yes Tested and Approved is earned by products that have passed rigorous testing by Novell Labs. Novell engineers work closely with the vendor to ensure its products meet Novell's strict quality standards. Novell publishes bulletins containing test results on each "Tested and Approved" product. These bulletins are available through your Novell Authorized Reseller, NetWire (to establish an account on NetWire, contact CompuServe at 800-524-3388, ext 200), the Network Support Encyclopedia (NSEPro), or by calling the Novell Product information directly at 801-429-5588 or 1-800-NETWARE.

Using UnixWare Applications Today

Prepackaged applications are available for UNIX, but the huge proliferation of these packages has been stymied by several factors:

▶ While DOS runs on Intel-based personal computers, the UNIX system runs on many different processors and comes in slightly different "flavors." Until now, no single UNIX system platform sold enough copies to warrant a flood of mass-market applications.

▶ The "install-and-run" mentality of DOS or Macintosh applications wasn't part of the UNIX culture until recently. An understanding of the UNIX system was often needed to install and configure an application.

▶ The UNIX system has been expensive. Both the cost of the operating system itself and the cost of the hardware has been beyond the means of most users and small businesses.

Traditionally, the UNIX system has had its greatest success in scientific and corporate environments, where applications are built by MIS professionals for use within their own companies. These users demanded advanced tools for creating applications. They required powerful features that would allow groups of computers to be networked together. On the whole, MIS professionals weren't as concerned about ease of use.

With the simplified UNIX SVR4.2 graphical user interface and a shift toward mass-market thinking in sales and distribution of UnixWare, the powerful features of UNIX applications are now accessible to users who are growing out of their DOS-based systems. With UnixWare, running applications can take on new dimensions. You can run UNIX, DOS, and Windows applications from the same computer at the same time. Using networking, you can store an application on a remote system, run it on another system, and use it from a display on still another system.

If UnixWare becomes the standard flavor of the UNIX system, application developers can make assumptions about the operating system so less configuration is needed to get their applications installed and running. Today, however, we are in a transition period. It is not obvious how to find prepackaged applications or how to write your own applications. After you find the UNIX application you want, you may discover that it is not tailored specifically for UnixWare; even though it is available for UNIX on the PC, it may have been developed for SCO (pronounced *scoh*) UNIX, Solaris, or UNIX SVR4. The application will probably run, but you may need to follow special procedures to install it.

FINDING UNIX APPLICATIONS

All major classes of personal productivity applications are available for UNIX, including spreadsheets, word processing, and database programs. However, if you go into your local computer software store today and say, "Show me where you keep your UNIX applications," you'll probably be met with a blank stare.

Although UNIX applications are not as easy to find as DOS applications, it doesn't mean they don't exist. More applications are being created every day to run natively on PC versions of UNIX in general and UnixWare in particular. Applications created for UNIX SVR4.2 and earlier releases of the UNIX system on Intel-based personal computers will also run on UnixWare.

Any application created specifically for UnixWare or UNIX SVR4.2 will probably install easily and run without any problems on UNIX SVR4.2 systems (for a given hardware architecture, such as Intel-based PCs). Sometimes these applications are listed as *iABI Compliant*. This means that an application meets the standards of the UNIX System V Application Binary Interface for Intel Processors. Any UNIX system, such as UnixWare, that complies with the iABI should be able to run the application without modification. The Application Binary Interface for Intel, as well as other processors, is maintained by Novell's UNIX System Laboratories.

Some UNIX system applications that were created for other, earlier versions of the UNIX system on Intel processors will also run on your UNIX SVR4.2 system. These applications include AT&T UNIX SVR3.2, Santa Cruz Operation (SCO) UNIX and XENIX, Interactive Systems Corporation (ISC) UNIX, and of course UnixWare applications. You can also run most DOS and Windows applications in UnixWare.

For information on applications supported by UnixWare, contact the USG Supported Applications hotline at (800) 722-UNIX.

NOTE

Interactive Systems Corporation (ISC) was bought by Sun Microsystems. Its shrink-wrapped UNIX system for Intel platforms is sold under the business unit called SunSoft and a product name of Solaris.

NOTE

If you have a choice, choose applications designed specifically for Unix-Ware or UNIX SVR4.2. There are several reasons why you may be happier with these applications:

▶ You may not be able to install pre-SVR4.2 UNIX applications using the Application Installer window. Although there are other ways to install applications, the Application Installer window makes the task easier. It also makes it easier to place the installed application's executable files in a convenient folder.

▶ Pre-SVR4.2 UNIX applications may not run without some special tweaking. Some pre-SVR4.2 systems incorporate subtle differences that make the applications developed for those systems incompatible with other systems.

▶ DOS and Windows applications that require protected mode do not run in UNIX SVR4.2. Also, DOS applications don't let you use some UNIX file system features (such as long file names) and don't take advantage of advanced UNIX features (such as the X Window graphical interface or UNIX networking).

Despite the previous warnings, remember that most UNIX system (for Intel processors), DOS, and Windows applications run on UNIX SVR4.2 and UnixWare in particular. But before you purchase any applications for your UNIX system, be sure that you will be able to run it; check with either the retailer or the manufacturer to make sure the application has been tested with UnixWare.

USING SCO UNIX APPLICATIONS

The first widely used PC-based version of the UNIX system was produced by the Santa Cruz Operation (SCO). SCO UNIX is based on an older version of UNIX System V: Release 3.2. Rather than move to UNIX System V Release 4, SCO seems to have decided to rely on its own value-added technology and strong support for a variety of hardware devices to move into the future. Many

UNIX System V Release 4 features are not supported in SCO UNIX, though they do offer point releases to include some Release 4 features.

SCO took advantage of the UNIX system's multiuser, multiprocessing capabilities and offered configurations that ran on relatively low-cost hardware. A popular SCO configuration consists of a single server machine with multiple character-based (dumb) terminals. A small office could run off of a single system or connect to other systems using UNIX system networking features. Because of the common use of dumb terminals, many of the most popular early SCO applications were character-based.

People who want to use the computer more like a workstation can purchase SCO's Open Desktop (ODT), a graphical user interface you can use from the console. Applications like FrameMaker and CorelDRAW are available for SCO ODT.

At first, SCO applications could not be used on other UNIX system platforms. SCO applications were dependent on special SCO value-added features that made it impossible to install and run the applications on any other UNIX operating systems. For example, SCO added the `custom` command for installing applications. Without that command, you couldn't install the application. SCO applications also had their own files for setting terminal and keyboard characteristics (`termcap` and `mapstrings`, respectively).

In UNIX System V/386, version 4, the special SCO features needed to support key applications were folded back into the base UNIX operating system at AT&T. These features are now included in the UnixWare system today, so most SCO applications will run on UnixWare. Your best bet for getting a SCO application to run on your UnixWare system is to purchase one that has already been tested in UnixWare. You can also contact the individual application vendor and ask if it runs on UnixWare. Special considerations for installing and running SCO applications are described in this chapter.

RUNNING APPLICATIONS WITH UNIX

The first time a UNIX user tries Macintosh or Windows, the user is usually surprised that double-clicking on a data file can start up an application.

Traditional UNIX system users are used to the separation between data files and applications. In the UNIX way of thinking, a data file is something that you can use with many different applications. You can edit a text file with the vi editor, change its contents with sed or sort programs, then format and print it with troff and lp programs. Every UNIX system user was a programmer of sorts, welding together programs with sets of pipes (|) and arrows (><) that would send the data files they fed into it to the right printer, file, or network.

UNIX novices would depend on the local guru to create *shell scripts* for them. For example, the guru might create a script called printit, which contained a set of commands and options that would format the type of document the user produced, then send it to the local printer.

With UNIX SVR4.2 and its graphical user interface, the model has changed. You can get applications that take you from one end of a task to another without patching together a set of commands. With document processing software, such as FrameMaker or WordPerfect, you can write a document, view the page layout, and print the document, all within a single application. To start the application, you simply double-click on the application's icon.

Another change is that data files can now be associated with an application. You can double-click on a data file icon and the text editor will start up with the data file on the screen ready to be edited. By using a data file icon's pull-down menu, you can print or delete the data file.

Because of these changes, casual computer users can now use the UNIX system. You can run applications and accomplish tasks without much understanding of how the system works.

Installing UNIX Applications

The easiest way to install UNIX applications is through the Application Installer window. It allows you to install from various types of media, store executable files in any folders you choose, and display information about any installed or yet-to-be-installed applications. Application Installer also supports installations over the network and from the file system.

Application Installer takes into account that UNIX applications can be packaged in different formats. It should work with applications in `pkgadd`, `installpkg`, or `custom` format. The `pkgadd` format is used by applications in UNIX SVR3.2 and later releases. The `installpkg` format was used for systems prior to SVR3.2. Most SCO applications use the `custom` format.

Unfortunately, not all UNIX applications have been updated to use the Application Installer method. If you have problems installing an application, review the application's compatibility and requirements, as described in the next section. Then read the section about solving installation problems later in this chapter.

You cannot install Windows or DOS applications through the Application Installer window. See Chapter 6 for information about installing and running DOS applications.

WARNING

PREPARING FOR INSTALLATION

Before you try to install an application on UnixWare, you should do the following:

▶ Check application compatibility. Contact the Novell hotline for a current list of applications that run on UnixWare. If the application is not included in that list, check with the vendor or manufacturer to make sure it has been tested on a UnixWare system.

See the beginning of this chapter for information on contacting Novell about UnixWare applications and hardware compatibility.

NOTE

▶ Check for any special procedures required. The installation guide that comes with the application usually will tell you if you need to do anything special before you install the application. For example, it might let you know that you need to set environment variables before installing the product. This chapter notes some of the special procedures that may be required for installing applications.

NOTE **See Chapter 8 for more information about environment variables.**

▸ Check the application's system requirements. You may need to prepare the system before you can install an application. For example, a remote mail application may not work unless a networking portion of the UNIX system, such as TCP/IP, is already installed. Some applications require a minimum amount of RAM. Check for hardware requirements; for example, applications that do a lot of calculations may require a math-coprocessor chip. Others may require a communications or video board or even a sound (multimedia) board.

▸ Make sure you can install from the medium the application comes on. Applications can come on floppy disks, cartridge tapes, or CD-ROMs. As long as you have the right size floppy disk drive (3.5- or 5.25-inch), you should be able to install any floppy disks. However, UnixWare supports only certain cartridge tape and CD-ROM drives. A CD-ROM is the most convenient form because it holds huge amounts of data. All of UnixWare can be installed from a single CD-ROM. Installing from a cartridge tape is not as fast as installing from a CD-ROM, but it is much quicker than installing from floppy disks. Floppy disks are the least convenient, but they are the most common media.

USING APPLICATION INSTALLER

To install an application using the Application Installer window, follow these steps:

1 · Insert the installation medium into the appropriate drive. Alternatively, you can install an application from the file system if it is in `pkgadd`, `installpkg`, or `custom` format and stored in an accessible folder.

2 · From the Desktop window, double-click on the Admin Tools icon.

3 · In the Admin Tools folder window, double-click on the App Installer icon. The system displays the Application Installer window, with information shown in two sections. The top section is for showing applications available from a particular medium (CD-ROM, floppy, cartridge tape, etc.). The bottom section shows software packages that are currently installed on the hard disk. An example of the Application Installer window is shown in Figure 3.2.

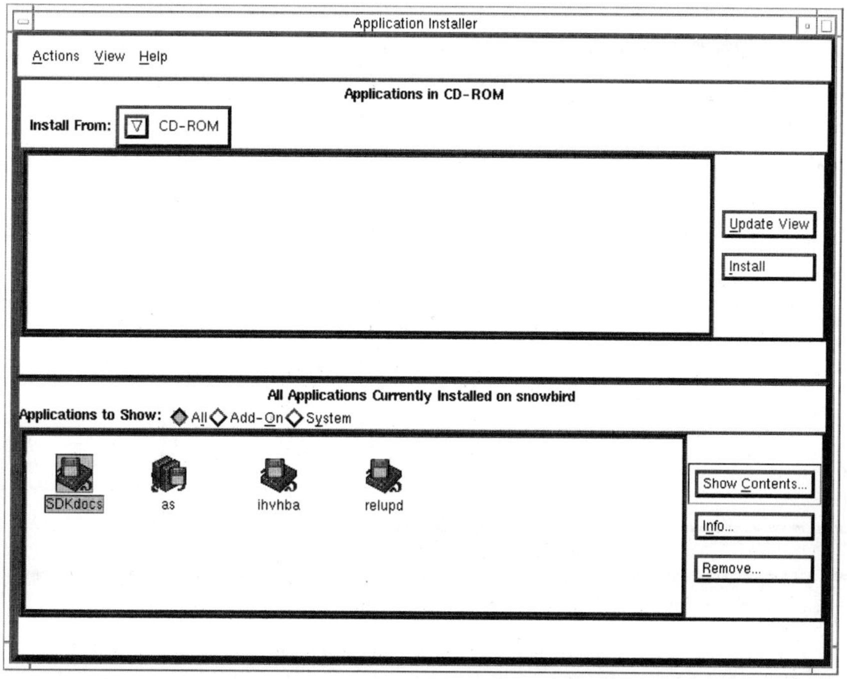

FIGURE 3.2

The Application Installer window showing installed applications

4 · Click on the button next to Install From, then click on the name of the medium you want to install from (CD-ROM, Network, Other, etc.). If you are installing from the file system, select Other as the medium. UnixWare tries to determine whether the application is in pkgadd, installpkg, or custom format. If it is in one of these formats, icons representing the applications that are contained on the medium appear in the top portion of the window. Figure 3.3 is an example of an Application Installer window containing icons that represent software packages on a CD-ROM (in this case, the UnixWare Software Development Kit).

FIGURE 3.3

The Application Installer window showing installable packages on CD-ROM

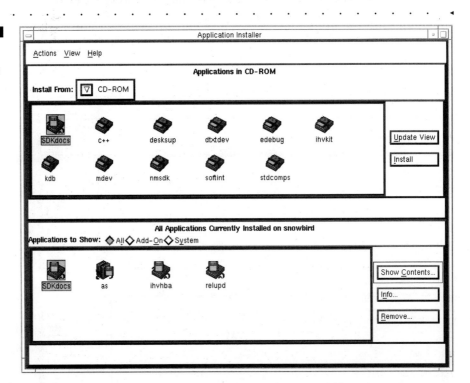

NOTE   If UnixWare can't determine the format of the package, you will see a message that the package is in an unknown format. You probably will need to install the application from the command line, following the instructions in the application's installation guide.

5 · Click on the icon of the application you want to install. (To select several icons, draw a box around the icons you want by pressing the left mouse button within the box, dragging it across the icons you want, and then releasing the mouse button. The icons will be selected.)

6 · Then click on Install. The Add Applications window appears.

7 · Answer any questions that are specific to the application. For example, you may be asked where you want to install the application, what the application's license number is, and if you want to install optional software (such as font packages and printer drivers).

When the installation is completed, you will see a message informing you that the application has been installed successfully. Consult the application's installation guide to see if you must run special commands to use the application. You may need to set up a user environment or configure a printer, for example.

After the application is completely installed, you can place it in a folder. If the application installation fails, read the section about handling installation problems later in this chapter.

Placing an Application in a Convenient Folder

Unlike DOS applications, which are typically installed in a single folder, parts of UNIX applications may be scattered throughout the file system. An application may put its executable files in `/usr/bin`, its libraries in `/usr/lib`, and a startup script in `/etc/rc2.d`.

By moving your application's file into a convenient folder, such as your Applications folder, you can make it easy to start an application, regardless of where its files are installed. The executable file that you place in another folder is not a copy. It is a link to the application in another part of the file system. This allows many users to link to the same executable file without taking up extra disk space on the system.

To place an application's executable file in your personal Applications folder, double-click on its icon in the bottom portion of the Application Installer window. If you double-click on a software package that contains other software packages, you will see another set of software applications. (For example, the UnixWare Application Server software contains a whole bunch of application packages). Double-click on the application package you want.

You see the Application Installer window for the application, which contains the icons that you can install on the Desktop. An example of applications from the Desktop package is shown in Figure 3.4.

F I G U R E   3.4

*The Application Installer:
desktop window showing
installable icons*

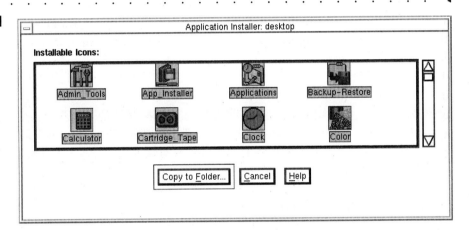

Click on the icon for the executable file, then click on the Copy to Folder button at the bottom of the window. A window appears, giving you options of which users' application folders you should install the icon into. The options are Self (your own), Current desktop users (any user currently configured to use the GUI), Current and future desktop users (same as the previous entry, plus as new desktop users are added, they get this application as well), Specific Users (displays a list of current users you can select).

Once you have made the selection, click on Apply (to copy the icon without closing the window) or OK (to copy the icon and close the window). The executable file is now installed in the Applications folder of whatever user you selected. You can run the application by double-clicking on its icon in the Applications folder window.

The Application Installer: desktop window includes icons for the Unix-Ware Desktop executable files. These files are already installed in convenient folders, such as the Applications or Games folders for each user. If you delete any of these basic icons by mistake, you can reinstall them through the Application Installer window, using the procedure just described.

NOTE

The application's executable file can go in any folder, not just into your Applications folder. You can move an executable file from any folder to any other folder using the drag-and-drop linking method. To link an executable file to another folder, open the folder that contains the file and the folder where you want to put that file. Then hold down the Ctrl and Alt keys as you drag-and-drop the executable file into its new folder (put the mouse cursor on the executable file's icon, hold down the left mouse button, drag the icon to the other window, and then release the mouse button). The executable file's icon appears in the other folder's window with dots beneath it to show that it is a link.

INSTALLING SCO APPLICATIONS

You may have problems installing a SCO application with the Desktop's Application Installer window for several reasons. The most common reason is that an environment variable required by the application has not been set. An environment variable may be needed to tell the application where to search for the files it needs to complete the installation or the type of operating system you are using. Check the application's installation instructions to see which environment variables it needs.

Some applications won't install because they were created for UNIX System V Release 3.2. The installation script for a particular application may actually check that the system is 3.2 and fail to install if it is not. To get around this problem, you can temporarily change the release number by setting the SCOMPAT variable before you install the application. To change this variable, open a Terminal window (open the Accessories folder window and click on the Terminal icon) and type

```
SCOMPAT=3.2;export SCOMPAT
```

If you changed your shell from the standard sh to csh, set the SCOMPAT variable with the command

```
setenv SCOMPAT 3.2
```

NOTE **You can also choose SCOMPAT from the Application Installer window by selecting Actions, then Option. The default version is set at 3.2 for the SCOCOMPAT Environment Variable. You can change the default version to match the version on the SCO application that you are installing.**

Another reason that a SCO application installation may fail is that its maximum file size is too big for the UNIX system as delivered. For example, to prevent runaway processes or a selfish user from creating unreasonably huge files that would grab all the storage from the hard disk, UnixWare sets a maximum for the size a file can grow to on the system. This value is called the ulimit. Any writes to a file beyond the ulimit will fail. UnixWare 2 increased its ulimit so it is large enough to handle any reasonable file size.

NOTE **The default ulimit size in UnixWare 2 allows a 2GB file size, as opposed to the 16MB default ulimit in UnixWare 1.1.**

Some SCO applications take advantage of the high ulimit value SCO uses on its system. Instead of installing files one at a time, they dump one big archive file onto the system and proceed to split it up into individual files. If you think an application installation is failing because the ulimit has been reached, log in to UnixWare as the root user and enter the command

```
ulimit 50000
```

This will increase the ulimit value to 50,000 blocks, which should allow more than enough room for the archive file.

If there doesn't seem to be enough disk space for the application, check the space in the /tmp directory (use the /etc/dfspace command). In UnixWare 2, /tmp is a separate memory file system, or *memfs*, with limited space. You may need to add space to the /tmp file system.

If you can't install a SCO application from the Application Installer window, try installing it by using its installation command. Check the application's installation instructions for the proper command. Then log in as the root user and enter the command.

INSTALLING APPLICATIONS ON NETWARE FILE SERVERS

UNIX applications tend to be hard disk space hogs. NetWare file servers are intended to store large amounts of data. It seems like a match made in heaven. Before you install UnixWare applications on a NetWare file server, however, the server must be configured to allow UNIX system name space. Configuring UNIX name space on a NetWare server is described in Chapter 4.

NOTE

The DOS name space is better behaved than the UNIX name space on NetWare file servers. If you install applications for UnixWare in the DOS name space (DOS and Windows applications only, please) you should have no problems. The only problem we've encountered is server names that exceed the 8.3 characters allowed for DOS file names. Long server names do not work if you try to use them to define a path for an application. One way around this is to make a symbolic link to the new volume. Name the link in 8.3 format.

Problems that come from installing UNIX applications on NetWare file servers usually stem from the way file systems are handled on the two systems. The application's installation script may check the NetWare file server for some "UNIX-kind-of-thing," not find it, and fail even though everything is fine. Here are some examples:

▶ An application script checks the place where it's told to install the files (on the NetWare file server) to see if it has enough inodes to support the installation. *Inodes* are the way the UNIX system identifies the physical location of each file. UNIX allocates lots of inodes. The UNIX name space on NetWare that comes with UnixWare 1.1, however, only counts inodes up to the maximum amount that have already been created on the system. To get around the problem of the UNIX name space on NetWare appearing not to have enough inodes, you can create and delete tons of files. The inode count on the NetWare file server will increase, and the installation script will work.

▶ If you "install" an application from a NetWare file server to one of your local folders (such as your Applications folder), it creates a link to the remote application. When your UnixWare system starts up, it checks that the files pointed to by the link exist. As a result, a NetWare authentication window may pop up on your login window before you have logged in. This isn't really a problem, it just looks strange.

 NOTE **Chapter 4 describes other strange authentication behavior you may encounter.**

▶ Permissions can be a problem. For example, UnixWare Read, Write, and Execute permissions don't map exactly into NetWare Read, Write, Create, Erase, Modify, File Scan, and Access Control access rights. Likewise, the UnixWare root user is not exactly the same as the NetWare Supervisor.

 NOTE **See Chapter 4 for information about handling NetWare and Unix-Ware permission conflicts.**

INSTALLING APPLICATIONS ON REMOTE UNIX SYSTEMS

You can install an application from your machine and have it stored on a remote system. To do this, first mount a remote file system, as described in Chapter 5. Then designate that file system as the install directory. The advantage of this approach is that you can put an application on one system and use the resources of other systems with it. For example, you may have a CD-ROM on one system and another system that has a lot of disk space but does not have a CD-ROM. With this method, you can install on the second system and use the software from there.

Any time the target file of a symbolic link disappears, the symbolically linked file is still in the directory, but its icon disappears from the folder window. This is most likely to happen when the files are shared across a network.

TECHNOTE

If you install (link) an executable file from the remote directory into a local folder, and the remote machine goes down (or the remote file system is no longer connected for some other reason), your executable file icon will disappear. Don't despair. It will reappear when the remote file system returns.

SOLVING INSTALLATION PROBLEMS

Some applications pose a challenge to install, despite your best efforts. Here are some of the more common problems that can occur:

- ▶ Running out of disk space. UNIX applications tend to take up more hard disk space than similar DOS applications. To check the amount of disk space you have available, either display the System Status window (accessible from the Admin Tools folder window) or type /etc/dfspace in a Terminal window. You might also run short of disk space during installation when you have your UNIX file system split across separate disk slices. Even if the disk has enough space, you can still run out of space in the root (/) slice, which can cause the installation to fail.

▶ Installing from the wrong command line or without the necessary permissions. An application that installs from the shell command line may not just install from any old shell. If an application directs messages to the console, you may not see them if you are using a Terminal window or a remote terminal.

NOTE **You can use the Message Monitor in the Applications window to view messages that are directed to the console. This allows you to install applications from a Terminal window or a remote terminal.**

It's usually safest to log in as the root user and install your application from the console. Usually, to install from the command line, you must be logged in as the root user. If you aren't logged in as root, installation may fail if the application needs to put files in restricted directories.

▶ Using different file system types. By default, UnixWare uses the **vxfs** file system type. Assigning a different file system type to part of your file system when you installed UnixWare can cause an application installation to fail. For example, if an application uses long file names and you installed on an **s5** file system type (which limits file names to 14 characters), some files may not be written to disk.

▶ Missing UnixWare software. Because it is designed to work on smaller systems, the UnixWare Personal Edition excludes some UNIX system commands and files. Some installation programs look for these missing commands and files. By installing the Software Development Kit (SDK), you get many of the commands and files the applications are looking for.

▶ Using the wrong command for the application's format. Several different UNIX commands have been developed for packaging software for installation. Each stores data in a different format. The most popular commands for installing applications are `pkgadd`, `installpkg`, `cpio`, `tar`, and `custom`. If your application was copied onto the installation media in the format intended for one of these commands, you must use the appropriate command to install it. Applications sometimes use a command, such as `tar`, that is available on all UNIX systems to read the application onto the system.

We've been told that the Application Installer window understands `tar` format, but we've never been able to get it to work.

NOTE

- ▶ Using a different operating system type. If the application gives you a choice of operating systems to select from, choose one of the following (listed in order of preference): UnixWare, SVR4.2, SVR4, SVR3.2, or SCO UNIX.

- ▶ Using different device names. Because different UNIX systems sometimes use different device names, hard-coded device names may fail to find the installation media. For example, for the cartridge tape, you can use `/dev/rmt/c0s0`; for floppy disks, use `/dev/rdsk/f03ht` or `/dev/rdsk/f13ht` for the first or second drive, respectively, if both drives are 3.5-inch drives. You may need to actually change the hard-coded device names in the installation scripts.

- ▶ The application's library uses outdated functions. Some applications use statically linked libraries that are compiled into their executable files. These libraries may include outdated functions, so the files fail to execute. For example, some SCO applications use old `stat` functions that can't stat files with inodes above about 65000. UnixWare allows inodes above that number. As a result, when you try to run the SCO application, you get a message saying that the application can't find itself.

Most applications come with an installation script that you can edit manually. If your problem is caused by something in the installation script, such as hard-coded disk space requirements, missing software commands, or hard-coded device names, you may be able to correct them by modifying the script.

Setting Up Your Applications to Run

On the UnixWare Desktop, your installed applications are represented by icons. Using icon classes, you can define what the application's icon looks like and how it behaves when you double-click on its icon. The icon class governs the following attributes:

- ▸ The icon that appears to represent that application, file, or folder
- ▸ The icon menu that appears for that file application, file, or folder
- ▸ The action that occurs when each icon menu item is selected
- ▸ The actions that occur when a file is dragged-and-dropped on the icon

TECHNOTE **Each time you open a folder window, the system checks both your personal and the system-wide icon class databases. It then matches each file in the folder with one of the entries in those databases and assigns these attributes to the file based on that icon class. In essence, as the graphical user interface adds a mask to the UnixWare system, the Icon Setup function adds a mask to all UNIX files by matching file attributes on the fly.**

As explained in Chapter 2, UNIX will assign generic icons to files that don't match certain criteria. For example, any file with Executable permissions that doesn't match any other icon class will be represented by a generic executable file icon. A generic datafile icon will be used for a file that does not match any other criteria and does not have Executable permissions.

The attributes are not, repeat, not welded to each file. You can assign a new icon class (and, therefore, different attributes) to a file by simply renaming the file, moving it to a different folder, or changing its permissions.

As an example, we will use a fictitious application named CoolDraw and say that it is a drawing program written for the X Window System (a graphical application). Let's assume you just installed this application and put its executable file into your Applications folder. When you opened your Applications folder window, this file had a generic executable file icon. This means that the system doesn't have an icon already defined for the application, as it does for WordPerfect and other commonly used applications.

VIEWING ICON CLASSES WITH ICON SETUP

You can see the icon classes available on your system by displaying the Icon Setup window. Icon classes are divided into two categories: Personal Classes and System Classes. The system icon classes apply to all of the desktop users on your computer. The personal classes only apply to the user who is running Icon Setup.

Any user can add a personal icon class, but only the owner can add to or change system icon classes. Double-click on the Admin Tools icon in the Desktop window, then double-click on the Icon Setup icon. The Icon Setup: Personal Classes window is displayed, as shown in Figure 3.5.

F I G U R E   3.5

The Icon Setup window
for personal icon classes

To see the icon classes for the entire system, click on View, then click on System Classes. The Icon Setup: System Classes window is displayed, as shown in Figure 3.6.

FIGURE 3.6

The Icon Setup window for system icon classes

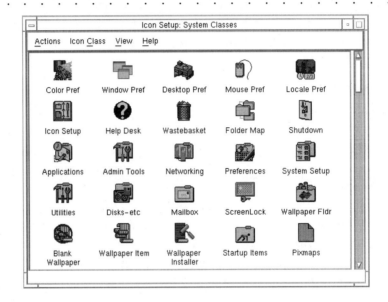

If you are not allowed to add to or change system classes, you can look on the bottom right-hand corner of the Icon Setup window while the system icon classes are being displayed. If you are not allowed to change system icon classes, it will say "Read Only."

To see the properties associated with any icon class (the icon that represents the class, what files it matches, etc.), double-click on the icon. A properties window appears with information on that class filled in.

 **WARNING**

The Icon Setup window is a graphical application with the mentality of an early UNIX system utility: it is extremely powerful, there's no way to guess what it does or how to use it, and if it's misused, it can really mess you up.

CREATING AN ICON CLASS FOR AN APPLICATION

Let's say you have a new application installed on your UNIX system and you want to assign an icon class to represent it. Using the example we used earlier, a drawing application called CoolDraw, follow these steps to assign an icon class:

1 · Display the view of the particular class to which you want to add a particular icon class by clicking on View, then clicking on either Personal Classes or System Classes. (For our example, we selected Personal Classes.)

2 · Click on Icon Class, then click on New.

3 · Click on one of the following: File (for a data file class), Folder (for a folder class), or Application (for an application). We selected Application for this example. The Icon Setup: New Personal Application window appears, as shown in Figure 3.7.

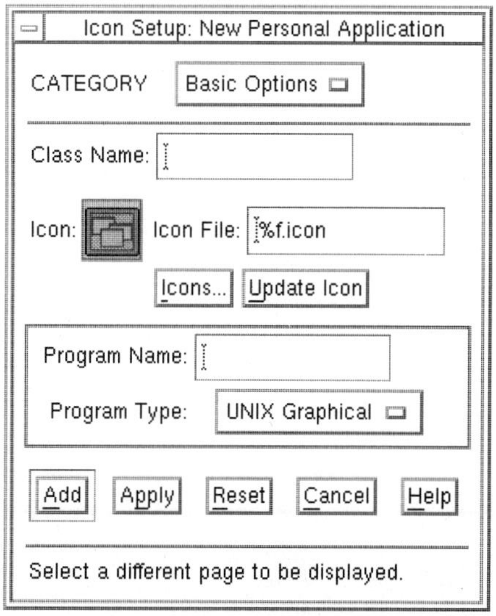

FIGURE 3.7

Adding a personal application icon class

4 · Add the following information to the display:

> ▸ **Class Name: CoolDrawRun.** This is just the name we want to give to this icon class.

> ▸ **Icon File: draw1.icon.** This is the name of a generic draw icon, provided by the system in the `/usr/X/lib/pixmaps` folder, that appears for any file that matches the class. Click on Update Icon to see the icon. If you want to use a different icon, click on Icons, select an icon from the window that appears, and click on OK. The new icon and its name will appear.

> ▸ **Program Name: CoolDraw.** This is the name the system matches against, so any file named `CoolDraw` is assigned to this class (if it is an application).

5 · Click on Add. The window disappears and a new icon representing the icon class you just added appears in the Icon Setup window, as shown in Figure 3.8.

F I G U R E   3.8

A new icon in the Icon Setup window

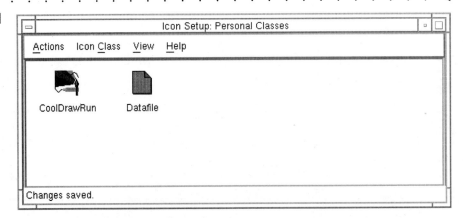

CREATING AN ICON CLASS FOR A DATA FILE

Let's assume that every time you create a picture with your CoolDraw application, you save it to a file with the suffix .cdp (for *CoolDraw picture*). By defining an icon class for .cdp files, you can specify an icon for them and the actions to take for those data files.

To create an icon class for data files used by our CoolDraw example, follow these steps:

I · From the Icon Setup window, click on Icon Class, then click on New.

2 · Click on File. The Icon Setup: New Personal File window appears, as shown in Figure 3.9.

F I G U R E 3.9

*Adding a personal file
icon class*

3 · Add the following information to the display:

  ▶ **Class Name:** CoolDraw Data. This is just the name we want to give to this icon class.

- ▸ Icon File: `drawfile1.icon`. This is the name of a generic draw file icon, provided by the system in the `/usr/X/lib/pixmaps` folder, that appears for any file that matches the class. Click on Update Icon to see the icon. If you want to use a different icon, click on Icons, select an icon from the window that appears, and click on OK. The new icon and its name will appear.

- ▸ Filename Extension: `*.cdp`. This says to match a file that begins with anything (`*`) and ends in `.cdp`, so any file whose name ends in `cdp` is assigned to this class.

- ▸ Program To Run: `exec "$HOME/Applications/CoolDraw" "%S" &`. This says to run CoolDraw with the full path of the file as input (`"%S"`). When this file is opened, UnixWare starts up the CoolDraw application, using the data file as input.

4 · Click on Add. The window disappears and a new icon representing the icon class you just added appears in the Icon Setup window.

CHANGING ICON CLASSES FROM THE COMMAND LINE

Some things you may want to do with icon class databases can't be done through the Icon Setup window. By editing the icon class database files, you can add extra actions to an icon menu or override the system classes. However, you must be very careful in making changes, because mistakes can cause trouble.

 **WARNING** **Editing icon class files directly, without using Icon Setup, is an advanced technique. If you make a mistake, you can override some or all of the system's icon classes, and the results can be bizarre. For example, UnixWare might give every file on the system the same icon.**

Each user's personal class database is in his or her home folder. However, you won't see the file on your Desktop, because its name begins with a dot: `.dtfclass`. The systemwide class database consists of files contained in the `/usr/X/lib/classdb` directory. You must have root user permissions to edit these files. Changes to these files apply to any user on the system. It's safest to add your own class file to this directory by copying an existing one and editing it to add your new information.

Figure 3.10 shows an entry that comes in everyone's `.dtfclass` file. If you look carefully, you can see how the file entry relates to what you saw in the Icon Setup window. The line

```
_FILETYPE  'DATA';
```

specifies the icon class as DATA, the only class in your personal class file. Because it is meant to represent a data file that isn't matched by any other class, it is matched after all of the system classes have been checked first.

▶ · ◀

```
                              Terminal
$ cat .dtfclass
INCLUDE system;
INCLUDE dtadmin;
CLASS 'DATA' DONT_DELETE
BEGIN
        _FILETYPE        'DATA';
        _CLASSNAME       'dtmgr:31Datafile';
        _ICONFILE        'datafile.icon';
        _PROG_TO_RUN     'dtedit';
        _PROG_TYPE       'UNIX Graphical';
        MENU _Open       '##DROP(%_PROG_TO_RUN) || exec %_PROG_TO_RUN "%F" &';
        MENU _Print      '$XWINHOME/bin/PrtMgr -p %_DEFAULT_PRINTER "%F" &';
END

INCLUDE system.post;
$ ▯
```

FIGURE 3.10

A .dtfclass (personal

class database) file entry

If you want to create your own entry, the lines of interest are the ones that begin with MENU. All MENU entries will appear on the icon menu when you click on the icon with the Menu mouse button (the right button). The lines

```
_PROG_TO_RUN        'dtedit';
```

```
MENU _Open        '##DROP(%_PROG_TO_RUN) ||
      exec %_PROG_TO_RUN "%F" &';
```

defines that when the data file is opened, the text editor (dtedit) is started
using the file name as an option (%F).

The line

```
MENU _Print       '$XWINHOME/bin/PrtMgr -p
      %_DEFAULT_PRINTER "%F" &';
```

says that choosing to print the file sends it to the printer. Because there is
no name or folder restriction, it will match any data file that isn't matched
by an earlier icon class.

Figure 3.11 shows an example of an icon class entry you could add to
your own personal .dtfclass file. With this addition, when you open
/usr/X/lib/pixmaps, which is a directory of icons, you see each icon
displaying itself as its icon file (_ICONFILE '%f'). When you click the Menu

FIGURE 3.11

Example of an entry added

to a .dtfclass file

```
$ cat .dtfclass
INCLUDE system;
INCLUDE dtadmin;
CLASS 'DATA' DONT_DELETE
BEGIN
        _FILETYPE        'DATA';
        _CLASSNAME       'dtmgr:31Datafile';
        _ICONFILE        'datafile.icon';
        _PROG_TO_RUN     'dtedit';
        _PROG_TYPE       'UNIX Graphical';
        MENU _Open       '##DROP(%_PROG_TO_RUN) || exec %_PROG_TO_RUN "%F" &';
        MENU _Print      '$XWINHOME/bin/PrtMgr -p %_DEFAULT_PRINTER "%F" &';
END

CLASS 'PIXMAPS'
BEGIN
        _FILETYPE        'DATA';
        _ICONFILE        '%f';
        _FILEPATH        '/usr/X/lib/pixmaps';
        _PATTERN         '*';
        MENU _Open       'exec /usr/X/bin/olpixmap %F &'; "%F" &';
        MENU _Mono       'exec /usr/X/bin/bitmaps %F &';
END




INCLUDE system.post;
$
```

mouse button on an icon, a menu appears containing an Open and a Mono Selection. Open lets you edit a color copy of the icon in the `olpixmap` editor; Mono lets you edit a black-and-white copy.

Starting Up Applications

After you have installed an application on your system, you can start it by opening its icon from the Desktop. You can also designate that an application start up automatically when you log in.

Another way to start up an application is to schedule it to run at a specific time, whether or not you are there. This feature is set through the Task Scheduler, which is in your Admin Tools folder. Since this feature is most useful for noninteractive tasks, such as backing up or transferring files, the Task Scheduler window is covered in Chapter 7, which is about backup and restore operations. The other methods for starting up applications are described in the following sections.

STARTING UP AN APPLICATION FROM THE DESKTOP

UnixWare makes it easy to start applications from the Desktop. Open the folder that contains the application and double-click on the application's icon. Most applications are installed in your Applications folder, so you can double-click on the Applications icon in the Desktop window, then double-click on the application's icon to open a window with that application running.

Another place to look for applications is in the `/usr/X/bin` folder. The system includes some X Window System utilties in that folder. Again, just double-click on the icon to start the application.

STARTING UP AN APPLICATION AT LOGIN

Every time the Desktop starts up, the system can run your favorite applications automatically, so you can start right in after you log in. For example, you might want your word processing program to start up automatically. The easiest way to set up applications to start up when you log in is through the Startup Items folder window. Another way to start up applications automatically is to add them to the `.olinitrc` file in your home folder. You will need to use this method if the application needs to be run with options.

Using the Startup Items Folder Window

To add applications to the Startup Items folder, simply drag-and-drop the application's icon into that window. To open the Startup Items folder window, double-click on the Preferences icon in the Desktop window, and then double-click on the Startup Items icon. Figure 3.12 shows an example of the window with icons for applications that will start up automatically.

Applications in the Startup Items folder window

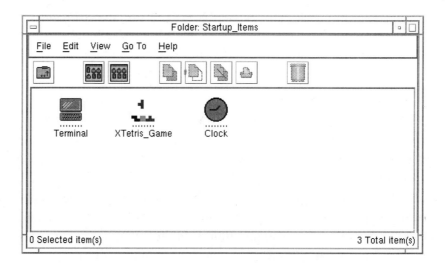

Starting Applications with the .olinitrc File

In some cases, an application that was simply dragged into the Startup Items folder won't start up. This is probably because the Startup Item feature simply runs the command, but the icon was configured to execute the command with options or execute a different command altogether. Use the Icon Setup window to determine the command executed for the icon, and add that command to your `.olinitrc` file. The advantages of adding a command to the `.olinitrc` instead of to the Startup Items folder is that you can string commands together and add command line options.

The `.olinitrc` file is another one of those files in your home folder that you can't see from your Desktop because it starts with a dot. To add applications to your `.olinitrc` file, open the file with any text editor. Then add the entries for your applications after the last line in the file. Type the command and add an ampersand (&) to the end of the line so the command is run in the background. It is very important that you run the command in the background, so that you won't hang up the Desktop. The following are some examples of commands added to the `.olinitrc` file to start up automatically at login:

```
cd $HOME/book;/usr/X/bin/xterm -sl 1500 &
/usr/X/bin/dtclock &
win +x &
```

The first line changes to the `book` directory in the home directory, to make it the current directory for the Terminal window session, and then starts up a Terminal window with the `-sl 1500` option. This saves the previous 1,500 lines during the Terminal session, so if you are listing a long file, you can scroll back to up to 1,500 saved lines in the window.

The other two commands in the example are for starting a clock to run on the Desktop (`dtclock`) and starting up Windows within a UnixWare window (`win +x`). Don't just drag and drop the Win icon into the Startup Items folder. It won't work.

FIXING APPLICATIONS THAT DON'T RUN

You may find that simply double-clicking on an application's icon won't start the application properly. Usually, you can solve the problem by starting the application from the command line. Some of the most common reasons an application fails to run and ways to resolve the problems are described in the following sections.

An Environment Variable Is Missing

The most common reason an application fails to run is that some shell environment variable needs to be set. For example, if you want to run the SCO ODT version of FrameMaker in UnixWare 1.1, you need to set the following environment variables:

```
FMARCH=scounix;export FMARCH
FMHOME=/usr/lib/frame3.1;export FMHOME
PATH=$PATH:$FMHOME/bin;export PATH
DISPLAY=:0;export DISPLAY
```

You could either type these lines into a Terminal window or, more commonly, add them to your `.profile` file in your home folder. You could then start FrameMaker by simply typing `maker` from the shell command line.

 NOTE **See Chapter 8 for more information about editing your `.profile` file. See the subsection about SCO applications that won't run, later in this section, for details on setting the PATH variable for SCO applications.**

The Licensing Fails

Different applications have different licensing mechanisms. Licensing failures you may encounter include the following:

▶ Too many people try to use a limited-use license.

▶ The license keys off of a system name and the system name has changed.

▶ The vendor gave you the wrong key to start the application (call the vendor before you try the application again).

The Terminal Type Is Wrong

In some cases, if the terminal type is set incorrectly, you could end up with garbled text on the screen. If you are using the shell from a Terminal window, the TERM variable should be set to xterm (TERM=xterm). TERM definitions are contained in the `terminfo` database (within the directory `/usr/ lib/terminfo/*`) or in the `termcap` database (in the file `/etc/termcap`).

Some applications supply their own `termcap` file or only support certain terminal types. Check the documentation that comes with the application to see if it requires a special TERM setting.

The Graphical Application Fails

Some applications come with both graphical and character-based versions. Usually, the two are started up with different commands. If, for some reason, the graphical application doesn't work, try opening a Terminal window and typing in the command for the character-based version.

A SCO Application Won't Run

When SCO features were brought into UNIX System V at AT&T, the intention was to be able to have SCO applications run on the system without modification. The major impediment to making this happen was that sometimes SCO and System V features just flat-out conflicted. If a SCO application doesn't run, you probably need to use one of the commands that tells the system, "Hey, there's a SCO application here; switch into SCO mode." Here are some of the ways you can let the system know:

► If you are running a SCO application, you may need to have `/usr/eac/bin` in your PATH before any other directories. If the SCO application tries to use the `cc` or `awk` commands, putting `/usr/eac/bin` in your PATH has the application find the SCO versions of those commands instead of the System V versions. Add `/usr/eac/bin` to you PATH by adding the following line to the `.profile` file in your home directory somewhere before the line $HOME/`.olsetup`:

```
PATH=/usr/eac/bin:$PATH;export PATH
```

NOTE **When you run a command from the command line, the directories listed in the PATH variable are searched for the command. The directories are searched in the order in which they appear in the PATH.**

▶ Certain shared libraries (files that contain code that is shared by different applications) conflict in System V and SCO. When an application is installed by `custom`, references to the correct shared library are made for all executable files in the application. If you have a SCO application that is not installed by `custom`, and it "dumps core" (fails and leaves a core file in the directory) when you try to run it, try running the following command from a Terminal window (as the root user), where *command* is replaced by the application you are trying to run:

`fixshlib` *command*

▶ UNIX has codes that applications send to input/output devices (such at networks, terminals, or floppy disk drives) to control those devices. These codes are sent by the `ioctl` system call. Unfortunately, the `ioctl` codes for SCO and UNIX System V devices sometimes conflict. If you run an application and there are `ioctl` errors, you should try running the following command from a Terminal window (as the root user), where *command* is replaced by the application you are trying to run:

`scompat` *command*

▶ When you press a function key or an arrow key on your keyboard, a code is sent to the application you are running. SCO has a different set of codes mapped to its function keys and arrow keys than UNIX System V. If you find that you are getting unexpected results from your application when you press function keys, try running the following command:

`mapstr /usr/lib/keyboard/scostrings`

Running Remote Applications

You can run applications located on a remote system in two ways. One way is to connect the remote system's files to your system and run the application locally. The other way is to run the application on the remote system, but direct the output to your display.

MOUNTING APPLICATIONS FROM REMOTE FILE SYSTEMS

If the applications you want to run are installed properly on a NetWare server or a remote UNIX system, you will be able to connect (mount) them to your UNIX system. (Some problems you may encounter in installing applications on NetWare servers are discussed earlier in this chapter.) In both cases, the application is using your system's processing power to run, and it is viewing your file system (which includes connections to remote systems).

To run an application stored on a NetWare file server, from your Desktop window, double-click on the NetWare icon. Select the server and volume where the application is located, then double-click on the application icon to start the application.

See Chapter 4 for more information about connecting your Unix-Ware system to a NetWare system.

In order to use an application stored on a remote UnixWare file system, you must be set up to share the directory that contains the application and then connect that directory to your system. You accomplish these tasks through the File Sharing window in the Networking folder. You can then open the folder window for the connected directory and double-click on the application icon to start the application.

See Chapter 5 for more information about connecting to remote UNIX systems.

SHARING APPLICATIONS WITH OTHER UNIXWARE SYSTEMS

UnixWare lets you share applications with other UnixWare systems connected to your system by using simple drag-and-drop actions. You work with the application from your own display and keyboard, but the remote system's processing power is used to run that application, and it is viewing the remote system's directories. So, for example, if you were to save a file using the application, the file would go in the remote system's directories. Also, if the remote system is a powerful computer, the application might perform better than if you were to run it locally.

Enabling Peer-to-Peer Communications and Application Sharing

By enabling peer-to-peer communications between systems, any user with a user account on a remote system can use any applications that system chooses to share. To turn on peer-to-peer communications, from your Desktop window, double-click on the Admin Tools icon, double-click on the Networking icon, and then double-click on the NetWare Setup icon. The NetWare Setup window appears, as shown in Figure 3.13. Click on the

F I G U R E 3.13

Enabling peer-to-peer
communications

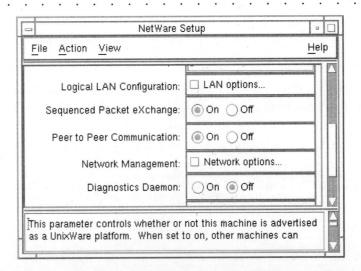

On button next to Peer to Peer Communication, click on Action, then click on Save Current Settings. Now you can share applications with other Unix-Ware systems on your network.

However, before you can use an application installed on another Unix-Ware system, peer-to-peer communications must also be enabled on that remote system, and the application must be added to that system's list of available applications. Go to the remote system and turn on peer-to-peer communications, as described in the previous paragraph. Then, from the Admin Tools folder window, double-click on the App Sharing icon. The App Sharing window appears, as shown in Figure 3.14.

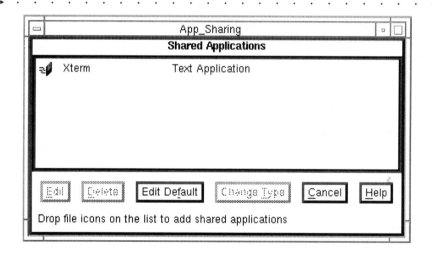

FIGURE 3.14

The App Sharing window

To make an application shareable, simply open the folder that contains the application and drag-and-drop it into the App Sharing window. The only selection you need to make is whether it is a Text Application or an X Application. If the wrong type appears, click on the Change Type button at the bottom of the window to change to the other type.

TECHNOTE

Scripts for remote applications are stored in the directory named `/usr/X/lib/app-defaults/.exportApps`.

A script is associated with any application you add to the App Sharing window. The script sets up a happy UNIX system environment for the script to start in: the PATH variable, the time zone, and whether it is an X or Text Application. You can see this script by clicking on the Edit button at the bottom of the App Sharing window while the application is selected. The last two lines are interesting because they show the actual commands that are run when the application is started.

Starting a Remote Application

After peer-to-peer communications are enabled, you can see which remote applications are available. Double-click on the Applications icon in the Desktop window, then double-click on the Remote Applications icon. The Remote Apps window appears, as shown in Figure 3.15.

FIGURE 3.15

The Remote Apps window

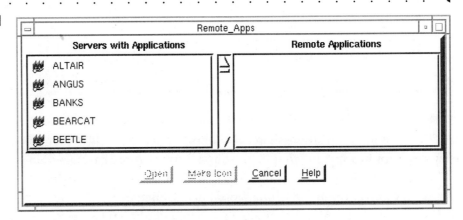

You must have a valid login and password on the remote system to use its applications. The login can be different from your local account.

NOTE

The names listed under Servers with Applications represent other Unix-Ware systems that have enabled peer-to-peer communications. Click on the name of the server that has the application you want to run. When an authentication window appears, type a valid UnixWare login and password to that UnixWare system.

Once the login and password are verified, a list of applications available from the remote UnixWare system appears. Click on the application you want to use, then click on Make Icon. An icon representing the remote application appears in your Applications window. To start the application, open your Applications folder window and double-click on the new icon.

SHARING APPLICATIONS WITH UNIX SYSTEMS

You can work with an application that is actually running on another UNIX system, as long as it is a graphical application (created for the X Window System) and you have a network connection to the remote system. As when you run an application on a remote UnixWare system, the application is using the remote system's processing power and viewing the remote system's directories. After you prepare your system, you can simply log into another system using a UNIX operating system, such as SunOS or SCO UNIX, and start the application with the DISPLAY environment variable set to your display.

As an example, suppose that a Sun workstation in your building has a really great application that isn't available in a UnixWare version yet (though, of course, it will be soon). If it is an X Window System application and you have a network connection to that system (through the Internet Setup window), you access that application from your UnixWare system.

Here is an example of the procedure you might follow to run a word processing application installed on a Sun workstation:

1 · To add the Sun's name and address to your system, double-click on the Networking icon in the Admin Tools window, then double-click on the Internet Setup icon. In the Internet Setup window, enter the workstation information, such as the following: `222.22.222.22 karenbox`.

2 · To allow the other system to display the application on your monitor, open a Terminal window (double-click on the Applications icon in the Desktop window, then double-click on the Terminal icon) and use the `xhost` command with the workstation name. For example, type `/usr/X/bin/xhost +karenbox`.

3 · While logged into the SUN workstation, open the console (shell) window and add your computer's name and network address to the `/etc/hosts` file. For example, add `111.11.111.11 mars`.

4 · At the command line, change the DISPLAY variable to redirect output to your terminal. For example, type `setenv DISPLAY mars:0`.

5 · Type the command to start the remote application, such as wordproc&, and the application shows up on your system.

NOTE **Sun workstations commonly use the `csh` shell. With a `ksh` or `sh` shell, you set the DISPLAY variable by using the format DISPLAY=mars:0.**

Remember that when you work with applications this way the application looks at the remote system's file system and not yours. If you save a file, it will be saved on the other system. Also, if the network is busy, your work could go very slowly. However, on a light network and with a powerful remote machine, the application could run faster than it would locally.

Creating Your Own Applications

The programming libraries and software development tools created for the
UNIX system have made it one of the richest environments for software development in the computing industry. You can develop graphical or character-
based applications. You can create applications for single-user or multiuser
environments. Applications can be designed to be used on your local machine
or to communicate across networks with other computers, remote applications, and users.

Here are some of the ways you can create your own applications:

▸ Write shell scripts. Even if you are not a programmer, you can
put together UNIX system commands to form applications
known as *shell scripts*. Using the wksh tool, you can even write
shell scripts that let you create your own Desktop windows. As
mentioned earlier in this book, a shell script is usually made up of
shell commands and simple programming functions, and you can
run the script from the command line, like any other command.

See Chapter 8 for more information about shell scripts.

NOTE

▸ Using a new tool available with UNIX SVR4.2, called the Windowing Korn Shell, you can create scripts that result in graphical
applications. The advantage is that you can define buttons, text
boxes, menus, and other graphical elements to operate the application graphically. The Windowing Korn Shell (or wksh) does its
job by offering extensions to the ksh command line interpreter.
It manipulates elements called *widgets*.

▸ Use the UnixWare Software Development Kit (SDK), a separate
add-on product you can purchase. The SDK provides the basic
software development tools you need to create UnixWare applications. The centerpiece of the SDK is the C language compilation
system, which includes the ANSI C compiler as well as other
tools for linking, compiling, and debugging C program code. The

ANSI C compiler translates your C program code into binary programs that run on UnixWare systems. The SDK set contains:

- ▸ Software packaging tools
- ▸ Enhanced debugger
- ▸ Kernel debugger
- ▸ Motif development
- ▸ Desktop manager development
- ▸ C++ compilation system
- ▸ C++ standard components
- ▸ Network management SDK
- ▸ IHV development kit
- ▸ Software development kit documentation

This chapter covered how to run applications on your UNIX system in general, and UnixWare in particular—from locating the types of applications it supports and installing them to sharing applications with remote systems and writing your own applications. However, even if you are moving to more powerful networked or multiuser applications, you may still need to run your DOS or Windows applications.

Using DOS and Windows on your UNIX system is covered in Chapter 6. The next chapter describes how to connect your UnixWare system to a NetWare system. Once you are part of a NetWare network, you will be able to run applications stored on the NetWare file servers, as described in this chapter.

Connecting
to NetWare

The most powerful advantage of UNIX System V Release 4.2MP (and its UnixWare 2 implementation) over earlier UNIX systems is its ability to tap into the NetWare networking environment. Getting into NetWare from UNIX can be as simple as connecting to your NetWare network, logging in to UNIX, and opening your NetWare folder.

Because UNIX and NetWare have different ways of storing files, dealing with users, and managing the security aspects of its file systems, it helps to understand what happens when you cross the boundaries between UNIX and NetWare. How do UNIX read/write/execute permissions relate to NetWare access rights, such as file scan, erase, and access control? How does NetWare authenticate who a UNIX user is when that user tries to access NetWare files?

This chapter describes what a UNIX user needs to know to access NetWare services. If you are not familiar with NetWare, we recommend you purchase one of the many NetWare books available today, such as those published by Novell Press.

 NOTE **Because not all UNIX System V systems incorporate the NetWare connectivity described in this chapter, the UnixWare implementation of UNIX is focused on. However, this technology is licensed to other UNIX vendors; therefore the NetWare connectivity in those other versions of UNIX will probably match the descriptions shown here.**

What Is NetWare?

From a UNIX user's perspective, NetWare is much different from what you are used to seeing in an operating system. Rather than being a platform for running applications, NetWare is an operating system that can glue together a diverse collection of computer systems and networking services.

NetWare provides the means for sharing information and computer peripherals among many different types of computers and applications. By allowing tight integration among DOS, UNIX systems, Apple Computer systems, and other operating environments, NetWare has become one of the world's most popular network operating systems.

NETWARE SERVICES

File service is the central feature of NetWare. The NetWare system is designed to pass information quickly and efficiently between application-oriented operating systems, such as UnixWare or DOS, and NetWare file servers. In fact, it is NetWare's ability to transform an office with several PCs and Macs into an inexpensive workgroup environment that has led to its success.

Along with file service, NetWare allows levels of security that were previously unknown in DOS environments. NetWare controls access to servers, including the files and directories a user can access and whether the user can view or change those files and directories.

To support file services, NetWare has backup and restore facilities. It also has features for monitoring the activities on NetWare servers, such as how many users have active connections to the server and the files currently in use on the system.

NetWare Release 3.12 servers maintain system security using login and password restrictions. The SUPERVISOR is a special login account used to set up and control security. Responsibility for other administrative tasks can be delegated to special workgroup and user account managers by the SUPERVISOR. The SUPERVISOR can also delegate individual responsibilities to a file server console operator, print server operator, and print queue operator.

Printing is another important NetWare service. The print service includes utilities for defining printers, managing print queues, defining print device definition files, and defining forms.

NETWARE LOADABLE MODULES

Support for hardware devices, as well as special file service utilities, is supplied to the NetWare operating system by *NetWare Loadable Modules* (*NLMs*). Some NLMs are included with NetWare; others are provided by third-party vendors to support their particular hardware or application.

NOTE

To see the NLMs available on a NetWare server, open your NetWare folder from the Desktop. Double-click on the icon for the server, double-click on the icon for the `sys` volume, and double-click on the icon for the system directory. NLMs for the server are typically listed in this directory (`/home/user/netware/server/sys/system`).

NetWare version 3.12 has four types of NLMs:

▸ **Disk drivers:** Manage the communications between hard disks and the NetWare system. Disk driver NLMs have a .DSK file name extension.

▸ **LAN drivers:** Handle communications between the network boards and NetWare. LAN driver NLMs have a .LAN file name extension.

▸ **Management utilities and server applications:** Let you modify configuration options. They include utilities for managing your hard disks and network applications, such as TCP/IP. Management utility and server application NLMs have an .NLM file name extension.

▸ **Name spaces:** Provide file system naming conventions that are used by operating environments other than DOS. The NFS.NAM, MAC.NAM, and OS2.NAM NLMs provide the Network File System file naming semantics for Network File System (UNIX), Mac, and OS/2 name spaces, respectively. The name space NLMs have a .NAM file name extension.

How UNIX/NetWare Connectivity Works

When you boot your UnixWare system, NetWare connectivity starts up automatically. The network is queried for available NetWare services. Servers on the network that communicate using the same frame type being used by UnixWare are connected into the UnixWare file system, where they can be accessed using the proper authentication of the user. The following sections go through the different components involved in NetWare connectivity.

CHECKING THE NETWORK FOR AVAILABLE SERVICES

UnixWare determines which NetWare services are available on your network by collecting Service Advertising Protocol packets (SAPs) from the network. SAPs contain information about services from NetWare servers, as well as services available from other UnixWare systems. The following is a list of some of the SAPs UnixWare gathers:

▸ **NetWare servers**: SAPs from every NetWare server on the network let UnixWare know which file system services are available on the network.

▸ **Novell Virtual Terminal**: UnixWare collects SAPs offering Novell Virtual Terminal (NVT) services from any UnixWare system on the network. Using NVT, users can log in to UnixWare from DOS workstations.

▸ **Simple Network Management Protocol (SNMP)**: SAPs from NetWare or UnixWare systems allow SNMP agents on the network to gather diagnostic statistics about systems on the network.

▸ **Advertising print servers**: SAPS from NetWare print servers advertise the availability of NetWare printers on the network.

▸ **Install servers**: SAPS from UnixWare Application Server systems offer remote UnixWare systems the ability to install UnixWare over the network from their systems.

▸ **UnixWare**: Every UnixWare system sends SAPs alerting other UnixWare systems that basic UnixWare features are available.

A user can access these services in a variety of ways through both the Desktop interface and the command line.

WHICH NETWARE SERVERS ARE SUPPORTED?

Using UnixWare, you can connect to the server versions of NetWare 3.12 and greater. (NetWare 4.x servers must be running bindery emulation.) In order to use the NetWare server from UnixWare in a way that supports UNIX semantics (long file names, ownership, read/write/execute permissions, etc.) the NetWare server must be running at least NetWare 3.12 and have the NUC.NLM installed (described later).

There are three different modes supported by the files systems on your NetWare server: DOS Mode, NetWare Mode, and UNIX Mode. DOS Mode requires no additional NLM installation, but is limited in how you can use it from UNIX. NetWare and UNIX Modes require some additional software and configuration, but can be used almost transparently from a UNIX system.

 NOTE   **See "Configuring the NetWare Server" later in this chapter for information on how to install the NLMs and configure user and group files to take full advantage of NetWare services from your UNIX system.**

NETWORKING SERVICE OVER IPX

NetWare systems use the IPX protocol, which communicates over many different lower level networking protocols, including Ethernet and Token Ring networks. UnixWare can communicate with these lower level protocols based on four different frame types: Ethernet II, Ethernet 802.3, Ethernet SNAP, and Ethernet 802.2. For Token Ring LANs, use the Ethernet SNAP or 802.2 frame type.

Along with access to NetWare file services, UnixWare implements several other networking services over IPX:

> ▶ **NetWare printing services:** Using the Printer Setup window, available on the UnixWare Desktop, you can configure your system to use a NetWare printer. An excellent interface in the Printer Setup window lets you browse through the NetWare servers UnixWare finds on the network and choose from their available print queues and printers.

▶ **MHS mail:** The MHS Setup window lets you connect your Unix-Ware mail service to MHS mail services on a NetWare server.

▶ **Application sharing:** Applications can be shared between Unix-Ware systems using the IPX/SPX protocols. The App Sharing window lets you offer your applications to other systems. The Remote Apps window lets you view and use applications that are offered by remote systems. When you actually run the remote applications, they execute on the remote system but display on the local system.

▶ **Remote UNIX system printing:** If your system has IPX/SPX connections to another UnixWare system, you can set up the systems to share printers. Although there is no graphical interface for sharing printers among UnixWare systems connected over IPX/SPX, you can use the command line to set up this type of printing. For details, see the `lpsystem` (1M) command using the `man` command or the Online Docs window (Command Reference book).

▶ **Novell Virtual Terminal (NVT):** With a UnixWare Application Server system, you can log in to that system over IPX and NVT's own protocol from a DOS workstation using NVT software. Likewise, you can get NVT services using Host Presenter software from a Microsoft Windows interface. The Novell terminal emulation software TNVT220 is now shipped with UnixWare. TNVT220 uses IPX/SPX as its transport.

The underlying networking architecture in UnixWare supports other networking protocols, in theory. These include SPXII, UDP, TCP, and ISO TP4 transport providers. At the moment, however, only IPX has been fully implemented for use in UnixWare/NetWare connectivity.

NETWARE DAEMON PROCESSES IN UNIXWARE

Daemon processes are a standard way of doing business in UNIX. As a multitasking system, UNIX can have many things running at the same time.

By having daemon processes running in the background, waiting for information to come in from the network, a lot of networking activity can go on without disturbing you and your work.

When NetWare connectivity starts up as you boot your UnixWare system, a handful of daemon processes start to manage your connections to the network. These daemons include nucd, npsd, sapd, and nwnetd.

The NetWare UNIX Client Daemon (nucd)

The nucd daemon handles most of the basic NetWare client operations from your UnixWare system. As NetWare file services are requested, the nucd daemon takes those requests and automatically mounts (connects) NetWare volumes to your system. After a timeout period during which the file server is not accessed, the nucd daemon will automatically unmount those NetWare volumes.

As messages come in from NetWare servers, the nucd daemon will take those messages and direct them to syslog (a standard UNIX message logging mechanism). The nucd daemon also produces its own messages, which are directed to the /tmp/nuc.start file during system startup. To get more verbose messages from nucd, it can be run with the −d option. Because nucd is run automatically at startup, you must edit the /etc/rc2.d/S27nuc startup script to add the −d option to the line in that script that starts the nucd daemon.

The NetWare Protocol Stack Daemon (npsd)

The UNIX networking architecture relies on a framework that is called *Streams*. With Streams, networking protocols (the rules that govern communication) can be plugged together in different ways. So, for example, higher level protocols, such as IPX and TCP, can be plugged on top of lower level protocols, such as Ethernet or Token Ring, as long as they maintain a standard set of services and ways of requesting those services.

The npsd daemon takes information about the protocols needed to provide NetWare connectivity and puts together the protocols needed to complete end-to-end communication between UnixWare and NetWare servers.

It then initializes the network and waits in the background for shutdown requests. When it receives a shutdown request, it takes down the protocol stack.

Like the nucd daemon, the npsd daemon can be run in a more verbose mode. Add a −v to the line that starts the npsd daemon in the startup script /etc/rc2.d/S25nw. Messages from npsd will then be sent to the console monitor.

The Service Access Protocol Daemon (sapd)

NetWare servers send out Service Access Protocol (SAP) packets to advertise the services it makes available to clients on the network. The sapd daemon listens to the network and gathers the SAPs so UnixWare knows what NetWare services are available. Likewise, sapd sends out SAPs to advertise the services that the local UnixWare system offers to clients on the network.

Using a −t option with sapd, you can enable or disable packet tracing. With the track command, you can then track the SAP packets on the network.

The NetWare TLI Application Services Daemon (nwnetd)

The nwnetd daemon, started at boot time, listens for requests on the IPX/SPX network for TLI services and starts up server processes to service the requests. In particular, the nwnetd daemon handles UnixWare-to-UnixWare services, such as remote execution and network installation, that communicate over NetWare protocols (IPX/SPX).

TLI stands for Transport Level Interface. The idea of TLI is to provide a standard that allows network developers to put an interface on top of a variety of different network types (TCP/IP, IPX/SPX, X.25, and others). Then standard applications written to the TLI interface can communicate over these networks without knowing the specifics about each network. For example, an application would simply say, "Connect me to system A, send data, receive data, and close the connection." TLI, along with related services, then resolves the addressing and translates the requests into the syntax understood by the particular network.

 **TECHNOTE**

For those who are familiar with the OSI networking standards, TLI implements the services defined at the fourth layer (the transport layer) of the OSI seven-layer model.

When the `nwnetd` daemon starts up, it reads the configuration file `/etc/nwnetd.conf`, which contains information about available network services. The default `/etc/nwnetd.conf` file contains one service: `exec`. When a request for an `exec` service comes into your system over the IPX/SPX protocol, `nwnetd` starts up the `nrexecd` daemon to handle the requests. Here's an example of listing in the `/etc/nwnetd.conf` file.

```
exec    stream   spx    nowait    root
   /usr/sbin/nrexecd    nrexecd
```

The file contains the following fields:

▶ The first field is the name of the requested service (**exec**).

▶ The second field (**stream**) shows that the daemon expects to talk to a Streams protocol stack.

▶ The third field (**spx**) defines the protocol stack as providing **spx** services.

▶ The fourth field (**nowait**) says to respond to the request immediately.

▶ The fifth field assigns the process to be run as **root**.

▶ The sixth field is the full path to the daemon that is started to respond to the request (**/usr/sbin/nrexecd**).

▶ The seventh field contains any arguments to the daemon (**nrexecd**).

Configuring the NetWare Server

When you access a NetWare server from UnixWare, you do it in a way that makes the NetWare volumes, directories, and files appear as though they are part of the local UnixWare system. In order to take full advantage of UNIX file and directory features (such as long file names, UNIX read/write/execute permissions, and file ownership), however, you must do some configuration on the NetWare server.

The two types of changes are configuring the name space and defining users (by setting up password, user, and group files). Information on changing your NetWare servers to enhance the name space and define users/groups is contained in the following sections.

> **Besides the configuration described in this chapter, UnixWare documentation recommends you add your UnixWare system's IP Address and Hostname to the `sys:etc\hosts` file on your NetWare server. We're not sure why this is needed since we are communicating with IPX and not TCP/IP, but adding it doesn't seem to hurt anything.**

CONFIGURING THE NETWARE NAME SPACE

When you configure the NetWare name space to become accessible to UnixWare systems, you have three choices: leave the servers as they are (Non-NFS Mode), update the name space to give priority to NetWare access rights over UnixWare permissions (NetWare Mode), or update the name space to give priority to UnixWare permissions (UNIX Mode or NFS Mode). Before you make this choice, you need to understand something about NetWare rights and UnixWare permissions.

> **See "UnixWare Permissions on NetWare Servers" later in this chapter for further information on rights and permissions.**

In all cases, files are stored on the NetWare server in its native format (DOS style). It is the mapping that differs between the different name space modes. Any time you view NetWare files and directories from UnixWare, it essentially puts a mask over the NetWare file system. Files and directories are still stored on the NetWare server with all the rights and attributes assigned to anything on the server. Those rights and attributes are then translated as closely as possible into UNIX semantics when you access the server from UnixWare.

In both the NetWare Mode and UNIX Mode cases, the name space is referred to as an NFS name space. This refers to Network File System, the mechanism used to share UNIX files and directories across a network.

NOTE **See the description of File Sharing in Chapter 5 for further information on NFS.**

Follow the procedure below to define which NetWare volumes on your NetWare server support NetWare or UNIX mode name spaces:

1 · On the NetWare server console, type VOLUMES. A list of mounted volumes and the name spaces they support appears. Volumes that support the NetWare Mode or UNIX Mode name spaces from UnixWare will have NFS listed in the Name Spaces column. For example,

```
Mounted Volumes              Name Spaces
     SYS                     DOS
     DOC                     DOS, NFS
     UNIXVOL1                DOS, NFS
```

2 · If you don't want the volume to support NFS (i.e., you want Non-NFS Mode only), type LOAD VREPAIR and remove the NFS name space. If, however, you want to add the NFS name space, proceed to the next step.

3 · If the NFS name space is not added to the volume, add it by typing the following:

```
ADD NAME SPACE NFS TO VOLUME VOL
```

where *VOL* is replaced by the name of the volume you want to add NFS to, or by the word **ALL** to add the name space to all volumes on the server.

4 · Now, to distinguish between a volume that uses a NetWare or
UNIX Mode name space, open the `sys:system\unistart.ncf`
file. Look for the line `load nuc` and see what follows it. If the
line is followed by the word `all`, then all NFS volumes will use
the UNIX Mode name space. Otherwise, specific volumes, or no
volumes, may be listed. In that case, only those specifically listed
will use the UNIX Mode name space. Those assigned as NFS but
not listed here will use the NetWare Mode name space when accessed from UnixWare. Here are some examples:

`load nuc all`

or

`load nuc unixvol1`

Using the VOLUMES listing shown earlier, the `load nuc all`
line would assign `DOC` and `UNIXVOL1` as UNIX Mode name
spaces. For `load nuc unixvol1`, only `UNIXVOL1` would be a
UNIX Mode name space, `DOC` would be a NetWare Mode name
space, and `SYS` would be a NetWare Mode name space.

The following sections on Non-NFS Mode, NetWare Mode, and UNIX
Mode describe how the rights and attributes for each of those modes relate
to how you access them from UnixWare.

Non-NFS Mode Name Space

No special configuration is required for NetWare to access the server's
DOS name space from UnixWare. There are, however, drawbacks to accessing DOS files and directories from UNIX.

File names on a DOS name space volume cannot exceed the DOS 8.3
character restriction (up to eight characters, plus an extension of up to
three characters, separated by a period). Some advanced UNIX features,
such as hard links and symbolic links, are not supported at all.

You cannot change the ownership on files or directories. All files appear
as though owned by authenticated user. Also, the support for changing

permissions is minimal. While UNIX lets you change permissions for the owner, group, and other, the DOS name space has no concept of group or other permissions.

There are certain special characters in DOS that you cannot use in file names (for example, */ [ ] :|<>+=;' "). Also, files do not distinguish between upper- and lowercase (so DOG is the same as dog).

 NOTE   **When this book went to press, the feature that allowed you to access a DOS name space on a NetWare server from UnixWare 2 was not working. Volumes that did not support the NFS name space in NetWare or UNIX mode could not be accessed. We hope the software will be corrected by the time you read this book.**

NetWare Mode Name Space

When a NetWare volume that is in NetWare Mode is viewed from Unix-Ware, traditional NetWare methods of file system security—such as effective rights, inherited rights masks, and trustee assignments—are in place. These methods will take precedence over traditional UNIX permissions. The idea here is that a NetWare administrator can maintain complete control of changes made to a NetWare volume by keeping it in NetWare Mode.

The differences between NetWare Mode and UNIX Mode affect what you are allowed to do when you try to create, view, modify, or delete files, or try to change their permissions. Here are a few tips that should help you understand what to expect when working with a NetWare Mode name space:

▸ Because Access Control rights take precedence over UNIX read, write, and execute permissions, you can't add or delete read or write (rw) permissions from a file.

▸ You can change the execute (x) permissions on a file if you are the owner.

▸ To open a file (click on an icon, click on File, then click on Open), you must have Read NetWare rights in the current folder.

- ▶ To create a new file (click on File, then click on New), you must have Create NetWare rights in the current folder.

- ▶ To copy a file (click on an icon, click on Edit, click on Copy, then select the target folder), you must have Read and File Scan NetWare rights in the current folder and Create NetWare right in the new folder.

- ▶ To rename a file (click on an icon, click on Edit, then click on Rename), you must have Modify NetWare rights for the file or folder.

- ▶ To move a file (click on an icon, click on Edit, click on Move, then select the target folder), you must have Read, Erase, and File Scan NetWare rights for the current file or folder and Create NetWare rights in the new folder.

- ▶ To link a file to another file (click on an icon, click on Edit, click on Link, then select the target file), you must have Read and File Scan NetWare rights for the current file or folder and Create NetWare rights in the new folder.

- ▶ To delete a file (click on an icon, click on Edit, then click on Delete), you must have Erase NetWare rights for the file or folder.

- ▶ To print a file (click on an icon, click on File, then click on Print), you must have Read and File Scan NetWare rights in the current folder.

The `ls` command, used to list information about files and directories, has been enhanced for UnixWare 2 to show when a user has Trustee rights or Access Control to a file listed from a NetWare server. A long listing (`ls -l`) of a file may be followed by + (for Access Control) or TA (for Trustee Assignment).

The server must be running NetWare 3.11 or later to be able to install the NetWare Mode name space.

NOTE

UNIX Mode Name Space

The way the files on a UNIX Mode name space appear to you from Unix-Ware is very similar to the way they would appear on a NetWare Mode name space. There are some striking differences, however.

If you have Access Control and Modify rights to a file stored on a Net-Ware server and it is configured with a UNIX Mode name space, you will be allowed to change the read and write (rw) permissions on that file from UnixWare, as well as the execute (x) permission. With a NetWare Mode name space, you would only be able to change the execute permissions.

Unlike a standard UNIX file system, however, if you do not have execute (x) permission for a folder you may still be able to do a search of that folder. In order to run an application from a NetWare server (i.e., to execute it), you must have at least read and execute (r_x) permissions.

When you try to change permissions on a NetWare file in UNIX mode, NetWare tries to assign access rights that approximate the requested UNIX permission. In order to do this, NetWare may change DOS file attributes to make the file's behavior match that of a UNIX file.

Ownership of a file or folder in UNIX Mode is determined by the Access Control rights. If you have them, you are shown as the owner on UnixWare. If not, you won't be shown as the owner, even if you have created the file. The mapped UID is shown as the owner (see the next section, "Assigning Users and Groups," for further information). You may appear as having group permission if you are part of the mapped group.

Here are a few other tips relating to the UNIX Mode name space:

▶ A new file or folder may inherit rights from its parent folder if the user id and group id of the user match those of the mapped ids on the parent folder. Otherwise, only Erase, Modify, and File Scan rights are allowed by the inherited rights mask.

▶ Standard file names can be used. You can have 255 characters and use upper- and lowercase. You can't use slash (/) or null characters in file names. If you look at the file on the DOS side, it will appear with a translated file name that fits the DOS naming style.

The server must be running NetWare 3.12 or later to be able to install the UNIX Mode name space.

ASSIGNING USERS AND GROUPS

In order to properly map your UnixWare users to the appropriate Net-
Ware users, you need to update three files on the NetWare server: passwd,
nfsusers, and nfsgroups. You must add this information if you want the
ownership of NetWare files to appear properly in UnixWare or if you want
to be able to use the UNIX chown and chgrp commands to change owner
and group assignments for files and folders.

A very good practice if you are maintaining a group of UNIX and Net-
Ware systems for a particular location is to keep the same list of users and
groups across all those systems. Then, for example, a user named chris with
a UID of 101 and a GID of 330 could have those names and numbers assigned on all systems on the network. If chris maintained the same password on all the computers, he could move easily among the computers,
maintaining the same permissions and not having to retype passwords.

If you're not sure of the UID for a UnixWare user, check the user account properties in the User Setup window in UnixWare or look in
the /etc/passwd file for the line containing the user name. To see
the GID for a group on your UnixWare system, check the group's
properties in the User Setup window or look in the /etc/group file
for the line containing the group name.

The following procedure describes how you can update the passwd,
nfsusers, and nfsgroups files on your NetWare server:

1 · Place a copy of the /etc/passwd file from your UnixWare system into the sys:etc\passwd file. Then edit that file to make
sure that there is only one entry for each user id in that file. The
user id is shown in the third field. So, in the example shown below, the UID for root is 0, chris is 101, and zorb is 102. No users

from other UnixWare systems should then be assigned to UID 0, 101, or 102 in `sys:etc\passwd` file.

```
root:x:0:3:0000-Admin(0000):/:/sbin/sh
chris:x:101:330::/home/chris:/usr/bin/ksh
zorb:x:102:330::/home/zorb:/usr/bin/ksh
```

2 · Assign the UnixWare UIDs to particular NetWare user names for the server in the `sys:etc\nfsusers` file. Again, all UIDs should be unique within this file. The `nfsusers` file should already contain entries for SUPERVISOR and NOBODY, which should not be removed. The following is an example of an `nfsusers` file.

```
   0        SUPERVISOR
  -2        NOBODY
 101        CHRIS
 102        ZORB
```

In this example, the users CHRIS and ZORB should be defined as NetWare users in the `sys:etc\nfsusers` file. If they are not, define them using the SYSCON utility.

3 · Assign the UnixWare GIDs to particular NetWare group names for the server in the `sys:etc\nfsgroup` file. As with UIDs, GID numbers should be unique in this file. The NOGROUP entry should not be changed. Here is an example of the `nfsgroup` file:

```
  -2        NOGROUP
 330        CLASSOC
 340        SALES
```

The group names should be existing NetWare group names, which you can add using the NetWare SYSCON utility. You can then add any of the new users to the NetWare groups. Those who are not assigned to a specific group are assigned to the group EVERYONE.

Starting Up NetWare Services

In most situations, you don't need to do anything to start up NetWare services from UnixWare. UnixWare finds the NetWare servers available on the network and lets you access the ones you want from the NetWare window on the Desktop or by using cd from the command line to move to the volume you want.

If you are not connecting your UnixWare system to a NetWare network, you should disable NetWare connectivity on startup. NetWare connectivity uses a lot of system processing power looking for NetWare services. Click on the Off button next to "NetWare UNIX Client" in the NetWare Setup window if you are not on a NetWare network or if you don't currently need NetWare services.

If you have a UnixWare Release 1.1 system and NetWare doesn't start up after you have rebooted your system, the problem might be that no NetWare servers are currently available. In UnixWare Release 1.1, to use any services on the network, at least one NetWare server needs to be up and running on the network. There is no such restriction in UnixWare 2.

Another possibility for startup problems is that UnixWare is using the wrong frame type for your NetWare servers. UnixWare checks for NetWare servers by trying up to four different frame types until it finds a NetWare server. You may want to force UnixWare to use a particular frame type for either of these reasons:

- ▶ Several different frame types are used on your network and UnixWare settles on a frame type that doesn't include the servers you want.

- ▶ The frame type used on your network is one of the last of the four checked, so it would be more efficient not to bother checking the other types each time UnixWare starts up.

Accessing NetWare Servers

Unlike other remote file services, such as the File Sharing window (based on the Network File System service), NetWare server access from UnixWare requires almost no configuration. When NetWare starts up on your system, it finds its own address from the nearest NetWare server and puts together a list of NetWare file servers you can access.

To see which NetWare file servers you can access on the network, you simply check the NetWare window by double-clicking on the NetWare icon in your Desktop window. The NetWare folder window appears, as shown in Figure 4.1.

Your system displays an icon for every file server it finds on the network that matches the frame type of the first server it finds. Each icon is tagged with the server name.

Sometimes a NetWare server is not listed. This happens when the frame type on your UnixWare system does not match the frame type on the Net-Ware server. (The default frame type for UnixWare is Ethernet 802.2.) To change the frame type, edit the file /etc/rc2.d/S24nw. Find the line that

FIGURE 4.1

NetWare servers in the
NetWare folder window

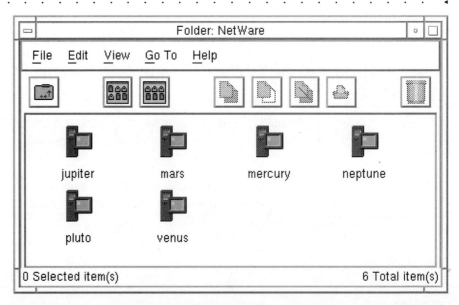

contains the nwdiscover command and add −f *frametype* to this command, where *frametype* is replaced by Ethernet_802.2, Ethernet_802.3, Ethernet_SNAP, or Ethernet_II.

VIEWING THE CONTENTS OF A SERVER

To view the contents of a particular NetWare server, double-click on that server's icon. There are a couple of things that might happen here, depending on the type of authentication scheme your system is using.

- ▶ No authentication required. If the single login feature is enabled, you may not have to authenticate at all. UnixWare takes your UnixWare login name and password and tries to use them to authenticate to the NetWare server. If this information matches login name and password on the server, the NetWare server may be immediately available.

- ▶ Authentication. If single login is not enabled or if your login and password don't match one on the server, you will see an Auto-Authenticator window, as shown in Figure 4.2.

Type in your user name for the NetWare server, press Tab to go to the Password box, type your user password, and press Enter.

For further information on authentication, see "Managing Authentication with NetWare Access" later in this chapter.

NOTE

If the login name and password match those set on the NetWare server, you will see a window with icons representing the volumes that are contained in that NetWare server. Figure 4.3 shows an example of a window with NetWare volume icons.

You may see another authentication window when you try to display individual NetWare volumes.

NOTE

FIGURE 4.2

Authenticating to a
NetWare server

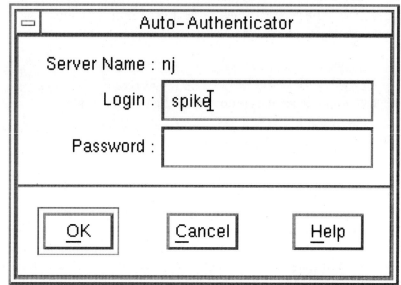

FIGURE 4.3

Displaying NetWare
volumes

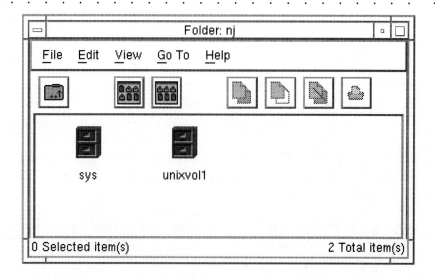

One of the volumes shown in Figure 4.3 is the basic NetWare SYS volume. The SYS volume contains four standard directories, plus an additional directory if your system includes the NUC NLM:

▶ The SYS:SYSTEM directory contains files and utilities for managing the NetWare server. Most of the contents of the SYSTEM directory must be managed by the SUPERVISOR.

▶ The SYS:PUBLIC directory contains utilities that can be used by NetWare users without requiring any special privileges.

▶ The SYS:LOGIN directory contains utilities related to logging in to NetWare.

▶ The SYS:MAIL directory contains user mailboxes and mail programs that are compatible with NetWare.

▶ The SYS:ETC directory is added if you're using the NUC NLM. It contains files for configuring the UNIX name space on NetWare. It also has utilities for translating files from DOS to UNIX and vice versa.

You may find other directories in the SYS volume. For example, there may be separate DOS directories in the SYS:PUBLIC directory. Often, separate directories appear for different applications. Also, there are probably directories for individual users so that they have a separate work space for storing their own files.

The other volume shown in Figure 4.3 is called unixvol1. We installed the UNIX name space on the NetWare server, then we created a volume named unixvol1. Next, we added the UNIX name space to the volume so we could create files and folders using UNIX file-naming conventions and modify permissions using UNIX-style commands.

If a server goes down, it automatically reconnects when it comes back up. You may need to authenticate again. However, if you are using the single login feature in UnixWare, it may just reconnect and let you continue your work.

Configuring NetWare Connectivity from the Desktop

On the UnixWare side, there is a lot you can do to configure your NetWare connectivity. The NetWare Setup window is the primary method of tuning the way you connect to NetWare. To access the NetWare Setup window from the Desktop window, double-click on the Admin Tools icon, double-click on the Networking icon, then double-click on the NetWare Setup icon. The NetWare Setup window appears, as shown in Figure 4.4.

The following are descriptions of the options you can enter on the NetWare Setup Window.

▶ **Server Name:** When your UnixWare system advertises the NetWare services it offers to the network, this is the name it uses to advertise those services. By default, your UnixWare system name is used. However, you can change this to another name (by editing the file `/etc/init.d/nw` and entering a name for *server_name*), as long as it doesn't conflict with other names on the network.

▶ **NetWare UNIX Client:** This simply turns on or off the entire NetWare connectivity feature. If this is off, you cannot access NetWare servers or use IPX-based applications (such as Application Sharing).

▶ **Enable IPX Auto Discovery:** Turn on this option to detect information about your network boards and about the NetWare network itself. If you add a new networking board, turn this option on, add the new board, then reboot. The new board should be detected and activated for NetWare.

▶ **IPX Internal LAN Address:** The number in this field represents the internal address of your LAN. Typically, this information is detected automatically and does not need to be typed in.

▶ **IPX Maximum Hops:** This value limits the number of nodes information can pass through (hop) from the UnixWare system on its way to a destination system. The maximum is 16, by default.

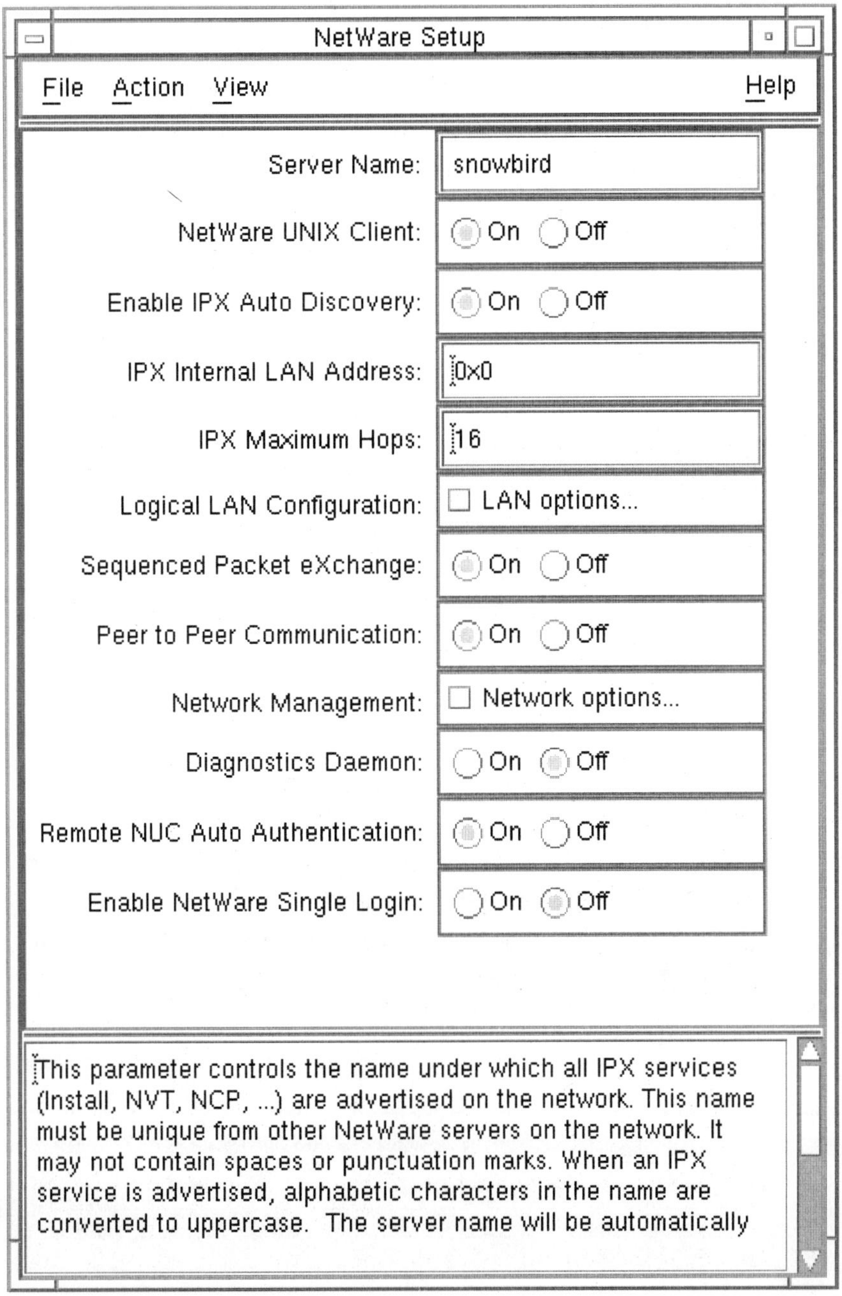

FIGURE 4.4
The NetWare Setup
window

NetWare Setup	
File Action View	Help

Server Name:	snowbird
NetWare UNIX Client:	● On ○ Off
Enable IPX Auto Discovery:	● On ○ Off
IPX Internal LAN Address:	0x0
IPX Maximum Hops:	16
Logical LAN Configuration:	☐ LAN options...
Sequenced Packet eXchange:	● On ○ Off
Peer to Peer Communication:	● On ○ Off
Network Management:	☐ Network options...
Diagnostics Daemon:	○ On ● Off
Remote NUC Auto Authentication:	● On ○ Off
Enable NetWare Single Login:	○ On ● Off

This parameter controls the name under which all IPX services
(Install, NVT, NCP, ...) are advertised on the network. This name
must be unique from other NetWare servers on the network. It
may not contain spaces or punctuation marks. When an IPX
service is advertised, alphabetic characters in the name are
converted to uppercase. The server name will be automatically

▸ **Logical LAN Configuration:** Click on this button to display the NetWare Setup: Logical LAN window, as shown in Figure 4.5. Typically, you don't need to change the information on this window. The IPX LAN Device shows the appropriate device for the network card you are using. The IPX LAN Frame Type defines the frame type. You may want to change frame type if the servers you want to connect to use a specific frame type. The IPX External LAN address and the LAN Speed are detected automatically and probably don't need to change.

▸ **Sequenced Packet eXchange:** Click on On to configure your system to use applications that require SPXII protocol. You can turn this off if you don't plan to use NVT or if you don't want to configure sockets for your system.

NetWare Setup

Logical LAN: 1

IPX LAN Device: /dev/TCM5X9_0

IPX LAN Frame Type: Ethernet 802.2

IPX External LAN Address: 0x1

LAN Speed (kilobytes/second):   10000

OK   Cancel   Help...

- ▶ **Peer to Peer Communications:** This enables peer-to-peer communications over IPX between you and other UnixWare systems on your network. By enabling this, you can share applications and install software among UnixWare systems using IPX protocol.

- ▶ **Network Management:** This enables network management features for your system using Simple Network Management Protocol (SNMP). SNMP is a networking feature that lets you centralize network management for many different heterogenous systems on the network.

- ▶ **Diagnostics Daemon:** By turning on the diagnostics daemon, you allow other nodes on the network to request diagnostic information from your system. When requested, your system will respond with an IPX Configuration Request Packet.

- ▶ **Remote NUC Auto Authentication:** This is on by default. When a user tries to access a NetWare server volume, instead of displaying an authentication window, the UnixWare system tries to authenticate using the current user's login name and user id. If this works, the user doesn't need to authenticate.

- ▶ **Enable NetWare Single Login:** This option can be used to enable the Auto Authentication feature for all users on your system.

After you have made changes to the NetWare Setup window, click on Actions, then click on Save Current Settings to activate the changes you have just made. If you don't like the changes you made, click on Restore Previous Settings (to go back to the most recently saved settings) or Restore Default (to restore the system's default settings).

Managing Authentication with NetWare Access

In order for you to access files from a NetWare server, you must authenticate to that server. If you have enabled single login and your password and login id match those on the NetWare server, authentication happens automatically. You will never have to type in your login and password.

If single login is not enabled, the first time you try to access a NetWare resource from the Desktop during a particular login session (by opening the folder for the NetWare server or printing to a NetWare printer), the Auto-Authenticator window appears.

Instead of authenticating at the time you try to access a NetWare server, you can manage your NetWare authentication through UnixWare's NetWare Access facility. The windows in the NetWare Access folder let you log in to and log out of NetWare servers. Once you have logged in to a server, you can see information about the volumes on that server and a list of users on your system that are logged in to the server.

To display NetWare Access information, double-click on the Admin Tools icon in the UnixWare Desktop window, double-click on Networking, and then double-click on the NetWare Access icon. The NetWare Access window appears, as shown in Figure 4.6. This window lists all the NetWare servers you can reach.

To authenticate to a server on the list, click on its name, and then click on the Login button at the bottom of the window. In the authentication window that appears, type your NetWare login name, press Tab, type your password, and click on Apply. In the NetWare Access window, your user name appears in the Authenticated list across from the server name. You

FIGURE 4.6

*The NetWare Access
window*

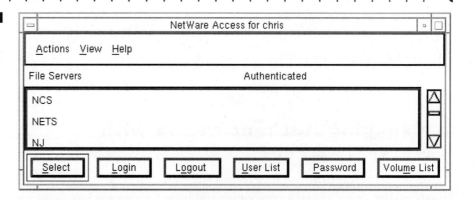

can now access files on that server and print to a printer connected to the server.

If you want to disconnect from a server, click on the server name and click on the Logout button. Your user name disappears from the list next to the server name.

To view information about the volumes on a particular server, click on the server name and click on the Volume List button. A list of volumes appears, as shown in Figure 4.7. For each volume, the Volume List window shows the total disk space available and the amount that has been used. The window also shows the total number of directories you are allowed on each volume (NetWare volumes have a limited number of directories), along with the number of directories that have been used.

Volume List for SLC-UNIVEL				
Volume	Total Bytes	Avail Bytes	Total Directories	Avail Directories
SYS	2375622656	127877120	483424	305219
NSE2	1387167744	68755456	135200	74570

| Cancel | Help... |

F I G U R E   4.7

Displaying NetWare server volume information

Once you open a NetWare server, by opening the server's icon or changing to the server's directory from a Terminal window, the server is mounted on your system. You can then check file system space on the NetWare server and volume using the standard UnixWare command /etc/dfspace from a Terminal window. You can also use the /etc/mount command to list mount information about the server and volume.

TECHNOTE

NETWARE AUTHENTICATION

As you use UnixWare, you may notice authentication windows popping up from time to time. Here is a list of times when you may see an authentication window:

▶ Printing to a NetWare printer. If you are printing to a NetWare printer and you are not already logged in to the NetWare server associated with the printer, an authentication window will pop up on your Desktop. The authentication window appears on your console monitor, even if another user queued the print job.

▶ Authenticating to different servers. Every time you try to access a different server, you will need to authenticate again.

▶ Authenticating for different users. If there are several users logged in to your system, each user who wants to access a NetWare server must authenticate.

You may also see authentication windows when you least expect them. An authentication window may pop up on either the graphical login window or on the Desktop immediately after you log in. This can happen when a directory representing a NetWare server or volume is in your PATH statement. The first time that directory is searched for a command, an authentication window appears. For example, if you set your PATH variable in the `.profile` file in your home directory to include the directory containing your WordPerfect application, which is installed on the NetWare server, the line in your `.profile` appears something like this:

```
PATH=$PATH:/home/chrisn/netware
    /spike/unixvol/wp/bin
```

When you run a command from a Terminal window, your standard UnixWare directories are searched for the command. If the command isn't found, you'll need to authenticate so that the WordPerfect `bin` directory can be searched.

Having NetWare volumes in your **PATH** variable can slow down your system's performance, especially if you run a command that is not found or if the NetWare volume is in the beginning of the **PATH** statement. See Chapter 8 for more information about setting up your **PATH** statement.

 **WARNING**

Trying to access a NetWare server from the command line can present authentication problems. If you try to access a NetWare server from a Terminal window or the console window, an authentication window appears on the Desktop and the command hangs. UnixWare doesn't seem to know where you are. For example, if you type a command such as

```
cd /home/chrisn/netware/spike
```

from a shell command line, the command hangs, waiting for the authentication window to be given the login name and password. Unfortunately, there may not be a Desktop graphical interface running at the moment. If you are logged in from a dumb terminal or an X-terminal, the Auto-Authenticator window may pop up on the console monitor's Desktop.

If you need to access a NetWare server from a nongraphical, command line interface, authenticate from the command line before trying to access the server. You can do this with the `nwlogin` command, as described in the next section.

We noticed that the active connections to NetWare servers are not always disconnected when the user logs off of UnixWare. Users are not logged out of NetWare when they log out of UnixWare. If you find your NetWare connections are failing, check to see if all the connections to the NetWare server are used. Delete any connections that you are no longer using.

 NOTE

Connecting to NetWare with UnixWare Commands

UnixWare comes with a set of commands that let you access NetWare from the command line. If you are an experienced DOS or UNIX system user, you might find it more comfortable to work from the command line than from the Desktop graphical interface. Most of these commands are the same, or at least similar to, the commands you use from a DOS workstation to connect to NetWare.

The first step is to authenticate to the NetWare server you want to access (`nwlogin`). Starting from your home directory, you simply change to the **netware** directory (`cd $HOME/netware`). From there, you can list the contents of the directory (`ls`) to see each server you can reach.

Once you are in the **netware** directory, you can move down the directory structure into the NetWare servers and volumes you want to access. You can use standard UnixWare commands to copy, move, delete, and edit files on the NetWare server. You can also run applications that are stored on the server.

The following sections describe some of the commands you can use to work with NetWare servers. Enter the commands from the command line of a UnixWare Terminal window.

AUTHENTICATING (nwlogin)

Authenticating to NetWare from the command line is a little tricky at first. Before you try to access any NetWare volumes from the command line in UnixWare, you should authenticate to the NetWare server containing the volume to let UnixWare know where you are trying to access NetWare from. When you try to use a NetWare resource, UnixWare displays an authentication window on the Desktop. In UnixWare 1.1, if you were working from a virtual terminal or a dumb terminal, you would just hang waiting for authentication. The authentication window may have appeared on someone else's screen, or it may not have come up at all. This problem seems to have been corrected in UnixWare 2.

To use the `nwlogin` command to authenticate to a NetWare server, use the command in one of the following forms:

```
nwlogin server/user
nwlogin user
```

In the first case, *server* is replaced by the name of the NetWare server and *user* is replaced by your NetWare user name. The second example lets you authenticate to the primary server you have defined using the `nwprimserver` command with the noted NetWare user name. You are prompted for the user's password:

```
Password for user on server server:
```

Enter the password for the server. Once you are authenticated, you can change into the server's directories and use printing services from the server.

LOGGING OUT OF SERVERS (nwlogout)

When you are finished using a NetWare server, or if you want to log in as a different NetWare user, you can log out from the server with the `nwlogout` command, using the following form:

```
nwlogout server
```

where *server* is replaced by the name of the server you want to log out of. After you have logged out, you can log in again as a different user with the `nwlogin` command.

VIEWING YOUR NETWARE CONNECTIONS (nwwhoami)

You can list all the servers to which you are currently authenticated by using the command

```
nwwhoami
```

Figure 4.8 shows an example of the output from the `nwwhoami` command.

FIGURE 4.8

Output from the
nwwhoami *command*

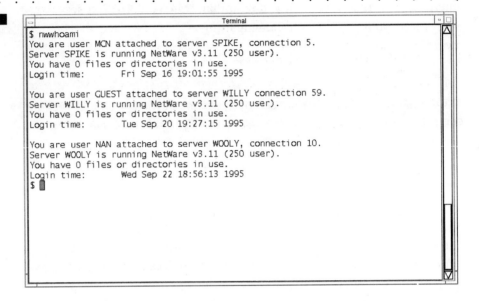

```
Terminal

$ nwwhoami
You are user MCN attached to server SPIKE, connection 5.
Server SPIKE is running NetWare v3.11 (250 user).
You have 0 files or directories in use.
Login time:       Fri Sep 16 19:01:55 1995

You are user GUEST attached to server WILLY connection 59.
Server WILLY is running NetWare v3.11 (250 user).
You have 0 files or directories in use.
Login time:       Tue Sep 20 19:27:15 1995

You are user NAN attached to server WOOLY, connection 10.
Server WOOLY is running NetWare v3.11 (250 user).
You have 0 files or directories in use.
Login time:       Wed Sep 22 18:56:13 1995
$
```

In the example, the output shows connections to three NetWare servers (SPIKE, WILLY, and WOOLY) from your login on your UnixWare system. Notice that you can be attached to different servers as different users (MCN, GUEST, and NAN). The Login time lines show the time and date you logged into each server. Other information listed by nwwhoami includes the version of the NetWare operating system, the number of connections allowed to the NetWare server (250), the number of your connection to the server (5, 59, and 10, respectively), and the number of files and directories you are currently using.

CHANGING YOUR NETWARE PASSWORD (setpass)

You can change the password set for you on a particular NetWare file server by using the setpass command. To use setpass, type the following:

setpass *fileserver*/*name*

where *fileserver* is replaced by the name of the NetWare file server and *name* is replaced by your user name on the NetWare server. You are prompted for the old password, the new password, then the new password again to confirm it.

If you are using the single login feature to automatically authenticate you to the server, you will want to make sure this password still matches your current UnixWare password. If not, then you will have to authenticate again.

MOUNTING A NETWARE VOLUME MANUALLY (mount)

The standard UnixWare mount command is used to connect NetWare servers to your system. Two different file system types are used to mount NetWare file systems: nucam and nucfs. The /.NetWare directory is a nucam file system type. A NetWare volume in UnixWare (for example, /.NetWare/spike/unixvol) is a nucfs type. A nucam file system is not intended to be mounted manually.

To mount a NetWare volume (nucfs file system) manually, you must run the mount command as the root user from a Terminal window:

```
mount -F nucfs spike/unixvol /.NetWare
    /spike/unixvol
```

If you have not already authenticated to this server, an authentication window will pop up after you enter this command.

AUTOMATICALLY UNMOUNTING INACTIVE VOLUMES (nucd)

During NetWare connectivity startup, the nucd daemon process is started to handle most of the NetWare connectivity processing in UnixWare. One of nucd's ongoing functions is to check all mounted NetWare volumes. When nucd finds a volume that is not being used, it unmounts that volume from your system.

When you open a NetWare server folder from your NetWare window or change to a server directory from a Terminal window and are authenticated, the server volume is automatically mounted on your system.

As long as you are using the volume (for example, the volume's folder or a file in that folder is open), the volume remains mounted. However, when the volume is no longer in use, `nucd` automatically unmounts it.

Using NetWare from DOS Merge

When you start up DOS Merge (by double-clicking on the DOS or Win icon in the Applications folder window), NetWare connectivity is automatically started from the DOS or Windows session. Two commands are run to start NetWare within a DOS Merge session: `j:\share\novell\ipxtli` and `j:\share\novell\netx`.

The `netx` command finds the nearest server and connects to it. To access the NetWare server, type `O:` from the DOS prompt. Then you can type `login user` (replacing *user* with your user name). When prompted, type the password, and you're logged in.

FORCING A SERVER CONNECTION ON DOS STARTUP

If you want to connect to a different server than the one `netx` picked, you can force the `netx` command to connect to a particular server. To force a connection to a particular server, you must edit the `/autoexec.bat` file as the root user to add a `PS` argument to the `netx` line.

For example, if you want to force the server `spike` to be the one you connect to when DOS starts up, open a Terminal window, obtain root user permissions, and open the `/autoexec.bat` file in an editor. Then change the `netx` line to look like this:

```
j:\share\novell\netx PS=spike
```

The next time you open a DOS Merge session, you will connect to the Net-Ware server named `spike`.

DISABLING CONNECTIVITY IN MERGE

If you don't want to connect to NetWare every time you open a DOS window, you can disable NetWare connectivity in DOS Merge. To disable this connectivity, edit the /autoexec.bat file (from a Terminal window as the root user). Add REM to the beginning of the ipxtli and netx lines in the file, so they appear as follows:

```
REM j:\share\novell\ipxtli
REM j:\share\novell\netx
```

See Chapter 6 to learn about changing your /autoexec.bat file so you can select whether or not to connect to a NetWare server each time you start a DOS or Windows session.

NOTE

UnixWare Permissions on NetWare Servers

Using NetWare files and folders from a UnixWare system means more than just mounting a NetWare file server. You may want to be able to use UnixWare features to change permissions, assign ownership, and copy, move, and link files and directories as though they were stored on your UnixWare system.

UnixWare and NetWare have their own methods for managing the ownership and permissions of files and directories. When you use a NetWare server from UnixWare, you effectively mask the NetWare permissions so everything on the server looks like UnixWare.

UnixWare lets you create two floppy disks, containing NetWare Loadable Modules (NLMs) that you can install on your NetWare servers. These NLMs add software to your NetWare servers that let you add UNIX (NFS) name spaces to the volumes on your servers. The contents of these floppies are referred to as the NUC (NetWare UNIX Client) NLM. The UNIX name space lets you store files that use long file names, implement UNIX read/write/execute permissions, and support UNIX features such as file linking.

In effect, the UNIX name space places a mask over the NetWare file system. Files are still stored with NetWare access rights, but those rights are mapped into UNIX system permissions so they can be manipulated with UNIX commands.

You will find it easier to work with NetWare servers from UnixWare if you understand NetWare Access Control, UnixWare permissions, and how UnixWare methods for working with files fit into the NetWare model.

INSTALLING UNIX NLMS ON NETWARE

Before you can install the UNIX name space on a NetWare server, you must create the two NLM floppy disks. The software to create these disks is contained in the UnixWare file system and must be placed on DOS floppy disks, as described below.

1 • From UnixWare, create two DOS floppy disks using the following command:

```
dosformat -v /dev/rdsk/f03ht
```

(This command assumes you are using a 3.5-inch floppy in drive A:. If it were drive B:, the device would be f13ht. Don't use 5.25-inch floppies, because the software won't fit.) Label one floppy *disk1* and the other *disk2*.

2 • Copy the contents of `/var/spool/nwsup/NWserv/nwuc/disk1` to the floppy you labeled *disk1*. The best way to do this is to open a window to both the floppy disk (from the Disks-etc window) and the `disk1` directory. Then select all contents and copy them to the floppy.

3 • Repeat step two for the second floppy disk (labeled *disk2*), copying the contents of `/var/spool/nwsup/NWserv/nwuc/disk2`.

4 · Install disk1, then disk2, on each NetWare server you want to communicate with from UnixWare, by selecting Product Options from the Install Screen.

A more detailed description of the process of installing these NLMs is contained in the NLM Installation and Administration document available through the UnixWare Online Docs. See Chapter 3, "Installing UnixWare NLMs on NetWare," in that document.

NOTE

NETWARE ACCESS CONTROLS

NetWare trustee right assignments govern the permissions of users and groups to particular files and directories. NetWare trustee rights are different from UnixWare file permissions. If you have trustee rights to a directory, those rights are propagated down the directory structure unless they are overridden by different trustee rights set in a subdirectory. Every file and directory in UnixWare has individual permissions associated with it, based on who creates it. When you use files and directories that are stored on a NetWare server from a UnixWare system, those resources appear to have UnixWare permissions, but they are stored by NetWare using NetWare rights.

Eight types of NetWare rights are assigned to the files and directories on a NetWare server:

- ▶ **Supervisor**: A user with supervisor rights to a directory has complete rights to any files and subdirectories in that directory. Supervisor rights to a directory also give the user permission to assign those rights to other users as well. Supervisor permissions are designated by the letter *S*.

- ▶ **Read:** With read permissions to a directory, you can use the files in the directory, but you cannot change them. Using a file consists of opening it, reading the contents, or executing it (if the file has execute permissions). If you have read permissions to a file, you can open and read the file, even if the directory containing it doesn't allow you to have read access. Read permissions are designated by the letter R.

▶ **Write:** You can open and write to all files and subdirectories in the directory for which you have write permissions. If you have write permissions to a file, you can change that file, even if you don't have write permissions to the directory. Write permissions are designated by the letter W.

▶ **Create:** You can create directories and files within a directory for which you have create permissions. With create permissions on a file, you can retrieve a deleted file. Create permissions are designated by the letter C.

▶ **Erase:** You can delete any files or directories for which you have erase permissions. You can delete a file for which you have erase permissions, even if you don't have erase permission for the directory. Erase permissions are designated by the letter E.

▶ **Modify:** A user with modify rights to a directory or file can rename or change attributes for the directory or file. Within a directory for which you have modify rights, you can rename or change attributes for all files and subdirectories. You can change a file's name and attributes if you have modify rights, even if you don't have modify rights for the directory containing it. Modify permissions are designated by the letter M.

▶ **File Scan:** You can see the file or directory for which you have file scan rights. For directories, this means you can see any files and directories within that directory. File scan permissions are designated by the letter F.

▶ **Access Control:** With Access Control rights, you can change trustee assignments and inherited rights masks. Trustee assignments are the rights assigned to a user or group to work with a particular directory or file. An inherited rights mask is assigned to each file and directory as it is created to define the rights users can inherit. In other words, a directory's inherited rights mask determines which of a directory's rights are in effect in its subdirectories. Access Control permissions are designated by the letter *A*.

NETWARE FILE ATTRIBUTES

In NetWare, files and directories also have *attributes*. Most NetWare file and directory attributes cannot be manipulated from UnixWare. Table 4.1 lists NetWare file attributes and whether or not you can modify them from UnixWare.

ATTRIBUTE	MODIFY FROM UNIXWARE?
File Attributes	
Archive Needed	No
Copy Inhibit	No
Delete Inhibit	No
Execute Only	No
Hidden	No
Indexed	No
Purge	No
Read Audit	No
Read Only	Yes
Read Write	No
Rename Inhibit	Yes
Shareable	Yes
System	No
Transactional	Yes
Write Audit	No

TABLE 4.1

NetWare file and directory attributes

TABLE   4.1

NetWare file and directory
attributes (continued)

ATTRIBUTE	MODIFY FROM UNIXWARE?
Directory Attributes	
Delete Inhibit	Yes
Hidden	No
Purge	No
Rename Inhibit	No
System	No

UNDERSTANDING UNIXWARE PERMISSIONS

Three types of UnixWare system permissions are associated with files
and directories: read, write, and execute. For each file and directory, permissions are assigned to three sets of users: the owner of the file, the group
assigned to the file, and all other users.

To see the permissions assigned to the files and directories in your current directory, open a Terminal window and type

```
ls -l
```

Figure 4.9 shows an example of the output.

The first column on the display contains ten characters. The first character indicates what the item is. A **d** represents a directory. In the example
shown in Figure 4.9, the first two items are directories. A – (dash) as the
first character means that the item is a file. The third, fourth, and fifth items
in Figure 4.9 are files.

The next nine characters in the column represent the three types of permissions for each of the three sets of users. For example, the first item in
Figure 4.9 is listed as

```
drwxr-xr-x  2 spike  doc  96 Sep 20 15:32 Info
```

After the **d** (for directory), the first three characters define the permissions
the owner (spike) has in the directory: read, write, and execute (rwx). The
next three characters define the permissions anyone in the group (doc)

```
┌─ ──────────────────────────────── Terminal ─────────────────────────┐ ·□
│ $ ls -l                                                              │△│
│ total 190                                                            │ │
│ drwxr-xr-x   2 spike    doc        96 Sep 20 15:32 Info              │ │
│ drwxr-xr-x   2 spike    doc        96 Sep 21 11:23 Old               │ │
│ -rw-rw-r--   1 spike    doc     18589 Sep 20 15:39 figure5.1         │ │
│ -rwxr-x---   1 spike    doc     11119 Sep 21 11:23 myscript          │ │
│ -rw-r--r--   1 spike    doc     66481 Sep 20 15:48 netware.wp        │ │
│ $ ▊                                                                  │ │
│                                                                      │ │
```

FIGURE 4.9

Output from the ls -l
command, showing
permissions for several
files and directories

assigned to the directory (Info) has in the directory: read and execute
(r-x). A dash indicates the permission in that position is not in effect. The
final three characters define the permissions everyone else who can log in
to the system has on the file: read and execute (r-x).

> **Other items in the file system can be represented in file and direc-
> tory listings. For example, in the /dev directory, you will find entries
> that begin with a b, which are block devices, and others that begin
> with a c, which are character devices.**

NOTE

In UnixWare, you can use a single, octal number, from 0 to 7, to represent each of the three sets of permissions on the file. You determine the
number by totaling the values for each type of permission in the set. Read
permission (r) has a value of 4, write (w) is 2, and execute (x) is 1. For the
Info directory in the example, the owner permissions are read (4), write (2),
and execute (1), which adds up to 7. Group and other permissions are both
read (4) and execute (1), so their permissions both equal 5. You put the
three numbers together, for permissions of 755.

In the last entry in Figure 4.9:

```
-rw-r--r--  1 spike   doc   66481 Sep 20
   15:48 netware.wp
```

The permissions for the file (`netware.wp`) are `rw-`, or 6, for the owner, and `r--`, or 4, for both the group and other users, for permissions of 644.

Permissions of 755 (on directories and commands) and 644 (on files) are common. These permissions let everyone search your directories, run your commands, and read your files, but they don't allow anyone but you to change them.

When you create files and directories in the course of your work, they are assigned default permissions. Your default permissions are determined by something called the `umask`. To see your `umask`, open a Terminal window and type

```
umask
```

By default, the numbers `022` should be returned by the command. Now subtract the `umask` number (022) from the maximum file permissions of 666 (when you create a file) or maximum directory permissions of 777 (when you create a directory) to determine the default permissions for the file or directory. With the default `umask` of 022, files are created with 644 permissions and directories have 755 permissions.

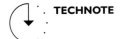 **TECHNOTE**   **The `umask` is set by the line `umask  022` in the `/etc/.profile` file for all users on the system. However, you can add a `umask` line to your own `.profile` file to override the system `umask` for any files and directories you create.**

To change the permissions on a file or directory, you must either own the file or be the root user. The command for changing permission on a file is `chmod`. The most common method is to use the permission numbers, as in

```
chmod 777 file1
```

where *file1* is the name of the file whose permissions you want to change. (Using 777 completely opens permissions to a file.)

You can also use chmod to change permissions individually, as in the following examples:

```
chmod u+w file1
chmod g-r file1
chmod o+x file1
chmod +w file1
chmod -x file1
```

The u stands for the user who owns a file, the g is for the file's group, and the o is for others. You can add or subtract certain permissions for the file by simply typing the letter for the user, group, or owner (u, g, or o), then a plus (+) or a minus (−) followed by a permission (r, w, or x). If you don't include the letter u, g, or o, the permissions apply to all three sets: owner, group, and other users.

COMPARING NETWARE RIGHTS AND UNIXWARE PERMISSIONS

The UNIX name space on the NetWare server maps permissions requested from UnixWare into the appropriate NetWare rights. This mapping takes place every time a file or directory is created from UnixWare on a NetWare server or whenever a permission change is requested.

To see how UnixWare permissions map into the NetWare file server, you can create several files and directories on a NetWare file server, change them to have various permissions, and check the resulting NetWare rights, as shown in the procedure below.

1 · From your UnixWare Desktop window, double-click on the Applications window, then double-click on Terminal to open a Terminal window.

2 · Change the directory to the NetWare server's directory. For example, for the server named mars, type

```
cd /.NetWare/mars
```

3 · If an authentication window appears, authenticate to the Net-Ware server.

4 · Change to the NetWare volume that contains the UNIX name space. For example, to change to `vol1`, type

```
cd vol1
```

5 · Change to any directory within that volume that allows you to write in it. For example, to change to the directory named `chris`, type

```
cd chris
```

6 · Create several files and directories, using the form

```
touch file1 file2 file3 file4
mkdir dir1 dir2 dir3 dir4
```

7 · Change the permissions on each file using the `chmod` command, as follows:

```
chmod 644 file1
chmod 600 file2
chmod 400 file3
chmod 100 file4
chmod 755 dir1
chmod 700 dir2
chmod 500 dir3
chmod 100 dir4
```

To see the permissions on the files and directories, type

```
ls -l
```

The output appears as follows:

```
total 8
drwxr-xr-x  2 chris  399  512 Feb 28 17:40 dir1
drwx------  2 chris  399  512 Feb 28 17:41 dir2
dr-x------  2 chris  399  512 Feb 28 17:41 dir3
d--x------  2 chris  399  512 Feb 28 17:41 dir4
-rw-r--r--  1 chris  399    0 Feb 28 17:38 file1
-rw-------  1 chris  399    0 Feb 28 17:38 file2
-r--------  1 chris  399    0 Feb 28 17:38 file3
---x------  1 chris  399    0 Feb 28 17:38 file4
```

CHECKING RIGHTS ON THE NETWARE SERVER

To compare the permissions of files and directories you just created on the NetWare server from UnixWare to the rights they have on the NetWare server, log in to the NetWare server from any DOS client and follow the procedure below:

1 · Log in to the NetWare server. For example, to log in to the server mars as user chris, type

```
login mars/chris
```

2 · Go to the directory where you created the files. For example:

```
cd vol1:\chris
```

3 · Type the following to see the NetWare rights:

```
ndir
```

The following is an example of the output:

```
Files         = Files contained in this path
Size          = Number of bytes in the file
Last Update = Date file was last updated
Owner         = ID of user who created or copied the file

MARS/VOL1: CHRIS\*.*
Files    Size  Last Update     Owner
-------- ----- --------------- -----
FILE1  u    0  2-28-95 5:38p   chris
FILE2  u    0  2-28-95 5:38p   chris
FILE3  u    0  2-28-95 5:38p   chris
FILE4  u    0  2-28-95 5:38p   chris

Directories = Directories contained in this path
Filter      = Inherited Rights Filter
Rights      = Effective Rights
Created     = Date directory was created
Owner       = ID of user who created or copied the file
```

```
MARS/VOL1: CHRIS\*.*
Directories  Filter      Rights        Created         Owner
------------ ----------- ------------- --------------- -----
DIR1         [SRWCEMFA]  [-RWCEMFA]    2-28-95 5:40p   chris
DIR2         [SRWCEMFA]  [-RWCEMFA]    2-28-95 5:40p   chris
DIR3         [SRWCEMFA]  [-RW-EMFA]    2-28-95 5:40p   chris
DIR4         [SRWCEMFA]  [-RW-EM-A]    2-28-95 5:40p   chris

     0  bytes (0  bytes of disk space used)
     4  Files
     4  Directories
```

Notice that with the directory dir4, even though read and write permissions were removed from the UnixWare side, read and write rights were maintained on the NetWare side. Removing read permissions did, however, remove the filescan (F) rights from dir4. Notice also that create (C) rights were removed from dir3 and dir4.

Using NetWare Tunable Parameters

UnixWare places limits on the number of users that can use NetWare simultaneously from UnixWare and the number of connections a single UnixWare user can have to different servers at the same time. On the NetWare side, the only parameter you need to change to support UnixWare is the one that supports your time zone.

CHANGING UNIXWARE PARAMETERS

The tunable parameters in UnixWare that relate to NetWare are defined in the file /etc/conf/mtune.d/nuc. The two parameters you may want to change are NUCLOGINS and NUCUSERS. By default, you can have eight different users logged into NetWare servers from your UnixWare system (NUCUSERS=8) and each user can be logged into up to 32 servers (NUCLOGINS=32).

For the Personal Edition version of UnixWare, you probably won't need to change either of these values. On a UnixWare Application Server system, you might have more than eight users trying to log in to NetWare servers. A larger system may also have the processing power to be working with many simultaneous connections to NetWare systems.

See Chapter 9 for descriptions of how to incorporate changes to tunable parameters into your UnixWare system.

The combination of the NetWare connectivity features in UnixWare and the NUC NLM available with NetWare provide a nearly transparent way of using NetWare services from a UnixWare system. Interfaces to NetWare servers are provided from both the UnixWare Desktop and the UnixWare command line interface.

As you connect to NetWare services from UnixWare, you may be required to authenticate to NetWare servers. You can authenticate from the Desktop or the command line. Because you can be logged in as different users on your UnixWare system, this chapter also described when authentication is required by multiple users.

What you can do in NetWare files and directories depends on your NetWare rights and UnixWare permissions. Because NetWare maps UnixWare permissions to NetWare rights, you should understand the relationship between these two different ways of protecting your files.

Finally, the chapter reviewed some of the command line utilities you can use to log in to NetWare servers and mount file systems manually.

The next chapter describes how to connect your UNIX System V system to other UNIX systems, using such networking facilities as TCP/IP and Basic Networking Utilities (BNU).

## CHAPTER 5

Connecting
to UNIX Systems

By networking your computer, you can exchange information with other computers. Most computers running UNIX have a variety of networking services available. Many of the networking features that must be purchased separately with other operating systems are built into UnixWare. After some setup, you can log in to remote systems, copy files, execute commands, and connect to file systems on remote computers.

Several networking technologies are built into UnixWare: Basic Networking Utilities (BNU), TCP/IP, and NetWare UNIX Client (connecting to NetWare servers). As the technology advances, the boundaries between these products begin to blur. However, in general, each of these products consists of a set of protocols (rules by which systems communicate) and utilities (specific applications for file transfer, remote login, file sharing, and other networking services). Some utilities, such as mail, cross product boundaries and allow you to use the utilities to communicate over many different network protocols.

The ability to connect seamlessly to NetWare servers is the strongest value-added networking feature of the UnixWare system. Once you have connected your UnixWare system to a network with NetWare servers, those servers appear in the NetWare window on your UnixWare Desktop.

NOTE   **UnixWare's NetWare connectivity is described in Chapter 4.**

▶ · ◀
Networking with the Desktop

Because the Desktop graphical interface for the UnixWare system is still relatively new and UNIX networking has grown for years, there are limits to what you can do strictly from the Desktop. If you have used UnixWare 1.1, however, you will notice that these capabilities have been greatly expanded in UnixWare 2.

This chapter describes the procedures for networking from the Desktop, as well as the commands you need to execute from the command line for special networking needs.

The primary Desktop windows you use to configure networking are all accessed from the Networking folder window (located in the Admin Tools folder window):

▸ **Dialup Setup:** This window lets you configure Basic Networking Utilities. With Dialup Setup, you define the networking devices (modems or direct connections) and remote systems with which you can communicate. You can also configure UnixWare to connect to character terminals with Dialup Setup.

▸ **Internet Setup:** This window lets you set up the systems you can communicate with over TCP/IP.

▸ **File Sharing:** This window lets you connect remote directories and files to your system and share your directories and files with remote systems. File Sharing is built on the Network File System (NFS). File Sharing relies on TCP/IP being installed on your system.

Once you have configured a remote system using Dialup Setup or Internet Setup, you can install an icon representing the remote system in any folder window. You can then log in to the remote system by double-clicking on the remote system icon. You can also copy a file to the remote system by dragging-and-dropping the file icon on the remote system icon.

Using Basic Networking Utilities

Basic Networking Utilities (BNU) provide the features that allow serial communications with other systems. BNU features, which were once an add-on package to UNIX, are now part of the UnixWare base system. You might also hear BNU referred to as uucp, the UNIX-to-UNIX copy program that is the cornerstone of BNU.

To use BNU, you typically connect the appropriate hardware to the COM1, COM2, or other serial ports on your computer. You can use one of the following types of networking hardware with BNU:

▸ A modem for networking over telephone lines

▸ A null modem cable for direct connections to another computer or terminal

▸ A network switch, such as Datakit

▸ A serial ports board, to expand the number of terminals, computers, or modems you can connect to your computer

After your hardware is installed, you set up configuration files to identify the network connections and remote systems available to your system. Then you can use any of the BNU commands to communicate over that hardware. From the Desktop, you can double-click on a remote system icon to connect with that system or drag-and-drop a file on it to transfer the file to that system. From a Terminal window, you can use cu to log in to the remote system, uucp to copy remote files, rexec to execute commands remotely, and other BNU commands.

The BNU services are connection-oriented. This means that each time your system needs to send data, it sets up a connection with the remote system. For example, when you transfer a file or log in to a remote system using a modem connection, your modem calls the modem connected to the remote system, sets up a connection, then sends data across that connection. This is in contrast to a connectionless network, such as TCP/IP, on which information is simply broadcast onto the wire and picked up by the appropriate computer.

The following sections describe how to set up modems and direct connections, as well as how to use BNU across those network connections.

COMMUNICATING OVER MODEMS

A modem is used for communications between computers over telephone lines. *Modem* is short for MOdulator and DEModulator. A modem modulates the data from one system to send it over telephone lines in analog form. Then the remote modem demodulates the data and relays it to the remote system.

To set up a connection between two systems with BNU, you need to configure the outgoing side (the system placing the call) differently than you configure the incoming side (the side accepting the call). Of course, both systems can be configured to handle both incoming and outgoing calls.

Figure 5.1 shows the basic setup that is required before you can establish a connection over modems to a remote system.

You set up networking from the bottom up and you use it from the top down. After you connect your modem, you identify the type of modem, the port it's connected to, and the names and addresses (or telephone numbers) of the systems you can reach over the modem. To use the connection, you typically run a command (such as cu or uucp) using the system name as an argument, and the connection is set up.

The advantage to the bottom-up approach to setting up a networking connection is that you can test each level before you move on to the next. For example, if you correct problems with modem settings and cables before trying to transfer a file, you will reduce the potential problem areas if the file transfer doesn't work.

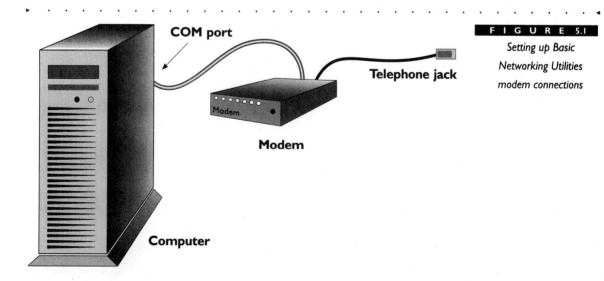

COM port

Telephone jack

Modem

Computer

FIGURE 5.1

Setting up Basic
Networking Utilities
modem connections

Setting up a modem can be tricky. The procedures outlined in the following sections include methods for checking the modem each step of the way, so you can pinpoint and correct any problems that come up.

CONNECTING THE MODEM

Most intelligent, Hayes-compatible modems let you change modem settings through the software. To make these changes, you must set up a direct connection to the modem. Unfortunately, you cannot currently do this through UnixWare's Dialup Setup window, so you need to enter commands at the command line (as the root user).

1 · Connect the cables. Most modems come with a serial RS-232 cable to connect from your serial port to the modem. A 9-pin connector should work, but if you have a choice, use a 25-pin connector. Some cables that are intended for use with DOS won't work for UnixWare.

2 · Connect the telephone wire from your modem to your telephone jack.

3 · Configure a direct connection. To do so, log in as the root user, open a Terminal window, and add an entry to the file called /etc/uucp/Devices. The entry has the format

```
Direct ttyXX,M - baud_rate direct_modem
```

Use tty00 for COM1 or tty01 for COM2. For example, to talk to a modem connected to the COM2 port at a baud rate of 9600 bps, enter

```
Direct tty01,M - 9600 direct_modem
```

4 · Connect to the modem. To actually change modem settings, you must call the modem using the cu command. For example, to call the modem configured in the previous step, from a Terminal window, type

```
cu -l tty01
```

In some cases, CU puts a port into a state in which you can't use it. You may find that you sometimes need to reboot to get the port working again.

 **WARNING**

5 · After you get a message that you are connected, type AT. If the modem connection is working, you will get the message OK. If you don't get an OK message, check the cables, check that the modem is plugged in, and make sure the entry in the Devices file is correct. Also check the permissions on the port, because a UnixWare application might have closed off the permissions on the port. You can type

```
ls -l /dev/tty01
```

(use tty00 for COM1) to see if there is write permission on the port. If there isn't, open the port by typing this command from a Terminal window:

```
chmod 666 /dev/tty01
```

6 · Change modem settings. Use the same CU command you typed in step 3 above to connect to the modem. Then change the settings as necessary to set up the modem to accept outgoing calls. Use the commands and settings specified in your modem manual. Some modems require special settings. Also, even Hayes-compatible modems have different ways of extending the AT command for their special features. For example, here are the settings used to set up a ZyXEL U-1496 series modem to accept outgoing calls:

```
ATS0=0
ATS15=130
ATS20=7
ATQ2
ATQ1 AT&W
```

The first command, ATS0=0, turns off auto-answering. Make it ATS0=1 to turn on auto-answering.

 TECHNOTE

We have also had some luck setting the modem to higher speeds. This entailed setting ATS20=2, which set the DTE speed (the speed between the computer and the modem) to 38.4 baud rate. We then set AT&N=0 to auto-negotiate the link rate between the modems. After that, the only requirement was to change the line speed for the `ttymon` entry on the incoming call side of the connection from 9600 to 19200. Depending on the quality of the telephone lines, we could actually get the 19200 baud rate. Otherwise, it would cycle down to a lower speed. Also, the 19200NP entry was preferable to the 19200 entry.

7 · To check that your settings are correct, type AT&V0 (for a ZyXEL modem; your modem may differ) to display all the modem settings.

8 · Before you try to make a call using UnixWare, try to place a call directly from the modem. Type the command ATDT followed by the telephone number, as in ATDT *1234567*, where *1234567* is the telephone number that will connect you to the remote modem. This tells the modem to use touch-tone dialing (T) to dial (D) the remote system. If the call is completed, you see a CONNECT message.

9 · Return to the UnixWare Terminal window by typing a tilde and a period (~.) to exit cu.

Identifying the Modem and Port

You can use the Dialup Setup window to configure most modem connections, including those for Hayes-compatible modems. Unfortunately, the Dialup Setup window procedure replaces the `Direct` entry for connecting directly to the modem, described in the previous section. You can add that entry again after you finish configuring your modem and port, or add the configuration to the `/etc/uucp/Devices` file yourself instead of using the Dialup Setup window.

To configure a modem and port on your system through the Dialup Setup window, follow these steps:

1 · In the Networking folder window, double-click on the Dialup Setup icon to see the Dialup Setup window, shown in Figure 5.2.

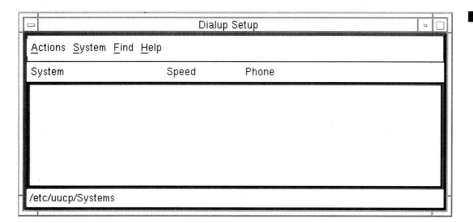

FIGURE 5.2

The Dialup Setup window

2 · In the Dialup Setup window, click on Actions to display the Actions menu, then click on Setup Devices. The Dialup Setup: Devices window appears.

3 · Click on Device to display the Device menu, then click on New. The Dialup Setup: Add New Device window appears, as shown in Figure 5.3.

4 · For the Port setting, click on the button for the serial port your modem is connected to: Com1 or Com2. If you are connecting to a serial port other than COM1 or COM2, click on Other. In the text box that appears, type the name of the device representing the serial port. If you have a serial port board connected to your system, check the manual that came with it to see which name the device uses to communicate with its ports.

The Dialup Setup: Add New
Device window

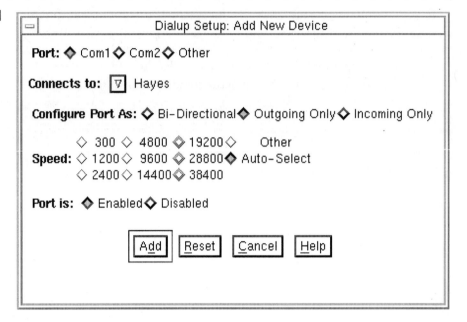

5 · For the Connects to setting, click on the arrow button to see the pop-up menu and select the appropriate type for your modem. For example, if it is a Hayes-compatible modem, choose Hayes from the pop-up menu.

6 · For Configure Port As, click on Bi-Directional, Outgoing Only, or Incoming Only. This step, which was not available in UnixWare 1.1, automatically configures the port monitor (Bi-Directional or Incoming Only) to listen for incoming calls. Before this feature was added, configuring the port monitor was difficult.

7 · For Speed, click on the highest speed supported by the modem. For some reason, not all the speeds you can select are actually available. For example, if you select 14400 the system changes that selection to 19200 because it doesn't support 14400.

8 · Click on Enable to enable the port for communication.

9 · Click on the Apply button. An icon for the port you selected appears in the Dialup Setup: Devices window. Figure 5.4 shows the window with a COM2 icon.

```
┌─────────────────────────────────────────────────┐
│ ⊟         Dialup Setup: Devices          ▫  □    │
│ ┌───────────────────────────────────────────────┐│
│ │ Actions  Device  Help                          ││
│ │                                                ││
│ │    ▤▟                                          ││
│ │    com2                                        ││
│ │                                                ││
│ └───────────────────────────────────────────────┘│
└─────────────────────────────────────────────────┘
```

FIGURE 5.4

The Dialup Setup: Devices window with a COM2 icon

The procedure for adding your modem and port to the Dialup Setup: Devices window creates an entry in the `/etc/uucp/Devices` file, which looks similar to this:

```
ACU /dev/tty01h,M - Any hayes
```

This `Devices` file entry points to the following entry for `hayes` in the `/etc/uucp/Dialers` file:

```
hayes    =,-,     "" \M\dAT\r\c OK\r
         ATDT\T\r\c CONNECT \r\m\c
```

The entry in the `Dialers` file defines the *chat script* that occurs when a call is made on the `/dev/tty01` entry. A chat script defines the interaction that goes on between your system and the remote system when you try to establish a connection. Essentially, this chat script waits for certain responses from the modem, calls the telephone number you configure for the remote system, and completes the connection.

If the Hayes entry doesn't suit you, you can add your own entry to the `Dialers` file to create your own chat script. The `Dialers` file also contains entries for other modems that may not be available in the Dialup Setup: Device Properties window. If you find one that you like, you can replace the word *hayes* in the `Devices` file with the word used in the `Dialers` file entry.

While you're in the `/etc/uucp/Devices` file, you may want to add (again) the `Direct` entry that was deleted by this procedure, as mentioned earlier.

Identifying the Remote System

After you have defined the port and modem connection, you need to identify the systems you plan to connect to using that modem. Follow these steps to define how to connect to a remote system:

1 · Display the Dialup Setup window (by double-clicking on its icon in the Networking folder window), and click on System to see the System menu. Then click on New. The Dialup Setup: Add New System window appears, as shown in Figure 5.5.

2 · For System Name, enter the name of the remote system. Typically, this is the name that would appear if you typed `uname -n` in a Terminal window on the remote system.

3 · For Connect Via, click on Modem to identify the device as a modem.

4 · For Speed, click on the speed (baud rate) of your modem. You can click on Auto-Select and have the system choose a speed for you, but there is less chance of error if you select a specific speed.

5 · For Phone Number, type the telephone number of the modem connected to the remote system. You can include the special

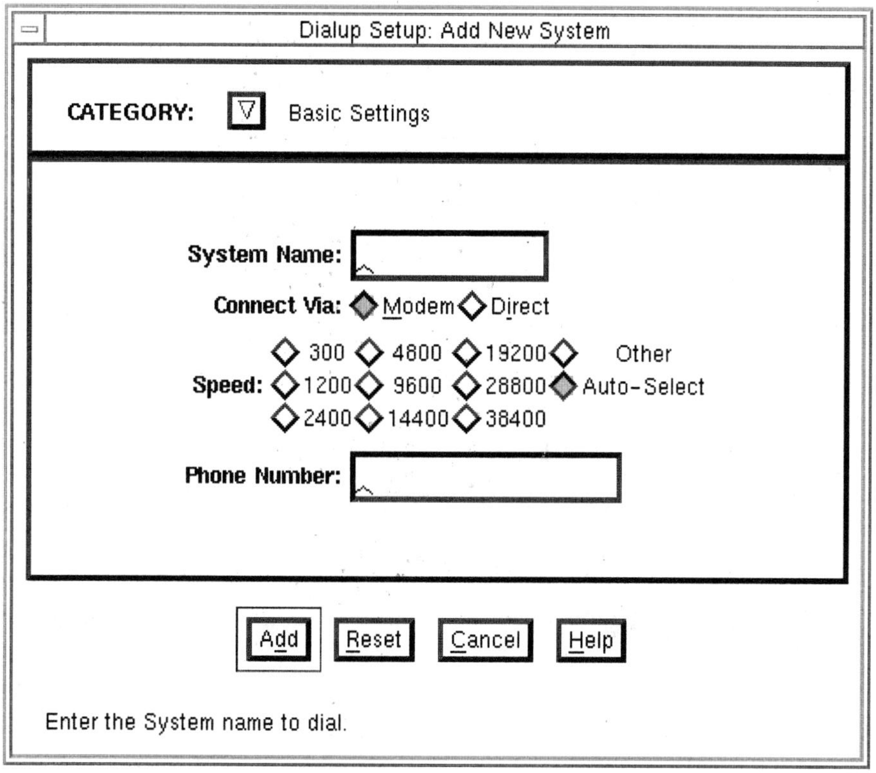

FIGURE 5.5

*Identifying a remote
system for modem
connections*

```
┌─────────────────────────────────────────────┐
│ ─    Dialup Setup: Add New System            │
├─────────────────────────────────────────────┤
│  CATEGORY:   [▽]  Basic Settings             │
│                                               │
│      System Name: [_____]          │
│      Connect Via: ◆Modem ◇Direct              │
│              ◇ 300  ◇ 4800 ◇19200◇  Other     │
│      Speed: ◇1200 ◇ 9600 ◇28800◆ Auto-Select │
│              ◇2400 ◇14400 ◇38400              │
│      Phone Number: [_____]         │
│                                               │
│        [Add] [Reset] [Cancel] [Help]          │
│                                               │
│  Enter the System name to dial.               │
└─────────────────────────────────────────────┘
```

codes for modems: an equal sign (=) to tell the modem to wait for a secondary tone and a dash (–) to tell it to pause.

6 · If you expect ever to call the remote system to copy files to or from the remote system, you should click on the CATEGORY button next to Basic Settings and select Login Sequence. Here you have the option of entering prompts and responses for the login sequence. This requires some explanation. Every UnixWare system has a user called nuucp. This user account is designed specifically to handle uucp file transfers. This sequence defines the sequence of events that occurs when uucp calls the remote system to make a file transfer. Typically, your system would call the

remote system and log in as nuucp. The remote system would
start the daemon process that would handle the file transfer. You
should typically add two sets of Prompt and Response messages
to handle this login procedure: use in:--in: for the first
Prompt and nuucp for the first Response. The next Prompt
should be word: and the last Response should be the password
of the remote system's nuucp user. (Each remote system's administrator must set the password for its nuucp user for this procedure to work.)

7 · Click on Add. The new system entry appears in the Dialup Setup
window, as shown in the example in Figure 5.6.

FIGURE 5.6

*The Dialup Setup window
with the remote system
listed*

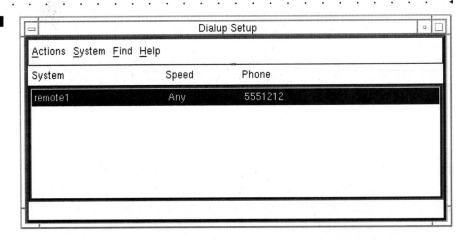

You can add more remote systems by repeating the same procedure.
The system entry you just added through the Dialup Setup window creates an entry in the /etc/uucp/Systems file that looks similar to this:

```
remote1 Any ACU 9600 5554311 in:--in: nuucp
    word: mypasswd
```

Any request for file transfers (uucp command) or remote logins (cu command) to remote1 will use this entry. In this example, when the command

is run, the system will find an ACU entry in the /etc/uucp/Devices file and place a call to 5554311 at 9600 baud. If you are logging in to the remote system, you will see the login prompt. If you are transferring files to the remote system, your system effectively waits for the login prompt, sends nuucp, waits for the password prompt, then sends mypasswd.

If you need to change the behavior of calls or file transfers to the remote system, you can edit the /etc/uucp/Systems file by hand (carefully), as described later in this chapter.

Because BNU is a batch type of networking system, remote requests are often stored up and sent sometime after the requests are made, whenever a connection is available. So, even though you place an outgoing call to that system, once the connection is made, the remote system may try to send data to you as well.

If you want to allow the remote system to send you files or execute commands on your system when you call that system, you can modify the /etc/uucp/Permissions file, as described later in this chapter. For outgoing calls, you may be interested in setting up MACHINE entries.

Setting Up Line Disciplines

The characteristics of a connection in BNU are determined by the line disciplines defined for the connection. Line disciplines include the speed at which information is exchanged (baud rate), whether or not parity is checked, and the size of the characters (typically 8-bit or 7-bit).

When you call a remote system, by using the cu command or by double-clicking on a remote system icon (which runs cu automatically), the cu command takes the current line settings from the Terminal window and tries to use them to establish a connection. To see what the line settings are for your current Terminal window, type

```
stty -a
```

Figure 5.7 shows an example of the output from the stty -a command.

FIGURE 5.7

Output from the stty -a
command

```
                                    Terminal
$ stty -a
speed 9600 baud;
rows = 24; columns = 77; ypixels = 534; xpixels = 930;
intr = DEL; quit = ^|; erase = ^h; kill = ^u;
eof = ^d; eol = <undef>; eol2 = <undef>; swtch = <undef>;
start = ^q; stop = ^s; susp = ^z; dsusp = ^y;
rprnt = <undef>; flush = <undef>; werase = <undef>; lnext = <undef>;
-parenb -parodd cs8 -cstopb hupcl cread -clocal -loblk -parext
-ignbrk -brkint -ignpar -parmrk -inpck -istrip -inlcr -igncr icrnl -iuclc
ixon -ixany -ixoff -imaxbel
isig icanon -xcase echo echoe echok -echonl -noflsh
-tostop -echoctl -echoprt -echoke -defecho -flusho -pendin -iexten
opost -olcuc onlcr -ocrnl -onocr -onlret -ofill -ofdel tab3
$
```

To change your current line settings, use the stty command. For example, to change the line disciplines in the previous example to use 7-bit characters and enable parity, type

```
stty parenb cs7
```

NOTE **Changing** stty **settings from a Terminal window has no effect on a remote login that occurs when you double-click on a remote system icon. You can, however, add an** stty **line to the** .profile **file in your home directory or to the** /etc/profile **file. Those** stty **settings will then apply when you run a** cu **command from the Desktop.**

NOTE **See Chapter 10 for a more complete discussion of how to change line disciplines.**

Understanding Incoming Modem Connections

In case something goes wrong with your modem connections, particularly on incoming calls, which are a little trickier, some explanation may be useful.

For pre-UNIX SVR4.0 users, `ttymon` replaces the `getty` (incoming) and `uugetty` (bidirectional) daemons that were previously used to monitor ports and spawn login processes. Do not simply add `getty` or `uugetty` entries to `/etc/inittab`, as you did in the old days. When you add a device with Dialup Setup and mark it as incoming or bidirectional, the system automatically configures the Service Access Facility (SAF) to start a `ttymon` daemon process. The `ttymon` daemon process is designed to listen to ports for incoming call requests and respond with some service. Typically, `ttymon` is configured to provide login services.

As explained earlier, the characteristics of a connection in BNU are determined by the connection's line disciplines. The `ttymon` daemon is set to try a particular set of line disciplines to match those of incoming calls. By default, the entry in `/etc/saf/`*<pmtag>*`/_pmtab` (where *<pmtag>* stands for the port monitor tag name) for a `ttymon` port monitor uses the 9600 line discipline entry. Your file's entry might look something like this:

```
# VERSION=2
tty00h:u::reserved:reserved:login:/dev/
   tty00h:bhr: 0:/usr/bin/shserv:60:9600:
   ldterm:login\: :::::#
```

When a connection request comes into `ttymon`, it uses the 9600 entry in the `/etc/ttydefs` file to match the connection. If that doesn't work, `ttymon` cycles through other entries until it finds one that matches. The next entry it tries is based on the last value in the current entry. For example, the 9600 entry in the `/etc/ttydefs` file looks like this:

```
9600: 9600 opost onlcr tab3 ignpar ixon
   ixany parenb istrip echo echoe erase
   echok isig cs7 cread : 9600 opost onlcr
   sane tab3 ignpar ixon ixany parenb istrip
   echo echoe erase echok isig cs7 cread
   ::4800
```

Therefore, the next entry it tries to use is 4800. That, in turn, points to the 2400 entry, and so on until it finds an entry that matches one that works with the calling system.

These entries are associated with the line speed. The problem with this arrangement is that the loop does not contain any *no parity* entries. This means that if the connection requires 8-bit, no parity, you will never get a usable connection.

One way to correct the problem of not matching parity is to edit the entry in the /etc/saf/*<pmtag>*/_pmtab file to change the 9600 number to 9600NP. This lets you cycle through the no parity entries. An alternative is to change the last field in the 19200 entry from 9600 to 9600NP and the last field in the 19200NP entry from 9600NP to 9600. This allows ttymon to cycle through all the parity and no parity entries.

Adding an nuucp Password

As explained earlier in the chapter, nuucp is a special system user account, created automatically when you install UnixWare. When a remote UnixWare system calls to copy a file to your system, it logs in as nuucp. Your system responds by starting up a process (uucico) to handle the file-transfer process.

Although the nuucp user account is already created, you still need to add a password for the nuucp user. Then you must tell the remote system's administrator what that password is so the remote system can call your system.

To change the nuucp password, type the following as the root user from a Terminal window:

```
passwd nuucp
```

When you are prompted, enter, and then reenter, a new password for nuucp.

Handling Calls from Unknown Systems

When a remote system you don't know (in other words, one that is not in your `/etc/uucp/Systems*` files) calls to transfer files or execute a command on your system, the request is logged and rejected. One way to prevent requests from unknown systems from being rejected is to add every system you want to have access to your system through BNU to the Dialup Setup window. Another approach is to allow requests to transfer files or execute commands on your system by any system that calls you. In this case, change the permissions of the `/usr/lib/uucp/remote.unknown` file so it is no longer executable, as follows:

```
chmod 444 /usr/lib/uucp/remote.unknown
```

Note that allowing remote systems access does not give them full permissions to run commands or change files on your system. The next section describes the default permissions to remote systems and how to change those permissions.

Assigning Permissions to Remote Systems

Once a connection is established to your system, the remote system can request to run commands on your system or access your files and directories. By default, your system is set up to allow known remote systems to place files in your `/var/spool/uucppublic` directory when they log in as the `nuucp` user. This is how files end up in a user's UUCP Inbox window in the Desktop. All users have the UUCP Inbox icon in their Mailbox folder linked to the `/var/spool/uucppublic/receive/user` directory on their system, where *user* is replaced by the user's login name. Also, by default, your system is set up to reject any requests for remote execution.

You can change the default permissions by becoming the root user and editing the `/etc/uucp/Permissions` file. The following are the two major `Permissions` file entry types:

- ▸ The `LOGNAME` option defines the login ID a remote system can use when it is requesting BNU services. By default, the only entry is LOGNAME=nuucp. LOGNAME defines what a remote system can access on your system when the remote calls you.

▶ The MACHINE option defines names of remote systems that are allowed specific permissions when your system initiated the call to the remote systems. In other words, MACHINE defines what a remote system can access on your system when you call the remote system.

Along with each LOGNAME or MACHINE entry is a set of options that assigns permissions to the entry. You can specify which directories can be read or written to, which commands can be run, and whether or not to send files you have queued for the remote system.

For example, this entry:

```
LOGNAME=myuucp READ=/ WRITE=/ REQUEST=yes
    SENDFILES=yes
```

defines a login ID called myuucp and its BNU permissions. When a remote system logs in as myuucp, it can read any files or directories (READ=/) or write to any files or directories (WRITE=/) in the entire file system that allow access to other users or to the myuucp login specifically. It can request the transfer of files from your system (REQUEST=yes), and it can request that any work your system has queued for it be sent (SENDFILES=yes).

For the LOGNAME=myuucp example to work, you must create a login for myuucp that is the same as the one for nuucp. In other words, the /etc/passwd file must include a myuucp entry that starts up a uucico command, as in

```
myuucp:x:110:10:0000- uucp(0000):/var/
    spool/uucppublic:/usr/lib/uucp/uucico
```

Another popular option to use with LOGNAME is CALLBACK. If you put CALLBACK=yes on a LOGNAME line, your system will call back the system that initiated the call. This is useful as a security feature, because you can be more sure that you are talking to the right system if you call it rather than if it calls you.

An example of a MACHINE entry is

```
MACHINE=larry:moe:curly REQUEST=yes
    COMMANDS=rmail READ=/home/stooge
    WRITE=/home/stooge
```

which determines what the systems named larry, moe, and curly can do on your system when you have initiated the call. The systems can request files from your system (REQUEST=yes), and they can read or write any of the files from the /home/stooge directory or any of its subdirectories (READ=/home/stooge and WRITE=/home/stooge). They can also request to run the rmail command on your system (COMMANDS=rmail).

Note that the COMMANDS option applies to requests from the remote systems regardless of who initiated the call. So, if the remote system curly had logged into your computer as myuucp, it would have permissions to run the rmail command.

For more information about the Permissions file options, which are extensive and complex, refer to the *Network Administration: Administering the Basic Networking Utilities* manual. This manual is in the *Dyna*Text Library (accessible through the Online Docs icon).

COMMUNICATING THROUGH DIRECT CONNECTIONS

An inexpensive way to network two systems on computers that are near each other is with a direct connection. A direct connection can simply be a cable between serial ports (typically, COM1 or COM2) on the two computers. The procedure for direct connections is similar to setting up modem connections (described above), but simpler.

Before you set up for outgoing calls on a direct connection, make sure you have the proper cables. For a direct connection, you must have a null modem cable (one where the send and receive pins are switched). The UNIX system is fussy about this cable. Some cables that work fine with DOS cause problems with UnixWare.

Setting Up for a Direct Connection

To configure the direct connection between two systems, follow these steps on both of the systems:

1 · In the Admin Tools folder window, double-click on the Networking icon. Then, in the Networking window, double-click on the Dialup Setup icon to display the Dialup Setup window.

2 · Click on Actions and select Setup Devices from the Actions menu.

3 · In the Dialup Setup: Devices window, click on Device to display the Device menu, then click on New.

4 · In the Dialup Setup: Add New Device window, select the port to which the direct-connection cable is attached: Com1, Com2, or Other.

5 · Click on the arrow button next to Connects to and select Direct from the pop-up menu.

6 · Click on Bi-Directional for the Configure Port As option.

7 · Click on the speed you want to use.

8 · Click on Enabled.

9 · Click on the Add button. An icon for the port you selected appears in the Dialup Setup: Devices window.

Identifying the Remote System with the Direct Connection

In order to communicate between the two directly-connected systems with commands such as cu or uucp, you must identify the other's system name on each of the two computers. To identify a remote system, follow these steps on each computer:

1 · Display the Dialup Setup window (by double-clicking on its icon in the Networking folder window), click on System, and then choose New from the System menu.

2 · In the Dialup Setup: Add New System window, fill in the fields, as described earlier for identifying a remote system for a modem connection. For Connection Via, select Direct. (No phone number is required because they are directly connected.)

3 · Click on Add. The new system entry appears in the Dialup Setup window. The system is now available for you to call.

Assigning Permissions for Direct Connections

A remote system with a direct connection has the same default permissions as one with a modem connection: it can request to run commands on your system or access your files and directories, as well as place files in your `/var/spool/uucppublic` directory.

If your computers are physically secure and have no other outside connections, you may want to relax the security requirements. To change the permissions, edit the `/etc/uucp/Permissions` file as the root user, as described earlier in this chapter.

USING BNU FROM THE DESKTOP

Once you have configured connections between your system and another system, you can communicate across those connections in a variety of ways. Using the Desktop, you can send files and call remote systems.

Any system that has been added through the Dialup Setup window can be installed as an icon in any folder you can access from the Desktop. That icon can be used to access the remote system for either remote login or file transfers.

You can install a remote system icon into a folder window with a simple drag-and-drop operation. Open a folder window for the folder into which you want to install the remote system's icon, and then open the Dialup Setup window. Move the mouse pointer onto the name of the remote system you want to install and drag-and-drop it into the folder window. An icon for the remote system appears in the folder window, as shown in Figure 5.8.

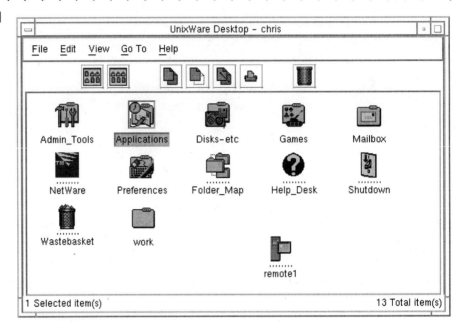

Transferring Files with a Remote System Icon

Once a remote system icon is installed in a folder window, you can use it to copy a file to the remote system. To copy a file, drag-and-drop the file on the remote system's icon. The Remote System - File Transfer window appears, as shown in Figure 5.9.

Type the name of the remote system user whom you want to receive the file. (By default, your system will send it to your user name on the remote system.) If this remote system can be reached over TCP/IP, you may have a choice of methods of copying the file (UUCP or TCP/IP). Click on Show Other Options to see if you have a choice of UUCP or Remote Copy (TCP/IP), or if only one method of transfer is available for the selected system. The UUCP method copies the file to the user's UUCP Inbox. Remote

```
 ┌─────────────────────────────────────────────────────┐
 │ ▭        Remote System – File Transfer               │
 ├─────────────────────────────────────────────────────┤
 │                                                       │
 │       System Name: │remote1          │  ┌────────┐    │
 │                    └─────────────────┘  │ Lookup…│    │
 │                                         └────────┘    │
 │  User Receiving File(s): │spike                  │    │
 │                          └───────────────────────┘    │
 │      File(s) Being Sent: abc                          │
 │                                                       │
 │   ☐ Show Other Options                                │
 │ ───────────────────────────────────────────────────  │
 │  ┌──────┐  ┌──────┐  ┌───────┐  ┌────────┐  ┌──────┐  │
 │  │ Send │  │ Save │  │ Reset │  │ Cancel │  │ Help │  │
 │  └──────┘  └──────┘  └───────┘  └────────┘  └──────┘  │
 │ ───────────────────────────────────────────────────  │
 │                                                       │
 └─────────────────────────────────────────────────────┘
```

FIGURE 5.9

Copying a file to a remote
system

Copy lets you copy it to any location that you have permission to access. (An additional field appears to enter the remote location.)

For the remote user to receive the file, the user must open the UUCP Inbox icon in his or her Mail folder. Or, if you used the Internet (Remote Copy) method, the user can find it in the folder you copied the file to. Typically, the UUCP method is easier because it doesn't require any additional permissions to be open to the remote system.

> **See the description of the Internet Setup window later in this chapter for information about opening permissions to remote users.**

NOTE

Logging In with a Remote System Icon

To log in to the remote system, double-click on the remote system's icon. A Remote System - Login window for the remote system appears, as shown in Figure 5.10.

Make sure the system name and remote login name are correct (it assumes you are using your local login name on the remote system). If this

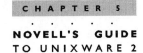

FIGURE 5.10

*Logging in to a remote
system*

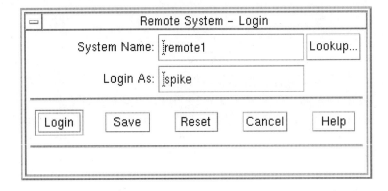

remote system can also be reached over TCP/IP, your system may automatically select TCP/IP as the method of completing the connection. If the remote system is set up to allow access to you from your system, you may be immediately logged in without needing to type a password.

USING BNU FROM A TERMINAL WINDOW

From a Terminal window, you can use all the standard BNU commands that have been available to UNIX system users for years. Although you don't need the Terminal window to use BNU, you may want some of the added flexibility this method provides. The following is a brief review of some of the most popular BNU commands. Refer to Online Docs (available through an icon in your Applications folder) or a UNIX system command reference manual for further information about these commands.

Copying Files (uucp and uuto)

The uucp command lets you copy files from one system to another using BNU connections. For example, the command

```
uucp myfile duke!/var/spool/uucppublic
```

copies the file named `myfile` from the current directory on your computer to the public directory on the system named `duke`.

The command

```
uucp jake!/home/jake/myfile
    duke!/home/spike/jake/myfile
```

illustrates how the source file can be on another system. In this case, `uucp` takes the file from jake's home directory on the system named `jake` and transfers it to a directory in spike's home directory on a system called `duke`. If the destination directory `jake` doesn't exist, `uucp` will try to create it.

The `uuto` command is a simplified version of the `uucp` command. For example, the command

```
uuto myfile duke!spike
```

sends the file to user spike on the system named `duke`. The `uuto` command mimics the behavior of dropping a file on a remote system's icon. It places the file in the remote user's UUCP Inbox.

Logging In Remotely (cu)

The `cu` command stands for *call UNIX*, but you can use it to call other types of systems and devices as well. As explained earlier in the chapter, you can use `cu` to communicate with your modem to change modem settings.

By entering the command

```
cu duke
```

you call a system called `duke` (`duke` must exist in your `Systems` file).

The command

```
cu -d -l tty01
```

turns on debugging (`-d`) and calls a direct connection to the device on the device `tty01`. A `Direct` entry for `tty01` (COM1) must exist in the

`Devices` file that points to either a `direct` or `direct_modem` entry in the `Dialers` file.

If you enter the command

```
cu 1234567
```

the system finds an ACU device and dials the number 1234567 to call a remote system.

Running Commands Remotely (uux)

The `uux` command lets you run a command on a remote system. The files that `uux` uses as input and output can be taken from your system, the remote system, or from yet another system. For example, the command

```
uux duke!"lp jake!/tmp/myfile"
```

runs the `lp` command on the system named `duke`, using the file `myfile` from the `/tmp` directory on the system `jake`.

The command

```
uux duke!"who -u > jake!/tmp/who.output"
```

runs the `who -u` command on `duke`, then sends the output to a file called `who.output` in the `/tmp` directory on `jake`.

Note that `uux` commands will not work unless the remote system is set up to allow the requested commands to be used and the files to be accessed. For the examples shown here, the remote system's `Permissions` files should include these commands:

```
MACHINE=duke COMMANDS=lp:who
MACHINE=jake READ=/tmp WRITE=/tmp
```

Checking the Status of BNU Requests (uustat and uulog)

To track the status of your `uucp` or `uux` requests, you can use the `uustat` and `uulog` commands. The `uustat` command shows you the status of

`uucp` requests. The `uulog` command prints information about `uucp` and `uux` requests that have already been logged. For example, the command

    uustat -a

shows all outstanding `uucp` requests to all remote systems.
   The command

    uustat -k dukeA2d8b

shows an outstanding `uucp` request being killed. The ID for the `uucp` request (`dukeA2d8b`) is determined from the output of the `uustat -a` command.
   The command

    uulog -x -s duke

displays all remote execution requests that have been logged for the remote system `duke`.

Checking System Names (uuname)

   The `uuname` command lists all the systems you can contact using BNU. You can also use `uuname` to print the name of the local system. The following are examples of the `uuname` command:

    uuname
    uuname -c
    uuname -l

   The first example lists all systems you can contact using BNU. The second example (`-c`) lists the systems you can contact using the `cu` command. The lists produced by the first two examples are usually the same. The third example (`-l`) lists your local system's node name. This is the name your system is typically known by to remote systems.

USING BNU OVER TCP/IP

If you have TCP/IP installed on your system, you can configure BNU to communicate over TCP/IP protocols. This means that, instead of connecting separate wires for BNU, you can use your TCP/IP connection (usually Ethernet or Token Ring) to connect to the remote system using `mail`, `uucp`, and other BNU commands.

The best way to configure BNU connections over TCP/IP is through the Internet Setup window, as described in the section about TCP/IP, later in this chapter. When you add a system using Internet Setup, then configure it to allow UUCP Transfers, several BNU files are created automatically. The `/etc/uucp/Sysfiles` file points to new `Systems` and `Devices` files configured for BNU services over TCP/IP. The file should include an entry similar to the `uucico` service shown below. You can also add the `cu` service by hand on the second line if you want to use `cu` to log in to the remote system.

```
service=uucico systems=Systems.tcp:Systems
    devices=Devices.tcp:Devices
service=cu      systems=Systems.tcp:Systems
    devices=Devices.tcp:Devices
```

These entries tell `uucico` (the `uucp` daemon) and `cu`, respectively, to look in the `Systems.tcp` and `Devices.tcp` files for additional `Systems` and `Devices` entries. `Systems.tcp` and `Devices.tcp` files are where the TCP/IP names, addresses, and devices are stored for use by BNU.

TECHNOTE **The `Sysfiles` file was originally created to let you have multiple `Systems` and `Devices` files on your system. It was considered a convenience for large computer installations that may get `Systems` lists from several different administrators. But `Sysfiles` also became a convenient way to separate sets of devices and system names that belong to a particular network architecture.**

Another file, `/etc/uucp/Systems.tcp`, is created to contain the TCP/IP names and addresses used by BNU. The file should include one or more entries that look like this:

```
duke Any TcpCico10103 - \x00020ace7b2d435a
```

In this entry, `duke` is the system name. The word `Any` indicates that BNU can use any available device named `TcpCico10103` (which points to an entry in the `Devices.tcp` file). Then, after a blank field (–), the Internet Protocol (IP) address for the remote system is indicated in hexadecimal form (`\x00020ace7b2d435a`). There is a separate entry for each system you can reach over TCP/IP protocols. In most cases, only the name and IP address will vary for each entry.

A third file created by Internet Setup is `/etc/uucp/Devices.tcp`. This file contains an entry identifying the TCP/IP device. The entry in the `Devices.tcp` file should appear similar to this:

```
TcpCico10103,eg tcp - - TLI \D nls.uucico
```

In this example, `TcpCico10103` is the tag used to identify the device. The `,eg` following the tag identifies the protocol used. First the system tries to use the `e` protocol, which assumes the underlying network does error checking and retransmission, so the `e` transmission doesn't need to perform these tasks. If `e` protocol is not acceptable, the system uses `g` protocol, which provides error detection and retransmission.

The `tcp` value defines the device used to make the connection as `/dev/tcp`. After two blank fields (– –), TLI identifies the network as a Transport Level Interface-compatible network. (TLI is a standard that was developed at AT&T so that people who develop networks to be used with UNIX can do so in a way that conforms to the Open System Interconnection transport specifications.) The `\D` tells the system to use the address in the fifth field in the `Systems` file (remember the strange hexadecimal number in the `/etc/uucp/Systems.tcp` file) as the address.

Finally, the `nls.uucico` identifies the network listener service dial script to negotiate for a server process for file transfers. This points to the following entry in the `/etc/uucp/Dialers` file:

```
nls.uucico    " "    " "NLPS:000:001:10103\N\c
```

The service code 10103 is how the uucico (file transfer) service is requested from the remote system.

CHECKING BNU

If any problems occur in your use of BNU, you can check your setup in several ways. The following sections offer some suggestions for uncovering the source of problems.

 NOTE   **For a complete set of troubleshooting tips, see Chapter 10.**

Running in Debug Mode

The connection server, a seemingly useless interface between BNU and the device, can cause trouble. You can run the connection server in debug mode to monitor outgoing calls and help determine why they are failing. To run the connection server in debug mode, add a −d option to the connection server command in the /etc/dinit.d/S80cs file, so it appears as

```
/usr/sbin/cs -d
```

After you reboot the system, all call requests handled by the connection server are logged into the files called /var/adm/log/cs.log and /var/adm/log/cs.debug. The cs.log file logs the success or failure of connections. The cs.debug file contains more detailed information about how the connection succeeds or fails. Check those files for information about why your connections may have failed.

There are many things you can find out about the connection request in the cs.debug file that may help you determine why a connection request failed. In cs.debug you can see the type of device the connection attempt was made on, the phone number or address being used, and the protocol assigned. You can also see the dialer script being used.

The `/var/adm/log/cs.debug` file grows quickly once you turn on debugging. We recommend that you monitor and delete this file on occasion if you are leaving connection server debugging on. Better yet, leave debugging on only for short periods of time.

NOTE

Connecting Terminals

Using serial communications to connect dumb terminals to your UNIX system is one of the most economical ways of using UNIX. A typical scenario for using dumb terminals with UnixWare is in a small office, such as a doctor's or lawyer's office, with one powerful personal computer, such as a Pentium system with a large hard disk and lots of RAM. The office can have all its billing, accounting, and scheduling running on the single computer, along with several dumb terminals that use the processed information: one at the reception desk for scheduling appointments, one in the back room for doing billing, and one near the examination rooms for checking patient records.

Because a typical personal computer has only one or two serial ports (COM1 and COM2), you need to add a serial ports board to your computer to attach several dumb terminals to your system. A serial ports board usually plugs into your system and has a connector to attach to 8 to 16 extra ports.

See Chapter 11 for the procedure for adding a ports board.

NOTE

The UnixWare Personal Edition lets you configure as many terminals as you want, but only two users can be logged in from those terminals at the same time. If you need to connect more than one or two terminals to your system, use the UnixWare Application Server. The cost of an Application Server system and dumb terminals is less than what you would spend on PCs and software for a half dozen or so users.

NOTE

Before you decide to buy several dumb terminals, make sure the applications you are using run in character mode. If your applications have only graphical versions, you may want to purchase separate PCs for everyone running the UnixWare Personal Edition, or you may want to get X-terminals for everyone. X-terminals let you offload some of the graphics processing while you are still using UnixWare as the primary operating environment.

UNDERSTANDING TERMINAL DEVICES

Entry points to devices, such as terminals, hard disks, and CD-ROM drives, are contained in the /dev directory. You don't usually access devices directly, but you often need to know the device names in order to configure your system properly.

Terminal device names usually follow one of two naming conventions. The traditional name for serial ports used by terminals is /dev/tty??, where ?? is replaced by 00 for port 1, 01 for port 2, and so on. Another naming convention, which began with UNIX System V Release 4, is to put serial devices in the /dev/term directory and name the device something like /dev/term/00 or /dev/term/01. Although the latter method is preferred, basic terminal devices are contained in both places (for example, /dev/tty01 is the same as /dev/term/01) to maintain compatibility. Most people use the old name.

If you list the tty devices with the command

```
ls -l /dev/tty*
```

you will see some entries that end with h and others that end with s. The h and s entries denote hardware flow control and software flow control devices, respectively. So, to allow hardware flow control on the COM1 device, you would use /dev/tty00h, as opposed to /dev/tty00.

To add a terminal device to your system, simply connect the terminal to one of the serial ports on your computer. Then configure the terminal as you would any device using the Dialup Setup window, designating the device as either incoming or bidirectional. Once Dialup Setup is configured, hit Enter a couple of times until you see a login prompt. Then you may login.

Using TCP/IP

TCP/IP refers to a family of protocols created to communicate over the Internet. The Internet is a wide-area network (WAN) developed by the U.S. Department of Defense. Once you connect to the Internet, you can communicate with thousands of individuals, companies, and universities worldwide.

As TCP/IP has grown to become one of the preferred methods for communications among UNIX systems, many useful network applications have grown with it. With TCP/IP, you have one of the most powerful tools for expanding beyond the boundaries of your system. Although TCP/IP literally refers to networking protocols used to transmit and route information to other systems, the term is popularly used to refer to a variety of networking services.

Tightly coupled with TCP/IP are utilities for file transfer, remote login, and electronic mail. Because of its popularity, many other applications have been created to integrate with TCP/IP. For example, the Network File System (NFS) uses TCP/IP as its *transport provider* to let you extend your file system to incorporate file systems from remote computers. The X Window System, the graphical system on which the UnixWare Desktop is based, uses TCP/IP to let you run graphical applications from your computer and have them appear on the screen for any computer you can reach over the network.

You can use UnixWare to send mail to other computers on the Internet. File transfer utilities, such as `ftp`, let you find and transfer files among computers. With the `telnet` and `rlogin` commands, you can log in to remote UNIX systems over the Internet. TCP/IP also lets you use the NFS facility to connect remote file systems to your file system.

Because TCP/IP is so rich in features, it's reasonable to use it even if you don't want to go to the effort and expense of connecting to the Internet. A small company can connect all its computers in one building with an Ethernet or Token Ring local area network (LAN), then use TCP/IP simply to share information among those computers.

The information presented here will help you understand the basic TCP/IP concepts and the TCP/IP features available in UnixWare. For more information about TCP/IP, you can refer to the many books and papers available on the subject.

REQUIREMENTS FOR SETTING UP YOUR TCP/IP NETWORK

Every TCP/IP product has different means of administering TCP/IP on the local system. TCP/IP standards focus more on how information is sent across the network than on how commands are run or configuration files are maintained. This means that different TCP/IP products can communicate with each other, even though the way you set up each product may not be the same.

UnixWare has a graphical interface for simple TCP/IP setup called the Internet Setup window. In addition, it has a rich set of TCP/IP administrative commands and configuration files. UnixWare releases after 1.0 include features for serial communications (PPP and SLIP) and for network management (SNMP).

TCP/IP is included with every UnixWare Personal Edition and Application Server system. In order to use it, however, you must install the hardware and software necessary for communicating over TCP/IP. You should install the networking hardware—Ethernet or Token Ring boards or modems—before you configure the software.

To use TCP/IP, you must have the following UnixWare software packages installed:

- ▶ **Network Driver Package:** Install the network driver package for the type of LAN hardware you have installed. For example, the Network Interface Card Support (`nics`) contains Ethernet and Token Ring drivers.

- ▶ **Internet Utilities:** TCP/IP protocols are in this package.

▸ **Network Support Utilities:** The network listener and other utilities are in this package.

▸ **Remote Procedure Call Utilities:** Remote Procedure Call (RPC) utilities are in this package.

▸ **Network File System (Optional):** NFS, an optional add-on to TCP/IP that lets you share file systems across the network, is contained in this package. NFS comes with the Application Server, but must be purchased as a separate add-on package for the Personal Edition.

In UnixWare 2, many of the above packages have been bundled together and cannot be removed separately. The primary package for using TCP/IP is the Internet Utilities package.

UNDERSTANDING TCP/IP CONFIGURATION

The Internet Setup window that comes with UnixWare provides a graphical interface to TCP/IP. If all the systems you communicate with are connected to a single LAN, and each system maintains a complete list of the other systems on the network, the Internet Setup window works very well.

In UnixWare 2, features have been added to the Internet Setup window for using Domain Name Service (DNS) and Network Information Service (NIS). Both of these services make it possible to take advantage of centralized network administration. The only major drawback is that there is no graphical interface for setting up the server side of DNS and NIS.

But don't despair. Despite the fact that the Desktop doesn't let you do everything you might want to do with TCP/IP, you should remember that under the hood you still have a full-blown UNIX system. You can access all of the latest TCP/IP features by leaving the graphical interface and executing commands from a Terminal window.

If you are responsible for maintaining a list of all TCP/IP system names and addresses for an entire organization, you should understand the basics of IP addressing and domains. These and other more advanced TCP/IP features are covered later in this chapter. If this list already exists and is kept by someone else, you can use the Internet Setup window without worrying about the details of domain structures and the like.

During TCP/IP installation, you are asked to add some basic information about your TCP/IP setup. In UnixWare 2, this feature has been enhanced greatly. If you are in a location where you have a domain name server, subnetworks, and routers, you can add all that information at installation and may never have to touch Internet Setup at all.

The menu that appears during TCP/IP installation is the same menu described in the "Using `bootp`" section later in this chapter. You can run that menu at any time by typing `/etc/inet/menu` as the root user from a Terminal window. Like many UNIX tools, the menu command can be used from different perspectives: initial TCP/IP configuration, gathering information from a `bootp` server, or updating your basic TCP/IP information.

USING THE INTERNET SETUP WINDOW

When you first open your Internet Setup window, what you see depends on what information you entered during TCP/IP installation. If you simply entered your system name, network address, and information about your networking card, you'll see the Local Systems List. The Local Systems List, at this point, will only show you your system name and address. If you also added the name of a domain name server during installation, you'll see the Domain Listing, which shows you the other systems in your domain.

To open the Internet Setup window, follow these steps:

1 · Double-click on Admin Tools in the UnixWare Desktop window. The Admin Tools window appears.

2 · Double-click on the Networking icon. The Networking window appears.

3 · Double-click on the Internet Setup icon. The Internet Setup window appears as shown in either Figure 5.11 or Figure 5.12, depending on whether or not you have configured DNS.

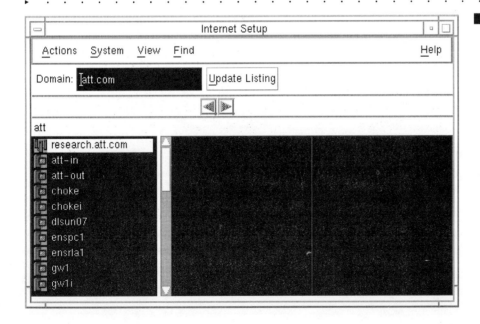

F I G U R E   5.11

Displaying the Internet Setup window (Local Systems Listing)

F I G U R E   5.12

Displaying the Internet Setup window (Domain Listing)

Once you have opened the Internet Setup window, there are several things you can do to configure TCP/IP. The following is a list of features available:

▸ **DNS Access:** You can add or modify information allowing you to connect to a domain name server system. From the Internet Setup window, click on Actions, then click on DNS Access to display the DNS Access window. From the DNS Access window, you can add the name of your local domain, plus the names and IP addresses of any domain name server systems.

NOTE   **For more information on domain name service, see "Domain Names" and "Configuring Domain Name Service" later in this chapter.**

▸ **NIS Access:** If you centralize administration of user, group, or various network information, you can configure access to an NIS server from the Internet Setup window. From the Internet Setup window, click on Actions, then NIS Access. The NIS Access window appears, allowing you to add the NIS domain name and the names of NIS servers that store the NIS information.

▸ **Remote User Access:** By selecting a system name from the Internet Setup window, clicking on Actions, and then clicking on Remote User Access, you can allow users from remote systems access to your system.

The purpose of Remote User Access is to allow users from remote systems to be able to log in or transfer files to your system without entering passwords. There are a couple of ways you can do this. One is to allow all users that have login accounts (of the same name) on both systems to access your system through that same login account. The other is to allow specific users access to your login account.

From the Remote User Access window, select either Remote Users with Local Accounts or Access to Your Personal Account. Then add the users who will either have access to their own accounts on your system or access to your account.

Selecting All Users or Specific Users adds information to your system's `/etc/hosts.equiv` **file. The entries in** `/etc/hosts.equiv` **consist of a system name and, optionally, user names.**

  **TECHNOTE**

▶ **UUCP Transfer Setup:** After you have added a system to Internet Setup, by default you are not able to use BNU utilities (`uucp`, `uuto`, and so on) to communicate to that system over a TCP/IP network. By clicking on Actions, then on UUCP Transfer Setup, you can accept or reject the ability to communicate with the remote system using BNU utilities. Note that this action does not allow you to use the `cu` command to call the remote system. See "Using BNU over TCP/IP" earlier in the chapter for further information on setting up BNU to work over TCP/IP.

▶ **Routing Setup:** By setting up the routing information, you can define how information is routed off of your current subnetwork. Click on Actions, then on Routing Setup to display the Routing Setup window. On that window you can set the *netmask* (which defines which part of the IP address applies to the host and which to the network) and the names and addresses of systems that route information to your local subnetwork to other networks.

▶ **Adding a System:** If you are maintaining a local system list, you can add a new system to that list by clicking on System, then clicking on New. The Add New System window lets you add the new system's name and IP address to your local system list. If DNS is configured on your system, you can add a system from your domain list to your local listing by clicking on System, then clicking on Copy to Systems List. By adding a system to your local system list, you will be able to contact that system even if you cannot access the DNS server for some reason.

▶ **Deleting a System:** You can delete a system name you previously added by clicking on the system's name, clicking on System, then clicking on Delete.

▸ **Copy to a Folder:** You can add a system to a folder by clicking on the system name, clicking on System, then clicking on Copy to Folder. Enter the name of the folder, then click on Copy. An icon representing the remote system is copied into the folder you chose. (You can get the same results by dragging-and-dropping the icon directly to a folder.)

▸ **Viewing System List and Domain Listings:** By selecting View, then clicking on Systems List or Domain Listing, you can change the list of systems that appears on your Internet Setup window. If you are in the domain listing, you can also move left or right along the listing of domains and systems on the screen by clicking on Shift to Left or Shift to Right.

Many of the above topics are discussed in more detail in the following sections. If you are simply hooking into an existing network, however, you might be able to skip right ahead to the sections that describe how to use TCP/IP to communicate with other systems.

UNDERSTANDING IP ADDRESSING AND DOMAINS

IP addresses, host names, and domains make it possible to uniquely identify every computer on the Internet. Every computer on the Internet has at least one IP address. Within an organization, you can have one or more domains in which each computer has a unique host name.

With a network address, you have access to a pool of IP addresses, which you assign as you add hosts to your local network. Within a domain, you can assign your own unique host name for each computer. If you ever expect to connect to the Internet, you should get an officially registered network address and domain name. There are several ways to obtain a network address. One way is to contact an Internet provider and get an address with them when you sign up for connection service to the Internet. The other way is to contact the InterNIC.

The InterNIC is the organization that has been sponsored by the U.S. National Science Foundation (NSF) to maintain IP addresses. To get information on obtaining IP addresses for you or your organization, send electronic mail to `info@internic.net` or call (619) 455-4600. An automatic email message is returned that will probably answer most of your questions.

The most complete and up-to-date selection of TCP/IP materials is available on the Internet. There are hundreds of documents called RFCs (Request for Comment), which define the Internet standards. You can get these documents by logging in to the following anonymous `ftp` sites:

Site	Directory
ftp.nisc.sri.com	/rfc
nic.ddn.mil	/rfc
nis.nsf.net	/internet/documents/rfs

A complete list of RFC locations is in `/innotes/rfc-retrieval.txt` located on the anonymous `ftp` site `isi.edu`.

The Internet is constantly changing. Hosts are taken off the network and directories are moved. By the time you read this text, some of the locations of RFCs may be different from those listed here.

NOTE

IP Addressing

When you are assigned a network number, you are essentially being assigned a pool of addresses. The network number belongs to a class of addresses: Class A, Class B, or Class C. The network number defines the first part of your pool of IP addresses, and you assign the last part (the host part) of the IP addresses.

An IP address consists of four parts, separated by periods. Here is an example of an IP address:

    148.52.77.88

Each part of the IP address represents an *octet* (an 8-bit field). The numbers in each field can range from all zeros (for a total of 0) to all ones (for a total of 255).

NOTE **If, like our editor, you're completely confused by this, don't despair. You simply have to think binary. You have 8 bits (1 1 1 1 1 1 1 1). Starting from the right, the first one represents 1, the next 2, then 4, 8, 16, 32, 64, 128. If all 8 bits in the octet are ones, the resulting decimal number is 128+64+32+16+8+4+2+1, or 255.**

From the first part of an IP address, you can tell the class of the address. A Class A address is from 0 to 127, Class B is from 128 to 191, and Class C is from 192 to 223. (Class D addresses, from 224 to 239, are *multicasting* addresses, used for joining a group of host computers. Class E addresses are reserved for future use. So you probably only need be concerned about Class A, B, and C addresses.)

The class of an address defines the number of host numbers in the pool that are available for you to assign. A Class A address uses the first part of the address as the network number, leaving you three parts to assign as host addresses. A Class B address uses the first two parts. A Class C address uses the first three parts.

If you have less than a couple hundred systems in your organization, you will probably be assigned a Class C address. This gives you 254 possible host numbers to assign. (0 and 255 are not legal host numbers.) If your organization has more than one physical network, but only one network address, you can configure your systems to do subnetworking, as described later in this chapter.

An example of a Class C network number is

```
202.129.15
```

If you received this as your network number, you could assign the following IP addresses to the systems in your organization's network:

```
202.129.15.1   mars
202.129.15.2   venus
202.129.15.3   saturn
202.129.15.4   mercury
```

Notice that with a Class C network type, you can assign only the last part of the address as a host number. If you had a Class B network number, such as

    131.57

you could assign up to about 64,000 host addresses for your network. In this case, valid IP addresses include

    131.57.181.202
    131.57.75.189
    131.57.111.14

Typically, however, 64,000 host addresses are too many to put on a single, physical LAN. Therefore, you would probably do subnetworking by assigning the third part of the network address as a subnet number and setting the *netmask* on each system in your organization, as explained in the section about subnetworking later in the chapter.

> **If a system has more than one network interface, it has more than one IP address. This concept is discussed further in the section about routing later in the chapter.**

NOTE

Domain Names

In order to use Domain Name Service (DNS) or to send electronic mail to systems on the Internet, you must be assigned a domain name. Domain names help form a logical hierarchy of systems on the Internet, so every system doesn't need to know the IP address of every system with which it wants to communicate.

The top-level domains form categories into which all other domains fall. Top-level domains include one for educational institutions (`edu`), one for government branches (`gov`), and one for commercial businesses (`com`). If you apply for a domain name as a business, you will probably be assigned to the com domain. Suppose you are a hotdog manufacturer and you choose the name redhots as your domain name. Your domain name would be:

```
redhots.com
```

 NOTE   **Case is not significant with domain names. The convention, however, is to use lowercase names, particularly with system names.**

Within your redhots.com domain, you could assign your own sub-domains and host names. For example, here are some subdomains you could assign to different locations within your organization:

```
nj.redhots.com
ny.redhots.com
utah.redhots.com
```

Finally, you can assign individual system names to each of the systems within each domain. Once you set up the systems within a subdomain, the system names might look like the following:

```
mars.utah.redhots.com
venus.utah.redhots.com
mercury.utah.redhots.com
```

Using this naming scheme, any system that could reach the Internet and find the com domain could send electronic mail to the full system/domain names shown above, provided they have connections to the Internet.

Configuring Domain Name Service

Setting up for DNS within your organization can be a complex task. Once it is set up, however, you no longer need to maintain lists of all system names and addresses on every system in your organization.

Most of the systems in your organization will be client systems. In other words, they will use the Domain Name Server to get information about the systems with which they communicate. One or more systems, however, must be designated as primary and secondary Domain Name Servers.

Configuring a Client to Use DNS

To configure a client system to use DNS, you need only identify the one or more Domain Name Server systems that control your domain, and the IP address for each. There are several ways you can do this.

If you know the names and addresses of your primary and secondary DNS servers when you install TCP/IP, you can add them during the installation process. Later, you can enter your DNS information through the Internet Setup window, as described earlier in this chapter.

If you are an old UNIX hacker, however, and like to go straight to the command line, you can update the /etc/resolv.conf file and the /etc/netconfig file. The /etc/resolv.conf file identifies the location of the DNS systems, while the /etc/netconfig file contains information needed to map the name to the address.

NOTE

When you use graphical means of setting up DNS client connections (the Internet Setup window or the /etc/inet/menu command), the resolv.conf and netconfig files are updated without you having to edit the files manually. You might want to view these files after you have added DNS information through the Desktop. This will give you a warm, fuzzy feeling that you set things up correctly.

This is an example of the /etc/resolv.conf file:

```
domain redhots.com
nameserver 127.0.0.1
nameserver 148.52.77.85
nameserver 148.52.77.89
```

In this example, redhots.com is the officially registered domain name. The first nameserver entry (127.0.0.1) shows the loopback address and tells the resolver to check the local system first. The other nameserver entries tell the resolver the names and addresses of primary and secondary Domain Name Servers the client can query for DNS.

For UnixWare 1.1 systems, the /etc/netconfig file may need to be modified to place the name-to-address resolving library that uses DNS in the name lookup field. (This procedure is not required for UnixWare 2.) Modify the `tcp`, `udp`, `icmp`, and `rawip` entries so they appear as follows:

```
tcp    tpi_cots_ord    v inet tcp /dev/tcp
   /usr/lib/resolv.so,/usr/lib/tcpip.so
udp    tpi_clts        v inet udp /dev/udp
   /usr/lib/resolv.so,/usr/lib/tcpip.so
icmp   tpi_raw         - inet icmp /dev/icmp
   /usr/lib/resolv.so,/usr/lib/tcpip.so0
rawip tpi_raw          - inet -    /dev/rawip
   /usr/lib/resolv.so,/usr/lib/tcpip.so
```

The parts shown in italics are changed from the original entries so that the `/usr/lib/resolve.so` part appears at the beginning of the field.

 NOTE **The process of configuring a Domain Name Server system is beyond the scope of this book. It involves configuring about a half dozen files and making decisions about the hierarchy of the domains you can reach. Refer to the** named **(IM) manual page in the Online Docs application for information on DNS configuration files.**

SUBNETWORKING

Let's say your organization has several physical LANs connected together and a Class B network number. If you add just the system names and addresses to your Internet Setup window, when the system tries to contact another system in the organization on a different LAN, by default, IP tries to communicate with that system on the local LAN. The solution is to set up your organization to do *subnetworking*.

Subnetworking, in effect, tells the local system to *not* use just the class to determine the network number. It says to use part of the host number as the network number also. It does this by *masking* a different amount of the IP address.

For example, suppose you have the Class B network address of 148.62 and you have your systems spread across three physical LANs. You could use the third part of the IP address as the subnetwork number. Your three subnetworks could then be defined as

```
148.62.1
148.62.2
148.62.3
```

You assign IP addresses to systems on each of the subnetworks and everything seems fine. But when a system from subnet 1 at address 148.62.1.1 tries to communicate with a system on subnet 2 at address 148.62.2.1, the communication fails. The reason is that the Internet protocol says, "hmmm… 148.62, that's on my network. I'll send out a request for host 2.1." You need your Internet protocol to recognize that 148.62.2 is another network. To do that, you set up a *netmask*.

To see the current netmask for your system, run the following command as root user from a Terminal window:

```
ifconfig -a
```

The output would include an entry that is something like this:

```
el30: flags=23<UP,BROADCAST,NOTRAILERS>
    inet 148.62.1.1 netmask ffff0000
    broadcast 148.62.255.255
```

The e130 is the name of the driver for the network interface card. The IP address you listen for on this interface is 148.62.1.1. The netmask is ffff0000 (which is hexadecimal to show that IP will mask the first two parts of the IP address). The broadcast defines that the last two parts of addresses that match the 148.62 network number are broadcast.

If you are using the Desktop, you can use the Internet Setup window to change your netmask, as described in "Using the Internet Setup Window" earlier in this chapter. The /etc/confnet.d/configure -i command, however, is a reliable way to change your netmask from the command line.

To use the configure -i command to configure the system to properly do subnetworking in the example given above, you would type the following command from a Terminal window as the root user:

```
/etc/confnet.d/configure -i
```

The following are the questions and answers generated by the command `configure -i` (answers are in bold):

```
These are the device(s) available on your
   system:
1  el3_0
Type the number of the device(s) to be
   configured with inet [?,??,q]: 1

Please enter the IP host name for device
   el3_0 (default: mars2): mars

Please initialize the IP address for host
   mars (default:148.62.1.1): 148.62.1.1

Configure host mars with default
   Ethernet(TM) ifconfig options?

Info message is long. (yes no ClassC
   BerkeleyC info; default: info): ClassC
```

Only one network device is available for our system (el3_0), so we choose that by typing 1. The system name for the interface is mars. The IP address is 148.62.1.1.

The last information requested about the ifconfig options is where you change your netmask and broadcast. In our case, the answer is ClassC. This sets the netmask to 255.255.255.0, which treats 148.62.1 as the network address and anything that follows in the fourth part of the address as the host address. It also sets the broadcast as 148.62.1.255.

If we selected BerkeleyC, the netmask would be the same, but the broadcast would be 148.62.1.0. The reason is that some Berkeley UNIX systems use all zeros in the host part for broadcast, while UNIX System V systems (such as UnixWare) use all ones (255) for broadcast.

When you restart TCP/IP, the new values take effect for the interface. Type ifconfig -a again from a Terminal window as root user to see the new interface.

The actual change to the interface is made by adding information to the file `/etc/confnet.d/inet/interface`. If you need to make a change that is not supported by the `configure` command, you can edit this file directly (carefully). The network interfaces are defined on the last couple of lines at the end of the file.

NOTE

Notice in the above example how `configure` recommends `mars2` as the host name. The `configure` command is not very sophisticated; it always assumes you are adding a board. So, it recommends that you use your current system name plus a number for the interface you are changing. For example, our system name is `mars`, so it recommends `mars2` for the second network board, then `mars3`, `mars4`, and so on. We simply type `mars`, because we are only modifying the current interface.

Setting up the subnetworks, however, isn't enough to allow systems on several LANs to communicate. You must provide a way for the networks to be physically and logically connected together, as described in the next section.

ROUTING

To communicate with TCP/IP from one network to another, you can designate a UnixWare system as a router. The routing system has network interfaces to more than one network. Usually, this means installing several networking cards, identifying each interface to your system, and broadcasting your system as a route to other networks.

Each interface on your system must have its own system name and IP address. Using the example of one Class B network with two subnetworks, you could assign the following names and addresses to two Ethernet interfaces:

```
mars   148.62.1.1
mars2  148.62.2.1
```

NOTE **By convention, 254 is often used as the host number for routing. In that case, the IP adddresses for mars and mars2 would be 148.62.1.254 and 148.62.2.254, respectively.**

You need to know which part of the IP address is the network part and which is the host part. The network class and the length of the network address tell you whether you need to set the subnetwork mask (which in this case you do).

Next, you need to decide which address is attached to which network interface. Here's a summary of the information you need to know about these two system names and IP addresses:

System name	Network address	Host address	Ethernet interface
mars	148.62.1	.1	el3_0
mars2	148.62.2	.1	wd0

Because the network address is a Class B (you can tell because it begins with 148) but the systems within that Class B network are on two different LANs, you need to change the netmask for each of the interfaces. The following are the basic steps for configuring these two interfaces:

1 · Install the Ethernet drivers.

2 · Configure the interface for the first Ethernet board.

3 · Configure the interface for the second Ethernet board.

4 · Check that the interfaces to each Ethernet board are working.

5 · Activate the router.

6 · Enable the system to do routing.

7 · Check the routing table.

The following sections describe each of these steps in more detail.

Installing the Networking Board Drivers

The Ethernet Hardware Support package contains the drivers for the most popular Ethernet cards. The driver for your Ethernet board may have already been installed during UnixWare installation. In our example, the board connected to the first LAN is an EtherCard PLUS Elite16 board (which uses the Western Digital, wd, driver), the second is a 3Com board.

Although the Network Interface Card Support (nics) package shipped with UnixWare supports more than 80 network interface card drivers, some drivers may still not be available. Contact your UnixWare support representative or check in the UnixWare forum on CompuServe to see if a new driver is available.

If you are adding a board and the driver is not installed for it yet, remove the Network Interface Card Support package, then reinstall it.

See Chapter 3 for instructions on removing and adding software packages.

NOTE

When you reinstall the software, make sure you add the total number of boards of each type you have installed. For example, you may have only configured one el3_0 board during installation, so you need to remove and reinstall the package to define one el3_0 and one wd. Reboot the computer after the package is installed.

Configuring the Networking Boards

To configure the interface for a network board, you run the configure -i command again as the root user from a Terminal window (the same command you ran to change the netmask earlier in this chapter). Follow these steps:

1 · Type the command

    /etc/confnet.d/configure -i

The two interfaces are listed (el3_0 and wd0 in our example).

2 · Type the number of the first interface (1 for el3_0 in our example).

3 · When you are prompted for the name of the host, type your system name (mars in our example) and press Enter.

4 · When you are prompted for the IP address for the system, type the IP address and press Enter, or just press Enter to accept the default (the default is 148.62.1.1 in our example, so you would just press Enter).

5 · When you are prompted for the interface configuration, type yes, no, ClassC, or BerkeleyC (ClassC in our example).

For our example, you would choose ClassC to set the netmask for Class C subnetworking on your Class B network number. In this way, IP knows to look beyond the local LAN if the first three parts of an IP address don't match those of the local LAN. Use the BerkeleyC option if you have a system on your LAN that requires that the host part of the broadcast be 0 rather than 255.

To configure your second network board, run configure again, but this time use the second interface. In our example, you would respond to the prompts as follows:

▸ Type 2 for the second interface.

▸ Type mars2 for the system name used by the interface.

▸ Type 148.62.2.1 for the IP address of the interface.

▸ Type ClassC to use Class C subnetworking for this Class B address.

▸ Type y to use the machine as a gateway. Basically, this means you want to allow other systems to route messages through your system, which is the point of this procedure.

When you are finished configuring your boards, reboot your system.

Checking the Interfaces

After you have rebooted the system, open a Terminal window, and as the root user, type

```
ifconfig -a
```

The output looks something like this:

```
lo0: flags=49<UP,LOOPBACK,RUNNING>
    inet 127.0.0.1 netmask ff000000
wd0: flags=23<UP,BROADCAST,NOTRAILERS>
    inet 148.62.1.1 netmask ffffff00
    broadcast 148.62.1.255
el3_0: flags=23<UP,BROADCAST,NOTRAILERS>
    inet 148.62.2.1 netmask ffffff00
    broadcast 148.62.2.255
```

This example shows the loopback driver (lo0), the Western Digital driver for the Elite16 board (wd0), and the 3Com driver (el3_0). The output provides the following information about the interfaces:

▶ UP: This tells us that the interface is up and running.

▶ 148.62.1.1: This is the address at which your system can be reached through the interface. Notice that the addresses are different for the two boards.

▶ ffffff00: This is the netmask for the interface. The first three pairs of *f*s are for the three parts of the IP address that represent the local network. (Each *f* represents four bits of ones.) The last two zeros represent the last part (the host part) of the IP address.

▶ 148.62.1.255: This represents the broadcast for the interface. The first three parts are the local network number. The last part (255), which is 8 bits all set to 1, tells the systems on the local network that the message is being broadcast to all hosts on the local network.

Activating the Router and Enabling Routing

To activate the router, you have to use the Internet Setup window. Click on Actions, then on Routing Setup. You'll see a little box next to the words Update Routing Tables Using Broadcasted Info. Make sure there is a check mark in the box. If there is, it means that your `route.d` daemon is running. Figure 5.13 shows an example of the Internet Setup window used for setting network routing and subnet mask information.

FIGURE 5.13

Setting routing and subnet mask information

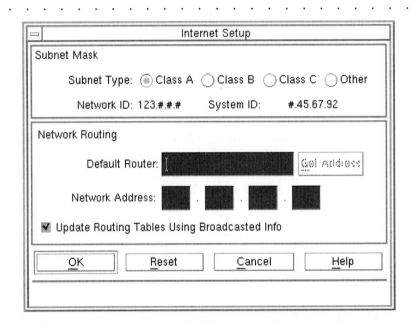

For your system to route between the two networks, however, you need to do more. You need to change the value of the IPFORWARDING tunable parameter to allow your computer to act as a gateway (i.e., route packets for other systems between the subnetworks). Double-click on the System Tuner icon (in the Admin Tools window). Click in the heading bar and select Networking Parameters. Scroll to the IPFORWARDING tunable parameter and change the value from 0 to 1 to make your system a gateway between the subnetworks connected to your system. Rebuild the kernel as requested, then reboot the system.

Checking the Routing Table

When the system comes back up, check the routing table. To make sure the new IP route is available, type the following command from a Terminal window as the root user:

```
# netstat -r
Routing tables
Destination Gateway    Flags Refcnt Use Interface
localhost   localhost UH    0      0   lo0
148.62.1    mar       U     3      0   el3_0
148.62.2    mars2     U     3      0   wd0
```

At this point, systems that can send information to any of the two networks to which you are connected can route their packets across those two networks.

USING TCP/IP FROM THE DESKTOP

You can install a remote system icon into a folder window for any remote TCP/IP system. Once that icon is installed, you can transfer files or log in to the remote system. Open a folder window for the folder into which you want to install the remote system's icon, and then open the Internet Setup window. Move the mouse pointer onto the name of the remote system you want to install and drag-and-drop it into the folder window. An icon of the remote system appears in the folder window.

USING TCP/IP FROM A TERMINAL WINDOW

Many TCP/IP utilities are available to pass information between you and the other systems you can reach using TCP/IP. The following is a brief review of some of the most popular TCP/IP utilities. Refer to the Online Docs application or any UNIX system commands reference manual for further information about the commands.

Using rlogin

With the `rlogin` command, you can establish a login session to a remote UNIX system. Use `rlogin` with a remote system name to log into a remote system. For example, the command

        rlogin mars

connects to the system called `mars` and tries to log in using your local user name. (`rlogin` assumes you have a user account on the other system.)

The command

        rlogin -l spike mars

tries to log you in as user spike on the remote system.

Once you are connected, type your user password and you will start up a login session.

If the remote system was set up to allow remote users (when your system was added to the Internet Setup window), you can log in to the remote system without typing a password. If the remote system is not a UnixWare system, have the remote administrator add your system name to the `/etc/hosts.equiv` file or add it yourself to the `.rhost` file in your home folder on the remote system.

 **WARNING**   **Any system you add to your `/etc/hosts.equiv` file is a potential security breach. Make sure that the security on the remote system is as good as your own, or don't allow the remote users to bypass passwords.**

The remote login environment uses the same TERM variable that was active from your local shell. For example, from a Terminal window, the TERM variable is `xterm`. Also, `rlogin` passes on the size of your Terminal window, so applications that control the whole screen, such as `vi`, can be used.

When you are finished, disconnect from the remote system by typing `.`, `^D`, or `exit` to end the session.

Using rcp

With the `rcp` command, you can copy files from one computer to another. After setting your `/etc/hosts.equiv` file to allow users to freely log in and copy files between the systems (as explained in the section about `rlogin`), `rcp` provides a quick way to transfer files.

To use `rcp`, your current user name must exist on the remote system you are accessing, and the remote system must allow remote execution by the `rsh` command.

For example, the command

```
rcp file1 mars:/home/spike
```

copies `file1` from the current directory to the directory `/home/spike` on the system named `mars`.

The command

```
rcp venus:/tmp/output mars:/tmp/venus.out
```

copies a file from one remote system (`venus`) to another remote system (`mars`). You must have logins on both systems set up to bypass password entry.

The command

```
rcp file1 spike@mars.redhost.com
```

shows how to transfer files to a particular user (spike) on a remote system (`mars`) in a particular domain (`redhost.com`). The file is copied to a point relative to the user's home folder (`/home/spike/file1`).

The command

```
rcp -p file1 mars:/tmp
```

copies `file1` to the `/tmp` directory on `mars` and passes through the current date and time.

And, finally, the command

```
rcp -r /home/spike/Work mars:/usr/project
```

uses the recursive option (−r) to copy all files from a particular directory (as well as directories on branches below it), to a directory on the remote system. When you use −r, the second argument must be a directory name.

NOTE **If you want to log in to remote systems other than UnixWare systems over TCP/IP, you may need to use the** telnet **command. To use** telnet, **simply type** telnet remote, **where** remote **is the name of the remote system. The** telnet **command is supported by all TCP/IP packages, but it doesn't allow you to bypass password entry by adding systems and users to the** /etc/hosts.equiv **file.**

Using rsh

With rsh, you can run a command on a remote system. First, rsh connects to the remote system, then it executes the command you request. For example, the command

    rsh mars /etc/dfspace

requests that /etc/dfspace be run on the remote system (mars), then sends the output from the command to your terminal.

The command

    rsh −l spike venus lp −dpsdoc /tmp/file

requests the remote command (lp −dpsdoc /tmp/file) to be run on the remote system as remote user spike (−l spike). (The file /tmp/file is on the remote system.)

NOTE **You can't use interactive commands, such as** vi, **with** rsh. **To run interactive commands with** rsh, **use** rlogin **to log in to the remote system, then run the command.**

As with other TCP/IP commands, host names are taken from your /etc/hosts file or from the Domain Name Server. Because the command is run by your login procedure on the remote system, any command you can run as that user you can run with rsh. Any file you can write to as that user you can write to with rsh.

Here's a neat trick for using rsh. First, create a symbolic link to rsh as the name of a remote system you log in to on a regular basis, as in

```
ln -s /usr/bin/rsh /home/spike/bin/venus
```

(for the remote system named venus). Next, either run the command from a Terminal window or double-click on it from a folder window. You are immediately logged into the remote system using rlogin. Make sure the location of the new file is in your PATH variable. In our example, /home/spike/bin was added to the PATH command in the .profile file.

Using ftp

The ftp command is the standard way of interactively transferring files between TCP/IP systems. It is also one of the primary tools for copying files from remote sites on the Internet. The rcp command is used with UNIX systems; the ftp command is available on all operating systems running TCP/IP.

Once you log in to the remote system, you can use any of a set of ftp commands to move around and transfer files between the systems. For a complete list of ftp commands, see the ftp(1) manual page in the Command Reference book available through the Online Docs application, or refer to any UNIX reference manual. Figure 5.14 shows an example of an ftp session.

In this example, ftp was used to connect to a remote system (ftp mars). After logging in, the user checked the current directory (pwd) and changed to the /tmp directory (cd /tmp). Then a file from the local system was placed on the remote system, with the command

```
put /home/spike/myfile /tmp/spikefile
```

F I G U R E 5.14

An example of an ftp
session

```
                                    Terminal
$ ftp mars
Connected to mars.redhot.COM.
220 mars FTP server (UnixWare 2.0) ready.
Name (mars:spike):
331 Password required for spike.
Password:
230 User spike logged in.
ftp> cd /tmp
250 CWD command successful.
ftp> put /home/spike/myfile /tmp/spikefile
local: /home/spike/myfile remote: /tmp/spikefile
200 PORT command successful.
150 Opening ASCII mode data connection for /tmp/spikefile.
226 Transfer complete.
721 bytes sent in 0.01 seconds (70 Kbytes/s)
ftp> get /home/bruiser/hisfile /tmp/bfile
local: /home/bruiser/hisfile remote: /tmp/bfile
200 PORT command successful.
150 Opening ASCII mode data connection for /tmp/bfile (791 bytes).
226 Transfer complete.
809 bytes received in 0 seconds (0.79 Kbytes/s)
ftp> help
Commands may be abbreviated.  Commands are:
!            debug          mget          pwd           status
$            dir            mkdir         quit          struct
account      disconnect     mls           quote         system
append       form           mode          recv          sunique
ascii        get            modtime       reget         tenex
bell         glob           mput          rstatus       trace
binary       hash           newer         rhelp         type
bye          help           nmap          rename        user
case         idle           nlist         reset         umask
cd           image          ntrans        restart       verbose
cdup         lcd            open          rmdir         ?
chmod        ls             prompt        runique
close        macdef         proxy         send
cr           mdelete        sendport      site
delete       mdir           put           size
ftp> quit
221 Goodbye.
$
```

Next, a file from the remote system was placed on the local system, with the
command

```
get /home/bruiser/hisfile /tmp/bfile
```

Finally, the user ended the session (quit).

During the ftp session, you can type help at any time to get a listing of
the ftp commands you can use.

CONNECTING TCP/IP OVER SERIAL PORTS (PPP)

The Point-to-Point Protocol (PPP) is a powerful tool for connecting to
the Internet or other TCP/IP sites using serial communications. Real computer nerds love this feature, because after they have worked for 12 hours
at the office, they can go home and connect to their computers at work over
modems with full networking capabilities.

PPP lets you use TCP/IP over modems instead of just over a LAN. Once PPP is configured, you can transfer files, execute commands remotely, and even use File Sharing (NFS) to advertise and mount remote directories.

You can set up PPP so that one system always calls the second system and keeps that connection up for a long period of time. Once the modem connection is established between the two systems, either side can request communications with the other. It can transfer files or mount file systems, regardless of which side established the connection.

UnixWare's PPP is built on top of the BNU facility. Therefore, the first step in using PPP is to configure a BNU connection. However, special information is required for PPP within the BNU databases. The following sections describe how to set up BNU, both on the incoming and outgoing side, for use with PPP.

Configuring an Incoming PPP Connection

To set up for an incoming PPP connection, you need to define the PPP interface (using the `/usr/sbin/pppconf` command) and define a special BNU connection and a PPP login. First, configure the incoming BNU modem connection, as described earlier in the chapter. Then, open a Terminal window, type `su`, and when prompted, type the root password.

From the Terminal window, type

```
/usr/sbin/pppconf
```

Respond to the prompts to allow an incoming PPP connection from another remote UnixWare system. For example, you might respond as follows:

- ► `1`, to configure a new PPP host.

- ► `1`, to add a PPP host.

- ► `148.52.78.1`, as the local address set for this PPP interface.

- ► `148.52.78.2`, as the remote IP address for the remote system's PPP interface.

- ▸ 255.255.255.0, as a Class C netmask (because we are using Class B addresses that we want to subnet).

- ▸ ppprmt, as the remote system's name. This name is used by BNU to establish the modem connection.

- ▸ y, to set negotiation parameters. If you type n, you skip most of the following questions.

- ▸ 100, to specify that the connection timeout after 100 minutes and be dropped. By default, the connection stays up forever.

- ▸ Press Enter, to accept the defaults for timeouts and compressions (for the next 15 questions). The values you can set are described inside the /etc/inet/ppphosts file.

- ▸ y, to add an entry for this system in the /etc/hosts file.

- ▸ ppprmt, as the name of the remote system for BNU use. This is the same name as for TCP/IP use, but these names can be different.

- ▸ q, to quit.

Run /usr/sbin/pppconf again to configure the incoming call parameters. The following are examples of the responses you might give:

- ▸ 2, to configure the incoming PPP parameters.

- ▸ 1, to add or modify the incoming PPP setup.

- ▸ pppuser, as the login name being defined for PPP. This is the name the remote system will try to log in as when it calls to establish the PPP connection.

- ▸ y, to create a login account for the new PPP user. This adds an account to the /etc/passwd file.

- ▸ ppp1pass, as the password for the pppuser account. The remote system must know this password to connect to your system.

When you are finished, reboot your system. When the system comes back up, check to make sure that the new PPP interface is there. Open a Terminal window as the root user and type

```
ifconfig -a
```

The output you see should include an entry similar to this:

```
ppp0: flags=11<UP,POINTOPOINT>  inet
   148.52.78.1 --> 148.52.78.2 netmask
   ffffff00
```

This shows that the PPP interface is up (UP), that it is a PPP interface (POINTOPOINT), that the local address is 148.52.78.1, and that the remote address is 148.52.78.2. The netmask is the Class C netmask for Class B addresses. Both addresses are Class B addresses on the same subnetwork.

The pppconf command places entries in several configuration files. The entries resulting from the responses shown for configuring a new PPP host and the incoming call parameters are shown below. (Each file name is shown in bold, with its corresponding entry indented underneath. A backslash indicates that the line is joined with the following line.)

```
/etc/inet/ppphosts
  148.52.78.2 - ppprmt idle=100*pppuser - -
/etc/hosts
  148.52.78.2 ppprmt
/etc/passwd
  pppuser:x:103::/usr/lib/ppp:/usr/lib/ppp/ppp
/etc/confnet.d/inet/interface
  ppp:0:148.52.78.1:/dev/ppp:148.52.78.2 \
  netmask 255.255.255.0:add_ppp:
```

The ppphosts file contains one entry that describes the interface and another that defines the user name for the PPP connection. You can add parameters to the interface definition based on descriptions in the ppphosts file.

The /etc/hosts file defines the system name and address for the remote PPP system. The /etc/passwd file entry creates a regular user account, except that instead of starting a shell when the `pppuser` logs in, the system runs the `/usr/lib/ppp/ppp` command to answer the call.

 **TECHNOTE**

To communicate with SCO systems using PPP, we needed to use `old`, `ipaddr`, and `rfc1172` options for the connection to work properly. We used this entry in the `ppphosts` file to communicate with a SCO system: `148.52.78.1 - remote1 old ipaddr rfc1172addr VJ accomp`.

Finally, a new entry is added to the `/etc/confnet.d/netdrivers` file to define the new PPP interface to TCP/IP. This is the file that contains the interfaces to your LAN board. The PPP entry defines the local and remote IP addresses for the interface, the device the system talks to (`/dev/ppp`), the netmask for the interface, and a pointer to an entry in the file `/etc/inet/strcf` (`add_ppp`).

Configuring an Outgoing PPP Connection

Setting up an outgoing PPP connection is similar to setting up an incoming connection, except that you need to add an entry for the outgoing system to call the incoming system in the `/etc/uucp/Systems` file. Follow these steps to set up an outgoing PPP connection:

1 · Configure your modem as you would for an outgoing connection, as described in the section about configuring your modem for BNU, earlier in this chapter.

2 · Open a Terminal window, type `su`, and type the password for the root user when prompted.

3 · Edit the `/etc/uucp/Systems` file to create an entry that will call the incoming system. Continuing with the example from before, the `Systems` entry might look this:

```
ppploc Any ACU 9600 1234567 "" \r\d "" \r\d in: --
    in: pppuser word: ppp1pass opyrigh
```

You would replace ppploc with the system name of the incoming system, 9600 with the line speed you want to use, 1234567 with the telephone number of the modem connected to the remote system, pppuser with the name of the PPP user you defined on the remote system, and ppp1pass with the password for that remote user.

4 · Type /usr/sbin/pppconf to configure the PPP interface. Enter the same information you did for the incoming system, but switch which is the remote address and which is the local address.

5 · Reboot the system.

6 · Log in as the root user again and type ifconfig -a to make sure the PPP interface is there.

7 · To establish a connection to the incoming system, type ping -s *system* as root user, where *system* is replaced by the incoming system name. You should hear the modem dial out, establish a connection, and return packets.

Once a PPP connection is established between two systems, you can use any TCP/IP utilities or applications across that connection in either direction. For example, you can use File Sharing to share and connect NFS file systems, rcp to transfer files, or mailx to send mail messages. Either side can make requests across the connection.

USING bootp

To save every new system from having to type essential TCP/IP information, you can configure one system on the network as a bootp server.

When TCP/IP is installed on a UnixWare system, it can automatically pick up information like the domain name, domain name server addresses, network frame type, netmask, broadcast address, and router IP address from the bootp server. If, later, there is a change to the network that effects all systems, such as a new domain name server on the network, you can use the bootp server to distribute the change.

Configuring a `bootp` client is done by running the `/etc/inet/menu` command. To get TCP/IP information from a `bootp` server, a client system runs the `/etc/inet/menu` command as root user from a Terminal window.

If there is more than one network card installed on your system, you are prompted to select which one you want to configure. Once you select one, you are asked if you want to configure your system as a gateway. If you do, you can type the frame type and the node name associated with the network that the card interfaces to. Every TCP/IP network interface to your computer must have a different node name. Typically, you would use a similar name (e.g., mars, mars2, mars3, etc.). To save the changes, click on Apply.

At this point, the main `bootp` window appears, as shown in Figure 5.15.

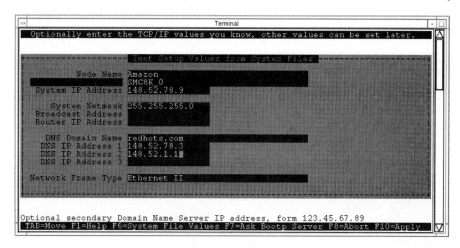

The `bootp` window is the same one that is displayed when you first install TCP/IP in UnixWare. If you cannot reach a `bootp` server from your system, this window appears with whatever information it can find from the local system.

When you view the `bootp` window, you will already have the Node Name, Device Handle, and probably also the System IP Address filled in. You can add any of the other information that is blank, or change it from whatever information was filled in by the `bootp` server.

NETWORK INFORMATION SERVICE

A way of sharing more general UNIX information over a TCP/IP network is through the Network Information Service (NIS). NIS, formerly called Yellow Pages, is a distributed database service that lets you share basic UNIX files, such as those that contain information about users, groups, and TCP/IP hosts.

NIS stores the information it shares in what are called *maps*. Maps are data files, non-ASCII, that contain information compiled from standard UNIX configuration files that are typically stored in the /etc directory of a UNIX system.

Originally, diskless workstations were a reason for using NIS. When UNIX workstation prices started at $10,000 and hard disks were fairly expensive, diskless workstations provided a lower-cost alternative to full-priced models. A minimal UNIX system could be booted from floppy disk, then essential information could be obtained from an NIS server, and other directories could be mounted from anywhere on the network.

Though there may be vendors that support diskless UNIX workstations, that feature is not supported in the UNIX System V base product. Therefore, NIS is primarily a tool for sharing information and keeping it up to date.

The following is a list of files, from the /etc directory, that could be shared from an NIS server to NIS clients. All of these files may not be used in the version of UNIX running on the client; however, you can share all of these files from a UnixWare system acting as an NIS server.

- **passwd**: Contains the name, user id, group id, home directory, and shell for every user that can access a system.

- **hosts**: Contains a list of node names and IP addresses for remote hosts that the local host can contact. These names and addresses are used by TCP/IP.

- **ethers**: Contains Ethernet addresses for hosts listed in the /etc/hosts file on some UNIX systems. (This file does not seem to be used in UnixWare.)

- **group**: Contains a list of group names, group ids, and lists of users available on the UNIX system.

- **networks**: Contains network names, network numbers, and aliases for Internet networks that are accessible to the system.

- **protocols**: Contains a list of supported IP network protocols.

- **services**: Contains a list of services available to remote TCP/IP clients. Entries contain the name of the service, socket number, and IP protocol that supports that service.

- **bootparams**: Contains a list of parameters needed to boot a diskless workstation.

- **netgroup**: Contains a list of systems that make up a network group.

 NOTE **For information on how to configure an NIS client or server, check the Network Administration guide available in UnixWare from the Online Docs application, located in the Applications folder. There is a full chapter on configuring NIS.**

Using File Sharing (NFS)

The UnixWare File Sharing window lets you share files and directories among systems in a way that makes them appear to be on the local system. File Sharing is built on the Network File System (NFS) software, which allows you to share resources among many different types of systems. It has built-in features that give you a lot of control over who has access to your resources.

The concept of File Sharing is very simple. One system agrees to share one of its files or folders (directories) with another system. The second system *mounts* the file system at a point in its directory tree. Users of the second system can then use the shared resource as they would any local file or folder, to open folders, move up and down the file system tree, or run programs.

> **File Sharing may not be included with the UnixWare Personal Edition. However, you can purchase the Network File System add-on package, which includes File Sharing. If you are not sure if File Sharing is on your system, it's easy to check. Double-click on the Admin Tools icon in the UnixWare Desktop window, then double-click on the Networking icon. If you see the File Sharing icon in the Networking folder window, this feature is available.**

NOTE

CHECKING FILE SHARING

With UnixWare, File Sharing relies on TCP/IP to provide the underlying network connections to the systems with which you share files. To use a remote resource, you must be able to reach the remote system, either by adding the system's name and IP address to the Internet Setup window or by using TCP/IP DNS.

File Sharing starts up automatically if it is installed in your system. The File Sharing window provides access to all File Sharing features available from the UnixWare Desktop. Before you can use the File Sharing window to share resources, however, you should check that File Sharing is running properly. Double-click on the Admin Tools icon in the your Desktop window, double-click on Networking, then double-click on the File Sharing icon to see the File Sharing Setup: Remote Share-Items window, as shown in Figure 5.16.

The first time you open this window, it should be blank. If there are any icons shown in the window, those items represent files or directories from remote systems that are ready to be mounted on your system. In the example shown in Figure 5.16, two remote directories are being shared: man and nucdoc. The icons show that man is not connected and nucdoc is connected.

Click on Actions to see the Actions menu, then click on Status. The Status window appears, as shown in Figure 5.17.

FIGURE 5.16

The File Sharing Setup: Remote Share-Items window

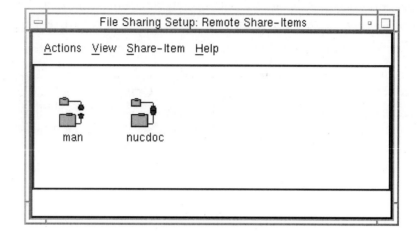

The Status window indicates whether the system is in a state where you can share (*advertise*) any of your files or folders or mount (*connect*) a remote system's files or folders on your system. It also shows, in the box near the bottom of the window, which remote systems are currently using any of your advertised resources.

From this window, you can click on the Stop NFS button at the bottom of the window to stop File Sharing or click on the Start NFS button to start it.

FIGURE 5.17

The Status window

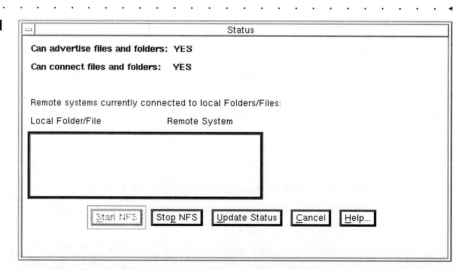

ADVERTISING A LOCAL FILE OR FOLDER

You can make any file or folder on your system available to other systems by advertising it through the File Sharing window. When you advertise the resource, you can also define the access one or more systems has to the resource.

When you share a directory, you are also sharing any files or directories that exist within that directory. In essence, you are sharing a point in the file system and making all the files in the directory tree below that point available to the remote system. So, if you shared your root directory (/), your entire system would be available to the remote system, although it would be protected by standard file system permissions.

To advertise one of your local files or folders so it can be used by remote systems, follow these steps:

1 · Double-click on the Admin Tools icon in the your Desktop window, double-click on the Networking icon in the Admin Tools folder window, and then double-click on the File Sharing icon.

2 · From the File Sharing window, click on View to display the View menu, and then click on Local. All local resources that are being shared are displayed.

3 · Click on Share-Item to see the menu, then click on New. The File Sharing: Add New Share-Item - Local window appears, as shown in Figure 5.18.

4 · In the Folder/File to share field, type the full path to the file or folder you want to share, or click on the Find... button next to the text box to browse through the file system until you find what you want to share.

5 · In the Icon Name field, type the name you want to use as a tag to identify the resource.

6 · For Advertise when NFS starts?, the default is yes. This means that the resource is advertised every time you start NFS. By default, NFS starts every time the system starts up. Click on no if

FIGURE 5.18

Sharing a local file or folder

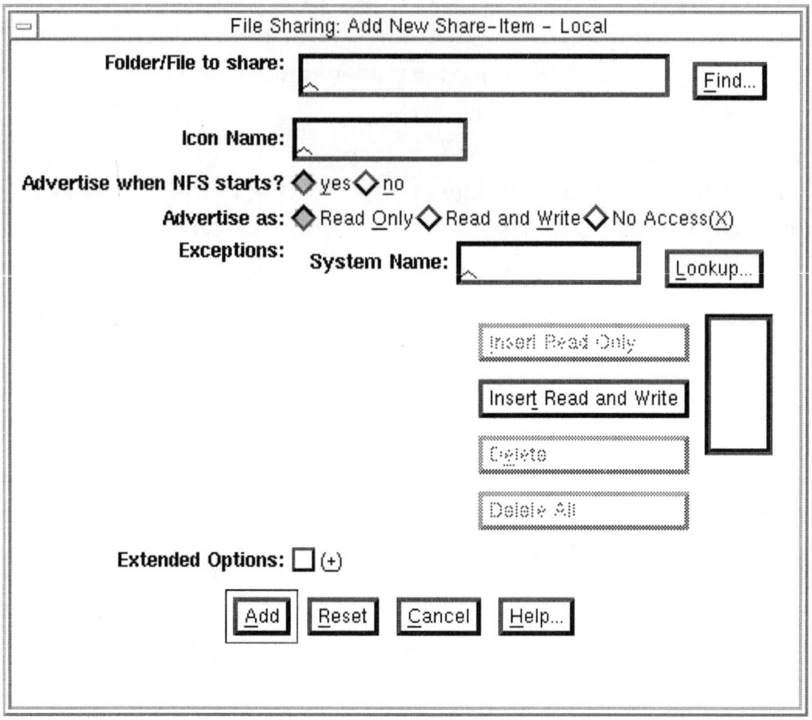

you do not want to advertise the resource on startup. (If you say no, each time you want to advertise it you'll need to open the File Sharing window, click on the icon, click on Actions, then click on Advertise.)

7 · Choose one of the three options for Advertise as. You can make the resource available to every system that can connect to your system with either Read Only permission or with Read and Write permission. Click on No Access if you want to specify individual systems to have access to the resource.

8 · If you selected No Access in the previous field, the Exceptions boxes and buttons let you select the systems that will have access to your resource. Type their names, or click on Search and choose from the system names in your Internet Setup window. Click on Insert Read Only or Insert Read and Write to add the system to the list. Use Delete or Delete All to remove systems from the list.

9 · If you want to add options to the share command, click on the Extended Options button. The text box that appears lets you type command line options that are passed to the share command. See the share(1M) command in the Command Reference, available through the Online Docs application for details.

10 · Click on the Add button at the bottom of the window to add the item to your list of advertised resources.

CONNECTING TO REMOTE FILES OR FOLDERS

Because File Sharing is peer-to-peer, you can offer your resources to another system, as well as use the other system's resources. To connect a remote resource to your system, follow these steps:

1 · Double-click on the Admin Tools icon in the your Desktop window, double-click on the Networking icon in the Admin Tools folder window, and then double-click on the File Sharing icon.

2 · From the File Sharing window, click on View to display the View menu, and then click on Remote. You see a list of all the remote resources that you are sharing.

3 · Click on Share-Item to see the menu, then click on New. The Add New Share-Item - Remote window appears, as shown in Figure 5.19.

4 · Click on the Lookup… button next to the Remote System Name box. A Remote Systems window pops up, listing the remote systems your system knows about. If your system is configured for DNS, you can choose a system from the domain listing by clicking on the category button near the top of the window, then clicking on the Domain Listing menu item.

FIGURE 5.19

Sharing a remote file or folder

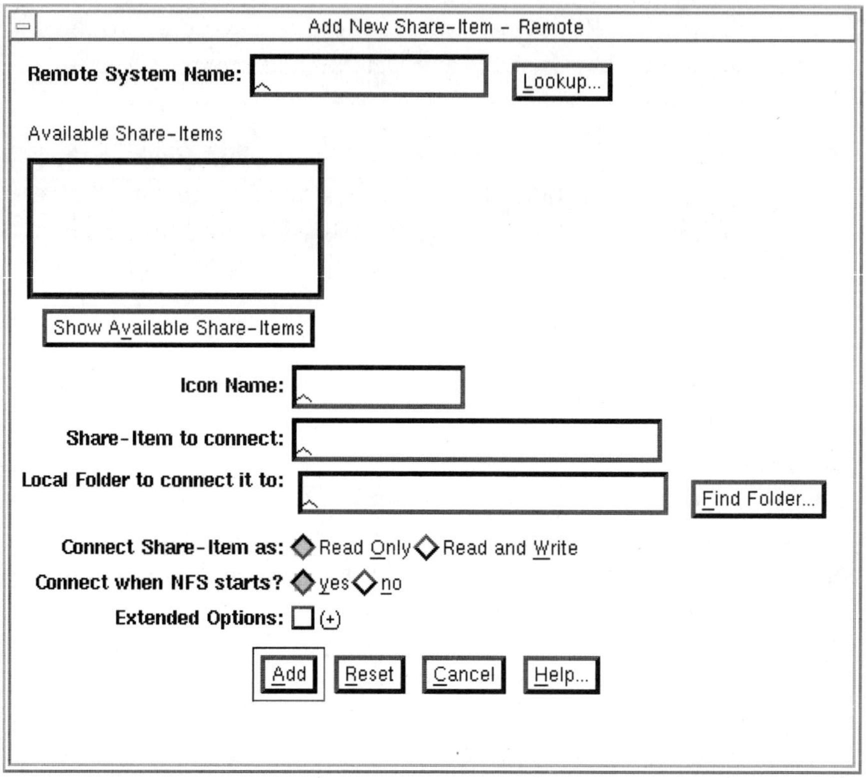

Add New Share-Item – Remote

Remote System Name: [　　　　　　　　] [Lookup...]

Available Share-Items

[Show Available Share-Items]

Icon Name: [　　　　　　]

Share-Item to connect: [　　　　　　　　　]

Local Folder to connect it to: [　　　　　　　　　] [Find Folder...]

Connect Share-Item as: ◆ Read Only ◆ Read and Write

Connect when NFS starts? ◆ yes ◆ no

Extended Options: ☐ (+)

[Add] [Reset] [Cancel] [Help...]

Next, click on the one you want. Then click on OK. The remote system name appears in the Remote System Name text box, and all available share items from that system appear in the Available Share-Items box. Alternatively, you can type the remote system name and click on Show Available Share-Items to see the files and directories available from the remote system.

5 · In the Available Share-Items box, click on the remote share item you want to connect to your system. The short name representing the share item appears in the Icon Name field. The Share-Item to connect field is filled in with the full path of the remote resource.

6 · In the Local Folder to connect it to field, type the name of the folder (directory) on your system you want to connect the remote resource to. If the folder you request doesn't exist, the system can create it for you. Alternatively, you can click on Find Folder… to search for a folder. In the Local Folders window that appears, you can move up and down the file system to find the folder you want. Use an empty directory, because once you connect the remote directory there, files in the local directory are inaccessible until the remote file system is unmounted.

7 · For Connect Share-Item as, click on either Read Only or Read and Write. If the share item was advertised as Read Only, you can only connect it to your system as Read Only.

8 · For Connect when NFS starts?, click on yes to automatically connect the resource to your system when NFS starts (usually this is at system startup time). Choose no if you want to connect it manually later.

9 · Click on the Extended Options box to see two options for using advanced NFS features. The Connection option lets you choose whether the mount is a soft mount (the default) or a hard mount. Use hard mounts only if it is imperative that writes to the remote share item not fail. If the resource can't be reached for some reason during a write operation, the system hangs until the resource returns. The Other command-line options field lets you fill in options that are passed to the `mount` command when the resource is connected to your system. See the `mount` (1M) command in the Online Docs application for information about `mount` command options.

10 · Click on the Add button at the bottom of the window to add the remote share item. If the local folder you selected doesn't exist, a pop-up window asks if you want to create it. Next, the folder is immediately connected to your system.

 **TECHNOTE** **In the Other command-line options field, add , bg to the end of the options shown. This tells the system to try to mount the resource in the background. If the remote share item is not available for some reason when you start your system, the bg option puts the request in the background so your system can continue its startup procedure and you can log in. If you don't use bg, your system hangs for some time trying to connect to the resource. If you are connected to an un-reliable network, add retrans=5 as a command-line option. This sets the number of NFS transmissions to 5. It seems to reduce the num-ber of failures.**

Networking services are closely integrated into the UnixWare operating system. As you learned in this chapter, UnixWare includes features for se-rial communications on COM ports (BNU), connecting to the Internet (TCP/IP), using NetWare servers (NetWare UNIX Client), and sharing files (File Sharing and the NFS facility).

As these networking products have evolved over years of UNIX system development, the distinctions among these products have become less de-fined. For example, you can use TCP/IP over serial lines, and you can use BNU over TCP/IP. More and more, you are able to use any networking serv-ice (file transfer or remote execution) over whatever medium you have available (modems, Ethernet, or direct connections).

Many of the features described in this chapter require you to run com-mands from a Terminal window. Once you make that leap, however, you will find a rich assortment of tools available for even the most complex net-working arrangements.

Chapter 6 contains information about how to run DOS and Microsoft Windows applications within the UnixWare Desktop graphical interface. It also helps you configure options and configuration files so DOS and Win-dows operate with maximum efficiency.

Using DOS
and MS Windows
with UNIX

DOS is the most popular operating system on the planet (possibly the universe). There is no way to get around this fact. And UNIX vendors have decided to join them instead of trying to beat them. Consequently, companies such as Locus Computing Corporation have been working long and hard to create an environment in which DOS and Windows applications can run right alongside your UNIX applications.

This chapter describes Merge, the DOS emulator created by Locus. Merge, supplied with UnixWare, allows you to run DOS and Windows applications in standard mode (not 386 enhanced mode) right on your Unix-Ware Desktop. Merge even lets you access a separate DOS partition, if you have one.

In this chapter you'll find out how to work with the DOS system, applications, and files, including Windows and Windows applications, from within the UnixWare Desktop. After an overview of how UnixWare coexists with DOS, the chapter provides information on installing Windows 3.1, loading DOS and Windows applications, running DOS and Windows sessions, working with DOS floppy disks from UnixWare, and running DOS and Windows applications from a remote system.

Using Merge to Get the Best of Both Worlds

This book was originally written on UnixWare, using DOS, Windows, and UnixWare applications. To write the text, we used WordPerfect for Windows while we ran UnixWare. When we needed to confirm how something in UnixWare functioned, we opened the appropriate UnixWare window. Then, with a click of the mouse, we were back in WordPerfect for Windows. To create our figures (*screen dumps*, in techie talk), we used a UnixWare application, even while WordPerfect for Windows was displayed in its window. The revised version of this book was written in a similar fashion, except that we used Microsoft Word. Figure 6.1 shows how Windows and the UnixWare Desktop window appear together under UnixWare.

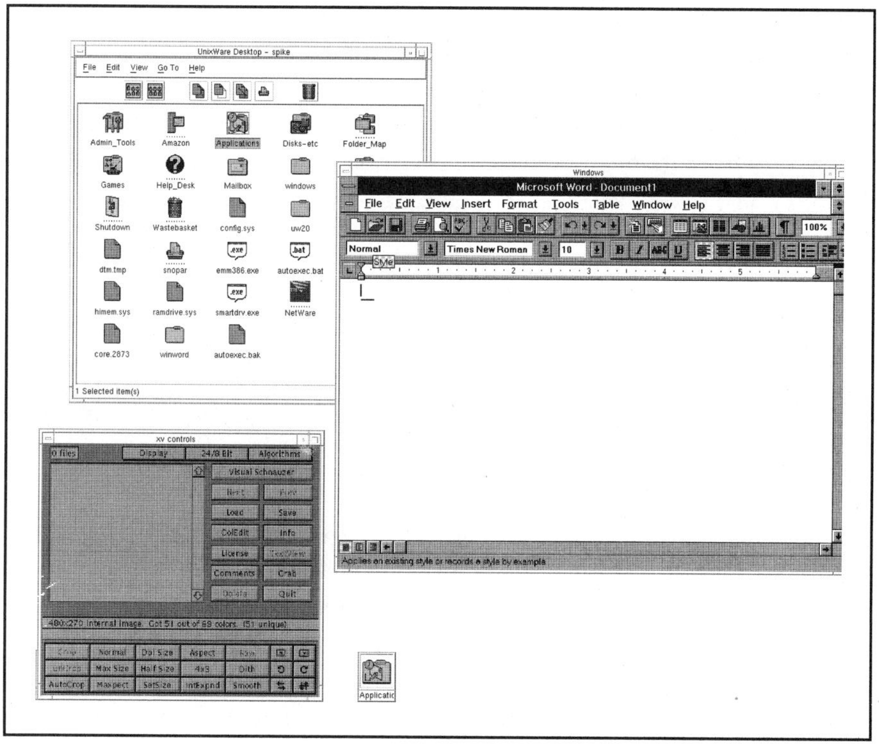

FIGURE 6.1

*Microsoft Word and
UnixWare running on the
Desktop*

To make this magic possible, Merge creates a pseudo-DOS environment
(in techie terms, it's called a *virtual computer*) within UnixWare that emu-
lates an 8086 computer. This means that you can load and run any DOS application that doesn't absolutely require an 80286 or better processor. The
only exception to this is Windows 3.1, which runs in standard (80286)
mode under UnixWare. Most DOS applications are completely compatible
with the older 8086 processor and therefore run fine under Merge. Merge
allows you to run as many DOS and Windows sessions as your computer's
memory allows.

NOTE

The number of simultaneous DOS and Windows sessions under Merge is limited by the amount of system resources, such as memory and swap space. For example, on our Gateway 2000 4D2/66 with 16MB of RAM and 32MB of swap space, we can open three DOS sessions along with one Windows session. On our Gateway 2000 P5-90 with 32MB of RAM and 64MB of swap space, we can open 11 DOS sessions and 1 Windows session simultaneously.

Merge provides a complete DOS environment, including a trimmed-down version of DR-DOS 6.0. (DR-DOS is an alternative version of DOS sold by Novell. Functionally it is similar to MS-DOS 5.0.) This DOS environment appears and acts as if your system is running only DOS. You can run DOS commands the same way you would run them on a stand-alone DOS system.

Microsoft Windows does not come with Merge. If you want to run Windows applications, you must purchase and install Windows separately.

Besides enabling you to access all DOS *and* UNIX directories on your hard disk, Merge provides access to your floppy disk drives, serial ports, and parallel ports, just as you have on a stand-alone DOS system. However, you must tell Merge that you're going to use your COM ports before you start a DOS session, because UnixWare and DOS can't both use your COM ports at the same time. Extended and Expanded memory are also supported.

If there is more than one user on the UNIX system running Merge, each one can customize their DOS sessions by having their own CONFIG.SYS and AUTOEXEC.BAT files in their respective home folders. If you don't like DR-DOS, you can even load a different version of DOS (MS-DOS 5.0, MS-DOS 6.0, MS-DOS 6.21, or the complete DR-DOS; Novell DOS 7.0 is not yet supported by Merge).

System Requirements for Running Merge

Using Merge with UNIX requires more system resources, such as memory and hard disk space, than running UNIX alone. The UnixWare Personal Edition is advertised to run on systems with only 8MB of RAM. A UnixWare Application Server is said to run with only 12MB of RAM. While technically this is true, we believe that you can never have too much RAM while running any version of UNIX. Never skimp on RAM if you plan to run UNIX on your computer.

When you run several DOS sessions along with a Windows session, you need more than the minimum amount of RAM. For good performance, we recommend a minimum of 16MB of RAM.

Of course, you must have enough free space on your hard disk to load Windows and Windows applications if you're going to use them. Windows will chew up about 6MB disk space plus its swap area, and Windows applications can really occupy space. Some Windows applications take 30MB or more of hard disk space.

 NOTE

Our smallest system (a laptop) has a 500MB hard disk, as does our older tower. Our new Pentium system has 1GB (1000MB) of hard disk space. The price of both RAM and hard disks has come down dramatically. Our advice is to buy as much RAM and hard disk space as you can afford.

INSTALLING MICROSOFT WINDOWS 3.1

Once you've started a DOS session as described below, Windows 3.1 installs as it would on a stand-alone DOS system. The trick is deciding where to install it, not how.

NOTE

Windows 3.0 is no longer commercially available. It will, however, work with Merge even though Merge is designed for Windows 3.1. Since the upgrade to Windows 3.1 is so reasonably priced, we highly recommend that you use Windows 3.1, even if you already have a copy of Windows 3.0. Windows 3.1 provides several benefits over Windows 3.0 when run under Merge, such as allowing you to run Windows on your UnixWare Desktop instead of in a separate full-screen window. If you insist on installing Windows 3.0, you'll have to look in the *User Handbook* that accompanies UnixWare 1.1 for instructions. In other words, use Windows 3.1.

When installing Windows, you must consider who needs access to the program. You can install Windows as a personal copy if you're the only user of Windows on your system. You can also install Windows onto a NetWare server or a shared directory, in which case each user installs Windows through a network installation procedure.

If you're installing a personal copy of Windows, use the C: drive for the installation. The C: drive is the same as your home directory under Unix-Ware. You have Write permission in this directory, so you can install Windows (or any other software) without worrying about changing file or directory permissions.

If you're installing a network version of Windows, you must have a license for each user accessing Windows. To install a shared copy of Windows, or to install Windows on your NetWare file server, use the /A option to the Windows SETUP command. After Windows is installed, users install their own copies using the /N option to SETUP. See *Getting Started with Microsoft Windows* (supplied with Windows) for additional information. With a network installation, users have only a few Windows configuration files in their personal directory. Most of the files for running Windows are accessed from the shared directory or the network file server, thereby saving several megabytes of disk space on each user's system.

To install Windows 3.1, you must first start a DOS session with 4MB of Standard (Extended) memory. The easiest way to do this is to double-click on the Win Setup icon in the Applications folder. This icon starts a DOS session with the correct type and amount of memory. It also provides some on-screen instructions for helping you load Windows.

With the DOS session started, insert Windows Disk 1 in the floppy disk drive and follow Microsoft's instructions. Read and keep the following in mind *before* you begin installing Windows 3.1:

- ▶ If your system is connected to a NetWare network, use the Win Setup icon for starting your DOS session. Otherwise, your system will try to authenticate to every NetWare server accessible by your system.

- ▶ You can ignore the message about SUBST.EXE running if it appears on your screen (press C to continue).

- ▶ Remember to use C: as the destination drive if you're installing a personal copy of Windows. For a network installation, use the O: drive (after logging in).

- ▶ To install Windows in a shared directory, use J:\SHARE as the drive and directory. Before starting, however, you must become the root user and change the permissions on /usr/merge/ dosroot/share or your installation will fail. To do this, open a UnixWare Terminal window, type su, and enter the root password when prompted. Then type

```
cd /usr/merge/dosroot
chmod 777 share
```

Press Ctrl-D to exit.

WARNING

Changing the permissions of /usr/merge/dosroot/share to 777 can cause a security problem on your system. After installing Windows, change the permissions back to their original values by becoming the root user and running the chmod command again, substituting 755 for 777.

▶ You can use either Windows Express Setup or Custom Setup.

▶ Sometime after the Windows installation begins, you will be prompted to switch to Merge's Zoom mode. Follow the instructions on the screen. The installation resumes in full-screen mode. Merge must change to full-screen mode so it can display Windows' graphics.

▶ When Windows asks whether it should modify your AUTO-EXEC.BAT and CONFIG.SYS files you can either have Windows make these changes for you or you can select the "let you make the modifications later" option. If you select the "later" option, be sure to add the Windows directory to your PATH in the AUTOEXEC.BAT file. To do so, you need to edit (or create) your AUTOEXEC.BAT file. If you installed a personal copy of Windows, edit the AUTOEXEC.BAT file in your UnixWare home directory (C:\ in DOS) and add the line

`PATH=C:\WINDOWS`

If you used a directory name other than WINDOWS, type that name instead. You don't need to add anything to your CONFIG.SYS file; however, some Windows applications don't install unless a CONFIG.SYS file exists in C:\. So even if you're not adding anything to the file, create a CONFIG.SYS file to play it safe. If you installed a shared or network copy, you need to perform this step after you install Windows in your personal directory using SETUP /N. If you don't already have an AUTOEXEC.BAT file, create one with a DOS editor and include the PATH line shown above. Also, add the shared directory to your PATH statement.

▶ When the Printers window is displayed, select your printer from the list and click on Install. When asked to select the port your printer is connected to, select LPT1.DOS.

▶ When the installation is completed, you are given a choice to reboot your system or return to a DOS prompt. Select Return to MS-DOS. When the DOS prompt appears, you are still in Zoom (full-screen) mode. Press Scroll Lock to return to the UnixWare Desktop. Exit DOS by pressing Scroll Lock again and clicking on Quit. In the confirmation window, click on Yes.

Windows, as installed, only runs in Zoom (full-screen) mode. If you prefer, you can configure Windows to run on the Desktop alongside UnixWare windows, as described in the next section.

CONFIGURING WINDOWS 3.1 TO RUN ON THE DESKTOP

If you want to run Windows on your Desktop along with your UNIX applications (as opposed to in a separate, full screen) you need to change the video driver from within Windows. Because you can change your video driver at any time, you can alternate between running Windows on your Desktop and running it in full-screen (Zoom) mode.

Normally, your mouse will not work in the DOS window on the Desktop. However, you can use the Focus option on the DOS menu to activate your mouse in DOS windows, as explained later in this chapter.

If Windows is installed on a network or in a shared directory, you must run `winxcopy` *win_dir*, where *win_dir* is the directory that contains the shared Windows files (such as J:\SHARE\WINDOWS), before you can configure Windows to run on the Desktop.

You change the video driver from within Windows by using the following procedure:

1 · From the Main window in Windows, double-click on the Windows Setup icon.

2 · From the Options menu in the Windows Setup window, select Change System Settings.

3 · Select Display in the Change System Settings window. The Display options are shown.

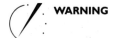 **WARNING** **Do not attempt to install a video driver that came with your video board. Other video drivers may make Windows inoperable. If you already selected the wrong video driver and Windows will not run, start a DOS session, change to the directory where Windows is installed, and type SETUP. If you get a message about SUBST.EXE running, press C to continue. Move the highlighting to Display and press Enter. Select one of the valid video drivers from the list. Save your change and exit SETUP. Windows should run with the selected video driver.**

4 · Scroll through the options to find the last one, Other display (Requires disk from OEM) and select it.

5 · In the text box, A:\ is highlighted. Change the A:\ to

J:\MERGE\WINDOWS

6 · Click on OK.

7 · Select DOS Merge Windows/X or, if your video resolution is 1024 × 768 or higher, choose DOS Merge Windows/X [Large Font].

8 · Click on OK. You should now see DOS Merge Windows/X (or DOS Merge Windows/X [Large Font]) in the Display box.

9 · Click on OK.

10 · When you see the Exit Windows Setup window, you can choose to continue using Windows as is (click on Continue) or to restart Windows (click on Restart Windows). If you choose Restart Windows, press the Scroll Lock key (if prompted) after you select that option to return to the Desktop.

The next time you start Windows, it will open as a window on the Unix-Ware Desktop.

 **WARNING**

The mouse tracking setting is something you do not want to change. When you run Windows on the Desktop, you *must* have the mouse tracking in Windows set for the slowest possible speed. Mouse tracking is normally changed in the Windows Control Panel. Stay out! The correct value is automatically set for you when you select the DOS Merge Windows/X video driver.

CHANGING THE DISPLAY RESOLUTION FOR WINDOWS

Merge automatically sets the size of the window in which Windows is running (the Windows window) to about 80 percent of your UnixWare screen. Using the `mrgconfig` command, however, you can custom set the size of the Windows window.

To change the resolution, you use the `mrgconfig` command. For example, if you have a 21-inch monitor running at 1280×1024, and you prefer to work in a much larger window than the one Merge chooses, you could run the following commands in a Terminal window:

```
mrgconfig win set windowsizeauto=false
mrgconfig win set windowswidth=1250
mrgconfig win set windowsheight=990
```

After running these commands, you must restart Windows to see the change.

The first command is necessary if you're specifically setting the width and height of your Windows window. Otherwise, Merge will continue to automatically set the window size for Windows. With these new settings, Windows fills the screen while still running on your Desktop. You can experiment with these numbers to find the setting that works best for your system.

OTHER CHANGES USING THE mrgconfig COMMAND

The `mrgconfig` command can be used in a Terminal window to change many aspects of your DOS or Windows session. To see all the parameters set by this command, look in the `.merge` directory in your home directory (for user spike it would be `/home/spike/.merge`). Note the dot in front of the directory name. This is a hidden directory in your home directory. Inside this directory are two files: `dos.cfd` and `win.cfw`. Use the `cat` command in a Terminal window to look at these files.

To use the `mrgconfig` command, you would enter one of the following:

```
mrgconfig dos set option=setting
```

or

```
mrgconfig win set option=setting
```

Replace *option* with the option you want to set and replace *setting* with the new value. For example, you can set the font size in the DOS window to either auto, small, or medium. To set it to medium, you would enter

```
mrgconfig dos set dosfont=medium
```

If you're using a high resolution video board, you may want to make this change.

Installing DOS Applications

With UnixWare, you can run DOS applications that are designed to run on an 8086 processor. Your Windows 3.1 applications must be designed to operate in standard mode. Windows applications that require enhanced mode, such as WordPerfect for Windows 6.*x*, MathCAD 4.0, and Visual C++ 7.0, will not run with Merge. Merge does not support applications that require protected-mode operation available with 80286, 80386, or 80486 processors. If your application gives you a choice of processors for which it can configure itself, always select 8086, or the application will not run.

You install most DOS and Windows applications the same way you would install them on a stand-alone DOS system. Start a DOS or Windows session (as described later in this chapter) and follow the application's installation instructions. However, before you begin an installation, you should consider who should have access to the application. The intended users determine on which drive and in which directory you install the application. Applications can be divided into three general categories:

▸ Personal applications, which are single-user versions of applications that only you will use. If other users on your system want to use the same application, they must install their own copies.

▸ Public applications, which are multiple-user versions of applications. If many users need to use the same application, a version with multiple licenses should be installed as a public application. Public applications are installed in a directory accessible to all users.

▸ Special applications, which include certain copy-protected applications that must be installed on a separate DOS partition (not under Merge).

The following sections describe the considerations for each type of application.

INSTALLING PERSONAL APPLICATIONS

If an application is intended for your use only, install it as a personal application in your own personal directory. As you install an application, certain information is usually requested by the installation program. You might be asked to designate the drive and directory where the application is to be installed, the video adapter type, the printer port, and the mouse type or port.

In addition, many applications give you the option of having them modify your AUTOEXEC.BAT and CONFIG.SYS files. A few DOS applications even offer to configure themselves to run in protected mode. It's important that you provide the application with the correct information. Use the following guidelines for answering the installation questions.

Drive and Directory Information

Most DOS and Windows applications prompt you for the name of the drive and directory where you want the application installed. In fact, many applications provide a drive and directory name for you. For example, the basic installation for WordPerfect 5.1 (DOS version) uses C:\WP51 as the installation directory. Always install applications on your C: drive since it's your home directory in UNIX and you already have permission to create files there.

For applications that don't suggest a drive and directory name, select an appropriate directory name and specify C:\ as the drive. For example, you might install Lotus 1-2-3 in C:\LOTUS or Quicken in C:\QUICKEN.

Some applications require that they be installed in the root directory. Using C: as the installation drive ensures that these applications install correctly.

Video Adapter Information

Some DOS applications detect and automatically configure the application for the type of video adapter (such as VGA or EGA) installed in your system. If the application you're installing doesn't automatically detect the type of video adapter you have, specify your video adapter type when prompted. Almost all systems sold today use a VGA type adapter.

Printer Port Information

As explained later in this chapter, when you print in Merge, you can direct your print requests either to a UNIX print spooler, which must be named `doslp`, or to a printer connected directly to your system's parallel port. By default, print requests are sent to the UNIX print spooler. With `doslp` properly configured, DOS and Windows print requests will be spooled just like UNIX print requests.

You can change the default destination for printer requests from the DOS Options window. See the section about configuring Merge, later in this chapter, for details.

Mouse Type or Port Information

If your mouse works when you use the UnixWare Desktop, it will work when you use Merge. This is because Merge knows about your UnixWare mouse and automatically installs a mouse driver to take advantage of it. You should not let your application install its own mouse driver. Your application may want to know what type of mouse is installed on your system. Merge considers your mouse to be a Microsoft bus mouse, regardless of the actual type of mouse connected to your system.

Changing the AUTOEXEC.BAT and CONFIG.SYS Files

Many DOS and Windows applications require that the BUFFERS and FILES statements in your CONFIG.SYS file be set to certain values, and some applications edit the CONFIG.SYS file for you. In fact, some applications edit your CONFIG.SYS and AUTOEXEC.BAT files without warning, so be sure to make a copy of these two files before installing any application.

If the application is well behaved, it will ask you whether it should modify the AUTOEXEC.BAT and CONFIG.SYS files before it does so. You can answer yes if asked, and let the application make the necessary changes.

INSTALLING PUBLIC APPLICATIONS

If you're installing an application that all users intend to share, install it in a directory that is accessible to all users. A good idea is to create subdirectories below J:\SHARE. However, only the root user can create directories or files in the J:\SHARE directory. For convenience, you could change the owner of the SHARE directory so one person could always install applications there. If you're the only person using the system, change the owner to your login ID. To change the owner of the SHARE directory to, for example, user spike, open a Terminal window, type su, and enter the root user password when prompted. Then type

```
chown spike /usr/merge/dosroot/share
```

User spike is now the owner of the SHARE directory and can install applications there.

After installing applications in the SHARE directory, add the directory to the PATH statement in the AUTOEXEC.BAT file in the system's root directory (this is the UNIX root directory). For example, if WordPerfect 5.1 was installed in the SHARE directory, you would add J:\SHARE\WP51 to PATH statement. You must be the root user to edit this file.

To get to the system AUTOEXEC.BAT and CONFIG.SYS files through UnixWare, open a Terminal window and type cd /. To get to them through a DOS window, at the DOS prompt, type D:, press Enter, and then type cd \.

You can edit the AUTOEXEC.BAT and CONFIG.SYS files using either a UNIX or DOS editor. If you edit the files with a UNIX editor (either in a Terminal window with vi or from the Desktop with the Text Editor), be sure to leave the Ctrl-M (^M) at the end of each line. The Ctrl-Ms do not appear when you edit the files with a DOS editor.

INSTALLING COPY-PROTECTED APPLICATIONS

Although it's less common today than several years ago, some software manufacturers still use schemes to prevent you from installing your software on more than one system or to prevent more than one user from running the software at the same time. The first line of defense against this type of software is, of course, not to buy it. However, if you must buy it because it's the only application that meets your particular needs, you can still install it (but not as easily as you can install non-copy-protected software).

Two popular methods for protecting software are key disks and special installation utilities. If your software comes with a key disk, you can install it as you would any other DOS application under Merge. When you run the application, insert the key disk as you would if you were running it on a stand-alone DOS system. No special procedures are required.

To prevent illegal copying of their software, some manufacturers use special programs for the installation and, sometimes, removal of their applications. Applications using these types of schemes often must be installed on an actual DOS partition, not on sections of your hard disk shared by both Merge and UNIX. You may not even know that the application uses such a scheme until you try to install it under Merge in the regular way. If this fails, try installing it on the DOS partition from within Merge (using the E: drive). If that fails, try rebooting your system with DOS and installing it on the DOS partition without running UnixWare. Both of these methods are described in the following sections.

Installing on the DOS Partition from UnixWare

To install a DOS application on the DOS partition, you must first have a DOS partition. When you install UnixWare, you are given the opportunity to create a DOS partition. If you don't have a DOS partition, and realize now that you need one, you must reinstall UnixWare and create one during the installation process. Reinstalling UnixWare is not a trivial task. You almost always want to avoid reloading operating system software if you can, especially the UNIX operating system. As far as the DOS applications go, you are better off finding some that work within Merge rather than reloading UnixWare.

If you already have a DOS partition, loading a DOS application on it using Merge is no more difficult than loading a DOS application in your C:\ directory. Simply open a DOS window or start Windows, and select drive E: as the location for the application. Drive E: in Merge is automatically mapped to what would be drive C: if you booted your system with DOS instead of UnixWare. You may have other DOS partitions mapped to F:, G:, and so on (this mapping is done through the DOS Options window, as explained later in this chapter). Your applications can be installed on any DOS partition by using the appropriate drive letter.

NOTE **You can install a second hard disk in your system on which you can place a DOS partition. However, because it's your second hard disk, you cannot make the DOS partition bootable.**

Installing on the DOS Partition from DOS

If you can't install your application from within Merge, you must shut down your system and reboot it with DOS. If your DOS partition is bootable (it was formatted with the FORMAT C: /S command), you can use `fdisk`, which is both a UNIX command and a DOS command, to set the active partition to either the DOS partition or the UNIX partition.

In a Terminal window, run the UNIX `fdisk` command and set the active partition to DOS. When you restart your computer, DOS will boot instead of UNIX. Install your application according to the manufacturer's instructions. In DOS, run FDISK and set the active partition to UNIX. Restart your computer, and UnixWare will boot. You can now use the application installed in the DOS partition in the same way that you use other applications in the DOS partition.

Some applications make your life particularly miserable by requiring that the application be run on the same drive on which it was installed. This can be a problem when you try to run an application under Merge (where the DOS partition is referred to as drive E:) that was installed under DOS (where the DOS partition is referred to as drive C:). To get around this and make the application easy to run from Merge, enter the following DOS command after booting your system with DOS but *before* installing the application.

    SUBST E: C:\

This command substitutes the drive name E: for C:. After installing the application, enter

    SUBST E: /D

to remove the substituted name from drive C:.

Now when you install the application, the application thinks it's being installed on E: and runs properly under Merge.

INSTALLING PROTECTED-MODE APPLICATIONS

Most DOS applications are designed to be compatible with an Intel 8086 processor. Some new applications let you set the type of processor installed in your system or will set the type themselves. A few applications run only on Intel 80286 and later processors.

Merge runs applications compatible with the 8086 processor. It does not support applications that require protected-mode operation available with 80286, 80386, 80486, or Pentium processors (except for Microsoft Windows 3.1, which runs in standard mode). If your protected-mode application gives you a choice of processors for which it can configure itself, you can install it using Merge in the regular way. Be sure to select 8086 when you are asked to specify the processor.

SETTING YOUR PATH

Some applications require that you add their directory to your PATH statement so they can be found by DOS. For other applications, it's preferable simply to work in the directory in which the application is installed. For example, you don't need to add Quicken's directory to your path. Run Quicken from the directory in which it was installed. From within Quicken, you can set where your account files are kept.

If you're going to change your PATH statement for personal applications, edit your personal AUTOEXEC.BAT file. For public applications, edit the system AUTOEXEC.BAT file located in the root directory.

REPLACING DR-DOS

The version of DR-DOS that comes with Merge is not the full DR-DOS product that you can purchase separately. It does not contain all the commands provided in the commercial package (nor does it include the DR-DOS documentation). However, the commands that are missing are those that either have something to do with memory or the hard disk, or are duplicated by UNIX commands. The commands that work with memory or the hard disk shouldn't be run in DOS when running under Merge (they didn't leave them out just so you would go buy the full package). These commands are not included in the DR-DOS that comes with Merge:

ASSIGN	DISKMAP	JOIN	SETUP	TREE
BACKUP	DISKOPT	LOCK	SSTOR	UNDELETE
CURSOR	DOSBOOK	PASSWORD	SUBST	UNFORMAT
DELPURGE	FASTOPEN	RESTORE	SUPERPCK	UNINSTAL
DELWATCH	FDISK	SCRIPT	TOUCH	

If you want to see exactly what *is* included, look in the `/usr/merge/dosroot/dos` directory. You can use either UnixWare or DOS commands to explore this directory. If you use DOS commands, don't forget to use backslashes (look in D:\USR\MERGE\DOSROOT\DOS).

If you would rather use MS-DOS (either version 5.0, 6.0, or 6.21) instead of DR-DOS, you can replace DR-DOS by using the `dosinstall` command. When replacing DR-DOS, DOS Merge requires that the floppy disks from which you're installing be bootable. You cannot, therefore, install MS-DOS directly from the DOS 5.0 Upgrade product. You must first create a bootable floppy disk from the DOS 5.0 Upgrade software, following the DOS 5.0 installation instructions. Once the proper floppy disks are created, use them with `dosinstall` to load DOS 5.0 on your system.

To replace DR-DOS, open a Terminal window, type `su`, and enter the root user's password when prompted. Next, type

```
dosinstall
```

This command first removes the existing version of DOS and prompts you for additional information about the version you're about to install. Follow the screen prompts about the version of DOS, number of floppy disks, and drive letter you're installing from. Finally, put in the first floppy disk. Change floppy disks when prompted. When you are finished, your MS-DOS will be installed.

Running DOS and Windows Sessions

When DOS is running under Merge, DOS and UNIX share the UNIX file system. This allows you to save your DOS files in the same directories as your UNIX files. It also allows you to use your UNIX files in your DOS applications and your DOS files in your UNIX applications.

STARTING DOS AND WINDOWS SESSIONS

DOS and Windows sessions are started independently in UnixWare. Each type of session has different memory requirements: a DOS session is begun with 1MB of Extended memory; a Windows session is begun with 4MB of Extended memory. DOS and Windows have separate icons in the Applications folder window.

The procedure for starting Windows in UnixWare is different from that in a stand-alone DOS system, where you always begin a DOS session first and then type WIN to start Windows (this sequence might be executed in the system's AUTOEXEC.BAT file). NOTE

You can start a DOS or Windows session in several ways:

▸ Open your Applications folder window and double-click on the DOS or Windows icon. Figure 6.2 shows the window with these icons.

▸ Double-click on an icon representing a DOS application. For example, if you have WordPerfect for DOS installed on your system, you can double-click on the `wp.exe` icon in the folder in which WordPerfect is installed.

▸ Use the DOS Options or Windows Options windows. Click the Menu button (the right mouse button) on the DOS or Windows icon in the Applications folder window. Select Options from the

The Folder: Applications window with DOS and Windows (Win) icons

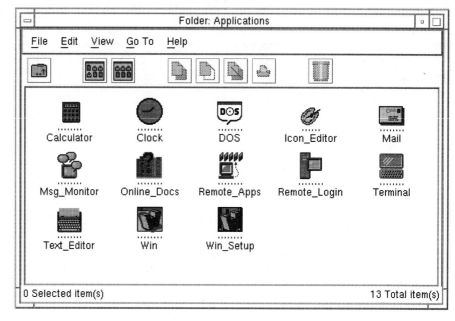

menu to see the Options window. Figure 6.3 shows the DOS Options window. The Windows Options window is shown in Figure 6.4. Click on Start.

 NOTE

For some unknown reason, the Options windows for both DOS and Windows are labeled DOS Options at the top. You can distinguish them from one another because the Windows Options window says *win* instead of *dos* in the text box. Despite what it says at the top, we will refer to this window as the Windows Options window, since that's its function.

▶ If you like working from the UnixWare system shell, you can start a DOS session by entering dos +x in a Terminal window. To start a Windows session from a Terminal window, enter win +x +m4.

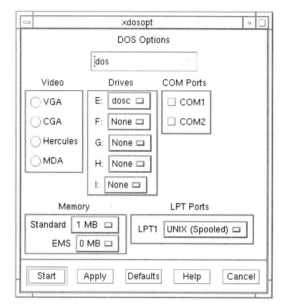

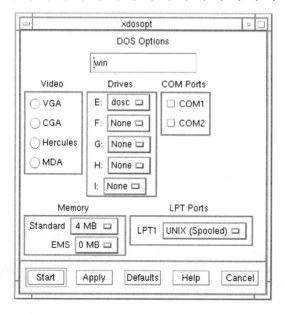

► You can also start a Windows session from a DOS window if you started the DOS window with at least 4MB of memory. However, you must start Windows with the /s switch (`win /s`) or Windows will attempt to start in enhanced mode and fail.

When a DOS or Windows session starts, the CONFIG.SYS and AUTO-EXEC.BAT files are read, just like on a stand-alone DOS system. Merge, however, allows several sets of these files to exist. Besides each user having his or her own CONFIG.SYS and AUTOEXEC.BAT files, Merge reads system CONFIG.SYS and AUTOEXEC.BAT files that affect all users.

Individual CONFIG.SYS and AUTOEXEC.BAT files, located in each user's home directory, offer great flexibility in customizing unique DOS environments. The system CONFIG.SYS and AUTOEXEC.BAT files are located in the UNIX root (/) directory and are read before your personal CONFIG.SYS and AUTOEXEC.BAT files.

ACCESSING DRIVES

Once you have a DOS session started, you navigate through directories as you normally would in DOS. In addition to the usual DOS drives (A:, B:, and C:), Merge provides special drives that allow you to access your UNIX directories (folders) and even the DOS partition if your system was set up with one.

As you would expect, you access your floppy disk drives by designating drives A: and B:. Drive C: gives you access to your home directory and the directories under it. For example, if your home directory is `spike`, then C: is the same as the UNIX directory `/home/spike` (or D:\HOME\SPIKE in DOS notation). This is the drive you should normally use while in a DOS session.

Drive D: refers to UnixWare's root directory. Through drive D:, you have access to all UNIX directories. Most likely, you won't be able to change or create files in many of the directories outside your home directory. However, you will be able to read many of the files.

For example, the system CONFIG.SYS and AUTOEXEC.BAT files are located on drive D:. Because the UNIX system permissions apply to the root directory, you and other users cannot normally edit the system CON-FIG.SYS and AUTOEXEC.BAT files or create new files in this directory. If you need to change the system CONFIG.SYS or AUTOEXEC.BAT file, and you know the UNIX root user password, you can edit these files by logging into UNIX as the root user and using a UNIX editor, such as `vi`.

If you don't know how to use `vi`, just change the permissions on the file you want to edit when you log in as the root user. Then use a DOS editor to make your changes. When you're finished, change the permissions back to the original values. For example, to change the permissions on CON-FIG.SYS after becoming the root user, type

```
chmod 666 config.sys
```

When you're finished editing, type

```
chmod 644 config.sys
```

Be sure that you don't delete the Ctrl-M (^M) at the end of each line in the CONFIG.SYS and AUTOEXEC.BAT files. You only see the Ctrl-M when you edit DOS files with a UNIX editor. To insert a Ctrl-M with `vi`, press Ctrl-V and then Ctrl-M.

Drive E: is special. It provides access to the first DOS partition on your hard disk; that is, what would normally be drive C: if you booted your system under DOS instead of UnixWare. Having access to your DOS partition is convenient if you created a DOS partition when you installed UnixWare. By specifying drive E:, you can access and run applications and utilities installed on the DOS partition, as well as save files there. You can access other DOS partitions (you may have extended partitions called D:, E:, and so on) by using the DOS Options window to assign the partitions to drive letters F: through I:, as described later in this chapter.

The DOS partition does not need to be bootable in order to be accessed by a DOS session under Merge; however, it must be formatted to allow you to load files and access E:.

 NOTE

Drive J: provides access to a special directory in UnixWare, /usr/merge/dosroot (D:\USR\MERGE\DOSROOT in DOS notation). This directory is accessible to all users. It's a good place to install applications that users share (public applications). Merge automatically includes the /usr/merge/dosroot directory in each user's PATH statement.

By default, the last drive letter defined is N: (LASTDRIVE=N). However, if your system is connected to a NetWare file server, drive O: is your NetWare login drive. The drive letters from K: to N: can refer to NetWare volumes or other DOS devices. Figure 6.5 shows an example of mapping DOS drives to the UNIX file system, NetWare servers, and DOS partitions, for a user named spike.

DOS drive mappings

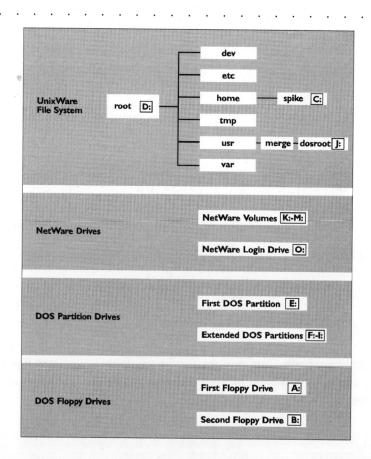

USING THE DOS MENU

When a DOS window is open, you can access the DOS menu by clicking the Menu button (the right mouse button). The menu includes the following options for controlling certain aspects of how you use Merge:

▶ **Zoom:** Puts DOS in full-screen mode (a new virtual terminal is created). In this mode, DOS Merge looks exactly like a stand-alone DOS system. In some cases, such as when a DOS application uses graphics modes or video modes other than VGA, you must use the Zoom option. Your mouse also works in Zoom mode (it normally doesn't work in a DOS window on the Desktop). To return from Zoom mode to the UnixWare Desktop, press the Scroll Lock key.

You can make your DOS applications zoom automatically when necessary by running the `mrgconfig` command. In a Terminal window, type `mrgconfig dos set autozoom=true` to set DOS to autozoom mode. You can see the Merge settings by looking at two files in the `.merge` directory in your home directory. These files are `dos.cfd` and `win.cfw`.

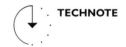

TECHNOTE

▶ **Focus:** Activates the mouse in the DOS window. When you use this option, the mouse doesn't work on the UnixWare Desktop. To switch the mouse back to working on the Desktop, press the Scroll Lock key to display the DOS menu and select Unfocus. Also, if you close the DOS window, by pressing Ctrl-Esc Ctrl-K, you regain use of the mouse on the Desktop.

▶ **Refresh:** Redraws the screen. Occasionally, your DOS window can become unreadable. If this happens, use the Refresh option.

▶ **DOS Colors:** Forces the DOS window to use DOS colors. On some systems, the UnixWare Desktop colors are used for DOS instead of the standard DOS colors. If this option is inactive (grayed), your system is already using the DOS colors.

▸ **Desktop Keys**: Sets the function keys to work as they do for the Desktop. When you start a DOS session, the function keys are automatically set to work as they do in DOS. If you select Desktop Keys and then display the DOS menu again, the option changes to DOS Keys. Select this option to change back to the DOS function keys.

▸ **Autofreeze On**: Stops the constant checking of the keyboard buffer for keystrokes by DOS applications. In the single-user, non-multitasking world of DOS, this checking usually doesn't cause any problems. UNIX, however, is a multiuser, multitasking system where something is always going on (even if you don't see anything happening). If DOS applications keep checking the keyboard buffer, they can use valuable computer processor time. By selecting this option, you can improve your UNIX performance.

▸ **Quit**: Closes the DOS window and exits from Merge. A confirmation window appears before the DOS window is closed. Select Yes to exit DOS or No to keep your DOS window open.

RUNNING DOS APPLICATIONS

You run applications in Merge the same way you would run them on a stand-alone DOS system. At the DOS prompt, enter the name of the application you want to run and press Enter. For example, to run WordPerfect, type wp and press Enter.

You can also start DOS applications directly from the Desktop. First, open the folder containing the application. Next, double-click on the icon representing the DOS file that runs the program. In the case of WordPerfect, the file's name is wp.com. In DOS, programs that you can run always end in either .COM, .EXE, or .BAT.

NOTE

Any file with a suffix of .exe is interpreted by UnixWare as a DOS application. Inside a UnixWare folder, it appears as a DOS executable icon or an icon for a specific application.

ACCESSING NETWARE SERVERS

To access NetWare servers from Merge, change to the O: drive (this is your NetWare login drive). From there, you can log in to a NetWare server. After you are logged in, use the NetWare MAP command to map servers to various DOS drive letters. See your *NetWare Utilities Reference* for details about using the MAP command.

If your system is not connected to a NetWare network, comment out two lines in your system AUTOEXEC.BAT file (located in the root directory). Figure 6.6 shows a typical system AUTOEXEC.BAT file before and after commenting out the two NetWare lines (one line contains the command `ipxtli`, and the other line contains the command `netx`).

FIGURE 6.6

System AUTOEXEC.BAT
file before and after editing

If your system is connected to a NetWare network, you may not always want your DOS or Windows session to connect to the network. You can change your AUTOEXEC.BAT file to ask you whether or not you want to connect to NetWare.

Unfortunately, DR-DOS does not provide an easy way to process questions in a batch file. However, you can use ASK.COM, which is included on the CD with this book, in your AUTOEXEC.BAT file, to process the networking question.

NOTE **ASK.COM is from the April 27, 1993, Volume 12, Number 8 issue of** ***PC Magazine.***

Copy ASK.COM into a directory that's in your PATH statement.

Figure 6.7 shows how to modify your system AUTOEXEC.BAT file using ASK.COM. Be sure to change the AUTOEXEC.BAT file located in the root directory, not the one in your home directory.

FIGURE 6.7

AUTOEXEC.BAT *file*
modified to prompt for a
network connection

```
                                    DOS

C:\TMP>type autoexec.bat
@echo off
path j:\dos;j:\merge;
@prompt $p$g
:LOOP
echo Connect to NetWare Servers (Y/N)?
ask
if errorlevel 90 goto LOOP
if errorlevel 89 goto YES
if errorlevel 89 goto LOOP
if errorlevel 78 goto NO
goto LOOP
:NO
cls
goto END
:YES
@if not exist j:\share\novell\ipxtli.com goto :END
j:\share\novell\ipxtli
j:\share\novell\netx
:END

C:\TMP>
```

After you make this change, the next time you start a DOS or Windows session, you'll be asked whether or not you want to connect to the network. Your session starts much quicker when you answer no. Also, if you try to connect to a NetWare server when the network is down, your DOS or Windows session does not start. If you know the network is down, answer no to the prompt.

DOS AND UNIX FILE-NAMING CONVENTIONS

DOS and UNIX have quite different conventions for naming files. UNIX is flexible about file names; DOS is very strict. For example, UNIX allows names such as `chapter.DOS.7`. DOS, of course, would choke on that name.

Because Merge lets you use the same files and directories that UNIX uses (in effect, DOS and UNIX share the same file system), Merge must have the means to deal with the long and unconventional file names that UNIX allows.

 **TECHNOTE**

UnixWare's default file system, `vxfs`, allows extremely long file names. Other UNIX file systems limit the number of characters in a file name. For example, the `s5` file system allows only 14 characters in a file name.

DOS restricts you to eight characters for the file name and, optionally, a period with a three-character extension. DOS file names never have more than eight characters to the left of the optional period and extension. Here are some examples of valid DOS file names:

- ▸ yourfile
- ▸ c.bat
- ▸ 123.exe
- ▸ somefile.7
- ▸ anyfile.111

The default file system in UnixWare allows very long file names, and there is no restriction on where periods, if used, can be located. The following are valid UnixWare file names:

- ▸ file1
- ▸ longfile12345
- ▸ a.chapter

> ▸ this_long.filename_is_okay

> ▸ file-name.with.two_periods

When Merge reads UNIX file names that don't conform to the DOS rules, Merge takes the liberty of changing them to legal DOS names. If the name is too long, Merge truncates it. In addition, an apostrophe and a unique index of one to three letters are added. Merge changes the name only in the following cases:

> ▸ The name contains a period with more than three characters following it.

> ▸ The name contains nonalphabetic characters that DOS doesn't recognize. For example, UNIX file names can have a space in them, but DOS file names cannot.

> ▸ The name contains uppercase letters.

> ▸ The name is too long.

The names are not actually changed on the hard disk. They only appear changed when you list the names with DIR in DOS or view them through a DOS application. The following are typical UNIX file names and what they turn into after Merge renames them (if you try this, your index characters after the apostrophe may be different):

UnixWare Name	DOS Merge Name
dos.chapter7	DOS'I8N.CHA
my file	MY_F'TN9
Applications	APPL'TS2
wpdictionary	WPDI'T5J

To use DOS commands, such as COPY and DEL, with these files, use the names you see in the DOS window. Do not use the original UNIX names.

You can see both the **UNIX** and **DOS** file names in the same listing with the `udir` command. This command works in both Terminal and DOS windows. A sample list is shown in Figure 6.8.

NOTE

F I G U R E 6.8

Sample list from the `udir` command in a Terminal window

```
                                                          Terminal
$ udir

Volume in drive D is snowbird
Directory of d:/home/spike

.                    .            spike   drwxr-xr-x  <DIR>     12-12-94   9:45p
..                   ..           root    drwxrwxr-x  <DIR>     12-06-94   5:19p
Help_Desk            HELP'D8K     bin     -rwxrwxrwx     11060  12-07-94  10:54p
Folder_Map           FOLD'D8L     bin     -rwxr-xr-x        11  11-23-94   6:24a
Wastebasket          WAST'D8O     bin     -rwxr-xr-x        14  11-23-94   6:24a
Shutdown             SHUT'D8Q     bin     -rwxr-xr-x         9  11-23-94   6:24a
Admin_Tools          ADMI'D8W     spike   drwxr-xr-x  <DIR>     12-06-94  11:02p
Mailbox              MAIL'D8X     spike   drwxr-x---  <DIR>     12-07-94   8:57p
Applications         APPL'D9A     spike   drwxr-xr-x  <DIR>     12-07-94  10:26p
Disks-etc            DISK'D9Q     spike   drwxr-xr-x  <DIR>     12-07-94  10:28p
Preferences          PREF'EAY     spike   drwxr-xr-x  <DIR>     12-06-94   8:43p
Games                GAME'ECU     spike   drwxr-xr-x  <DIR>     12-07-94  10:54p
windows              WINDOWS      spike   drwxr-xr-x  <DIR>     12-11-94  10:43p
Amazon               AMAZO'EZ     spike   -rwxr--r--        19  12-06-94  11:46a
config.sys           CONFIG.SYS   spike   -rw-r--r--        76  12-11-94   8:51p
tmp                  TMP          spike   drwxr-xr-x  <DIR>     12-12-94   9:35p
snopar               SNOPAR       spike   -rwxr-xr-x         0  12-07-94   9:49p
uw20                 UW20         spike   drwxr-xr-x  <DIR>     12-11-94  10:54p
dtm.tmp              DTM.TMP      spike   -rw-r--r--      1140  12-07-94  11:02p
outp                 OUTP         spike   -rw-r--r--    148489  12-12-94   8:42p
config.old           CONFIG.OLD   spike   -rw-r--r--         0  12-06-94   5:11p
emm386.exe           EMM386.EXE   spike   -rw-r--r--    110174  3-10-92    3:10a
ramdrive.sys         RAMDRIVE.SYS spike   -rw-r--r--      5873  3-10-92    3:10a
smartdrv.exe         SMARTDRV.EXE spike   -rw-r--r--     43609  3-10-92    3:10a
himem.sys            HIMEM.SYS    spike   -rw-r--r--     13824  3-10-92    3:10a
autoexec.bat         AUTOEXEC.BAT spike   -rw-r--r--        69  12-11-94  10:42p
netware              NETWARE      root    drwxr-xr-x  <DIR>     12-06-94   2:03a
autoexec.sav         AUTOEXEC.SAV spike   -rw-r--r--        69  12-12-94   8:45p
winword              WINWORD      spike   drwxr-xr-x  <DIR>     12-12-94   8:15p
autoexec.bak         AUTOEXEC.BAK spike   -rw-r--r--        35  12-11-94   8:51p
       30 File(s)                 17465344 bytes free
$ █
```

RUNNING UNIX COMMANDS FROM A DOS WINDOW

You can run UNIX commands in a DOS window either by using the on command provided by Merge or by linking the UNIX command to the on command. The on command is located in \USR\MERGE\DOSROOT\DOS with the rest of the DOS commands. Use it by typing

>   on unix *unix_command*

or

>   on – *unix_command*

where *unix_command* is the name of the UNIX command you want to run. You can use either the word unix or the minus sign (–) after on.

For example, try entering the following in a DOS window:

>   on unix cal

or use the form

>   on – cal

This line executes the UNIX command cal, which displays a calendar for the current month and year in your DOS window. You can run any noninteractive (one that doesn't require input from you) UNIX command in this manner.

By linking UNIX commands to the on command, you can run UNIX commands without having to enter on unix or on – before them. As an example, use the following steps to create the l (the letter *l*) command for DOS. This command will display the files in the current directory in the same format that the UNIX ls –F command produces. (Many UNIX systems have l built in as an alias for ls –CF.) The output from l is nicely formatted and differentiates between files and directories.

1 • Enter l in a Terminal window to see if the command already exists on your system. If you see a "not found" message, you need to create your own alias. The next steps make an alias by creating

a small shell script. If you see a listing of files when you enter the
l command, skip to step 4.

2 · In a directory that is in your PATH statement, such as your personal `bin` directory, create a file with the following line (use any UnixWare editor, such as `vi` in a Terminal window or Text Editor from the Desktop):

```
ls -F
```

See Chapter 8 for information about creating your own `bin` directory and adding it to your PATH statement.

NOTE

3 · Name this file l (the letter *l*). Make the script executable by entering

```
chmod 755 l
```

The file is now an executable shell script.

4 · In the Terminal window, type `su` and enter the root user's password when prompted.

5 · Create a link by entering

```
ln -s /usr/lib/merge/dosside/on.exe
   /usr/lib/merge/dosside/l.exe
```

6 · Exit by pressing Ctrl-D.

7 · Open a DOS session. At the DOS prompt, enter l. A UNIX style directory listing is displayed.

In general, if you link `/usr/lib/merge/dosside/on.exe` to a UNIX command that is available from your path, you can run it in a DOS window.

Some UnixWare system commands are already linked for you:

cat	cp	du	grep	ls	spell
chmod	df	egrep	in	mv	tail
cmp	diff	fgrep	lp	pv	wc

All these commands can be run from within a DOS window. See Chapter 8 and your online commands reference book for details on using these commands.

PRINTING IN MERGE

You print in Merge the same way you would print on a stand-alone DOS system, including by using the DOS PRINT command or the Print Screen key. Set your applications to print to lpt1. To make lpt1 work, however, you need to create a print spooler named doslp. In UnixWare, use the Printer Setup window. The Printer Setup window is accessed from the Admin Tools folder window. (See Chapter 11 for details on using the Printer Setup window.) Set up the doslp print spooler as you would any Unix-Ware print spooler, except select DOS printer as the printer type. The DOS printer selection passes through whatever comes from your DOS application.

In your applications, set the printer type to the printer model being used by the print spooler. For example, if you have a TI microLaser Pro 600 Post-Script printer as the destination for print spooler doslp, select TI micro-Laser Pro 600 as the printer type in your applications.

If you have several print spoolers defined in UNIX, each connected to a different type of printer, you can use the DOS command line to direct your print requests to any of those printers. For example, you might have one PostScript printer connected to doslp and another printer that supports PCL (such as an HP LaserJet) connected to a print spooler named lppcl. Any applications that support PostScript should be configured to print to lpt1. Applications that only support PCL should be configured for lpt2. To connect lpt2 to the PCL printer, enter the following at the DOS prompt:

```
PRINTER LPT2 UNIX "lp -dlppcl"
```

This command directs all output to `lpt2` (from your applications) to the UNIX print spooler `lppcl`. For the second argument (LPT2 in the example), you can substitute LPT1 or LPT3. If you omit the second argument, the command assumes LPT1. The part between the quotation marks must be in lowercase letters. The rest can be uppercase or lowercase. If you use this command to direct output to `lpt2`, set your application to print to `lpt2` as well.

If you're an advanced user and are familiar with the `lp` command, you can include options to `lp` when using printer command. For example, if you want to use `psnec`, which is connected to a PostScript printer, you can direct output from `lpt2` to this printer and let it know that the data is PostScript by entering

```
PRINTER LPT2 UNIX "lp -Tpostscript -dpsnec"
```

If you sent PostScript output to `psnec` without using the `-Tpostscript` option to `lp`, you would get the raw PostScript code as the printed output.

If you are getting partially printed pages from your printer, you need to increase the printer timeout. For a DOS session, the default timeout is 15 seconds. To increase the printer timeout to, say, 30 seconds for printer `lpt1`, enter the following at a DOS prompt:

```
PRINTER LPT1 UNIX /T30
```

CONFIGURING MERGE

Through the Options and Windows Options windows, you can set certain characteristics for how your DOS (or Windows) session will operate, such as the video mode, how much Expanded memory (EMS) DOS or Windows uses, and how print jobs are handled. The DOS and Windows icons display separate Options boxes with the same options but different settings.

To display the Options box, open your UnixWare Applications folder and click the Menu button on the DOS (or Windows) icon. Choose Options from this menu to see the DOS or Windows Options window (see Figures 6.3 and 6.4, earlier in this chapter).

The Options windows contain five sections: Video, Drives, COM Ports, Memory, and LPT Ports. You can change the settings in any of these sections. Then you can either click on the Apply button to close the window and save the new settings, or click on the Start button to start a session with the chosen options. However, if you don't click on Apply, the selected options are not saved, and your next session uses the old settings. Each of the Options settings is described in the following sections.

Selecting the Video Mode

The Video section lets you select the mode for your DOS or Windows session. Your choices are VGA, CGA, MDA, and Hercules. This is useful if you have software that only operates in a certain mode and doesn't set the mode automatically. For example, some older games need to be run in CGA mode. If you want to run such a game, change the Video setting to CGA before starting your session.

Mapping Drive Letters

The Drives settings let you map the drives you created in DOS to Merge drive letters. This is a useful feature if you have more than one DOS partition on your hard disk. For example, when you partition your hard disk, you can create a primary DOS partition, which is always C:, and an extended partition, which can be divided into one or more logical drives, such as D:, E:, and so on.

The primary DOS partition is automatically assigned to E: in Merge. Use the Drives section to assign the other partitions to Merge drive letters. Click on the Merge drive letter you want to assign. Select the DOS drive you want assigned from the list displayed (dosC is DOS drive C:, dosD is DOS drive D:, and so on).

 NOTE   **By default, your DOS partition, if you have one, is *not* mapped to your E: drive in Merge. You must map it, as instructed above, before you can access your DOS partition from Merge.**

Activating COM Ports

If you will use a modem, serial printer, or other device that needs a COM port in your DOS or Windows session, you must turn on the port through the Options window.

For serial devices other than your mouse, click on the COM port to which the device is connected. For example, if you want to connect a modem to COM1 for use while in DOS or Windows, click on COM1 in the COM Ports box. If your mouse is connected to COM2, *do not* click on COM2 in the COM Ports box. The mouse is already taken care of.

WARNING

When you connect a COM port for use with Merge, you cannot access the COM port from UnixWare. We suggest that you connect a COM port for use in Merge only as you need it. Do not permanently apply the change.

Selecting the Amount of Memory

The Memory section of the Options windows allows you to select between Standard and EMS memory for your DOS or Windows session. Standard memory is the same as Extended memory. EMS memory is Expanded memory. When you first open the DOS Options window, 1MB is selected for Standard memory. This is why you shouldn't start a DOS session and then type WIN to start Windows. Windows sessions should always be started with at least 4MB of Standard memory. You can increase the amount of Standard memory used by clicking on the arrow next to the Standard setting and selecting a value from the list.

When you open the Windows Options window from the Windows icon, 4MB is selected for Standard memory. No EMS memory is initially selected for either a DOS or a Windows session.

NOTE

The Expanded memory that Merge supports is compatible with the LIM EMS 4.0 specification.

If you are running DOS applications that use Expanded memory, you can select the amount of EMS memory (1, 2, 4, or 8MB) in addition to the 1MB of Standard memory. To change the amount of memory, click on the arrow next to EMS and select from the amounts listed.

In the DOS Options window, choose the amount of memory carefully, however. Do not select more than you need, or your DOS session may not run. Some systems will not start a DOS session if too much EMS memory is selected. For example, on our 80486 33MHz Gateway 2000 with 16MB of RAM, we cannot start a DOS session with more than 2MB of EMS memory. However, on our 80486 66MHz Gateway 2000, also with 16MB of RAM, we have no trouble starting a DOS session with 4MB of EMS memory selected.

A safe approach would be to begin with 1MB of EMS memory and see how your applications run. If you have problems running an application that uses EMS memory, increase the EMS memory to 2MB and test your applications again. Repeat this procedure until your DOS session starts and your applications run properly. Keep in mind that UNIX is also running, and it will use as much memory as it needs (which always seems to be more than you have).

Choosing a Printer Port

The LPT Ports section offers a choice between printing through the UNIX print system (`lp`) or printing directly to a printer connected to a parallel port on your system. If you choose to use the UNIX print facility, you must have a print spooler with the name `doslp` defined in UNIX, as explained earlier in this chapter, in the section about printing in Merge. With `doslp` set up properly, and UNIX (Spooled) selected for LPT1, you only need to set your applications to print to LPT1, which is usually the default. UNIX spools your print requests and eventually sends them to the printer designated by `doslp`.

If you have a parallel printer connected to your system, you can direct your print requests to it by selecting DOS (Direct):lp0 (or lp1 or lp2, depending on whether your printer is connected to the first, second, or third parallel port). You still set your application to print to LPT1. Merge sends your print requests to the port set in the LPT Ports section of the Options window.

ENDING A DOS OR WINDOWS SESSION

The quickest ways to exit a DOS session are to type `quit` at the DOS prompt or press Ctrl-Esc followed by Ctrl-K. Either method closes the DOS window immediately. If you prefer, you can use the DOS menu. Click the Menu button with the mouse pointer in the DOS window to display the DOS menu. Then select Quit from the menu. When you see the window asking you to confirm that you want to quit, click on Yes to close the DOS window.

To exit a Windows session, exit from Windows in the normal manner (by selecting File ➤ Exit Windows or double-clicking on the Close box). Your Windows session ends, and you're returned to the UnixWare Desktop.

Working with DOS Files on Floppy Disks

To work in a complete DOS or Windows environment, you start a DOS or Windows session. But if you just want to transfer a file from a DOS floppy disk onto your UNIX system or perform some other operation on a DOS floppy, you don't need to start a DOS session. You can perform operations such as copying and erasing files on a DOS floppy directly from the UnixWare Desktop or from a Terminal window. UnixWare is smart enough to recognize when a DOS floppy disk has been inserted into a drive.

USING THE DESKTOP TO WORK WITH DOS FILES

The UnixWare Desktop lets you copy DOS files between UNIX folders and DOS floppies, erase DOS files from DOS floppies, and create directories on DOS floppies. You can also format DOS floppies from the Desktop.

Copy, erase, and directory operations are accomplished through the Folder: Disk_A (or Disk_B) window. To open this window, double-click on the Disks-etc icon in your Desktop window. The Disks-etc window includes icons for each floppy drive, Disk_A and Disk_B, as shown in Figure 6.9. Click on the icon for the drive that has the DOS floppy disk. You see the DOS Floppy window, with an icon for each file on the floppy disk, as shown in Figure 6.10.

▶ . . . . ◀

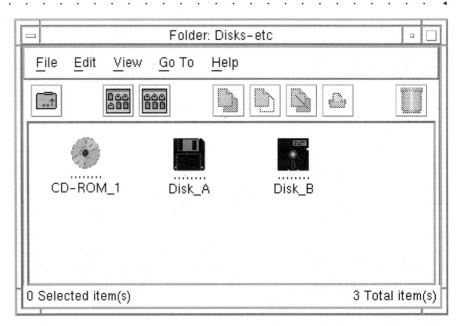

NOTE   **If you have only one floppy drive installed in your system, Disk_B will not appear in the Disks-etc folder window.**

. . . . . .

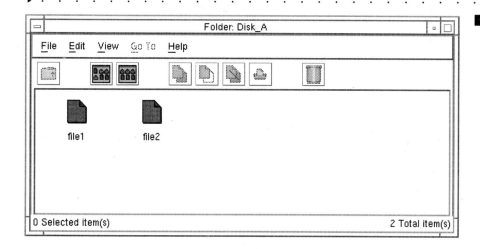

FIGURE 6.10

The Folder: Disk_A window

Copying DOS Files with the UnixWare Desktop

The easiest way to copy files from a DOS floppy disk to a UnixWare folder is to use drag-and-drop. First, open the DOS floppy disk by clicking on the floppy disk's icon in the Disks-etc window. Next, open the UnixWare folder you want to copy files to. Then, press the Ctrl key as you drag-and-drop the file from the window with the DOS files to the UnixWare folder window.

You can also use the Edit: Copy window to copy DOS files to your Unix-Ware system. To use the Edit: Copy window to copy a DOS file, follow these steps:

I · Open the Folder: Disk_A (or Disk_B) window by double-clicking on the Disks-etc icon in your Desktop window and then double-clicking on the icon for the disk drive that contains the DOS floppy disk.

2 · Click on the file that you want to copy. To select several files at once, press and hold down the Ctrl key as you click on file icons with the mouse.

3 · Click on Edit at the top of the window to see the Edit menu, and then click on Copy. You see the Edit: Copy window, as shown in Figure 6.11.

FIGURE 6.11

The Edit: Copy window

4 · Select the folder into which you want the files copied.

5 · Click on the Copy button to copy the selected file into the selected folder.

Copying Files to a DOS Floppy

You copy files to a DOS floppy disk the same way you copy files from a DOS floppy disk, that is, you use the drag-and-drop technique. Simply open the floppy disk as mentioned above and open the UnixWare folder. Next, hold down the Ctrl key and drag-and-drop the desired file's icon to the floppy disk's window. To see how this works, follow these steps to create a file and copy it to a DOS floppy:

1 · Open a Terminal window (if you already have one open, make sure you're in your home directory by typing cd) and type

```
mkdir tmp
cd tmp
echo hello > file1
```

In this example, the first line creates a directory called tmp. The third line creates a file called file1, which contains the word hello. If you want to see the contents of the file, type cat file1.

NOTE

2 · In your UnixWare Desktop window, you should see a folder icon called tmp. Double-click on this icon. The folder opens and shows an icon for the file just created.

3 · Double-click on the Disks-etc icon in your Desktop window.

4 · Place a formatted DOS floppy disk in one of your floppy drives.

5 · Click on the disk icon representing the drive with the DOS floppy to open the DOS Floppy window.

6 · Drag-and-drop the file from the tmp folder into the DOS Floppy window. The file is copied to the DOS floppy disk.

Erasing DOS Files

From the DOS Floppy window, you can erase files from a DOS floppy disk. Display the window for the drive with the DOS disk and click on the file that you want to remove. Then click on Edit to see the Edit menu. Click on Delete.

Formatting DOS Floppies

To format a floppy disk, open the Disks-etc folder window and click with the Menu button (the right mouse button) on the icon for the drive that contains the DOS floppy. From the icon menu, select Format. You see the Format window, as shown in Figure 6.12.

FIGURE 6.12

The Format window

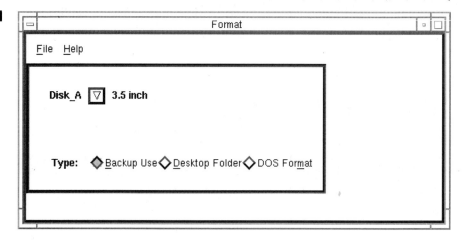

The window shows the capacity or density of the floppy disk and is usually correct for the type of disk in the drive. If the density is not correct, set it accordingly.

The Type options let you choose from three ways of formatting a floppy:

▶ **Backup Use:** Formats a standard UNIX floppy disk. The disk can then be used with the Desktop's Backup utility or with cpio or tar from a Terminal window.

▶ **Desktop Folder:** Creates a UNIX floppy disk that can be mounted as a file system. Although this is easy to do on a Unix-Ware system, it's quite difficult on a standard UNIX system. If you plan to use floppies to share UNIX files between UnixWare and non-UnixWare systems, use the Backup Use option for formatting UNIX floppies. Click on File at the top of the window to see the File menu. Then click on Properties and select either Veritas (VxFS) or s5 as the file system type to format the floppy disk.

▶ **DOS Format:** Formats a floppy disk for use with DOS. The format is DOS 2.0 compatible, and is therefore compatible with all versions of DOS since 2.0.

After selecting the format type, click on File at the top of the window to see the File menu. Then click on Format.

WORKING WITH DOS FILES FROM THE COMMAND LINE

From a Terminal window, you have access to the DOS-specific commands `doscat`, `doscp`, `dosdir`, `dosformat`, `dosmkdir`, `dosls`, `dosrm`, and `dosrmdir`. These commands let you do just about everything you need to without starting a DOS session. However, if you're more comfortable with the DOS command line than you are with the UNIX command line, you may want to use a DOS session for these tasks.

Further information on all these commands is available through the UNIX online documentation. See the DOS(1) manual page.

NOTE

The doscat Command

Use the `doscat` command to view the contents of a DOS text file. For example, if you have an AUTOEXEC.BAT file on a floppy disk, you can read it from a Terminal window by typing

```
doscat a:autoexec.bat
```

This is like using the TYPE command in DOS.

The doscp Command

Use the `doscp` command to copy files between a DOS floppy and your UNIX system. The files can be either UNIX files or DOS files. For example, to copy a file called `myfile` to the DOS floppy in drive A:, type

```
doscp myfile a:
```

To copy a file called DOSFILE from a DOS floppy in drive A: to the `/tmp` directory in UnixWare, type

```
doscp a:dosfile /tmp
```

The dosdir and dosls Commands

Use the `dosdir` and `dosls` commands to view the files and directories on a DOS floppy disk. The `dosdir` command lists the contents of the disk, as the DIR command would in DOS. The `dosls` command produces a UNIX style listing. To see what is on the floppy disk in drive A:, type

```
dosdir a:
```

or

```
dosls a:
```

The dosformat Command

Use the `dosformat` command to format a DOS floppy disk. The syntax (format) for the `dosformat` command is a little tricky. You must know the UNIX device name for the drive and type of floppy disk you're formatting. For example, assume your system has two high-density floppy drives. Drive A: is for 3.5-inch floppies, and drive B: is for 5.25-inch floppies. To format a 3.5-inch, high-density disk (1.4MB), type

```
dosformat /dev/rdsk/f03ht
```

To format a 5.25-inch, high-density disk (1.2MB), type

```
dosformat /dev/rdsk/f15ht
```

To format a 3.5-inch, double-density disk (720KB), type

```
dosformat /dev/rdsk/f03dt
```

To format a 5.25-inch, double-density disk (360KB), type

```
dosformat /dev/rdsk/f15d9t
```

As you can see, the UNIX device names are not pretty. An easy way to format DOS floppy disks from a Terminal window is to use shell script, so you don't need to remember the correct device names. For example, you might create a shell script called `dformat` to format 1.4MB floppies in drive A: with the following commands:

```
dosformat -f /dev/rdsk/f03ht
echo ^M
```

The `-f` after the `dosformat` command causes the floppy in drive A: to be formatted immediately; that is, without displaying a prompt for inserting the floppy and waiting for Enter to be pressed. This means that you must insert the floppy before you execute the script. The second line sends a carriage return (Ctrl-M) to the screen. This just puts the prompt at the next line instead of after the Formatting... message that appears.

To format other floppy disk types with a shell script, substitute the appropriate device name and create a script with a new name. See Chapter 8 for more information about shell scripts.

The dosmkdir and dosrmdir Commands

Use the `dosmkdir` command to create directories and the `dosrmdir` command to remove directories on a DOS floppy. Unless you need to duplicate a hard disk's directory structure on a DOS floppy disk, these commands are not very useful. It's easier to use several DOS floppies for transferring files.

If you need to create a directory, say DIR1, on a DOS floppy in drive A: type

```
dosmkdir a:dir1
```

To remove the same directory, type

```
dosrmdir a:dir1
```

The dosrm Command

Use the `dosrm` command for removing files from a DOS floppy. For example, to remove a file called `oldfile` from the floppy in drive A:, type

```
dosrm a:oldfile
```

Accessing Remote DOS and Windows Applications

If you have another UNIX system connected to your system, either directly or through a network, Merge allows you to have two simultaneous logins on your system. This means that you to can be using the console (the monitor and keyboard attached to your computer) and have another user log in over a network with an ASCII serial terminal, an X-terminal or another UNIX system. If an X-terminal or UnixWare system is used, the user can access Windows and graphical applications. Otherwise, only character-based applications can be accessed.

See Chapter 5 for information about connecting systems.

NOTE

Several steps are required to allow a remote UnixWare system access to Windows. The remote system is referred to as the *client*. Your system is referred to as the *server*. You must configure the server (your system) first. If you have a Personal Edition, you must first install Server Merge, a separate licensing product that allows multiple users to access and run Merge.

SETTING UP THE SERVER

On your UnixWare system, you must *advertise* Windows for sharing with remote systems. Follow these steps to set this up:

1 · Open the Application Sharing window (by double-clicking on the Admin Tools icon in the UnixWare Desktop window, then double-clicking on the Application Sharing icon).

2 · Open the Applications folder window, where the Win icon is located (by double-clicking on the Applications icon in the Unix-Ware Desktop window).

3 · Drag-and-drop the Win icon from the Applications folder to the Application Sharing window. A Win entry is created in the Application Sharing window.

4 · Close the Applications folder.

5 · Click on the Win entry in the Application Sharing window to highlight it, then click on the Change Type button to change the application type to X Application.

6 · Click on the Edit button to display a Text Editor window.

7 · Use the scroll bar to move to the end of the file. Find the line

```
"X_Application") "/home/login/Applications/Win";;
```

and add "+x" near the end of the line, including the quotation marks as shown, so that the line looks like this:

```
"X_Application")  "/home/login/Applications/Win"
     "+x";;
```

Replace the word *login* with your login ID.

8 · Click on File at the top of the Text Editor window and then click on Save on the File menu.

9 · Click on File and select Exit from the menu.

Before a remote user can run Windows from the server, that user must have a user account on your system, and the user account must have Windows in its DOS path. This is set in the user's AUTOEXEC.BAT file, located in their home directory. Be sure this file exists and contains a line similar to this:

```
PATH=C:\WINDOWS
```

If Windows isn't installed in C:\WINDOWS, replace `C:\WINDOWS` with the directory where Windows is installed.

The server is now set up to allow remote access to Windows.

ACCESSING WINDOWS FROM THE CLIENT

To access Windows from the client (a remote UnixWare system), follow these steps:

1 · Open the Applications folder window and double-click on the Remote Applications icon to open the Remote Applications window.

2 · In the Servers with Applications section, locate the server you just set up for sharing Windows. If necessary, use the scroll bar.

3 · Click on the server's name to select it. An authentication window is displayed.

4 · Use the authentication window to log in to the server. Enter your login ID, press Tab, and enter your password. Then click on Authenticate. In the Remote Applications section, the applications available on that server are shown.

5 · Click on Win, and then click on the Make Icon button. This installs an icon for Windows in your Applications folder.

6 · Click on Cancel to close the Remote Applications window.

7 · To start Windows, click on the Win icon in your Applications folder. Note that the name of the server and application are shown under the icon.

Merge allows you to run DOS and Windows applications while Unix-Ware is running. You can run DOS and Windows sessions full-screen (as they would appear on a stand-alone DOS system) or run them as windows on the UnixWare Desktop. Merge also allows you to access your DOS partitions (if you created them when you installed UnixWare) from DOS and Windows sessions.

UNIX provides many DOS-compatible commands. These commands let you work with DOS floppy disks. You can see file listings, copy files to and from, delete files on, and format DOS floppies while working from a Terminal window in UnixWare.

## CHAPTER 7

Backup and Restore Operations

Backups are the things that we hate to do most with our computers, but cherish the most when things go wrong. Sooner or later, we all accidentally erase a file, trash our hard disk, or have a power surge destroy our work. It happens to us, our coworkers, and to everyone else having anything to do with computers. It's a variant of Murphy's Law: The more important the information is on your computer, the greater the chance that it will be lost when something goes wrong with your computer.

NOTE
Recently, while we were working at Novell's office in Sandy, Utah, there was a power failure. Unfortunately, the building-wide UPS (uninterruptable power supply) went out and the non-UPS-protected circuits stayed on. So while the monitors worked, all the computers went dead. Many of us sweated long moments while we waited to assess our damage. Some of us, but not all, got lucky—we only had to do a shutdown and reboot to reset our hard disk controllers. After that, everything on our systems was intact. Moral of the story: Don't count on technology to protect you. Make backups!

This chapter will help you formulate a plan for backing up and storing your data. It will also show you several ways to perform backups and to restore your data *when* you lose it. (Notice we didn't say *if* you lose it. We all pay tribute to Murphy sooner or later.)

Planning Your Backup System

Backups are easy to make, but most people ignore the possibility that the next time they turn on their computer, it won't boot because the motor on the hard disk decided to take a vacation. Losing important data quickly teaches us the value of the time we spend entering data into our computers. In many small- and medium-sized business environments, the costs associated with entering and maintaining accounting, ordering, inventory, billing, and other information far outweigh the costs of the computing equipment. Even in large businesses, these costs are not trivial. The last thing that any company (or individual) needs or wants is to reenter by hand data lost due to either hardware or user mishap.

A good backup plan is the first and best line of defense against losing data. Whether you're a student, part of a business, or just a casual computer user, you should have a regular schedule for doing backups. Businesses should keep backups in a fireproof safe. In addition, some backups should be kept off-site, such as in the company's safe deposit box, or, at the very least, taken home by a company executive. Nonbusiness users have less demanding needs for storing backups, but they should make backup copies all the same.

If your computer is truly personal, that is, used only by you for non-business reasons, the backup plan can be very simple. Before you turn your computer off, copy the files you just created or changed to a floppy disk. Label the floppy with the file names and the date and put it away.

If you're working in a business environment, you can't afford to be casual about your backups. There are many schemes for doing backups. The one presented here is used by many businesses and offers good protection. The scheme requires carefully labeling your media (tapes or floppy disks) and doing backups every day. As you'll see, many tapes are used in the cycle. Sometimes you don't know when a certain file was damaged, so you need to go back to the latest tape containing good data. The procedure given provides 12 weeks of backed up data.

CHOOSING YOUR MEDIA

The most common medium used for backing up data in all but the smallest businesses is tape. Large computers (minicomputers and mainframes) often use 9-track tape on large reels. For personal computers, it's much more convenient to use cartridge tapes. UnixWare supports ¼-inch cartridge tape drives, such as the Wangtek 5125EQ and 5150EQ and Archive 2060L and 2150L.

You may think that the capacity of the tape drive must match the size of your hard disk. This isn't true. You'll never use the tape to back up the entire hard disk. Your data files take up only part of your disk space. UNIX is on the disk, too. You don't need to back up UNIX. If you lose UNIX, which rarely happens, you can reload the operating system from the purchased medium (tape or CD-ROM).

A tape drive that's large enough to back up all your data, without requiring you to change tapes, is your best choice. This allows you to do an unattended backup after business hours. For example, we have two systems that each have 700MB of hard disk space. One system has an older 60MB tape drive; the other system has a 120MB tape drive. These tape drives are more than adequate for backing up these systems. However, many UNIX applications, such as FrameMaker, come on 150MB cartridge tapes that can be read only on 150MB and higher capacity drives. For this reason, you probably should purchase at least a 150MB tape drive.

For very small businesses, it may be reasonable to use floppy disks for your backups. If your backup fits on a few floppies, it may not be worth the expense to install a cartridge tape drive in your system. The drawback is that the process is more labor-intensive, because you must wait while the backup is being performed so you can change floppies when required.

If you are going to use floppy disks, do yourself a favor and only use the 3.5-inch, high-density type (all new computers have this type of floppy drive). The floppies themselves are more durable than the 5.25-inch type, and they hold 1.44MB of data. The four popular floppy disk types and their capacities are as follows:

Disk Type	Capacity
3.5-inch high-density	1.44MB
3.5-inch double-density	7.2MB
5.25-inch high-density	1.2MB
5.25-inch double-density	3.6KB

Although this chapter refers to cartridge tape backups, the information applies to backups on floppy disks as well. Consider each cartridge tape as a set of floppies. The number of floppies in each set depends upon the amount of data you need to back up.

LABELING YOUR MEDIA

Start with 10 cartridge tapes. Label them as follows:

Monday	Tuesday	Wednesday	Thursday	Friday 1
Friday 2	Friday 3	Month 1	Month 2	Month 3

Each time you use one for a backup, pencil the date on the label. Each tape will be used many times, so leave room for future dates.

The tapes will be used in a cycle. Follow this procedure to complete a cycle:

▸ Friday: The cycle begins on a Friday. Use the Friday 1 tape to back up all the data on your hard disk.

▸ Monday: Use the Monday tape to back up just the data that has changed that day.

▸ Tuesday–Thursday: On each day, use the corresponding tape and back up the data that has changed that day.

▸ Friday: Use the Friday 2 tape and back up all your data files again.

▸ Monday–Thursday: Reuse last week's tapes and repeat the procedure for these days, backing up only the data that has changed.

▸ Friday: It's now the third Friday. Use the Friday 3 tape and back up all your data files.

▸ Monday–Thursday: Again, reuse last week's tapes and back up just the files that have changed.

▸ Friday: It's the fourth Friday. Use the Month 1 tape and back up all the data files. This completes one cycle.

Repeat this procedure. When you get to the fourth Friday, use the Month 2 tape to complete the second cycle. Repeat the cycle, using the Month 3 tape to end the third cycle. At the end of the third cycle, you have a complete record of 12 weeks of data.

DECIDING WHAT TO BACK UP

In general, an application that you install can be reinstalled from the original medium (such as floppy disk or tape) if something goes wrong with the application. Don't waste time backing up an application's program files. The exception is that you may want to back up a program once immediately after it's installed if the installation was an ordeal. For example, WordPerfect for UNIX 5.1 installs in a directory called wp. You can make a tape of this directory and store it with the master tape that comes with WordPerfect.

The files that your applications create, referred to as data files, are the ones that you want to back up regularly. Also, you may, on occasion, create your own shell scripts and other data files. You should also back up these files regularly.

Each user has a directory in the /home directory where his or her personal files are kept. If your login name is spike, for example, your personal files are located in /home/spike. To back up the files belonging to every user on the system, you can simply back up /home. However, if you or other users installed personal applications in their home directories, you'll be backing up those, too.

 NOTE **In UnixWare, your home directory (or folder) corresponds to your UnixWare Desktop window.**

You may also have data that is accessible to more than one user. For example, you might have accounting data stored in the /usr/Accounts directory. Back up this directory as well.

Performing Your Backups

UNIX provides several methods for backing up data. Later in this chapter, backing up from the command line with `cpio` is discussed, and Chapter 8 discusses the `tar` command. UnixWare provides an easy method for backing up your files. Through the Backup window, you can do immediate as well as scheduled backups. You can also choose to do complete backups or incremental backups. Incremental backups back up only the files that have changed since the last time you performed a backup.

To open the Backup window, double-click on the Admin Tools icon in your Desktop window and then double-click on the Backup-Restore icon. The Backup window appears, as shown in Figure 7.1.

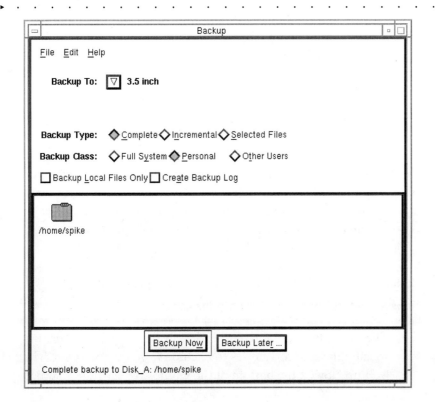

PERFORMING AN IMMEDIATE BACKUP

An immediate backup is relatively simple. You select the medium to use and the files to back up, and let it run.

As an example, suppose that you want to do an immediate backup of just your personal files. Here are the steps to follow:

1 · In the Backup window, click on the arrow next to Backup To to see a pop-up menu with your choices for a backup device. The options you see depend on how your system is configured.

2 · Select the type of media to use. When the pop-up menu disappears, your choice is shown as the Backup To setting. When you select either Disk A or Disk B, the type of floppy disk for that drive is shown. For example, if you select Disk A, 3.5 inch may appear as the Backup To choice.

3 · Select the type of backup to perform. UnixWare provides three options: Complete, Incremental, and Selected Files. Complete backs up every file in the Backup Class. Incremental backs up only those files that have changed since the last backup. Selected Files lets you select the specific files and directories you want to back up. Because you want to back up every file in your personal directory, click on Complete.

4 · Choose the Backup Class for the backup. Full System backs up all files from the root directory, which you probably never want to do. Personal backs up just your own personal files. Other Users allows you to select another user's files to back up. Click on Personal to back up the files in your home directory.

 NOTE **If you installed personal applications in your home directory, choosing Personal for the Backup Class backs up your personal applications as well as your personal data files.**

5 · Click on Edit at the top of the window and select Exclude to specify files and directories to exclude from the backup. Click on Backup Now at the bottom of the window to start the backup.

Before an immediate backup begins, the medium is checked for data. If data is found, a warning window appears asking if you want to overwrite the data. Click on Overwrite to continue with the backup and overwrite the data on the floppy disk or tape, or click on Exit to cancel the backup procedure.

PERFORMING A SCHEDULED BACKUP

A scheduled backup is more complicated than an immediate backup, but only the first time. Once you set up how you want it done, you can save the specifications for the backup in a backup script. After that, you can open the backup script and it will fill in the Backup window with the same settings for you.

You won't need to use backup scripts for your regular backup plan, but you may want to create them for occasional scheduled backups. Backup scripts are discussed later in this chapter.

NOTE

As an example, suppose that you want to do a scheduled, incremental backup of two users' files. Here are the steps to follow for this type of backup:

1 · In the Backup window, select the media type from the Backup To pop-up menu.

2 · For the Backup Type, choose Selected Files. You don't need to select a Backup Class.

3 · Open the Admin Tools window and click on the Parent Folder button in the tool bar (left-most button). This displays the /home folder.

4 · Use the mouse to drag-and-drop your home folder into the box at the bottom of the Backup window.

5 · Drag-and-drop one other user's home folder into the same box in the Backup window.

NOTE   **If you don't have another user on your system, you can do a sched-uled backup of just your home directory by following the instructions given in the previous section up through step 4 and then continuing with the following steps.**

6 · With the selected users' folders in the Backup window, click on Backup Later at the bottom of the window. The Task Scheduler: Add Task window appears, as shown in Figure 7.2. The name for the task is already entered in the first field.

FIGURE 7.2

The Task Scheduler:

Add Task window

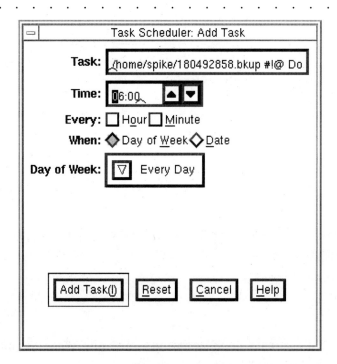

7 · In the Time box, you set when you want the backup to run. Click in the Time box and use the arrows to change the time shown, or type the time directly in the box. You must enter the

time in 24-hour format. For example, if you want the backup to start after work, say at 8:00 p.m., you must enter 20:00 in the Time box.

8 · To choose a specific day, make sure Day of Week is selected for the When setting. Then click on the arrow in the Day of the Week box. Select the day you want the backup to be performed from the pop-up menu.

9 · Click on the Add Task button at the bottom of the window.

This backup task is run automatically at the designated time, *provided* that you remember to put the selected medium (either a floppy disk or a cartridge tape) in the appropriate drive. With all scheduled backups, you must remember to put in the medium before the backup is set to take place. Otherwise, when you return, you'll have an error message on your screen instead of a backup in your floppy disk or tape drive.

DELETING A TASK

If you change your mind about a scheduled backup, you need to delete the backup task you added through the Task Scheduler window. Before continuing, if you added the sample task, delete it now by following these steps:

1 · From the Desktop window, double-click on the Admin Tools icon, and then double-click on the Task Scheduler icon in the Admin Tools folder window. The Task Scheduler window appears, as shown in Figure 7.3. Your backup task should be listed there.

2 · If it's not already selected, click on your backup task to select it.

3 · Click on Edit at the top of the window and select Delete from the menu. The backup task disappears from the window. However, the task isn't permanently removed until you save the task file.

FIGURE 7.3

The Task Scheduler window

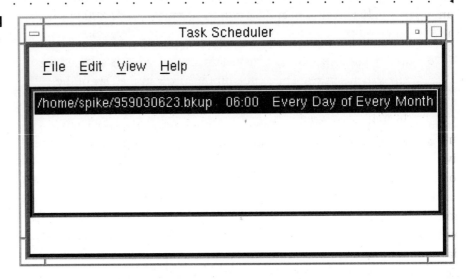

4 · Click on File at the top of the Task Scheduler window and select Save from the menu. The Task Scheduler window closes.

OTHER TASK SCHEDULER FUNCTIONS

The Task Scheduler window is where you maintain your tasks. When you need to edit or delete a backup task, use this window.

If you want to make a change to the task, such as what time it should execute, select Properties from the Edit pop-up menu. Change the settings in the Edit Properties window, then click on Apply. In the Task Scheduler window, click on File and select Save from the menu to save your changes.

You can also schedule other types of tasks to run at convenient times. For example, if you have a large file to print, instead of tying up the printer during regular hours, you can schedule the file to print in the middle of the night. After you create a shell script for the print job (see Chapter 8), display the Task Scheduler window and click on Edit. In the Edit Properties window, enter the full path for the task. For example, if you have a script called `print.doc` in your personal `bin` directory, and your user name is spike, enter `/home/spike/bin/print.doc`. Then set when you want to run the task, as you do for backup tasks, and click on Apply. Finally, select the Save option from the Task Scheduler window's File menu to save the scheduled task.

IMPLEMENTING THE COMPLETE BACKUP PLAN

Using the backup procedures described in the previous sections, you can implement your full backup plan. For the backup plan, you need to create five backup tasks, one for each day of the week. Use the procedure for performing scheduled backups described in the previous section.

By opening various folders and dragging-and-dropping the files and folders you want backed up into the Backup window, you can control exactly what gets backed up. Repeat the process of creating a backup task for each day. Select Incremental for Monday's through Thursday's backups and Complete for Friday's backup. You can specify any hour that you know you won't be using your system for the Time setting. Generally, the early morning hours are best. Once your tasks are created, you only need to remember to change the media each day.

Getting Fancy with Other Backup Options

Several additional options exist for backing up files. For your regular backup plan, the other options are not required. However, for occasional, nonscheduled backups, these options might come in handy.

BACKING UP LOCAL FILES ONLY

In the Backup window, below Backup Class, there is a check box labeled Backup Local Files Only. If you select this box, directories that are mounted from remote systems are not included in your backup.

USING BACKUP LOGS

Next to the Backup Local Files Only check box is the check box for Create Backup Log. If you select this option, UnixWare saves a backup log that lists every file in your backup, even if you only specified folders to be backed up. The backup log, named `backuplog`, can be used to verify that certain files were backed up on a certain date.

If you selected Personal as the Backup Class, the log is saved in your home directory (look for it in your Desktop window). If you selected Full System or Other Users as the Backup Class, the log is saved in the `/etc` folder.

USING BACKUP SCRIPTS

A *backup script* is a file that saves all the settings for a backup. If you occasionally perform the same backup procedure (it isn't part of your regular backup plan), you may want to save the settings for later use. Three options on the Backup window's File menu let you open and save backup scripts: Open, Save, and Save As.

Saving a Backup Script

After selecting your backup media, type, and class, follow these steps to save your settings as a backup script:

1 · Click on File to display the File menu. If this is the first time you're saving the script, you can choose either Save or Save As from the menu. Both will display the Backup: Save Script window, as shown in Figure 7.4.

2 · For the Path setting, your home folder is shown. You can select another folder for the file from the Folder(s) box.

3 · To specify the file, either type its name in the File text box or select a file from the File(s) box.

FIGURE 7.4
The Backup: Save Script
window

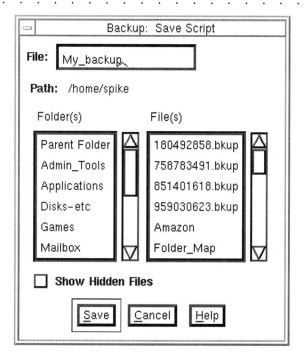

4 · Click on Save. (If you change your mind and don't want to save
the file, click on Cancel.) The backup script file is saved with a
`.bkup` extension, which is used by the backup utility to recognize the backup script file.

Opening a Backup Script

Once you have some backup scripts saved, you can recall them by clicking on Open in the File menu. The Backup: Open Script window appears,
as shown in Figure 7.5.

From the Folder(s) and File(s) boxes, select the backup script you want
to use, and then click on Open. The settings are transferred to the Backup
window. You can use the settings as they are or change them for this backup.
If you change them, you can also save them as another backup script by

FIGURE 7.5

The Backup: Open Script
window

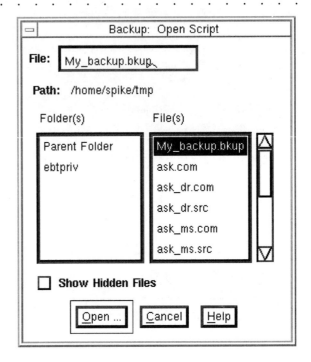

clicking on Save As on the File menu and selecting a new file name for the script. The original script remains unchanged.

Restoring Your Data

Restoring is what you hope you never need to do with your backup tapes or floppy disks (it usually means you did something you shouldn't have and lost one or more files). However, we all need to restore something sooner or later.

You restore files through the Restore window, shown in Figure 7.6. You can display this window in several ways:

- ▶ Click with the Menu button on the Backup-Restore icon in the Admin Tools folder window, and then click on the Restore option on the icon menu.

- ▶ Click with the Menu mouse button (right button) on the Disk or Cartridge Tape icon (whichever icon matches the medium from which you're restoring files) in the Disks-etc folder window, and then select Restore from the icon menu.

- ▶ From the Backup window, click on File to display the File menu, then click on Go to Restore.

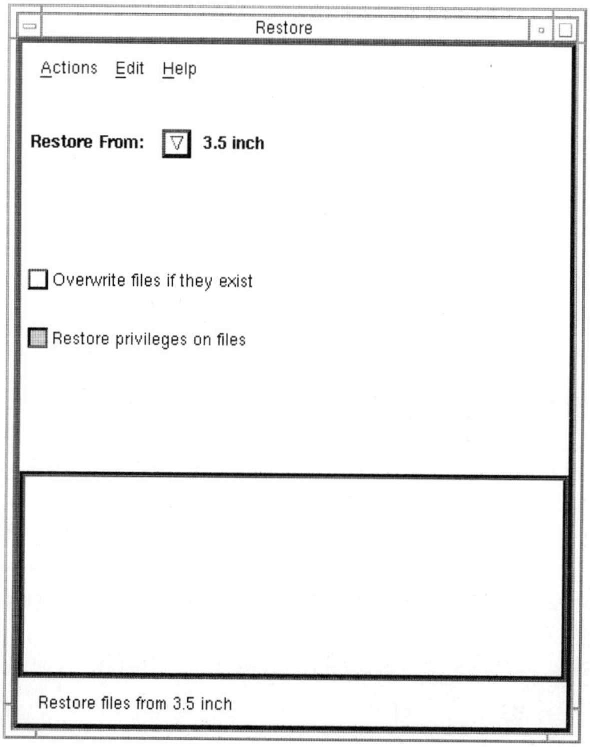

FIGURE 7.6

The Restore window

The Restore window allows you to restore all the files from your tapes or floppies or to select specific files to restore. Follow these steps to restore files:

1 · From the Restore From pop-up menu, select the type of media from which you're restoring.

2 · Decide whether or not you want the restored files to overwrite files on your hard disk if they already exist. For example, if you have the file `/home/spike/letters/Chris` on your hard disk, and the same file exists on your backup, you can choose whether or not you want the file on the backup to replace the one on your hard disk. If you want to overwrite your files, click in the check box marked Overwrite files if they exist. (By default, this box is not checked.) If you leave the check box blank, the backup files are not restored at all.

3 · Click on Actions at the top of the window and select the appropriate option from the Actions menu:

▸ Choose Restore to restore all the files in your backup. Unix-Ware will copy the files from your backup to your hard disk.

▸ Click on Actions and Show Files to view specific files for restoring. UnixWare displays a list of the backed up files. Initially, all the files are highlighted, indicating that they are all selected to be restored. You can click on individual files to unselect them. If you need to restore only a few files, click on Edit, select Unselect All from the Edit menu, and then click on the individual file or files you want to restore. (The Select All option on the Edit menu selects all the files on the cartridge tape or floppy disk.)

4 · Click on Actions, and then select Restore from the menu.

There is a second check box, located below the Overwrite files if they exist check box, which lets you restore privileges on the files you restore. By default this box is checked. As far as we can tell, this check box has no effect when restoring files.

Backing Up and Restoring from the Command Line

As nice as UnixWare's Backup window is, in some cases it may be easier or more efficient to back up your files from the command line in a Terminal window.

Backups made from the Backup window always include the full path of the file, which means that if you back up a file named `Chris.ltr`, which is located in the `letters` directory (in your home directory), the file on your backup has the full name of `/home/`*userid*`/letters/Chris.ltr`, where *userid* is your login name. When you restore this file, you must restore it in the same directory from which you backed it up.

However, it is often useful to restore files to a directory other than where they originally resided. For example, you may have already modified the file on your hard disk, but need the older version to get some data you deleted from your current file.

To create backups that you can restore anywhere, you need to use either the UNIX `cpio` or the UNIX `tar` command. This section discusses the `cpio` command. See Chapter 8 for information on the `tar` command.

Let's assume that your login ID is spike and you want to back up the following directories using `cpio`:

```
/home/spike/letters
/home/spike/wpdata
/home/spike/quickendata
```

To back up these directories, you enter the following commands in a Terminal window (double-click on the Applications icon in the Desktop window, then double-click on the Terminal icon to open a Terminal window):

```
cd /home/spike
find letters wpdata quickendata -depth -print |
   cpio -ocdB > /dev/rmt/c0s0
```

The first line makes sure you're in the correct directory. The second line uses the `find` and `cpio` commands to back up the three directories to a non-SCSI cartridge tape (/dev/rmt/c0s0). To back up to your first floppy disk drive, substitute /dev/rdsk/f0t for /dev/rmt/c0s0. To back up to your second floppy disk drive, use /dev/rdsk/f1t.

If you want to back up all the files in the directory, you don't use a list as shown in the previous example. The command line would look like this:

```
find . -depth -print | cpio -ocdB >
    /dev/rmt/c0s0
```

The period after find means start the find command from the current directory and include everything.

 NOTE **The examples here use cartridge tape as the backup medium. Substitute the correct name of the drive for your medium.**

With this type of backup, you can create a directory in which to restore the files without worrying about overwriting the originals. To restore the files to a directory called backup in your home directory, open a Terminal window and type

```
cd /home/spike
mkdir backup
cd backup
cpio -icdvB < /dev/rmt/c0s0
```

The first line makes sure you're in the correct directory to start. The second line creates the directory backup. The third line uses the cpio command to read the cartridge tape. As the files are restored, they are listed on the screen.

Sometimes, you just want to see what is included in a backup. If the backup was created with the cpio command (UnixWare's Backup window also uses the cpio command), enter this command in a Terminal window:

```
cpio -it < /dev/rmt/c0s0
```

Using a Network for Backing Up

In some situations, you may not need to worry about backing up your files to tape or floppy disks. If you're connected to a network, you may be able to use its file server for your backups.

This type of backup is ideal for scheduling with the Task Scheduler. Create a script with the command line that copies your files to the file server (described in this section) and have the Task Scheduler run the script before the file server is backed up. Your files will be included in the file server's scheduled backups.

BACKING UP TO A REMOTE UNIX SYSTEM

If you have another system on your network on which UNIX is installed, you can use the remote copy command, `rcp`, to copy your files from your computer to the remote computer. Naturally, you need a user account on the remote system. The system administrator should be able to set up a login name and password for you.

First, create a file called `.rhosts` in your home directory on the remote system. In this file, put the name of the system you will be backing up *from*. The `.rhosts` file enables you to copy your files to the file server without needing to enter your password.

Let's assume your user account on the remote system is spike and it's located under the home directory. The remote system name is `bigdisk`. Furthermore, the files you want to back up on your system are in the directory `/home/spike/newbook`. You could use the following command to copy all the files and subdirectories, if any, in the indicated directory from your system to a directory on the remote system:

```
rcp -r /home/spike/newbook
   bigdisk:/home/ spike/newbook
```

In this example, the directory names are the same on both computers, but they don't need to be. The following would work as well:

```
rcp -r /home/spike/newbook
   bigdisk:/home/ spike/book.backup
```

BACKING UP TO A NETWARE FILE SERVER

A major advantage of UnixWare over other flavors of UNIX is its built-in connectivity for NetWare. If your UnixWare system is on a network with NetWare servers, you have automatic access to those servers, providing, of course, you have accounts on those servers.

With UnixWare, you don't actually log in to the NetWare file server to copy files there. You do, however, need to authenticate to the server.

The NetWare Access icon is located in the Networking folder, which is located in your Admin Tools folder. Double-click on it to open the NetWare window. Now, double-click on the server you want to authenticate to. Enter your login and password when the authentication window appears.

To copy your files to the NetWare file server, use the UnixWare copy command, `cp`. For example, if your NetWare file server is called `netserve` and your user name is spike, the following command copies all your files in `newbook` to a directory called `book_bak` on the NetWare file server:

```
cp /home/spike/newbook/* /.NetWare/
   netserv.nws/sys.nwv/users/spike/book_bak
```

You can automate this process by using the `nwlogin` command. Create a script similar to this:

```
/usr/bin/nwlogin spike/zorb
cp /home/spike/newbook/* /.NetWare/
   netserv.nws/sys.nwv/users/spike/book_bak
```

Next, use the Task Scheduler, located in the Admin Tools folder, to schedule the running of this script. See Chapter 11 for more information on the Task Scheduler.

Copy files to a NetWare server from a Terminal window, not from a virtual terminal. In a Terminal window, you will be able to see an authentication window if it appears.

NOTE

If you're careful and make sure that you're authenticated before you leave your office for the day, you can schedule this type of backup for late night or early morning. Create a script with a line similar to the example above and use the Task Scheduler to schedule it to run every day (see Chapter 8 for details on creating scripts). You should check with the administrator of the NetWare file server, however, to make sure you're not trying to back up your files onto the server while the server is trying to back up itself. The NetWare server may, in fact, be inaccessible during certain times. Plan your backup to run before the file server's backup routine is run and when you know the file server is accessible.

This chapter has pointed out the importance of planning and maintaining a schedule for backing up your files. You can create backups through the Desktop's Backup-Restore facility or by using the command line in a Terminal window. By adhering to a backup schedule, you minimize the risk of losing valuable data due to hardware failure or human error.

With the Desktop's Backup-Restore facility, you can set up scheduled backups that run when there is little computer use, such as during the early morning hours. Then all you need to do is be sure to insert the correct medium before leaving work for the day.

## CHAPTER 8

The UNIX Shell

The UNIX shell (sometimes referred to as the *command line*) enables you to do everything that the UnixWare Desktop and other UNIX graphical user interfaces allow you to do, plus a great deal more. Besides running purchased applications from the shell, you can run hundreds of commands that come with UNIX, including commands for text processing and printing (such as `vi` and `lp`), maintaining your system (such as `usermod` and `diskadd`) and manipulating files and directories (such as `mv` and `cp`). UNIX even includes utilities for backing up your files (such as `tar` and `cpio`).

With the number of commands that come with UNIX, the issue isn't whether or not you can do something; it's deciding which way to do it. This multiplicity of ways to accomplish a task is not only one of UNIX's strong points, it's one of the factors contributing to UNIX's reputation for being difficult to use. Fortunately, UnixWare shields you from the shell by providing the Desktop, which includes facilities for doing most of what you need to do on your system.

However, even if you run all your applications from the Desktop or another UNIX GUI, you may still find yourself going to the shell (with Unix-Ware you open a Terminal window or switch to a *virtual terminal*—more about virtual terminals later). For example, you may find situations in which it is easier to switch to a Terminal window or virtual terminal and enter a few commands than to traverse through the windows on the Desktop, such as when you check files and directories, log in to remote systems, format floppy disks, and check your mail. The Desktop certainly provides a means to do these tasks. You just might find it faster to use the shell.

If you're an experienced UNIX user, you will want to have ready access to the shell. The UNIX developers we know always have at least two Terminal windows open on their Desktop at all times. If you're new to UNIX and use UnixWare mainly to run your applications, you can probably skip this chapter and never miss the shell.

Configuring Your Terminal Environment

In the old days, the UNIX system had no graphical user interface. Setting up a working environment meant defining how you used the system through the shell from a character terminal. With UnixWare, you can set up the shell environment that suits your work from a Terminal window, virtual terminal, or non-Desktop login.

Most of your shell environment configuration is stored in hidden files in your home directory. You can't see these files in your Desktop window because their names begin with a period. To display a list of hidden files in your home directory, open a Terminal window and type

```
ls -a
```

Every time you log in, your system reads your `.profile` file and executes the commands it contains. Most of your shell environment is defined in the `.profile` file. For example, the `.profile` file runs the `.olsetup` file, which includes the PATH statement (which sets the directories Unix-Ware searches for the commands you run) and the MAIL statement (which defines the location of your mailbox).

Each time you start up a shell, your system reads a file that is defined by the ENV variable in your `.profile` file. Typically, if you start a `wksh` or `ksh` shell, the `.kshrc` file is read and the commands in it are executed. A `csh` shell uses the `.cshrc` file.

With UnixWare 2, `ksh` is the default shell.

NOTE

Some individual shell commands have their own files that are read when the command starts up. One such file is the `.exrc`, which is read by the `vi` command each time that command is run.

If you are running virtual terminals (separate shell sessions), there is a file in which you define information that's applied to your virtual terminal sessions. The file is called `.vtlrc`. Within that file you can, for example, map your function keys to any keystrokes you choose.

EDITING UNIX FILES

To correct problems or enhance functionality, you often need to directly edit a file, both as a regular user and as the root user. As a regular user, you can just double-click on a text file and it appears in a Text Editor window. However, if you're working in a Terminal window, it may be easier to enter a command to start a Text Editor window. For example, to edit the file `.Xdefaults` (located in your home directory), enter

```
dtedit .Xdefaults
```

A Text Editor window will open with the `.Xdefaults` file ready for editing.

If you need to edit a file as the root user (certain files need root permissions for editing), first become the root user by entering `su` and, when prompted, the password for the root user. Then open the file for editing. To edit the `/etc/shells` file, for example, type

```
DISPLAY=:0;export DISPLAY;/usr/X/bin/dtedit
   /etc/shells
```

CONFIGURING THE .profile FILE

When a user account is added to the system, a `.profile` file is placed in the user's home directory. At first, the `.profile` file contains only two entries for a Desktop user. The first sets the location of your mailbox. The second starts the Desktop. Actually, there are many other lines in `.profile` beginning with a pound sign (#). These are comment lines and do not execute any commands.

Opening Your .profile File

To open your `.profile` file, open a Terminal window and type

```
cd
/usr/X/bin/dtedit .profile
```

You can replace /usr/X/bin/dtedit with another UNIX editor if you prefer.

Figure 8.1 shows the default .profile file. It sets your mailbox (where incoming mail is received) to

/var/mail/${LOGNAME:?}

where ${LOGNAME:?} is automatically replaced by your user name. When you use the Mail window or mailx command, the mailbox represented by your MAIL variable is read. The last line starts the UnixWare Desktop.

```
$ cat .profile
LANG=C export LANG        #!@ Do not edit this line !@
#         This is the default standard profile provided to a user.
#         They are expected to edit it to meet their own needs.
#
#         If you have a profile that is attempting to read from the
#         terminal or is using the stty(1) command to set terminal
#         settings, you may find that GRAPHICAL LOGIN does not give
#         you a desktop metaphor session.
#
#         To update your profile, you should surround any section
#         that reads from the terminal or performs stty(1) commands
#         with the following 'if' statement:
#
#         if [ "$XDM_LOGIN" != "yes" ]
#         then
#                  :
#                  read from the terminal or stty(1) commands
#         fi

MAIL=/var/mail/${LOGNAME:?}
. $HOME/.olsetup          #!@ Do not edit this line !@
$
```

F I G U R E 8.1

The default .profile file

Setting the PATH Variable

The PATH variable in your .profile file is set to the names of the directories that are searched when you type a command. For example, you might add this entry to your .profile file to add directories to your path:

```
PATH=$PATH:/usr/X/bin:/usr/bin2:$HOME/bin:/
    etc:;export PATH
```

The next time you log in, your new PATH entry is in effect. When you type a command, all directories previously defined by $PATH are checked first. Next, the added directories (usr/X/bin, /usr/bin2, $HOME/bin, and /etc) are checked. Finally, the current directory is checked, as indicated by the colon (:) before the semicolon (;). After the path is set, it must be exported (export PATH) so that it will be known by all the shells that are started.

The directories added in the PATH line shown here are very useful. The /usr/X/bin directory is where graphical applications are stored. The /usr/bin2 directory is a directory you can create to store utilities that are shared by anyone who uses the system (there already is a /usr/bin directory). The $HOME/bin directory is a directory you can create in your home directory to store utilities for your own use. Finally, /etc contains some administrative utilities that are useful to casual users (such as dfspace to display disk space in the file system and mount to see which directories are mounted). After it is set, the PATH must be exported (export PATH) so the new PATH is used when the shell starts up.

Setting Shell Variables

You can also set some variables that apply to specific shells. For example, if you use the ksh (or wksh) shell, you can use the ENV variable to tell the system to read the .kshrc file for settings that are specific to the ksh shell. The HISTSIZE variable indicates how many previously entered command lines to save (the ksh shell lets you recall old command lines, edit them, and run them again). The following example shows the ENV variable set to read the `.kshrc` file and `HISTSIZE` set to save the previous one thousand commands:

```
ENV=$HOME/.kshrc;export ENV
HISTSIZE=1000;export HISTSIZE
```

Changing the Command Line Prompt

The default command line prompt in a Terminal window is a pound sign (#) for the root user and a dollar sign ($) for other users. You can change the prompt to any characters by adding a `PS1` entry to your `.profile` file.

If your system is on a network and you have several Terminal windows open, logged in to several systems, you can easily become confused about who you are and where you are. To help you get your bearings, set your prompt to the system name. For example, if your system name is superman and your user name is spike, add the following entry:

```
PS1="superman-spike:";export PS1
```

Other .profile File Configurations

You can set many other variables and run more commands within the `.profile` file. Individual applications may add information to this file. For example, FrameMaker defines an FMHOME variable in your `.profile` file as the location of your FrameMaker directories (such as `/usr/frame`). Then it adds `$FMHOME/bin` to your PATH, so your shell can find your FrameMaker commands.

The system also sets several variables for you before it even checks your `.profile` file. You can override any of these variables by resetting them in `.profile`. Many of these variables are set in the `/etc/profile` file.

To check your environment and see what variables are set, type `env` from a Terminal window.

If you want to be able to use multiple virtual terminals, you must add the line `/usr/bin/vtlmgr -k` to your `.profile` file. See the section about accessing multiple virtual terminals in this chapter for more information.

NOTE

Figure 8.2 shows a sample .profile from one of our systems.

Sample .profile *from a working system*

```
                                   Terminal
$ cat .profile
#          If you have a profile that is attempting to read from the
#          terminal or is using the stty(1) command to set terminal
#          settings, you may find that GRAPHICAL LOGIN does not give
#          you a desktop metaphor session.
#
#          To update your profile, you should surround any section
#          that reads from the terminal or performs stty(1) commands
#          with the following 'if' statement:
#
#          if [ "$XDM_LOGIN" != "yes" ]
#          then
#                  :
#                  read from the terminal or stty(1) commands
#          fi
MAIL=/var/mail/${LOGNAME:?}
WPOSDB=/opt/po;export WPOSDB
XAPPLRESDIR=~/app-defaults/;export XAPPLRESDIR
FMHOME=/usr/frame;export FMHOME
CDPATH=.:/home/zorb:/home/zorb/work;export CDPATH
PATH=$FMHOME/bin:$PATH; export PATH
PATH=$PATH:/usr/X/bin:$HOME/bin:/usr/bin2:/opt/bin:/sbin:;export PATH
PATH=$PATH:/usr/doctools/bin;export PATH
PATH=$PATH:/opt/gw/wpoffice/ofunix40/ofbin;export PATH
SHELL=/usr/bin/ksh;export SHELL
EDITOR=vi;export EDITOR
HISTSIZE=5000;export HISTSIZE
ENV=$HOME/.kshrc;export ENV
PS1="ZorBix> "
/usr/bin/vtlmgr -k
setcolor -o lt_magenta
setcolor yellow
tput init
. $HOME/.olsetup              #!@ Do not edit this line !@
$ 
```

CONFIGURING THE .Xdefaults FILE

The .Xdefaults file contains Desktop configuration information, such as color and mouse preferences. For UnixWare 2.0, the .Xdefaults file should only be changed by Desktop applications. Do not add configuration lines, which are called *resources*, to this file. Instead, you can create a file called .Xdefaults-*nodename* in which you can add resources. The *nodename* is

the name you gave your system when you installed UnixWare. For example, if your system name is bluebird, the name of the file would be .Xdefaults-bluebird.

You would typically use the .Xdefaults-*nodename* file to customize an application. For example, by adding the resources shown in Figure 8.3, you can customize the colors and characteristics for a Terminal window. Be sure to type the resources exactly as shown. Use a tab after the colon on each line.

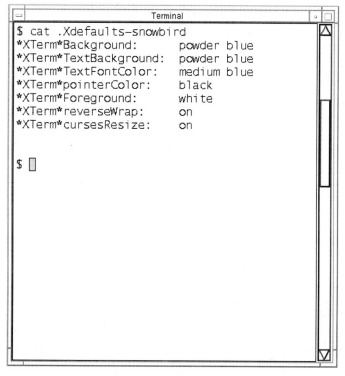

FIGURE 8.3

Resources for configuring
a Terminal window

The first five lines in Figure 8.3 set the various colors in the Terminal window. Many other color names can be used. For the complete list of colors see the /usr/X/lib/rgb.txt file. You can experiment with the colors all you like. Each time you make a change, enter the following line to instantly update your Terminal window colors:

```
/usr/X/bin/xrdb -load ~/.Xdefaults-nodename
```

The last two lines in Figure 8.3 set some useful characteristics for the Terminal window. The first allows you to backspace to the end of a previous line, instead of having the cursor stop when it reaches the left edge of the first column. The second allows you to resize the Terminal window while using a curses application such as vi.

CONFIGURING THE .kshrc FILE

Each time a ksh or wksh shell starts up (such as when you open a Terminal window), the system can read a file that defines shell-specific information. If you set ENV=$HOME/.kshrc in your .profile file (as described earlier), create a .kshrc file in your home directory. Then you can add entries to allow you to use command shortcuts from the shell.

Adding Aliases to Your .kshrc File

Aliases let you set a shorthand notation to execute a long command line. By adding the appropriate alias line to your .kshrc file, you will be able to type just one or two letters (more if you choose) to change to a specific directory or to run a command.

Here are some examples of lines you might add:

```
alias x=cd "/usr/X/bin;pwd"
alias book="cd /$HOME/work/uw20/book;pwd"
alias m="mailx"
```

After setting these aliases, the next time you open a shell, you could simply type x to change directories to /usr/X/bin and list the current directory. To change to the work/uw20/book directory under your home directory, you would type book. Or you could type m to start the mailx command.

Using Functions in Your .kshrc File

If you want to be able to input information with an alias, you can use *functions*. Figure 8.4 shows examples of the c and b functions you can set in your .kshrc file. The c function shown in the example lets you change to a directory by typing c *dir*, where *dir* is replaced by the name of the directory. The function also saves the previous directory name. The b function in the example lets you return to the previous directory (saved by the c function) by simply typing b from the shell.

```
                          Terminal
$ cat .kshrc
c()
{
        if [ $# != 1 ]
        then
                cd $HOME
                echo $PWD
                return
        fi
        SAVEDIR=$PWD
        echo "Enter b for: $SAVEDIR"
        cd $1
        pwd
}

b()
{
        cd $SAVEDIR
        echo $PWD

}
$
```

FIGURE 8.4

Examples of .kshrc *file*

functions

If you need to convert numbers into hexadecimal notation, you can add this function to your .kshrc file:

```
HEX()
{
  for i in $* ;
  do echo"$i in Hex: \t\c";
  echo 16o $i p | dc;
  done ;
}
```

Then you could simply type HEX *num,* where *num* is replaced by the number you want to convert.

CONFIGURING THE .exrc FILE

The vi command is a standard UNIX system text editor. The .exrc file, if it exists in your home directory, is read every time you start vi. If you use vi, create the .exrc file to set options, create abbreviations, or map useful keystrokes into single keystrokes. Figure 8.5 shows an example of a useful .exrc file.

```
Terminal
$ cat .exrc
set nu
set wrapmargin=18
set showmode
abbr uW UnixWare is very cool.
abbr Nv Novell is a registered trademark of Novell, Inc.
map , cwAllworthy^[
map > i"^[ea"^[
$ []
```

Using set Commands in Your .exrc File

The `set` commands define options that are used with your `vi` session. In the example, the `set nu` entry shows the line numbers alongside your text as you work in `vi`. The `set wrapmargin=18` entry makes `vi` automatically go to the next line when your cursor reaches 18 characters from the right margin. The `wrapmargin` setting is a convenient way to set the width of documents. For example, if you use `vi` to compose mail messages, you might use the `wrapmargin` setting to make sure your mail messages are not too wide. The `set showmode` entry displays your current typing mode, such as replace mode, insert mode, or change mode, in the bottom-right corner of your window as you work.

Using Abbreviations in Your .exrc File

With abbreviations, you can define short keystrokes that expand into long strings of characters while you are in editing mode. After typing **a** (add) or **i** (insert) to go into editing mode, type the abbreviation, and it will expand into the longer phrase. In the example in Figure 8.5, the first abbreviation set is `abbr uW UnixWare is very cool`. If you type uW, the characters are replaced by the words *UnixWare is very cool*. The `abbr Nv` line sets the characters Nv to be replaced by the Novell trademark phrase.

Using map Entries in Your .exrc File

Using `map` entries, you can map a single character into several characters when you are in command mode. Mapping is very useful if you are doing repetitive editing that includes one or more `vi` commands. For example, suppose that you want to change the name of your company from NoGood Corporation to Allworthy Corporation. Once you have set up the first `map` entry in Figure 8.5, `map , cwAllworthy^[`, you could move the cursor to the word *NoGood* in your text file and type a comma (,) to change the word (`cw`) to *Allworthy* and escape (`^[`) back to command mode.

To enter ^[for escape, you must press Ctrl-V, then Esc.

NOTE

The second map entry in the example, `map > i"^[ea"^[`, lets you `add quotation marks around a word by typing` > with the cursor on the first character of the word. `vi` goes into insert mode (`i`), types a quotation mark (`"`), types escape (`^[`), goes to the end of the word (`e`), begins append mode (`a`), types another quotation mark (`"`), then types escape again.

CONFIGURING THE .vtlrc FILE

If you use virtual terminals, the `.vtlrc` file is read each time you switch to another virtual terminal. The following is an example of a `.vtlrc` file:

```
mapstr
setcolor yellow
setcolor -o lt_red
```

The `mapstr` command makes sure the functions are mapped properly for each virtual terminal. The `setcolor yellow` command makes the text you type at the virtual terminal appear in yellow. The `setcolor -o lt_red` command puts a light red border around the edge of the virtual terminal screen.

NOTE   **To see all the possibilities for the `setcolor` command, just type `setcolor` in a Terminal window. However, if you type `setcolor` at the console or at a virtual terminal, you'll actually see the colors that you can set, not just the words.**

Using Terminal Windows and Virtual Terminals

UnixWare provides several ways to get to a UNIX shell (command line). One way to get to a shell while the Desktop is running is to open a Terminal window. Another way is to use a virtual terminal (VT). If you're a non-Desktop user, you always have access to the UNIX shell since the Desktop doesn't start when you log in. Also, when you log in as the root user, by default, you only have access to the command line; the Desktop does not automatically run.

USING TERMINAL WINDOWS

When you log in from the graphical login window, the only way to get to the shell is through a Terminal window. As you've learned, it's a simple matter to open a Terminal window: just open your Applications folder and double-click on the Terminal icon.

The Terminal window gives you some graphical control over the command line, which you don't have if you use a virtual terminal. For example, you can cut and paste text while in a Terminal window. In addition, you can configure certain characteristics of a Terminal window.

The Terminal menu, shown in Figure 8.6, allows you to customize certain aspects of a Terminal window. To display this menu, click the Menu mouse button anywhere in the Terminal window.

Terminal
Edit ▷
Redraw
Soft Reset
Full Reset
Properties...
Interrupt
Hangup
Terminate
Kill

FIGURE 8.6

The Terminal window

menu

The menu lists nine options:

- **Edit:** Lets you cut and paste text between various windows on the Desktop. When you click on the Edit option, the Edit submenu is displayed.

- **Redraw:** Redraws the contents of the Terminal window. This is sometimes necessary if the Terminal window becomes unreadable. Clicking on Redraw clears things up.

- **Soft Reset:** Resets the scrolling region of the Terminal window to its normal state (as it first appears).

- **Full Reset:** Clears the Terminal window and resets it to its normal state.

- **Properties:** Allows you to change certain characteristics of the Terminal window. When you click on the Properties option, the Properties window is displayed.

- **Interrupt, Hangup, Terminate, Kill:** Send different signals to whatever is running in the foreground of Terminal window. Their effect depends on the application receiving the signal. Hangup and Kill usually stop the application and close the Terminal window. The Interrupt and Terminate options send interrupt and terminate signals, respectively, to the application currently running. (In practice, we have found that Interrupt and Terminate don't have much effect on applications.)

NOTE **If you need to stop an application (which could be a command you entered), try pressing the Delete key first. In most cases, your application will stop and you'll get the UNIX prompt back. If this doesn't work, try using Kill from the Terminal window menu. This will close your Terminal window, but you can easily open another one (or many) from your Applications folder window.**

The Edit submenu and Properties window offer some useful options for your work in a Terminal window. These options are described in the following sections.

Cutting and Pasting in a Terminal Window

The Edit option lets you cut and paste text among various windows on the Desktop. For example, you can cut text from a Terminal window and paste it into a Text Editor window.

You can highlight and copy text from a window in most applications and paste it into your Terminal window. However, you can't copy text from your Terminal window and paste it into another application's document. For example, you can highlight text in a FrameMaker document and paste it into a file you're editing with `vi` (a UNIX editor) in the Terminal window. But you can't paste text from the Terminal window into the FrameMaker document.

The submenu that appears when you click on the Edit option lists the following choices:

▸ **Stay Up:** Keeps the Edit submenu open while you use its other options. This is handy if you are performing several cut-and-paste operations. Then you don't need to display the Terminal menu and click on Edit for each cut and paste. After you select Stay Up, the option changes to Dismiss. Click on Dismiss to close the Edit submenu.

▸ **Send:** Inserts the highlighted text at the cursor position. Send is a shortcut for using both Copy and Paste. Before using this option, you should make sure that the Terminal window is ready to accept input. For example, if you are using `vi` in the Terminal window, enter the append or insert mode before you highlight the text to be copied. Then you can highlight the text you want to copy to the Terminal window and choose Send from the Edit submenu.

▶ **Copy:** Copies the highlighted text to the clipboard. The *clipboard* is a temporary holding area in memory. If you copy something to the clipboard and turn off your computer, the data in the clipboard is lost. Text in the clipboard can be pasted to another Terminal window or to a different location in the same window.

▶ **Paste:** Inserts text copied to the clipboard at the cursor position. First, copy text to the clipboard using the Copy option. Next, prepare the receiving window for input. For example, if you're using vi, enter append or insert mode. Then you can choose Paste.

Changing Terminal Window Properties

When you select the Properties option on the Terminal menu, you see the window shown in Figure 8.7. Through this window, you can change how text is displayed in a Terminal window and other characteristics of the Terminal window. The changes, however, are not permanent. The next time you start the Desktop or click on the Terminal icon to display a Terminal window, the default settings are in effect.

FIGURE 8.7

*Terminal window
properties*

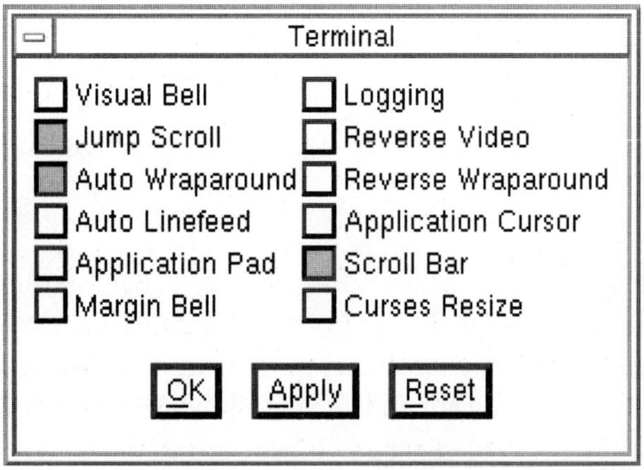

You can set the following properties for a Terminal window:

- **Visual Bell:** If you turn on this property (the default setting is off), the window flashes to get your attention instead of beeping at you. For example, when you press a key that the Terminal window doesn't understand (such as the Esc key), you won't hear a beep, but the window will flash.

- **Jump Scroll:** If you turn off this property (the default setting is on), the Terminal window scrolls a line at a time when it receives large amounts of data instead of scrolling a full window at a time.

- **Auto Wraparound:** If you turn off this property (the default setting is on), the characters at the end of a line are not displayed. When Auto Wraparound is on, the characters entered at the end of a line wrap to the beginning of the next line. Whether Auto Wraparound is turned on or off, all the characters are read by the Terminal window as having been entered.

- **Auto Linefeed:** If you turn on this property (the default setting is off), a carriage return is issued after a newline, vertical tab, or new page code.

- **Application Pad:** If you turn on this property (the default setting is off), the numeric keypad is active and can be used for input for the Terminal window.

- **Margin Bell:** If you turn on this property (the default setting is off), the Terminal window beeps when the cursor gets close to the right margin.

- **Logging:** If you turn on this property (the default setting is off), UnixWare captures all the input to and output from the Terminal window into a log file called `XtermLog.XXX`, where *XXX* is replaced by a random series of characters. Although you can open multiple Terminal windows on your Desktop simultaneously, only one Terminal window can be logged at a time.

▶ **Reverse Video:** If you turn on this property (the default setting is off), the background and foreground colors of the Terminal window are reversed.

▶ **Reverse Wraparound:** If you turn on this property (the default setting is off), when you backspace to the beginning of a line, the cursor will continue backspacing to the end of the previous line. With Reverse Wraparound off, the cursor stops at the beginning of a line when you backspace.

▶ **Application Cursor:** If you turn on this property (the default setting is off), the arrow keys are active in a Terminal window. With Application Cursor off, you can't use the arrow keys.

▶ **Scroll Bar:** If you turn off this property (the default setting is on), the scroll bar won't appear along the right edge of the Terminal window.

▶ **Curses Resize:** If you turn on this property (the default setting is off), you can resize a Terminal window while a `curses`-based application, such as `vi`, is running. If you use `vi` in a Terminal window, it's useful to turn on Curses Resize.

USING VIRTUAL TERMINALS

You can also get to a shell (command line) by switching to another virtual terminal (VT). Using VTs is like having several computers in one. When you switch to a new VT, you are presented with a full-size, blank screen. Although you can't start the Desktop in a new VT, because you can run only one Desktop session at a time, you can do anything in a VT that you could do at the shell command line. You may find that it's more convenient to switch to a VT than to open a Terminal window.

Accessing One Virtual Terminal

To access virtual terminals, you must disable the graphical login window, either just for your current session or permanently. To permanently disable the graphical login window, open a Terminal window, enter `su -`, and enter

the root user password when prompted. Be sure to include the hyphen (−) so the root `.profile` file is read and your path is set up properly. At the prompt, enter

```
/usr/X/bin/disable_glogin
```

You shouldn't see a message on the screen. This takes care of the graphical login window for the next time you boot your system, but you must still disable the graphical login window for this current session.

When you permanently disable the graphical login window, the console login prompt is displayed the next time you boot your system. Type your login name at this prompt. Next you're prompted for your password. Enter it. After a few moments, the Desktop appears.

— NOTE

To disable the graphical login window for the current session, exit the Desktop. When the graphical login window appears, click on Exit. At the console login prompt, enter your login name. Then enter your password when prompted. The UnixWare Desktop is displayed after a few moments.

From the Desktop, press Alt-SysRq p, that is, press and hold down the Alt key, press the SysRq (System Request) key, and then release both keys and press the p key. The Desktop should disappear, and you should see the screen in which you originally logged in (the shell). By repeatedly pressing Alt-SysRq p, you can switch back and forth between the UnixWare Desktop and the virtual terminal. This procedure gives you access to one VT besides the Desktop. Actually, you can access eight VTs with your system, as explained in the next section.

Accessing Multiple Virtual Terminals

By adding a line to your `.profile` file (located in your home directory), you can access up to eight VTs. Using any UnixWare editor, add the following line to your `.profile` file. You must add this line *before* the last line in the `.profile` file.

```
/usr/bin/vtlmgr −k
```

This entry starts the virtual terminal manager. The −k is for security. It ensures that all your virtual terminals are closed when you log off. Otherwise, it's possible for someone else to press Alt-SysRq p and access your system after you've logged off.

The next time you log in, you can access any of eight VTs in addition to your UnixWare Desktop. To access a specific VT, press Alt-SysRq *Fn* where *Fn* is a function key from F1 to F8 (F1 for your first VT, F2 for the second VT, and so on). With several VTs open, you can switch among them with Alt-SysRq p and Alt-SysRq n. Alt-SysRq p displays the *previous* VT while Alt-SysRq n displays the *next* VT.

To go directly to the original login screen, press Alt-SysRq h (h is for your home VT). The UnixWare Desktop is always VT number 1. From any VT you can press Alt-SysRq F1 to get to the Desktop.

If you try to log off your system from the home VT (the VT you logged in from) while other VTs are open, you see a message asking if you want all the VTs closed for you. If you indicate yes, you are immediately logged off and all open VTs are closed. If you say no, you are placed back at a VT so you can close it yourself. To close a VT (or log off your system from the shell), type `exit` or press Ctrl-D at the prompt.

Using UNIX Commands

The UnixWare Desktop allows you to perform many of the same functions as the basic UNIX commands, but you may actually find it more useful and convenient to run the commands from the shell. For example, with the Desktop, you can open any folder window to see its contents. You can also display a graphical representation of a directory tree in the Folder Map window. And you can perform basic file functions, such as copying, moving, and deleting files, through these windows. However, the same tasks are extremely simple to do from the shell. Try some of the examples presented here. You then can decide for yourself whether you prefer using the Desktop or the shell for simple tasks.

UNDERSTANDING UNIX CONVENTIONS

If you are a DOS user, you will find that many UNIX and DOS commands are similar. In fact, many UNIX commands (such as `fdisk`, `cd`, and `mkdir`) are exactly the same as their DOS equivalents. However, different conventions are used to enter UNIX commands. Table 8.1 summarizes the differences between UNIX and DOS conventions. The following sections describe the conventions and concepts you need to understand how to use UNIX commands.

CONVENTION	UNIX	DOS
Options/switches	Command options are preceded by a dash, as in `-l`	Command switches are preceded by a slash, as in `/W`
Arguments	Commands allow multiple arguments	Commands allow one argument
Uppercase and lowercase	Case-sensitive (commands usually lowercase)	Not case-sensitive (uppercase and lowercase are not distinguished)
File names	Flexible file name rules	Strict file name rules (8.3—eight-character file name, dot, three-character extension)
File ownership and permissions	Owner of file sets permissions (read-write-execute)	No file ownership concept; files can be made read-only
Path separators	Slash (/) character	Backslash (\) character

T A B L E   8.1

Summary of differences between UNIX and DOS conventions

UNIX Options and DOS Switches

In both UNIX and DOS, when you want a command to behave a certain way, you follow the command with one or more special characters. In UNIX, this is called an *option* (or sometimes a *flag*); in DOS it is called a *switch*.

UNIX uses the dash (-) character to indicate an option. For example, the `ls` command is used for listing the contents of directories. The −1 option is for a long listing. The command is entered as `ls −1`.

A switch in DOS, on the other hand, uses the slash character (/). For example, you can use the DIR command with the /W switch to indicate a wide directory listing (DIR /W).

UNIX and DOS Arguments

Both UNIX and DOS commands accept *arguments*. An argument is what you want a command to operate on. For example, in DOS, if you enter DIR A:, the command is DIR, and the argument is A:.

Many UNIX commands accept multiple arguments. For example, to delete a file in UNIX, you use the `rm` command. With the `rm` command, you can name several files, for example, `rm file1 file2 file3`.

To delete a file in DOS, you use the DEL command. The DOS command DEL accepts only one argument. To remove three files in DOS (without using the ? or * wildcards), you need to enter the DEL command three times.

Uppercase and Lowercase Commands

In UNIX, it matters whether you enter uppercase or lowercase letters. Some commands have both lowercase and uppercase options. For example, the `ls` command has both −f and −F options. You must enter the correct case. Also, the files `myfile` and `MYFILE` are different files in UNIX.

In DOS, case doesn't matter. Both `myfile` and `MYFILE` refer to the same file. The same is true with commands. You can enter `dir` or `DIR` to get a directory listing in DOS.

File Name Length

In UNIX, file names can be much longer than in DOS. If you install Unix-Ware with the default file system type (`vxfs`), you can have file names with more than 200 characters. In addition, you can put one or more periods anywhere in the name.

DOS has strict rules about file names. A DOS file name has up to three parts. The name of the file can have a maximum of eight characters. This can be followed by a period and a three-character extension. The period and extension are optional. DOS file name rules are often referred to as 8.3 (pronounced *eight-dot-three*).

For more information about file names, see Chapter 6.

 NOTE

File Ownership and Permissions

UNIX uses the concept of file ownership to restrict who can do what to a file. When a user creates a file, the user *owns* the file. The owner can set the permissions on the file to either allow or restrict access, allow it to be changed or not, and decide whether or not it can be run as a program. These permissions are set as read, write, and execute.

DOS has no concept of file ownership. All DOS files are available to anyone using the system. However, DOS does allow files to be set as read-only.

Path Separators

To specify a path in UNIX you use the slash (/) character. For example, the home directory for user spike is `/home/spike`.

DOS uses the backslash (\) character to specify paths. For example, to specify the subdirectory TEMP in the WINDOWS directory, you enter \WINDOWS\TEMP.

COMPARING UNIX AND DOS COMMANDS

Table 8.2 provides a cross-reference for some frequently used UNIX and DOS commands. If you are a DOS user, review the table before you use UNIX commands, and particularly before you call for support or try to troubleshoot your system. The first column is the UNIX command that you may be asked to use by UnixWare support. The second column gives the equivalent or closest DOS command. The third column gives a brief description of the command's function. Each of the UNIX commands listed in the table is described in more detail in the following sections.

TABLE 8.2

Comparing UNIX and DOS
commands

UNIX COMMAND	DOS COMMAND	FUNCTION
ls	DIR	Lists the contents of a directory
more or pg	MORE	Stops text from scrolling off the screen when the window fills
cat	TYPE	Shows the contents of a file
cd	CD	Moves you around the file system
pwd	CD	Displays your current directory
cp	COPY	Copies a file from one place to another
grep	FIND	Searches for text within a file
mkdir	MD	Creates a directory
rm	DEL or ERASE	Removes a file or directory

MANAGING FILES AND DIRECTORIES

You can do just about everything you need to do with your files and directories by using the following commands:

- ▶ The pwd command prints a working directory.
- ▶ The ls command displays a directory list.
- ▶ The cd command changes to another directory.
- ▶ The cp command copies a file.
- ▶ The mv command moves a file.
- ▶ The rm command removes (deletes) a file.

► The `mkdir` command creates a directory.

► The `rmdir` command removes a directory.

► The `grep` command searches for text within a file.

► The `cat` command displays the contents of a file on the screen.

► The `pg` and `more` commands display the contents of a file but stop the output when the window fills.

Each of these commands is described in the following sections.

The pwd Command

One of the simplest UNIX commands is `pwd` (print working directory). For DOS users, the UNIX `pwd` command is similar to the DOS CD command when it's used alone.

When you enter `pwd` at a command line prompt, the current directory is displayed. This is handy because it helps you keep track of where you are in the file system. For example, if your user name is spike and you use the `pwd` command while you're in your home directory, you see

        /home/spike

In this example, `/home/spike` represents the full path to your current directory, which is `spike`.

The ls Command

Use the `ls` (list) command to display a list of files and directories in any directory. For DOS users, the UNIX `ls` command is similar to the DOS DIR command.

To see the files and directories in the current directory, just enter `ls`. You can also specify a directory other than your current directory. For example, if you're in your home directory and want to see which files are in the `/etc` directory, enter

        ls /etc

The `ls` command has many options. Each gives you a different type of listing. Try entering `ls  -F` in a Terminal window. The `-F` option differentiates between nonexecutable files, executable files, links, and directories as the contents of the directory are displayed. Figure 8.8 shows the output of using `ls  -F` to display the contents of a user's home directory.

F I G U R E 8.8

Output of `ls` `-F` *for a*
user's home directory

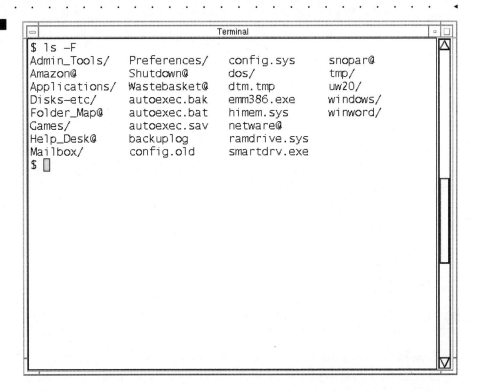

```
                                              Terminal
$ ls -F
Admin_Tools/    Preferences/    config.sys      snopar@
Amazon@         Shutdown@       dos/            tmp/
Applications/   Wastebasket@    dtm.tmp         uw20/
Disks-etc/      autoexec.bak    emm386.exe      windows/
Folder_Map@     autoexec.bat    himem.sys       winword/
Games/          autoexec.sav    netware@
Help_Desk@      backuplog       ramdrive.sys
Mailbox/        config.old      smartdrv.exe
$
```

In the example in Figure 8.8, some names are followed by symbols. These represent the file types as follows:

▸ If a name is followed by a slash (/), it's a directory.

▸ If a name is followed by an asterisk (*), it's an executable file.

▸ If a name followed by an at sign (@), it's a link.

▶ If the name isn't followed by one of these symbols, it's a nonexecutable file.

Other useful ls options are −a, −t, and −l. The a option shows all files, including hidden files. The −t option sorts the entries by each file's time stamp. The −l option shows a long listing. You can use several options together. For example, to see a long listing that includes all files, sorted by the time they were created, enter

```
ls -lat
```

The cd command

The cd (change directory) command is used for moving around the UNIX file system. For DOS users, the UNIX cd command is similar to the DOS CD command.

For example, if you're in your home directory and want to move to your mailbox directory, enter

```
cd mailbox
```

This works because the mailbox directory is below your current directory. You can also move to specific directories anywhere in the file system. For example, to move to the /usr/lib directory, enter

```
cd /usr/lib
```

If you're moving around the file system quite a bit, looking in many directories, using cd can be easier and faster than opening multiple folder windows on the Desktop.

The cp Command

Use the cp (copy) command to copy a file. For DOS users, the UNIX cp command is similar to the DOS COPY command.

For example, you may want to make a copy of a file called myfile, which happens to be in your current directory, before you edit it. To make a copy called `myfile.bak`, enter

```
cp myfile myfile.bak
```

The original file, `myfile`, remains unchanged.

You can also copy a file into another directory with the `cp` command. For example, to copy a file called `spike.file` from the home directory of user spike to the `/tmp` directory, enter

```
cp /home/spike/spike.file /tmp
```

With `cp`, you can copy several files at the same time. For example, to copy the files `thisfile`, `thatfile`, and `anotherfile` to the directory `/doc/allfiles`, enter

```
cp thisfile thatfile anotherfile /doc/allfiles
```

You can rename a file while copying it to another directory by providing the file name along with the directory name. For example, to copy `spike.file` from the home directory to the `/tmp` directory and rename the file `spike.tmp`, enter

```
cp /home/spike/spike.file /tmp/spike.tmp
```

The mv Command

Use the `mv` (move) command to move a file to a new location. Early DOS versions did not have an equivalent command for moving a file (you had to first copy and then delete the file). DOS 6.0 and later versions now have the MOVE command.

For example, to move a file called `junk` from your current directory to the home directory of user spike, enter

```
mv junk /home/spike
```

You can also move a file to a new name, which renames the file without making a copy. Using `mv` this way is similar to the DOS REN command for renaming files. To rename a file in your current directory with the `mv` command, just specify a new file name. For example, to change the name of a file from `thisfile` to `thatfile`, enter

```
mv thisfile thatfile
```

The contents of `thisfile` are now located in a file called `thatfile`. The file called `thisfile` no longer exists.

The rm Command

The `rm` (remove) command lets you remove files. For DOS users, the UNIX `rm` command is similar to the DEL and ERASE commands in DOS.

You can specify a directory with the file name or just specify the file if the file is located in your current directory. For example, to remove a file called `junkfile` from your current directory, enter

```
rm junkfile
```

If you remove a file with the `rm` command, there is no way to get it back (unless you have a backup copy). However, if you remove files using the UnixWare Desktop, you can retrieve them from the Wastebasket.

WARNING

To remove a file from a directory other than your current directory, specify the directory name with the file name. For example, if you're in your home directory and want to remove a file called `scripts` from the `/tmp` directory, enter

```
rm /tmp/scripts
```

Keep in mind that you must have permission to remove a file. If the file is in one of the directories you own, you'll have no trouble removing it. However, if you try to remove a file from a directory owned by another user, you'll get a "permission denied" message, unless the other user specifically gave you permission to remove the file. Figure 8.9 shows an example of what happens when you try to remove another user's file without the proper permissions.

FIGURE 8.9

*Attempting to remove a
file without permission*

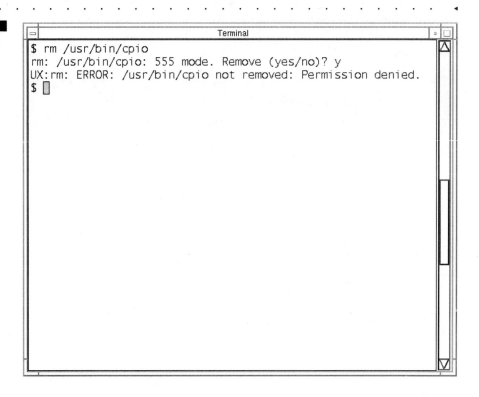

```
┌─  Terminal                                            ▫ □
│ $ rm /usr/bin/cpio
│ rm: /usr/bin/cpio: 555 mode. Remove (yes/no)? y
│ UX:rm: ERROR: /usr/bin/cpio not removed: Permission denied.
│ $ ▯
```

WARNING   **Running rm -r as the root user will erase all files from your system.**

With the -r option, rm can remove directories. For example, to remove
a directory called junkdir, even if it contains files, type

    rm -r junkdir

The mkdir and rmdir Commands

Use the mkdir (make directory) and rmdir (remove directory) commands
for making and removing directories, respectively. Use the mkdir command
to create directories in which you organize your files. In general, you want to

keep related files in one directory. For example, it's a good idea to keep all your saved mail messages in the `mailbox` directory. To make a directory, enter

```
mkdir dir_name
```

where *dir_name* is the directory you want to create.

If you are finished with a directory (when you're at the end of a project, for instance), you should remove it (after you've made a backup, of course) to keep your file system from becoming cluttered. To remove a directory with `rmdir` command, the directory must be empty of all files and sub-directories. To remove a directory, enter

```
rmdir dir_name
```

where *dir_name* is the directory you want to remove.

NOTE

Occasionally, you might find that although a directory appears empty, you cannot remove it with the `rmdir` command. The directory may contain hidden files, sometimes called *dot* files because the first character of the file is a dot (.). Dot files can only be seen when you use the `-a` option to the `ls` command. To see all files in a directory, including dot files, enter the command `ls  -a` while in the directory.

The grep Command

Use the `grep` command to search for text within a file. For DOS users, `grep` is similar to FIND.

For example, to search for the word *PATH* within your `.profile` file, enter

```
grep PATH .profile
```

This command finds the word *PATH* in all uppercase letters. To find text in either uppercase or lowercase letters, use the `-i` option. For example, to find *PATH* or *path* (or any combination of uppercase and lowercase letters), type

```
grep -i path .profile
```

The cat Command

The cat command shows the contents of a file. You can only view files containing ASCII text. For DOS users, cat is similar to the DOS TYPE command.

 NOTE **Files containing ASCII text are sometimes called *flat files* or *text files*.**

To see how this command works, type

```
cat ~/.profile
```

You will see the text in your .profile file, which contains information about setting up your environment when you log in. You can open the file in an editor, but using the cat command is quicker if you just want to see the file's contents.

The pg Command

Use the pg (page) command if a file you're displaying on your screen is so long that its text scrolls by before you've had a chance to read it. For DOS users, pg is similar to the DOS MORE command. When you use pg, after the window fills, the output stops until you press Enter to continue the listing.

To see how this command works, type

```
cat /etc/gettydefs
```

Even on a slow computer, you can't read the beginning of this file because it scrolls by so quickly. Now type

```
pg /etc/gettydefs
```

When the window fills with text, the text stops scrolling, and a colon prompt (:) appears in the lower-left corner. To continue viewing the file, press Enter. To exit the pg command, press the Del key.

You can use pg to skip around in a file by entering a number at the colon prompt. When you press Enter, you jump directly to that line.

The pg command also lets you search forward and backward in the file for specific words. To search forward, type a slash (/) and the word. To search backward, type a question mark (?) and the word. For example, to search forward for the word *terminal*, type

```
/terminal
```

> **If you attempt to use the cat or pg commands on a binary file, strange things happen in your Terminal window. Try typing cat /usr/bin/cpio in a Terminal window. The special codes in a binary file cause the strange output.** — NOTE

The more Command

You can use the more command as an alternative to the pg command when a listing is longer than the size of a window. For example, you can *pipe* the output of ls into more by typing

```
ls | more
```

As when you use pg, when the window fills, the output stops. With more, press the spacebar to continue the listing. The | is the pipe symbol. The next section explains how pipes work with UNIX commands.

USING PIPES, REDIRECTION, AND METACHARACTERS

Pipes and redirection enable you to combine UNIX commands in order to accomplish tasks that you normally can't do with individual UNIX commands. For DOS users, pipes and redirection are used the same way in UNIX as they are in DOS. Some of the UNIX *metacharacters*, such as ? and *, are often called *wildcards* in DOS.

Piping Commands

As a simple example of using pipes, suppose that you want to count the number of files and directories in your current directory. You could use the ls command to list the files and directories on the screen, and then count them yourself. And, in fact, if there are only a few files and directories, this is a perfectly acceptable method. But if you try counting the contents of the /etc directory, you will see that you need a better way.

The UNIX command called wc (word count) can help you count your files and directories. However, you must give wc something to count. You do this by *piping* the output from another command, such as ls, to it. So, to see how many files and directories are in /etc, enter

```
ls /etc/ | wc
```

The character separating the two commands is the pipe symbol. Most keyboards show it as a broken vertical line. Figure 8.10 shows the output from piping the output of the ls command to the wc command.

F I G U R E   8.10

Piping the output of the
ls command to the wc
command

```
Terminal
$ ls /etc/ | wc
 192  192  1358
$ 
```

A more complex example of using pipes involves trying to print a document using troff. troff is a text-formatting command that understands certain complex macro packages. Figure 8.11 shows a typical way to format and print a memo file called my_memo with troff:

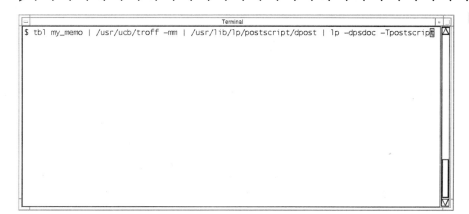

```
Terminal
$ tbl my_memo | /usr/ucb/troff -mm | /usr/lib/lp/postscript/dpost | lp -dpsdoc -Tpostscript
```

F I G U R E   8.11

Using a troff
formatting command line

This line formats the document my_memo by first processing any tables in the document (tbl my memo). Next, the output from tbl is piped to the troff command, where the file's troff macros are processed (| /usr/ucb/troff -mm). The output from troff is piped to dpost, where it is turned into PostScript (| /usr/lib/lp/postscript/dpost). Finally, the PostScript output is piped to lp, which sends the job to the printer connected to printer queue psdoc (| lp -dpsdoc -Tpostscript). Using troff, as you might guess, can be tricky.

Redirecting Output

Redirection lets you send the output of a command to a file or UNIX device. The symbol for redirecting output is >. A typical example would be using the ls command to list the contents of a directory and redirecting the output to a file. This creates a file containing the listing instead of having the listing appear on the screen. Try entering this command from your home directory:

```
ls > junk
```

To see the contents of the file created, named junk, enter

```
cat junk
```

Notice how the output is in a single column instead of in several columns, as it usually is when you use the ls command. To create a multiple-column listing in the file, enter

```
ls -C > junk
```

Use the cat command again to see the contents of the file junk.

Using Metacharacters

UNIX contains a rich set of *metacharacters*, which are characters that have special meanings to the shell. For example, if you enter

```
ls *
```

you don't get a listing of a file with an asterisk (*) as its name. The asterisk is a special character that matches all file and directory names. You can use the asterisk with other characters to narrow the list of files displayed with the ls command. Try entering

```
ls /etc/b*
```

This command lists only the files that begin with the letter *b* in the /etc directory. The asterisk matches any and all characters after the *b*. The asterisk is perhaps the most frequently used metacharacter.

The question mark (?) is another common metacharacter. It matches any single character in the position of the question mark. For example, try entering the following two commands:

```
ls /bin/a?
ls /bin/a*
```

Figure 8.12 shows the output from these commands. Notice how the listing using the asterisk is much longer than the listing from the question mark. The question mark matches only a single character in the second position of the file name. The asterisk matches any and all characters following the first letter.

```
                               Terminal
$ ls /bin/a?
/bin/ar  /bin/as  /bin/at
$ ls /bin/a*
/bin/acctcom          /bin/adminuser     /bin/as          /bin/autodetect
/bin/addmrgconfig     /bin/alpq          /bin/at          /bin/awk
/bin/admin            /bin/apropos       /bin/atq
/bin/adminrole        /bin/ar            /bin/atrm
$ []
```

FIGURE 8.12

Using the * and ?

metacharacters

RUNNING COMMANDS IN THE FOREGROUND AND BACKGROUND

When you type the name of a command and press Enter, the command immediately runs. You do not see the UnixWare prompt again until the command has finished executing. For example, if you enter `ls /etc`, the listing is displayed on the screen, and when it's finished, your prompt reappears so you can enter additional commands. Executing commands in this manner is referred to as running them in the *foreground*.

Because UNIX is multitasking, you can also run commands in the *background*, that is, while you do other things at the command line. This allows you to continue working while giving UnixWare something to do that may take some time. As an example, say you wanted to search for a file. Because the UnixWare file system is quite large, searching for a specific file can take some time. Enter the following commands:

```
cd /usr
find . -name dtadmin -print
```

Notice how long the `find` command takes to locate any files with the name `dtadmin`.

By running this task in the background and redirecting the output to a file instead of to the screen, you can continue with other tasks while Unix-Ware is searching for the file. To run a command in the background, place an ampersand (&) at the end of the line. Now try entering these commands:

```
cd /usr
find . -name dtadmin -print > /tmp/junk &
```

The command prompt returns immediately and you can enter other commands, but the file search is still taking place. You might even be able to hear your hard disk or see the hard disk light blink while the search is going on. To see if the command is still running in the background, type `jobs` and press Enter. Anything running in the background of the current Terminal window is shown, along with its status. Figure 8.13 shows the status of the file search both while the command is running and when it's finished.

USING OTHER UNIX COMMANDS

The commands discussed so far are fairly common, and anyone using a UNIX system should become somewhat familiar with them. The commands covered in the following sections are less frequently used. Some of

```
 ─                                      Terminal                                      ◦ □
$ find . −name dtadmin −print > /tmp/junk &
[1]     4052
$ jobs
[1] + Running               find . −name dtadmin −print > /tmp/junk &
$
[1] + Done                  find . −name dtadmin −print > /tmp/junk &
$ ▯
```

F I G U R E   8.13

*A background file search
while running and when
completed*

these commands perform functions that are not available through the Unix-Ware Desktop. For example, the diff and dircomp commands compare files and directories and cannot be done from the Desktop.

For more information on any of the commands discussed in this chapter, see the manual pages that come with UnixWare. Simply type man **followed by the command. For example, to see the manual page for the** chmod **command, type** man chmod **and press Enter.**

NOTE

The chmod, chown, and chgrp Commands

The chmod, chown, and chgrp commands change the permissions, owner, and group, respectively, for a file or directory. Before you change file or directory attributes, you can check the current ones by using the −l option to the ls command (enter ls −l). Figure 8.14 shows an example of using this command to list the owners, groups, and permissions for several files.

FIGURE 8.14

A file and directory listing
showing owners, groups,
and permissions

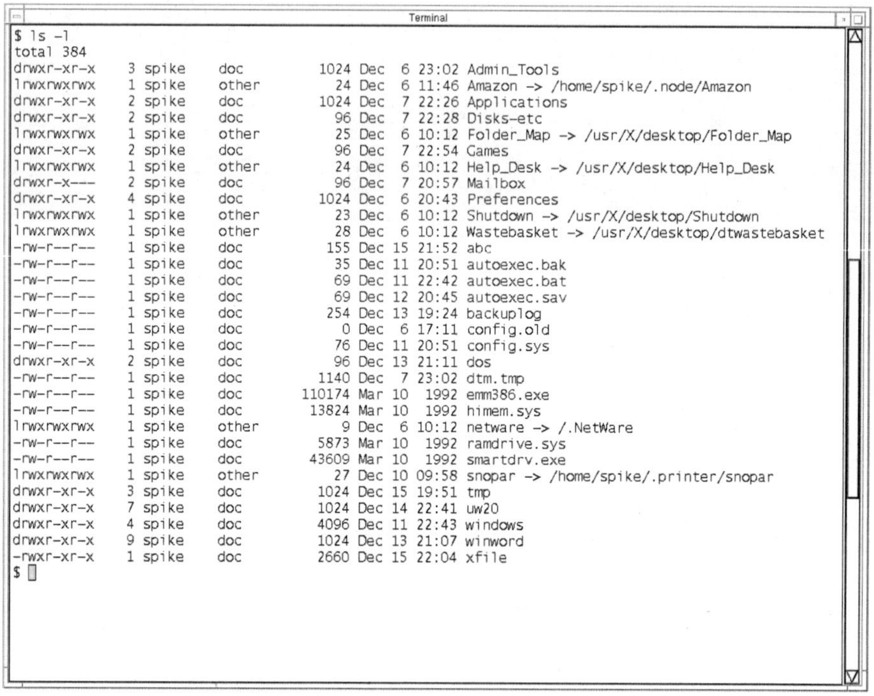

```
                                                       Terminal
$ ls -l
total 384
drwxr-xr-x   3 spike    doc        1024 Dec  6 23:02 Admin_Tools
lrwxrwxrwx   1 spike    other        24 Dec  6 11:46 Amazon -> /home/spike/.node/Amazon
drwxr-xr-x   2 spike    doc        1024 Dec  7 22:26 Applications
drwxr-xr-x   2 spike    doc          96 Dec  7 22:28 Disks-etc
lrwxrwxrwx   1 spike    other        25 Dec  6 10:12 Folder_Map -> /usr/X/desktop/Folder_Map
drwxr-xr-x   2 spike    doc          96 Dec  7 22:54 Games
lrwxrwxrwx   1 spike    other        24 Dec  6 10:12 Help_Desk -> /usr/X/desktop/Help_Desk
drwx-x---    2 spike    doc          96 Dec  7 20:57 Mailbox
drwxr-xr-x   4 spike    doc        1024 Dec  6 20:43 Preferences
lrwxrwxrwx   1 spike    other        23 Dec  6 10:12 Shutdown -> /usr/X/desktop/Shutdown
lrwxrwxrwx   1 spike    other        28 Dec  6 10:12 Wastebasket -> /usr/X/desktop/dtwastebasket
-rw-r--r--   1 spike    doc         155 Dec 15 21:52 abc
-rw-r--r--   1 spike    doc          35 Dec 11 20:51 autoexec.bak
-rw-r--r--   1 spike    doc          69 Dec 11 22:42 autoexec.bat
-rw-r--r--   1 spike    doc          69 Dec 12 20:45 autoexec.sav
-rw-r--r--   1 spike    doc         254 Dec 13 19:24 backuplog
-rw-r--r--   1 spike    doc           0 Dec  6 17:11 config.old
-rw-r--r--   1 spike    doc          76 Dec 11 20:51 config.sys
drwxr-xr-x   2 spike    doc          96 Dec 13 21:11 dos
-rw-r--r--   1 spike    doc        1140 Dec  7 23:02 dtm.tmp
-rw-r--r--   1 spike    doc      110174 Mar 10  1992 emm386.exe
-rw-r--r--   1 spike    doc       13824 Mar 10  1992 himem.sys
lrwxrwxrwx   1 spike    other         9 Dec  6 10:12 netware -> /.NetWare
-rw-r--r--   1 spike    doc        5873 Mar 10  1992 ramdrive.sys
-rw-r--r--   1 spike    doc       43609 Mar 10  1992 smartdrv.exe
lrwxrwxrwx   1 spike    other        27 Dec 10 09:58 snopar -> /home/spike/.printer/snopar
drwxr-xr-x   3 spike    doc        1024 Dec 15 19:51 tmp
drwxr-xr-x   7 spike    doc        1024 Dec 14 22:41 uw20
drwxr-xr-x   4 spike    doc        4096 Dec 11 22:43 windows
drwxr-xr-x   9 spike    doc        1024 Dec 13 21:07 winword
-rwxr-xr-x   1 spike    doc        2660 Dec 15 22:04 xfile
$
```

The first position in the first column of the `ls -l` listing shows whether
the item is a file, a directory, or a link. An `l` as the first character indicates
that the item is a link, a dash(-) shows that the item is a file, and a **d** indicates that the item is a directory. The remaining nine positions are actually
three sets of characters, with three characters in each set. They represent the
permissions for the file. The first set of three is for the owner of the file or
directory, the second set of three is for the group to which the file or directory belongs, and the last set of three is for all other users that may access
the file or directory (usually just referred to as *other*).

The permissions can include **r** for read, **w** for write, and **x** for execute. A
dash means the permission isn't granted. Each set of three characters can
have an **r** or dash in the first position, a **w** or dash in the second position,
or an **x** or dash in the third position.

Look at the permissions on the last line in Figure 8.14. The first set of permissions is rwx. This means that the owner of the file, spike (shown in column three), has read, write, and execute permissions for the file. The second set of three characters is r-x. This means that members of the file's group, doc (shown in column four), can read or execute the file, but they cannot make changes (write) to the file. The last set of three characters is the same as the second set. Any other users on the system can also only read and execute the file.

To change these permissions, you must be the owner of the file. You change the permissions through a number scheme in which the first position in a set of three characters has a value of 4, the second position has a value of 2, and the third position has a value of 1. Add the numbers together to get the permission for a set of three characters. The dash gets no value. For example, if the owner's permissions are rwx, the value is 7 (4+2+1). If the permissions are r-x, the value is 5 (4+1). The directory in line three of Figure 8.14, therefore, has permissions of 755 (7 for the owner, 5 for the group, and 5 for other). Table 8.3 shows typical permissions and their number values.

PERMISSIONS	NUMBER VALUE
rwx rwx rwx	777
rwx rwx r-x	775
rwx r-x r-x	755
rwx --- ---	700
rw- rw- rw-	666
rw- r-- r--	644
rw- --- ---	600
r-- r-- r--	444

T A B L E   8.3

Common file and directory permissions and number values

You use the permission number values with the `chmod` command to change permissions. For example, to change a file named `myfile` to `rw-` permissions for the owner, group, and other, enter

```
chmod 666 myfile
```

Each 6 represents `rw` (4+2). To change the same file so that the owner has `rw-` permissions, but the group and other have no permissions, enter

```
chmod 600 myfile
```

The permissions for `myfile` would look like this: `rw-------`. If you have files that you don't want anyone else to read, change the file's permissions to 600 as shown.

Typically, two permissions are used for files. Permissions of 644 allow the owner to read and write (change) the file and everyone else to only read the file. If a file is meant to be an executable, such as a shell script, make the permissions 755. Everyone will be able to execute the file, but only the owner can change it.

You can use metacharacters, such as * and ? with the `chmod` command. To change every file in your current directory to have permissions of 644, enter

```
chmod 644 *
```

You must be particularly careful when changing permissions of directories. The permission characters used for directories have almost the same meaning as they do for files. The most important exception is the `x` character. A directory must have the `x` character set for you to be able to enter the directory or view its contents.

Typical permissions for a directory are 755. This allows the owner to read the contents of the directory, write in the directory, and enter the directory. If, for example, you change a directory's permissions to 644, no one would be able to use `cd` to enter the directory.

To change the owner of the file (or directory), use the `chown` command. For example, to change the owner of the `autoexec.bat` file (line 14 in Figure 8.14) to `gretch`, enter

```
chown gretch autoexec.bat
```

WARNING

Keep in mind that if you change the owner for a file, the original owner can no longer use `chmod`, `chgrp`, or `chown` on the file.

To change the group to which a file (or directory) belongs, use the `chgrp` command. For example, to change the group of the `autoexec.bat file` to `docgroup`, enter

```
chgrp docgroup autoexec.bat
```

NOTE

Permissions, ownership, and group assignments can be changed through the UnixWare Desktop as well. To do so, select a file (or directory) in a folder, click on Edit at the top of the window, and then click on Properties in the File menu. In the Edit: Properties window, click on the appropriate boxes to change the owner access, group access, and other access. See Chapter 2 for more information about changing file permissions from the Desktop.

The cpio, find, and tar Commands

The `cpio` and `tar` commands are used for grouping sets of files, usually for storing on floppy disk or tapes. The `find` command is often used in conjunction with the `cpio` command. You can also create an archive file with the `cpio` command.

NOTE

For more information about the `cpio` command, see Chapter 7.

The `tar` command is often used by applications for installing their files. For example, the UnixWare version of WordPerfect 5.1 uses the `tar` command during installation.

To use the `tar` command to back up some files to your first floppy disk drive, enter

```
tar -cvf /dev/rdsk/f03ht file1 file2...
```

 NOTE   **To back up files to a floppy, the floppy must first be formatted. See Chapter 11 for information on formatting UNIX floppies.**

The `c` means copy the files to the indicated device; the `v` (verbose) means display the file names on the screen as they're copied; the `f` followed by a space and `/dev/rdsk/f03ht` indicate the device to which the files are copied. In this case, `/dev/rdsk/f03ht` is the device name for the first floppy drive (`f0`), which is a 3.5-inch (`3`), high-density drive (`h`). The `t` indicates that the entire disk is to be used; otherwise, track 0 on cylinder 0 is skipped.

To store the files on a cartridge tape, use `/dev/rmt/c0s0` as the device:

```
tar -cvf /dev/rmt/c0s0 file1 file2...
```

To copy the files *from* a floppy disk or tape on which `tar` was used, use an `x` (for extract) in place of the `c`. For example, to copy the files from a `tar` floppy disk to your hard disk, enter

```
tar -xvf /dev/rdsk/f03ht
```

To see what is on a `tar` floppy disk or tape, without copying the files to your hard disk, substitute a `t` for the `x`. For example, to read a `tar` floppy in your first floppy drive, enter

```
tar -tvf /dev/rdsk/f0t
```

The `tar` command offers a handy shortcut for entering the `f` and the device name. You can enter a number that represents the device instead of its full name. The `/etc/default/tar` file matches a set of numbers to various devices on your system. Figure 8.15 shows the contents of this file.

For example, the line containing number 6 (`archive6`) is matched to `/dev/rdsk/f03ht`. This device is a name for the first floppy drive, which

```
                                    Terminal
$ cat /etc/default/tar
#ident   "@(#)/etc/default/tar.sl 1.1 UW2.0 11/23/94 55447 NOVELL"
#ident "$Header: /sms/sinixV5.4es/rcs/s19-full/usr/src/cmd/tar/tar.dfl,v 1.1 91/
02/28 20:11:52 ccs Exp $"
#          device          block    size
archive0=/dev/rdsk/f0q15dt    15     1200
archive1=/dev/rdsk/f1q15dt    15     1200
archive2=/dev/rdsk/f05ht      15     1200
archive3=/dev/rdsk/f15ht      15     1200
archive4=/dev/rdsk/f03dt      18     720
archive5=/dev/rdsk/f13dt      18     720
archive6=/dev/rdsk/f03ht      18     1440
archive7=/dev/rdsk/f13ht      18     1440
archive8=/dev/rmt/c0s0        20     0
#archive9=/dev/null #reserved
#
# The default device in the absence of a numeric or "-f device" argument
archive=/dev/rdsk/f0t         15     1200
$ []
```

is a 3.5-inch, high-density, floppy drive. The mapping allows you to copy
files to /dev/rdsk/f03ht by entering

        tar -cv6 file1 file2...

instead of

        tar -cvf /dev/rdsk/f03ht file1 file2...

To copy files to the cartridge tape, you can use

        tar -cv8 file1 file2...

The shortcut notation also works for copying files from the floppy disk or
cartridge tape and just reading the floppy or tape.

The last line of /etc/default/tar indicates the default device; that is,
where tar attempts to read from or write to if you omit the number or -f
option. In this case, tar uses /dev/rdsk/f03ht.

The dfspace Command

By using the `dfspace` command, you can see how much space you have left on each file system. At the shell prompt, enter

`/sbin/dfspace`

Figure 8.16 shows the output from the `dfspace` command.

FIGURE 8.16

Output from the dfspace command

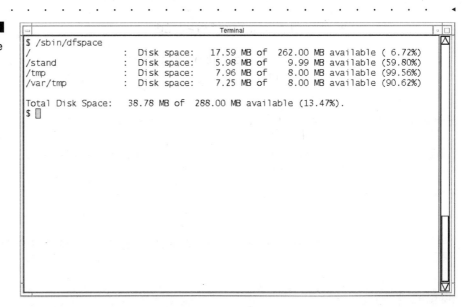

```
$ /sbin/dfspace
/                    :  Disk space:    17.59 MB of   262.00 MB available ( 6.72%)
/stand               :  Disk space:     5.98 MB of     9.99 MB available (59.80%)
/tmp                 :  Disk space:     7.96 MB of     8.00 MB available (99.56%)
/var/tmp             :  Disk space:     7.25 MB of     8.00 MB available (90.62%)

Total Disk Space:     38.78 MB of   288.00 MB available (13.47%).
$ 
```

If `/sbin` is in your path, you can just enter `dfspace`. (We use this command so often that we programmed one of the function keys on our Gateway 2000 keyboard to run it.)

NOTE **The UnixWare Desktop offers a way to check how much hard disk space you've used. Double-click on the System Status icon in the Admin Tools folder. The System Status window shows the total amount of disk space and the amount of space used for each file system. If you want to know how much space you have left, you must do a calculation.**

The diff and dircmp Commands

The `diff` and `dircmp` commands allow you to compare files and directories, respectively. To tell if two files are the same, enter

diff *file1 file2*

where *file1* and *file2* are the two files you want to compare. For example, to compare the files `addressfile` and `addressfile.old`, enter

diff addressfile addressfile.old

Figure 8.17 shows an example of the output. The arrow next to the output indicates the file in which the information was found. If the arrows point to the left, the information was found in the first file you specified (`addressfile` in this case). If the arrows point to the right, the information was found in the second file you specified (`addressfile.old`). In this example, the Large Software Company address was found only in `addressfile.` The Small Computing Corporation address was only in `addressfile.old.`

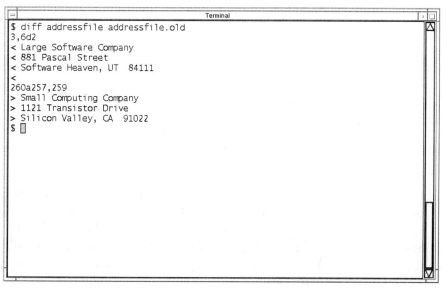

```
$ diff addressfile addressfile.old
3,6d2
< Large Software Company
< 881 Pascal Street
< Software Heaven, UT  84111
<
260a257,259
> Small Computing Company
> 1121 Transistor Drive
> Silicon Valley, CA  91022
$ 
```

FIGURE 8.17

Output of the `diff`
command

You can use `diff` to compare binary files as well as ASCII files, but the actual differences are not shown. If the binary files are different, you will see a message that says the files are different. If the binary files are identical, no message appears.

Use the `dircmp` command to compare entire directories. Everything in the first directory is compared with everything in the second directory, including files and subdirectories. The output usually flashes quickly on the screen and then scrolls off. To make sure you see all the output, add | pg to the end of the command. This pipes the output to the `pg` command, which limits the output to one window at a time. For example, to compare `dir1` with `dir2`, enter

```
dircmp dir1 dir2 | pg
```

Figure 8.18 shows the output from using `dircmp` on `newbook` and `oldbook`. The first part of the listing shows the files in each directory that were not found in the other directory. In this example, `chap4` and `chap5` are only found in the `newbook` directory. The file `appA` is only in the `oldbook` directory.

FIGURE 8.18

Output of the dircomp
command

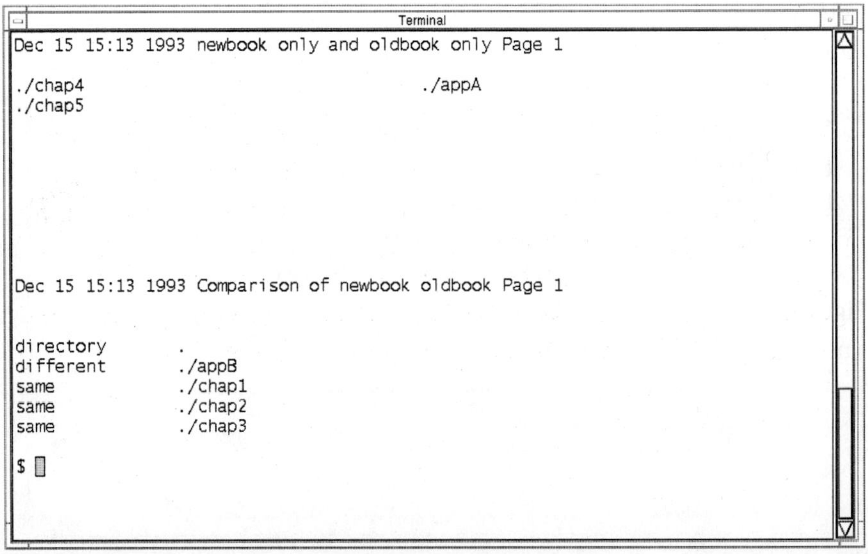

```
Dec 15 15:13 1993 newbook only and oldbook only Page 1

./chap4                                          ./appA
./chap5




Dec 15 15:13 1993 Comparison of newbook oldbook Page 1

directory      .
different      ./appB
same           ./chap1
same           ./chap2
same           ./chap3

$
```

The next part of the output compares the files common to both directories. The output shows that the file appB is different in each directory, and files chap1, chap2, and chap3 are the same in both directories.

When you have many files in the directories you're comparing, you can suppress the information about what is the same by using the -s option to dircmp. To compare dir1 and dir2 without showing the files that are the same in each directory, enter

```
dircmp -s dir1 dir2 | pg
```

The dircmp command can be extremely helpful for checking a backup of a directory against the original on the hard disk. For example, suppose that you have a directory called mybook, which you recently backed up, and you want to check to see which files have changed since the backup. You can restore the backup to a directory with a different name, such as mybook.bak. Then run the dircmp command on the two directories. You'll see which files have been edited since the backup was created.

The lp Command

The lp command is your entry point to the UNIX printing system. After setting up your printers, you can print directly from the shell. By using certain options to the print command, you can print all sorts of files.

NOTE

You can set up your printer through the UnixWare Desktop. Open the Admin Tools folder window and double-click on the Printer Setup icon. See Chapter 10 for more information about setting up printers.

For the following examples, assume you have a PostScript printer configured as psdoc (psdoc is a UNIX print queue). To print the plain ASCII (non-PostScript) file called myfile from the shell, enter ·

```
lp -dpsdoc myfile
```

The `-d` option tells `lp` which print queue you want used to print your file (`psdoc`, in this example).

Many text processing applications, including FrameMaker and Word-Perfect, let you create a PostScript file on your hard disk instead of printing it on the printer. If you have such a file, called, for example, `myfile.ps`, you can print it by entering

```
lp -Tpostscript -dpsdoc myfile.ps
```

The `-Tpostscript` option to `lp` tells `lp` that the file is PostScript, and since `lp` knows that the printer connected to `psdoc` is a PostScript printer, `lp` passes the file directly through to the printer without changing it.

The mailx Command

The UnixWare Desktop includes an extensive mail facility that enables you to read, send, and maintain your mail messages. This mail facility is based on the `mailx` command. Some people (like us) find that it's more convenient to use `mailx` from the shell than to negotiate the many Mail windows in the Desktop.

When you enter `mailx` at the shell, you either see a list of messages or a message that says you have no mail. Figure 8.19 shows an example of a mail message list.

Each mail message has a code letter at the far left. Old mail messages have an O. New mail messages have an N. Unread mail messages have a U. If you have new mail messages, an arrow points to the first new message to indicate that it is the current message. If you press Enter, the current mail message is displayed on the screen, one page at a time. When you are finished, the `mailx` prompt is displayed.

At the end of the list, the cursor waits next to a question mark. This is the `mailx` prompt. At the prompt, you can enter certain one-character commands. To delete the message you just read, press d. To see the list of messages again, press h. To read a specific mail message, enter the number. Press Enter after you type the character at the `mailx` prompt.

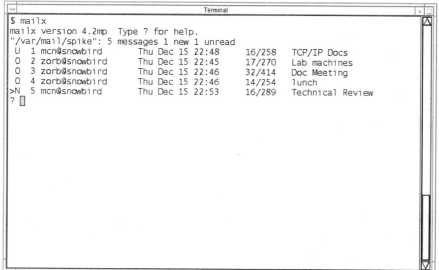

FIGURE 8.19

Running the mailx
command from the shell

In some cases, you may want to save a mail message to a file. To save a mail message, use s and a file name at the mailx prompt. For example, to save the mail message just read to a file called doc.info, enter

    s doc.info

The file doc.info is created in your current directory. You could specify a location for the file if you don't want it saved in the current directory. For example, each Desktop user's home directory has a directory called mailbox. If your user name is spike and you want to save your mail message in a file called doc.info in your mailbox directory, enter

    s /home/spike/mailbox/doc.info

To exit mailx and save any changes you made, use q. If you want to exit mailx and not have any deletions or other changes saved, use x.

The type Command

The type command locates commands in the file system by checking every directory listed in your PATH statement. For example, to see where the dfspace command is located, enter

    type dfspace

If the command is found, its full path is displayed. Figure 8.20 shows the output when type finds the dfspace command. If the message dfspace not found was displayed, dfspace is not in your path or it is not on your system. The type command only checks your path.

FIGURE 8.20

Output of the type *command locating the* dfspace *command*

```
 Terminal
$ type dfspace
dfspace is /sbin/dfspace
$ 
```

 NOTE

To see what your path is, enter echo $PATH at the command line. The /etc directory is not in a non-root user's PATH by default. However, because /etc contains some useful utilities, including links to utilities located in other directories, such as /sbin/dfspace, you should add it to your PATH in your .profile file.

The file Command

The `file` command gives you information about a file's type. For example, if you type

```
file /usr/bin/cpio
```

you see the following information about `cpio`:

```
ELF 32-bit LSB executable 80386 Version 1
```

This information shows you, among other things, that `cpio` is an executable, binary file, which means it is not an ASCII file and that you cannot open it in a text editor.

If you type

```
file /etc/hosts
```

you see the following:

```
/etc/hosts:  ascii text
```

You could, if you had the correct permissions, edit the `/etc/hosts` file with a text editor because it contains ASCII text.

You usually use the **type** command before the `file` command so you know where the file is. The `file` command only looks in your current directory for the file. In the previous example, unless you're in the `/usr/bin` directory, you must enter the full path for `cpio`. If you were in a directory other than `/usr/bin` and entered just `file cpio`, you would get the following error message:

```
UX:file: ERROR: Cannot open cpio: No such
    file or directory
```

This message indicates that the `file` command could not find the file named `cpio`.

Using Shell Scripts

Quite often, you may need to run several, if not many, UNIX commands in a row. You could enter each one from the shell, one at a time. However, if you wanted to run the same set of UNIX commands again, you would need to type them in all over again. The solution is to use a shell script (it's like a batch file in DOS). A *shell script* is simply a collection of UNIX commands saved in a file.

Although shell scripts can be complex, they are also very useful for simple tasks. For example, you could create a one-line shell script that allows you to format floppy disks while you continue doing other work in a Terminal window. The following sections describe how to set up a directory for your shell scripts and create scripts. You can use any of the examples of shell scripts presented here as shown or modify them to suit your needs.

ORGANIZING YOUR SHELL SCRIPTS

Before creating shell scripts, you should create a directory in which to store them. We recommend that you create a directory in your home directory called bin. You can call the directory anything you like, but bin is traditionally used as a name for a directory containing executable files.

To create a bin directory, open a Terminal window and type the following:

```
cd
mkdir bin
```

Entering cd as the first command ensures that you are in your home directory before creating the new directory. The second line creates the bin directory.

Next, add the bin directory to your PATH statement. If you don't add the bin directory to your path, you will either have to be in the bin directory or enter the full path to run your scripts. Having bin in your path lets you execute your scripts from any directory in the system.

Open the `.profile` file, which is located in your home directory, using any UnixWare editor. Locate your PATH line. A typical PATH line may look something like this:

```
PATH=$PATH:/usr/X/bin;export PATH
```

Edit your PATH line to include $HOME/bin. If you started with a PATH line shown above, your new PATH line would look like this:

```
PATH=$PATH:/usr/X/bin:$HOME/bin;export PATH
```

Be certain to include all the punctuation shown. A colon (:) is used between each directory in the PATH line. A semicolon (;) is used to separate the PATH statement from the **export** statement.

If you don't have a PATH line in your `.profile` file, you must add one. If you're creating a PATH line for the first time, make it look like this:

```
PATH=$PATH:$HOME/bin;export PATH
```

Save and close your `.profile` file. You must log out and log in again for your new path to take effect.

CREATING SHELL SCRIPTS

You can use any UnixWare editor to create a shell script. For example, to create a shell script to format floppy disks while you're working in a Terminal window, open an editor and type this line:

```
/usr/sbin/format /dev/rdsk/f03ht >
    /dev/null &
```

In this example, device **f03ht** is used. This device formats a 3.5-inch, high-density floppy disk in drive A:. Substitute **f13ht** for **f03ht** to use drive B:. For a 5.25-inch floppy disk in drive A:, use **f05ht**. For a 5.25-inch floppy disk in drive B:, use **f15ht**.

Give the file a short, easy-to-remember name, such as **uformat** (for UNIX format). With **uformat** created, you can type **uformat**, press Enter (after putting a floppy in the appropriate drive), and continue working. The floppy disk is formatted in the background.

If you have two floppy disk drives, you can create a shell script for each one. You might name one script `uformatA` and the other `uformatB`. The only difference in these scripts would be the name of the device.

After creating a script, be sure to change its permissions so you can run the file as a script. For example, if you created the disk-formatting script called `uformat`, to make the file executable for yourself and other users on your system, open a Terminal window and enter

```
chmod 755 uformat
```

The following sections present examples of shell scripts that we find useful. You can create the scripts that interest you. Give the scripts the names suggested here or use other names. You can store the scripts in your `bin` directory, as recommended, or put them in whatever directory you set up for your scripts.

A Clear Window and Directory List Script

Here is a simple, two-line script that clears the Terminal window and then gives you a directory listing:

```
clear
ls -F
```

The first line clears the window. The second provides the directory listing. You might name this script `cl`. A variation of this script, `cll`, clears the screen and does a long listing. Just replace the second line with `ls -Fl`.

A File-Locator Script

A shell script that finds files provides a shortcut for typing in a somewhat long line. You can use the script to locate a file on your hard disk. If you start at the root directory, this script will search every directory looking for the file you name:

```
find . -name "$*" -print
```

You might name this script `Find`. Use a capital `F` in the name to distinguish it from the UNIX `find` command, which is used in the script. (Unlike in DOS, in UNIX the case is important. The file `Find` is different from the file `find`.)

To see how the script works, open a Terminal window and change to the root directory by typing `cd /`. Now type `Find lp`. UnixWare begins looking for a file with the name `lp`. Soon, you'll begin to see various lines, all containing the file name `lp`. If you're connected to a network, you may get messages indicating that you don't have permission to look in certain directories. Figure 8.21 shows the partial output from running `Find lp` on an Application Server version of UnixWare.

```
                                    Terminal
$ cd /
$ Find lp
./etc/default/lp
./etc/inst/save/etc/lp
./etc/conf/drvmap.d/lp
./etc/conf/mdevice.d/lp
./etc/conf/node.d/lp
./etc/conf/pack.d/lp
./etc/conf/sdevice.d/lp
./etc/conf/.sdevice.d/lp
./etc/conf/mod.d/lp
./etc/init.d/lp
./etc/lp
./etc/security/tfm/users/lp
./etc/conf.unix.old/mod.d/lp
./dev/lp
./usr/bin/lp
./usr/lib/lp
./usr/sadm/sysadm/add-ons/lp
./usr/share/lib/terminfo/1/lp
./var/sadm/pkg/lp
UX:find: ERROR: Cannot read dir ./var/spool/cron: Permission denied
./var/spool/lp
./var/spool/lp/admins/lp
UX:find: ERROR: Cannot read dir ./var/spool/lp/fifos/private: Permission denied
UX:find: ERROR: Cannot read dir ./var/spool/lp/fifos/public: Permission denied
UX:find: ERROR: Cannot read dir ./var/spool/lp/requests/snowbird: Permission den
ied
UX:find: ERROR: Cannot read dir ./var/spool/lp/tmp: Permission denied
UX:find: ERROR: Cannot read dir ./var/spool/uucp: Permission denied
./var/lp
UX:find: ERROR: Cannot read dir ./var/audit: Permission denied
UX:find: ERROR: Cannot read dir ./home/zorb/Mailbox: Permission denied
UX:find: ERROR: Cannot read dir ./home/mcn/Mailbox: Permission denied
UX:find: ERROR: Cannot read dir ./proc/1/object: Permission denied
UX:find: ERROR: Cannot read dir ./proc/192/object: Permission denied
UX:find: ERROR: Cannot read dir ./proc/67/object: Permission denied
UX:find: ERROR: Cannot read dir ./proc/250/object: Permission denied
UX:find: ERROR: Cannot read dir ./proc/274/object: Permission denied
UX:find: ERROR: Cannot read dir ./proc/214/object: Permission denied
UX:find: ERROR: Cannot read dir ./proc/338/object: Permission denied
```

F I G U R E   8.21

Output of the Find *shell script*

A Self-Searching Shell Script

You can create an interesting shell script that contains both the instructions to search and the data to search through in the same file. You might use this type of script to hold names and addresses. It makes for a quick on-line database in which you can enter the information in any order.

Here is an example of the search instructions followed by part of a large name and address file:

```
exec /usr/bin/egrep -i "$1"
  /home/spike/bin/a

Excell Widgets: (213) 778-1234, FAX (213)
  778-1235
Excell Widgets: John Jones, Technical
  Support
Excell Widgets: 1 Techno Blvd.
Excell Widgets: Computer City, CA 98001

Joe Smith: (718) 888-1111

Gretchen Jones: HOME (212) 321-4321
Gretchen Jones: WORK (212) 888-1100
```

When you create this file, you must change the first line to indicate the directory where the file is kept and the name of the file. This example is kept in /home/spike/bin and the file name is the letter a.

To use this script, type a plus the data that you want to find. For example, to search for Gretchen's telephone number, enter a gretchen (you do not need to type Gretchen with a capital *G* to find her number). Every line in the file containing the word *gretchen*, either in uppercase or lowercase, is displayed.

By repeating the name at the beginning of the line, you group all the information for one person or company in an easy-to-read manner. You could just as easily have an entry like this:

```
Bill Smith, (617) 222-9009, 1982 George
  St., Sandy, UT 84070
```

Keep in mind that when the search is made, every line with the word you're searching for will be displayed.

A Copy Floppies Script

DOS provides a convenient way to make an exact copy of a floppy disk; namely, the DISKCOPY command. In UNIX it's not so simple. You must copy the floppy to your hard disk and then write it back to a new floppy disk. The script shown in Figure 8.22 makes the job trivial. You can use this script to make copies of both UNIX and DOS floppy disks.

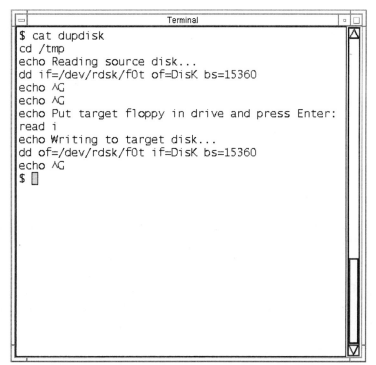

```
$ cat dupdisk
cd /tmp
echo Reading source disk...
dd if=/dev/rdsk/f0t of=DisK bs=15360
echo ^G
echo ^G
echo Put target floppy in drive and press Enter:
read i
echo Writing to target disk...
dd of=/dev/rdsk/f0t if=DisK bs=15360
echo ^G
$
```

F I G U R E   8.22

A shell script for copying floppy disks

Here's what each line in the shell script does:

- The first line,

  ```
  cd /tmp
  ```

  changes directory to /tmp, which is a temporary directory that is emptied each time you reboot your system. This is where the copy of the floppy is stored.

- The second line,

  ```
  echo Reading source disk...
  ```

  displays a message indicating that the floppy disk is being read.

- The third line,

  ```
  dd if=/dev/rdsk/f0t of=DisK bs=15360
  ```

  uses the UNIX dd command to copy an image of the floppy to a file called DisK. This script uses f0t as the device, which is floppy drive A:. If you want to use B: as your floppy drive, substitute f1t for f0t on the third and ninth lines (two places) in the script.

- The fourth and fifth lines,

  ```
  echo ^G
  echo ^G
  ```

  sound two beeps (one echo ^G for each beep) to let you know it's time to change floppies. If you're using vi to create the script, you must press Ctrl-V and then Ctrl-G to produce the ^G you see in the file. If you're using the UnixWare Desktop Text Editor, just press Ctrl-G to create the ^G.

- The sixth line,

  ```
  echo Put target floppy in drive and press Enter:
  ```

  prompts you to change floppies.

► The seventh line,

```
read i
```

senses when you press Enter.

► The eighth line,

```
echo Writing to target disk...
```

displays a message indicating that the system is writing to the new floppy.

► The ninth line,

```
dd of=/dev/rdsk/f0t if=DisK bs=15360
```

uses the **dd** command to copy the data previously stored in the file **DisK** to the new floppy.

► The last line, another `echo ^G`, emits one beep to indicate that the process is finished.

To use this script, first put the floppy disk to be copied in the appropriate drive. Then type **dupdisk** in a Terminal window and press Enter. When you hear two beeps, change floppies and press Enter. When you hear one beep, the copy has been made.

A System-Checking Script to Run from the Desktop

The system-checking shell script lets you get information about your system by choosing the item you want to check from a menu. It can check your disk space, which file systems are mounted, the system name, who is logged in, and the size of your files.

This script is more complicated than the other shell scripts in this chapter. It makes use of programming techniques usually used in traditional programming languages, such as C and Pascal. You don't, however, need to know how *while loops* and *case statements* work in order to use the script.

This example also serves to show you how to assign an icon to a shell script. If you create an icon for a script, you can have it appear in a folder window or your Desktop window and you can run it from there.

Follow these steps to create the script and an icon, which we'll locate in your Applications folder.

1 · Use any UNIX editor to create the script shown in Figure 8.23. Put the script in your Applications folder and name it sycheck.

F I G U R E 8.23

*System-checking shell
script*

```
                                                    Terminal
$ cat syscheck
while true
do
        echo "

                        Personal System Checker

                1) Check system disk space
                2) Check mounted file systems
                3) Check the system name
                4) Check who is logged in
                5) Check the size of your files
                6) Exit

        "
        echo "Select the information you want to check: \c"
        read check
        echo ""
        case $check in
        1)
                /etc/dfspace
                ;;
        2)
                /etc/mount
                ;;
        3)      /usr/bin/uname -a
                ;;
        4)      /usr/bin/who -u
                ;;
        5)      du $HOME|pg
                ;;
        6)
                break
                ;;
        *)
                echo "**** You must enter a number from 1 and 6.   ***** \c"
                continue
                ;;
        esac
done
exit 0
$
```

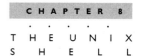

2 · Double-click on Admin Tools in your Desktop window, then double-click on Icon Setup. The Icon Setup: Personal Classes window is displayed, as shown in Figure 8.24.

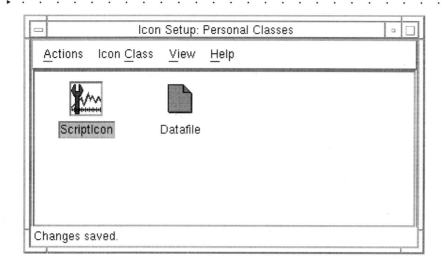

F I G U R E 8.24

Icon Setup: Personal
Classes window showing
new icon

3 · In the Icon Setup: Personal Classes window, click on Icon Class to display the Icon Class menu. Next click on New, and in the pop-up window click on Application. The Icon Setup: New Personal Application window is displayed.

4 · Click in the Class Name text box and enter ScriptIcon.

5 · Click on the Icons button to display the Icon Setup: Icon Library window. Click on diagnose.icon and then click on OK.

6 · Click in the Program Name text box and enter `syscheck`.

7 · Next to Program Type, click on UNIX Graphical to display the pop-up menu. Select UNIX Character.

8 · At the top of the window, click on Basic Options, and in the pop-up menu, click on File Typing.

9 · Click in the "it is in the following folder" text box and enter $HOME/Applications. Click on the OK button.

10 · Open the Applications folder. The diagnostic icon should appear with syscheck as its label. Click on Edit to display the Edit: Properties menu. Click on the three Execute boxes to make the script executable by everyone on your system. Click on Apply. Finally, double click on the syscheck icon to run your shell script.

 NOTE **For a complete description of the Icon Setup window, see Chapter 3.**

If you do not create an icon for the syscheck script, you won't be able to run it from the Desktop. You can, however, create the shell script and run it from a Terminal window by just typing its name.

Explanation of syscheck Script

The first two command lines are

```
while true
do
```

The while part encases the rest of the script's commands between the do and the done. The true part repeatedly runs the script until you select Exit (option 6) from the script's menu to quit.

The echo " line prints to the screen everything before the next quotation mark. The menu part of the script follows, ending with the " line to stop printing to the screen.

The next echo line

```
echo "Select the information you want to
    check: \c"
```

prints to the screen the prompt for selecting a menu item. The \c at the end of the line forces the cursor to stay on the same line as the prompt. Without the \c, the cursor would automatically move down to the next line.

The `read check` line reads what you enter at the keyboard. The information is saved in a variable called `check`.

The next `echo` line, `echo " "`, just prints a blank line to the screen. The next line,

```
case $check in
```

begins the `case` statement. It checks the value of the variable `check`. All the lines that follow, up to `esac` (which is *case* backwards), are part of the `case` statement. If the value of `check` is not 1, 2, 3, 4, 5, or 6, the line beginning with `*)` is executed. This line just reminds you that you must enter a number from 1 to 6. When a number from 1 to 6 is entered, the line beginning with that number is executed. Each line runs the command associated with the corresponding menu item. You can substitute other commands if you choose. Don't forget to change the menu item description to match the command you're using.

Using Manual Pages

UNIX *manual pages* (usually referred to as *man pages*) contain descriptions of every command, programming interface, file format, and device in the UNIX system. The `man` command lets you read man pages from a Terminal window.

Most versions of UNIX available today support the `man` command and come with a complete set of man pages. UnixWare's Personal Edition (PE) and Application Server (AS) both come with the `man` command and man pages. However, with the PE, the man pages are not automatically installed. You must select the manual page package to install the man pages.

VIEWING MANUAL PAGES

Each type of man page is given a section number. For example, generalpurpose commands are in section 1 and system calls are in section 2. Table 8.4 lists each man page type and its section number.

MANUAL PAGE SECTION	SECTION NUMBER
General-purpose user commands	1
Basic networking commands	1C
C++ Commands	1C++
Form and menu language interpreter	1F
System maintenance commands	1M
Commands (Motif reference)	1X
System calls	2
BSD system compatibility library	3BSD
Standard C library	3C
C++ library	3C++
ETI-curses library	3curses
Data link provider interface utility routines	3dlpi
Desktop library	3Dt
Executable and linking format library	3E
General-purpose library	3G
Identification and authentication library	3I
Math library	3M
Metric access support library	3mas
Networking library	3N
Standard I/O library	3S
Synchronization routines for the threads library	3synch
Threads library	3thread
Multibyte/wide character conversion library	3W

MANUAL PAGE SECTION	SECTION NUMBER
Library functions (Motif reference)	3X
System file formats	4
C++ file formats	4C++
Data link provider interface data structures	4dlpi
Miscellaneous facilities	5
File formats (Motif reference)	5X
Special files (devices)	7
Data link provider interface message formats	7dlpi
Transport provider interface message formats	7tpi
DDI/DKI driver data definitions	D1
DDI/DKI driver entry point routines	D2
PDI driver entry point routines	D2I
DDI/DKI kernel utility routines	D3
PDI driver utility routines	D3I
DDI/DKI kernel data structures	D4
PDI data structures	D4I
DDI/DKI kernels defines	D5

T A B L E   8.4

*Manual page sections and
numbers (continued)*

To use the man command, you simply enter man plus the name of the man page you want to view in a Terminal window. For example, to view the cpio man page, enter

```
man cpio
```

To view the man page on the man command, enter

```
man man
```

If a man page of the same name exists in more than one section, you must include the section. Type the section number before the man page name.

For example, there is a `passwd` man page in section 1 and in section 4. To view the section 1 `passwd` man page, just type

    man passwd

However, to view the `passwd` man page in section 4, you must type

    man 4 passwd

If the man page contains more than a full window of text, use the spacebar to view additional text. In the lower-left corner of the window you'll see the word *More* and the percentage of the file displayed, as shown in Figure 8.25. You can stop viewing a man page at any time by pressing the Del key.

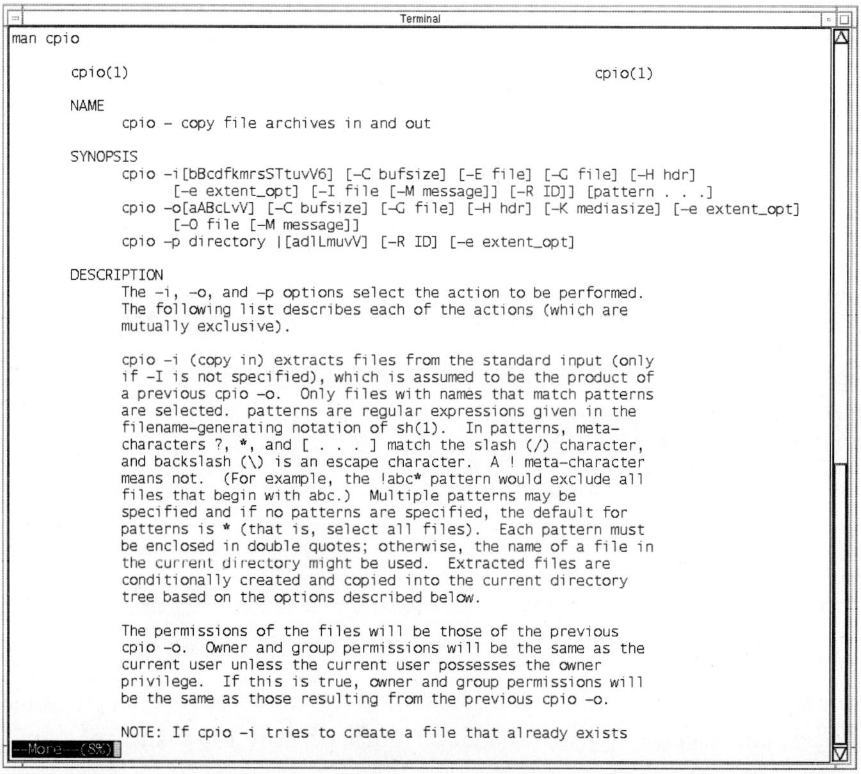

FIGURE 8.25

Using the man *command to view the* cpio *man page*

```
Terminal
man cpio

        cpio(1)                                                    cpio(1)

        NAME
             cpio - copy file archives in and out

        SYNOPSIS
             cpio -i[bBcdfkmrsSTtuvV6] [-C bufsize] [-E file] [-G file] [-H hdr]
                  [-e extent_opt] [-I file [-M message]] [-R ID]] [pattern . . .]
             cpio -o[aABcLvV] [-C bufsize] [-G file] [-H hdr] [-K mediasize] [-e extent_opt]
                  [-O file [-M message]]
             cpio -p directory |[adlLmuvV] [-R ID] [-e extent_opt]

        DESCRIPTION
             The -i, -o, and -p options select the action to be performed.
             The following list describes each of the actions (which are
             mutually exclusive).

             cpio -i (copy in) extracts files from the standard input (only
             if -I is not specified), which is assumed to be the product of
             a previous cpio -o.  Only files with names that match patterns
             are selected.  patterns are regular expressions given in the
             filename-generating notation of sh(1).  In patterns, meta-
             characters ?, *, and [ . . . ] match the slash (/) character,
             and backslash (\) is an escape character.  A ! meta-character
             means not.  (For example, the !abc* pattern would exclude all
             files that begin with abc.)  Multiple patterns may be
             specified and if no patterns are specified, the default for
             patterns is * (that is, select all files).  Each pattern must
             be enclosed in double quotes; otherwise, the name of a file in
             the current directory might be used.  Extracted files are
             conditionally created and copied into the current directory
             tree based on the options described below.

             The permissions of the files will be those of the previous
             cpio -o.  Owner and group permissions will be the same as the
             current user unless the current user possesses the owner
             privilege.  If this is true, owner and group permissions will
             be the same as those resulting from the previous cpio -o.

             NOTE: If cpio -i tries to create a file that already exists
--More--(5%)
```

There are two ways to use UnixWare. Normally, you use the UnixWare Desktop to graphically run applications, manipulate files, and administer your system. Sometimes, however, either because it's easier to use the UNIX shell (command line) or because the functionality you want is not available through the UnixWare Desktop, you find yourself opening a Terminal window or a virtual terminal and entering commands at the UNIX prompt.

Before UnixWare was available, almost all versions of UNIX were used and administered from the shell. Notable exceptions are NeXT, SCO, and Sun. These were among the few versions of UNIX available with graphical interfaces. These early graphical interfaces often expected you to do many basic tasks, particularly administrative tasks, from the command line. To properly configure and maintain UNIX systems, you needed to be more than casually acquainted with UNIX commands. As a result, books have proliferated on the subject. This chapter introduced some of UnixWare's (and UNIX's) many commands. For more information about using the UNIX shell, see any of the many books available on the subject—Stan Kelly-Bootle's *Understanding UNIX, Second Edition* (SYBEX Inc.), for instance.

## CHAPTER 9

Improving
System Performance

Most early UNIX systems ran on large mainframes or minicomputers. Because many users often worked on the computer at the same time, a system administrator had to make sure the UNIX system performed in a way that allowed everyone to get their work done. To meet that need, UNIX utilities were developed to monitor how a system was used and to let the administrator change how resources were distributed.

Though many UNIX systems today are run on personal computers with only one or two users, the tools for monitoring and tuning UNIX are still there. With the addition of the UNIX System V graphical user interface (GUI), many of these administrative tools are available through graphical windows. Even if yours is a single-user UNIX system, monitoring and tuning can help you see if you need to increase your computer's RAM, add another processor, or otherwise improve your hardware.

If you are a system administrator managing many users, computers and networks, you can use monitoring data to support requests to management for more computer resources. You can gather real numbers to show when and how your systems are being overloaded.

Using UnixWare, you have a choice between graphical monitoring and tuning tools and the old, standard UNIX command line tools for improving your system performance. The following system performance tools and procedures are described in this chapter:

▸ **System Monitoring**. The System Monitor window lets you check how the system is performing across several different variables. You can watch graphs of CPU usage, memory consumption, process switching and other information relating to how UNIX resources change over time. You can also display system monitoring information from the command line using the UNIX `sar` and `rtpm` commands.

▸ **Managing Processes**. Sometimes runaway processes can deteriorate the performance of your system. Using commands such as `ps`, you can check for runaway processes and clean up those processes as needed.

▸ **Console Monitoring.** The Message Monitor monitors many of the error messages that appear on the console and displays them on a window in the graphical user interface.

▸ **System Tuning.** The System Tuner window lets you change your system's tunable parameters. These parameters limit how system resources can be used, such as how many processes a user can run at a time or how large a file the user can create. You can also use command line tools, such as `idtune`, for displaying and changing tunable parameters.

▸ **Distributing the Workload.** There are ways of improving the general performance of the system by distributing how and when work is done. This section contains tips on improving performance by changing your habits on how you use your UNIX system.

Fully understanding UNIX system monitoring and tuning requires in-depth knowledge of the UNIX system. You need to know, for example, how UNIX allocates memory, what the different system calls do, and how UNIX queues and runs processes. Because covering these topics completely could fill an entire book, this chapter focuses on common performance problems, then describes how to monitor and correct them. For comprehensive coverage of the topics presented here, we recommend you refer to a book on UNIX system internals, such as *Understanding UNIX, Second Edition* from SYBEX Inc.

NOTE

System Monitoring

Nearly every action that goes on in the UNIX kernel, whether it's writing to the hard disk, accessing the CPU, or manipulating memory, activates data points. You can monitor these data points to get a feel for how your UNIX system is performing.

The UNIX tools for monitoring your system described in this chapter draw on the same data points. Depending on the interface you are using (the GUI or the command line), however, you have a choice of how to display monitoring data. The System Monitor window provides monitoring data in a graphical form that can be displayed on the Desktop. The `rtpm` command displays data in graphical and text form, though it will work on most dumb terminals. The `sar` command lets you output monitoring data in text form.

Each of the monitoring tools is described separately in the following sections. Because the tools draw on many of the same data points, information on how to interpret the data for these tools is contained in the section "Understanding Monitoring Data" later in the chapter.

USING THE SYSTEM MONITOR WINDOW

Like many of the graphical tools that come with UnixWare, you can start up the System Monitor from an icon in the Admin Tools window in the UnixWare Desktop. When you double-click on that icon, you see a System Monitor window, as shown in Figure 9.1.

Essentially, what you do with this window is select the system performance values you want to monitor, assign a color to each of them, and watch as the lines move up and down on the graph to reflect how the values change over time. For example, click the mouse on CPU Usage - User time, then click on the blue color bar under List of Colors. A blue line appears in the graph, progressing from left to right and waving up and down as the percentage of CPU time dedicated to user processes changes over time. Repeat this procedure (using different colors) for CPU Usage - System time and CPU Usage - Wait I/O time.

NOTE **Notice that the scales for CPU Usage values are all set to 100. This is because the CPU values all represent a percentage (100% scale) of the available CPU capacity. Other values can be charted on scales from 10 to 10,000. To change the scale of a value, click on the value, then click on a number under the scale heading.**

Because the graph is just a line moving across the screen, you can only see roughly what the values are. To see the specific number at any point in the graph, click on that point in the graph. A number appears, showing you the exact value for that point in time.

If you forget what a particular line on the graph represents, look at the List of System Monitor options on the window. The option is displayed in the same color as the line it represents on the graph above.

F I G U R E 9.1

*Displaying the System
Monitor window*

Using the Tool Bar to Set Options and Alarms

You'll notice that there is a bar containing three icons and a text box under the menu bar near the top of the window. This is called the tool bar. The icons are, from left to right, Options, Alarm, and Playback.

Click on the Options icon and the System Monitor: Options window appears, as shown in Figure 9.2.

FIGURE 9.2

The System Monitor:

Options window

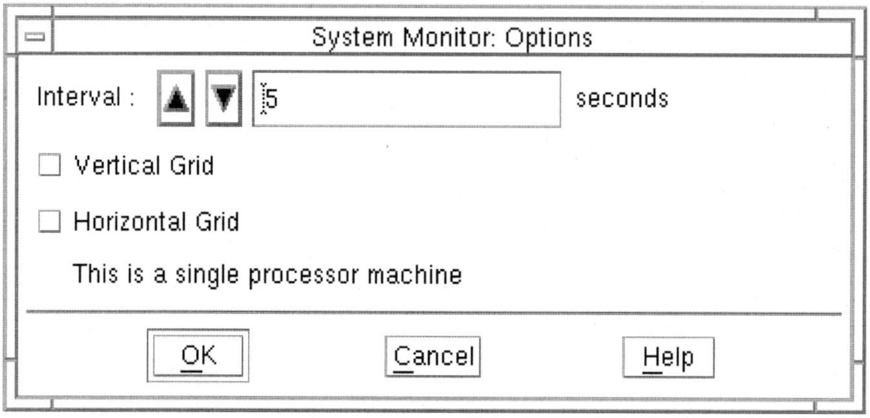

```
┌─────────────────────────────────────────────────┐
│ ▭         System Monitor: Options                 │
│                                                   │
│  Interval :  ▲  ▼  │5                │  seconds    │
│                                                   │
│  ☐ Vertical Grid                                  │
│                                                   │
│  ☐ Horizontal Grid                                │
│                                                   │
│     This is a single processor machine            │
│                                                   │
│      OK          Cancel           Help            │
└─────────────────────────────────────────────────┘
```

The System Monitor: Options window lets you turn horizontal and vertical grid lines on and off for the graph area on the main System Monitor window. There is also an option to change the interval at which the data are sampled. By default, the interval at which data samples are taken is every five seconds. Click on the up or down arrows to increase or decrease the interval. An interval that is too short (such as one second) may cause the System Monitor window itself to become a drag on system performance.

From the System Monitor window, click on the Alarm icon to bring up the System Montitor: Alarm Setup window, as shown in Figure 9.3. This window lets you set alarms for each of the System Monitor values.

Alarms are used to alert you when a value goes above or below the limit (either high or low) that you choose. Click on one of the monitor options, then click on either Beep or Flash Header, depending on how you want to

The System Monitor:

Alarm Setup window

be alerted when the alarm value is reached. Type a number into either the Alarm Above or Alarm Below text boxes. Then click on Set Alarm. Clicking on OK saves the settings and closes the window.

From the System Monitor window, click on the Playback icon and, when prompted, fill in the name of a file containing previously saved System Monitor logged data. The log data will play back on the graph.

Logging System Monitor Data

Using the log and playback features, you can save system monitoring data and play it back at a later date. Logging information can be saved to any file you choose, then replayed by simply recalling the file.

To start logging data, click on the Actions button in the menu bar. Then, from the pull-down menu, click on "Log data to file." When a dialog window appears, type in the file name you want to use. The default file name is `sys_mon.log.0` and is stored in your home directory.

When you have saved enough monitoring data, you can turn off logging. Click on the Actions button in the menu bar. Then click on "Stop logging data" to end the logging session.

To play back the logged data, either use the Playback icon (on the tool bar) or click on the Actions button in the menu bar and select "Playback log data." When prompted, type in the name of the file containing the logged data. Click on OK and a new window is displayed showing you the saved data.

Changing System Monitor Colors

The colors shown in the System Monitor window can be assigned to particular monitoring entries. Definitions for these colors are stored in the `/usr/X/lib/app-defaults/System_Monitor` file. Use a UNIX text editor to open this file and add color definitions.

To assign colors to the first five monitoring entries, you could add the following lines to the `/usr/X/lib/app-defaults/System_Monitor` file (separate the resource name from the color with tabs):

```
*SarOption0*foreground:    blue
*SarOption1*foreground:    magenta
*SarOption2*foreground:    yellow
*SarOption3*foreground:    green
*SarOption4*foreground:    red
```

The next time you open the System Monitor window, the first five entries will be assigned the colors blue, magenta, yellow, green, and red. The entries assigned to those colors would be CPU Usage - User time, CPU Usage - System time, CPU Usage - Wait I/O time, CPU Usage - Idle Time, and Free memory pages, respectively.

SYSTEM MONITORING WITH THE sar COMMAND

The UNIX system activity reporter (`sar` command) is the oldest and most commonly used of the performance monitoring tools described in this chapter. Using sar, you can report on activity relating to processor utilization, buffers, hard disks, terminals, system calls, swapping and switching, file access, queues, processes, file system types, messages and semaphores, paging, and kernel memory.

When you run the sar command, using any of the couple dozen or so options, it outputs text data at your terminal showing your system activity over a set period of time. If run without specifying time intervals, sar outputs statistics taken at 20-minute intervals from the time you booted the system to the current time.

From the time it is booted, the system gathers system activity statistics and stores them in the /var/adm/sa directory. Each day's statistics are gathered in a file named sa*dd*, where *dd* is replaced by a two-digit number representing the current day of the month (i.e., sa01, sa02, etc.). The sar command takes statistics from these files and outputs them as you request.

With the multiprocessor release of UnixWare 2, sar has been enhanced to output statistical information for any or all of the processors on your system. As you may guess, the total output of the sar command can be quite extensive.

The best way to get a feel for the output of the sar command is to use the −A option. This outputs all sar reports, displaying information for all time intervals since the system was last booted. In the following examples, we ran the command sar −A | more. This command pipes all reports to the more command so that you can page through the statistics using the space bar or use the Enter key to advance a line at a time. Figure 9.4 (shown in the next section) shows the first page of output from the sar −A command.

The sar reports can also be output separately using individual options. Look at the usage line for sar (type sar −?). The following is an example of the sar usage line:

```
usage:
sar [-P 0,1...|ALL] [-ubdycwaqvtmpgrkAR]
    [-o file] t [n]
sar [-P 0,1...|ALL] [-ubdycwaqvtmpgrkAR]
    [-s time] [-e time] [-i sec] [-f file]
```

The order of the report options shows how reports are output with the −A option. In other words, the reports are shown in the following order: ubdycwaqvtmpgrk. So sar −u would print the first report shown, sar −b the second, and so on.

The sar CPU, Buffer, and Hard Disk Reports

The first three reports output by the sar −A command are the processor utilization report, the buffer activity report, and the hard disk activity report. Examples of these three reports are shown in Figure 9.4. To print these reports individually, you could use the −u, −b, and −d options to sar, respectively.

The processor utilization report (%usr, %sys, %wio, and %idle) shows CPU activity from the time the computer was booted (9:54:02 a.m.) to the current time (shortly after 11:20 a.m.). As you can see, there wasn't much activity during this time. The %idle shows that the CPU was not active

F I G U R E   9.4

sar *reports: CPU, buffer,*
and hard disk

```
                                                                Terminal
$ sar -Almore

UNIX_SV snowbird 4.2MP 2.0 i386      12/08/94

09:54:02    %usr    %sys    %wio   %idle
10:00:04       0       0       0      99
10:20:02       0       0       0     100
10:40:00       0       0       1      99
11:00:00       1       1       1      98
11:20:01       0       0       0      99
Average        0       0       0      99

09:54:02  bread/s lread/s %rcache  bwrit/s  lwrit/s  %wcache  pread/s pwrite/s
10:00:04       0       1     100       1        1        3        0       0
10:20:02       0       0      96       0        0       13        0       0
10:40:00       0       2      93       0        0       14        0       0
11:00:00       0       2      99       0        0        5        0       0
11:20:01       0       0     100       0        0        9        0       0
Average        0       1      96       0        0        8        0       0

09:54:02 device       %busy    avque    r+w/s   blks/s   avwait   avserv
10:00:04 sd011            0      4.3        0        0     30.4      9.2

10:20:02 sd011            0      1.5        0        0      3.1      6.4

10:40:00 sd011            0      1.5        0        0      4.0      8.4

11:00:00 sd011            0      1.2        0        0      1.5      6.1

11:20:01 sd011            0      1.4        0        0      2.1      5.2

Average  sd011           0      1.8        0        0      6.1      7.3
--More--
```

from 98% to 100% of this time period.

The %wio shows the percentage of time the processor was waiting for block I/O and was idle as it waited. In other words, the CPU is waiting for a hard disk or some other device to respond before it can proceed. The %usr and %sys columns show the percentage of CPU time dedicated to processing requests from user space (applications and utilities) and system kernel space (the operating system itself).

The buffer activity report (bread/s, lread/s, %rcache, bwrit/s, lwrit/s, %wcache, pread/s, and pwrite/s) shows information about the transfer of information from system buffers and disks. The bread/s and bwrit/s columns show the number of data transfers (reads and writes) per second between system buffers and block devices (such as hard disks). The number of times per second that data are read or written to system buffers is shown the lread/s and lwrit/s columns.

The percentage of times data are found in cache (as opposed to having to go to hard disk) is shown in the %rcache and %wcache columns. Finally, the pread/s and pwrit/s columns show the number of times per second transfers are made by means of raw physical device (i.e., read and written in characters, as opposed to blocks of data).

The hard disk activity report (%busy, avque, r+w/s, blks/s, avwait, and avserv) shows the activity of the hard disk devices on your system. The hard disk device name (in this case /dev/sd001) is listed under the device column. If there were other hard disks on the system, they would also be listed for each interval time.

The %busy column shows the percentage of time the hard disk was busy servicing read and write requests. The ratio of total time for all requests to complete to the total time the disk was busy servicing requests (i.e., the average time a request was queued) is reflected in the avque column. The r+w/s column shows the number transfers per second of data between the system and the hard disk.

The blks/s column reflects the number of blocks of data (512 bytes) transferred between the system and the disk per second. The average time that a transfer waits idly on the queue (in milliseconds) is shown in the avwait column. The average time (in milliseconds) it takes the disk to complete a transfer request is shown in the avserv column.

 NOTE **You can use the −R option with the hard disk report (sar −dR) to display the total time the disk was active (%busy column). The avwait and avserv columns are not shown with the −R option.**

The sar Terminal, System Call, Swapping and Switching, and File System Access Reports

The next four reports output by the sar −A command are the terminal, system call, swapping and switching, and file system access reports (see Figure 9.5). You can print these reports individually, with the −y, −c, −w, and −a options to sar, respectively.

FIGURE 9.5

sar *reports: terminal,*
system call, swapping and
switching, and file system
access

```
                                              Terminal
 09:54:02    rawch/s   canch/s   outch/s   rcvin/s   xmtin/s   mdmin/s
 10:00:04        0         0         0         0         0         0
 10:20:02        0         0         0         0         0         0
 10:40:00        0         0         4         0         0         0
 11:00:00        0         0        66         0         0         0
 11:20:01        0         0        52         0         0         0
 Average         0         0        29         0         0         0

 09:54:02    scall/s sread/s swrit/s  fork/s lwpcr/s  exec/s rchar/s wchar/s
 10:00:04       35       6       3     0.09    0.00    0.09    9787      91
 10:20:02       20       3       3     0.01    0.00    0.02     149      83
 10:40:00       34       7       5     0.06    0.00    0.06    1307     848
 11:00:00       51      12       6     0.10    0.00    0.10    2388     791
 11:20:01       30       9       2     0.03    0.00    0.03     241     615
 Average        34       8       4     0.05    0.00    0.05    1633     551

 09:54:02    swpin/s   pswin/s   swpot/s   pswot/s vpswout/s   pswch/s
 10:00:04      0.00      0.0      0.00      0.0       0.0        14
 10:20:02      0.00      0.0      0.00      0.0       0.0        14
 10:40:00      0.00      0.0      0.00      0.0       0.0        16
 11:00:00      0.00      0.0      0.00      0.0       0.0        16
 11:20:01      0.00      0.0      0.00      0.0       0.0        11
 Average       0.00      0.0      0.00      0.0       0.0        14

 09:54:02    iget/s  namei/s  dirbk/s   %dnlc
 10:00:04       0       2        0        98
 10:20:02       0       0        0        76
 10:40:00       0       4        1        91
 11:00:00       0       5        0        94
 11:20:01       0       4        0        99
 Average        0       3        0        94
 ─More─
```

The terminal report (`rawch/s`, `canch/s`, `outch/s`, `rcvin/s`, `xmtin/s`, and `mdmin/s`) shows the activity that goes on with the terminal devices on your system (for example, `/dev/tty00`, `/dev/tty01`, etc.). The `rawch/s` and `outch/s` columns show input and output to terminal devices, respectively. Input characters processed canonically are shown in `canch/s`. Hardware interrupts that are transmitted and received are displayed by `xmtin/s` and `rcvin/s`, respectively. The `mdmin/s` column shows modem interrupts.

The system call report (`scall/s`, `sread/s`, `swrit/s`, `fork/s`, `lwpcr/s`, `exec/s`, `rchar/s`, and `wchar/s`) shows how many of the most basic UNIX system calls were run per second. The total number of system calls is shown under the `scall/s` column.

The number of read, write, fork and exec system calls are shown in the `sread/s`, `swrit/s`, `fork/s`, and `exec/s` columns. The number of characters read by the read system call and written by the write system call are shown under the `rchar/s` and `wchar/s` column, respectively.

The system swapping and switching report (`swpin/s`, `pswin/s`, `swpot/s`, `pswot/s`, `vpswout/s`, and `pswch/s`) reports on transfers from memory to swap space. Swap space is the area on a hard disk where data that doesn't fit in memory is stored temporarily until it is needed again.

The `swpin/s` and `swpot/s` columns report the number of transfers to and from swap space. The number of pages transferred for swapins and swapouts is shown in the `pswin/s` and `pswot/s` columns, respectively. The `vpswout/s` column shows the total number of virtual pages transferred because of swapouts. The `pswch/s` column shows process switches.

The file system access report (`iget/s`, `namei/s`, `dirbk/s`, and `%dnlc`) displays activities relating to system routines that access the file system. The `iget/s` column shows the number of files from S%, SFS, and UFS file systems that are located by inode entry. The number of file system path searches is shown in the `namei/s` column. The number of S5 file system directory block reads issued is shown in the `dirblk/s` column. The `%dnlc` column shows the number of times the directory name lookup cache is hit (i.e., information is found there instead of the request having to go to the hard disk).

The sar Run Queue, System Tables, and File System Type Reports

The next three reports output by the sar -A command are run queue, system tables, and file system type reports (see Figure 9.6). You can print these reports individually, with the -q, -v, and -t options to sar, respectively.

FIGURE 9.6

sar reports: run queue,

system tables, and file

system type

```
┌──────────────────────────────────── Terminal ──────────────────────────────┐
│ 09:54:02    prunq %prunocc     runq %runocc    swpq %swpocc                  │
│ 10:00:04                       2.0   100                                     │
│ 10:20:02                       2.0   100                                     │
│ 10:40:00     1.0        0      2.0   100                                     │
│ 11:00:00     2.3        0      2.0   100                                     │
│ 11:20:01                       2.0   100                                     │
│ Average      1.6        0      2.0   100                                     │
│                                                                              │
│ 09:54:02 proc-sz fail lpw-sz fail  inod-sz fail   file-sz fail   lock-sz     │
│ 10:00:04  35/400  0   0/66   0     183/4000  0    224/     0     7/          │
│ 10:20:02  35/400  0   0/66   0     183/4000  0    224/     0     7/          │
│ 10:40:00  44/400  0   0/75   0     205/4000  0    247/     0     8/          │
│ 11:00:00  50/400  0   0/81   0     211/4000  0    267/     0     8/          │
│ 11:20:01  50/400  0   0/81   0     208/4000  0    267/     0     8/          │
│ Average   42/400  0   0/73   0     198/4000  0    245/     0     7/          │
│                                                                              │
│ 09:54:02 file system    inodes inuse   alloc   limit   fail    %ipf          │
│ 10:00:04 s5                 0           0       0       0      100           │
│          sfs/ufs            0           0       0       0      100           │
│          vxfs             183         555    4000       0       50           │
│          other              0           0       0       0      100           │
│                                                                              │
│ 10:20:02 s5                 0           0       0       0      100           │
│          sfs/ufs            0           0       0       0      100           │
│          vxfs             183         492    4000       0       50           │
│          other              0           0       0       0      100           │
│                                                                              │
│ 10:40:00 s5                 0           0       0       0      100           │
│          sfs/ufs            0           0       0       0      100           │
│          vxfs             205         462    4000       0       46           │
│          other              0           0       0       0      100           │
│                                                                              │
│ 11:00:00 s5                 0           0       0       0      100           │
│          sfs/ufs            0           0       0       0      100           │
│          vxfs             211         236    4000       0       44           │
│          other              0           0       0       0      100           │
│                                                                              │
│ 11:20:01 s5                 0           0       0       0      100           │
│          sfs/ufs            0           0       0       0      100           │
│          vxfs             208         222    4000       0       43           │
│          other              0           0       0       0      100           │
│                                                                              │
│ Average   s5                0           0       0       0      100           │
│          sfs/ufs            0           0       0       0      100           │
│          vxfs             198         393    4000       0       45           │
│          other              0           0       0       0      100           │
│ ─More─                                                                       │
└──────────────────────────────────────────────────────────────────────────┘
```

The run queue report (`prunq`, `%prunocc`, `runq`, `%runocc`, `swpq`, and `%swpocc`) shows how long requests wait in the run queue. The `prunq` column shows the size of the processor private queue that is in memory and ready to run. The percentage of time the processor private run queue is occupied is shown in the `%prunocc` column. The `runq` column shows the size of the run queue of processes in memory that are ready to run. You must use the `-p` option for the `prunq` and `%prunocc` columns to display any queue information.

The percentage of time the run queue is occupied is shown in the `%runocc` column. The `swpq` column shows the average number of processes in the swap queue when occupied. The `%swpocc` column shows the percentage of time there were processes in the swap queue. If there were no processes in the queue during the interval period, `swpq` and `%swpocc` are empty.

The system tables report (`proc-sz`, `fail`, `lpw-sz`, `fail`, `inod-sz`, `fail`, `file-sz`, `fail`, and `lock-sz`) shows the status of various system tables. The entries and sizes for each table are separated by a slash (/). The tables reported on are process (`proc-sz`), lightweight process (`lpw-sz`), inode (`inod-sz`), file (`file-sz`), and file and record locking (`lock-sz`) tables. A fail column next to each table column shows any overflows that occur for each table.

The file system type report (`file system`, `inodes inuse`, `alloc`, `limit`, `fail`, and `%ipf`) displays statistics for the different file system types that exist on your UNIX system. Information is reported for the System V (s5), sfs/ufs, and Veritas (vxfs) types. The `file system` column notes either `s5`, `sfs/ufs`, `vxfs`, or `other` file system types.

The `inodes inuse` column shows the number of inodes for each file system type that are currently in use by processes. The number of in-use and free inode table entries that are currently allocated is shown in the `alloc` column. The `limit` column shows the maximum number of inodes that can be allocated (though the number can be bumped up if necessary). The `fail` column shows the number of times the system tried, but failed, to allocate an inode. The `%ipf` column shows the percentage of inodes with reusable pages that were removed from the free list by an `iget` call.

The sar Message and Semaphore, Page Fault, Page Request, and Unused Memory Reports

The next four reports output by the sar -A command are message and semaphore, page faults, page request, and unused memory reports (see Figure 9.7). You can print these reports individually, with the -m, -p, -g, and -r options to sar, respectively.

```
                                          Terminal                                    □  □
             sfs/ufs            0             0        0        0      100
             vxfs              211           236     4000        0       44
             other              0             0        0        0      100

11:20:01 s5                     0             0        0        0      100
             sfs/ufs            0             0        0        0      100
             vxfs              208           222     4000        0       43
             other              0             0        0        0      100

Average  s5                     0             0        0        0      100
             sfs/ufs            0             0        0        0      100
             vxfs              198           393     4000        0       45
             other              0             0        0        0      100


09:54:02     msg    sema
10:00:04    0.00    0.00
10:20:02    0.00    0.00
10:40:00    0.00    0.00
11:00:00    0.00    0.00
11:20:01    0.00    0.00
Average     0.00    0.00

09:54:02  atch/s atfree/s atmiss/s pgin/s  ppgin/s  pflt/s  vflt/s slock/s
10:00:04    1.36    0.07    0.15    0.05    0.07    1.22    0.64    0.00
10:20:02    0.27    0.04    0.04    0.02    0.03    0.21    0.16    0.00
10:40:00    2.52    0.22    0.63    0.47    0.67    1.40    1.45    0.00
11:00:00    4.12    0.41    0.71    0.39    0.62    2.39    1.86    0.06
11:20:01    0.58    0.09    0.08    0.06    0.11    0.47    0.30    0.00
Average     1.84    0.18    0.35    0.22    0.34    1.13    0.92    0.02

09:54:02  pgout/s ppgout/s  vfree/s  pfree/s  vscan/s
10:00:04    0.00    0.00    0.00    0.00    0.00
10:20:02    0.00    0.00    0.00    0.00    0.00
10:40:00    0.00    0.00    0.00    0.00    0.00
11:00:00    0.02    0.04    1.32    0.13   12.04
11:20:01    0.00    0.00    0.00    0.00    0.00
Average     0.00    0.01    0.31    0.03    2.81

09:54:02  freemem freeswap
10:00:04    2859    19329
10:20:02    2939    19267
10:40:00    2659    19069
11:00:00     994    17584
11:20:01     973    17407
Average     1955    18391

—More—
```

The message and semaphore report (msg and sema) shows the number of message and semaphore primitives sent per second.

The page fault report (atch/s, atfree/s, atmiss/s, pgin/s, ppgin/s, pflt/s, vflt/s, and slock/s) displays information on page faults. The atch/s and atfree/s columns show page faults that are satisfied by reclaiming a page currently in memory or by a page on the free list, respectively.

The atmiss/s column shows page faults, per second, that are not fulfilled by a page-in memory. Page-in requests per second are shown in the pgin/s column. The ppgin/s column shows the number of pages paged in per second. Page faults from protection errors are in the pflt/s column. Address translation page faults are in the vflt/s column. Faults caused by software lock requests requiring physical I/O are shown in the slock/s column.

The page request report (pgout/s, ppgout/s, vfree/s, pfree/s, and vscan/s) shows paging activity relating to the page-stealing daemon. The pgout/s and ppgout/s columns show the number of page-out requests and the number pages actually paged out per second, respectively. The vfree/s column shows the virtual pages per second placed on the free list by the page-stealing daemon, while the pfree/s column shows the physical pages per second placed on the free list by the daemon. The vscan/s column shows the virtual pages per second scanned by the daemon.

The unused memory report (freemem and freeswap) show the available memory and swap space on the system. The freemem column shows the pages of memory available to user processes. The freeswap column shows the disk blocks available for page swapping.

The sar Kernel Memory Allocation (KMA) Report

The final report output by the sar -A command is the kernel memory allocation report (see Figure 9.8). You can print this report individually, with the -k option to sar.

FIGURE 9.8

sar *report: kernel memory*
allocation

```
┌──────────────────────────── Terminal ──────────────────────┐
│ 09:54:02 size        mem      alloc       succ      fail     │
│ 10:00:04    16      81920      80608      51439        0      │
│             32      69632      53344      45684        0      │
│             64      86016      15680      13232        0      │
│            128     122880      84608      69354        0      │
│            256     147456     139776     109770        0      │
│            512      24576       7168       6720        0      │
│           1024     221184     208896     207876        0      │
│           2048    1163264    1142784    1141232        0      │
│           4096     147456     110592      96640        0      │
│           8192      98304      81920      68016        0      │
│            176     102400      95040      88388        0      │
│             80      53248      46320      39481        0      │
│           1360      61440      51680      49768        0      │
│            336      32768      29568      28661        0      │
│            672     811008     383040     375112        0      │
│           Ovsz          0     573440     548592        0      │
│           Total   3223552    3104464    2939965        0      │
│                                                              │
│ 10:20:02    16      81920      80608      51439        0      │
│             32      69632      53344      45684        0      │
│             64      86016      15744      13288        0      │
│            128     122880      84608      69394        0      │
│            256     147456     139776     109770        0      │
│            512      24576       7168       6720        0      │
│           1024     225280     212992     211972        0      │
│           2048    1175552    1157120    1155568        0      │
│           4096     147456     110592      96640        0      │
│           8192      98304      81920      68016        0      │
│            176     102400      95392      88708        0      │
│             80      53248      46320      39481        0      │
│           1360      61440      51680      49768        0      │
│            336      32768      29904      28949        0      │
│            672     811008     340704     333532        0      │
│           Ovsz          0     573440     548592        0      │
│           Total   3239936    3081312    2917521        0      │
│                                                              │
│ 10:40:00    16      98304      85360      54690        0      │
│             32      69632      61056      52476        0      │
│             64      86016      26880      21756        0      │
│            128     122880      95488      78378        0      │
│            256     163840     147200     116118        0      │
│            512      24576       8192       7688        0      │
│           1024     282624     268288     267024        0      │
│           2048    1507328    1497088    1495536        0      │
│ ─More─                                                       │
└──────────────────────────────────────────────────────────────┘
```

The kernel memory allocation report (`size`, `mem`, `alloc`, `succ`, `fail`) shows the kernel memory used and allocated for each size allocated. The size column shows the different sized memory pools, in bytes, that have buffers allocated on the system. Buffer pools allocated by the system run in order from 16 to 8192, with the oversize buffer pool noted as Ovsz. Those allocated by individual applications are also shown in the example (176, 80, 1360, 336, and 672).

The mem column shows the amount of memory, in bytes, that is allocated for the pool, and alloc is the number of bytes allocated from that pool. The memory that was requested and allocated successfully is shown in the succ column. Those requests that failed are noted in the fail column.

SYSTEM MONITORING WITH THE rtpm COMMAND

The real-time performance monitor command, rtpm, provides a graphical and text-based display for performance monitoring that doesn't require you to have the X Window System running. The rtpm command was created using the *curses* library functions, which allows it to display on most dumb character terminals. Though rtpm can run on the console, a virtual terminal, or a dumb terminal, the output of rtpm is referred to in this section as the rtpm window.

Like the System Monitor window, rtpm lets you graphically present performance data as it happens. Though rtpm doesn't let you show as many performance variables graphically at a time as the System Monitor window, it does provide much more text-based information that is continuously updated. To graphically display any text-based variable graphically, move the cursor to the variable and press Enter. A moving bar or line graph of that variable appears at the top of the window.

To start the rtpm command, become the root user and type rtpm from the shell command line. There are two options you can use with rtpm if you choose. The −h *history_buffer_size* option defines how many history data points rtpm saves for plotting the data. By default, rtpm saves one data point for each column in the display. The other option is simply an integer representing the number of seconds between each data sample. By default, this interval is 2 seconds.

We do not recommend using an interval of 1 second. The information you get is no more useful than that gathered at 2-second intervals and the tool itself can begin to drag on system performance.

NOTE

Once you type the rtpm command, a display appears that is similar to the one shown in Figure 9.9.

FIGURE 9.9

The rtpm window

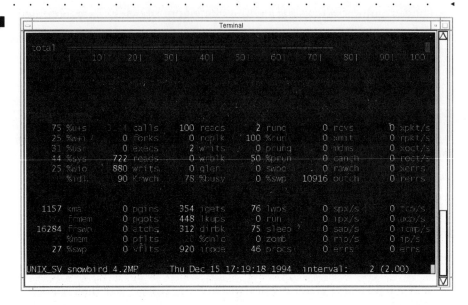

Sections of the rtpm Window

There are three sections of the rtpm window. The top of the window is where performance data runs across the window in bar graphs or line graphs like a stock ticker. In the middle, the text-based performance information appears and is updated at the set interval. The bottom line of the window is a status line. The status line contains basic information, such as the system's name, the date/time stamp, the interval you set for collecting performance data, and the actual interval used. (If the UNIX system is running slowly, the actual interval will be longer than the set interval.)

The top of the window can have up to two data options plotting data across the window for a normal 80-character display. By default, the data displayed is the percentage of user time and system time. If yours is a multiprocessor system, data appears for each CPU that is active on your system.

In the middle of the window, you start out with 12 categories of information displayed in text format. Each category has five or six entries associated with it. At every interval (by default, 2 seconds) the number to the left of each entry is updated. The number reflects, for the interval period, either the number of times an event occurred or the percentage of time the resource was used (or not used). The exception is error totals, which accumulate over the entire time `rtpm` is running.

The following is a list of the 12 categories on the `rtpm` window and what they contain:

- **CPU.** For each central processing unit, you can see statistics that reflect how busy the processor is. This information is shown as a percentage of consumption. The `%usr` and `%sys` entries reflect the amount of the CPU's time that is consumed by processing requests from user space (applications and utilities) and kernel space (within the operating system), respectively. The `%u+s` entry shows the total of these two numbers. The `%wio` is the percentage of time the CPU is waiting for input or output from the disk and `%idl` is the percentage of time the CPU is idle because there are no requests waiting for the CPU. The `%w+i` shows the percentage of time during the interval that the CPU is inactive (this is the sum of the `%wio` and `%idl` values).

- **MEMORY.** Statistics under this heading show you how the RAM (random access memory, the physical memory) and swap space (the area on the hard disk that is used when data overflows the RAM) are being consumed. The `kma` is the number of 4KB pages of memory currently in use by the kernel memory allocator, while `frmem` is the number of free memory pages. The `frswp` is the number of pages of free swap space available and the `%swp` shows the percentage of swap space currently being used. The `%mem` shows the total percentage of memory currently in use.

- **CALL/s.** This heading lists some of the basic system call activities (requests for services in the kernel). The `calls` entry shows the total number of system calls made during the interval period. The `forks` and `execs` entries show the number of fork and exec calls made per second. The `reads` and `writs` entries show the number of read and write calls per second, respectively. The total number of characters read and written per second (in KB) is shown in the `Krwch` entry.

▸ **PAGING/s.** Each time a page of data is accessed from the hard disk, statistics are incremented under this heading. The `pgins` and `pgots` show the number of pages per second that are written to or read from the disk. The number of `atchs` represent the number of times per second that pages are found in cache memory and attached, rather than having to go to the hard disk. The `pflts` entry shows the number of protection faults and the `vflts` entry shows the number of validity faults per second.

▸ **IO/s.** This heading shows the number of operations performed on the hard disk. The `reads` and `writs` show how many read and write operations are done per second. Likewise, `rdblk` and `wrblk` are the number of disk blocks read and written per second, respectively. The instantaneous queue length is reflected by the value of `qlen`. The `%busy` value shows the percentage of time the hard disk was busy. You can display each of these values for all hard disks on the system.

▸ **FILESYS/s.** Operations relating to file system activities are reflected in this heading. The `igets` value is the number of inode get operations. The `lkups` is the number of file table lookups. The `dirbk` entry is the number of directory block reads per second. The `%dnlc` shows the percentage of time a file or directory name is found in the directory name lookup cache. (If the `%dnlc` is low, system performance may slow because of having to go to the hard disk too often to resolve directory lookups.) The `inode` entry reflects the number of inodes currently in use.

▸ **QUEUE.** These statistics describe process switching and queuing information. The `runq` is the mean length of the run queue. The percentage of time the run queue was occupied is shown in the `%run` value. The length of the processor local run queue is shown in `prunq` value, while the length of time the processor local run queue was occupied is represented by `%prun`. The mean length of the swap queue is shown in `swpq` and the percentage of time the swap queue was occupied is reflected in `%swp`.

▶ LWPS. Process and light weight process statistics are under this heading. The `lwps` entry shows the total number of light weight processes. The `run` value is the number of runable light weight processes. Sleep light weight processes are shown in `sleep`, and zombie processes are shown in `zomb`. The total number of processes in the system is shown in `procs`.

▶ TTY/s. These statistics reflect activity between terminals and the system. The `rcvs` heading shows the number of receiver interrupts per second. The number of transmitter interrupts per second is displayed by the `xmit` value. Modem interrupts per second are shown in the `mdms` value. The number of canonical characters written to terminals per second is shown in `canch`, while the number of raw characters written is reflected by `rawch`. Finally, the number of output characters to the terminal per second is shown in `outch`.

▶ NETWARE. Under this heading are statistics relating to NetWare protocol activities. Each of the following represents the number of packets transferred for each protocol: SPX packets (`spx/s`), IPX packets (`ipx/s`), SAP packets (`sap/s`), and RIP packets (`rip/s`). The `errs` entry shows the number of failed transfer requests for all protocols.

▶ ETHER. These statistics relate to Ethernet activities. They can help you judge the amount of activity on your Ethernet network and see if too much traffic is causing errors. The Ethernet packets transferred and received are listed under `xpkt/s` and `rpkt/s`, respectively. Ethernet octets transferred and received are shown under `xoct/s` and `roct/s`, respectively. Total transfer and receive errors are listed under `xerrs` and `rerrs`, respectively.

▶ TCP/IP. Activities concerning TCP/IP are covered under this heading. There are separate headings to display the number of packets transferred (per second) by each protocol that make up the TCP/IP protocol suite. They include the TCP (`tcp/s`), UDP (`upd/s`), ICMP (`icmp/s`), and IP (`ip/s`) protocols. The number of packet transfer errors is listed under `errs`.

Most of these headings have more than five or six metrics (statistical measurements) associated with them. Also, the metrics associated with each heading may be available for multiple CPUs or hard disks. To change the display from showing the twelve headings to showing all data relating to a particular heading, move the cursor so the heading is highlighted and press Enter. The middle portion of the window displays all the data for the heading.

Interpreting Colors on the rtpm Window

If system activity changes as you run `rtpm`, you'll notice that some numbers change color as their values go up or down. These colors tell you whether the number is in an acceptable range, has become dangerously high (or low), or has exceeded acceptable limits.

In the top of the window, safe levels are green, dangerous levels are yellow, and excessive levels are red. For the middle of the window, safe levels are white, dangerous are yellow, and excessive are red.

Notice that error totals are red and remain that color. If the system is running very slowly, you may notice that entries under the CPU heading (for example, `%u+s`) or the MEMORY heading (for example `%mem`) turn red. This indicates that you are overloading your CPU or running out of RAM. If these cases are persistent, you need to think about upgrading your hardware. Other recurring yellow or red conditions may need to reallocate the resources you have by tuning your system (see "Understanding Monitoring Data" later in the chapter for further information).

Manipulating the rtpm Window

From the keyboard, you can move around the `rtpm` window and change the information that is displayed in the top or middle of the window.

To move the cursor so it highlights different entries in the middle of the window, you can use arrow keys, vi-style cursor movement, or emacs-style cursor movement. (vi and emacs are popular UNIX text editors.) Use the h, j, k, or l keys (vi-style) or ^f, ^b, ^p, or ^n (emacs-style) to move the cursor keys to the entry you are interested in.

Once an entry in the middle of the window you are interested in is highlighted, press either the space bar or the Enter key. If, instead, a header is highlighted, the middle of the window fills with metrics relating to that header. If an entry under the header is highlighted, a running graph of the entry appears at the top of the window.

If you selected a header (i.e., the center of the window displays only metrics for the header), you can redisplay the main window by pressing the Escape key. If you selected an entry under the heading, you can change whether the entry (which is now shown in graph form at the top of the window) is shown as a bar graph or a line graph by typing the letter p. Typing p toggles between the bar graph and line graph. You can clear all data from the top of the window by pressing the c key.

To change the sampling interval (which is two seconds, by default), press the + or − keys. The + key increases the interval by one second; the − key reduces the interval by one second.

UNDERSTANDING MONITORING DATA

It's nice to watch all the system monitoring numbers run across your screen, but they are not very valuable unless you use them to improve the performance of your system. CPUs, memory, and hard disk subsystems each have finite limits on what they can handle. Using the data from UNIX monitoring tools, you can see if these or other areas are being overloaded.

Because the performance monitoring tools described in this chapter measure many of the same items, the information in this section applies to any of them (System Monitor window, sar command, or rtpm command). For the examples, however, we are using the rtpm window because this is the easiest way to see many metrics at the same time.

To follow along with the examples in this section, you should open two Terminal windows. In one of the Terminal windows (which should be at least 80 characters wide), obtain root permissions by typing su and (when prompted) the root password. Type rtpm. The rtpm window appears, as shown in Figure 9.10.

F I G U R E   9.10

Displaying the rtpm window

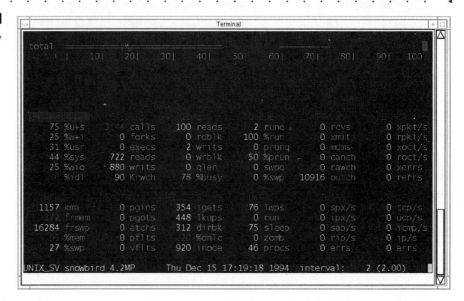

The following sections describe how some of the common performance problems that can occur on your system are reflected in the data that appear on the rtpm window.

Overloading the CPU

There are several indications that your system slowing down may be caused by overloading requests for processor time. Under the CPU heading on the rtpm window, the %u+s value may stay around 100%. This shows that the processor is constantly busy and is the first indication that you may be overloading the CPU.

The fact that the CPU is busy near its capacity, however, doesn't mean that your system is CPU-bound (i.e., keeping your applications from processing). For example, a continously running process, such as a screen saver or a statistical gathering package, may be keeping the CPU constantly busy. But if another process comes along that has equal or higher priority, the CPU may be freed up quickly for that process.

So how can you tell if your processor can't handle the load you are putting on it? Look at the QUEUE heading. If there are a lot of jobs waiting in the run queue (see the runq value), it probably means the processor isn't handling things fast enough.

Besides having too many processes, another problem that can cause CPU overload is having very high priority processes running. Most processes on the system are designated as time-sharing processes (TS). TS processes are those that have basically the same shot at the CPU. The average system will also have some fixed class processes (FC). FC processes run at a higher priority and keep TS processes from getting processor time.

For example, the X server process (/usr/X/bin/X) runs in fixed class mode. If you were to run the command ps -ef | grep FC while the UnixWare Desktop was running, you would see something like the output shown in Figure 9.11.

In Figure 9.11 you can see that the command is a fixed class process by the FC shown in the CLS column (the scheduling class for the process). You can see that the X process has consumed 5 minutes and 44 seconds worth of CPU time. If you are doing a lot of work from the Desktop, the X server activity might keep time sharing processes from getting much CPU time. If there are other FC processes running on your system, the system might

```
                                        Terminal
$ ps -ef|grep FC
    UID    PID  PPID  CLS PRI  C    STIME TTY       TIME COMD
   spike  3828  3826   FC  80  0 20:49:45 vt01      5:44 X :0 -xnetaccess on
$ []
```

F I G U R E 9.11

Displaying a fixed class

process

become very slow. Some specially configured systems also may have real time processes (RT) running. Those processes basically take over the CPU.

Running Short of Memory

Having too little memory (RAM) is one of the major reasons for slow system performance. If the system is actively using more memory than it has in RAM, it must move the data it needs back and forth between swap space on the hard disk and RAM.

Though the minimum amount of RAM for UnixWare is 8MB, if you get 32MB of RAM you'll probably be a lot happier. In particular, graphical and heavy computational applications will gobble up your RAM very quickly.

In your `rtpm` window, look under the MEMORY heading. The `%mem` value may very well be in the 90% to 100% range if you are running the Desktop. To understand if that's a problem, however, it helps to understand how memory is handled in UNIX.

Information that is placed in RAM for running processes comes in several forms. When you start an application, its code is read into RAM from the hard disk so the code is ready to run. This part of the application, which doesn't change, is called the *text* area. The other part of the application in RAM is *data*. The data portion may change during processing.

When UNIX needs space in RAM, but RAM is full, UNIX can throw away any pages of information that are no longer needed. It can also look at text and data pages in RAM that are not busy at the moment. Any text pages can be discarded and retrieved later from the original code on the hard disk. Any data pages that have not been modified can be thrown out if they haven't been modified, or copied to *swap* space if they have been modified. Modified data can be retrieved from swap and returned to RAM as needed.

The point is that just because your memory appears full, it doesn't mean you're going to have performance problems. Performance problems occur when there is a lot of swapping. So, more important than MEMORY information in `rtpm` is the PAGING information. Watch the `pgots` (paging out to swap or disk) and `pgins` (paging in from swap or disk). Also, `vflts` (validity faults) shows how often the system tries to load a page from RAM and fails because it is not present. A lot of page faults mean the system probably has to get the page from disk or swap.

If you find you are doing a lot of swapping, there are a few ways to fix the problem. Adding RAM is probably the best idea. Also, you should find and restrict applications that are taking up a lot of space in memory. (To do this, type `ps -efl | pg` and compare the size of running processes in the `SZ` column.) Or, if you're a real kernel hacker, you could try to reduce the amount of memory allocated to the kernel (shown in 4K pages in the `kma` value) by changing tunable parameters to free up more memory for applications.

Slow Disk Response

To check if you are having performance problems due to slow hard disk response, look at the I/O column of the `rtpm` window. By moving the cursor to the I/O heading and pressing Enter, you can see information for every hard disk on your system.

The first thing you look for is the `%busy` entry. If the hard disk is continuously busy, you may have a problem. The `reads` and `writs` values will also appear high if the disk is very busy.

In general, the best you can do if your disk is overloaded is to spread the load across several hard disks (possibly by moving user accounts to other hard disks) or to move the hard disk that is being heavily accessed to another computer.

Managing Processes

Every application, utility, daemon, or kernel process running concurrently on your system must battle against each other for processor time. If you have many users on your system, or if you are simply running a lot of processes, and you notice the system response slowing down, you may be able to speed things up by managing the process table.

A process is a running instance of a program. In UNIX, you can view the processes that you and other users are running on the system by using the ps command. To display a list of the processes running on your system, type ps -ef | pg. An example of output from this command is shown in Figure 9.12.

In Figure 9.12, the -e option to ps displays every process on the system, while the -f option displays a full listing. Because there is probably more than a pageful of processes running, we pipe the output to the pg command (| pg) so you can go through the output one page at a time.

In this example, we are running UnixWare with only one user logged in (spike). Even if the only thing the user is doing at the moment is running the ps command from a Terminal window, you can see a lot of other activity

```
Terminal
$ ps -ef|pg
   UID   PID  PPID  CLS PRI  C    STIME TTY      TIME COMD
  root     0     0  SYS  79  0 21:14:41 ?        0:03 sysproc
  root     1     0   TS  70  0 21:14:41 ?        0:01 /sbin/init
  root   277     1   TS  80  0 21:15:42 ?        0:00 /usr/sbin/rpcbind
  smtp   254     1   TS  80  0 21:15:40 ?        0:00 /usr/lib/mail/surrcmd/smtpd
  root    71     1   TS  88  0 21:15:00 ?        0:00 /usr/lib/mousemgr
   bin   196     1   TS  80  0 21:15:27 ?        0:01 /usr/X/bin/fs
 spike   232   229   TS  70  0 21:15:35 ?        0:00 /usr/X/bin/xdm
  root   302     1   TS  80  0 21:15:43 ?        0:00 /usr/lib/nfs/biod
 spike   438     1   TS  80  0 21:17:42 ?        0:00 mwm -xrm *showFeedback: -kill
  root   218     1   TS  80  0 21:15:30 ?        0:00 /usr/sbin/in.routed -q
 spike   230   229   FC  49  0 21:15:32 vt01     6:33 /usr/X/bin/X -xnetaccess on -auth /dev/X/A:0-a0003-

  root   229     1   TS  80  0 21:15:32 ?        0:00 /usr/X/bin/xdm
  root   343     1   TS  80  0 21:15:46 ?        0:00 hostmibd
  root   257     1   TS  80  0 21:15:41 ?        0:00 in.snmpd
  root   280     1   TS  80  0 21:15:42 ?        0:00 /usr/lib/netsvc/rwall/rpc.rwalld
  root   271     1   TS  80  0 21:15:42 ?        0:00 cat /dev/osm
  root   282     1   TS  80  0 21:15:43 ?        0:00 /usr/lib/netsvc/rusers/rpc.rusersd
  root   284     1   TS  80  0 21:15:43 ?        0:00 /usr/lib/netsvc/spray/rpc.sprayd
  root   303     1   TS  80  0 21:15:43 ?        0:00 /usr/lib/nfs/nfsd -a
  root . 306     1   TS  80  0 21:15:43 ?        0:00 /usr/lib/nfs/nfsd -a
  root   317     1   TS  80  0 21:15:44 console  0:00 /usr/lib/saf/ttymon -g -v -p Console Login: -d /de
v/syscon -l console
  root   316     1   TS  85  0 21:15:44 ?        0:00 /usr/lib/saf/sac -t 300
  root   305     1   TS  80  0 21:15:43 ?        0:00 /usr/lib/nfs/mountd
  root   309     1   TS  80  0 21:15:43 ?        0:00 /usr/lib/nfs/statd
  root   308     1   TS  80  0 21:15:43 ?        0:00 /usr/lib/nfs/pcnfsd
  root   304     1   TS  80  0 21:15:43 ?        0:00 /usr/lib/nfs/bootparamd
  root   310     1   TS  80  0 21:15:43 ?        0:00 /usr/lib/nfs/lockd
 spike   404   232   TS  70  0 21:17:39 ?        0:00 -ksh
 spike  1075  1074   TS  70  0 10:14:29 pts/4    0:00 ksh
  root   326   316   TS  80  0 21:15:45 ?        0:00 /usr/sbin/inetd
  root   335     1   TS  80  0 21:15:45 ?        0:00 /usr/sbin/keymaster -n
  root   336   316   TS  80  0 21:15:46 ?        0:00 /usr/lib/saf/listen -m inet/tcp0 tcp 2>/dev/null
  root   337     1   TS  80  0 21:15:46 ?        0:00 /usr/sbin/cron
  root   340     1   TS  80  0 21:15:46 ?        0:00 /usr/sbin/cs
 spike   420   404   TS  80  0 21:17:40 ?        0:06 /usr/X/bin/dtm
  root   356     1   TS  80  0 21:15:48 ?        0:00 /usr/lib/lpsched
  root   362   356   TS  80  0 21:15:48 ?        0:00 lpNet
 spike   429     1   TS  80  0 21:17:41 ?        0:00 colorserver
 spike   436     1   TS  80  0 21:17:42 ?        0:00 dsdm
 spike  1074     1   TS  80  0 10:14:28 ?        0:00 /home/spike/Applications/Terminal -T Terminal
 spike  1084  1075   TS  59  0 10:15:42 pts/4    0:00 ksh
 spike   917     1   TS  80  0 09:31:21 ?        0:00 /usr/X/bin/xidlelock
 spike  1083  1075   TS  59  0 10:15:42 pts/4    0:00 ps -ef
(EOF):
```

is going on. The processes shown in this output basically fall into four categories: system processes, networking processes, GUI processes, and the user's processes.

When UNIX first starts up, it initiates some processes that must always be running. The `init` process is what is responsible for starting up all the other system background processes on the system. Most of those background processes are owned by the root user (UID column). And, in our case, the daemon processes that handle networking requests are owned by root.

The standard UNIX daemons shown running here include `cron` (the daemon that starts up process requests set to run at a particular time) and `lpsched` (which schedules printer requests). Any processes beginning with `/usr/lib/nfs` relate to Network File System features (i.e., mounting and sharing directories with remote systems). Other networking processes include the `rpcbind`, `smtpd`, `in.routed`, `hostmibd`, `in.snmpd`, `rcp.rwalld`, `rpc.rusersd`, `rpc.sprayd`, `sac`, `inetd`, `listen`, `cs`, and `lpNet` daemons.

Most of the other processes shown here relate to the user's graphical user interface and whatever processes the user is running. For example, `fs` handles screen fonts, `mousemgr` controls the mouse driver, `colorserver` works with the screen colors. Basic GUI functions are done by `xdm` (X display manager), `mwm` (Motif window manager), `dtm` (Desktop manager), `dsdm` (drag-and-drop manager), and `X` (the main X server process).

The user in this case has a Terminal window open in which the `ps -ef` command is run. The terminal lock program is also turned on in the background to lock the screen after a set idle time.

There are two points to this discussion. The first is that you should understand that there is a lot happening on the system that can impact performance even though you are not requesting those things directly. The other is that, when we describe later how to kill runaway processes you need to be careful about what you kill. Killing the wrong process can blow away an entire set of features.

For example, you'll notice that the X process (`/usr/X/bin/X`) gobbles up a lot of CPU time (see the TIME column). But if you kill that process, your entire GUI, your Terminal windows, and any other processes run from the GUI are killed. Or, as another example, killing the wrong nfs process can make NFS unusable.

So, as a rule, try to understand what processes should normally be running on your system.

SEARCHING FOR RUNAWAY PROCESSES

When you are looking for the cause of performance problems on a multi-user UNIX system, the best way to begin is to see what processes users are running. It's possible that an errant user kicked off a background process that is spinning away without the user even knowing it. Or a user may be doing something that may be better done at another time.

In the old days of UNIX, programmers compiling large programs or users formatting large documents using the troff or nroff commands would often be the culprits when system performance began to drag. Today, GUI programs tend to be the larger resource hogs. Spreadsheet and word processing applications can be big drains on the CPU and even bigger drains on systems with limited RAM.

Using the ps -ef command, as shown earlier, you can list all the processes that are running on the system. Check the TIME column for CPU times in excess of one minute. Check the STIME column for when the process started. If it seems to have grabbed a lot of CPU time in a short period of clock time, you have a potential for a runaway process.

In most cases, the best course of action is to contact the user and find out if there is a problem. In some cases, you can recommend that some programs be run at times when the system is less busy. For example, you might suggest that very large file transfers or database report generators be run at night when the system is not busy.

If you do find a runaway process, however, you kill that process using the kill command. Type kill -9 *PID*, where *PID* is replaced by the process ID for the process. The process ID is listed in the PID column of your ps output.

USING THE timex COMMAND TO REPORT ON A PROCESS

If you are interested in how long a particular command takes to execute, you can run the command with the `timex` command. The `timex` command reports the amount of total clock time a command takes to execute, as well as the amount of user and system time it takes.

An example of the `timex` command is shown below. This example shows the time it takes to execute an `nroff` command to format a midsize document.

```
$ timex /usr/ucb/nroff -mm doc > doc.out

real      24.31
user      17.39
sys        0.55

$
```

The command took 24.31 seconds to complete. It took most of its time in user space (17.39 seconds) and used only 0.55 seconds of time in system space.

A good option to use with the `timex` command is the `-s` option. With `-s`, you not only report on the time used by the command, you also get a `sar` report that shows activity on the entire system during the time the command was executed. This is a good way to get an indication if the system is being dragged on while you are running the command.

Console Monitoring

One of the problems with using a UNIX graphical user interface on a PC is that messages intended for the system console may become lost while the GUI is running. System console messages alert you of such things as write errors to your hard disk or problems reaching the network.

UnixWare has a window available on the Desktop that lets you monitor most of the messages intended for the console monitor. The window is called the Message Monitor window. In particular, the window shows you those messages, that are directed to the operating system messages file (/dev/osm). (These messages are also stored in the file named /var/adm/log/osmlog.)

One advantage of the Message Monitor window is that you don't have to have the full window displayed for it to be useful. You can set the window so that when it is iconized and a new message comes in, the icon changes to alert you of the new message.

To open the System Monitor window in UnixWare, first open the Applications folder from the UnixWare Desktop Window. Then double-click on the Msg Monitor icon. A window appears, as shown in Figure 9.13.

The first messages that appear on the Message Monitor window are those that relate to the system starting up normally. After that, most messages will relate to problems being encountered on the system.

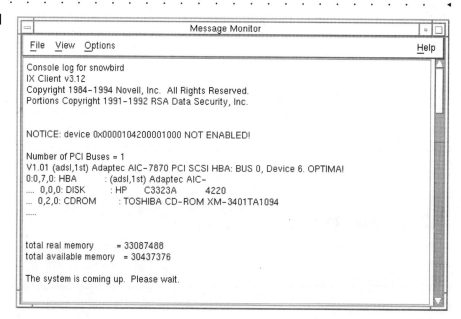

The best way to use the Message Monitor window is to set one of the options to have it alert you when a message comes in. Click on the Options button, then click on one of the following options: Deiconify, Flash, Color Change, or Off.

If you select the Deiconify option, when a message comes in while the Message Monitor is iconified, the Message Monitor window opens to its full size again. If you select Flash, the small balloons on the iconized window blink when a message comes in. The Color Change option causes the icon to change to a solid color when a message comes in. The Off option causes no change to the Message Monitor icon or window when a message comes in.

System Tuning

Every computer has limits. A hard disk is a set size. There is only so much space in RAM. The processor can only handle a limited number of processes before it slows down. Because all these resources must be shared on a multiuser system like UNIX, boundaries are set up that prevent any user, process, or system feature from consuming too much of the pool of resources.

The way you set limits on how resources are allocated in UNIX is with tunable parameters. There are literally hundreds of tunable parameters in the UNIX system. Tunable parameters define how many processes a user can run at a time, how large a file can be created, and how many terminal windows you can have open, to name a few. They also determine things like the amount of memory the system can consume to store the data structures it needs to operate.

Changing tunable parameters is not something you should do lightly. In fact, except in a few cases, such as those described later in this chapter, only a UNIX expert should change tunable parameters. A mistake made tuning a system could result in the system running poorly or not at all.

Before you change tunable parameters to try to improve system perform-ance, try some of the following suggestions:

▸ Read the "Understanding Monitoring Data" section of this chap-ter and determine if simply improving your computer hardware will correct some of the problems.

▸ Spread out the computer's work load by doing such things as run-ning large background jobs during off-hours or dividing heavily used disk partitions across different hard disks.

There are both graphical and command line methods of changing tun-able parameters. The System Tuner window lets you select from different categories of tunable parameters and change them within the acceptable range of values for each parameter. The `idtune` command can be used to change a parameter from the command line. The following sections de-scribe how to use these tools.

 NOTE   **For a complete description of the tunable parameters used in Unix-Ware, see the *System Performance Administration* manual in the Unix-Ware online documentation. Each tunable is also described in the System Tuning window when you select the tunable.**

USING THE SYSTEM TUNER WINDOW

To open the System Tuner window, double-click on the System Tuner icon in the Admin Tools window. The System Tuner window appears, as shown in Figure 9.14.

The first window shows the Device Driver Parameters. To see other cate-gories of parameters, click on the button in the Device Driver Parameters bar. Select from one of the options on the list. The parameters relating to that category appear.

To see more information about any parameter, click in the text box next to the parameter name. A description will appear to the right of the parameter.

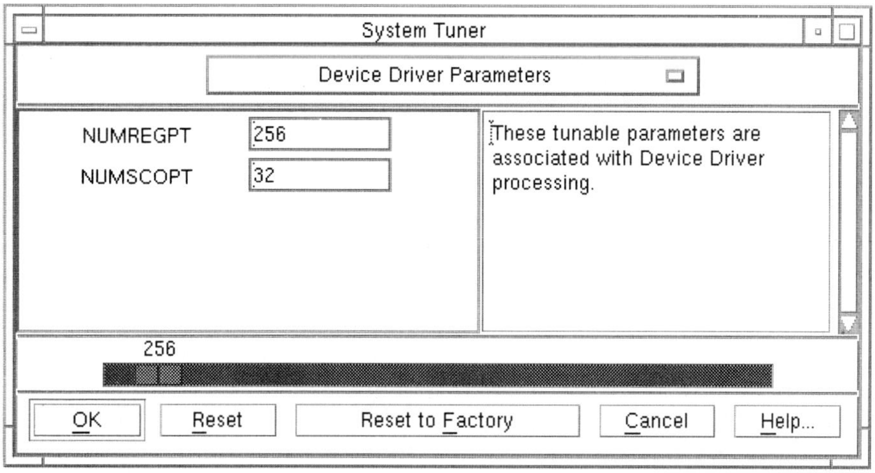

FIGURE 9.14

Displaying the System
Tuner window

There are two ways to change the parameter values. One way is to click in the text box next to the parameter and type in the new value. The other way is to move the slider bar at the bottom of the window to the value you want. The bar only lets you select a number that is in the acceptable range of values. Likewise, if you go above or below the value allowed for the parameter, the window automatically changes it to the minimum or maximum value when you save the parameters.

If you make a mistake changing a parameter, you can reset it to the original setting as the system was delivered by clicking on the Reset to Factory button. To reset values to the last values before the parameters were changed, click on Reset.

When you have a set of parameter values you are happy with, click on OK. The new parameters are set and the window asks you if you want to reboot the system now. If you say yes, the system will be rebooted immediately and the kernel will be rebuilt. If you say no, the kernel is rebuilt the next time you reboot the system.

We suggest that you don't reboot immediately. Instead, rebuild the kernel as described later in this chapter before you reboot the system. This lets you make sure you can build a working kernel while the system is still running.

USING TUNABLE COMMANDS

Tunable parameters are contained in the file `/etc/conf/cf.d/mtune`. Don't edit this file directly, however, because it is created automatically from individual tunable parameter files in the `/etc/conf/mtune.d` directory. The recommended way to work with tunable parameters from the command line is with the `idtune` commands.

To print or change the value of an individual tunable parameter, you can use the `idtune` command with various options. This command can only be run by the root user, and, like any tool that changes tunable parameters, should be used with caution.

The `idtune` command is not in the standard PATH for the root user. To run `idtune` in order to print the value of a parameter (for example, the NBUF parameter), type the following as root user from a Terminal window:

```
# /etc/conf/bin/idtune -g NBUF
256      256      20      3000
#
```

The NBUF parameter shows the number of buffer headers allocated at a time. There are four columns of information shown. The first column (256) displays the value that is currently set for the parameter. The second column (256) shows the default value. The third column (20) is the minimum value you're allowed to set the parameter to. The fourth column (3000) is the maximum value you can set the value to.

To change the value of a tunable parameter, use the `-c` option of `idtune`. For example, to change the maximum number of processes a user can run at a time from the default (80) to 100, type the following bold text as root user from a Terminal window (the nonbold text is what you see on the screen):

```
# /etc/conf/bin/idtune -c MAXUP 100
UX:idtune: INFO: Tunable Parameter MAXUP is
    currently autotuned. Is it OK to change
    it to 100? (y/n) y
#
```

Some tunables are set automatically, based on system resources. MAXUP is one of those parameters. As you see, the system asks you if you want to override the autotuned value. Type y and the new value is assigned.

You can force idtune to update the parameter, without being prompted for a confirmation, by using the −f option. Or you could change the value of the parameter by using the −m option, but only if the current value is smaller than the new value you are trying to set.

WHEN TO TUNE

There are several common problems that are appropriate to fix by changing tunable parameters. One fairly common problem you may encounter is running out of processes. When you see messages like this at the console:

```
NOTICE: newproc: pid_assign failed
NOTICE: fork1: newproc failed
```

it means you have passed the limit on the number of processes you can have running at the same time.

By default, the number of processes allowed for each user is 80. If the same user is logged in more than once, everyone logged in as that user must share those 80 processes. You can increase the number of processes per user by changing the MAXUP value from 80 to a larger number. The total number of processes allowed on the system is 400. If you need to surpass that number, you can increase the value of NPROC to some number greater than 400.

Another problem you may experience is that a file you try to create is too large. The system limits the maximum size file you can create. This prevents a runaway process from creating a file that consumes the entire hard disk. When the file size passes about 8MB in UnixWare 1.1 or 2GB in UnixWare 2, you will see a message similar to this:

```
ERROR: Write error (96/1024 characters
    written): File too large
```

The SFSZLIM parameter limits the maximum size file a process can create. You can increase that value or remove the limitation altogether by setting SFSZLIM to the value of 0x7FFFFFFF. You can also override this value using the ulimit command from a Terminal window or with the ULIMIT line in the /etc/default/login file.

REBUILDING THE KERNEL

After you have changed any of your tunable parameters, we recommend you rebuild the UNIX kernel before you restart the system. When you change the tunable parameters, the idbuild command is run automatically when you reboot the system. However, running it before you reboot lets you see messages regarding any errors that may have been encountered. If you build a kernel that won't boot, you can fix the problem while the system is still running.

Type the following command, as root user from a Terminal window, to rebuild the UnixWare kernel, incorporating the new kernel values:

```
/etc/conf/bin/idbuild -B
```

Finally, close all open files and reboot the system with either the Shutdown icon or by typing the following command:

```
init 6
```

Performance Improvement Strategies

There are a lot of commonsense strategies you can use to improve your system performance without changing any of your tunable parameters. Using many standard UNIX system tools, you can distribute your workload to maximize your system performance. You can also improve the hardware on your system.

Adding Hardware

If your UNIX system is running slowly simply from too much demand, the best way to improve performance is to add hardware. The section "Understanding Monitoring Data" in this chapter provides some tips on determining what part of your computer hardware may be overloaded. The following are the things you can upgrade:

- ▸ **RAM:** You can add additional memory chips if your system is doing a lot of heavy computational or graphical processing.

- ▸ **Processors:** If your computer is a multiprocessing system, you can add additional processors. UnixWare 2 can support up to 32 processors. Or you may decide you need a Pentium instead of a 486 system.

- ▸ **Hard disks:** Adding a hard disk to spread out the disk I/O can aid performance.

- ▸ **Network Interface Cards: If your system is doing a lot of network access, your network interface card may be a bottleneck. TCP/IP and IPX/SPX allow you to have several network interface cards on your UnixWare system.**

RUNNING COMMANDS DURING OFF-HOURS (cron)

By running commands that consume a lot of system resources during off-hours you can make it easier for users to get their work done during the busier hours of the day. Using the `crontab` command or the UnixWare Task Scheduler window, you can set up tasks to run at any time of the day or night.

Some of the tasks you may want to run during off-hours include

- ▸ Backups of your files and directories
- ▸ Large database reports
- ▸ Large file transfers

An example of using the Task Scheduler window to do system backups is shown in Chapter 7, "Backup and Restore Operations." Though the example is shown for backups, other commands can be run instead of backups on that window.

From the command line, you can use the `crontab` command to set up commands to be run later by the `cron` daemon. First, you create a "crontab" file that specifies the command you want to run and the times you want it to run, then install that file with the `crontab` command.

For example, suppose you have a backup script called `allbackup` in your personal `bin` directory that backs up all your files. You want it to run once a week, early Sunday morning. So, you create a file called `spikecron`, using any text editor, and have it include the following information:

```
20 4 * * 0 /home/spike/bin/allbackup
```

Next, you could install the command by typing `crontab spikecron`. This installs the file so the `cron` daemon can read it. When the `cron` daemon does read it, it sees that `/home/spike/bin/allbackup` is to be run at 4:20 a.m. (20 4) every Sunday morning (0).

 NOTE   **If you get a message that says you are not allowed to add a `crontab` file, you need to make sure that your user name is added to the `/etc/cron.d/cron.allow` file. You need to have root permissions to add a user to the `cron.allow` file.**

RUNNING APPLICATIONS ON OTHER COMPUTERS

Another way to improve the performance of your UNIX systems is to spread your processing across several different computers. You can do this by running a command on a processor that is less busy than yours and then working with either the display of that application or the output of it on your local system.

See the "Running Remote Applications" section of Chapter 3 for in-formation on distributing your applications across other processors. See the "Using `rsh`**" section of Chapter 5 for information on running applications on a remote system over TCP/IP connections.**

Using the monitoring and tuning tools that come with UNIX, you can take some of the mystery out of performance problems on your UNIX system. There are both graphical and command line tools for checking and fixing performance problems.

For system monitoring, UnixWare and other UNIX systems have the standard `sar` (system activity report) command, as well as the `rtpm` (real-time performance monitor) command and the System Monitor graphical window. To tune your system, UNIX provides the `idtune` command and the System Tuner window for changing tunable parameters.

Besides changing tunable parameters, there are other ways of improving system performance problems. This chapter describes cases where you may want to upgrade your hardware or spread your workload by running commands during off-hours or by running applications on other processors over a network.

If you have done everything as you should, but UnixWare still isn't working right, you may need to dig a little deeper. Chapter 10 describes ways of troubleshooting problems on your UnixWare 2 system.

Troubleshooting

"**S**oftware is soft," as a great operating system visionary once said. You can usually make it do what you want. The trick is to know where and how to look for what you need. Within UNIX is an armory of tools for troubleshooting your system. This chapter provides an entry into this area, which was once the private domain of UNIX system gurus.

Most UnixWare problems occur for simple reasons. The ownership of a file or a port may be wrong. Or you may have left a floppy disk in the drive so the system won't start. Other problems may be more complicated, requiring a greater understanding of configuration files or the use of special commands.

Read the troubleshooting tips contained in this chapter when you run into problems with UNIX. The troubleshooting techniques are grouped into categories: installation, basic information, permissions, networking, the Desktop, devices, and printing.

If your problems are more general in nature, such as poor overall system performance, refer to Chapter 9 for information on how to monitor and tune your UNIX system.

Before You Start Troubleshooting

Because the graphical interface for UNIX System V provides access primarily to configuring and executing utilities in UnixWare, most of your UnixWare troubleshooting must be done from a command line (usually from a Terminal window). Some of the solutions described here involve running utilities and editing system files. Before you try to solve problems, you should know the following:

► The basics of using the UNIX shell. Read Chapter 8 if you are not already familiar with the shell. You can also refer to any of the hundreds of UNIX books on the market. There is also a quick reference to common UNIX commands shown in Appendix D.

▶ The basics of UNIX file system permissions. You need to understand the concepts of user and group permissions. You also need
to know about read, write, and execute permissions on files, applications, directories, and devices. These concepts are described
in Chapters 1, 2, and 3.

▶ How to use a UNIX text editor. You can edit UnixWare files with
the Text Editor window that comes with the Desktop or a UNIX
system editor, such as vi or ed. vi is a very powerful visual editor, but it's not easy to learn.

The Text Editor is easy to use. However, although you can perform basic
administration tasks as the owner, you must be the root user to edit many
of the system files from the Text Editor. Other UNIX editors also require you
to be the root user in order to make changes to system files. So, if you want to
use the Text Editor window, you can follow these steps to edit a system file:

1 · Double-click on the Applications icon in the Desktop window.

2 · Double-click on the Terminal icon in the Applications folder. A
Terminal window opens and presents you with a command line
prompt.

3 · Obtain root permissions by typing su – and entering the root
user password when prompted.

**If you can't remember if you currently have root permissions, type id
in a Terminal window. This command shows you your current permissions. For example, if the output is uid=0(root) gid=3(sys), you
currently have the root user and sys group permissions.**

NOTE

4 · To open a Text Editor window as root user, type the following
while you still have root permissions:

```
/usr/X/bin/dtedit&
```

If `dtedit` fails because it cannot access the display, you may need to type something like

```
DISPLAY=:0;export DISPLAY
```

to make sure the system knows where to display the editor. To use `vi` to edit the file, just type `vi` *file* (where *file* is replaced by the name of the file you want to edit) in the Terminal window.

Be cautious when you edit UNIX system files. UNIX is built on many configuration files, and an error in some of them can wreck your system. Unless you are a very experienced UNIX system user, stick with the changes recommended in this chapter; experiment only with the greatest care.

Troubleshooting Installation

If UNIX won't install on your computer, the rest of this book isn't very useful. Every different version of UNIX has its own way of doing software installation. General tips for installing UnixWare are included in Appendix A. The following sections offer suggestions for solving some specific problems you may encounter during UnixWare installation.

HARDWARE CONFIGURATION

The most common reason for installation failures is incompatible or improperly configured hardware. First get the right hardware. Appendix A contains information on how to get up-to-date hardware lists for UnixWare. If it doesn't work, read the remainder of this section to understand how to get the hardware right.

Before you begin installation, the boards in your computer must be configured properly. Although you can install certain add-on boards later, it's best to have all your boards installed when you begin UnixWare installation. If your board is installed properly, UnixWare can configure it for the system during installation.

Here are some points to review if your hardware board won't install correctly:

- ▶ The hardware board for the installation medium (cartridge tape or CD-ROM drive) must be supported and configured properly. You will find it particularly annoying if the installation device is not accessible. You can spend about 10 minutes installing the UnixWare boot floppy, only to find that the primary installation medium is not available.

- ▶ If you are installing from an external SCSI device, such as an external tape drive, make sure that device is on *before* you turn on your computer to install UnixWare. Otherwise, UnixWare may not find the device later.

- ▶ Make sure all your boards are placed firmly in their slots.

- ▶ Know all the IRQ (interrupt) and address settings for your boards. You may need them during installation. In UnixWare 2, this is less of an issue than it was in earlier releases because UnixWare can now automatically detect what boards are installed and what their addresses are.

- ▶ Remove any boards you are not using from the computer. There's no reason to risk address conflicts and use memory resources for a board you don't need.

- ▶ Use low memory addresses for add-on boards if your system is configured with more than 16MB of memory. There have been problems with memory addresses of F00000 and above on earlier versions of UnixWare systems with more than 16MB of memory.

SCSI DEVICES

SCSI (Small Computer System Interface) devices send information much faster than standard devices. You can chain together several SCSI devices from a single slot in your computer.

SCSI Device Configuration

SCSI devices are connected together in a daisy chain. The SCSI device at each end of the daisy chain must have a terminator. There are always two, and only two, terminators on a SCSI daisy chain.

You can have up to seven devices daisy-chained to a single SCSI board. On each SCSI device, you must set a switch or jumper (internal device) to a number between 0 and 6. That number represents one of the seven possible devices on the chain. The same number can't be used twice on the chain. If you're booting from a SCSI hard disk, the lowest number is assumed to be the boot drive (number 0). Figure 10.1 illustrates three different SCSI device configurations:

▸ A single internal hard disk connected to a SCSI card, with terminators on both the hard disk and the card.

▸ A second hard disk added to the chain between the first hard disk and the card, with no terminators on the second hard disk. Additional internal SCSI devices, such as an internal CD-ROM or an internal SCSI tape drive, could be connected to the chain between the two terminated devices.

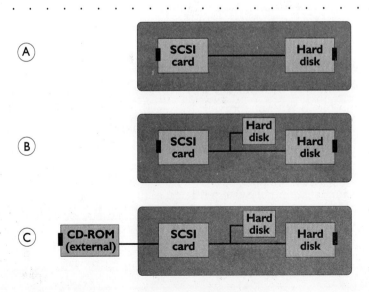

▶ An external SCSI CD-ROM player attached to the port on the back of the SCSI card. The terminators are removed from the SCSI card and added to the external CD-ROM.

Working with SCSI Devices

After you have physically installed the SCSI board and other hardware devices into your computer, you need to tell UNIX about these devices. The /etc/scsi directory contains a set of commands for managing SCSI devices. The commands include pdiadd, pdirm, and pdiconfig. To run any of these commands, open a Terminal window, type su, type the root user password when prompted, and type cd /etc/scsi.

UnixWare typically detects the SCSI boards on your system. If for some reason it doesn't, you can add the board using the pdiadd command. The following procedure describes how to add a SCSI controller board with a single hard disk attached to it:

1 · Open a Terminal window, type su, and enter the root user password when prompted.

2 · Type cd /etc/scsi.

3 · Type ./pdiadd adsc. (The adsc is for an Adaptec SCSI controller.)

4 · Reboot the system.

5 · If there is a hard disk attached to the device, you can add that hard disk using the "Hard Disk: Adding a Second Hard Disk" procedure described in Chapter 11.

6 · Reboot the system again.

The full syntax of the pdiadd command is

```
./pdiadd -d DMA -v Int -i I/O_addr -m mem_addr
```

Replace DMA with the DMA channel, Int with the interrupt vector (IRQ), I/O_addr with the I/O address, and mem_addr with the memory address.

Use `pdirm` to remove an active host bus adapter from your system. `pdirm` has the same form and options as `pdiadd`.

Use `pdiconfig` to list the current configuration of devices. You can use the information in `pdiconfig` to fix the UnixWare kernel if it gets out of sync with the hardware connected to your SCSI device. Run the following commands if you have changed some SCSI devices and they don't work properly:

```
./pdiconfig | ./diskcfg
/etc/conf/bin/idbuild -B
init 6
```

Here are some points to review if you're having problems installing your SCSI device with UnixWare:

▸ Turn on all external SCSI devices (such as a CD-ROM or cartridge tape drive) before you turn on your computer to install UnixWare. If you forget to turn it on, UnixWare may not know it's there.

▸ You may need to disable shadow BIOS on computers that use SCSI host adapters with particular disk controllers. The manuals that come with your computer should describe how to disable shadow BIOS.

SYSTEM WON'T START

You have already successfully installed and booted your UNIX system, but for some reason it won't start now. Go through the checklist below before calling for help:

▸ Of course, you have already checked that your power cord, monitor, keyboard, and mouse are plugged in properly, so we don't even have to mention that.

▸ Open each floppy drive to make sure no floppies are in them. Pop out any floppies in the drives and press the Ctrl-Alt-Del keys simultaneously or press the Reset button to reboot the system.

▶ Changed any system files? If you have changed any of the basic system files, such as the `inittab` or the `passwd` files, your edits may have corrupted them, and this is why the system won't start. If you have made emergency boot recovery floppies, you can use them to boot your system, then possibly correct the damaged files. If that doesn't work, call your UnixWare support representative for information about how to correct the corrupted files.

▶ Added a new hardware board? If you have just installed a board and it is defective or set improperly, the system may not start. Power down the system, then remove the last board you put in and restart the system. If the system starts, check the settings on the board.

▶ Changed devices? The software side of adding a new hardware device can also cause problems if the devices are not configured properly. Sometimes, when you reconfigure devices, you can build a kernel that cannot be booted. Try booting the system from the previous UnixWare kernel as follows:

1 · Reboot the system.

2 · When you see the message "Booting UnixWare," quickly hit the Delete key.

3 · When you are prompted for which kernel to boot, at the # prompt, type

```
unix.old
go
```

The previous kernel should start. If you want to boot a different kernel (for example, one named my_special_unix), type

```
KERNEL=my_special_unix
go
```

4 · Check for bad driver entries among any of the files you may have changed in the `/etc/conf` directories.

If you have recently taken a UnixWare partition or entire disk backup, you can choose to restore the tapes. Restoring a 500MB disk takes approximately 30 minutes. This is much faster than having to reinstall and reconfigure UNIX. See Chapter 7 for information on how to restore from a backup medium.

Changing Basic Information

When you add basic information to your system, such as the system name or user names, many system files are changed. Unfortunately, if you change a name any time after installation, the change may not make it through to every necessary file.

The best way to avoid problems with system names, user names, network addresses, and other basic information is to get them right the first time. However, if you do need to change this information later, you must make sure that all the files that rely on that information are up to date.

 NOTE **Some of the problems described in this section may be seen as bugs. Therefore, they may be fixed by new releases or by updates. In the worst case, however, you may find that UnixWare has automatically updated configuration files with the proper information. No harm is done.**

CHANGING THE SYSTEM NAME

The preferred way of changing your system name (after initial installation of your system) is to use the `setuname` command. To change your system name, type the following as the root user from a Terminal window:

```
setuname -n name
```

Replace *name* with the new name for your system. Next, reboot the system. When the system restarts, you may see error messages relating to some networking services. Don't worry; you can update the files to reflect the new name, as described in the next section.

Although many configuration files are updated automatically when you run `setuname` and reboot your system, you will need to update some files manually. If you communicate with other systems, some of their configuration files will need to be changed to add your system's new name.

Changing the System Name in Local Files

After you have changed your system name with `setuname` and rebooted, check the files listed below for the old system name. Open a Terminal window, get root permissions, and edit the following files with your favorite text editor. In each case, change your old system name to your new system name.

- `/etc/inet/hosts`: Contains your system name and IP address. This file is used by TCP/IP.

- `/etc/inet/inetd.conf`: May contain an entry for the SMTP mail protocol that lists your system name.

- `/etc/net/ticlts/hosts`: Used by protocols that provide connectionless networking services.

- `/etc/net/ticots/hosts`: Used by protocols that provide connection-oriented networking services.

- `/etc/net/ticotsord/hosts`: Used by protocols that provide connection-oriented networking services.

The other basic UnixWare files that contain the system name should have been updated properly when you ran the `setuname` command and rebooted your system. This includes the `/etc/nodename` file.

Individual applications, particularly those that involve networking, also may store your system name. Some applications, such as FrameMaker, use your system name as part of the basis for a license. So, if you change your system name, you may need to contact the application's vendor for a new license.

Another way to find the places where your old system name is stored is to just search the entire system, using the `find` and `grep` commands. Open a Terminal window, obtain root permissions, and run the following command:

```
find / -xdev -print | xargs grep system
```

where *system* is replaced by the old system name you want to find. If you have a very large hard disk or remote directories mounted on your system, you may want to restrict this search to certain directories, such as `/etc` and `/sbin`.

Changing the System Name in Remote Files

The remote systems you communicate with relate your system name to information that lets them contact you and allow you a certain level of access to their file systems. The following are some remote system files that may need to be updated to reflect your new system name. These apply to remote UnixWare systems; other types of systems may use different files.

▶ `$HOME/.rhosts`: Allows users of the same name on a remote system to have direct access to their login on the local system. UnixWare users can create `.rhost` files in their home directories. A remote user may have added your system name to this file.

▶ `/etc/hosts.equiv`: The systemwide equivalent of the `.rhosts` file.

▶ `/etc/inet/hosts`: May list your system name.

▶ `/etc/uucp/Systems`: Where BNU stores remote system names. There may be other `Systems` files in this directory. For example, `Systems.tcp` stores system names used by BNU over TCP/IP protocols.

If the system is a remote UnixWare system, you can also use the Unix-Ware Desktop to update your system name on remote systems. For example, if the remote system is using any of your NFS share items, use the File Sharing window to change your system name. The Internet Setup window lets you change your system name for use by TCP/IP. The Dialup Setup window lets you change BNU (uucp) files that may contain your system name. See Chapter 5 for more information about using the File Sharing, Internet Setup, and Dialup Setup windows.

You may also want to check the Domain Name Server system's databases for any instances of your system name.

NOTE

CHANGING USER NAMES

In UnixWare Release 1.0, if you change the name of the system owner, the database that stores ownership information is not updated. As a result, the new user name does not have ownership permissions. In fact, nobody on the system has ownership permissions.

If you change the owner's name on your system, log in as the new user name and check that the new owner has ownership permissions. To see these permissions, double-click on the User Setup icon, click on the new user name, and select Permissions from the Actions menu.

If the new owner doesn't have ownership permissions, open a Terminal window and enter the following command as the root user:

```
/usr/X/adm/make-owner newuser olduser
```

where *newuser* is replaced by the new owner's name and *olduser* is replaced by the old owner's name.

CHANGING USER ACCOUNT INFORMATION

Most of the user account information set up for the owner when you install a system doesn't need to be changed. To see the properties set for your account, double-click on the User Setup icon in your Admin Tools folder window. In the User Setup: User Accounts window, click on the icon with your login name on it. Then select the Properties option from the Account menu. In the User Setup: User Account Properties window, click on Show Other Options.

You can change any of the information in this window, but there are a few potential problems you should try to avoid. Typically, the home folder is a directory name that matches the login ID. So if you change the Login ID entry, you should probably change the Home Folder entry. The system will move all your files to the new location.

You may find that after you add the login ID, you want to change its user ID (UID) number or group. Some networking applications work better if the UIDs for the same user on two systems match. Also, you may want to add groups later so you can restrict access to certain files by a particular group of users.

Changing UID and group ID (GID) information in UnixWare 2 works fine. In UnixWare 1.1, however, the danger in changing your UID and/or GID is that simply changing those items doesn't change all the files you own to the new assignments. As a result, the next time you log in, you won't be able to add or change any files in your home folder.

Don't try to shortcut changing the UID or GID by changing the home folder name at the same time, and then clicking on Apply. The result will be that all files will move to the new location, but with the old permissions.

The best way to get around this problem is to change your home folder location after you change your UID or GID. Here's the order:

1 · From the User Account Properties window, change the UID and/or select a new group.

2 · Click on OK.

3 · Reopen the window and change the location of the home folder.

4 · Click on Apply.

Because all the files are moved to the new folder, all the new UID and group permissions are transferred as well.

BASIC SYSTEM FILES YOU SHOULDN'T TOUCH

A standard practice for old UNIX hackers is to ignore graphical interfaces or administrative commands and edit basic system files manually. Although you can do this with some UnixWare system files (in fact, we even recommend it for certain situations), some files should never be edited directly.

The following files are very basic system files that UNIX administrators used to edit without a thought. Don't do it with UnixWare. Here's why:

▸ /etc/passwd: Defines all user names, along with other basic user information. Standard practice used to be to add users directly to this file. Now editing the /etc/passwd file causes it to get out of sync with the /etc/shadow file. The shadow file contains encrypted passwords for each user. (Don't edit the shadow file either, by the way.) You should use the Desktop (User Setup window) or the useradd command to add new users. These interfaces add the new user to the /etc/passwd file, and they also can automatically create files and directories for the new user.

Changing /etc/passwd and /etc/shadow also throws the security database out of sync. Running the creatiadb command usually corrects this problem.

NOTE

▸ /etc/inittab: Kicks off every process that starts when UnixWare comes up. If you needed to add a terminal to your system in the old days, it was standard practice to add a getty or uugetty command line to the inittab file to send a login prompt to a particular port. Now, however, every time you add a device to your system and rebuild the UnixWare kernel, the /etc/inittab file is overwritten. Don't despair, however. The entire file is overwritten by /etc/conf/init.d/kernel. You can change this file as you would the inittab file. The next time you rebuild your kernel and reboot, the new inittab file is created from the kernel file.

▸ /etc/vfstab: Contains entries for remote share items added to the File Sharing window. If you change one of the entries in the vfstab file, two entries appear in the File Sharing window for the share item. You should make any changes to share items through the File Sharing window.

▸ /etc/conf/sdevice.d: In earlier UnixWare versions, if you needed to enable or disable a device you would edit the device entry in the sdevice.d directory and flag the device 'Y' or 'N.' Now, even if you change fields for a device file in sdevice.d, the resmgr in /stand overwrites these entries in sdevice.d. This happens each time you boot your system. The device files in sdevice.d are updated to reflect the devices actually auto-detected at boot. You should only use the Device Configuration Utility (DCU) to modify device configuration information.

Troubleshooting Permissions Problems

While security is one of the strongest features of UnixWare, it is also one of the most common reasons for things not working. If you are coming from a DOS environment, your response to an error message might be, "What do you mean I don't have permission? It's my darn computer!" The following sections describe some common permissions errors and what you can do about them.

CAN'T OPEN AN APPLICATION OR A DATA FILE

You may find that an application doesn't appear as an application icon on the Desktop. In some cases, when you create or install an application and the file doesn't have execute permission, it will appear as a data file. If you double-click on the icon, the Desktop tries to open the file in the Text Editor.

To change the permissions on the icon, select Properties from the File menu. In the File Properties window, click on Execute permissions, then click on Apply. The application should appear as an executable icon. If you are not the owner of the file, you will need to open a Terminal window, and as the root user, change the permissions on the file.

If you can't open a data file because permission is denied when you try to open that file, it may be owned by another user on the system or owned by the root user for system administration purposes. Try to open the file as the root user, as described in the section about what to do before you start troubleshooting, earlier in the chapter.

CAN'T OPEN A DEVICE (PORT)

In some cases, the permissions on a device (such as `/dev/tty01` for the COM2 port) may be closed, so you may not be able to communicate with the hardware connected to it. For example, if you configure a printer to use your COM2 port, UnixWare changes the port to be owned by the printer service (`lp`), and only `lp` can read from or write to the port. If you then try to connect a modem to the port, the port may still be owned by `lp`, and any attempts to communicate with the modem will fail.

You may need to change the permissions of the port manually. Open a Terminal window, and as the root user, change the permissions of the port. For example, to open the permissions on the COM2 port, type the following:

```
chmod 666 /dev/tty01
```

Unfortunately, simply opening the permissions on a port does not always ensure that the port will be accessible. Security features added in a previous UNIX release broke some basic port features and have yet to be fixed completely. If changing permissions doesn't allow you access to a port, try rebooting the computer. That often fixes the problem temporarily.

 **WARNING**

CAN'T OPEN A REMOTE FILE

A file may appear to be accessible, but because the file actually resides on a remote system, you may not be able to read or change the file. Networking features, such as NFS and NetWare, allow remote systems to impose their own security on a shared resource.

For example, if a remote UnixWare system shares a directory as read-only, even though the permissions on a particular file may appear open when the directory is mounted on your system, you won't be able to change the file. Similarly, access to a NetWare volume is determined by the user's authentication on the NetWare volume.

 NOTE **See Chapters 4 and 5 for more information about permissions and security issues relating to networking with UnixWare.**

Troubleshooting Networking

Most of the sophisticated tools for troubleshooting the networking features in UnixWare haven't worked their way up to the graphical interface yet. So, if your modem won't place a call, you can't reach a remote system on TCP/IP, or remote login doesn't work, you'll need to open a Terminal window and get to work.

In many cases, an in-depth understanding of UnixWare networking services is required for troubleshooting networking problems. Read Chapter 4 before you begin trying to correct problems with connecting to NetWare systems. Read Chapter 5 first if you need help with UnixWare networking services.

TROUBLESHOOTING BNU (SERIAL COMMUNICATIONS)

BNU contains a set of log files and commands that are useful for troubleshooting communications problems. In some cases, you need to turn on debugging to generate information about communications activities. In other cases, the information is stored automatically.

The Connection Server

Outgoing calls on BNU connections are handled by the connection server. By reading the log of messages from the connection server, you can see which services were requested, by whom, and when. To get more detailed information about connection server activities, you can set up the connection server to output debugging information into a debug log.

To read the connection server log file, open a Terminal window, obtain root permissions, and page through the file by typing the following:

```
pg /var/adm/log/cs.log
```

Figure 10.2 shows an example of the output you might see.

```
Terminal
# pg /var/adm/log/cs.log
01/08/95 22:52:46;    338; *** CONNECTION SERVER starting ***
01/10/95 21:42:10;   1178; *** CONNECTION SERVER starting ***
01/10/95 21:55:18;    332; *** CONNECTION SERVER starting ***
01/10/95 22:22:26;    364; *** CONNECTION SERVER starting ***
01/10/95 22:52:49;    389; *** CONNECTION SERVER starting ***
01/10/95 23:00:34;   1268; *** CONNECTION SERVER starting ***
01/10/95 23:12:23;   1185; *** CONNECTION SERVER starting ***
01/11/95 19:10:26;    402; *** CONNECTION SERVER starting ***
01/15/95 16:43:39;    372; *** CONNECTION SERVER starting ***
01/15/95 17:39:42;    610; Request by process uid<0> gid<5>
01/15/95 17:39:42;    610;    for service<cu> on host</dev/tty01> FAILED
01/15/95 17:39:42;    610; cs: ioctl() set signal error; errno=22
01/15/95 17:40:05;    612; client exited unexpectedly, signal=22
01/15/95 17:40:05;    612; Request by process uid<0> gid<5>
01/15/95 17:42:55;    618; client exited unexpectedly, signal=22
01/15/95 17:42:55;    618; Request by process uid<0> gid<5>
01/15/95 17:43:36;    620; client exited unexpectedly, signal=22
01/15/95 17:43:36;    620; Request by process uid<0> gid<5>
01/15/95 17:56:20;    626; Request by process uid<0> gid<5>
01/15/95 17:58:20;    631; Request by process uid<0> gid<5>
01/15/95 17:58:51;    634; Request by process uid<0> gid<5>
#
```

F I G U R E   10.2

Output from the `cs.log`
command

Along with the date and time of each activity, the log shows each service that is requested, the user ID and group ID that made the request, the host from which the service is requested, and whether the attempt succeeded or failed.

For more in-depth information about connections, you can turn on debugging for the connection server. To turn on debugging, you must change the `/etc/init.d/cs` file to add a `-d`. The command line that starts the connection server should read as follows:

/usr/sbin/cs -d

The next time you boot your system, debugging information from the connection server will be output to the /var/adm/log/cs.debug file. An example of the output from the connection server debug file is shown in Figure 10.3.

▸ · ◂

```
━━━━━━━━━━━━━━━━━━━━━━━━━━━━━━━━━ Terminal ━━━━━━━━━━━━━━━━━━━━━━━━━━━━━━━━━
# pg /var/adm/log/cs.debug

01/16/95 21:38:25;    462; cs: connection server child forked
01/16/95 21:38:25;    462; cs: request-type: DIAL_REQUEST
01/16/95 21:38:25;    462; cs: dial_connect() reads from fd=3
01/16/95 21:38:25;    462; sr: NETPATH: <NULL>
01/16/95 21:38:25;    462; cs: dial Call structure set up as follows:
01/16/95 21:38:25;    462; cs: baud<-1>
01/16/95 21:38:25;    462; cs: speed<-1>
01/16/95 21:38:25;    462; cs: modem<-1>
01/16/95 21:38:25;    462; cs: dev_len<-1>
01/16/95 21:38:25;    462; cs: c_iflag<0x1806>
01/16/95 21:38:25;    462; cs: c_oflag<0x1804>
01/16/95 21:38:25;    462; cs: c_cflag<0x5ad>
01/16/95 21:38:25;    462; cs: c_lflag<0x30>
01/16/95 21:38:25;    462; cs: c_line<0x0>
01/16/95 21:38:25;    462; cs: line<NULL>
01/16/95 21:38:25;    462; cs: telno<venus>
01/16/95 21:38:25;    462; cs: service<cu>
01/16/95 21:38:25;    462; cs: class<NULL>
01/16/95 21:38:25;    462; cs: protocol<NULL>
conn(venus)
Call Failed: SYSTEM NOT IN Systems FILE
# ▊
```

The example shows an attempt to place a call to a remote system (venus) that fails because the system isn't listed in any of the BNU systems files (/etc/uucp/Systems*).

NOTE **The connection server debug option turns out reams of information. We recommend that you turn off the connection server debugging when you don't need it or delete the cs.debug file occasionally.**

CHECKING THE STATUS OF FILE TRANSFERS

BNU (uucp) operates in batch mode by queuing file transfers and remote execution requests to happen at a later date. In some cases, it may not be clear what has happened to your request. Did the request fail, or is it simply waiting to be sent later? You can find out by checking the list of remote systems you can reach, checking the BNU log files, and running status commands.

Checking System Names

You can't reach a system using BNU if it's not configured on your system. To see the list of systems you can reach over BNU, type the following command from a Terminal window:

```
uuname
```

If the system you are trying to reach is not shown on the list, add the system, as described in Chapter 5. If the system can be reached over TCP/IP, add the system through the Internet Setup window.

Creating BNU Log Files

Some log files are automatically created with BNU when you install your system. Others need to be created before you can collect information about some types of BNU processing. Most of the BNU log files are contained in subdirectories of the directory /var/spool/uucp. Go to that directory and type ls -a to see a set of hidden directories that contain BNU log files. Figure 10.4 shows an example of the output you may see.

In your listings, you will also see a directory for each remote system to which you transfer files.

NOTE

You can open the hidden directories and review their contents or run the commands shown in the following sections to list information from the files.

F I G U R E   10.4

Hidden directories in the

/var/spool/uucp

directory

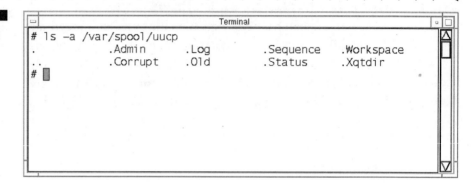

```
                                      Terminal
# ls -a /var/spool/uucp
.                 .Admin        .Log          .Sequence     .Workspace
..                .Corrupt      .Old          .Status       .Xqtdir
#
```

In order to gather performance information and accounting information, you must create log files for each of those areas. To create these log files, type the following:

```
cd /var/spool/uucp/.Admin
touch perflog account
chown uucp perflog account
chgrp uucp perflog account
```

The `perflog` file gathers statistics relating to `uucico`, the daemon that handles file transfers. The `account` file collects information that can be used to account for file transfer usage.

Checking File Transfers with the uustat Command

To check the status of file transfer requests waiting to be sent, use the `uustat` command. After you have sent a file to a remote system (by using the `uuto` command or by dropping a file icon on a remote system icon), check the status of the file transfer by typing the following:

```
uustat -a
```

Figure 10.5 shows an example of the output.

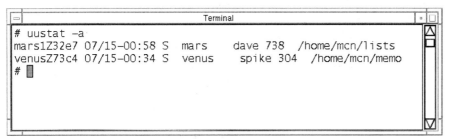

FIGURE 10.5

Output from the

uustat –a *command*

The output in this example shows two file transfers. The job identification for the first job is `mars1Z32e7`. The job was sent on 7/15 at 12:58 a.m. The remote system is `mars`, and the job is being sent to the user named dave. The file being sent is `/home/mcn/lists`.

By using `uustat` with the `–m` option, you can see the status of any recent attempts to transfer files. It lists each system and notes the result of the most recent attempt to contact the system. Figure 10.6 shows an example of the results of using the `uustat –m` command.

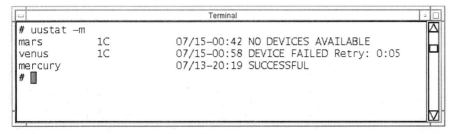

FIGURE 10.6

Output from the

uustat –m *command*

The output shows three entries. The first entry, for the system `mars`, shows that an attempt to transfer a file (using the `auto` command) failed because, although the system is configured for communications over the LAN, the remote system is currently shut down. The second entry shows that attempts to call the system `venus` failed because, although the system is configured for modem communications, the modem is not currently connected to the local system. The third entry shows a successful file transfer to the system mercury.

If you decide you want to cancel any of the queued file transfers, you can do so with the uustat −k command. Take the job identifier for the file transfer request from the uustat −a command. For example, to cancel the file transfer request for the remote system named mars (in Figure 10.6), you would type the following:

```
uustat −k mars1Z32e7
```

Trying the Remote Connection with the uutry Command

At regular intervals, BNU will retry the remote systems that have queued jobs. If you want to try a connection to the remote system immediately, use the uutry command. For example, to try to establish a connection to a remote system named remote1, type the following command:

```
/usr/lib/uucp/uutry −r −x9 remote1
```

Figure 10.7 shows an example of the output from the uutry command.

F I G U R E 10.7

Output from the uutry command

```
                              Terminal
# /usr/lib/uucp/uutry −r remote1
/usr/lib/uucp/uucico −r1 −sremote1  −f −x9 >/tmp/remote1 2>&1&
tmp=/tmp/remote1
force flag set (ignoring uucico limit)
mchFind called (remote1)
name (remote1) not found; return FAIL
name (OTHER) not found; return FAIL
attempting to open /var/uucp/.Admin/account log.
Open failed, errno=2
mkdir − /var/spool/uucp/remote1
Job grade to process − Z
chdir(var/spool/uucp/remote1/Z)
exit code 101
Conversation Complete: Status FAILED

TM_cnt: 0
3985 Killed
#
```

In this example, the `uutry` command starts the `uucico` process to the system `remote1`. The `/tmp` files and log files are identified. The connection fails, however, because the modem still isn't connected.

Checking BNU Requests with the uulog Command

As the root user, you can open a Terminal window and use the `uulog` command to see a listing of all recent connection requests. The output shows every BNU request, along with information about the success or failure of the request.

If you want to watch the progress of a connection while it is occurring, open two Terminal windows. In one window, start `uuto`, `uutry`, or the other BNU command you want to use to reach the system. In the other Terminal window, type the following command:

```
uulog -f remote1
```

In this example, the system to which the request will be made is called `remote1`.

The `uulog` command starts and displays any remote requests as they occur. The command stays active until you press the Delete key.

Checking BNU (uucp) Mail Messages

The BNU daemon processes send mail with information about BNU activities to the `uucp` user account. Occasionally, you should either log in as `uucp` or open a Terminal window as the root user and check the `uucp` mail.

By default, two kinds of mail messages are sent to the `uucp` login. The first type is messages containing the status of queued file transfers, so you can see what has not been transferred and how many times the transfer has been retried. The second type of message shows the result of cleaning up `uucp` spool directories.

To check and clear the `uucp` mailbox, as the root or `uucp` user, open a Terminal window and type the following:

```
mailx -f /usr/mail/uucp
```

You can work with the mail messages as follows:

▸ To page through each message, press Enter.

▸ To show a listing of the messages, type h.

▸ To delete a message, type d#, where # is replaced by the message number.

▸ To quit the mailbox, type q.

TROUBLESHOOTING TCP/IP

If you are operating a TCP/IP network of any complexity, you'll probably need to do some troubleshooting at some point. You may not be able to reach a system you used to be able to reach, or a certain TCP/IP service may not be working.

Luckily, along with TCP/IP's complexity comes a barrel full of utilities designed to help you unravel what is going on. The following sections describe some common problems and suggest ways of fixing them.

TCP/IP Not Running

The best way to find out if TCP/IP is running is to use the ifconfig command with the -a option to see which interfaces are currently active. Type the following command from a Terminal window as the root user:

```
ifconfig -a
```

Figure 10.8 shows an example of the output of the ifconfig -a command. This example shows that the interfaces that are currently active for TCP/IP (inet) are the loopback driver (lo0) and one Ethernet board (el30). Both interfaces are active (UP).

If the ifconfig command does not display any results, this means that there are no interfaces available. You can try rebooting your system. Sometimes the interfaces will come back. Or you can try stopping and restarting

```
┌─────────────────────────── Terminal ──────────────────────────┐
│ # ifconfig -a                                                  │
│ lo0: flags=49<UP,LOOPBACK,RUNNING>                             │
│         inet 127.0.0.1 netmask ff000000                        │
│ e130: flags=23<UP,BROADCAST,NOTRAILERS>                        │
│         inet 123.45.67.92 netmask ffff0000 broadcast 123.45.67.255 │
│ #                                                              │
│                                                                │
│                                                                │
└────────────────────────────────────────────────────────────────┘
```

TCP/IP from the startup script by typing the following from a Terminal window as the root user:

```
sh -x /etc/init.d/inetinit stop
sh -x /etc/init.d/inetinit start
```

The -x option in the example is optional. It simply says to print debugging information as the startup script runs.

Use the `ifconfig -a` command again to see if the interfaces are available. If the loopback interface and interfaces to each Ethernet board on your system are not listed, check the interfaces next.

Remember that you are known to the outside world as the IP address and system name associated with each interface. An interface is typically an Ethernet board or a serial connection (for PPP). Make sure the correct device driver is installed on your system for the board. (Most popular Ethernet drivers can be installed from the UnixWare Ethernet Hardware Support package.) Then, to add or change an interface, type the following command:

```
sh /etc/confnet.d/configure -i
```

The `configure` command lets you choose an interface (typically an Ethernet or Token Ring device name), the system name you are using with that interface, and the IP address associated with that interface. It also asks you an obtuse question about using default Ethernet `ifconfig` options. If you are on a single LAN, with no connections to outside systems, answer yes. (See the section about routing problems for further information.)

 NOTE   **Unfortunately, the** configure **command assumes you are adding an extra board. It tries to add a new name for the interface, even if you are just modifying the original interface. For example, if your system name is** mars, **it tries to add an interface with the name** mars2. **If you are changing the configuration for the first board, type your local system name instead of pressing Enter to accept the system name** configure **is suggesting.**

If after you run configure you still don't have a working interface, you may have a corrupted /etc/confnet.d/inet/interface file. We do not recommend editing this file by hand, but you can check it to see if any of the interface entries at the end of the file look strange. If you put a comment character (#) in front of a strange-looking interface entry, the other entries may work.

Another way to view information about your TCP/IP interface is with the netstat -i command. Its output includes the system name by which you are known to the interface. Figure 10.9 shows an example of the output of the netstat -i command.

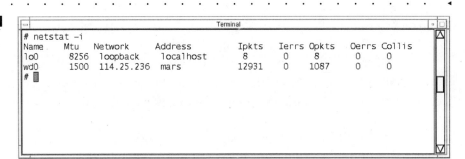

```
# netstat -i
Name    Mtu    Network     Address      Ipkts   Ierrs Opkts   Oerrs Collis
lo0     8256   loopback    localhost    8       0     8       0     0
wd0     1500   114.25.236  mars         12931   0     1087    0     0
#
```

Can't Contact Remote System

If you see a message similar to this:

```
remote1: unknown host
```

when you try to log in or transfer files to a remote system, it means that the system isn't listed in your /etc/hosts file (it is not set up in the Internet Setup window). If you are using Domain Name Service, the system can't be found by the Domain Name Server either. Check that you requested the correct remote system name. If you did, add the system to the Internet Setup window or to your Domain Name Server.

If you see a message similar to this:

```
remote1: Connection timed out
```

it probably means that the remote system is down or has been disconnected from the network. Another possibility is that you have the wrong IP address.

First, check to see if you can reach the system at all. Type the following from a Terminal window as the root user:

```
ping -s remote1
```

Replace *remote1* with the name of the system you want to reach.

If you can reach the system, you'll get several messages from the remote system, such as this:

```
64 bytes from remote1 (148.52.77.85)
   icmp_seq=1. time=0. ms
```

If you can't connect to the remote system, the ping command hangs. For example, you may see something like this:

```
PING remote1: 56 data bytes
```

Press the Delete key to see a summary report. It may look something like this:

```
----remote1 PING Statistics----
19 packets transmitted, 0 packets received,
   100% packet loss
```

If the report shows this type of failure, you may want to call the owner of the system and see if it is up. If the remote system is up, but your system still can't reach it, check the routing to the other system, as described in the next section.

Can't Route to Other Networks

If your system is set up to do routing or is connected to a system that does routing, you can check the routes available for communications with remote systems. The netstat command has several options for producing different routing information.

To list each of the different networks connected directly to your computer, use the −r option. In a Terminal window, type

```
netstat -r
```

Figure 10.10 shows an example of the output of the netstat −r command.

In this example, the local network is 148.52, reached through the 729 interface board. A system named jupiter is connected to the local network

F I G U R E 10.10

Output from the

netstat −r *command*

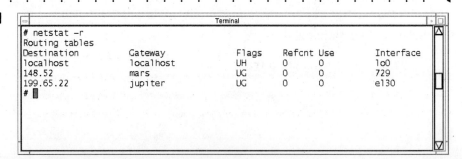

```
# netstat -r
Routing tables
Destination        Gateway            Flags    Refcnt Use        Interface
localhost          localhost          UH       0      0          loO
148.52             mars               UG       0      0          729
199.65.22          jupiter            UG       0      0          e130
#
```

(accessible through board e130). Through `jupiter`, you can reach network `199.65.22`. That network may or may not be directly connected to `jupiter`, but `jupiter` does provide a route to the network.

If the network of the remote system you are trying to reach is not shown on this list, your system won't be able to route information to that remote system. You might be able to set up a PPP connection to the remote system (if there is a modem connected to the remote system) or establish a connection to another part of the Internet.

See Chapter 5 for more information about PPP and Internet connections.

NOTE

Services Not Available

You might find that your connection to a remote system is active, but a particular service is not available to you from that system. For example, you may want to run `finger` to find user information on the remote system, but when you try it, the connection is refused.

Many TCP services are listed in the `/etc/services` file and activated from the `/etc/inet/inetd.conf` file. Other services are turned on automatically.

If you try to request a service from a remote system you can otherwise contact and you receive a message similar to this:

```
[remote1] connect: Connection refused
```

you can ask the administrator on the remote system to turn on the service you are requesting.

To turn on or off services in the `inetd.conf` file, open a Terminal window, obtain root user permissions, and open the `/etc/init/inetd.conf` file with your favorite text editor. Edit the file to either remove the comment character from in front of the service line you want to activate or add a comment character to a service you want to deactivate. Figure 10.11 shows an example of activating the `finger` service and deactivating the `talk` service.

Editing the
/etc/init/inetd.conf
file to activate the finger
service and deactivate the
talk *service*

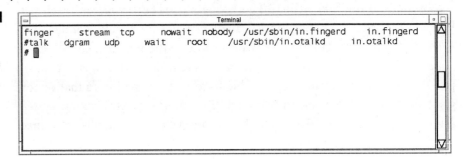

```
finger      stream  tcp     nowait  nobody  /usr/sbin/in.fingerd    in.fingerd
#talk  dgram  udp     wait     root    /usr/sbin/in.otalkd    in.otalkd
#
```

If the remote system's administrator changed the finger and talk lines to read as shown in Figure 10.11, you could use the following finger command from your system:

finger spike@remote1

But if you used this command:

talk spike@remote1

you would fail to get a connection.

TROUBLESHOOTING MAIL

UnixWare provides three methods for sending mail: BNU, TCP/IP, and MHS. When you use the Mail window or the mailx command, UnixWare sends mail based on the type of addressing used on the messages.

If you simply send a message to a user name, with the address in the format

user

the system tries to send the message to that user name on the local system. (The exception is that you may have defined a user alias to represent a *user@system* or *system!user* type of address.)

The ! style of addressing is used by BNU (uucp). When UnixWare sees this address form:

> system!user

it looks for how to reach the system based on system entries in the Dialup Setup window (/etc/uucp/Systems). You can even hop across systems to send mail, provided the permissions allow it on each system. For example,

> mars!jupiter!venus!spike

is a valid mail address for BNU.

The TCP/IP style of addressing has the form

> user@system

The system must be listed in your Internet Setup window or available from your Domain Name Server. If you are using Domain Name Service, you can use the full domain name with the address. For example,

> spike@mars.candl.COM

is a system and full domain name. Unfortunately, simply using the @ type of addressing doesn't guarantee delivery with TCP/IP. Mail might fail because UnixWare tries to use BNU delivery, as explained in the next section.

If MHS mail is your method of managing your mail, you use an address style similar to the TCP/IP addressing style. However, instead of using system names, you use the name of the MHS workgroup on which the user has a mailbox, in the form

> user@mhsworkgroup

To use MHS for UnixWare, you need to set up MHS for each UnixWare user through the MHS Setup window. You also need to have MHS set up for the user on a NetWare server.

There are two keys to getting mail to work. First, you must be able to reach the remote systems over the interface. (See Chapter 5 for descriptions of BNU and TCP/IP communications.) The second is to make sure that compatible mail delivery systems are being used on both ends of the communication.

TROUBLESHOOTING NETWARE CONNECTIONS

In the course of using UnixWare's NetWare connectivity, you may run into problems starting up the connection, or you may not have access to NetWare servers that you know are available. The following sections suggest how to deal with these situations.

Problems Starting Up NetWare Connections

When you first boot up your UnixWare system, if you see the message

```
NetWare IPX startup is disabled
```

it means that NetWare connectivity is not working. The primary reason the NetWare daemon (npsd) does not start is that your UnixWare system can't find a NetWare server.

Make sure that at least one NetWare server is active on your network. If it's not, turn on the NetWare server and try to restart NetWare connectivity. To restart NetWare connectivity, start the NetWare UNIX Client service. From a Terminal window, obtain root user permissions, and then type the following:

```
sh -x /etc/init.d/nw start
sh -x /etc/init.d/nuc start
```

Then open your NetWare window. If NetWare is working, you will see icons for one or more servers in this window. If the icons don't show up immediately, wait; it may take a few minutes.

When NetWare connectivity is not started properly (no servers are on the line), none of the other services that use IPX/SPX will work with UnixWare. For example, you can't use the Remote Applications window to share applications with remote systems because this facility uses IPX/SPX. NOTE

NetWare Servers Not Appearing

You may know that certain NetWare servers are available, but they don't appear in your NetWare window. One possible explanation is that the server is using a different frame type. A single physical network can include NetWare servers that use different frame types.

You can find out the frame types for all the NetWare networks connected to your computer by typing nwdiscover -a as the root user. NOTE

When UnixWare starts up NetWare connectivity, it searches the network for the nearest NetWare server using the ETHERNET_II frame type. If it finds a server of that frame type, then it looks for other servers using that frame type on the network and displays icons for those servers as well. If UnixWare doesn't find a server, it checks ETHERNET_802.3, ETHERNET_SNAP, and ETHERNET_802.2 frame types, respectively, for a server.

To see what your primary NetWare server is set to, type the command nwprimserver -g as root user. To change your primary server, type nwprimserver -s *server*, replacing *server* with the new server. NOTE

If the servers you want are not using the first frame type found, you won't be able to access those servers. The way around this problem is to force the frame type you want.

Using the NetWare Setup window, you can change the Frame Type used, so servers of the new frame type are found. From the Networking window, double-click on the NetWare Setup icon, then click on the button next to Logical LAN Configuration. Click on the button next to IPX LAN Frame

Type to see the available frame types. Click on the one you want, then click on Apply to make it active.

In pre-UnixWare 2 systems, to force the frame type used for NetWare connectivity, open the `/etc/rc2.d/S27nuc` startup script from a Terminal window as the root user with any text editor. Once the file is open, change the line where the `npsd` daemon is started to add the `-f` `frame_type` option:

```
/usr/sbin/npsd -f frame_type >> $LOG 2>&1
```

Replace the *frame_type* with ETHERNET_II, ETHERNET_802.3, ETHERNET_SNAP, or ETHERNET_802.2. The next time the startup script is run (typically when the system is started), the new frame type is used.

Troubleshooting the Desktop

Because the Desktop graphical interface is your primary means of using the system, it is important to have it working as well as possible. You will find tips that will help get your Desktop running faster later in this chapter. The following sections describe potential Desktop problems and how to fix them.

MISSING BASIC DESKTOP ICONS

You may open your Desktop window and not see one or more of your basic Desktop icons, such as the Preferences or Applications icon. You can restore the original icons, plus any files or folders in subfolders of that icon's window, by using a simple drag-and-drop method.

To restore a basic Desktop icon, open both the Desktop window and the `/usr/X/desktop` window. Next, hold down the Ctrl and Shift keys together as you drag-and-drop the missing icon from the `/usr/X/desktop` window into the Desktop window. The icon is restored to your Desktop window. When you open that icon, any icons within that icon's window are restored. For example, if you were restoring the Preferences icon in your Desktop, when you double-click on Preferences, the Preferences folder window appears with each of its icons restored (Color, Mouse, Fonts, and so on).

Several of the basic Desktop icons need to be reinstated using a link command (`ln`) from a Terminal window. First use the `cd $HOME` command to change to your home directory, then use the `ln` command with the `-s` option. For example, to restore the Folder Map icon, open a Terminal Window, obtain root user permissions, and type the following:

```
cd $HOME
ln -s /usr/X/desktop/Folder_Map Folder_Map
```

To restore the Wastebasket icon, enter this command:

```
ln -s /usr/X/desktop/dtwastebasket
   Wastebasket
```

CAN'T SEE FILES BEGINNING WITH PERIODS

The UNIX system includes files that begin with periods, such as the `.profile` file, but when you open a folder window, files beginning with periods do not appear. In a Terminal window, simply type `ls -a`. The `-a` option lists files that are hidden; in other words, it lists files in the current directory that begin with periods.

Even though you can't see files beginning with periods, you can still access those files from a folder window. To open a file that begins with a period, open the Text Editor window (double-click on Applications, then double-click on Text Editor). In the Text Editor window, select Open from the File menu. In the Text Editor: Open window, files beginning with periods (such as `.profile` and `.Xdefaults`), appear as files you can select. Move up and down the directory structure using the Folder entries until you find the file you want.

DESKTOP APPEARS SCRAMBLED

If the Desktop interface doesn't look right, chances are you changed the video driver used for your Desktop with the Display Setup command. Changing the video driver with an incorrect entry can make the Desktop appear blurry or completely scrambled.

If, after running Display Setup, the graphical login window appears scrambled, press the Alt-X key combination to get to a login prompt you can see. Next, log in as the root user and run the following command: /usr/X/lib/display/setvideomode. (You probably can't run Display Setup because the video is scrambled.) Remember that setvideomode options are based on the type of chips on the graphics card, the screen resolution, and the type of display you are using.

NOTE   **If your display is really garbled, you can return to the default VGA settings (640 × 480 resolution with 16 colors) by typing the following: /usr/X/lib/display/setvideomode −default.**

REMOTE GRAPHICAL APPLICATION WON'T START

As explained in Chapter 3, you can start an application from the command line on a remote system and have it display on your system. If you tried this and it failed, the problem might be that you have not turned on access to your display.

For example, suppose that you logged in to a remote system named remote1 and typed

```
DISPLAY=mars:0;export DISPLAY;
   /usr/X/bin/dtclock
```

to start a clock from the remote system so it appears on your display (your system is named mars). But you get this message:

```
Xlib: connection to mars refused by server
```

Chances are your display is not accessible to mars.

To make your display available to all remote systems, open a Terminal window on your local Desktop and type `xhost +`. You can make the display available to a particular remote system by following the command with the remote system's name. For example, to make the display accessible to the system named `remote1`, type

```
xhost + remote1
```

THE DESKTOP HANGS

If the activities of a particular application hang, the entire Desktop may become inaccessible. For example, if you try to open a file that is on a remote file system and between the time you view and select the file, the connection is broken to the remote system, the Desktop will hang waiting for the file to open.

You can just press the Reset button to start up again, but you may have other alternatives. If you have virtual terminals running, you can switch to another virtual terminal (by pressing Alt-SysRq p) and type `exit` at the shell prompt. The system will tell you there are other virtual terminals running (which include the Desktop) and ask you to type `y` to close them. Once the Desktop is closed, you can log in again.

If you think a particular application is hanging up the Desktop, you can try to stop just that process, and the rest of the Desktop may become accessible again. For example, suppose that you think that your WonderWord application is hanging your Desktop. The name of the application is `ww`. Switch to a virtual terminal (press Alt-SysRq p) and, from the command line, type

```
ps -aef | grep ww
```

Next, kill the process ID of the `ww` process listed (the second field from the left) by typing

```
kill -9 pid
```

where *pid* is replaced by the process ID of the ww process. Press the keys Alt-SysRq p to return to the Desktop and see if it is working properly.

CHANGES TO DESKTOP RESOURCES (.Xdefaults) DON'T TAKE EFFECT

Some applications require you to add resources to the .Xdefaults file. These entries may define the colors on the application, special mouse actions, or fonts, to name a few types of resources.

If you add resources to the .Xdefaults file manually, and the resources don't take effect, check the .Xdefaults file again. If you mistyped the resource name in the .Xdefaults file, the X server will silently ignore the resource. You won't see any error messages.

A resource name should be in the form

```
resource:<Tab>value
```

Correct the error and restart the Desktop.

RUNNING OUT OF TERMINAL WINDOWS AND LOGIN PORTS

When you install your UNIX system, there are a set number of pseudo terminals available. Every time someone on your system opens a Terminal window or uses an rlogin command to log in to your system, another one of these pseudo terminals is used. Standard pseudo terminals are represented by devices in the /dev/pts directory (named as files 0 through 255). SCO-compatible pseudo terminals are represented by /dev/ptyp*XX* devices, where *XX* is replaced by the number of the device.

By default, there are 256 standard pseudo terminals configured for a UnixWare AS and 64 configured for a UnixWare PE. There are 32 SCO-compatible pseudo terminals by default.

If you have a large UnixWare Application Server system, with several X-terminals connected to it, you could possibly run out of these devices. Fortunately, you can increase the number of pseudo terminal devices by changing some tunable parameters.

To increase the number of standard pseudo terminals from 256 to 330, for example, open a Terminal window, obtain root user permissions and type the following command:

```
/etc/conf/bin/idtune -f NUMREGPT 330
```

Next, rebuild the kernel by typing the following:

```
/etc/conf/bin/idbuild -B
```

Reboot the system. After the system has rebooted, type

```
ls -l /dev/pts
```

to see if the new number of ports was properly configured. In this case, you should see device names of 00 through 329. To change the number of SCO-compatible pseudo terminals, change the NUMSCOPT tunable parameter, using the same format of the idtune command shown previously.

TECHNOTE

The changes to tunable parameters are actually made in the /etc/conf/mtune.d/ptm file. In that file, a note suggests that the NUMSCOMPAT and NUMREGPT parameters must also be changed in the acp and nsu pkginfo files, respectively. It doesn't seem to be necessary to change these parameters, but if you want to change them, the files the note refers to are /var/sadm/pkg/acp/pkginfo and /var/sadm/pkg/nsu/pkginfo, respectively. The parameters are DFLT_SCO_AS (or PE) and DLFT_REG_AS (or PE), respectively.

CAN'T RESIZE A TERMINAL WINDOW

There are times in UnixWare 2 when you try to resize a Terminal window and it won't resize. The problem is that after you run some utilities that take control of the window, such as vi, a bug prevents you from changing the window size, even after your vi session has ended. To prevent this from happening, after you open the Terminal window and before you run vi, click the right mouse button on the window, click on Properties, then click on Curses Resize. After that you should be able to resize the window as you please.

Troubleshooting DOS and Windows

As explained in Chapter 6, Merge allows you to run DOS and Windows sessions within UnixWare. Because you are actually using DOS and Windows within a UnixWare window, you need to set up DOS and Windows slightly differently than you would if UnixWare weren't on the system.

You may find that you can't start Windows in UnixWare. You may also have problems with DOS and UnixWare sharing your COM ports.

WINDOWS WON'T START

If you installed Windows but you can't start it, the problem may stem from an unsupported video driver. The other possibility is that UnixWare does not have enough swap space for Windows. Procedures for fixing these problems are described in the following sections.

Unsupported Video Driver

The drivers that come with video boards for Windows may not work with UnixWare. When you install Windows, choose VGA, DOS Merge Windows/X, or DOS Merge Windows/X [Large Fonts] for your video driver.

If you installed a video driver that isn't working, you need to change to a driver that does work. Start a DOS session (by double-clicking on the DOS icon in the Applications folder window) and change to the directory where Windows is installed. Type **SETUP** (press C to continue if you see a message regarding SUBST.EXE), move the highlighting to Display, and press Enter. Select one of the valid video drivers (VGA, DOS Merge Windows/X, or DOS Merge Windows/X [Large Fonts]) from the list. Finally, save the change and exit **SETUP**. Windows will work with the new video driver.

This subject is discussed in greater detail in Chapter 6.

Not Enough Swap Space

During UnixWare installation, swap space is created to suit the amount of hard disk space and RAM in your system. If you double-click on the Win icon and Windows does not start, you may need more swap space.

To check how much swap space is being used, open a Terminal window and type the following:

```
/usr/sbin/swap -s
```

The output might look something like this:

```
total: 26872 allocated + 6304 reserved =
    33176 blocks used, 16384 blocks available
```

The total amount of swap space is the number of blocks used plus the number of blocks available. To determine the number of megabytes of swap space available, divide the number of blocks available by 2048.

To temporarily gain swap space, close some of your open windows and try starting Windows again. If you still don't have enough swap space to start Windows, try changing the total amount of swap space.

To change the total amount of swap, type the following from a Terminal window as root user:

```
dd if=/dev/swap of=/extraswap count=2048
    bs=4096
swap -a /extraswap
```

This temporarily adds an extra 8MB of swap. To add the extra swap permanently, you can create a script in the /etc/rc2.d directory to run every time the system is booted. Create a script called **S99moreswap** that includes the following line:

```
swap -a /extraswap
```

COM PORT DOESN'T WORK

Because UnixWare and DOS are sharing the COM ports, those ports must have the proper permissions associated with them on the UnixWare side so they work properly in DOS. If you can't access a port in DOS, open a Terminal window and check the permissions of the port. For example, to see the COM1 port permissions, type

```
ls -l /dev/tty00
```

The permissions should read as follows:

```
crw-rw-rw 1 root  root 3, 0 Jul 21 02:00
  /dev/tty00
```

If these are not the permissions on the port, type the following from a Terminal window as the root user:

```
chmod 666 /dev/tty00
chown root /dev/tty00
chgrp root /dev/tty00
```

Merge also requires that you select the COM port in the DOS Options window before starting a DOS or Windows session. Otherwise, you won't be able to use the COM port in that session.

Troubleshooting Devices

All hardware devices on your computer are accessible through entries in the /dev directory. The entries in the /dev directory look a lot like other files when you list them. However, when information is sent to these special files, that information is directed to the associated hardware device.

Devices are built into the UNIX kernel, based on information in the /etc/conf directory and its subdirectories. Typically, installing the operating system or various hardware devices will automatically create the configuration information that is used to build the /dev entries needed to access the hardware from UNIX.

Any direct editing of device configuration files can seriously damage your UNIX system. You could damage it to the point where you couldn't build a UNIX kernel or, worse, you could build one that wouldn't boot. The procedures we recommend in the following sections should be done with great care.

COM PORT DEVICES NOT AVAILABLE

If your computer has COM3 or COM4 ports installed, UnixWare, in its default configuration, will not recognize that they are there. You can, however, configure those ports into UnixWare.

The interrupts assigned to each of the four possible COM ports for DOS are COM1=4, COM2=3, COM3=4, and COM4=3. However, because Unix-Ware can't have two COM ports at the same IRQ, it assigns COM3 to be at IRQ 9 and COM4 to be at IRQ 5.

Because the IRQs for the COM3 and COM4 boards would probably be set physically to 4 and 3, respectively, you might need to reset them to the IRQs expected by UnixWare. If either of the default IRQs for COM3 and COM4 are being used, you can reconfigure them.

In UnixWare 2, you can change the definitions for the COM3 and COM4 ports using the Hardware Setup window (available from the Admin Tools window). In UnixWare 1.1, however, to make your COM3 and COM4 ports available with UnixWare, you must open a Terminal window as the root user and type the following:

```
cd /etc/conf/sdevice.d
```

Then open the async file using your favorite text editor (vi, ed, or /usr/X/bin/dtedit) and change the last two lines of the file so that the first field is a Y instead of an N, for COM3 and COM4, respectively. The four entries for COM1 through COM4 would then appear as shown in Figure 10.12.

FIGURE 10.12

The `async` file with edited
entries to make COM3 and
COM4 available to
UnixWare

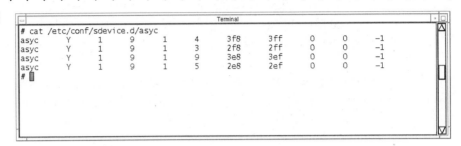

```
# cat /etc/conf/sdevice.d/async
async     Y     1     9     1     4     3f8     3ff     0     0     -1
async     Y     1     9     1     3     2f8     2ff     0     0     -1
async     Y     1     9     1     9     3e8     3ef     0     0     -1
async     Y     1     9     1     5     2e8     2ef     0     0     -1
#
```

 NOTE
The sixth field in the `async` file shows the IRQ. Because IRQs 9 and 5
are often assigned to other devices, you may need to change these
numbers for COM3 and COM4 to other available IRQs.

Save your changes to the file. Next, type the following command:

`/etc/conf/bin/idbuild -B`

Wait for several minutes while the kernel is rebuilt. Finally, reboot the system. When the system comes up, all of your COM ports should be accessible.

FLOPPY DRIVE NOT ACCESSIBLE

If you add a floppy disk drive to your computer after UnixWare is installed, you need to make the new drive accessible to UnixWare. After you have added the floppy disk drive hardware to your computer, you need to use the setup facility that comes with your computer to configure the floppy drive into your system. Check the manuals that come with your computer for instructions.

With your new floppy drive installed and configured for your computer, start up the system. From a Terminal window, type the following command as the root user:

`/usr/sadm/sysadm/bin/mkdtab`

This ensures that an icon for the floppy disk is automatically created in your Disks-etc folder so you can use it from the Desktop. Reboot your computer. The floppy disk should now be accessible.

Troubleshooting Printing

Methods for troubleshooting printing vary depending on how your system is connected to the printer. With UnixWare, printers can be connected directly to serial or parallel ports, or you can print to remote printers that are connected to other UNIX systems or NetWare servers.

CHECKING THE PRINTER CONTROL WINDOW

Once a printer is attached and configured using the Printer Setup icon, send a print job to the printer. If printing fails, first check that the printer is accepting print jobs by checking the Printer Control window. From the Admin Tools window, double-click on the Printer Setup icon, and then click on the icon for the printer you want to check. Select Control from the Printer menu.

In the Control Printer window, make sure that Accept and Enabled are both selected. If they are not, select them and click on Apply to make the change.

Try sending the print job again. If it still doesn't print, read the sections that follow, which describe printing problems relating to particular printer types.

TROUBLESHOOTING PARALLEL PRINTERS

If your printer is connected to your parallel port (lpt1) and configured properly through the Printer Setup, first check to see that it is enabled, as described in the preceding section. If that isn't the problem, next test that the printer works in DOS.

Insert a bootable DOS floppy in the first floppy disk drive and reboot. Try printing to the parallel port while in DOS. If that works, then reboot your system in UNIX, open a DOS window, and try to print to the `doslp` printer from within DOS in UNIX.

If the `doslp` printer doesn't work, the address of the parallel port on your computer is probably not the address UnixWare expects it to be. By default, the beginning and ending addresses are `378` and `37F` for the `lp` device. Check the manual that came with your computer for the address of your parallel port.

In UnixWare 2, you can change the printer device definitions using the Hardware Setup window (available from the Admin Tools window). In UnixWare 1.1, however, you must change the printer device definition manually. Open a Terminal window, and type the following as the root user:

```
cd /etc/conf/sdevice.d
```

Next, open the `lp` file in this directory in an editor (such as `vi`) and change the numbers `378` and `37F` to the new addresses for the parallel port.

Then make the change in the kernel by typing this command:

```
/etc/conf/bin/idbuild -B
```

After the kernel is rebuilt, reboot the system and try using the printer again.

TROUBLESHOOTING SERIAL PRINTERS

Printing to serial ports can fail because of communications, port permissions, or cable problems. UnixWare is more particular about the type of cable you use for your printer than DOS is. Check that your have a proper serial cable. All hardware handshaking signals must be supported by the cable for it to work with UnixWare.

Checking Communication Parameters

You can check that the communications parameters set up in UnixWare match those used by your printer. To view the printer communications parameters, from the Admin Tools window, double-click on the Printer Setup icon, and then click on the icon for the printer you want to check. Select Properties from the Printer menu and click on Serial Configuration. The Properties: Serial Configuration window appears, as shown in Figure 10.13.

Properties : Serial Configuration						
Baud Rate	○ 300	○ 1200	○ 2400	○ 4800	◉ 9600	○ 19200
Parity	○ even	○ odd	◉ none			
Stop Bits	◉ 1	○ 2				
Character Size	◉ 8	○ 7				
OK		Reset		Cancel		Help

Check that the Baud Rate, Parity, Stop Bits, and Character Size settings are the same as the values that the printer is expecting. If you need to change any of the values, make your selections and click on Apply.

Checking Port Permissions

The other problem you may encounter with serial printing has to do with the permissions on the port. If you are using a serial port on which you previously had a modem or some other device configured, the port permissions may have changed to permissions that make it inaccessible to your printer.

Check the permissions on your serial printer port by generating a long list on the port. For example, if you are using the COM2 port, type the following:

```
ls -l /dev/tty01
```

For the port to be accessible to the printer, the owner and group should be lp and the owner and group should have read/write access. If necessary, use the chown, chgrp, and chmod commands to change the permissions.

For example, to assign these permissions to COM2, type the following from a Terminal window as the root user:

```
chown lp /dev/tty01
chgrp lp /dev/tty01
chmod 660 /dev/tty01
```

TROUBLESHOOTING REMOTE UNIX PRINTERS

On the local, UnixWare side, remote printing between UNIX systems tends to be fairly robust. Follow the procedure outlined in Chapter 11 for setting up a remote UnixWare printer.

To avoid printing problems, remember to enable remote access between the two systems and to make sure the underlying TCP/IP connection is properly configured. If the remote system uses a BSD print spooler (such as a Sun system), make sure you note that when you add the printer using the Printer Setup window.

If the remote system is another UNIX System V system, but without a Desktop interface, use the `lpsystem` command from the remote system. Log in as the root user and type the following command:

```
lpsystem -T s5 system
```

where *system* is replaced by the name of your system. This allows the remote system to accept print jobs from your system.

TROUBLESHOOTING NETWARE PRINTERS

The Browse feature on the Printer Setup window makes it easy for you to look through the available NetWare servers to find the printer you want to use. In general, if your networking connections are in order and you set up the printer properly on the NetWare side, printing should work fine.

However, two strange bits of behavior are sometimes exhibited during printing from UnixWare to NetWare. On occasion, a print job is lost and discarded. The mail message you receive indicates that the print job was canceled by the administrator. This is probably not what happened. The print job is just gone. In this case, we suggest you simply resubmit the print job.

If you are using a UnixWare 1.1 system, you may also experience a problem printing to a PostScript printer on a NetWare server. When you print to PostScript printers, you must designate no banners. For some reason, printing a banner page throws the printer into a state where it simply prints a bunch of PostScript code.

To designate no banners on a print job sent from the command line, add -onobanner to the lp command line, as in

```
lp -dprinter1 -Tpostscript -onobanner file.ps
```

To designate no banners when you print using the drag-and-drop method from the Desktop (by dropping a file icon on a printer icon), click on the No button next to the Print banner page setting in the Printer: Request Properties window.

Improving System Performance

No matter how many features a computer system has, using it will be a very frustrating experience if the system runs slowly. Because UnixWare is so flexible and can have so many things happening at the same time, performance can be a problem.

Performance is simply how quickly your system does the things it is asked to do: copy a file, redraw the screen, run an application, and so on. With the right hardware and by following some of the suggestions offered here, you can have your UnixWare system blazing in no time.

For in-depth information regarding monitoring your system and tuning it to improve system performance, see Chapter 9.

NOTE

USING THE RIGHT HARDWARE

The importance of acquiring the right computer hardware to get maximum performance out of UnixWare cannot be stressed enough. With at least a 486 processor, your computer's amount of RAM has the next most significant impact on your system performance. If there are many users on the system simultaneously, and you find that performance is degraded, adding RAM will probably help.

NOTE **We always have at least 16MB of RAM for a single-user UnixWare configuration. See Appendix A for descriptions of the minimum hardware configurations we recommend.**

Besides the RAM used by the central processing unit, increasing the RAM on the video board can significantly increase the speed of the Desktop graphical interface. For example, going from 1 to 2MB of RAM on your video board can significantly increase the rate at which the Desktop is redrawn (when moving windows or listing files in a Terminal window, for example).

MAXIMIZING DESKTOP PERFORMANCE

The main way to improve your Desktop performance is to eliminate any unnecessary activities on the Desktop. Here are some ways to reduce the amount of work UnixWare needs to do:

► Iconize windows you want to see on startup. When you first log in and start up the Desktop, the icons and windows from your last saved Desktop session appear on your screen. If you left the Desktop with a lot of windows open and these windows have many icons in them, it could take a long time for everything to appear. The best solution is to iconize any windows you want to see each time you log in. Iconized windows come up much faster than those that aren't iconized. You'll be able to start your work much quicker this way.

▸ Iconize scrolling windows. Iconizing can also help the performance of scrolling windows, such as the Terminal window. For example, if you are listing a very long file or installing files from
tape so that hundreds of them are listed in the Terminal window
as they are installed, iconize the Terminal window. Iconizing
makes the action you requested go much faster, because the process doesn't need to wait for the screen to be redrawn over and
over again.

▸ Don't use graphic backgrounds. Fancy backdrops on your screen
also slow down the speed of the Desktop. A simple color in the
background redraws much faster than a complex graphic.

▸ Close unnecessary windows. In general, you should not have any
window open or process running that you don't need. Double-
click on the window button in the upper-left hand corner of a
window to close it.

KILLING PROCESSES

Although you don't want to run unnecessary processes, you need to be
careful when it comes to killing them. Some processes are needed to run the
Desktop or other applications that are going on in the background.

To see which processes are currently running on your system, open a Terminal window and type the following:

```
ps -ef
```

If you see a process that you know is not needed or is running out of control, you can kill it by typing the following as the root user:

```
kill -9 pid
```

where *pid* is replaced by the process ID of the process.

Instead of killing individual processes, however, a more effective way of
getting rid of unnecessary processes is to turn off an entire feature you don't
need. For example, if you are not using a particular networking feature, you

can kill all processes associated with that feature, as described in the next section.

RUNNING IN STAND-ALONE MODE

If you are working with UNIX on a computer that is not connected to a network, there are a lot of processes running that you don't need. Turning off some or all of these processes can significantly improve your system's performance.

Most of the networking features in UNIX are started up automatically. These features place daemon (background) processes that wait around to service requests. If you are not using these networking features, you are just chewing up processor time that could be better spent running your applications faster.

The /etc/init.d directory contains most of the scripts that start up networking features in UnixWare. They are linked to files in startup directories (such as /etc/rc2.d) from which they are actually run. You can deal with these files from either location.

The following are the scripts that you might want to turn off in some circumstances:

- ▸ nfs: Starts and stops the Network File System (NFS) features
- ▸ inetinit: Starts and stops TCP/IP features for communicating with the Internet
- ▸ rpc: Starts features related to Remote Procedure Calls, such as NIS
- ▸ nuc: Starts the NetWare Unix Client for connecting to NetWare servers
- ▸ cs: Starts the connection server, which handles outgoing connections for Basic Networking Utilities, such as modem connections over serial lines

If you are not connected to a NetWare server, it's a good idea to stop the nuc script, which does a lot of processing. The NFS services, started with the nfs script, spin off lots of processes, too, so it is also a good one to stop.

You can turn off each script individually or, if you have no networking connections, you can turn them all off using the `netrun` command, which is described in Appendix B. If you decide to stop several of these startup scripts, you need to be careful about dependencies. You should stop the scripts in the order shown below. Also, if you decide to restart scripts, do it in the opposite order you stopped them because some depend on others. For example, for NFS to work, Internet Utilities must be running. To restart everything cleanly, however, you might need to reboot your system.

To turn off a single script, open a Terminal window and, as the root user, type

```
cd /etc/init.d
```

Then enter

```
sh -x script stop
```

where *script* is the name of the script you want to turn off. The `-x` is optional. It shows you the processes as they are stopped. When the script is completed, the prompt (#) returns. You can repeat the `sh` command for each script that you want to stop.

To permanently disable a startup script, change the name of the script in the `rc2.d` directory to any name that doesn't begin with an *S* or a *K*. For example, to permanently disable the NetWare UNIX Client software, as the root user from a Terminal window, type

```
mv /etc/rc2.d/S27nuc /etc/rc2.d/xS27nuc
```

For your own information, you may want to check which processes are running before and after you turn off the services. When we stopped all the scripts listed here, our system went from running 55 processes to running 32 processes (with the Desktop running). Your numbers will vary, but you get the idea.

NOTE

SETTING YOUR PATH

When you use UnixWare from a Terminal window and you type the name of a command to run, UNIX searches the directories set by your PATH variable to find and run that command. UNIX assigns you a path, so each user has at least the standard UnixWare directories in the PATH statement, such as /usr/bin.

When you set up your system, one of your tasks is to set up your own PATH statement so it includes any directories that contain your applications. For example, if you have FrameMaker installed in /usr/frame, with the application (maker) in the /usr/frame/bin directory, you would add /usr/frame/bin to your PATH statement. Then, whenever you type maker from a Terminal window, UNIX will search through the directories in the PATH statement until it finds maker in /usr/frame/bin.

The order of the directories in the PATH statement is also significant. UnixWare searches from the first directory to the last to find the requested command. So, if the command was located in the first and the last directory in the PATH statement, when you request the command, UNIX runs the command in the first directory.

To determine the current path, open a Terminal window and type echo $PATH. The output looks something like this:

```
/usr/bin:/usr/merge/dosroot/ubin:
     /usr/ccsbin:/usr/X/bin:/usr/frame/bin
```

This output shows that the standard UNIX directories (/usr/bin, /user/merge/dosroot/ubin, and /usr/ccsbin) are searched first, then directories added by the user (/usr/X/bin and /usr/frame/bin) are searched. The PATH entry you might use in your .profile file in your home directory is this:

```
PATH=$PATH:/usr/X/bin:/usr/frame/bin
```

The PATH variable can have a significant impact on performance when you run commands from the command line. Here are a few of the points you should consider when you set your PATH variable:

▸ Be careful about putting remote system directories (those on Net-Ware servers or mounted file systems) in your PATH statement. Searching those directories can take a long time.

▸ Large directories or those on remote systems should usually be put at the end of your PATH statement. In that way, every time you run a common, local command, UNIX won't need to spend a lot of time going through directories that take a long time to search.

▸ Don't put directories that you never use in your PATH statement. If you type a command that is not in any directory in your PATH statement, UNIX searches all directories in your path before it comes back with a failure message. If the directories are large or are physically located on other systems (such as a NetWare server or NFS-mounted file system), they can take a long time to search.

▸ To use a command that is in the second of two directories in your PATH statement, type the full path to use the command. For example, type /usr/X/bin/myscript if there is also a command called myscript in /usr/bin.

KEEPING EMPTY DISK SPACE

Try to keep at least 10 percent of your disk empty. When your system gets close to running out of space, access to your disk slows considerably. If you find yourself running low on disk space, consider adding a new hard disk. In the meantime, however, there a some things you can do to free up disk space.

To see how much disk space is available on your system, from a Terminal window, type the following:

```
/etc/dfspace
```

Figure 10.14 shows an example of the output from /etc/dfspace.

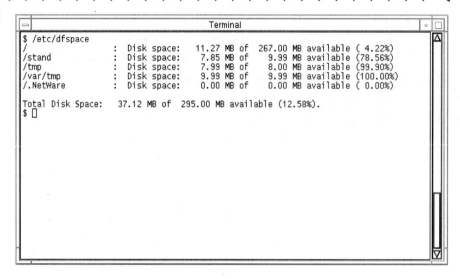

```
  $ /etc/dfspace
  /                    :  Disk space:    11.27 MB of  267.00 MB available ( 4.22%)
  /stand               :  Disk space:     7.85 MB of    9.99 MB available (78.56%)
  /tmp                 :  Disk space:     7.99 MB of    8.00 MB available (99.90%)
  /var/tmp             :  Disk space:     9.99 MB of    9.99 MB available (100.00%)
  /.NetWare            :  Disk space:     0.00 MB of    0.00 MB available ( 0.00%)

  Total Disk Space:   37.12 MB of  295.00 MB available (12.58%).
  $ []
```

To keep from running out of disk space, one thing you can do is to periodically clear out system files that grow:

- The /usr/mail directory: Contains the mailboxes for users on your system. Some system user accounts get mail automatically. For example, the root user receives a mail message after a new software package is installed. The uucp user receives mail about the status of queued file transfers. List the contents of the /usr/mail directory. Then either remove files you don't need or read them as the root user from the Terminal window by typing mailx -f /usr/mail/*file*, where *file* is replaced by the name of the mailbox file.

- The /var/adm/sulog file: Contains a history of when users obtain root access.

- The /var/adm/log/cs.log file: Contains a history of activities by the connection server. Also see if there is a cs.debug file, which can become very large if you turned on debugging for the connection server.

▸ The `/var/spool/uucp` directory: Contains several hidden directories with log files. As the root user from a Terminal window, type `ls -a /var/spool/uucp` to see the hidden directories. The directories `.Admin` and `.Log` may contain large log files you can delete.

Other temporary files and log files in the system can be cleaned out automatically by simply rebooting your system. Rebooting is a good thing to do every once in a while, as explained in the next section.

You can also locate where there are large files and directories on the system. Enter the following command from a Terminal window as the root user:

```
du /home | sort -rn | pg
```

This runs the disk usage command (`du`) on the `/home` directory, where users typically keep their personal data files and applications. The command checks all directories under the `/home` directory for disk space and sorts them from largest to smallest. Press Enter to page through these entries.

Next, go to the largest of the directories and type the following command:

```
ls -l
```

See which are the largest files in the list. Then delete the files, or ask the user to delete or move the ones that are not needed.

If you are connected to a network, consider moving some of your data or applications to another system or a NetWare file server. You can run applications remotely and display them on your Desktop or bring over files as you need them.

REBOOTING YOUR SYSTEM

UnixWare is a complex system. Sometimes, especially if the system has been up for a while, it might start to behave strangely. Performance slows down, networking isn't working properly, or you notice other erratic behavior. The universal cure-all is a system reboot.

The preferred method for shutting down your system is to double-click on the Shutdown icon in the Desktop window. However, as mentioned in Chapter 1, UNIX does have a system reboot state that you can get to with the `init` command. To reboot your system, close any files you have open on the Desktop and complete any activities in progress, such as file transfers. Remove any floppies in your floppy disk drives. Open a Terminal window, and type the following command as the root user:

    init 6

There are some computers that go down with this procedure, but don't come back up. If this happens to you, simply press the Reset button after the system goes down.

 NOTE **With the Veritas file system (`vxfs`), which is the one that comes with UnixWare, you can simply power down or hit the Reset button while UnixWare is running to have it come up later without losing any data. Old UNIX system users are very nervous about doing this, however, because in the past this often resulted in loss of data or at least a very long file system check. If you have the guts to hit the Reset button, go for it.**

Troubleshooting Booting from Multiple Partition Hard Disks

In UnixWare 1.1 there was a nasty problem involving the `fdisk` command that has supposedly been fixed in UnixWare 2. Apparently, it was possible that `fdisk` would corrupt the partition table and make one or more partitions nonusable when your system had a 1GB or larger hard disk. Though we never experienced this problem with UnixWare 1.1, we have experienced it with UnixWare 2.

To avoid this problem, we highly recommend using a *boot manager* program instead of `fdisk` for switching among partitions. We use OS Boot

Select Version 1.32, which we downloaded from CompuServe (file name: OS-BS132.EXE). A boot manager shows a small menu when your computer boots and gives you a choice of which partition you want to boot from.

When installing the boot manager, be sure to make the UNIX partition the *active* partition. You'll then be able to boot either DOS or UNIX from the boot manager menu. Another hint is to make the DOS partition the *default* partition. This causes DOS to boot when you don't enter a number for the boot manager menu before it times out. Because DOS boots much more quickly than UNIX, we find this more efficient than booting UNIX by default.

Once you have a problem due to a corrupt partition table, all is not lost. With the help of two software programs, we were able to reconstruct the damaged part of our partition table and once again boot our machine.

Here's what we did: We booted our computer with DOS and ran FIPS (GNU software, available on the Internet) to view the partition table and confirm that the partition table was corrupted. This software is actually used for shrinking an existing DOS partition when you want to add a partition to a hard disk without repartitioning the entire disk. Our partition table looked similar to Figure 10.15.

Part.	bootable	Start Head	Cyl.	Sector	System	End Head	Cyl.	Sector	Start Sector	Number of Sectors	MB
1	no	0	0	0	00h	0	0	0	0	0	0
2	no	0	0	0	00h	0	0	0	0	0	0
3	no	1	0	1	06h	63	301	32	32	618464	301
4	yes	0	302	1	63h	63	499	32	0	0	0

FIGURE 10.15
Corrupted partition table viewed with FIPS

The problem is with the three zeros on the right side of the bottom row. In fact, when you run FIPS, it will tell you that you have a problem with the starting sector number.

The hardest part of our procedure was trying to figure out what those numbers should be. The Start Sector is the number of sectors for the previous partition (in this case, 618464) plus 32. So the Start Sector number for the bottom row is 618496.

To calculate the number of sectors, you need to know the size of the damaged partition. In our case, the number was 198. Multiply by 2048 and you have the number of sectors (405504). Now all you need is to edit the partition table. Enter Norton Utilities.

Although we used Norton Utilities DISKEDIT, you can use any program that lets you edit the partition table. When we ran DISKEDIT and edited our partition table, it looked like Figure 10.16.

FIGURE 10.16

Repaired partition table
viewed with DISKEDIT

System	Boot	Starting Location			Ending Location			Relative Sectors	Number of Sectors
		Side	Cylinder	Sector	Side	Cylinder	Sector		
unused	No	0	0	0	0	0	0	0	0
unused	No	0	0	0	0	0	0	0	0
BIGDOS	No	1	0	1	63	301	32	32	618464
386/ix	Yes	0	302	1	63	499	32	618496	405504

The bottom rows under Relative Sectors and Number of Sectors show the calculated values restored. To confirm the fix, we exited DISKEDIT and used the DOS FDISK to view the partition table.

The final step was installing the boot manager program mentioned above. We were careful to use the boot manager program for setting the active partition, not `fdisk`. Once installed, we rebooted and, to our relief, both DOS and UNIX were now bootable.

Using many of the basic tools built into the UNIX system, and with some patience, you can track down and fix almost any problem. If done carefully, using the commands and editing the system files described in this chapter will help you debug problems with printers, networking, and even the kernel. However, most of the procedures described in this chapter are for users who are more advanced. A new user should use care in troubleshooting.

Along with troubleshooting techniques, this chapter presented some ideas for improving your system's performance. Following these suggestions can help make your UNIX system operate more efficiently.

At this point, you've seen a lot of what UNIX can do. Now turn to Chapter 11 for a wrap-up of the most important tasks you can do with UNIX (in general) and UnixWare (in particular).

## CHAPTER II

Quick Reference by Task

Administering a UNIX system has never been a picnic on the beach, that is, until UNIX was bestowed with a graphical user interface (GUI). Actually, it's still not a picnic on the beach. It's more like a picnic in the woods on a rainy day, with a few ants. Anyway, Sun, SCO, and Novell have all tried to make the system administrator's life a little easier by allowing the administrator to use the GUI for most administration, as well as regular user tasks.

This chapter summarizes the most common tasks that can be performed through the UnixWare Desktop. Step-by-step instructions are given for each task. Be sure to read through the entire procedure before you actually start a task.

Many of the tasks, especially those involving programs located in the Admin Tools window, require that you have system owner permissions. The instructions assume that you have the correct permissions to run the programs and open the files required for the task.

An Overview of the Tasks

Tasks are organized alphabetically. The following tasks are covered in this chapter:

TASK	PURPOSE	LOCATION
Application Installer	Adding and removing applications	Desktop, Admin Tools
Application Sharing	Advertising and unadvertising to remote systems	Desktop, Admin Tools
Backup-Restore	Backing up and restoring files	Desktop, Admin Tools
Clock	Setting alarms	Desktop, Applications

TASK	PURPOSE	LOCATION
Dialup Setup	Setting up modems and direct connections	Desktop, Admin Tools, Networking
Disk A (or Disk B)	Floppy disk formatting, copying, deleting, and creating directories	Desktop, Disks-etc
Display Setup	Changing your video characteristics	Desktop, Admin Tools
File Sharing Setup	Advertising to and mounting from remote systems	Desktop, Admin Tools, Networking
Get Inet Browser	Using FTP to get Mosaic from Novell server	Desktop, Admin Tools
Hard Disk	Adding a second hard disk to your system	Terminal window
Help	Accessing online help	Any window
Icon Editor	Creating your own icons	Desktop, Applications
Internet Setup	Adding a remote system name so your system and the remote system can communicate over TCP/IP	Desktop, Admin Tools, Networking
Login	Enabling and disabling the graphical login window	Terminal window
Mail	Sending and receiving mail messages	Desktop, Applications
Message Monitor	Viewing console messages from the Desktop	Desktop, Applications

TASK	PURPOSE	LOCATION
Online Docs	Accessing the *Dyna*Text browser	Desktop, Applications
Password Setup	Changing your UnixWare password	Desktop, Preferences
Printer Setup	Adding a print queue to your system	Desktop, Admin Tools
Printing	Printing a file from the UnixWare Desktop	Any window
Processor Setup	Activating processors on a multiprocessor system	Desktop, Admin Tools
Remote Applications	Running applications located on a remote UnixWare system	Desktop, Applications
Serial Ports Board	Adding a serial ports board	Terminal window
Shutdown	Shutting down your system	Desktop
System Monitor	Monitoring your system's performance	Desktop, Admin Tools
System Status	Checking your system's resources	Desktop, Admin Tools
System Tuner	Fine tuning your system's performance	Desktop, Admin Tools
Task Scheduler	Scheduling commands to run at fixed times	Desktop, Admin Tools
Text Editor	Editing and creating text files	Desktop, Applications

TASK	PURPOSE	LOCATION
User Setup	Adding users and groups to your system	Desktop, Admin Tools
Wastebasket	Restoring deleted files and folders	Desktop

For additional information, refer to the UnixWare online help or the relevant chapters in this book.

Some tasks require the use of the Menu mouse button. The right mouse button is the Menu button on both two- and three-button mice.

Application Installer: Adding, Removing, and Viewing Application Properties

Software packages that you can add to your UnixWare system include the following:

► Third-party UNIX applications, such as FrameMaker and Word-Perfect for UNIX

► UnixWare add-on packages, such as the Software Development Kit

► UnixWare updates, such as the update disk that comes with UnixWare or packages that are available though online services such as CompuServe

See Chapter 3 for details on running applications with UnixWare.

ADDING APPLICATIONS

There are a number of ways to add applications to UNIX systems. Applications for UnixWare are usually in **pkgadd** format. However, Application Installer usually detects other formats and installs the software correctly. If you have any problems installing non-**pkgadd**-format software, then follow the manufacturer's instructions for installation. This section describes how to install applications in the **pkgadd** format to UnixWare.

The window used for adding applications is the Application Installer window. This window is shown in Figure 11.1.

1 · From the UnixWare Desktop window, double-click on the Admin Tools icon.

2 · From the Admin Tools folder window, double-click on the App Installer icon.

F I G U R E 11.1

The Application Installer window

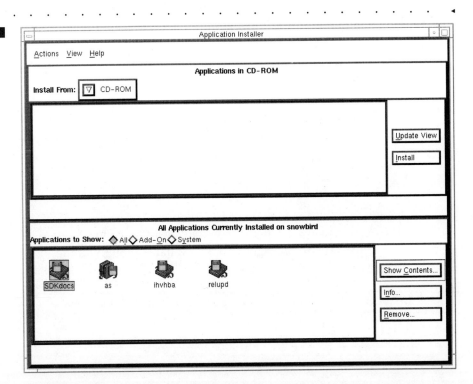

3 · In the Application Installer window, click on the down arrow next to Install From.

4 · In the pop-up menu, click on the medium on which the application you want to install is provided, such as Disk_A or CD-ROM.

5 · Wait while the medium is cataloged. In the top box in the Application Installer window you will see an icon for each package on the medium.

6 · Click on the icon for the application you want to install. If the application is on more than one floppy disk or cartridge tape, you'll be prompted to insert the next floppy or cartridge tape. To select more than one package, press and hold the Ctrl key as you click on the icons.

7 · Click on the Install button on the right side of the window. The Add Application window is displayed. Your package may or may not ask you questions before it is installed.

8 · After the installation is complete, click on Actions in the Application Installer window, then click on Exit.

REMOVING APPLICATIONS

The Application Installer window can also be used to remove applications.

1 · From the UnixWare Desktop window, double-click on the Admin Tools icon.

2 · From the Admin Tools folder window, double-click on the App Installer icon.

3 · In the Application Installer window, take one of the following actions, depending on whether or not the icon of the application appears in the box showing current applications:

> ▸ If you see the icon for the application you want to remove, click on it, then click on the Remove button on the right side of the window.

> ▸ If you don't see the icon for the application you want to remove, double-click on the icon for the set that contains the application. For example, to remove the *Dyna*Text online documentation, double-click on the AS icon (if you have the Application Server) or the PE icon (if you have the Personal Edition). The next window that appears shows the contents of the set. In that window, click on the *Dyna*Text icon, and then click on the Remove button at the bottom of the window.

4 · In the confirmation window, type y and press Enter to confirm that you want to remove the application.

VIEWING APPLICATION PROPERTIES

In an application's Properties window, you can view certain attributes of the application, such as its owner and permissions.

I · From the UnixWare Desktop window, double-click on the Admin Tools icon.

2 · From the Admin Tools folder window, double-click on the App Installer icon.

3 · In the Application Installer window, take one of the following actions, depending on whether or not the icon of the application appears in the box showing current applications:

> ▸ If you see the icon for the application, click on it, then click on the Info button on the right side of the window.

> ▸ If you don't see the icon for the application, double-click on the icon for the set that contains the application. The next

window that appears shows the contents of the set. In that window, click on the application icon and then click on the Properties button at the bottom of the window.

4 · After viewing the properties, click on Cancel.

Application Sharing: Advertising and Unadvertising to Remote Systems

You *advertise* applications on your UnixWare system so they can be run (shared) by remote systems. If the remote system is another UnixWare system, users of that system can run your advertised applications by clicking on an icon for the remote application, located in a folder on their Desktop.

See Chapter 3 for details on sharing applications with remote systems.

NOTE

ADVERTISING APPLICATIONS

You use the App Sharing window to share applications. This window is shown in Figure 11.2.

1 · From the UnixWare Desktop window, double-click on the Admin Tools icon.

2 · From the Admin Tools folder window, double-click on the App Sharing icon.

3 · From the Desktop, open the folder window that contains the icon for the application you want to share.

4 · From the folder window, drag-and-drop the icon for the application you want to share into the App Sharing window. An entry is created for the application.

FIGURE II.2

The App Sharing window

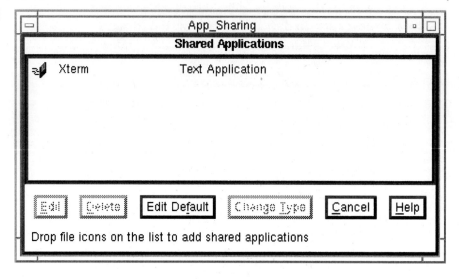

5 · In the App Sharing window, the application you just added should be highlighted. If it's not, click on it.

6 · If the application is a graphical application, which means that it does not require a Terminal window in which to run, click on the Change Type button to change the type from Text Application to X Application.

7 · Click on the Cancel button to close the window.

NOTE **See the Remote Applications section later in the chapter for steps for running shared applications from a remote system.**

UNADVERTISING APPLICATIONS

The App Sharing window can also be used for deleting applications from the list of shared applications, or *unadvertising* them.

I · From the UnixWare Desktop window, double-click on the Admin Tools icon.

2 · From the Admin Tools folder window, double-click on the App Sharing icon.

3 · In the App Sharing window, click on the application.

4 · Click on the Delete button.

5 · Click on Cancel to close the App Sharing window.

Backup-Restore: Backing Up and Restoring Files

You can use UnixWare's Backup-Restore facility to back up files from your system and restore them. You can initiate the backup process immediately or schedule it for a later time.

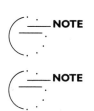

See Chapter 7 for details on backing up and restoring files with UnixWare. NOTE

With the Backup-Restore feature, backed up files can only be restored to their original location. If you need to create backups that can be restored to a directory other than the original directory, use one of the UNIX backup commands (`cpio` or `tar`) from a Terminal window. See Chapters 7 and 8 for more information. NOTE

BACKING UP FILES IMMEDIATELY

The Backup window is used for backing up your files. This window is shown in Figure 11.3.

1 · From the UnixWare Desktop window, double-click on the Admin Tools icon.

2 · From the Admin Tools folder window, double-click on the Backup-Restore icon.

FIGURE II.3

The Backup window

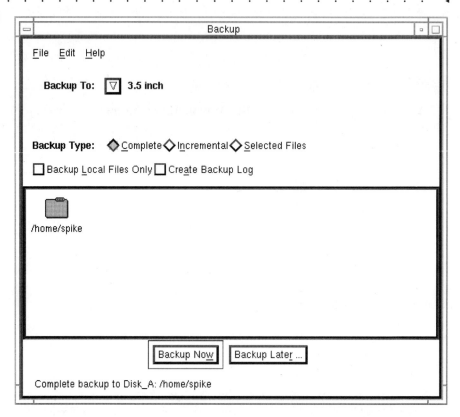

3 · In the Backup window, set the Backup To option. If the media type is not correct, click on the down arrow, then select the medium to which you want to back up your files. Be sure the medium is in the drive.

NOTE **If you have a CD-ROM player installed in your system, you'll notice that it shows up as a media option. However, you cannot use a CD-ROM player for backing up and restoring files.**

4 · Set the Backup Type option:

> ▸ Click on Complete to back up all files shown in the Backup box.

> ▸ Click on Incremental to back up just the files that have changed since your last backup.

> ▸ Click on Selected Files to select files to back up. Drag-and-drop file or folder icons into the Backup box to back up just those files or folders, along with any subfolders.

5 · Set the Backup Class option:

> ▸ Click on Full System to back up the entire hard disk.

> ▸ Click on Personal to back up the files in your home folder.

> ▸ Click on Other Users to back up files belonging to another user (you can only back up one user's files at a time with Backup-Restore).

6 · Click on the Backup Now button at the bottom of the window. Wait for the back up procedure to be completed.

7 · At the top of the window, click on File.

8 · In the File menu, click on Exit.

SCHEDULING BACKUPS

A *scheduled backup* is a backup that is set to occur at a specified time. For example, you can set a backup procedure to begin in the early morning hours when the system is not being used.

The Backup and Task Scheduler: Add Task windows are used for scheduled backups. Figure 11.4 shows the Task Scheduler: Add Task window.

I · From the UnixWare Desktop window, double-click on the Admin Tools icon.

2 · From the Admin Tools folder window, double-click on the Backup-Restore icon.

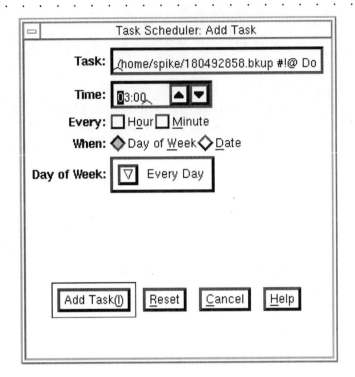

3 ·   In the Backup window, set the Backup To option. If the media
      type is not correct, click on the down arrow, then select the cor-
      rect medium for your backup.

4 ·   Set the Backup Type option:

      ▸ Click on Complete to back up all files shown in the Backup box.

      ▸ Click on Incremental to back up just the files that have
        changed since your last backup.

      ▸ Click on Selected Files to select specific files to back up.
        Drag-and-drop file or folder icons into the Backup box to
        back up just those files or folders, along with any subfolders.

5 ·   Click on the Backup Later button at the bottom of the window.

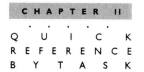

6 · In the Task Scheduler: Add Task window, the Task text box is already filled in. Set the Time option. Use the arrows to change the time shown, or click in the Time box and type the time in 24-hour format.

7 · Set the When option. To schedule a backup to run repeatedly on the same day of the week, select Day of Week. Click on the arrow next to Day of Week. In the pop-up menu, select the day on which the backup should be run.

8 · Click on the Add Task button at the bottom of the Task Scheduler: Add Task window.

RESTORING ALL FILES IN THE BACKUP

You use the Restore window to restore files from your backup media. This window is shown in Figure 11.5.

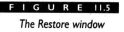

FIGURE II.5

The Restore window

 **WARNING**

When you're restoring files saved through the Backup window, be sure to move any files that you don't want overwritten.

1 · From the UnixWare Desktop window, double-click on the Admin Tools icon.

2 · From the Admin Tools folder window, click the Menu mouse button on the Backup-Restore icon and then click on Restore.

3 · In the Restore window, set the Restore From option. If the media type shown is not correct, click on the down arrow, then select the medium from which you want to restore your files. Be sure the medium is in the drive.

4 · Click on Actions.

5 · In the Actions menu, click on Restore. Wait for the restore operation to complete.

6 · Click on Actions.

7 · In the Actions menu, click on Exit.

RESTORING SELECTED FILES

The Restore window can also be used for restoring selected files.

1 · From the UnixWare Desktop window, double-click on the Admin Tools icon.

2 · From the Admin Tools folder window, click the Menu mouse button on the Backup-Restore icon and then click on Restore.

3 · In the Restore window, set the Restore From option. To change the media type shown, click on the down arrow, then select the medium from which you want to restore your files. Be sure the medium is in the drive.

4 · Click on Actions and then click on Show Files. The files on the medium you're restoring from are shown in the Restore window. All the files are highlighted.

5 · Click on the files you don't want restored. If there are many files on the medium and you only want to restore a few, click on Edit, then click on Unselect All. Next, click on just the files you want restored.

6 · Click on Actions.

7 · In the Actions menu, click on Restore.

8 · When the restoration process is completed, click on Actions.

9 · In the Actions menu, click on Exit.

Clock: Setting Alarms

Use the clock to set an alarm to go off at a specified time. For example, you can use an alarm to remind you of the time that you have a scheduled appointment. The alarm is not accompanied by sound. Only the Alarm window is displayed when the alarm goes off.

You use the Clock window and the Clock: Set Alarm window to set your alarms. These windows are shown in Figures 11.6 and 11.7.

1 · From the UnixWare Desktop window, double-click on the Applications icon.

2 · From the Applications folder window, double-click on the Clock icon.

3 · Click the Menu mouse button anywhere inside the Clock window.

4 · In the Clock menu, click on Set Alarm.

5 · In the Clock: Set Alarm window, enter the message you want to appear on the screen when the alarm goes off.

FIGURE II.6

The Clock window

FIGURE II.7

The Clock: Set Alarm window

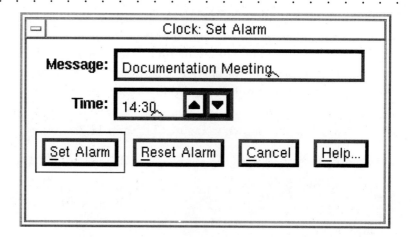

6 · Enter the time for the alarm. You must set the alarm using 24-hour time. For example, to set the alarm for 4:00 in the afternoon, enter 16:00 for the time.

7 · Click on Set Alarm.

After setting an alarm, you can minimize the Clock window or even close the window. The alarm will still work. NOTE

When the alarm goes off, an Alarm window appears with your message. Click on Rearm if you want the alarm to repeat the next day, or click on Disarm to cancel the alarm.

Dialup Setup: Modems and Direct Connections

To communicate with remote UNIX systems using your modem, you need to define the modem device, the remote system, and the port within UnixWare. For communications over a direct connection between systems, you need to define the direct connection, the remote system, and the port.

See Chapter 5 for details on setting up for remote communications. NOTE

SETTING UP A MODEM

You use the Dialup Setup window, the Dialup Setup: Add New System window, and the Dialup Setup: Copy To Folder window to set up remote serial communications. These windows are shown in Figures 11.8, 11.9, and 11.10.

1 · From the UnixWare Desktop window, double-click on the Admin Tools icon.

2 · From the Admin Tools folder window, double-click on the Networking icon.

3 · From the Networking folder, click on the Dialup Setup icon.

4 · In the Dialup Setup window, click on System.

5 · In the System menu, click on New.

6 · In the Dialup Setup: Add New System window, enter the name of the remote system in the System Name text box.

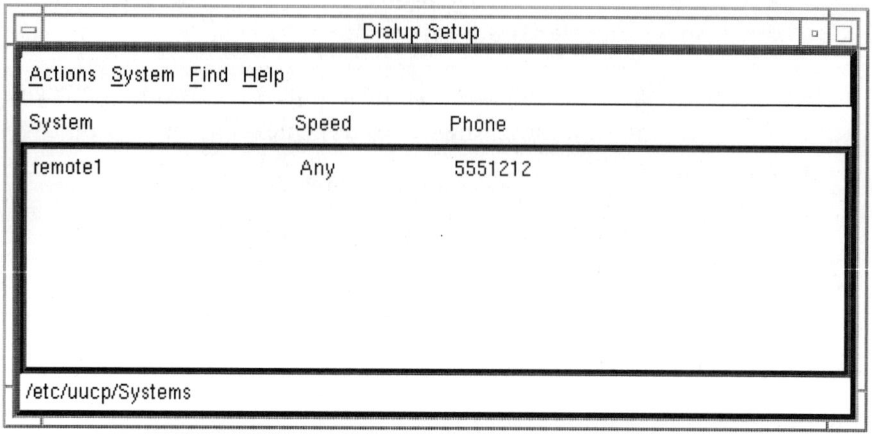

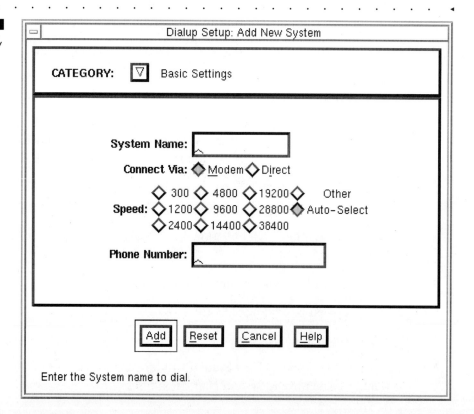

FIGURE 11.8

The Dialup Setup window

FIGURE 11.9

The Dialup Setup: Add New
System window

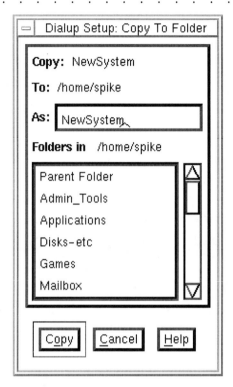

FIGURE 11.10
The Dialup Setup: Copy To
Folder window

7 · For the Connect Via option, make sure that Modem is selected.

8 · Set the Speed option. Click on the speed that matches your modem's speed. You can also leave this setting at Auto-Select and let the system select the correct speed.

9 · Enter the phone number for the modem connected to the remote system.

10 · To set up this connection for file transfers, click on the arrow next to CATEGORY at the top of the window, then click on Login Sequence.

11 · In the Prompt text box, enter the letters ogin (do not enter the leading *l* for the word *login*).

12 · In the Response text box, enter nuucp and then click on the Add button near the Current Login Sequence line.

13 · In the Prompt text box, enter the letters assword (do not enter the leading *p* for the word *password*).

14 · In the Response text box, enter the nuucp password for the remote system. Obtain this password from the administrator of the remote system.

 NOTE **To create an nuucp password on another system, from the remote system, open a Terminal window and, as the root user, type passwd nuucp. Type the new password, and then enter it again.**

15 · Click on the Add button at the bottom of the window.

16 · In the Dialup Setup window, click on System.

17 · In the System menu, click on Copy To Folder.

18 · From the Dialup Setup: Copy To Folder window, click on Copy to create an icon for the remote system in your UnixWare Desktop window. To create an icon in another folder, enter the path for the folder.

19 · In the Actions menu, click on Exit.

CONFIGURING SERIAL PORTS

Before you can communicate with a remote UNIX system over a modem or direct connection, you must use Dialup Setup to configure one of your system's serial ports (most personal computers come with two serial ports, COM1 and COM2) for use with a modem.

Use the Dialup Setup: Devices window along with the Dialup Setup: Device Properties or Dialup Setup: Add New Device window to configure a serial port. The Dialup Setup: Devices and Dialup Setup: Add New Device windows are shown in Figures 11.11 and 11.12.

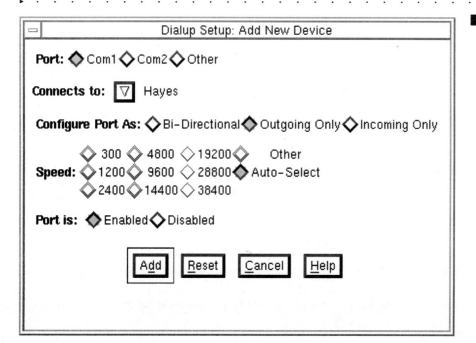

1 · From the UnixWare Desktop window, double-click on the Admin Tools icon.

2 · From the Admin Tools folder window, double-click on the Networking icon.

3 · From the Networking folder, double-click on the Dialup Setup icon.

4 · In the Dialup Setup window, click on Actions.

5 · In the Actions menu, click on Setup Devices.

6 · In the Dialup Setup: Devices window, take one of the following actions, depending on whether or not an icon for the port you want to use appears in the window:

  ▸ If the port icon appears in the window, click on it, click on Device, and then click on Properties.

  ▸ If an icon for the port does not appear in the window, click on Device, then click on New.

NOTE **Step 6 displays either the Device Properties window or the Add New Device window, depending on which bullet item you followed. Both windows are identical except for their title. Below, we'll refer to either window as the Device Properties window.**

7 · In the Dialup Setup: Device Properties window, make sure the port you want to configure is selected for the Port option.

8 · Set the Connects to option. Click on the down arrow, and in the pop-up menu, click on the type that most closely matches your modem (most modems either are Hayes-compatible or can be set to be Hayes-compatible) or choose Direct to configure the port for a direct connection.

9 · Set the Configure Port As option. Choose from the following:

  ▸ **Bi-Directional:** Sets port for both incoming and outgoing communications

> ► **Outgoing Only:** Sets port for outgoing communications only

> ► **Incoming Only:** Sets port for incoming communications only

10 · Set the Speed option. Click on the speed that matches your modem's speed. You can also leave this setting at Auto-Select and let the system select the correct speed.

11 · Set the Port is option. Click on Enabled to enable the port for use or click on Disabled if you don't want the port to be used at this time.

12 · Click on OK.

13 · In the Dialup Setup: Devices window, click on Actions.

14 · In the Actions menu, click on Exit.

ACCESSING NON-UNIX SYSTEMS

To access non-UNIX systems, such as CompuServe or other electronic bulletin boards, use the Dialup Setup: Devices window to install the port's icon in your UnixWare Desktop window.

1 · From the UnixWare Desktop window, double-click on the Admin Tools icon.

2 · From the Admin Tools folder window, double-click on the Networking icon.

3 · From the Networking folder, double-click on the Dialup Setup icon.

4 · In the Dialup Setup window, click on Setup Devices.

5 · In the Dialup Setup: Devices window, click on Device.

6 · In the Device menu, click on Copy To Folder.

7 · In the Dialup Setup: Copy To Folder window, click on Copy to create an icon for the remote system in your Desktop window.

8 · In the Dialup Setup window, click on Actions.

9 · In the Actions menu, click on Exit.

To dial out, double-click on the port's icon. Enter or select the information requested (phone number, speed, parity, character size, and duplex mode). Then click on Dial.

Disk A or B: Floppy Disk Formatting and Copying and Deleting Files

UnixWare provides facilities for working with floppy disks in your floppy drives (drive A: or drive B:). You can format disks for DOS or UNIX and copy and delete files on floppies. (See Chapter 6 for details on working with floppy disks.)

NOTE **We have found that you cannot share files with UNIX floppies between a UnixWare system and a NeXT computer. Instead, we use DOS floppies to copy files between our UnixWare system and NeXT computers.**

FORMATTING A FLOPPY DISK

Before a floppy disk can be used with a computer, it must be formatted for the operating system on which it will be used. The Disk A (or Disk B) icon enables you to format floppy disks for use with either UnixWare or DOS. It's a good idea to keep a supply of both UnixWare-formatted floppies and DOS-formatted floppies on hand.

Use the Disks-etc folder window and the Format window to format floppy disks. These windows are shown in Figures 11.13 and 11.14.

I · From the UnixWare Desktop, double-click on the Disks-etc icon.

2 · From the Disks-etc folder window, click the Menu mouse button on the Disk A (or Disk B) icon.

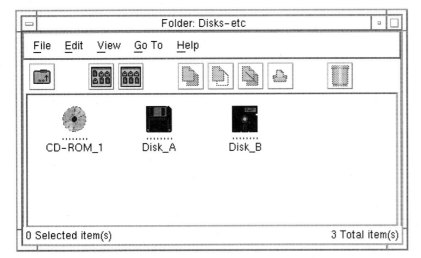

FIGURE 11.13
The Disks-etc folder
window

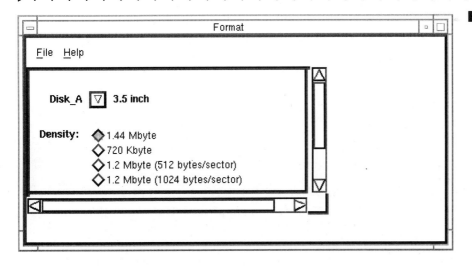

FIGURE 11.14
The Format window

3 · In the Disk A (or Disk B) icon menu, click on Format.

4 · In the Format window, make sure that the floppy disk drive containing the floppy you want to format is selected. Click on the arrow if you need to select the other floppy drive.

5 · Set the Type option:

> ▸ Click on Backup Use for regular UNIX format.
> ▸ Click on Desktop Folder for a mountable UNIX floppy.
> ▸ Click on DOS Format for a DOS 2.0 compatible format.

NOTE **The Desktop Folder type is a convenient way to format floppies to be mounted as file systems. Using file systems on floppies is an easy way to exchange files between UnixWare systems. You can drag-and-drop files between the floppy and your hard disk through the Desktop. However, mounting a floppy as a file system on a non-UnixWare UNIX system requires advanced UNIX commands. Generally, for sharing files on floppies, use the Backup Use type of formatting.**

6 · Click on File.

7 · In the File menu, click on Format. Wait for the formatting process to be completed.

8 · Click on File.

9 · In the File menu, click on Exit.

COPYING A UNIXWARE FILE TO A DOS FLOPPY

From the UnixWare Desktop, you can copy UnixWare files onto DOS floppies for use with either another UnixWare system or a DOS system. To copy files from your UnixWare system to non-UnixWare UNIX systems, you must use UNIX commands, such as `cpio` or `tar`.

See Chapters 7 and 8 for more information on the UNIX commands.

— NOTE

Use the Folder: Disk A (or B) window to copy files on floppy disks. This window is shown in Figure 11.15.

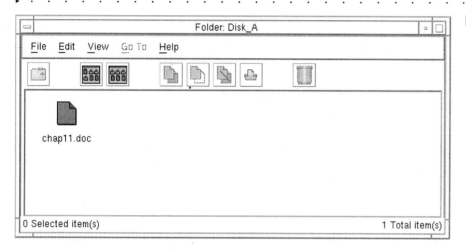

I · Insert a formatted DOS floppy in the appropriate drive.

2 · From the UnixWare Desktop window, double-click on the Disks-etc icon.

3 · From the Disks-etc folder window, double-click on the icon representing the floppy drive you're using. For example, if you're using the first floppy drive, double-click on the Disk A icon.

4 · From the UnixWare Desktop window, open the folder window containing the file you want to copy to another system.

5 · From the folder window, press the Ctrl key as you drag-and-drop the file you want to copy to the Folder: Disk A (or B) window (if you don't press the Ctrl key, the file is moved instead of copied).

COPYING FILES FROM A DOS FLOPPY TO A UNIXWARE SYSTEM

You can copy the files from a DOS floppy disk to a folder on a UnixWare system the same way that files are copied from a UnixWare system to a DOS floppy, that is, by dragging-and-dropping.

Use the Folder: Disk A (or B) window to copy a file from a floppy disk. This window is shown back in Figure 11.15.

1 · Insert the DOS floppy containing the file you want to copy in the appropriate drive.

2 · From the UnixWare Desktop window, double-click on the Disks-etc icon.

3 · From the Disks-etc folder window, double-click on the icon representing the floppy drive you're using. For example, if you're using the first floppy drive, double-click on the Disk A icon.

4 · From the UnixWare Desktop window, open the folder window to which you want to copy the DOS file.

5 · In the Folder: Disk A (or B) window, press the Ctrl key as you drag-and-drop the file you want to copy to the UnixWare folder (if you don't press the Ctrl key, the file is moved instead of copied).

To copy the files to a DOS system, insert the floppy into a drive on the DOS system and use the COPY or XCOPY command to copy the files. For example, to copy all the files on a floppy in drive A: to the C:\MYDOC directory, enter

```
COPY A:*.* C:\MYDOC.
```

NOTE **If your system is connected to another UnixWare system on a network, it may be quicker to copy files across the network than to use floppies. To use the network, install an icon for the remote system in the Internet Setup window. Drag-and-drop the file you want to copy onto the remote system icon, fill in the information, and click on Send.**

DELETING A FILE ON A FLOPPY

You can also use the Folder: Disk A (or B) window to delete files on a DOS floppy disk.

1 · Insert the DOS floppy containing the file you want to delete in the appropriate drive.

2 · From the UnixWare Desktop window, double-click on the Disks-etc icon.

3 · From the Disks-etc folder window, double-click on the icon representing the floppy drive that contains the disk.

4 · In the Folder: Disk A (or B) window, click on the file or files that you want to delete.

5 · Click on Edit.

6 · In the Edit menu, click on Delete.

Directories must be empty before they can be erased from the DOS floppy. However, if you just want to delete all files and directories from a floppy, it may be faster and easier to use the FORMAT command in a DOS window. By default, DR-DOS does a quick format; that is, if the floppy has already been previously formatted, it just erases the pointers to the files so DOS thinks the floppy is blank. When you use this floppy to store data, the old files are overwritten.

NOTE

Display Setup: Changing Your Video Characteristics

Display Setup lets you change the resolution displayed on your Desktop. The higher the resolution, the smaller the windows appear, therefore letting you see more windows at one time. A large monitor (17-inch and up) is recommended for running at very high resolutions, such as 1280 × 1024.

It's also necessary to run Display Setup when you change the video card in your computer unless you're running at the lowest resolution (standard VGA).

You use the Display Setup window to change your display resolution. This window is shown in Figure 11.16.

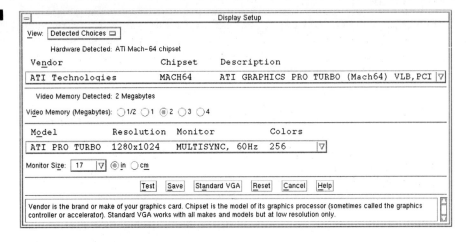

1 • From the UnixWare Desktop window, double-click on the Admin Tools icon.

2 • From the Admin Tools folder window, double-click on the Display Setup icon.

3 • Double-click on the Display Setup icon to display the Display Setup window.

4 • Click on the long button in the top part of the window to display the various brands of graphics cards. UnixWare attempts to detect the type of card in your computer.

5 • Select your video card from the list.

6 • Click on the amount of video memory on your video card. UnixWare attempts to detect the correct amount.

7 · Click on the button under Model.

8 · Select the resolution and number of colors for your display.

9 · Click on the button next to Monitor Size.

10 · Select the monitor size you're using.

11 · Click on Test and then click on Continue to make sure your selections are valid.

12 · If necessary, repeat steps 4 through 11 until you get a configuration that tests properly.

13 · Click on Save to save this configuration.

14 · Click on Cancel to close the Display Setup window.

The changes take effect the next time you start the Desktop.

File Sharing: Advertising to and Mounting from Remote Systems

UnixWare lets you offer (*advertise*) your files and folders so they can be *mounted* by remote systems. It also lets you mount folders from remote systems onto your system.

See Chapter 5 for details on advertising your system's files and folders and mounting files and folders stored on remote systems.

ADDING AN ITEM TO SHARE FROM YOUR SYSTEM

Use the File Sharing Setup: Local Share-Items and File Sharing: Add New Share-Item - Local windows to set up files and folders so that they can be mounted by a remote system. These windows are shown in Figures 11.17 and 11.18.

F I G U R E 11.17

The File Sharing Setup:
Local Share-Items window

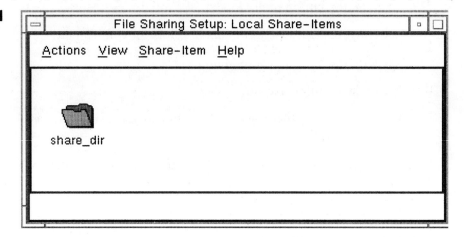

F I G U R E 11.18

The File Sharing: Add New
Share-Item - Local window

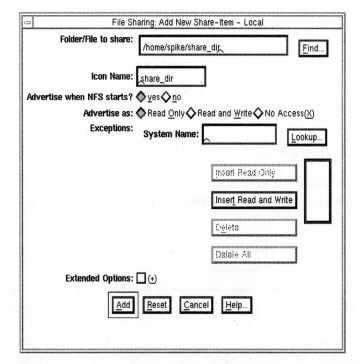

1 · From the UnixWare Desktop window, double-click on the Admin Tools icon.

2 · From the Admin Tools folder window, double-click on the Networking icon.

3 · From the Networking folder, double-click on the File Sharing icon.

4 · In the File Sharing Setup window, click on View.

5 · In the View menu, click on Local.

6 · In the File Sharing Setup: Local Share-Items window, click on Share-Item.

7 · In the Share-Item menu, click on New.

8 · In the File Sharing: Add New Share-Item - Local window, enter the name of the folder or file that you want to share. For example, you should enter `/home/spike/share_dir` if you have a folder called `share_dir` in your home directory and your user name is spike.

9 · Enter a name for the icon. This icon appears in the File Sharing window. Choose a name that will remind you which folder the icon represents. The icon can have the same name as the folder.

10 · Set the Advertise when NFS starts? option:

▸ Click on yes to automatically advertise the folder when NFS starts (typically when you boot your system).

▸ Click on no if you want the folder advertised only when you specifically open the File Sharing window and advertise it.

11 · Set the Advertise as option:

▸ Click on Read Only if you don't want users on remote systems writing to the folder (they can only read the files).

> Click on Read and Write to allow other users to write to the folder.

> Click on No Access if you want only specific remote systems to have access to the folder. Then enter the name of the system that you want to have special permissions. Click on Insert Read Only or Insert Read and Write, depending on the permissions that you want to give the remote system.

12 · Click on Add. The folder is automatically advertised.

 NOTE **Note that the icon is an open folder, indicating that the folder is advertised.**

13 · Click on Actions.

14 · In the Actions menu, click on Exit.

ADDING AN ITEM TO BE SHARED FROM A REMOTE SYSTEM

When you mount a remote system's folder, the folder appears on your system as if the folder is actually part of your file system. The fact that the folder and files it contains are located on a remote system is transparent.

Use the File Sharing Setup: Remote Share-Items and Add New Share-Item - Remote windows to mount folders and files on other systems. These windows are shown in Figures 11.19 and 11.20.

1 · From the UnixWare Desktop window, double-click on the Admin Tools icon.

2 · From the Admin Tools folder window, double-click on the Networking icon.

3 · From the Networking folder, double-click on the File Sharing icon.

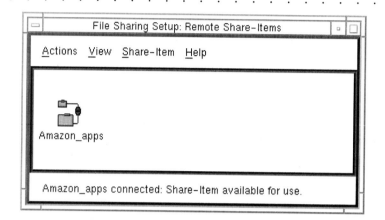

F I G U R E II.19

The File Sharing Setup:
Remote Share-Items
window

F I G U R E II.20

The Add New Share-
Item - Remote window

4 · In the File Sharing Setup: Remote Share-Items window, click on Share-Item.

5 · In the Share-Item menu, click on New.

6 · In the Add New Share-Item - Remote window, enter the name of the remote system advertising a file or folder you want to use. After a short delay, while your machine contacts the remote system, the available share items from the remote system are listed in the Available Share-Items box.

7 · Enter a name for the icon. This icon will appear in the File Sharing window. Choose a name that will remind you which file or folder the icon represents. The icon can have the same name as the file or folder on the remote system.

8 · Enter the name of the share item on the remote system. This information is in the Available Share-Items box.

9 · Enter the name for the folder on your system to which the remote share item should connect. This folder does not need to already exist. It will be created automatically by this procedure.

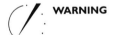 **WARNING** **Use care in selecting a local folder when you are connecting a remote share item. If you select a folder that contains files, those files will not be accessible when the remote share item is connected. We recommend that you create a new folder for each remote share item.**

10 · Set the Connect Share-Item as option:

▸ Click on Read Only if you don't want to be able to write on the remote system.

▸ Click on Read and Write to be able to write on the remote system. The remote share item must be advertised as read and write for you to be able to write on the remote system.

II · Set the Connect when NFS starts? option:

- ► Click on yes to automatically connect to the remote share item when NFS starts (typically when you boot your system).
- ► Click on no if you want the remote share item connected only when you specifically open the File Sharing window and select it.

When you boot your system, it attempts to connect all remote share items set to be connected when NFS starts. If it can't contact a system, it keeps trying, preventing your system from booting until NFS times out. For this reason, if you are connecting remote share items from systems that aren't always available, you may not want the share items connected when NFS starts.

NOTE

12 · Click on Add.

13 · If you choose a local folder that does not exist, a message window appears, asking if you want the folder created. Click on Create.

Notice that the icon indicates that the remote share item is connected.

NOTE

14 · In the File Sharing Setup window, click on Actions.

15 · In the Actions menu, click on Exit.

After file sharing is set up, you can open folders from the Desktop to access the files and folders on the remote system.

ADVERTISING AND UNADVERTISING LOCAL SHARE ITEMS

The File Sharing Setup window can also be used to advertise or unadvertise a share item.

I · From the UnixWare Desktop window, double-click on the Admin Tools icon.

2 · From the Admin Tools folder window, double-click on the Net-working icon.

3 · From the Networking folder, double-click on the File Sharing icon.

4 · In the File Sharing Setup window, click on View.

5 · In the View menu, click on Local.

6 · Click on the icon for the share item.

7 · Click on Actions.

8 · In the Actions menu, click on the action you want to take: Advertise or Unadvertise.

9 · Click on Actions.

10 · In the Actions menu, click on Exit.

CONNECTING AND UNCONNECTING REMOTE SHARE ITEMS

The File Sharing window can also be used to connect and unconnect a remote share item.

1 · From the UnixWare Desktop window, double-click on the Admin Tools icon.

2 · From the Admin Tools folder window, double-click on the Net-working icon.

3 · From the Networking folder, double-click on the File Sharing icon.

4 · Click on the icon for the share item.

5 · Click on Actions.

6 · In the Actions menu, click on the action you want to take: Connect or Unconnect.

7 · Click on Actions.

8 · In the Actions menu, click on Exit.

DELETING A SHARE ITEM

You can also delete a share item, either one that is advertised by your system or one that is mounted from a remote system.

1 · From the UnixWare Desktop window, double-click on the Admin Tools icon.

2 · From the Admin Tools folder window, double-click on the Networking icon.

3 · From the Networking folder, double-click on the File Sharing icon.

4 · In the File Sharing Setup window, click on View.

5 · In the View menu, click on the appropriate view: Local to delete local share items or Remote to delete remote share items.

6 · Click on Share-Item.

7 · In the Share-Item menu, click on Delete.

8 · In the confirmation window, click on Delete.

9 · In the File Sharing window, click on Actions.

10 · In the Actions menu, click on Exit.

CHECKING NFS STATUS

NFS is the mechanism that UnixWare's File Sharing facility uses. The information appears in the Status window. This window is shown in Figure 11.21.

1 · From the UnixWare Desktop window, double-click on the Admin Tools icon.

FIGURE II.21

The Status window

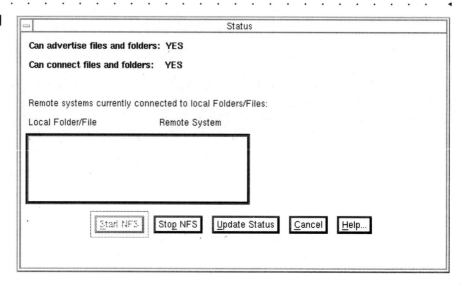

2 · From the Admin Tools folder window, double-click on the Networking icon.

3 · From the Networking folder, double-click on the File Sharing icon.

4 · In the File Sharing Setup window, click on Actions.

5 · In the Actions menu, click on Status. The Status window appears. After a short delay, the status of NFS on your system is shown.

6 · In the Status window, click on Cancel to exit.

Get Inet Browser: Using FTP to Download Mosaic

You use the Get Inet Browser icon located in the Admin Tools folder window to display the Get Internet Browser window, shown in Figure 11.22.

```
┌─────────────────────────────────────────────────────────────┐
│ ─  │             Get Internet Browser              │  □  │ □ │
├─────────────────────────────────────────────────────────────┤
│ Internet Browsers help you locate and retrieve network resources │
│  (documents, data, software, etc) from all over the Internet. Typically, │
│  you navigate through the Internet by following hyperlinks -- terms, │
│  icons or images in documents that point to related documents. │
│                                                               │
│ An Internet Browser is available from the anonymous ftp site  │
│  at ftp.summit.novell.com. It is not part of the UnixWare 2.0 │
│  Product, and is neither supported nor endorsed by Novell.    │
│  It is provided only for your convenience.                    │
│  You must have a working Domain Name Server and               │
│  Internet connection in order to retrieve the Internet Browser. │
│                                                               │
│ Click Instructions to display information on how to retrieve and │
│  install the Internet Browser.                                │
│                                                               │
│ ┌───────────────┐  ┌───────────┐  ┌───────────┐             │
│ │  Instructions │  │   Exit    │  │   Help    │             │
│ └───────────────┘  └───────────┘  └───────────┘             │
└─────────────────────────────────────────────────────────────┘
```

F I G U R E II.22

The Get Internet Browser
window

This window gives you instructions on downloading a copy of Mosaic from a Novell server in Summit, New Jersey.

The Get Inet Browser icon does not open an application that retrieves Mosaic for you. To download and install Mosaic, follow these instructions.

To use the following instructions, you must already have a working Domain Name Server and Internet connection.

NOTE

1 · From the UnixWare Desktop window, double-click on the Applications icon.

2 · From the Applications folder window, double-click on the Terminal icon.

3 · In the Terminal window, enter the following to create and change to a temporary directory:

```
cd
mkdir /tmp/tmp_browser
cd /tmp/tmp_browser
```

4 · Enter the following to connect to the Novell FTP server:

```
ftp ftp.summit.novell.com
```

5 · When the FTP server requests your login, enter `ftp`.

6 · When the FTP server requests your password, enter your complete e-mail address, for example:

```
spike@cnl.com
```

7 · To change to the directory where Mosaic is located, enter:

```
cd /WWW
```

8 · To indicate that you want a binary type file transfer, enter the word `binary`.

9 · To retrieve the file, enter:

```
get pkg.Browser.tar.Z
```

10 · When the file transfer is complete, enter the word `quit`.

11 · To uncompress the file, enter:

```
zcat pkg.Browser.tar.Z | tar -xmof -
```

12 · After the downloaded file is uncompressed, you can install Mosaic. From the UnixWare Desktop window, double-click on the Admin Tools icon.

13 · From the Admin Tools folder window, double-click on the App Installer icon.

14 · In the Application Installer window, click on the Install From arrow. Select Other.

15 · In the Folder text box, enter /tmp/tmp_browser.

16 · Click on Update View.

17 · Click on Install.

18 · From the Terminal window, enter:

```
rm -rf /tmp/tmp_browser
```

Mosaic is now located in your Applications Folder. To start Mosaic, open the Applications folder and double-click on the Inet Browser icon.

Hard Disk: Adding a Second Hard Disk

Whether your first hard disk is an IDE or SCSI type drive, you can easily add a second hard disk.

If the hard disk you're adding is the same type as your first hard disk, or you already installed a controller matching the hard disk type, you just need to add the second hard disk. For example, if your first hard drive is an IDE type, and you installed a SCSI CD-ROM drive, you can plug a new SCSI hard disk into the SCSI controller being used for the CD-ROM drive.

Most IDE controllers allow you to install at least one additional hard drive. Just plug a new IDE drive into the existing controller.

You must use a Terminal window to add a controller and second hard disk. This task can only be done from the command line. See Chapter 8 for details on using the UNIX command line.

> **Add the largest hard disk your budget allows. UNIX applications and data files tend to be larger than their DOS counterparts.**

NOTE

ADDING A SECOND HARD DISK

Before you add a hard disk to an existing controller, you should connect all new hardware. Be sure to follow the manufacturer's instructions for setting jumpers and, with SCSI devices, ID numbers.

1 · From the UnixWare Desktop window, double-click on the Applications icon.

2 · From the Applications folder window, double-click on the Terminal icon.

3 · From the Terminal window, become the root user by typing `su`. Enter the root password when prompted.

4 · In the Terminal window, type `/sbin/diskadd 1`. The `fdisk` screen appears (although this screen is not labeled). The total disk space is shown at the top.

5 · In the `fdisk` screen, make the following entries:

▶ Type 1 to create a partition.

▶ Type 1 to select UNIX System as the partition type.

▶ Type 100 to use 100% of the new disk for UNIX.

▶ Type 4 to update the partition information.

6 · At the prompt

`Do you wish to skip surface analysis?`

type n. Wait while the hard disk is checked for defects.

7 · At the prompt

`How many slices/filesystems do you want created
  on the disk (1-13)?`

type 1 to use the new hard disk as one file system.

8 · At the prompt

`Please enter the absolute pathname (e.g., /usr3)
  for slice/filesystem 1 (1-32 chars)`

type the name you want to use for the file system; for example,
/usr2. (Use a short name for less typing when you want to access the hard disk.) You must use a slash (/) in front of the name.

9 · At the prompt

```
Enter the filesystem type for this slice (vxfs,
   ufs, s5, sfs), type 'no' if no filesystem is
   needed, or press <ENTER> to use the default
   (vxfs)
```

press Enter. (Unless you have a specific reason for using one of
the other file system types, use the default, vxfs type.)

10 · At the prompt

```
Specify the block size from the following list
   (1024, 2048, 4096, 8192) or press <ENTER> to
   use the first one
```

press Enter. The list of block sizes varies with the size of the hard
disk being added.

11 · At the prompt

```
Should /usr2 be automatically mounted during a
   reboot? Type "no" to override auto-mount or
   press <ENTER> to enable the option
```

press Enter. The name you see is the one you're using for the file
system (/usr2 in this example).

12 · At the prompt

```
You will now specify the size in cylinders of
   each slice. (One megabyte of disk space is
   approximately 1 cylinders.) How many cylinders
   would you like for /usr2 (0-115)? Hit <ENTER>
   for 0 cylinders
```

type the higher number shown in the parentheses. The name
you're using for the file system will be shown instead of /usr2.
The higher number you see for the cylinders depends on the size
of your hard disk. In this example, the number is for a small disk
(120 MB).

 **WARNING**

Do not press Enter without entering a number at this prompt or your disk will not be usable.

13 · Several confirmation messages are displayed. At the prompt

`Is this allocation acceptable to you?`

type y.

14 · At the prompt

```
Creating the /usr2 filesystem on /dev/rdsk/1s1.
  Allocated approximately 24908 inodes for this
  file system. Specify a new value or press
  <ENTER> to use the default
```

press Enter. The name you're using for the file system is shown instead of /usr2. The number of inodes allocated depends on the size of your hard disk.

MOVING FILES TO THE SECOND HARD DISK

If your first hard disk is almost full, you can move many of the files in your home directory to the new hard disk and create links so you can easily access them.

1 · From the UnixWare Desktop window, double-click on the Applications icon.

2 · From the Applications folder window, double-click on the Terminal icon.

3 · From the Terminal window, change to the file system on your second hard disk. For example, if the file system is named /usr2, type cd /usr2.

4 · Create a new directory. For example, if your user name is spike, type mkdir spike.

5 · Change to the new directory. For example, type cd spike.

6 · Create a new directory under this one. For example, type
`mkdir work`.

7 · Copy the directories from your home directory to the new directory. For example, to copy an existing directory named `dir1`, type

`cp -r /home/spike/dir1 /usr2/spike/work`

Repeat this for each directory.

8 · Confirm that all your files have been copied. When you're positive the directories and files in your home directory have been copied to the new directory, you can remove them from your home directory.

Once you remove directories, you cannot get them back. Be absolutely positive that all files have been moved. To be safe, create a backup of your home directory on floppy disk or tape before performing these steps.

 **WARNING**

9 · Change to your home directory. For example, type `cd /home/spike`.

10 · Remove the directory and everything it contains. For example, to remove `dir1`, type `rm -rf dir1`. Remove one directory at a time. It's a good idea to frequently check that you're in the directory you think you're in by typing `pwd` *before* you start removing anything.

11 · Create a link from your home directory to the new hard disk. For example, to link the `work` directory (and therefore, everything in it), type

`ln -s /usr2/spike/work /home/spike`

Now when you change to the `work` directory from your home directory, you're really working on the new hard disk. When you need new directories for projects, create them in the `work` directory.

Help: Accessing Online Help

UnixWare has an extensive online help system as well as online documentation. You can open any application that comes with UnixWare and click on that application's Help button to view help on that application. In addition, there is a Help Desk window with icons for each application and some general topics, such as linking files. The Help Desk window is shown in Figure 11.23.

The Help Desk window

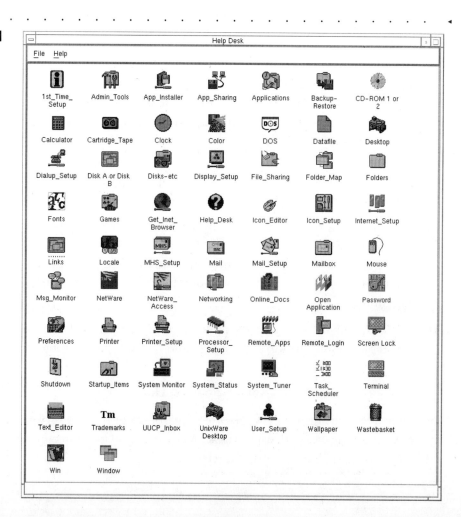

1 · From the UnixWare Desktop window, double-click on the Help
Desk icon.

2 · From the Help Desk window, double-click on the application's or
topic's icon for which you want to view help.

Icon Editor: Creating Your Own Icons

The Icon Editor lets you create your own icons for applications you install or create. You can also use the icons you create to represent files and
directories on your system.

You use the Pixmap Editor and Pixmap Editor: File windows to create
and save icons. These windows are shown in Figures 11.24 and 11.25.

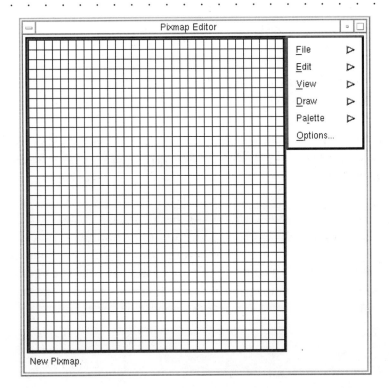

F I G U R E II.24

The Pixmap Editor window

FIGURE 11.25

The Pixmap Editor: File
window

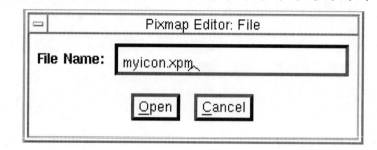

1 · From the UnixWare Desktop window, double-click on the Applications icon.

2 · From the Applications folder window, double-click on the Icon Editor icon.

3 · In the Pixmap Editor window, click on the squares to fill them in. You can drag along several squares as well. To erase a square, click on Edit and then Clear. Either click on a single square to erase or drag the mouse over several squares. You can draw various shapes by clicking on Draw and selecting the desired style, such as Lines, Segments, Ovals, etc.

NOTE **Edit, Draw, and Palette have options that let you keep their pop-up menus on the screen. Just click on Stay up. To get rid of the menu, click on Dismiss.**

4 · To save your icon, click on File and then click on Save. The icon is saved as `Untitled.xpm` in your home directory (you could see your new icon in your Desktop window). To save your icon under a different name, click on File and Save As. The Pixmap Editor: File window is displayed. Enter the desired name and click on Save.

5 · To exit the Icon Editor, double-click on the button in the upper left-hand corner of the Pixmap Editor window.

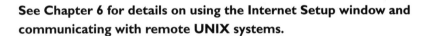

Internet Setup: Communicating with Remote Systems

To allow two systems to communicate over TCP/IP and use TCP/IP utilities, such as `rlogin`, `rcp`, and `telnet`, and BNU (Basic Networking Utilities), such as `cu` and `uucp`, you must add remote systems through the Internet Setup window or configure Domain Name Service.

See Chapter 5 for information on setting up Domain Name Service.

You can also use the Internet Setup window to install an icon representing a remote system in a Desktop window, delete a remote system name from your systems list (`/etc/hosts` file), copy a systems list from another system, and change the properties for a remote system entry in your `/etc/hosts` file.

See Chapter 6 for details on using the Internet Setup window and communicating with remote UNIX systems.

ADDING REMOTE SYSTEM NAMES

Use the Internet Setup and Internet Setup: Add New System windows to add remote TCP/IP system names. These windows are shown in Figures 11.26 and 11.27.

1 · From the UnixWare Desktop window, double-click on the Admin Tools icon.

2 · From the Admin Tools folder window, double-click on the Networking icon.

The Internet Setup window

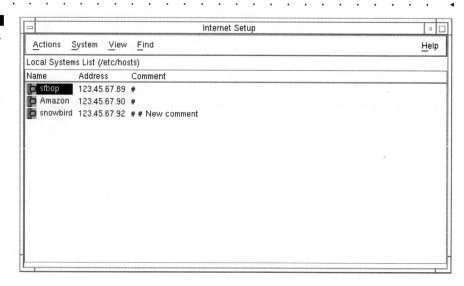

The Internet Setup: Add
New System window

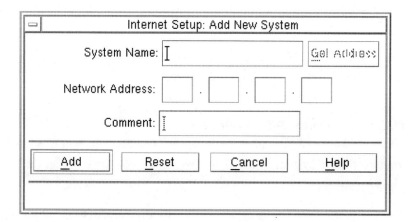

3 · From the Networking folder, double-click on the Internet Setup icon.

4 · In the Internet Setup window, click on System.

5 · In the System menu, click on New.

6 · In the Internet Setup: Add New System window, enter the name of the remote system.

7 · In the Network Address text boxes, enter the full Internet address of the remote system. Use the four boxes to enter the four parts of the Internet address.

8 · Optionally, enter a comment, such as the remote system's owner.

9 · Click on Add.

10 · In the Internet Setup window, click on Actions.

11 · In the Actions menu, click on Exit.

INSTALLING A REMOTE SYSTEM ICON

After you have added a remote system, you can install an icon for that remote system in your UnixWare Desktop window. Use the Internet Setup: Copy To Folder window to add remote system icons. This window is shown in Figure 11.28.

FIGURE 11.28

The Internet Setup: Copy To Folder window

1 · From the UnixWare Desktop window, double-click on the Admin Tools icon.

2 · From the Admin Tools folder window, double-click on the Networking icon.

3 · From the Networking folder, double-click on the Internet Setup icon.

4 · From the Internet Setup window, click on System.

5 · In the System menu, click on Copy To Folder.

6 · The folder in which the icon will be copied is shown next to To. If you want to copy the icon to a different folder, use the Folders in box to select the folder. If necessary, use the scroll bar to find the desired folder.

7 · Enter the name for the icon in the As box if you want a different name than shown.

8 · Click on Copy.

9 · In the confirmation window, click on OK.

You can use the installed icon to log in to a remote system or send files to the remote system. To log in to the remote system, double-click on the system's icon. You must have a login account on the remote system to log in.

 NOTE **You can also install an icon by dragging-and-dropping a remote system entry into a folder window.**

DELETING A REMOTE SYSTEM

When you no longer need to communicate with one of the remote systems you set up in UnixWare, you can delete it.

1 · From the UnixWare Desktop window, double-click on the Admin Tools icon.

2 · From the Admin Tools folder window, double-click on the Networking icon.

3 · From the Networking folder, double-click on the Internet Setup icon.

4 · In the Internet Setup window, click on the system name you want to delete.

5 · Click on System.

6 · In the System menu, click on Delete.

7 · In the confirmation window, click on OK.

8 · Click on Actions.

9 · In the Actions menu, click on Exit.

CHANGING REMOTE SYSTEM PROPERTIES

You can change the properties of an existing entry in your systems list.

1 · From the UnixWare Desktop window, double-click on the Admin Tools icon.

2 · From the Admin Tools folder window, double-click on the Networking icon.

3 · From the Networking folder, double-click on the Internet Setup icon.

4 · In the Internet Setup window, click on the system name you want to modify.

5 · Click on System.

6 · In the System menu, click on Properties.

7 · In the Properties window, make your changes.

8 · Click on OK.

9 · In the Internet Setup window, click on Actions.

10 · In the Actions menu, click on Exit.

SENDING A FILE TO A REMOTE SYSTEM

After you've created an icon for a remote system, you can send a file to that system with a simple drag-and-drop operation. Use the Remote System - File Transfer window to send a file to a remote system. This window is shown in Figure 11.29.

1 · Open the folder window that contains the icon for the file you want to send.

2 · Open the folder window that contains the remote system's icon.

3 · Drag-and-drop the file icon onto the remote system icon.

4 · In the Remote System - File Transfer window, enter the name of the user you want to receive the file.

F I G U R E 11.29

The Remote System - File Transfer window

5 · Click on Show Other Options to set the method of delivery:

 ▸ Click on UUCP to use this delivery method. With UUCP, you don't need a login account on the remote system to send the file. The receiver is notified by mail that a file has been received. If the receiving system is a UnixWare system, the file goes to the user's UUCP_Inbox folder, which is located in the Mailbox folder on the Desktop. If the receiving system is not a UnixWare system, the user must run the `uupick` command to receive the file.

 ▸ Click on Remote Copy to use the Internet as your delivery method. With Internet, you must have a login account on the receiving system, and your system name must appear in the `.rhosts` or `/etc/resolv.conf` file on the remote system. Enter the name of the directory where you want to send the file. Your login account must have write permissions for the directory to which you're sending the file.

6 · Click on Send.

7 · In the confirmation window, click on OK.

8 · In the Remote System - File Transfer window, click on Cancel.

Login: Enabling and Disabling the Login Window

When UnixWare is first installed, the graphical login window is used by default. Although the graphical login window is cute and convenient to use for logging in, it has the disadvantage of restricting how you can use virtual terminals (you must type `newvt` in a Terminal window instead of having them automatically start from your `.profile` file. To make the best use of virtual terminals, which can be very handy, you must disable the graphical login window.

NOTE   **See Chapter 8 for information about using virtual terminals with UnixWare.**

You must enter commands in a Terminal window to disable or enable the graphical login window.

1 · From the UnixWare Desktop window, double-click on the Applications icon.

2 · From the Applications window, double-click on the Terminal icon.

3 · In the Terminal window, enter su. When prompted, enter the root user password.

4 · Enter cd /usr/X/bin.

5 · Enter ./disable_glogin. Be sure to include the period and slash (./) before the command.

6 · Enter Ctrl-D (press and hold the Ctrl key and then press the D key).

The next time you boot your system, the graphical login window won't appear. To enable the graphical login window, repeat these steps, but in step 5, enter ./enable_glogin.

Mail: Sending and Receiving Messages

You can use UnixWare's Mail facility to manage your electronic mail, including sending, reading, and deleting mail messages.

If you're an experienced UNIX user, you may want to use the mailx command in a Terminal window instead of using the Desktop to send mail messages. Like most UNIX utilities, the mailx command is less intuitive than its graphical counterpart, but it works much faster once you learn it.

For details on using the `mailx` command, see **Chapter 8.**

NOTE

SENDING MAIL

The windows used for sending mail are the Mail and Mail: Compose Message window. These windows are shown in Figures 11.30 and 11.31.

1 · From the UnixWare Desktop window, double-click on the Applications icon.

2 · From the Applications folder, double-click on the Mail icon.

3 · From the Mail window, double-click on the Compose New Message icon (the left-most icon).

4 · From the Mail: Compose Message window, in the To text box, enter the e-mail address for the person you want to receive the mail message.

5 · Optionally, in the Subject text box, enter the subject of the mail message.

6 · Optionally, in the Cc text box, enter the electronic address(es) for the people to whom you want to send copies of the message.

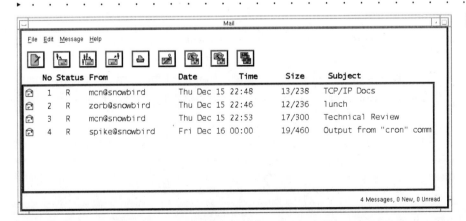

FIGURE 11.30

The Mail window

FIGURE 11.31

The Mail: Compose

Message window

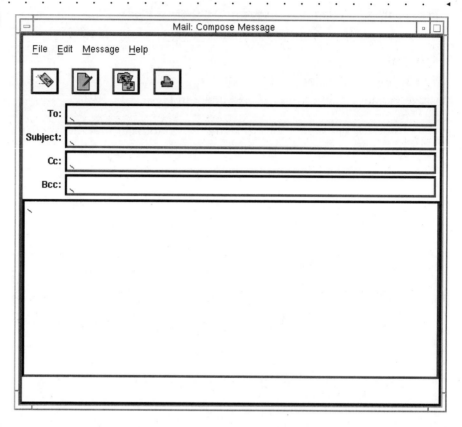

7 · Optionally, in the Bcc text box, enter the electronic address(es) for the people to whom you want to send blind copies. The addresses do not show up in the actual mail message, so the people receiving the message are not aware that copies were sent to these people.

8 · Enter the text of the message. You can use the options on the Edit menu for editing your message.

9 · Click on the Send icon (the left-most icon).

10 · Click on File.

11 · In the File menu, click on Exit.

12 · In the Mail window, click on File.

13 · In the File menu, click on Exit.

READING MAIL MESSAGES

The windows used for reading your mail are the Mail and Mail: Read windows. The Mail: Read window is shown in Figure 11.32.

F I G U R E 11.32

The Mail: Read window

Mail: Read: 3

File Edit View Message Help

From mcn Thu Dec 15 22:53 MST 1994
From: mcn@snowbird
To: spike
Date: Thu, 15 Dec 1994 22:53 MST
Subject: Technical Review

Spike,

The TCP/IP docs will be ready for Tech review in 1 week

4 Messages, 0 New, 0 Unread

1 · From the UnixWare Desktop window, double-click on the Applications icon.

2 · From the Applications folder, double-click on the Mail icon.

3 · From the Mail window, double-click on the message you want to read.

4 · In the Mail: Read window, read your message, then click on the Next arrow (the right-pointing arrow) to read your next message, or click on the Previous arrow (the left-pointing arrow) to read your previous message.

5 · Continue to click on the Next arrow until you've read all your messages.

6 · Click on File.

7 · In the File menu, click on Exit.

DELETING MAIL MESSAGES

After you're finished reading a message, you may want to delete it.

1 · From the UnixWare Desktop window, double-click on the Applications icon.

2 · From the Applications folder, double-click on the Mail icon.

3 · From the Mail window, click on the mail message you want to delete.

4 · Click on the Delete icon (the fourth icon from the right).

5 · Click on File.

6 · In the File menu, click on Exit.

Message Monitor: Viewing Console Messages from the Desktop

The Message Monitor lets you view error messages generated by Unix-Ware. The messages viewed are those sent to the device `/dev/sysdat`. Most of the messages sent to the system console are also sent to the device `/dev/sysdat` and therefore can be viewed by the Message Monitor. The console messages are stored in a file called `/etc/.osm`. You can `cat` this file to view console messages.

You use the Message Monitor window for viewing messages. This window is shown in Figure 11.33.

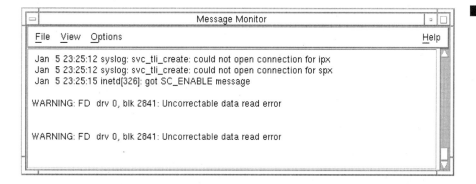

F I G U R E   11.33

The Message Monitor window

1 · From the UnixWare Desktop window, double-click on the Applications icon.

2 · From the Applications folder, double-click on the Msg Monitor icon.

If you don't want to leave this window open on your Desktop, you can iconify it by clicking on the small square button in the upper right-hand corner of the window. When the Message Monitor receives an error message, it automatically displays the full window so you can read the message.

NOTE

3 · Use the Options menu to change the behavior of the icon when a message is received. Click on Options and then Notification for the menu. Your choices are:

> ▸ **Deiconify:** Causes the Message Monitor window to open to full size when new messages arrive.

> ▸ **Flash:** Causes the icon to flash when new messages arrive.

> ▸ **Color Change:** Causes the icon to change color when new messages arrive.

> ▸ **Off:** Turns off all notification of when new messages arrive.

Online Docs: Accessing the DynaText Browser

UnixWare includes the complete text of several books, including the Command Reference books, the Desktop User Handbook, and the System Owner Handbook. The online documentation is in addition to the online help, which is provided for the applications included with UnixWare.

You use the *Dyna*Text Library window and the relevant book window to view online documentation. These windows are shown in Figures 11.34 and 11.35.

I · From the UnixWare Desktop window, double-click on the Applications icon.

2 · From the Applications folder, double-click on the Online Docs icon.

3 · In the *Dyna*Text Library window, under Collections, click on the type of documentation you want to view. Typically, your choices are *Dyna*Text Browser, Reference, and Use & Admin.

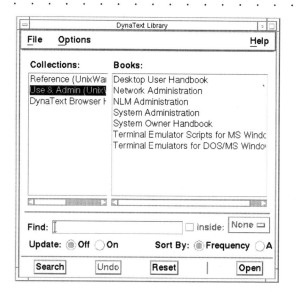

The DynaText Library
window

The Desktop User
Handbook window

4 · Under Books, double-click on the book you want to access. A window with the Table of Contents on the left and the actual text on the right is displayed.

5 · Click on the Table of Contents item to display the text for that topic.

6 · Click on File and Close Book to close the current book.

7 · Click on File and Quit to close the *Dyna*Text view.

Password Setup: Changing Your UnixWare Password

If you think someone might know your password, or your password is about to expire, change your password. Passwords automatically expire in 168 days from the time they are entered. Seven days before the expiration date, you are warned that your password will expire. When you see the warning, change your password.

A password should be at least six characters long and should contain at least one special character, such as a semicolon (;), colon (:), bracket ([or]), brace ({ or }), or another punctuation mark.

Use the PassWord window to create a new password for yourself. This window is shown in Figure 11.36.

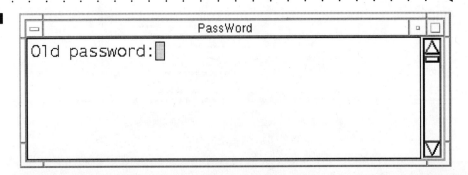

1 · From the UnixWare Desktop window, double-click on the Preferences icon.

2 · From the Preferences window, double-click on the Password icon.

3 · In the PassWord window, enter your old password at the prompt. The characters do not appear on the screen.

4 · Enter your new password at the prompt. Again, you won't see the characters on the screen.

5 · Reenter your new password at the prompt. If you correctly enter your new password a second time, the PassWord window closes; your password has been changed.

Printer Setup: Setting Up and Managing Printers

To print on your UnixWare system, you must define a *print queue* to which print requests are sent. When you set up a printer on UnixWare, you are actually setting up a print queue. The print queue defines the port or network the printer is connected to and the type of printer being used.

SETTING UP A LOCAL PRINTER

A *local* printer is one that is connected to your system. Use the Printer Setup and Printer Setup: Add Local Printer windows to set up your printer. Figures 11.37 and 11.38 show these windows.

1 · From the UnixWare Desktop window, double-click on the Admin Tools icon.

2 · From the Admin Tools folder window, double-click on the Printer Setup icon.

3 · From the Printer Setup window, click on Printer.

FIGURE 11.37

The Printer Setup window

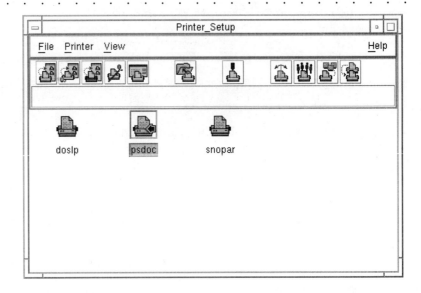

FIGURE 11.38

The Printer Setup: Add Local
Printer window

4 · In the Printer menu, click on Add Local Printer.

5 · In the Printer Setup: Add Local Printer window, in the Local Printer Name text box, enter a name for the print queue. This is an arbitrary name. You use this name in your applications when you want to print. When you're printing from the command line, this name goes with the −d option to lp. For example, lp −dpsdoc myfile, where psdoc is the printer name.

If you are setting up a print queue for use with Merge printing, you must name the printer doslp and select DOS printer as the Model.

NOTE

6 · Under Printer Model, select the type of printer on which the print job will be printed. For example, if the print request is eventually printed on a PostScript printer, select one of the PostScript options. For a serial or parallel PostScript printer, be sure to select the appropriate entry.

When setting up a local PostScript printer, select the appropriate serial or parallel option. If your PostScript printer does not reverse the page order for you (like, for example, the original Apple Laser-Writer), select the option that includes w/page reversal. Most new PostScript printers output their pages face down so they are in the correct order when removed from the printer. For these printers, do not select the w/page reversal option.

NOTE

7 · Select the Connection Type. If your printer is connected to a serial port, select Serial. If your printer is connected to a parallel port, select Parallel.

8 · Select the port, either LPT1 or LPT2 for parallel printers or Other for serial printers. If you select Other, enter the device name of the port in the text box that appears.

9 · Select the mail and banner options, as appropriate.

10 · Click on the Add button. This creates the print queue you defined and adds a printer icon in the Printer Setup window.

11 · If you want this printer to be the default printer, take the following actions:

- ▸ In the Printer Setup window, click on the printer icon you just created.

- ▸ Click on Printer.

- ▸ In the Printer menu, click on Make Default.

 NOTE **This procedure sets up the user's default printer, which is used automatically when the user prints with the Print option on a window's File menu and from applications that come with UnixWare, such as the Text Editor and Mail. Because none of these printing methods allows you to select a printer, it's a good idea to specify a default printer so you can print from these sources.**

By default, no one else on your network can access your local printer. If you want other users to be able to use your printer, do the following:

1 · Click on Printer.

2 · In the Printer menu, click on Set Remote Access.

3 · In the Printer Setup: Set Remote Access window, you can either allow access by all systems except those specified, or deny access to all systems except those specified. Select the appropriate option.

4 · If you selected the option to *allow* access by all systems, do the following to select which systems *cannot* access your printer. If you selected the option to *deny* access by all systems, do the following to select which systems *may* access your printer.

- ▸ On the left side of the window select one of the network options. When the system name you want appears, click on it.

- ▸ Click on Add.

- ▸ Repeat the above steps until you have selected all the desired systems.

5 · Click on the Add button.

6 · In the Printer Setup window, click on File.

7 · In the Actions menu, click on Exit.

SETTING UP A REMOTE UNIX PRINTER

A *remote* UNIX printer is one that is connected to a remote UNIX system (either System V or BSD) that you can access from your system. Use the Printer Setup and Printer Setup: Add Remote UNIX Printer windows to set up a remote printer. The Printer Setup: Add Remote UNIX Printer window is shown in Figure 11.39.

```
┌──────────────────────────────────────────────────────┐
│ ▭  │  Printer_Setup : Add Remote UNIX Printer  │      │
│ Local Printer Name  [                    ]            │
│ Printer Model                                         │
│ ┌────────────────────────────────────────────┐ ▲     │
│ │ Canon Bubble Jet 10ex                       │ ▓     │
│ │ Canon Bubble Jet 130e                       │       │
│ │ Canon Bubble Jet 200                        │       │
│ │ Canon Bubble Jet 300                        │ ▼     │
│ └────────────────────────────────────────────┘       │
│ Remote Operating System Type    ◉ System V  ○ BSD     │
│ Remote System [                         ]             │
│ ◁├──────────────────────────────────────────┤▷        │
│ │ Domain Name Server >             │                  │
│ │ Network Information Service >    │                  │
│ │ System Files >                   │                  │
│ │                                  │                  │
│ │                                  │                  │
│ │                                  │                  │
│ │                                  │                  │
│ │                                  │                  │
│ Remote Printer Name [                  ]              │
│ ┌─────────┐ ┌─────────┐ ┌─────────┐ ┌─────────┐      │
│ │   Add   │ │  Reset  │ │ Cancel  │ │  Help   │      │
│ └─────────┘ └─────────┘ └─────────┘ └─────────┘      │
└──────────────────────────────────────────────────────┘
```

FIGURE 11.39

The Printer Setup: Add Remote UNIX Printer window

NOTE **If you're trying to configure a print queue that will access a printer on a non-UnixWare remote system, use the `lpsystem` command on the remote system to allow for remote access. See the section about printer configuration in Appendix A for more information.**

1 · From the UnixWare Desktop window, double-click on the Admin Tools icon.

2 · From the Admin Tools folder window, double-click on the Printer Setup icon.

3 · From the Printer Setup window, click on Printer.

4 · In the Printer menu, click on Add Remote UNIX Printer.

5 · In the Printer Setup: Add Remote UNIX window, in the Local Printer Name text box, enter a name for the print queue. This is an arbitrary name. You use this name in your applications when you want to print. When you're printing from the command line, this name goes with the −d option to lp, for example, lp −dpsdoc myfile, where psdoc is the printer name.

NOTE **If you are setting up a print queue for use with Merge printing, you must name the printer `doslp` and select `DOS printer` as the Type.**

6 · Under Printer Model, select the type of printer on which the print job will be printed. For example, if the print request is eventually printed on a PostScript printer, select one of the PostScript options. For a remote PostScript printer, you can select any of the PostScript options.

7 · Select the remote operating system type, either System V or BSD. Select System V if the remote system's operating system is UNIX System V Release 4.0 or higher. Select BSD if the remote system's operating system is a Berkeley version of UNIX. UnixWare is System V Release 4.2.

8 · In the Remote System text box, enter the name of the remote system. This is the name of the remote system you'll be sending the print requests to. You can select from a list by selecting one of the network options and selecting the remote system for the list displayed.

9 · Enter the name of the remote printer. This is the name of the print queue on the remote system.

10 · Click on the Add button. This creates the print queue you defined and adds a printer icon in the Printer Setup window. The Add window closes.

11 · If you want this printer to be the default printer, take the following actions:

> In the Printer Setup window, click on the printer icon you just created.

> Click on Printer.

> In the Actions menu, click on Make Default.

12 · In the Printer Setup window, click on File.

13 · In the File menu, click on Exit.

SETTING UP A NETWARE PRINTER

A NetWare printer is one that is connected to a NetWare network that you can access from your system. Use the Printer Setup and Printer Setup: Add NetWare Printer windows to set up a NetWare printer. The Printer Setup: Add NetWare Printer window is shown in Figure 11.40.

1 · From the UnixWare Desktop window, double-click on the Admin Tools icon.

2 · From the Admin Tools folder window, double-click on the Printer Setup icon.

3 · From the Printer Setup window, click on Printer.

FIGURE 11.40

The Printer Setup: Add
NetWare Printer window

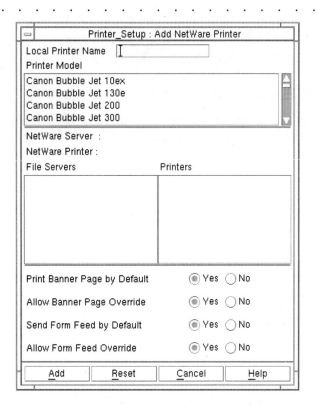

FIGURE 11.40

The Printer Setup: Add
NetWare Printer window

4 · In the Printer menu, click on Add NetWare Printer.

5 · In the Printer Setup: Add NetWare Printer window, in the Local
Printer Name text box, enter a name for the print queue. This is
an arbitrary name. You use this name in your applications when
you want to print. When you're printing from the command
line, this name goes with the −d option to lp, for example, lp
−dpsdoc myfile, where psdoc is the printer name.

NOTE   **If you are setting up a print queue for use with Merge printing, you
must name the printer doslp and select DOS printer as the Type.**

6 · Under Printer Model, select the type of printer on which the print job will be printed. For example, if the print request is eventually printed on a PostScript printer, select one of the PostScript options. For a remote PostScript printer, you can select any of the PostScript options.

7 · Enter the name for the NetWare server on which the remote printer is configured. You can also just click on one of the NetWare servers listed.

8 · Enter the name for the remote NetWare printer. You can also click on a NetWare server and then click on one of the printers shown.

9 · Select the Banner and Form Feed options, as appropriate.

10 · Click on the Add button. This creates the print queue you defined and adds a printer icon in the Printer Setup window. The Add window closes.

11 · If you want this printer to be the default printer, take the following actions:

   ▸ In the Printer Setup window, click on the printer icon you just created.

   ▸ Click on Printer.

   ▸ In the Actions menu, click on Make Default.

12 · In the Printer Setup window, click on File.

13 · In the File menu, click on Exit.

SETTING THE DEFAULT SYSTEM PRINTER

You can set two types of default printers on your UnixWare system. (The default printer is actually the default print queue.) Through the Printer Setup window, users can set their own default printer, as described in the preceding sections. The other default printer is the system default. You must set the system default printer from a Terminal window as the root user.

1 · From the UnixWare Desktop window, double-click on the Applications icon.

2 · From the Applications folder window, double-click on the Terminal icon.

3 · From the Terminal window, become the root user by typing `su`. Enter the root user's password when prompted.

4 · In the Terminal window, type `lpadmin -d printer`, where *printer* is replaced by the name of the printer you want to make the system default.

5 · To verify that the printer you specified is the system default printer, type `lpstat -t`. This command shows your system default printer and the status of all print queues defined on your system.

INSTALLING A PRINTER ICON

Use the Printer Setup: Copy to Folder window to install a printer icon in your Desktop window. This window is shown in Figure 11.41.

1 · From the UnixWare Desktop window, double-click on the Admin Tools icon.

2 · From the Admin Tools folder window, double-click on the Printer Setup icon.

3 · From the Printer Setup window, click on File.

4 · In the File menu, click on Copy To Folder.

5 · In the Printer Setup: Copy to Folder window, use the scroll bars to find and select the folder in which to install the icon. By default, your home folder (the UnixWare Desktop window) is selected.

Printer_Setup : Copy to Folder

Copy : psdoc

To : /home/spike

- spike
- zorb
- mcn
- joe

- Admin_To
- Mailbox
- Applicatio
- Disks-etc
- Preference
- Games
- tmp
- uw20

Selection

/home/spike

| OK | Cancel | Help |

FIGURE 11.41

The Printer Setup: Copy to
Folder window

6 · In the Printer Setup window, click on File.

7 · In the File menu, click on Exit.

You can also install a printer icon by dragging-and-dropping the printer icon onto a folder.

DELETING A PRINTER

If a particular printer is no longer available to you, remove it from the Printer Setup window.

1 · From the UnixWare Desktop window, double-click on the Admin Tools icon.

2 · From the Admin Tools folder window, double-click on the Printer Setup icon.

3 · From the Printer Setup window, click on Printer.

4 · In the Printer menu, click on Delete.

5 · In the confirmation window, click on Delete.

NOTE **If you have print requests pending for the printer, you will be asked whether you want to delete the printer anyway.**

6 · In the Printer Setup window, click on File.

7 · In the File menu, click on Exit.

CHANGING PRINTER PROPERTIES

After you set up a printer, you can change its definition by making changes in the Properties window for that printer.

1 · From the UnixWare Desktop window, double-click on the Admin Tools icon.

2 · From the Admin Tools folder window, double-click on the Printer Setup icon.

3 · From the Printer Setup window, click on Printer.

4 · In the Printer menu, click on Properties.

5 · In the Properties window for the printer, make your changes.

6 · Click on OK.

7 · In the Printer Setup window, click on File.

8 · In the File menu, click on Exit.

CONTROLLING PRINT QUEUE CHARACTERISTICS

Use the Printer Setup: Control Printer window to control whether the print queue accepts or rejects new requests and to disable or enable the printer. This window is shown in Figure 11.42.

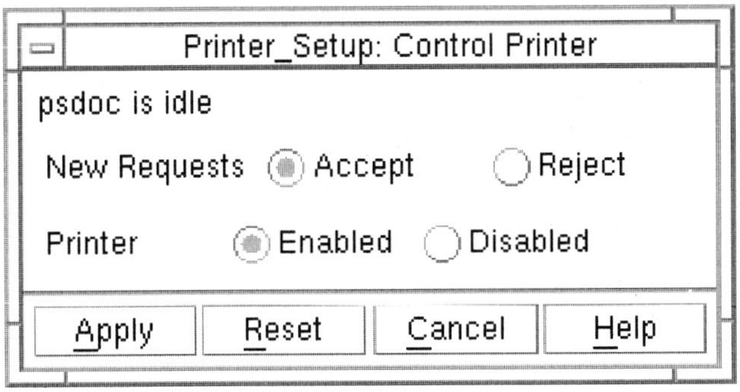

FIGURE 11.42
The Printer Setup: Control
Printer window

```
┌─────────────────────────────────────────────┐
│  ▭        Printer_Setup: Control Printer       │
├─────────────────────────────────────────────┤
│  psdoc is idle                                 │
│                                                │
│  New Requests  ◉ Accept      ○ Reject         │
│                                                │
│  Printer        ◉ Enabled    ○ Disabled       │
│                                                │
│  ┌────────┐ ┌────────┐ ┌────────┐ ┌────────┐  │
│  │ Apply  │ │ Reset  │ │ Cancel │ │ Help   │  │
│  └────────┘ └────────┘ └────────┘ └────────┘  │
└─────────────────────────────────────────────┘
```

1 · From the UnixWare Desktop window, double-click on the Admin Tools icon.

2 · From the Admin Tools folder window, double-click on the Printer Setup icon.

3 · From the Printer Setup window, click on Printer.

4 · In the Printer menu, click on Control.

5 · In the Printer Setup: Control Printer window, set the New Requests option. When this option is set to Accept, the print queue accepts new requests to its queue. When it's set to Reject, you cannot send print requests to the queue.

6 · Set the Printer option. When this option is set to Enabled, the print queue sends its requests to the designated printer. If you set this option to Disabled, the requests are not set to the designated printer, but the printer still accepts print requests to print later.

7 · Click on the Apply button.

8 · Click on the Cancel button.

9 · In the Printer Setup window, click on File.

10 · In the File menu, click on Exit.

This level of control is especially useful when you need to service or replace your printer. You can leave the New requests option set to Accept and set Printer to Disabled. Print requests are queued but not printed. When you reconnect the printer and enable it, all the queued jobs are sent to the printer.

Printing: Printing a File from the Desktop

Before you can print from the UnixWare Desktop, you must set up a printer through the Printer Setup window and install the printer's icon in a window.

The Printer: Request Properties window is used for printing files from the Desktop. This window is shown in Figure 11.43.

FIGURE 11.43

The Printer: Request
Properties window

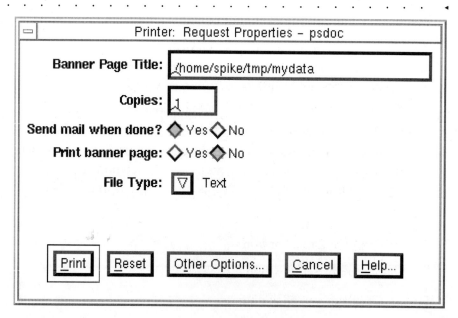

1 · From the UnixWare Desktop window, double-click on the icon for the folder containing the file you want to print. For example, if you have a PostScript file called `mydoc.ps` in the `newdoc` folder, double-click on the `newdoc` icon.

2 · From the Desktop window, open the folder that contains the icon for the printer that you want to use.

3 · Drag-and-drop the icon for the file that you want to print onto the printer icon. Make sure that the printer is the correct type for the file. For example, you can't send a PostScript file to a non-PostScript printer.

4 · In the Printer: Request Properties window, change the title for the banner page if you want to print a banner page with a different title than shown.

5 · Set the number of copies you want to print. To print multiple copies, type the number in the Copies box.

6 · Set the Send mail when done? option. By default, UnixWare will put a message in your mailbox when your print job is finished. If you don't want this message sent, click on No.

7 · Set the Print banner page option.

8 · Set the type of file to be printed. The default is Text, for printing an ASCII (text) file. To choose a different type, such as Post-Script, click on the arrow and click on the correct type in the pop-up menu.

9 · Click on Print.

Processor Setup: Activating Processors on Multiprocessor Systems

UnixWare supports up to 32 processor chips in your computer. (Additional Processor Upgrades must be purchased if you want to activate more than two processors on an Application Server. The Personal Edition only supports up to two processors.) Use the Processor Administration window for activating additional processors. This window is shown in Figure 11.44.

I · From the UnixWare Desktop window, double-click on the Admin Tools icon.

2 · From the Admin Tools folder window, double-click on the Processor Setup icon.

FIGURE 11.44

The Processor Administration window

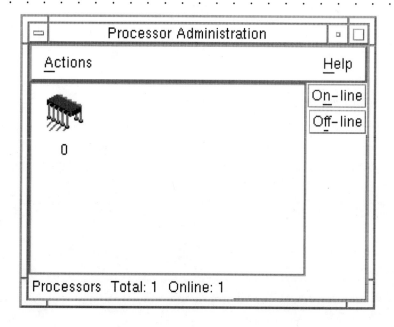

Processor Administration

Actions   Help

On-line
Off-line

0

Processors Total: 1 Online: 1

3 • From the Processor Administration window, click on the processor icon you want to activate or deactivate.

4 • Click on On-line to activate the processor, or click on Off-line to deactivate the processor.

5 • Click on Actions.

6 • In the Actions menu, click on Exit.

Remote Applications: Running Applications on Other Systems

UnixWare's Remote Applications facility is the other side of its Application Sharing facility. If a user on a remote UnixWare system uses the App Sharing window to advertise an application, you can run that application on your system from the Remote Apps window, shown in Figure 11.45. You must also fill in the Authentication window before you can access the remote application. This window is shown in Figure 11.46.

1 • From the UnixWare Desktop window, double-click on the Applications icon.

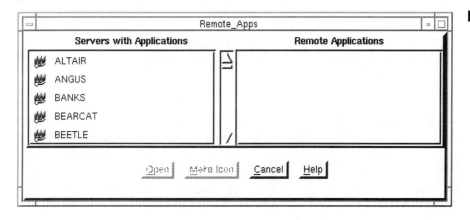

FIGURE 11.45

The Remote Apps window

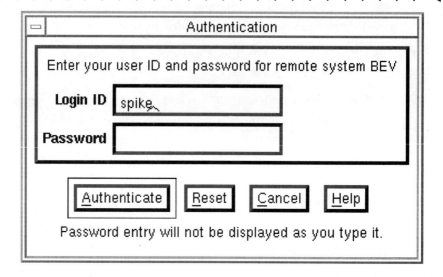

2 · From the Applications folder window, double-click on the Remote Apps icon.

3 · In the Remote Apps window, the Servers with Applications box lists the remote servers currently advertising applications. Click on the remote system that has the application you want to run.

4 · In the Authentication window, enter your login ID and password, then click on Authenticate. If you are already authenticated to the remote system, the Authentication window does not appear.

NOTE **The Authentication window is for your login and password on the remote UnixWare system. Don't worry that this window looks like a NetWare Authentication window.**

5 · In the Remote Apps window, the Remote Apps box lists the applications advertised by the server you chose. Click on the remote application you want to run.

6 · Click on Open to start the application, or click on Make Icon to create an icon for the application in your Applications folder window.

7 · Click on Cancel.

Remember, the application is actually running on the remote system. This means that any files that are opened or saved are opened and saved on the remote system, not your local system. This is an advantage if your system is low on space and you want to store files on the remote system as well as run the application from there. However, it can be a problem if you want to work with files stored on your local system. For example, if you have some WordPerfect files on your local system and run WordPerfect from a remote system, you cannot edit your local files with the remote version of WordPerfect. One way around this is to use File Sharing to mount your file system on the remote system.

See Chapter 3 for details on running remote applications.

 NOTE

Serial Ports Board: Adding Serial Ports to Your System

The Application Server version of UnixWare allows many simultaneous users. Given enough serial ports, you can connect as many users as your license permits to your system.

Most personal computers are equipped with only two serial ports. However, there are many companies that sell serial ports boards, which expand the number of serial ports on your system. Typical ports boards add 8, 16, or 32 serial ports.

INSTALLING A SERIAL PORTS BOARD

This section takes you through the steps for installing the Star Gate ACL II+ serial ports board in a Gateway 2000 computer. The ACL II+ adds eight serial ports. The package consists of an adapter board to be plugged into the bus of your computer, an external box containing the extra ports, and a cable to connect the adapter board and the ports box. Special software (the driver) supplied by Star Gate makes the ports board work.

 NOTE **These steps are for version 2.03 of the ACL driver from Star Gate (the version number is printed on the floppy disk accompanying your ports board). If you have an earlier version of the driver, such as version 2.01 or 1.20, contact Star Gate for an updated driver, or download it from their bulletin board (BBS). You can reach their BBS at (216) 349-2904.**

1 · Insert the floppy disk containing the ACL driver in the appropriate disk drive.

2 · From the UnixWare Desktop window, double-click on the Applications icon.

3 · From the Applications folder window, double-click on the Terminal icon.

4 · From the Terminal window, become the root user by typing `su`. Enter the root password when prompted.

5 · In the Terminal window, type `pkgadd -ddiskette1` if you inserted the floppy in drive A:, or `pkgadd -ddiskette2` if you inserted the floppy in drive B:.

6 · At the prompt to insert the floppy disk, press Enter.

7 · At the prompt to choose which packages you want to add, press Enter. When the package has been added, a series of configuration questions appear.

8 · At the prompt

`Should the driver poll or be interrupted? (i or p)`

type `i`.

9 · At the prompt

    How many boards will be installed? (1-4)

type 1.

10 · At the prompt

    Adding board 1. What board type is this board?

type 2 (for ACL II/ACL II+).

11 · At the prompt

    What I/O address is board 1 to use? (200, 300,
      600, or 700)

type 200.

12 · At the prompt

    What size is the dual port on board 1? (16, or 64)

type 16.

13 · At the prompt

    What memory address is board 1 to use?

type D0000.

14 · At the prompt

    What IRQ is board 1 to use? (3, 4, 5, 9, 10, 11,
      12, or 15)

type 15.

You can use Hardware Setup to check which IRQ is available. Enter that number here and be sure to check the switch settings on the board. See the board's manual for instructions on setting the switch.

NOTE

15 · At the screen showing the configuration options, type Y to confirm that the board should be added. You'll see several messages regarding the progress of the installation.

16 · When prompted about adding another package, press q.

17 · Remove the floppy from the drive.

18 · From the Desktop window, double-click on the Shutdown icon.

19 · From the UnixWare Desktop Shutdown window, click on Shutdown.

20 · From the UnixWare Desktop End Desktop Session window, click on Save Session & Exit (to save your current Desktop configuration) or click on Exit (to exit without saving the current Desktop configuration).

21 · When you are prompted to press Ctrl-Alt-Del to reboot your system, turn off the power (don't reboot yet).

 NOTE

If you are not comfortable working inside a computer, have someone help you insert the adapter board. Although this procedure is not particularly dangerous, you could break something in your computer if you're not careful.

22 · Install the adapter board inside your computer:

▸ Remove the screws holding on the cover from the back of the computer. With desktop models, be very careful not to catch and pull any wires as you slide off the cover. Desktop models have five screws; towers have six screws. Carefully remove the cover.

▸ Find an empty bus slot. Remove the blank plate that blocks the opening from the bus slot to the back of the computer. Save the screw.

▸ Carefully insert the adapter board into the bus slot. Be sure the board is lined up with the connector and firmly push the board. If you don't feel the board going in, do not force it. Take the board out, line it up, and try again. When the board is inserted all the way, the flange with the screw hole should line up with the hole from which you removed the screw.

▸ Replace the bus slot screw.

▸ Replace the cover. With desktop models, be careful not to catch any wires as you slide the case on. Replace the cover's screws.

23 · Turn the power to the computer back on. When the computer boots, it will rebuild the UnixWare kernel. This takes several minutes. Go get some coffee.

CONFIGURING A PORT ON A SERIAL PORTS BOARD

After you've installed the ports board driver and adapter board, you can configure the ports for use with a terminal or modem.

1 · From the UnixWare Desktop window, double-click on the System Setup icon.

2 · From the System Setup window, double-click on the Dialup Setup icon.

3 · In the Dialup Setup window, click on Actions.

4 · In the Actions menu, click on Setup Devices.

5 · In the Dialup Setup Devices window, click on Device.

6 · In the Device menu, click on New.

7 · In the Dialup Setup Device Properties window, click on Other for the Port option.

8 · In the text box that appears, enter `/dev/` followed by the name of the port you want to use. For connecting a terminal or a modem that will be used for dialing out, use one of the following names: `ttya00`, `ttya01`, `ttya02`, `ttya03`, `ttya04`, `ttya05`, `ttya06`, `ttya07`. These names refer to ports 1 through 8, respectively. If you're connecting a modem for dialing in, replace the lowercase a with an uppercase A in the names, as in ttyA01.

9 · Set the Connects To option. Click on the arrow and then click on Direct.

10 · Set the Configure Port As option. Click on Incoming Only.

11 · The speed setting should be 9600. Don't change it.

12 · The Port is option should be Enabled. Don't change it.

13 · Click on Add.

14 · Click on Actions.

15 · In the Actions menu, click on Exit.

16 · In the Dialup Setup window, click on Actions.

17 · In the Actions menu, click on Exit.

18 · From the UnixWare Desktop window, double-click on the Applications icon.

19 · From the Applications folder window, double-click on the Terminal icon.

20 · From the Terminal window, become the root user by typing su. Enter the root user password when prompted.

21 · Type /sbin/acl/enable. The port is now ready to use. After you connect a terminal to the port (with the correct cable type), a login prompt will appear on the terminal's screen.

USING A STRAIGHT CABLE TO CONNECT TO A TERMINAL

When you are connecting a terminal or modem to a serial port either on a ports board or on your PC, you must use the correct type of serial cable. A terminal is considered a DTE device. The ports on the Star Gate ports board are configured as DTE by default. When you connect two DTE devices, you must use a null modem cable (some of the wires are crossed; for example, pin 2 on one end of the cable goes to pin 3 on the other end of the cable). A modem, on the other hand, is a DCE device. When connecting a DCE device to a DTE device, you use a straight cable (the wires go straight through: pin 1 to pin 1, pin 2 to pin 2, and so on).

If you only have a straight cable and want to connect a terminal to one of the ports on the ports board, you need to change the port from DTE to DCE. This is done with a utility supplied by Star Gate.

1 · From the UnixWare Desktop window, double-click on the Applications icon.

2 · From the Applications folder window, double-click on the Terminal icon.

3 · From the Terminal window, become the root user by typing `su`. Enter the root user password when prompted.

4 · In the Terminal window, type `/etc/acl/select dce`.

5 · When the list of ports is displayed, type the name of the port you want to change.

6 · Type `q` to quit.

7 · Type `/sbin/acl/disable`.

8 · Enable the port by typing `/sbin/acl/enable`. The port will now work with a terminal with a straight cable.

Shutdown: Shutting Down Your System

In business environments, computers are frequently left on at all times. This is actually good for the computer, because the electrical surges that occur every time the system is turned off and then on place a certain amount of stress on the electrical components of the computer.

Eventually, however, you're going to need to turn off your system. To ensure the integrity of your files, you should use the correct shutdown procedure to bring down your system before you turn the power off.

Use the UnixWare Desktop Shutdown and the UnixWare Desktop End Desktop Session windows to shut down your computer system. These windows are shown in Figures 11.47 and 11.48.

1 · From the UnixWare Desktop window, double-click on the Shutdown icon.

2 · In the UnixWare Desktop Shutdown window, click on Shutdown.

3 · In the UnixWare Desktop End Desktop Session window, click on Save Session & Exit to save your current Desktop configuration, or click on Exit to exit without saving the current Desktop configuration.

F I G U R E 11.47

The UnixWare Desktop

Shutdown window

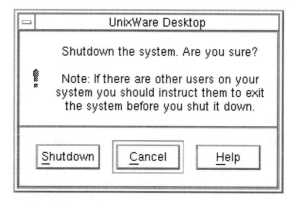

F I G U R E 11.48

UnixWare Desktop End

Desktop Session window

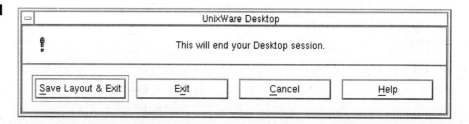

4 · When prompted to press Ctrl-Alt-Del to reboot your system, turn off the power.

System Monitor: Monitoring Your System's Performance

To optimize your system's performance, you must first know what its performance is. Use the System Monitor window to view graphs of certain system performance parameters, such as how much CPU time is being used. This window is shown in Figure 11.49.

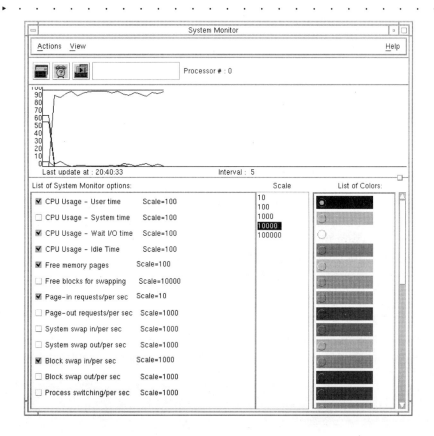

FIGURE 11.49

The System Monitor
window

1 · From the UnixWare Desktop window, double-click on the Admin Tools icon.

2 · From the Admin Tools folder window, double-click on the System Monitor icon.

3 · Click on the parameters you want to view. For example, click on CPU Usage - User time. A graph line immediately appears in the top half of the window.

4 · Click on a color under List of Colors to change the color of the graph line.

5 · For some items, you can change the scale. Under Scale, click on the scale value desired.

6 · To close the System Monitor, click on Actions.

7 · In the Actions menu, click on Exit.

System Status: Checking and Changing System Configuration Information

As you use your UnixWare system to create files and install more applications, the amount of free hard disk space decreases. It's useful to know when you're running low on space so you can take appropriate measures, such as deleting unnecessary files or adding another hard disk.

The System Status window shows you how much of your hard disk is being used, along with other system configuration information, such as total RAM, system date, time, time zone, floppy disk drives installed, and other devices installed (such as a cartridge tape). You can use the System Status window to set the date, time, and time zone. This window is shown in Figure 11.50.

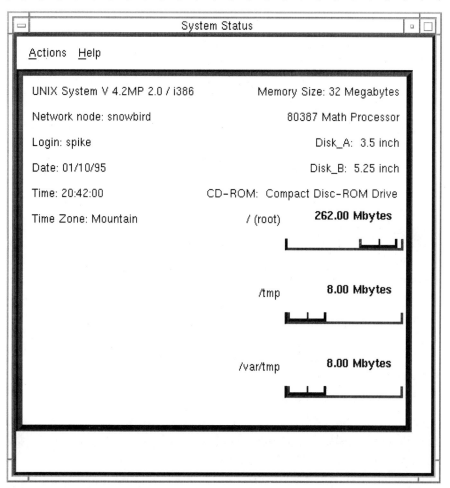

FIGURE 11.50

The System Status window

1 · From the UnixWare Desktop window, double-click on the Admin Tools icon.

2 · From the Admin Tools folder window, double-click on the System Status icon.

3 · In the System Status window, check your hard disk space and any other items of interest.

4 · To set the date, time, or time zone, click on Actions, and then click on Properties. Click on the up and down arrows to increase or decrease the values in the Date or Time box. Click on the arrow next to Time Zone to change the system's time zone.

 NOTE **It's very easy to check your disk space from a Terminal window. Just enter /sbin/dfspace. Your total disk space and amount remaining are shown.**

System Tuner: Fine Tuning Your System's Performance

After viewing your system's performance using the System Monitor window, you can make changes to the parameters that control your system's performance. Use the System Tuner window to make these changes. This window is shown in Figure 11.51.

I · From the UnixWare Desktop window, double-click on the Admin Tools icon.

2 · From the Admin Tools folder window, double-click on the System Tuner icon.

3 · Click on the large Device Driver Parameters button at the top of the window.

 NOTE **The label on this button changes as you select various parameters to change. When the System Tuner window first appears, this button's label is Device Driver Parameters; in Figure 11.51, it's File System Parameters.**

4 · Click on the category of tunable parameters you want to change. Wait while the system displays the parameter list.

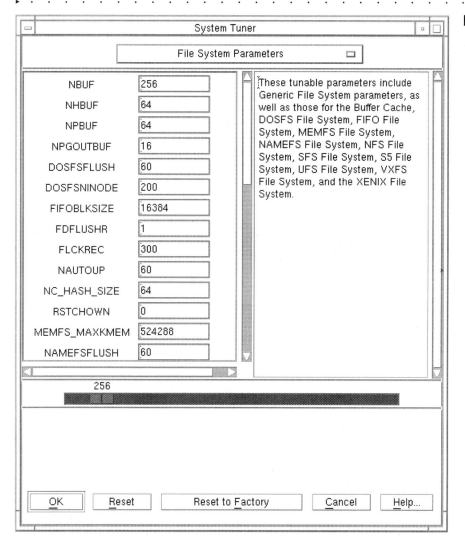

FIGURE 11.51

The System Tuner window

5 · Click in the text box for the parameter you want to change and either move the slider at the bottom of the window or enter the new value.

6 · Repeat steps 5 and 6 for each parameter you want to change.

7 · Click on OK to save your changes and exit, or click on Cancel to exit without saving your changes.

Task Scheduler: Scheduling Commands to Run

The Task Scheduler lets you schedule commands and shell scripts to run at a convenient time, which is not necessarily when you're working at your computer. For example, you could schedule a large printing job or a backup procedure to run late at night.

Noninteractive tasks (tasks that can be run without user input) are best suited for scheduling. Most often, tasks are created with shell scripts. In a shell script for a scheduled task, it's always best to use full path names for any commands or files used. For example, to use the `lp` command to print a PostScript file called `mydoc`, located in a directory called `docs` in your home directory, on printer `psdoc`, create a shell script containing the following line:

```
/usr/bin/lp -Tpostscript -dpsdoc
    /home/spike/docs/mydoc
```

NOTE **See Chapter 8 for details on using shell scripts. See Chapter 7 for details on using the Task Scheduler window to schedule backups.**

SCHEDULING A TASK

Use the Task Scheduler and Task Scheduler: Edit Properties windows to schedule tasks. These windows are shown in Figures 11.52 and 11.53.

1 · From the UnixWare Desktop window, double-click on the Admin Tools icon.

2 · From the Admin Tools window, double-click on the Task Scheduler icon.

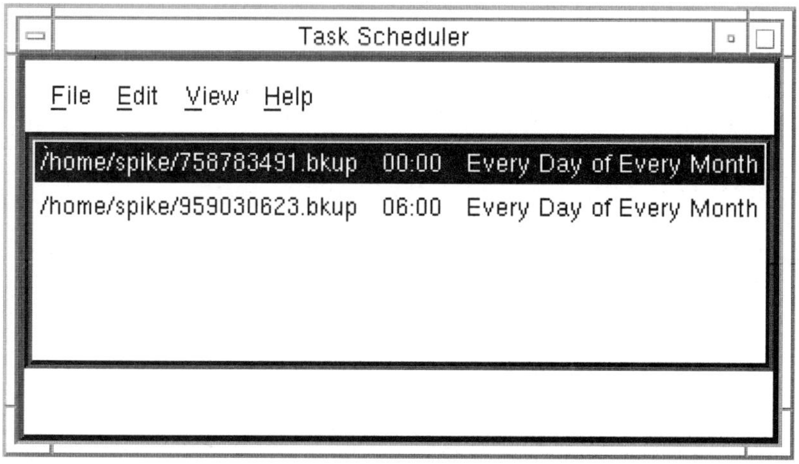

FIGURE 11.52

The Task Scheduler window

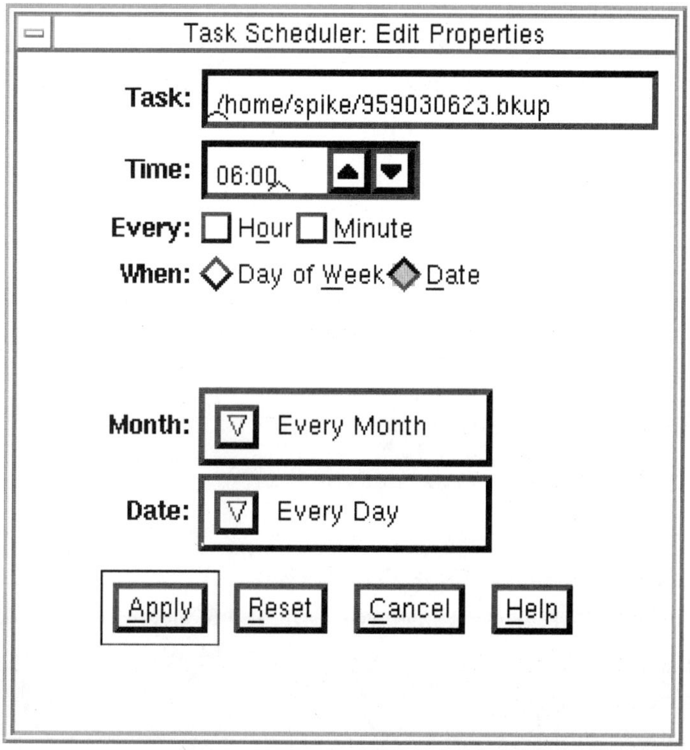

FIGURE 11.53

The Task Scheduler: Edit Properties window

3 · In the Task Scheduler window, click on Edit.

4 · In the Edit menu, click on Insert.

5 · In the Task Scheduler: Edit Properties window, enter the full path for the task. For example, suppose you have a script called `backup.doc` in your personal `bin` directory, and your login is `spike`; enter `/home/spike/bin/backup.doc`.

6 · Enter the time (in 24-hour notation) at which you want to run the task. For example, to run the task at 11:30 p.m., enter 23:30.

7 · If you want to task to run every hour or every minute, click on the appropriate box for the Every option.

8 · If you want to schedule the task for a specific day of the week or a specific calendar date, click on the appropriate box for the When option:

- ▶ Click on Day of Week, and the Day of Week selection box appears. Click on the arrow and select the day from the list.

- ▶ Click on Date, and the Month and Date selection boxes appear. Click on the arrows and select the date you want the task run.

9 · Click on Apply.

10 · In the Task Scheduler window, click on File.

11 · In the File menu, click on Save.

12 · Click on File.

13 · In the File menu, click on Exit.

DELETING A SCHEDULED TASK

If you want to remove a task you scheduled, delete it from the Task Scheduler window.

1 · From the UnixWare Desktop window, double-click on the Admin Tools icon.

2 · From the Admin Tools window, double-click on the Task Scheduler icon.

3 · In the Task Scheduler window, click on Edit.

4 · In the Edit menu, click on Delete.

5 · Click on File.

6 · In the File menu, click on Save.

7 · Click on File.

8 · In the File menu, click on Exit.

Text Editor: Editing and Creating Text Files

Use the Text Editor for creating or changing text files. *Text files* (also called ASCII files) are files that contain only readable ASCII characters. Files created by applications, such as WordPerfect, are not text files. They contain various control codes that cannot be displayed on the screen. However, WordPerfect (and other applications) does allow you to save a file as an ASCII file. In this case, the file loses the formatting information, but you can use a UNIX editor, including the Text Editor, to edit the file.

EDITING EXISTING TEXT FILES

Use the Text Editor, Text Editor: Open, and Text Editor: Save windows to edit an existing text file. These windows are shown in Figures 11.54, 11.55, and 11.56.

FIGURE 11.54

The Text Editor window

FIGURE 11.55

The Text Editor: Open
window

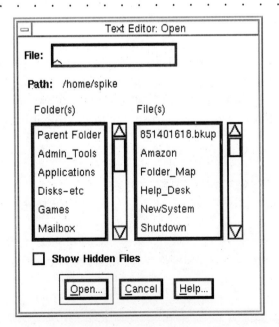

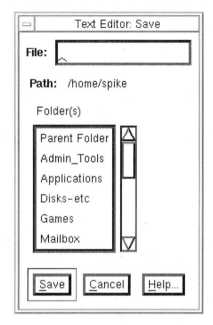

1 · From the UnixWare Desktop window, double-click on the Applications icon.

2 · From the Applications folder window, double-click on the Text Editor icon.

3 · In the Text Editor window, click on File.

4 · In the File menu, click on Open.

5 · In the Text Editor: Open window, click on a folder name in the Folder(s) box to see the files contained in that folder listed in the File(s) box. To move up one folder in the directory tree, click on Parent Folder. If you know the path for the file you want to edit, you can enter it in the File text box.

6 · Click on Open. Another Text Editor window opens with the selected file ready for editing.

7 • In the Text Editor window, make your changes to the file. For Cut, Copy, Paste, and other functions, click on Edit and choose the appropriate option from the Edit menu.

8 • When you are finished editing the file, click on File.

9 • In the File menu, click on Save.

10 • Click on File.

11 • In the File menu, click on Exit.

CREATING A NEW FILE

You can use the Text Editor window for creating new text files as well as editing existing text files.

1 • From the UnixWare Desktop window, double-click on the Applications icon.

2 • From the Applications folder window, double-click on the Text Editor icon.

3 • In the Text Editor window, type the text.

4 • When you are ready to save the file, click on File.

5 • In the File menu, click on Save As (or you can click on Save, since the file has not yet been saved).

6 • In the Text Editor: Save window, click on the folder in which you want to save the file.

7 • Enter a file name in the File text box.

8 • Click on Save.

9 • In the Text Editor window, click on File.

10 • In the File menu, click on Exit.

User Setup: Adding and Managing Users and Groups

When UnixWare is first loaded, only a root user and system owner are created. If other people will log in to your system, each one should have their own user account. You also may want to assign users to groups. Users and groups are set up through the User Setup facility.

See Chapter 1 for details on adding user accounts and groups in UnixWare.

NOTE

ADDING USERS

Use the User Setup: User Accounts, User Setup: Add New User Account, and User Setup: User Permissions windows to add user accounts. These windows are shown in Figures 11.57, 11.58, and 11.59.

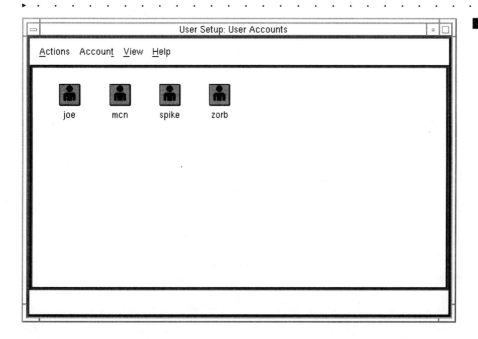

The User Setup: User Accounts window

F I G U R E   II.58

The User Setup: Add New
User Account window

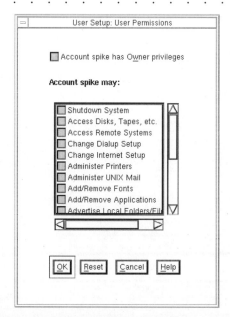

F I G U R E   II.59

The User Setup: User
Permissions window

1 · From the UnixWare Desktop window, double-click on the Admin Tools icon.

2 · From the Admin Tools window, double-click on the User Setup icon.

3 · In the User Setup: User Accounts window, click on Account.

4 · In the Account menu, click on New.

5 · From the User Setup: Add New User Account window, click on Show Other Options (near the bottom of the window). The window will grow and more options will appear below Show Other Options (Figure 11.58 shows the full window).

6 · In the Login ID text box, enter the login ID for the new user.

7 · For the Type option, Desktop is already selected. If you don't want this user to be a Desktop user, click on Nondesktop.

8 · If you're in a corporate environment with an IS department, ask your IS administrator whether or not you should enable NIS management of your system. If yes, then click on Manage User Info via NIS.

9 · Optionally, in the Comment text box, enter the full name of the user.

10 · In the User ID text box, enter the user ID number for the new user. If you have a network where users have logins on several systems, their user ID number should be the same on each system. For a stand-alone system, you can use the ID number shown.

11 · In the Shell text box, change the entry so it reads /usr/bin/ksh (we prefer to use the K Shell over the other shells available). If for some reason /usr/bin/ksh is not available on your system, use /usr/bin/wksh.

12 · In the Groups box, click on the group this user should belong to. Use the scroll bar to display additional groups.

13 · In the Locales box, click on the locale this user should use. The default is the C locale, which is correct for English in the United States.

14 · Click on Add.

15 · In the User Setup: Confirmation window, click on Yes.

16 · In the Password Manager window, enter a temporary password for the new user. When you're finished setting up the account, tell the new user to use Password Setup to select a new password.

17 · In the User Setup: User Accounts window, click on Actions.

18 · In the Actions menu, click on Exit.

CHANGING PERMISSIONS FOR A USER

If you want to change the default permissions assigned to this user, do the following:

1 · From the UnixWare Desktop window, double-click on the Admin Tools icon.

2 · From the Admin Tools window, double-click on the User Setup icon.

3 · In the User Setup: User Accounts window, click on the icon for the user whose permissions you want to change.

4 · Click on Account.

5 · In the Account menu, click on Permissions.

6 · In the User Setup: User Permissions window, click on the lines for the permissions you want to change for this user. If you want this user to have system owner permission, click on the first box.

7 · Click on OK.

8 · If you made the user a system owner, click on the Yes button in the confirmation window.

9 · In the User Setup: User Accounts window, click on Actions.

10 · In the Actions menu, click on Exit.

DELETING A USER

If a user will no longer be logging in to your system, you can delete that user's account.

1 · From the UnixWare Desktop window, double-click on the Admin Tools icon.

2 · From the Admin Tools window, double-click on the User Setup icon.

3 · In the User Setup: User Accounts window, click on the icon for the user account you want to delete.

4 · Click on Account.

5 · In the Account menu, click on Delete.

6 · In the User Setup: Confirmation window, click on Yes to delete the user and all of the user's files. If you don't want to delete the user's files, click on Remove User's Files to unselect it. Then click on Yes.

7 · In the User Setup: User Accounts window, click on Actions.

8 · In the Actions menu, click on Exit.

ADDING A GROUP

After you first install UnixWare, use the User Setup window to create the group you want to belong to. If you do this before you create many files in your home directory, you won't need to spend time changing the group for these files later. Furthermore, when adding users to your group, all their files will belong to the correct group. Maintaining correct groups is not important if you're the only user using your system. In a multiuser environment, however, setting up groups for users makes it easier for members of a group to share files.

Use the User Setup: Groups and User Setup: Add New Group windows to set up groups. These windows are shown in Figures 11.60 and 11.61.

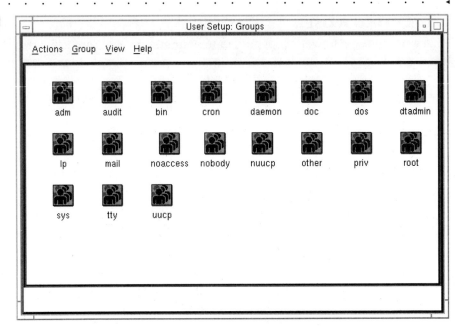

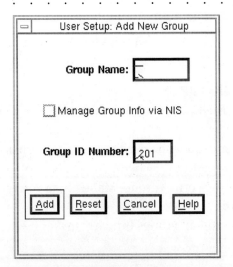

1 · From the UnixWare Desktop window, double-click on the Admin Tools icon.

2 · From the Admin Tools window, double-click on the User Setup icon.

3 · In the User Setup: User Accounts window, click on View.

4 · In the View menu, click on Groups.

5 · In the User Setup: Groups window, click on Group.

6 · In the Group menu, click on New.

7 · In the User Setup: Add New Group window, enter the new group's name and ID number in the text boxes.

8 · If you're in a corporate environment with an IS department, ask your IS administrator whether or not you should enable NIS management of your system. If yes, then click on Manage Group Info via NIS.

9 · Click on Add.

10 · In the User Setup: User Accounts window, click on Actions.

11 · In the Actions menu, click on Exit.

DELETING A GROUP

You can remove any existing groups you don't need from your system.

1 · From the UnixWare Desktop window, double-click on the Admin Tools icon.

2 · From the Admin Tools window, double-click on the User Setup icon.

3 · In the User Setup: User Accounts window, click on View.

4 · In the View menu, click on Groups.

5 · In the User Setup: Groups window, click on the icon for the group you want to remove.

6 · Click on Group.

7 · In the Group menu, click on Delete.

8 · In the User Setup: Confirmation window, click on Yes.

9 · In the User Setup: User Accounts window, click on Actions.

10 · In the Actions menu, click on Exit.

Wastebasket: Restoring Deleted Files

The Wastebasket holds files and folders you delete through the Unix-Ware Desktop. From the Wastebasket window, you can restore these deleted items to their original locations. The Wastebasket window is shown in Figure 11.62.

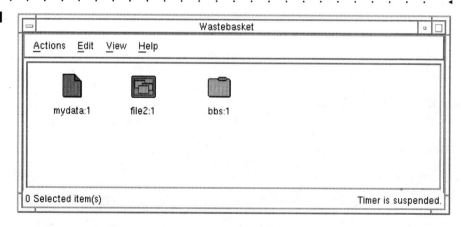

FIGURE 11.62

The Wastebasket window

RESTORING FILES AND FOLDERS

Only files and folders deleted through the Desktop, either by dragging-and-dropping onto the Wastebasket or by clicking on the icon and then selecting the Delete option from the File or icon menu, can be restored. If you delete a file or folder with the `rm` or `rmdir` command in a Terminal window, the file or folder cannot be restored. It is permanently deleted.

1 · From the UnixWare Desktop window, double-click on the Waste-basket icon.

2 · In the Wastebasket window, click on the file or folder you want to restore. To select more than one icon, press the Ctrl key and the left mouse button on the icon after selecting the first one.

3 · Click on Edit.

4 · In the Edit menu, click on Put Back. All the selected icons are restored to their original location.

5 · Click on Actions.

6 · In the Actions menu, click on Exit.

EMPTYING THE WASTEBASKET

When you're running low on hard disk space, check your Wastebasket. Deleted files still take up space until you empty your Wastebasket. Once the Wastebasket is emptied, the files and folders can no longer be restored.

1 · From the UnixWare Desktop window, double-click on the Waste-basket icon.

2 · In the Wastebasket window, click on Actions.

3 · In the Actions menu, click on Empty.

4 · In the confirmation window, click on Yes.

5 · Click on Actions.

6 · In the Actions menu, click on Exit.

This chapter provides a quick reference to a variety of specific tasks—ranging from installing new applications to adding a second hard disk to your system to emptying the Wastebasket. Most of these tasks are accomplished through the UnixWare Desktop, but some must be performed from the command line (Terminal window). Because many of the tasks involve system maintenance types of activities, they can only be performed by the system owner. Other users do not have the correct permissions to run certain commands and open certain files.

The appendices that follow provide information about installing and configuring UnixWare, using shell scripts downloadable from CompuServe, playing the games that are included with UnixWare, and a brief description of all the commands included with UNIX.

Installing and
Configuring UnixWare

This appendix is intended to help you install a real UNIX system on your PC. Like the rest of the book, this appendix focuses on installing the UnixWare version of UNIX System V Release 4.2. UnixWare's form and menu installation interface simplifies the traditionally difficult process of installing and setting up the UNIX operating system. Graphical windows present you with simple choices for setting up the look and feel of the Desktop, as well as for more complex tasks, such as configuring networking.

The *UnixWare Installation Handbook* that accompanies the software does a good job of helping you install the system. This appendix explains the most critical installation decisions you need to make when you set up a UnixWare system. The setup process includes choosing the hardware, installing the software, configuring the system, and reviewing the setup.

Installation Guidelines

Although the installation procedure is relatively simple, setting up UnixWare can have its difficult moments. You will have fewer of those moments if you follow a few basic guidelines:

- ▶ Choose computer hardware that has been tested with your version of UNIX. For UnixWare, you can obtain a list of supported hardware from NSEPro (Novell's NetWare Support Encyclopedia) and Novell's Market Messenger. You can also call Novell's Fax Back system for the latest hardware information. To access this system, call (800) 414-LABS (in the US or Canada) or (801) 429-2776 (from other countries). Even though many PC hardware components and peripherals that aren't on these lists will work, those that are included have been tested and certified by Novell. Sometimes subtle hardware differences can cause installation problems.

- ▶ Check if any settings on the hardware need to be changed. For example, you may need to change your motherboard if you add RAM. If you add peripheral boards, you might need to change

IRQs and addresses so board settings don't conflict. Also, during installation, UnixWare expects certain hardware to be at certain addresses and may not find the hardware if it is at a different address. Check the *UnixWare Installation Handbook* for further information.

► Use the Desktop GUI as much as possible for configuring your system. Often, the Desktop condenses several UNIX steps into one mouse click. Its error checking can sometimes keep you from hanging yourself. This doesn't mean that you will be able to avoid the command line completely. Because the UNIX system is extremely rich in features, and the Desktop GUI is still fairly new, going to a command line may be required for some configuration.

Editing configuration files with a text editor such as `vi` is the traditional UNIX way to configure a system. However, with UnixWare installation, this method may introduce errors that are difficult to track down. For example, you should never, *ever*, edit your `/etc/passwd` file directly (a common practice among pre-UNIX System V Release 4 UNIX system administrators).

Choosing Computer Hardware

Choosing the correct computer hardware is the most important factor for a successful UnixWare installation. Of course, the hardware you choose depends on whether you are using UnixWare as a network or a stand-alone system, the size of your system, and your particular needs.

For the examples in this book, we used a mini UnixWare/NetWare configuration, which is illustrated in Figure A.1. Our setup consists of three computers: a tower PC (running UnixWare), a notebook PC with docking station (running UnixWare), and a desktop PC (running NetWare). The computers are networked together with Ethernet. Table A.1 shows the specifications of each of these computers.

▸ · ◂

F I G U R E   A.1

A mini UnixWare/NetWare configuration

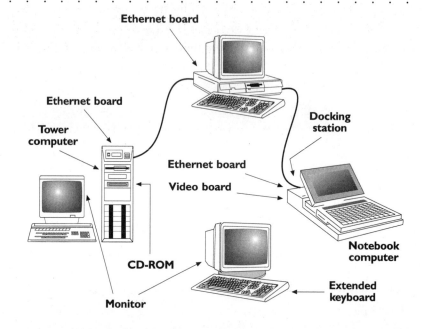

T A B L E   A.1

Specifications of the computers in the sample UnixWare/NetWare configuration

	Tower PC (Gateway2000 P5-90)	Notebook PC (Ergo Computing)	Desktop PC (Generic PC clone)
Processor	Intel Pentium (90MHz)(with PCI local bus motherboard)	Intel 486DX2 (50MHz)	Intel 386SX (16MHz)
Bus	ISA	ISA	ISA
RAM	32MB	16MB	4MB
Hard disk	1GB 9ms (SCSI)	210MB 16ms (IDE)	80MB 28ms
Hard disk controller	Adaptec 2940 (local bus SCSI)	IDE	IDE
Floppy drives	A: 3.5" (1.4MB); B: 5.25" (1.2MB)	A: 3.5" (1.4MB)	A: 5.25" (1.4MB)

	Tower PC (Gateway2000 P5-90)	Notebook PC (Ergo Computing)	Desktop PC (Generic PC clone)
Video	ATI GX PCI; 2MB RAM (local bus)	Trident TVGA-8900LC2; IMB RAM	CGA board
Monitor	NEC MultiSync 5D	NEC MultiSync 5D	CGA monitor
CD-ROM	Toshiba XM3401	None	None
Ethernet board	3Com EtherLink III 3C509	3Com EtherLink III 3C509	3Com EtherLink III 3C509
Ethernet cables	Coaxial (BNC)	Coaxial (BNC)	Coaxial (BNC)
Mouse	Microsoft Serial	Microsoft Serial	None
Operating system	UnixWare	UnixWare	NetWare
Hard disk partitions	First: Novell DOS (200MB); Second: UnixWare (300MB)	First: MS-DOS (30MB); Second: UnixWare (170MB)	First: MS-DOS (5MB); Second: NetWare (75MB)
Modem	Courier HST with ASL	None	None

T A B L E   A.1
Specifications of the
computers in the sample
UnixWare/NetWare configu-
ration (continued)

HARDWARE COMPONENTS

In our system configuration, of the two computers that run UnixWare, one uses a Pentium processor and the other a 486 processor. The Pentium tower PC stays at the office and has enough slots to handle our extra peripherals (CD-ROM, an extra floppy drive, and so on). The 486 notebook PC is portable, yet powerful enough to operate as a desktop system. The 386-based desktop PC is an inexpensive system to use as a NetWare file server. Its purpose is to store our files; performance is not an issue.

Processor

You can never have too much processing power for UnixWare. A 386 processor (with a 387 math coprocessor) is the minimum processor required, but you'll become frustrated with the speed of a 386 system if you use the computer often. We chose a Pentium processor and a 486 processor with high clock speeds (90MHz for the tower and 50MHz for the notebook) for running UnixWare. For a small configuration like ours, the NetWare file server works fine with a 386 processor.

None of our computers supports multiple processors. If you need a computer that will be used for high volume and many users, you may want to consider pricing a multiprocessor computer. Adding a processor is an easy and relatively inexpensive way of improving your system's performance as your needs grow.

Random Access Memory (RAM)

RAM is another item you don't want to skimp on with UnixWare. UNIX applications in general, and graphical applications in particular, use a lot of RAM. When RAM is full, UnixWare does something called *swapping*, which means that it puts the overflow of information on the hard disk. If you start up several applications and your computer slows down considerably while the hard disk light is flashing, UnixWare is probably swapping. If this happens often, you may want to add more RAM to your system.

The UnixWare documentation recommends that you have at least 8MB of RAM for a UnixWare Personal Edition and 12MB of RAM for an Application Server. We suggest having at least 16MB of RAM. If you expect to have many users logged in at a time using the graphical interface, you will probably want even more RAM than 16MB. We have 32MB of RAM on our Pentium and 16MB on our 486 computer.

Unlike DOS, UnixWare automatically takes advantage of any amount of RAM you have installed in your system. Load it up.

Hard Disk

Your hard disk should be large enough to store the UnixWare system plus any applications and data files you want to keep on your local system. If you are in a networked environment, you can store applications and files on other UnixWare or NetWare systems. We've never heard anyone complain about having too much disk space, although we've often heard people cursing when an installation fails or when they can't save a file because their hard disk is full. Make sure you have enough disk space for your needs.

For a stand-alone UnixWare Personal Edition (PE) system, you should have at least a 340MB hard disk. Usually, this will give you enough room for UnixWare, a healthy-sized separate DOS partition (an area of the disk devoted exclusively to DOS), a couple of large applications, and a fair number of data files.

A UnixWare Application Server (AS) system should have at least a 500MB hard disk. You may want more room if the hard disk is providing space for applications and data for other UnixWare PE systems. If you plan to use your system as an install server you must add 70MB to 80MB to your disk requirements. If you plan to install the UnixWare online documents (*Dyna*Text) you will need to add an additional 70MB to your disk requirements (Application Server only).

For UnixWare 2, Novell recommends a minimum 120MB hard disk to install UnixWare, 140MB to install the default set of packages. This won't be enough space, however, if you install all software packages included with the UnixWare Application Server.

If you want to install several operating systems on your computer, you will want an even larger hard disk. We have three operating systems on our hard disk: UnixWare, DOS/Windows, and OS/2. We divided our 1GB, HP SCSI (9.5ms) hard disk into three partitions: one for each operating system. Now we can use either a boot manager to let us select which operating system to use as the computer comes up, or the `fdisk` command to select the active partition and reboot to have the operating system on that partition come up.

Hard Disk Controller

Many new PC systems, such as the Gateway 2000, have slots on the motherboard where you can attach local bus hard disk controllers. The throughput is much faster with local bus controllers, so any operations that read and write to the hard disk are performed more quickly.

The hard disk controller in our Gateway 2000 system is a SCSI controller: Adaptec Model 2940 (PCI bus). Adaptec worked closely with the UnixWare developers, so their controllers are well supported in UnixWare.

IDE disk controllers are also fast and have tested well with UnixWare. In the past, SCSI controllers have been faster than most IDE controllers, but the newer, enhanced IDE controllers approach or surpass SCSI controllers. An advantage to using SCSI controllers, however, is that they give you the option of purchasing SCSI peripherals (such as a cartridge tape and CD-ROM) without needing to buy an additional controller.

Floppy Drives

When we purchased our Gateway computer, we had Gateway swap the two floppy disk drives so the 3.5-inch floppy drive is drive A: and the 5.25-inch floppy drive is drive B:. In our experience, 3.5-inch floppy disks are more durable and easier to deal with. Also, the industry is moving away from 5.25-inch floppy disks. The 3.5-inch floppy drive must be drive A: if you are going to boot from 3.5-inch floppy disks.

 NOTE **Currently, UnixWare is not available on floppy disk. You must install from CD-ROM, cartridge tape, or a UnixWare Application Server system over a network.**

Video

We connected an ATI GX PCI local bus video card to the second local bus slot on our motherboard (Gateway 2000). This video board has 2MB of RAM and is functionally equivalent to the Graphics Pro Turbo video board. Window redrawing and text scrolling are much faster with a local bus video board than with an AT bus video board.

For the nonlocal bus system, any supported VGA board is fine. In our notebook computer, we have a Trident TVGA-8900LC2 board. The ATI Graphics Ultra Pro is a good choice for UnixWare. This model is fast and supports high resolution (1280×1024) and 256 colors.

In general, boards that support higher resolution let you fit more windows onto your screen. The dots are smaller, so the windows and icons are also smaller.

As UnixWare is delivered, the video is set to standard VGA, 640×480 resolution. Immediately after you install UnixWare and log in for the first time, a setup window pops up, allowing you to change the display resolution. You can choose to change the resolution at this time or run the Display Setup utility from the Admin Tools window. Display Setup lets you define the type of video board (by the video chip set used), the screen resolution, number of colors (16, 256, 64KB or 16.7MB), monitor size, and video RAM.

Monitor

Because UnixWare lets you have many windows open and lots of applications running at a time, it's a shame to be limited by the area on a small monitor. Although a large monitor can be nearly as expensive as the PC itself, if you are spending a lot of time using your computer, your eyes will thank you for the space.

Make sure you have a monitor that runs at the resolution and scan rate your video board supports. We use NEC MultiSync 5D 20-inch monitors. NEC 5Ds support high resolution (1280×1024) and are noninterlaced (which causes less flicker).

CD-ROM

Get a CD-ROM for your computer. The industry is moving more and more toward CD-ROMs. Software companies like the CD-ROM because it's a cheap medium for their software. As a user, try installing a UNIX operating system from 50 or so floppy disks a few times and you'll be begging for a CD-ROM drive.

We use a Toshiba XM3401 CD-ROM on our Gateway 2000 computer. It's a dual-speed, SCSI-based CD-ROM drive. If you are using a SONY cd33a, non-SCSI CD-ROM, you need to set the JP4 jumper to 1.

Ethernet or Token Ring Boards and Cables

If you have two or more UnixWare systems in a location, connect them with some Ethernet or Token Ring boards and cables. Once you do, you can use many of the networking features built into the operating system to share information between the systems. You can also connect UnixWare to Net-Ware systems using Ethernet.

After checking the UnixWare hardware compatibility list for Ethernet or Token Ring boards, choose one that matches your bus type (such as ISA, EISA, or MCA) and cable type (such as thin coaxial, twisted-pair, or thick coaxial). We chose the 3Com EtherLink III 3C509, parallel tasking, 16-bit network adapter for coaxial cable. This board has both AUI (15-pin) and BNC connectors. The 3C509 is a high-performance (because of its parallel tasking feature), low-cost Ethernet board.

Mouse

You can use a PS/2, bus, or serial mouse with UnixWare. Having a PS/2 or bus mouse saves you from using one of your serial ports (COM1 or COM2). We use the serial type because it came with our systems.

Both two-button and three-button mice are supported. Though nothing in UnixWare absolutely requires a three-button mouse, there are times that we find we need a three-button mouse in some graphical applications. The left button may be for selecting, the right button for opening a menu, and the center button for sweeping a box around an area of the screen.

CONFIGURING COMPUTER HARDWARE

Although most motherboards and peripheral boards can be installed and used without modification, in some cases the boards must be configured to work properly with UnixWare. When you add peripheral boards, it is essential that each board on your PC be assigned a unique IRQ. The UNIX ID checking command, /etc/conf/bin/idcheck -r -v *irq* (where *irq* is the value of the IRQ that you wish to use), lets you see if a particular IRQ is already assigned. For example, to check if IRQ 5 is available, you would enter /etc/conf/bin/idcheck -r -v 5. In Appendix B, we've provided a shell script, based on idcheck, that checks all IRQs on your system and tells you which are and are not assigned. The script is called irqcheck. Once your run irqcheck, the output looks similar to the following:

```
1    ---    kd
2    ---    ** THIS IRQ AVAILABLE **
3    ---    asyc
4    ---    asyc
5    ---    dcd
6    ---    fd
7    ---    lp
8    ---    rtc
9    ---    ** THIS IRQ AVAILABLE **
10   ---    el3
11   ---    ** THIS IRQ AVAILABLE **
12   ---    ** THIS IRQ AVAILABLE **
13   ---    fp
14   ---    dcd
15   ---    ** THIS IRQ AVAILABLE **
```

The output above shows that IRQs 2, 9, 11, 12, and 15 are available on the current computer. You can assign peripheral boards to any of these IRQs. If you have a cartridge tape drive, UnixWare expects it to be at IRQ 5, by default. We assigned our Ethernet board to IRQ 10 (el3). If you don't use IRQ 5 for a tape drive, you can use it for another device.

If you have a non-SCSI cartridge tape, it *must* be set to IRQ 5 if you want to install UnixWare from cartridge tape.

NOTE

The Hardware Setup window is a new utility with UnixWare 2. This window lets you display and update information related to your computer hardware. You can access computer hardware information by double-clicking on the Hardware Setup icon in the Admin Tools window on the UnixWare

Desktop. Select Hardware Device Configuration, and a listing of your hardware devices, IRQs, addresses, and related information is displayed.

Checking Computer Hardware

Before you install additional peripheral boards, check that your hardware works as it's delivered from your manufacturer. Most PCs come with DOS installed on the hard disk. We strongly recommend booting the computer in DOS and checking all hardware accessories. The system should boot and all peripherals (floppy disk, hard disk, CD-ROM, and so on) should be accessible.

If there is a problem at this point, contact your PC vendor immediately. If everything runs smoothly, power down, then add any other peripherals that might not have come installed on the computer (such as Ethernet boards) one at a time. Check each peripheral in DOS before continuing.

It is particularly important that the installation drive (such as cartridge tape or CD-ROM) is installed properly. Otherwise, you will not be able to install UnixWare.

Once you are satisfied that the hardware is configured and working properly, you can begin installing the UnixWare software.

Installing UnixWare Software

This section describes how to install an Application Server (AS) version of UnixWare. If you're installing a Personal Edition (PE) system, you won't be asked all the questions you are asked during an AS installation (the PE contains a subset of the packages included in the AS). If you don't see some of the prompts described here, you don't need to provide that information for your system setup.

Each UnixWare system is made up of separately installable packages. Some packages are required (such as the Base System) and others are optional (such as TCP/IP). During installation, you can select which packages you want to install. Table A.2 lists the UnixWare packages.

PACKAGE	UNIXWARE VERSION	DESCRIPTION
Access Control Lists Utilities (acl)	AS and PE	Provides utilities for granting different access permissions for selected users and groups
Enhanced Application Compatibility (acp)	AS and PE	Provides features that let you run applications created for other UNIX systems, including SCO UNIX, XENIX, and Interactive UNIX
Application Server Documentation (ASdocs)	AS	Contains online versions of UNIX guides and reference manuals; these books can be viewed using the *DynaText* online document browser
Adobe Type Manager (atm)	AS and PE	Contains support for storing and managing Adobe Type I scalable fonts (used on the Desktop and in some applications)
ATM Basic Fonts (atm13)	AS and PE	Contains scalable Type I fonts used on the Desktop, such as Courier, Helvetica, and Times Roman
Auditing Utilities (audit)	AS and PE	Provides auditing facilities that allow you to record security-related information on your system
Base System (base)	AS and PE	Contains the required parts of the UnixWare system
Backup/Restore (bkrs)	AS	Contains backup and restore options you can use with the Operations, Administration, and Maintenance (OA&M) facility (accessible through the Extra Admin icon in the System Setup folder window)
BSD Compatibility (bsdcompat)	AS	Contains commands, header files, and libraries found in BSD-compatible UNIX systems

PACKAGE	UNIXWARE VERSION	DESCRIPTION
Optimizing C Compilation System (ccs)	AS and PE	Contains the basic programming environment that is used with UNIX
Advanced Commands (cmds)	AS	Contains commands intended for experienced users and administrators
Desktop Manager (desktop)	AS and PE	Provides the graphical user interface
Distributed File System Utilities (dfs)	AS	Contains support for running X Window applications on remote system displays
Graphics Display Support (display)	AS and PE	Provides you with drivers needed to support different types of video boards
Applications and Demos (dtclients)	AS	Provides the X Window System, which is the foundation for the UnixWare Desktop graphical user interface
Graphics Utilities (dtxt)	AS and PE	Contains an optimized version of the X Window System server
Graphics Supplemental Fonts (dtxtfonts)	AS and PE	Contains the complete set of ISO 8859-1 bit-mapped fonts and Type 1 Utopia scalable outline fonts. These are fonts available with X Window System version X11R5
*Dyna*Text Document Browser (dynatext)	AS and PE	Contains a graphical application for viewing online UnixWare documents
Internet Utilities (inet)	AS and PE	Contains TCP/IP protocols and utilities used to communicate over LANs, as well as over the Internet
Printer Support (lp)	AS and PE	Supports UnixWare printing services

PACKAGE	UNIXWARE VERSION	DESCRIPTION
Language Supplement (ls)	AS and PE	Provides support for general keyboard and font mappings required for non-English versions of UnixWare
Traditional Manual Pages (manpages)	AS and PE	Contains online versions of the traditional UNIX manual pages; manual pages can be viewed using the man command
Advanced Merge (merge)	AS and PE	Includes DOS Merge and DR-DOS 6.0 for running DOS and Microsoft Windows applications in a UnixWare window
Network Management (netmgt)	AS and PE	Provides the framework required to use SNMP network management over UnixWare and NetWare networks
Network File System Utilities (nfs)	AS	Contains features to support file sharing using the NFS facility
NFS Set (nfsset)	AS	Contains commands used to share and connect file systems using the NFS file system
Network Interface Card Support (nics)	AS and PE	Contains drivers needed to support a wide range of network interface cards (Ethernet and Token Ring) that can be used with TCP/IP and IPX/SPX networking features
Network Information Service (nis)	AS	Allows you to set up distributed databases of information that can be used to configure UnixWare users and network configuration files over a network
Network Support Utilities (nsu)	AS and PE	Supports basic UnixWare networking features

PACKAGE	UNIXWARE VERSION	DESCRIPTION
NetWare Networking (nwnet)	AS and PE	Provides NetWare networking features, such as NVT2, for sharing NetWare resources and services over a network
NetWare Integration Kit (nwsup)	AS and PE	Provides capabilities for creating diskettes that can be used to install UNIX (NFS) name spaces on NetWare servers. This allows UnixWare to access NetWare servers using full UNIX semantics
Operations, Administration & Maintenance (oam)	AS	Provides the OA&M facility, a forms- and menu-based administrative interface
OS Multiprocessor Support (osmp)	AS and PE	Supplies utilities for adding and deleting multiple processors on computers that support multi-processing architecture
Additional Platform Support (platform)	AS	Provides software required to support features specific to particular hardware platforms; there are utilities for Compaq, AST Manhattan, and Tricord platforms
Remote Procedure Calls Utilities (rpc)	AS	Contains the RPC utilities needed to support TCP/IP and other network services
Server Utilities (server)	AS	Contains the utilities required for setting up your application server to act as an install server
Terminfo Utilities (terminf)	AS	Contains support for connecting different kinds of terminals to your UnixWare system

You can see a list of UnixWare packages installed on your system by typing `pkginfo` from a Terminal window.

NOTE

In general, we recommend installing all the packages that come with your AS or PE system. Developers of the applications you use tend to hook into all kinds of utilities and files in the operating system, even if they don't really need to. Installing all the packages that come with your version of UnixWare reduces the risk of applications failing. (If necessary, get more disk space rather than install less of the operating system.) You can save disk space without risking applications failing by installing less of the online documentation.

Each new release or update of an operating system like UnixWare carries with it its own installation quirks and packaging changes. Be sure to read the *Installation Handbook* that accompanies UnixWare so you don't miss any important steps.

NOTE

After you've finished answering all the questions and the software is installed, reboot your computer. If the installation doesn't work or you encounter errors as the computer reboots, go to Chapter 10 for suggestions on installation troubleshooting.

USING INSTALLATION MEDIA

The UnixWare installation media consist of one or more boot floppies and a high-capacity medium. The boot floppies let you start the minimum UNIX system needed to install the full operating system. The high-capacity medium is either a cartridge tape or a CD-ROM. UnixWare also supports a network installation, where you can download the operating system from an AS system over the network.

You start the UnixWare installation procedure by putting the first floppy in floppy drive A: and booting the computer (turn it on or press the reset button). The system tells you when it needs information from you and when you need to put in another floppy, the CD-ROM, or the tape. Installing UnixWare over the network is the fastest, easiest way, followed by installing from a CD-ROM.

NOTE **Most UnixWare configurations have only one boot floppy. You probably have a second boot floppy only if you're installing from 5.25-inch diskettes or if the particular locale you are installing to requires a second floppy. Also, certain HBA controllers require that you install a driver from the HBA floppy that comes with UnixWare.**

ANSWERING INSTALLATION QUESTIONS

The answers to the questions you are asked during installation define how your hard disk is set up, the type of keyboard and mouse you are using, the parts of the system you are installing, and the user account for the owner of the system. Other information you will need to supply is specific to different areas of the operating system, such as the network address (for TCP/IP networking).

Using a Host Bus Adapter

If your system uses a SCSI controller, you might need to install HBA (host bus adapter) driver software. Many of the common HBA drivers are contained on the HBA floppy disk that comes with UnixWare. Others may be available from the UnixWare forum on CompuServe or directly from the hardware manufacturer.

After UnixWare is finished with the first boot floppy, you are asked to insert the HBA floppy. If you are not sure if you need the HBA floppy, insert it anyway. It won't hurt. UnixWare decides which drivers, if any, it needs.

Choosing a Keyboard

Because UnixWare supports different languages, it gives you the opportunity during installation to select a keyboard type that is appropriate to each supported language. The default is US (ASCII). If you want to be able to generate non-ASCII keyboard characters and you are in the United States, select US (Latin 1). For other language versions, you should generally select the language name to get the right keyboard.

Checking Hardware Support

UnixWare detects most hardware you might have connected to your computer. During installation, you get a chance to view, and optionally change, the hardware configuration. UnixWare asks if you want to view the DCU (Device Configuration Utility). If you say yes, then select Hardware Device Configuration, a list of detected hardware is displayed.

In general, we recommend you don't change this hardware information. Just look at it to get a warm, fuzzy feeling that UnixWare can see all the hardware that is installed. If you change this information in a way that is incorrect, the devices may be inaccessible.

Selecting Upgrade or New Installation

If you are installing UnixWare 2 on a computer that already contains a UnixWare installation (UnixWare 1.1.2 or UnixWare 2), you have a choice of upgrading the current system or completely overwriting the current system. The UnixWare installation procedure asks if you want to do a nondestructive or a destructive installation.

The destructive installation is easy. It just destroys the entire old Unix-Ware system and installs the new one.

The nondestructive installation gives you more options. You can choose whether or not to combine system configuration files. So, for example, you won't have to add all your users again to the /etc/passwd file or all the remote systems you communicate with to the /etc/hosts file. You also can choose to have the system delete any software packages from earlier versions of UnixWare that are obsolete. You need to have a total of 70MB of free disk space (20MB in /, 45MB in /usr, and 5MB in /var) to be allowed to perform an upgrade installation.

Changing Hard Disk Partitions

Part of the new, or destructive, installation requires you to *partition* your hard disk. This gives you an opportunity to divide the space on your hard disk between UnixWare and different operating systems.

You can also divide the UnixWare portion of your hard disk into different *slices*. Before the days when you could install multiple operating systems on a single hard disk, what we now call UNIX slices were called UNIX partitions. Now that several operating systems can coexist on the same hard disk, the terminology has changed. A *partition* defines operating system boundaries; a *slice* defines a separate space within a UnixWare partition. Having separate slices allows you to assign a specific amount of disk space to a particular area of the UnixWare file system.

TECHNOTE

The UnixWare `fdisk` utility sometimes has trouble recognizing existing partitions for some other operating systems (such as OS/2). Therefore, UnixWare installation may overwrite existing partitions. We recommend that you install UnixWare and set up all partitions before installing other operating systems on your hard disk.

You can assign part of your hard disk to be a bootable DOS, NT, OS/2, or other operating system partition. If you're creating a DOS partition, make it your first partition. For a 500MB hard disk, we typically assign about 200MB to DOS and 300MB to UnixWare. Because UnixWare tends to be more demanding of space, make UnixWare your larger partition.

By default, the space assigned to the UnixWare partition is divided across four slices: `/stand`, `/var/tmp`, `/tmp`, and `/`. The `/stand` slice contains the bootable UnixWare operating system. The `/tmp` and `/var/tmp` slices are used by the system and by applications to save temporary files. The remainder of the UnixWare partition is the root (`/`) slice. The default slices are usually fine.

TECHNOTE

If you are an advanced UNIX user, you may want to further divide your root (`/`) slice into separate slices. For example, you may want to assign a different file system type to a slice or define a specific slice for which you want to do a full image backup.

Set the UnixWare partition as the *active* partition. That means that when you start up the system, UnixWare rather than the operating system on the other partition (such as OS/2 or NT) will run. If you want to run another operating system, change the active partition using the `fdisk` command.

See Chapter 6 for more information about the `fdisk` command.

NOTE

Selecting Packages to Install

UNIX has been around for a long time. Many features, such as networking, that were add-ons for other systems or earlier UNIX systems are now built into UnixWare systems. To make the massive amounts of software more manageable, UnixWare divides the operating system into packages, many of which you can choose to install or not install.

On the whole, we recommend you install as many of the packages as you can comfortably fit on your hard disk. However, if you are tight on disk space, here are a few suggestions regarding the optional software packages:

▸ **OA&M package (`oam`):** You can save a lot of disk space by not installing this package. This package contains the `sysadm` interface, which is a forms and menus interface for UNIX system administration. Most of the functions in this interface can be done more effectively from the UnixWare Desktop or the command line. Also, because this interface is not being enhanced, some of its procedures are not up to date. For example, you cannot add a graphical user through OA&M. OA&M does contain some useful features for managing ports and terminals, however.

▸ **Networking packages:** If you plan to use UnixWare as a standalone system, without networking, you can save a lot of space by excluding the various networking packages. Networking packages include Network Support Utilities (`nsu`), Network Interface Card Support (`nics`), Network Management (`netmgmt`), NetWare Networking (`nwnet`), NetWare Integration Kit (`nwsup`), Distributed File System (`dfs`), Remote Procedure Calls (`rpc`), Network File System Utilities (`nfs`), and Network Information Service (`nis`).

▸ Application Server Documentation (**ASdocs**): If you are short
on space, there are several ways of handling the online documentation to conserve space. One way is to not install the **ASdocs**
package at all and just use the hard copy documentation, the
manual pages and, of course, this book. Other options are to access documentation directly from the CD-ROM when you need it
or to install the documentation on one UnixWare system and access it from other systems on the network. In any case, it saves a
lot of space to not have it all residing on your local hard disk.
You can also choose not to install the Traditional Manual Pages
(**manpages**).

Assigning an Owner

UnixWare introduces the concept of a system *owner*. During installation,
you are asked to assign an owner name, login ID, and user number. This
user has the rights to change the system in ways that are not available to all
users. For example, the owner can add other users, change the networking
configuration, and install software packages.

Always assign the login ID as a name with all lowercase letters, preferably
eight characters or less. For example, *chrisn*, *larrys*, *shs*, and *jones* are good
login IDs. Also, if you (the owner) are connecting your system to other systems on which you have a login account, assign a user number that matches
your user number on the other systems.

 **TECHNOTE**

**If you are an experienced UNIX system user, many of your favorite
utilities may be missing in a PE system. (We always get annoyed that
our PE systems don't have the env command, to see shell environment variables, and the head command, to look at the top part of a
text file.) With the AS, however, you will find all the UNIX System V
commands you're used to.**

Configuring Networking

Depending on which software packages you installed, you may be asked for other information. In particular, networking packages (such as TCP/IP and NIS) require additional information to be installed properly.

If you are installing an Ethernet board, we strongly recommend you have the information available to install that board. You should know the type of board, the I/O base address, the IRQ level, and the type of cable. If you don't do it here, you need to provide the information later by reinstalling the Network Interface Card Package.

TCP/IP information is also good to have when you are installing the TCP/IP package. You should know the name you want to give your system and the Internet address. If you are using domain name service, you should supply the name and address of the domain name server system during installation as well.

By configuring the NIS package, you can centralize some of your user administration. UnixWare gives you the option of configuring this during installation.

Completing Installation

When all of the UnixWare software is installed, the system is rebooted. If no errors are encountered, your system should be immediately ready for use. Log in as the system owner and configure your system as described later in this chapter.

Using UnixWare on a Laptop

With today's powerful laptop computers, you can run UnixWare on a computer that goes with you as effectively as you can with one that is planted on your desk. Because your laptop may have a limited number of slots and may act as both a networked system (while you're at work) and a stand-alone system (while you're on the road), there are a few things you should consider about laptops and UnixWare.

CHOOSING LAPTOP PERIPHERALS

A *docking station* provides a means of expanding your laptop system into a desktop system. The docking station for our laptop has only two slots. We use one for an Ethernet card and the other for a video card. Because the slots may be smaller than those on a regular desktop system, make sure you get cards that fit.

We tried network installations over Ethernet from a UnixWare AS system, which worked very well. We also popped out the Ethernet board and put in a cartridge tape controller. We were able to install from cartridge tape as well.

Our laptop computer automatically senses the video card and uses it when the laptop is attached to the docking station. With the video and Ethernet cards installed, the computer performs as well as any comparably configured desktop model.

TAKING YOUR LAPTOP ON THE ROAD

When you take your laptop on the road and leave your docking station behind, you lose the abilities to use higher resolution video and to connect via Ethernet. Before you unplug from your docking station, there are a few things you should do to have your laptop work more efficiently as a stand-alone system.

One step is to change the video resolution. If you changed your video resolution to suit a video board in your docking station, you need to change the resolution to match your laptop screen. Run the Display Setup window to change the resolution to a basic VGA mode. This procedure is described in Chapter 2.

You also should disable networking features. There is no reason to wait for networking to try to start up and fail if the computer is no longer attached to the network. To disable NetWare connectivity, from the UnixWare Desktop window, double-click on the Admin Tools icon, double-click on Networking, and then double-click on the NetWare Setup icon. In the NetWare Setup window, click on OFF for the NetWare UNIX Client and Peer to Peer Communication options.

To disable file sharing features, double-click on the Admin Tools icon, double-click on Networking, and then double-click on the File Sharing icon. Select each shared item and set it to not start automatically when NFS starts.

See Chapters 6 and 10 for more information about disabling networking features.

NOTE

When you return to your docking station later, remember to turn the networking features back on.

Configuring UnixWare

After you install UnixWare and log in as the system owner for the first time, UnixWare recommends some initial configuration procedures you may want to do. A window pops up that lists what are called "First Time Setup" procedures. The following sections step you through what we feel are the most important of these procedures. Most of these procedures are covered in more detail in other parts of this book.

CREATING EMERGENCY BOOT FLOPPIES AND TAPE

If you have ever had a hard disk malfunction in a way that prevented your hard disk from booting, you'll understand the value of creating emergency boot floppies. Basically, this procedure lets you create boot floppies so that if for any reason you can't boot UnixWare from hard disk, you can start UnixWare from floppy disks and possibly correct the hard disk problem. This procedure also lets you create an emergency recovery tape that backs up key configuration files, the entire UnixWare partition, or the entire disk and that can be restored later.

The procedure for creating emergency boot floppies and tapes is in Chapter 10, "Troubleshooting."

INCREASING DISPLAY RESOLUTION

UnixWare is delivered with the Desktop set to run at a low resolution, standard VGA mode, so most displays will work with the Desktop the first time you start it up. To more specifically set your display to match the capabilities of your video board, run the Display Setup window in the Admin Tools folder. The procedure for running Display Setup is in Chapter 11.

QUICK-STARTING NETWORKING

The UnixWare Desktop simplifies the complex task of setting up networking. It has support for NetWare connectivity, TCP/IP, File Sharing (NFS), and Basic Networking Utilities (BNU) built in. Networking with UnixWare is discussed in depth in Chapters 4 and 5 of this book. Here, we summarize how to get networking up and running.

Connecting to NetWare Servers

In most cases, you do not need to take any actions to set up your system to connect to NetWare because UnixWare is designed with NetWare connectivity in mind. If you are connected to a local area network (LAN) and can reach at least one NetWare server, you can access NetWare services.

To connect to a NetWare server, double-click on the NetWare icon in the UnixWare Desktop window. Double-click on the NetWare server you want to access to see available volumes. Then, continue to traverse directories within volumes by double-clicking on directory icons.

In order to make NetWare connectivity work, UnixWare makes some assumptions about your network configuration. For example, several different frame types may be used on your network. UnixWare chooses one frame type and connects to all servers that are communicating using that frame type. See Chapter 4 for information about what to do if servers that you know are on your network are not appearing in your NetWare window.

Setting Up TCP/IP

TCP/IP is the most popular networking protocol for connecting UNIX desktop systems. Using TCP/IP, you can send mail, transfer files, and log in to remote systems.

The least you have to do to use TCP/IP is identify the names and Internet Protocol (IP) addresses for each host computer you can access on a single LAN or identify the domain name server system that centrally stores the names and addresses of many systems.

You add host names and addresses to your system using the Internet Setup window. To get to the Internet Setup window, double-click on the Admin Tools icon in the UnixWare Desktop window, double-click on the Networking icon in the Admin Tools folder, and then double-click on the Internet Setup icon.

Setting Up File Sharing

Once you have TCP/IP configured for your system, you can access directories from other systems using the File Sharing feature. File sharing lets you connect a directory from a remote system to a point in your file system. You can then use the files and directories within the connected directory in the same way that you use the files and directories stored on your local system.

See Chapter 5 for information about how to use UnixWare's File Sharing feature.

Setting Up Basic Networking Utilities

Traditional UNIX system networking relies on Basic Networking Utilities (BNU) for networking over serial connections using modems or direct connections. Over the years, BNU has expanded to let you configure a variety of networking interfaces, such as TCP/IP, to hook into BNU facilities. Often, BNU is referred to simply as uucp, which is the UNIX-to-UNIX copy command. To be able to use remote electronic mail services and BNU commands (such as cu to log in to a remote system or uucp to copy files remotely), you must configure BNU.

You set up BNU connections using the Dialup Setup window. To get to the Dialup Setup window, double-click on the Admin Tools icon in the Unix-Ware Desktop window, double-click on the Networking icon in the Admin Tools folder, and then double-click on the Dialup Setup icon.

CONFIGURING PRINTERS

Although you only need to connect to one printer to use your UnixWare system effectively, you should have at least two printers configured for your system: one for use by UNIX applications and one for use by DOS.

You can define local printers, which are connected directly to a parallel or serial port on your computer, and remote printers, which are connected to a remote UnixWare or NetWare system that you can reach over the network.

Adding a Printer

The Printer Setup window is where you define the printers you can reach with your UnixWare system. To get to this window, from your UnixWare Desktop window, double-click on the Admin Tools icon, then double-click on the Printer Setup icon.

When you configure a printer that's connected to your system, all you need to know is the printer name, the type of printer it is, the port it's connected to, and which remote systems and users that can reach your system over the network can use the printer.

For remote UNIX printers, you need to specify the remote system name, the remote printer name, and the type of operating system (System V or BSD) running on the remote system. NetWare printers are easier to configure. You simply click on Browse and search the available file servers, print queues, and print servers to access your NetWare printers.

Once a printer is added to your system, there are a few things you can do to make it more accessible. These include setting remote access, setting your personal default printer, and installing a printer icon in a folder.

Setting Remote Printer Access

Any time you are sharing printers with a remote UNIX system, you must allow remote printer access between the two systems. This is true whether you are using a printer connected to that system or it is using a printer connected to your system.

The Printer Setup: Set Remote Access window lets you enable printer access between your system and a remote system, as well as identify the remote operating system. In order for you to share printers with the remote UNIX system, you must also enable remote access to your system from the remote system.

If you're trying to configure a print queue on your UnixWare system that will access a printer on a non-UnixWare remote system, use the `lpsystem` command on the remote system to allow for remote access. For example, to allow the UnixWare system called `docsys` to access the printers on a non-UnixWare remote system, enter the following on the remote system:

```
lpsystem -ts5 -R5 -T10 docsys
```

The system name `docsys` must be in the `/etc/hosts` file on the remote system. The `-ts5` option indicates that the system trying to access the printers on the remote system is a UNIX System V system. The `-R5` option specifies how long to wait before trying to reconnect if the connection between `docsys` and the remote system is dropped. The `-T10` option specifies how long the connection between `docsys` and the remote system should be idle before the connection is dropped by the remote system. For more information about the `lpsystem` command, see the `lpsystem` manual page available through the Online Docs window.

Setting Your Personal Default Printer

You should select one of the printers connected to your system as your default printer. When you print a document from the Desktop, UnixWare sends the file to your default printer.

Each user can set his or her own personal default printer. In the Printer Setup window, click on the printer that you want to be your default and then choose the Make Default option from the Actions menu.

The default personal printer is in effect for the Desktop. It has no meaning from the command line (within a Terminal window).

Setting the Default System Printer

Before the UnixWare Desktop was created, there was no concept of a personal default printer in UNIX. There was, and still is, a way to set a default system printer. Some UNIX applications will automatically direct printing to the default system printer. Also, once the default system printer is set, any user on the system can direct a print request to the default printer, without identifying that printer by name, simply by typing

```
lp file
```

where *file* is the name of the file to be printed.

To set your default system printer, from the UnixWare Desktop window, double-click on the Applications icon, then double-click on the Terminal icon. In the Terminal window, type su to become the root user and enter the root user's password when prompted. Then type the following:

```
lpadmin -d printer
```

where *printer* is replaced by the printer you want to set as the default.

Note that the default system printer applies to the command line. It cannot be set or accessed from the Desktop.

TECHNOTE

The lpadmin command can be used for many printer setup features besides setting default system printers. Experienced UNIX system users can use lpadmin to configure a wide variety of printers, as they always have with UNIX. Those printers will then be accessible from the UnixWare Desktop.

Installing a Printer Icon

You can *install* an icon for an added printer into a folder. By installing a printer icon into a folder containing documents you want to print, you can print those documents by simply dragging-and-dropping them on the printer icon.

To install a printer icon into a folder, add the printer to your system, then drag-and-drop the icon from the Printer Setup window to the folder window of your choice. The printer icon appears in the folder window, ready for you to drop files on it to print.

> **To drag-and-drop icons in UnixWare, move the mouse cursor to the icon you want to drop on top of another icon, press and hold down the left mouse button, move the mouse (and hence the icon) to a new location, and then release the mouse button. See Chapter 2 for more information about functions you can perform by dragging-and-dropping and other mouse techniques in UnixWare.**

NOTE

CONNECTING AN EXTRA TERMINAL

Any UnixWare system can be changed into a multiuser system by connecting a character terminal to a serial port on the computer. UnixWare doesn't restrict the number of terminals you can connect to your system; however, it may restrict the number of users that can be logged in at one time. The UnixWare Personal Edition allows two users to be logged in to the system at the same time. The UnixWare Application Server allows many users to be logged in simultaneously.

The only limitation on the number of terminals you connect is the number of serial ports on your computer (which you can increase by adding a serial ports board). Another factor you need to consider is that adding terminals can slow down your system's performance. Typically, however, using UNIX from a dumb terminal consumes much fewer system resources than running UNIX from graphical X-terminals.

> **For details on adding terminals, see Chapter 5. For instructions on adding a serial ports board, see Chapter 11.**

NOTE

Reviewing Your Setup

Once you have set up your system to your satisfaction, you should review your system's configuration. Because the state of your computer changes as you use it, it's a good idea to occasionally monitor its setup and performance data.

After you have installed and configured UnixWare, you should check the amount of disk space you have remaining to use for data and applications. The System Status window displays information about the space on your hard disk, as well as other pertinent system information.

To view disk space and other system status information, double-click on the Admin Tools icon in the UnixWare Desktop window, then double-click on the System Status icon. The System Status window appears, as shown in the example in Figure A.2.

*Displaying system status
information*

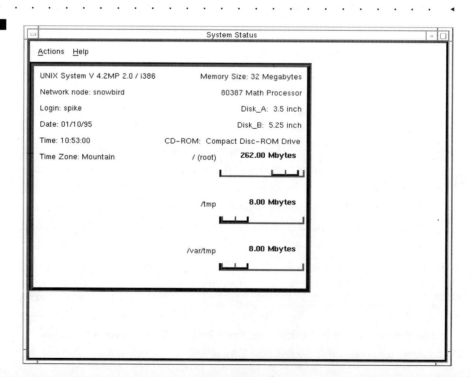

The slider bars on the right side of the window show the disk space available on the / (root) file system, as well as any other file systems you may have mounted (/tmp and /var/tmp in this example). The position of each slider bar shows how much space is currently being used.

You need to decide if the space remaining on your hard disk is sufficient to hold the data you expect to put on the system. A good rule is to never go below 10 percent of the disk space. If you run out of disk space while you are working, you can lose data.

The System Status window contains other information worth noting:

- ▶ **Network node:** The name used to identify your system to other systems on the network

- ▶ **Login:** The user name under which you are currently logged in

- ▶ **Date, Time, and Time Zone:** The current system date, time, and the local time zone

- ▶ **Memory Size:** The amount of RAM installed on your computer

- ▶ **Disk:** The location (Disk_A or Disk_B) and size (3.5 or 5.25 inches) of your floppy disk drives

- ▶ **CD-ROM:** An indication that there is a Compact Disc-ROM drive available on your computer

 **TECHNOTE**

You can also enter commands at the command line to see system information. Run the /etc/dfspace command from a Terminal window to show a more complete listing of available disk space. Along with the amount of space on your local hard disk(s), dfspace also shows space available on file systems connected to your system. Run the /etc/mount command to see all mounted file systems.

Once your system is up and in full use, you may want to run some of the system monitoring tools to get a feel for whether the system is holding up well enough for the demands put on it. See Chapter 9 for further information on how to monitor your system's performance and, if necessary, make some tuning adjustments.

After you've set up your system, you can tailor the UnixWare Desktop to suit your own preferences, as described in Chapter 2. You can also configure your terminal environment, as described in Chapter 8. See Chapter 9 for tips on getting maximum performance from your UnixWare system.

Using the
UNIX Utilities

This appendix describes some of the useful shell scripts and utilities we have created for our work with UnixWare. These utilities are located on the Novell and SYBEX forums on CompuServe and on SYBEX's `ftp` server.

After you have installed the utilities, you can run any of them by opening a Terminal window and typing its name (along with any other required information, such as file names) at the command line prompt.

Downloading the Scripts

You can download the scripts from Novell's CompuServe forum in either of two ways:

- ► Enter `GO NETWIRE`, choose the option that includes the words *Tech Files*, and download the file named `uwutil.exe`.

- ► Enter `GO UNIXWARE`, select General Library, and download the file named `uwutil.exe`.

To download the scripts from SYBEX's CompuServe forum, enter `GO SYBEX`, select Novell, and download the file named `uwutil.exe`.

NOTE **To get a CompuServe account, call CompuServe customer service at (800) 848-8990 or (614) 457-8650.**

If you don't have a CompuServe account, but do have access to the Internet, you can download the scripts through anonymous `ftp` from the SYBEX `ftp` server (`ftp.sybex.com`). The scripts are in the directory called `/pub/books/1720/`.

To use `ftp` to get the scripts, follow these steps:

1 · Type `ftp ftp.sybex.com`

2 · At the Name prompt, type `anonymous`.

3 · At the Password prompt, type your e-mail address.

4 · Type cd /pub/books/1720 to change to the directory where the scripts are kept.

5 · Type get uwutil.exe.

6 · To close your connection, type bye.

Organizing the Utilities

After downloading the scripts and programs, you have to "unzip" the files. Within Merge, create a new directory (scripts is a good name for it) and put nwutil.exe in the directory. Now type nwutil. The files will automatically unzip from nwutil.

Before moving any files, become the root user. Type su in a Terminal window and enter the root password when prompted. NOTE

Go to a terminal window, change to the new directory, and separate the scripts into directories as follows:

▶ Put the scripts that must be run as the root user (fd, irqcheck, lpfix, and netrun) in the /sbin directory. Type the following:

```
mv $HOME/bin/fd /sbin
mv $HOME/bin/irqcheck /sbin
mv $HOME/bin/lpfix /sbin
mv $HOME/bin/netrun /sbin
```

▶ Put ask.com in /usr/merge/dosroot/dos. Type the following:

```
mv $HOME/bin/ask.com /usr/merge/dosroot/dos
```

▶ Put autoexec.bat in the root (/) directory. Save a copy of the existing autoexec.bat first. Type the following:

```
mv /autoexec.bat /autoexec.old
mv $HOME/bin/autoexec.bat /
```

► · ◄

Modifying the Utilities

Many of the scripts must be edited before you can use them. They contain placeholder names, which you must replace in order for the script to work properly. For example, the scripts for printing contain the placeholder *printer_name*. Replace this with the actual name of your printer, as instructed in the usage section of the script.

To edit the scripts, use either the Text Editor from the UnixWare Desktop or a UNIX editor, such as `vi`, from a Terminal window. One compiled program (`ask.com`) is also included. It does not contain readable text and cannot be edited.

► · ◄

Utility Descriptions

The downloadable scripts are described in the following sections. They are presented in alphabetical order.

Most of the scripts contain built-in usage messages. When you type just the name of a script that requires an argument, you will see a message on the screen indicating the correct way to use the script (for example, try typing `netrun`). The scripts that don't require an argument (such as `cl`) will run immediately after you type in the script name and press Enter.

Although you cannot damage your system by running any of the scripts before reading about them, we recommend you review the description of each script in this appendix before using it.

ASAMPLE

The `asample` script is for creating a self-searching database, such as an online name and address file. We use this script for names, phone numbers, addresses, and related information.

Using asample

Before using `asample`, take the following steps:

1 · Rename the script to something easy to type, such as just the letter `a` (for address).

2 · Change the line beginning with `exec` so that the path indicates the actual location of the script on your system and its name. In the sample, the script is located in `/home/spike/bin`, and the script's name is `a`.

3 · Replace the sample information in the script with your own information.

To make retrieving the information easy, we use the person's name or company name at the beginning of each line containing information about that person or company, as shown in the sample data. In this way, when you search for the person or company, every line of information about that person or company is displayed.

To use the script, assuming you named it `a`, type `a` and the name of the person or company you want to find. For example, using the sample data, if you want the information for Excell Widgets, type `a excell`. The four lines with Excell data will appear. You can also type `a widgets` to get the same information. If you type `a jack`, only the line with Jack's name in it will appear. The entire file is scanned when you use this script. It doesn't matter which case you use for the letters, because the search isn't case-sensitive.

If your data contains two names that differ only slightly, you may want to narrow the search. For example, if you have information for Excell Gadgets as well as Excell Widgets, you can search for Excell Widgets by typing `a "excell widgets"` (you must use quotation marks when you are searching for more than one word).

Listing for asample

```
#! /usr/bin/sh
if
  test $# -ne 1
then
  echo usage: $0 'data_to_search_for'
  exit 1
fi

exec /usr/bin/egrep -i "$1"
  /home/spike/bin/a

Excell Widgets: (213) 778-1234, FAX (213)
  778-1235
Excell Widgets: Jack Smith, Technical Support
Excell Widgets: 1 Techno Blvd.
Excell Widgets: Computer City, CA 98001

Joe Smith: (718) 498-1111

Lyn Green: Home (212) 321-4321
Lyn Green: Work (212) 888-1100
```

ASK.COM

The ask.com utility is used in the autoexec.bat file in the root directory. It allows you to decide each time you open a DOS window whether or not you want to connect to NetWare. By using ask.com, your autoexec.bat file can ask a yes or no question and accept input (y or n) from the keyboard. Be sure ask.com is located in /usr/merge/dosroot/dos so it can be found by DOS.

The ask.com utility is a binary file, that is, it is not an editable script. It is intended to be run from a DOS session. You cannot run ask.com in a Terminal window in UnixWare.

There's no listing here for ask.com (since it's a binary file). However, the source code and instructions for creating ask.com are presented in Chapter 6.

AUTOEXEC.BAT

The sample `autoexec.bat` file can be used in your `root` directory. It lets you decide each time you start a DOS or Windows session whether or not you want to connect to a NetWare server.

Using autoexec.bat

No changes need to be made to `autoexec.bat`. However, you should save a copy of the `autoexec.bat` file currently in your `root` directory before installing the new one. If you have changed your current `autoexec.bat` file, add those changes to the new one before you use it.

After you add the new `autoexec.bat` file to your system, when you open a DOS or Windows session, you will see the question

```
Connect to NetWare Servers (Y/N)?
```

Press the Y key for yes or the N key for no. If you press any other key, the question is repeated. Do not press Enter after pressing the Y or N key.

Listing for autoexec.bat

```
@echo off
cls
path j:\dos;j:\merge;
prompt $p$g
:LOOP
echo Connect to NetWare Servers (Y/N)?
ask
if errorlevel 90 goto LOOP
if errorlevel 89 goto YES
if errorlevel 79 goto LOOP
if errorlevel 78 goto NO goto LOOP
:NO
cls
goto END
:YES
if not exist j:\share\novell\ipxtli.com
   goto :END
j:\share\novell\ipxtli
j:\share\novell\netx
:END
```

CL

cl is a small script that clears your Terminal window and then gives you a listing of the current directory's contents. It provides a quick way to clear the screen and then run ls -F.

Using cl

To use cl, simply type cl in a Terminal window.

Listing for cl

```
#! /usr/bin/sh
clear
ls -F
```

DEC

The dec script is used for converting hexadecimal (base 16) values into decimal (base 10) numbers. For example, the hexadecimal number A is 10 in decimal. To convert decimal numbers into hexadecimal numbers, use the hex script.

Using dec

To use dec, type dec followed by the hexadecimal number you want to convert. For example, to convert the hexadecimal number A to decimal, type dec A.

Listing for dec

```
#! /usr/bin/sh
if
   test $# -eq 0
then
   echo usage: $0 'hexadecimal_number'>&2
   exit 1
fi
for i in $* ;
```

```
do
  echo "$i in Decimal: \t\c";
  echo 16i $i p | dc;
done
```

DUPDISK

The `dupdisk` script provides an easy way to duplicate UNIX or DOS floppies. It copies the entire image of a floppy to the hard disk, prompts you to change floppies, and then writes the image to the new floppy.

Using dupdisk

The new floppy must be formatted before using `dupdisk`. However, for copying either UNIX or DOS floppies, the floppy can be formatted for either UNIX or DOS. For example, to duplicate a UNIX floppy, you can use a floppy formatted either as a UNIX or a DOS floppy.

To use `dupdisk`, first insert the floppy to be copied into your first floppy drive. (This would be the drive designated as drive A: in DOS.) Next, in a Terminal window, type `dupdisk`. When the floppy has been copied to the hard disk, your system sounds its bell twice. Now insert the blank, formatted floppy (either UNIX or DOS format) and press Enter. You hear one bell when the copy to the floppy is complete.

After copying a floppy with `dupdisk`, the file `DisK` is left in your `/tmp` directory. You can use this file to create another copy of the floppy by inserting another formatted floppy in the drive and typing the second from last line of the script in the Terminal window: `dd of=/dev/rdsk/f0t if=DisK bs=15360`.

To change `dupdisk` so that it works with your second floppy drive, change `f0t` to `f1t` in the two lines beginning with `dd`.

Listing for dupdisk

```
#! /usr/bin/sh
cd /tmp
echo Reading source disk...
dd if=/dev/rdsk/f0t of=DisK bs=15360
```

```
echo ^G
echo ^G
echo Put target floppy in drive and press
   Enter:
read i
echo Writing to target disk...
dd of=/dev/rdsk/f0t if=DisK bs=15360
echo ^G
```

 NOTE **If you create this script with the UNIX editor vi, type Ctrl-V followed by Ctrl-G to put each ^G in the script.**

FD

You must have a DOS partition on your computer (as the first partition)
to use the fd script. Use fd to shut down your UnixWare session and reboot your computer from your DOS partition. fd runs the fdisk command
and loads it with the correct keystrokes to make the DOS partition active.
It then automatically reboots your computer. Because the DOS partition is
active, your system boots DOS instead of UnixWare.

Using fd

Before using fd, you must become the root user (type su in a Terminal
window and enter the root user's password when prompted). Next, type fd
and press Enter.

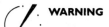 **WARNING** **Before running fd, be sure to close any files you may have open, so
that you won't lose any of your work. For example, if you're working
with an editor or word processor, save your work and exit the application before running fd.**

Listing for fd

```
#! /usr/bin/sh
fdisk <<eof
2
```

```
1
4
eof
init 6
```

FINDER

The `finder` script lets you search the current directory and all directories below the current directory for a file or directory name.

Using finder

To use `finder`, type `finder` followed by the file or directory name you want to find. For example, to find the file called `chap1`, type `finder chap1`.

If you use `finder` when your current directory is the root directory, or search large, remotely mounted file systems, the search can take a very long time to complete.

NOTE

Listing for finder

```
#! /usr/bin/sh
if
   test $# -ne 1
then
   echo usage: $0 'file_name'>&2
   echo "    or">&2
   echo "    "$0 'directory_name'>&2
   exit 1
fi
find . -name "$*" -print
```

FINDPAT

The `findpat` script is similar to the `finder` script, except that it looks for a pattern within a file instead of a file or directory name. `findpat` searches the files in the current directory and all the directories below it.

Using findpat

To use findpat, type findpat followed by the text you want to find. For example, to find the text *local bus*, type findpat "local bus". If the text you're looking for contains only one word, you don't need to type the quotation marks.

Listing for findpat

```
if
   test $# -ne 1
then
   echo usage: $0 '"text to search for"'
   exit 1
fi

find . -type d -print | while
   read dname
do
   grep "$1" $dname/*
done
```

FORMATD

Use formatd for formatting a DOS floppy while you're working in a Terminal window. The formatting is done in the background so you can continue working while the floppy is being formatted.

Using formatd

To use formatd, just type formatd. The script is set to format a high-density (1.4MB), 3.5-inch floppy in the first floppy drive. You can easily change the script (or create new ones) to accommodate your other floppy drives.

In the script, f03ht is the device name for a 3.5-inch floppy drive in-stalled as the first floppy drive. To format other density floppies, change the device name as follows:

Floppy type	Device name
720KB	f03dt
1.2MB	f05ht
360KB	f05d9

To use any of these device names for the second floppy drive, change the zero (0) after the letter f to a one (1).

Listing for formatd

```
#! /usr/bin/sh
dosformat -f /dev/rdsk/f03ht &
sleep 1
echo ^M
```

If you create this script with a UNIX editor, type Ctrl-V followed by Ctrl-M to put the ^M in the script.

NOTE

FORMATU

The formatu script is for formatting a UNIX floppy while you're work-ing in a Terminal window. The formatting is done in the background so you can continue to work while the floppy is being formatted.

Using formatu

To use formatu, just type formatu. The script is set to format a high-density (1.4MB), 3.5-inch floppy in the first floppy drive. You can easily change the script (or create new ones) to accommodate your other floppy drives.

In the script, f03ht is the device name for a 3.5-inch floppy drive installed as the first floppy drive. To format other density floppies, change this device name per the list shown in the section about the formatd script. To use any of these device names for the second floppy drive, change the zero (0) after the letter f to a one (1).

Listing for formatu

```
#! /usr/bin/sh
/usr/sbin/format /dev/rdsk/f03ht >
  /dev/null &
```

GETFLOP

The getflop script is for extracting data from a UNIX floppy that has been created using cpio. Using it with makeflop (which creates a cpio UNIX floppy) is an easy way to back up and restore files to a floppy. See Chapter 8 for more information about using cpio.

Using getflop

To use getflop, just type getflop. The floppy in the first floppy drive is read and the data is extracted into the current directory. To read the second floppy drive, change f0t to f1t.

Listing for getflop

```
#! /usr/bin/sh
cpio –idcvC1024 < /dev/rdsk/f0t
```

GETTAPE

The gettape script is for extracting data from a cartridge tape that has been created using cpio. Using it with maketape (which creates a cpio UNIX cartridge tape) is an easy way to back up and restore files to a cartridge tape. See Chapter 8 for more information about using cpio.

Using gettape

To use `gettape`, just type `gettape`. The cartridge tape is read and the data extracted into the current directory.

Listing for gettape

```
#! /usr/bin/sh
cpio -ivcdC512000</dev/rmt/c0s0
```

HEX

The `hex` script is used for converting decimal (base 10) values into hexadecimal (base 16) numbers. For example, the decimal number 10 is A in hexadecimal. To convert hexadecimal numbers into decimal numbers, use the `dec` script.

Using hex

To use `hex`, type `hex` followed by the decimal number you want to convert. For example, to convert the decimal number 10 to hexadecimal, type `hex 10`.

Listing for hex

```
#! /usr/bin/sh
if
   test $# -eq 0
then
   echo usage: $0 'decimal_number'>&2
   exit 1
fi
for i in $* ;
do
   echo "$i in Hex: \t\c";
   echo 16o $i p | dc;
done
```

IRQCHECK

Use the `irqcheck` script to check your system for available interrupts (IRQs) before you install a new add-in card in your computer (each card must use a unique IRQ number). An example of the output is shown here:

```
1    kd
2    ** THIS IRQ AVAILABLE **
3    asyc
4    asyc
5    el3
6    fd
7    lp
8    rtc
9    ** THIS IRQ AVAILABLE **
10   ** THIS IRQ AVAILABLE **
11   ** THIS IRQ AVAILABLE **
12   ** THIS IRQ AVAILABLE **
13   fp
14   usc
15   ** THIS IRQ AVAILABLE **
```

Using irqcheck

Before using `irqcheck`, you must become the root user (type **su** in a Terminal window and enter the root user's password when prompted). Next, type `irqcheck` and press Enter.

Listing for irqcheck

```
i=1
while
  test "$i" -le 15
do
  v='/etc/conf/bin/idcheck -r -v $I'
  if
    [ $v ]
  then
    ccho "$i\t$v"
  else
    echo "$i\t"'** THIS IRQ AVAILABLE **'
  fi
  i='expr $i + 1'
done
```

L

The l (*el*) script is a shortcut for using the ls -F command. The output is a file listing that indicates which entries are directories (followed by a slash, /), which are executable files (followed by an asterisk, *), and which are links (followed by an at sign, @). Unmarked entries are regular files. See the section about using the ls command in Chapter 8 for more information.

Using l

To use l, type l and press Enter. In addition, you can use any of the valid options to the ls command with the l script. For example, to see hidden files (files that begin with a period), type l -a.

Listing for l

```
#! /usr/bin/sh
ls -F $*
```

LL

The ll (*el-el*) script is a shortcut for using the ls -l command. The output is a file listing that shows the permissions, size, date, and other information for each entry. See the section about using the ls command in Chapter 8 for more information.

Using ll

To use ll, type ll and press Enter. In addition, you can use any of the valid options to the ls command with the ll script. For example, to see hidden files (files that begin with a period), type ll -a.

Listing for ll

```
#! /usr/bin/sh
ls -l $*
```

LPFIX

The lpfix script shuts down the lp print scheduler, which controls the UnixWare printing system. This is sometimes necessary when printing from your system fails for no apparent reason. We've occasionally used this script after canceling a very large print job and then finding we could no longer print. Using this script resets the printing system and allows printing to resume.

Using lpfix

Before using lpfix, you must become the root user (type su in a Terminal window and enter the root user's password when prompted). Next, type lpfix and press Enter. A listing of all pending print jobs is displayed (the lpstat -t command does that), and then the print system is turned off and back on.

Listing for lpfix

```
#! /usr/bin/sh
lpstat -t
/usr/sbin/lpshut
/usr/lib/lp/lpsched
```

MAKEFLOP

The makeflop script is for backing up files or directories on a cpio UNIX floppy (use getflop to extract data from the floppy). See Chapter 8 for more information about using cpio.

Using makeflop

To use makeflop, type makeflop followed by the names of the files or directories you want to write to the floppy. For example, to back up all the files in /home/spike/doc, type makeflop /home/spike/doc. If you were user spike and your current directory was your home directory (/home/spike), you could just type makeflop doc to back up the files.

To back up a single file, type `makeflop` and the file name. You can also mix file names with directory names. For example, you could type

```
makeflop file1 file2 dir1 dir2
```

The floppy must be a UNIX formatted floppy. To edit the script so the second floppy drive is used instead of the first, change `f0t` to `f1t`.

If the backup requires more than one floppy, you will be prompted to insert another floppy. Press Enter after inserting the next floppy.

Listing for makeflop

```
#! /usr/bin/sh
if
   test $# -eq 0
then
   echo usage: $0 'file1 file2 ... dir1 dir2 ...'>&2
   exit 1
fi
find $* -print | cpio -ovcB -O /dev/rdsk/f0t
```

MAKETAPE

The `maketape` script is for backing up files or directories on a `cpio` cartridge tape (use `gettape` to extract data from the tape). See Chapter 8 for more information about using the `cpio` command.

Using maketape

To use `maketape`, type `maketape` followed by the names of the files or directories you want to write to the tape. For example, to back up all the files in `/home/spike/doc`, type `maketape /home/spike/doc`. If you were user spike and your current directory was your home directory (`/home/spike`), you could just type `maketape doc` to back up the files.

To back up a single file, type `maketape` and the file name. You can also mix file names with directory names; for example, you could type

```
maketape file1 file2 dir1 dir2
```

If the backup requires more than one tape, you will be prompted to insert another tape. Press Enter after inserting the new tape.

Listing for maketape

```
#! /usr/bin/sh
if
  test $# -eq 0
then
  echo usage: $0 'file1 file2 ... dir1 dir2 ...'>&2
  exit 1
fi
find $* -print | cpio -ovcC512000 -O
  /dev/rmt/c0s0
```

MANPRINT

The manprint script is for printing troff manual pages, using the man macros, to a PostScript printer. If you don't know what troff is, you'll probably never need to use this script. However, if you work for a company that gets source code for UNIX from Novell (UNIX source code used to come from UNIX System Laboratories until Novell bought them in 1994), you may have occasion to print manual pages from their troff source. This script is handy if you don't have DOCTOOLS installed, which is supplied by Novell specifically for printing their documentation.

Using manprint

Before using manprint, replace *printer_name* in the script with the actual name of your printer.

To use manprint, type manprint followed by the manual pages you want printed. If they are not in the current directory, include the full path to the manual pages. Add -onobanner after -Tpostscript if you don't want a banner page to print.

Listing for manprint

```
#! /usr/bin/sh
if
   test $# -eq 0
then
   echo usage: $0 'manpage1 manpage2 ...'
   exit 1
fi
cat $* | tbl | /usr/ucb/troff -man |
   /usr/lib/lp/postscript/dpost | lp
   -dprinter_name -Tpostscript
```

MM

The mm script is for printing troff memos, using the mm macros, to a PostScript printer. As with the manprint script, if you're not dealing with troff or Novell source code, you probably won't need this script.

Using mm

Before using mm, replace *printer_name* in the script with the actual name of your printer.

To use mm, type mm followed by the memos you want printed. If they are not in the current directory, include the full path to the memos. If you don't want a banner page to print, add -onobanner to the end of the line after -Tpostscript.

Listing for mm

```
#! /usr/bin/sh
if
   test $# -eq 0
then
   echo usage: $0 'memo1 memo2 ...'>&2
   exit 1
fi
cat $* | grap | pic | tbl | /usr/ucb/troff
   -mm | /usr/lib/lp/postscript/dpost | lp
   -dprinter_name -Tpostscript
```

NETRUN

The `netrun` script is extremely useful if you are using your UnixWare system as a single-user system and don't need the networking features. The speed of your system is increased considerably by turning off networking services. `netrun` is also used for turning networking back on.

Using netrun

Before using `netrun`, you must become the root user (type `su` in a Terminal window and enter the root user's password when prompted). Next, type `netrun stop` or `netrun start` to stop and start the networking services, respectively. Turning networking back on could take several minutes. Be patient while the script does its work.

Listing for netrun

```
#! /usr/bin/sh
if
   test $# -ne 1
then
   echo usage: $0 'start'>&2
   echo "    or">&2
   echo "    "$0 'stop'>&2
   exit 1
fi

cd /etc/init.d
case $1 in
   start)
      sh nfs start
      ch nw start
      sh nuc start
      sh inetinit start
      sh rpc start
      sh cs start
      ;;
   stop)
      sh nuc stop
      sh nw stop
      sh inetinit stop
      sh rpc stop
      sh cs stop
```

```
   sh nfs stop
   ;;
 *)
  echo usage: $0 'start'>&2
  echo "    or"
  echo "    "$0 'stop'>&2
   exit 1
   ;;
esac
```

OWNCHG

The ownchg script changes the owner and group of all the files and directories in the current directory and the directories below it. This script is useful when you need to change the owner and group for many files and directories at the same time.

Using ownchg

Before you use ownchg, change the owner (spike) and the group (doc) to the names of the owner and group you want to assign to the files and directories.

To use ownchg, change to the directory in which you want the owner and group to begin changing. Next type ownchg.

Listing for ownchg

```
#! /usr/bin/sh
# Change owner
find . ! \( -type d \) -exec chown spike {}
   \;
find . -type d -exec chown spike {} \;
# Change groups
find . ! \( -type d \) -exec chgrp doc {} \;
find . -type d -exec chgrp doc {} \;
```

PD

Use the pd script to print ASCII text files to your printer. For example, you can use pd to print a copy of your .profile file. You can rename this script to represent your printer.

If you can access more than one printer, you can create a printing script for each one. Give the scripts names that identify the printer to which they print.

Using pd

Before using pd, change *printer_name* to the name of your printer. The print job is piped to pr before it's printed. pr formats the job so the page number, file name, and date appear at the top of the page. In addition, a 1-inch margin is left at the top and bottom.

Listing for pd

```
#! /usr/bin/sh
if
   test $# -eq 0
then
   echo usage: $0 'file1 file2 ...'>&2
   exit 1
fi
pr $* | lp -dprinter_name
```

PERMCHG

The permchg script changes the permissions of all the files and directories in the current directory and the directories below it. This script is useful when you need to change the permissions for many files and directories at the same time.

Using permchg

Each time you use permchg, you'll want to make sure that the permissions are set correctly inside the script. As written, the script changes all directories to 755 (the first `find` command) and all files to 644 (the second `find` command).

To use `permchg`, change to the directory in which you want the permissions to begin changing. Next, type `permchg`.

Listing for permchg

```
#! /usr/bin/sh
find . -type d -exec chmod 755 {} \;
find . ! \( -type d \) -exec chmod 644 {} \;
```

PSD

The `psd` script is similar to the `pd` script, except that it prints PostScript files to your PostScript printer (this script is only for use with PostScript printers). As with `pd`, you might want to have several versions of the `psd` script, one for each PostScript printer you can access. You can rename each script to represent the printer.

Using psd

Before using `psd`, change *printer_name* to the name of your PostScript printer. Then type `psd` followed by the names of the files you want printed.

Listing for psd

```
#! /usr/bin/sh
if
  test $# -eq 0
then
  echo usage: $0 'file1 file2 ...'>&2
  exit 1
fi
for i in 'ls $*'
 do
  cat $i | lp -onobanner -Tpostscript
  -dprinter_name
 done
```

NOTE

Notice that this script has a `for` loop where `pd` doesn't. Due to a bug in UnixWare 1.1, multiple PostScript files cannot be printed on a single command line, as can text files (with `pd`). Each file must be processed separately. The `for` loop executes the `cat` line individually for each file. For UnixWare 2, you can make a copy of the `pd` script, rename it `psd`, and add `-Tpostscript`, as shown in this script.

READFLOP

The `readflop` script is for viewing the data on a UNIX floppy that has been created using `cpio`. The data is *not* extracted from the floppy. This script is a convenient way to check the contents of a `cpio` floppy without restoring its contents. See Chapter 8 for more information about using `cpio`.

Using readflop

To use `readflop`, insert a `cpio` UNIX floppy in the first floppy drive and type `readflop`. To read the second floppy drive, change `f0t` to `f1t`.

Listing for readflop

```
#! /usr/bin/sh
cpio -it</dev/rdsk/f0t
```

READTAPE

The `readtape` script is for viewing the data on a cartridge tape that has been created using `cpio`. The data is *not* extracted from the tape. This script is a convenient way to check the contents of a `cpio` tape without restoring its contents. See Chapter 8 for more information about using `cpio`.

Using readtape

To use `readtape`, insert a `cpio` cartridge tape in the tape drive and type `readtape`.

Listing for readtape

```
#! /usr/bin/sh
cpio -it</dev/rmt/c0s0
```

SYSCHECK

The `syscheck` script provides various information about your system. Through the Icon Setup window, you can create an icon for the script and run it from the UnixWare Desktop. You can also modify it to run different commands. See Chapter 8 for more information about `syscheck` and running it from the Desktop.

Using syscheck

To use `syscheck`, type `syscheck` and press Enter. When the menu appears, type the number of the menu item you want and press Enter.

Listing for syscheck

```
#! /usr/bin/sh
while true
do
  echo "


        Personal System Checker

      1) Check system disk space
      2) Check mounted file systems
      3) Check the system name
      4) Check who is logged in
      5) Check the size of your files
      6) Exit

"
  echo "Select the information you want to
check: \c"
  read check
  echo ""
  case $check in
  1)
```

```
                    /etc/dfspace
                    ;;
              2)
                    /etc/mount
                    ;;
              3)    /usr/bin/uname -a
                    ;;
              4)    /usr/bin/who -u
                    ;;
              5)    du $HOME | pg
                    ;;
              6)
                    break
                    ;;
              *)
                    echo "**** You must enter a number from
              1 to 6. ***** \c"
                    continue
                    ;;
         esac
    done
    exit 0
```

Playing
with UnixWare

UNIX is an ideal platform for playing games, especially multiuser games. For example, you can play bridge across a network with players anywhere in the world. Although they're not included with UnixWare, multi-user games are available "off the net." (The *net* is how UNIX hackers refer to the Internet.) See Chapter 5 for details on accessing the Internet.

UnixWare does include two single-user graphical games: Xtetris and Puzzle. Xtetris is a UNIX version of the familiar DOS game called Tetris. Puzzle is a UNIX version of the little plastic game with 15 movable squares, each numbered 1 through 15. These games are located in the Games folder (see Figure C.1), which is accessed from the UnixWare Desktop window.

F I G U R E C.1

The Folder: Games window

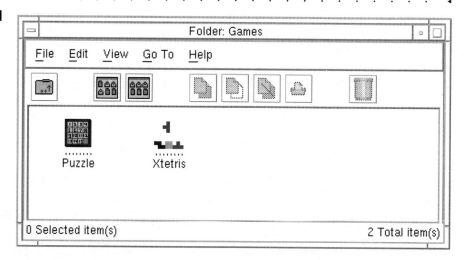

Playing Xtetris

To start Xtetris, from the UnixWare Desktop window, double-click on the Games icon, then double-click on the Xtetris icon in the Games folder window. The Xtetris window appears, as shown in Figure C.2.

FIGURE C.2

The Xtetris window

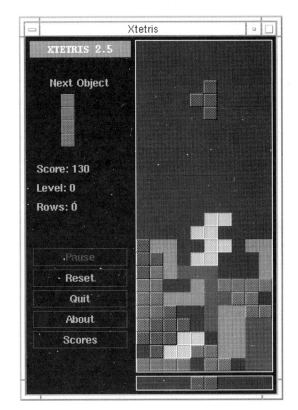

To play the game, use the numeric keypad to control the pieces. Table C.1 shows what the various keys do.

KEY	ACTION
8	Rotate piece counterclockwise
5 or 2	Rotate piece clockwise
4	Move piece left
6	Move piece right
Spacebar	Drop piece to bottom

TABLE C.1

Xtetris keyboard actions

OBJECT AND STRATEGY OF XTETRIS

The object of Xtetris is to score as many points as possible before the game pieces, called *objects*, stack up and touch the top of the playing area. The more objects you can make drop before they touch the top, the more points you score. When you manipulate the objects so they form a solid row, the row disappears, giving you more room for additional objects. Filling in a row also scores additional points.

To manipulate the objects as they fall, use the 4 and 6 keys to move the objects left and right. Use the 8, 5, or 2 keys to rotate the objects so they interlock without spaces.

XTETRIS WINDOW LAYOUT

The upper-left side of the Xtetris window displays the next game piece. Knowing the next piece helps you plan your strategy for placing the current piece. The following information appears beneath the next object:

- **Score:** Keeps track of your accumulated score

- **Level:** Displays the playing level

- **Rows:** Keeps track of how many rows you've completed

When you've completed a certain number of rows, the level changes. Each higher level increases the speed of the game.

Below the game information are the game controls:

- **Start:** Begins the game. Pieces start falling from the top of the game area.

 NOTE   **Once you click on the Start button, it changes to a Pause button.**

- **Pause:** Temporarily pauses the game, and the button becomes the Start button again. To resume, click on Start.

- **Reset:** Cancels the current game and clears the game area. Press Start to begin a new game.

▶ **Quit:** Closes the Xtetris window, even if you're in the middle of a game.

▶ **About:** Displays the Xtetris authors' names and the copyright notice.

▶ **Scores:** Shows a window with the best score. As a higher score is achieved, it replaces the previous high score.

Playing Puzzle

To start Puzzle, double-click on the Puzzle icon in the Games folder window. The Puzzle window appears, as shown in Figure C.3.

Puzzle is quite simple to play. It has only two controls: Scramble, to start a new game, and Solve, to have your computer solve the puzzle for you.

To solve the puzzle yourself, click on a number square next to the empty space. The number square takes the place of the space. The object is to align the numbers sequentially from left to right, as shown in Figure C.4.

The Puzzle window

▶ . . . . ◀

Solved Puzzle game

You can move several squares at the same time by clicking on any square in the same row or column as the space. All the squares from the one you clicked on to the space will move.

Once you've solved Puzzle, click on Scramble to start a new game.

Command
Reference
Summary

Every experienced UNIX user realizes that, without the *man pages* (manual pages), you're dead in the water. Even with UnixWare, where most common system administration and user tasks can be done from the GUI, the man pages are invaluable for the many tasks that can only be done from the command line. For example, certain file manipulations can only be done from the command line using commands such as diff, sort, and awk. Auditing, too, can only be started from the command line. And if you're doing any development work, make, the C compiler (cc), and the rest of the development tools are accessible only from the command line.

The UNIX man pages are the life-blood of the UNIX guru. Whether on-line or printed, to get the most out of your UNIX system, you need the man pages. For example, the simple ls command has 24 options. We don't know anyone that has memorized all 24 options. Then again, with the man pages handy, we don't know anyone stupid enough to try to memorize all 24 options.

Most, if not all, UNIX systems have the complete set of man pages available online. In UnixWare, for example, you can access the man pages two ways. From the Desktop you can open the Applications folder, double-click on the Online Docs icon, and then access the Command Reference. And from the command line you can type man plus the man page name (for example, man cpio) to view the corresponding man page.

NOTE **See Chapter 8 for complete information on using the man command.**

This appendix provides something different. It lists only the name, short description, and syntax for each UNIX System V Release 4.2, section 1, 1C, 1F, and 1M man pages (the commands). It allows you to quickly (well, sort of quickly) peruse the entire set of section 1 man pages. If you see something for which you want more information, use the man command to view the entire man page.

accept
Accept print requests

```
accept destinations
```

acctdisk
Overview of accounting and miscellaneous accounting commands

```
/usr/lib/acct/acctdisk
```

acctcms
Command summary from per-process accounting records

```
/usr/lib/acct/acctcms [-a [-p] [-o]] [-c] [-j] [-n]
[-s] [-t] files
```

acctcom
Search and print process accounting file(s)

```
acctcom [options] [file ... ]
```

acctcon, acctcon1, acctcon2
Connect-time accounting

```
/usr/lib/acct/acctcon [options]
/usr/lib/acct/acctcon1 [options]
/usr/lib/acct/acctcon2
```

acctdusg
Overview of accounting and miscellaneous accounting commands

```
/usr/lib/acct/acctdusg [-u file] [-p file]
```

accton

Overview of accounting and miscellaneous accounting commands

```
/usr/lib/acct/accton [file]
```

acctmerg

Merge or add total accounting files

```
/usr/lib/acct/acctmerg [-a] [-i] [-p] [-t] [-u] [-v]
[file] ...
```

acctwtmp

Overview of accounting and miscellaneous accounting commands

```
/usr/lib/acct/acctwtmp "reason"
```

acctprc, acctprc1, acctprc2

Process accounting

```
/usr/lib/acct/acctprc
/usr/lib/acct/acctprc1 [ctmp]
/usr/lib/acct/acctprc2
```

acctsh: chargefee, ckpacct, dodisk, lastlogin, monacct, nulladm, prctmp, prdaily, prtacct, runacct, shutacct, startup, turnacct

Shell procedures for accounting

```
/usr/lib/acct/chargefee login-name number
/usr/lib/acct/ckpacct [blocks]
/usr/lib/acct/dodisk [-o] [files ...]
/usr/lib/acct/lastlogin
/usr/lib/acct/monacct number
/usr/lib/acct/nulladm file
/usr/lib/acct/prctmp
/usr/lib/acct/prdaily [-l] [-c] [mmdd]
/usr/lib/acct/prtacct file ["heading"]
```

```
/usr/lib/acct/runacct [mmdd] [mmdd state]
/usr/lib/acct/shutacct ["reason"]
/usr/lib/acct/startup
/usr/lib/acct/turnacct on | off | switch
```

addbib

(BSD) create or extend a bibliographic database

```
/usr/ucb/addbib [-a] [-p promptfile] database
```

adduser

Create a login for a new user

```
adduser login_name name user_ID logdir Yes | No
```

admin

Create and administer SCCS files

```
admin [-i[name]] [-b] [-n] [-rrel] [-t[name]]
   [-fflag[flag-val]][-dflag[flag-val]] [-alogin]
   [-elogin] [-m[mrlist]] [-y[comment]] [-h] [-z] file ...
```

adminrole

Display, add, change, delete roles in the TFM database

```
adminrole [-n] [-a [cmd:path[:priv[:priv ... ]]][,...]]
   role ...
adminrole [-a [cmd:path[:priv[:priv ... ]]][, ...]] role ...
   [-r cmd[:priv[:priv ... ]][, ...]] role ...
adminrole [-d] role ...
adminrole
```

adminuser

Display, add, change, delete administrators in the TFM database

```
adminuser [-n] [-o role[, ...]]
  [-a cmd:path[:priv[:priv ...]]][, ...]]
  user ...
adminuser [-o role[, ...]
  [-r cmd[:priv[:priv ...]]][, ...]]
  [-a cmd:path[:priv[:priv ...]]][, ...]] user ...
adminuser [-d] user ...
adminuser
```

alarm_agent

Compaq Insight Manager (CIM) alarm agent

```
alarm_agent [-p time] [-i] [-s OK | NOTOK]
  [-t OK | NOTOK]
```

alpq

Query the alp STREAMS module

```
alpq
```

apropos

(BSD) locate commands by keyword lookup

```
/usr/ucb/apropos keyword ...
```

ar

Maintain portable archive or library

```
ar [-V] -key [arg] [posname] afile [name ... ]
```

arch

(BSD) display the architecture of the current host

```
/usr/ucb/arch
```

arp

Address resolution display and control

```
arp hostname
arp -a [unix [kmem]]
arp -d hostname
arp -s hostname ether_address [temp] [pub] [trail]
arp -f filename
```

as

Assembler

```
as [-VTm] [-Q yn] [-Y key,dir] [-o objfile] [-t cpu]
    file ...
```

at

Execute commands at a later time

```
at [-f script] [-m] time [date] [+ increment]
at -l [job  ...]
at -r job  ...
at -d job
```

atq

Display the jobs queued to run at specified times

```
atq [-c] [-n] [username ...  ]
```

atrm

Remove jobs spooled by at or batch

```
atrm [-afi] arg ...
```

attradmin

Attribute map database administration

```
attradmin [-A attr_name [-l local_attr]]
attradmin -A attr_name -a -r remote_attr -l local_attr
attradmin -A attr_name -d [-r remote_attr] -l local_attr
attradmin -A attr_name -I attr_descr
attradmin -A attr_name [-Dcf]
```

auditcnv

Create default audit mask file

```
auditcnv
```

auditfltr

Convert audit log file for intermachine portability

```
auditfltr [[-iN] [-oX]] | [-iX -oN]
```

auditlog

Display or set audit log file attributes

```
auditlog [-P path][-p node] [-v high_water]
   [-x max_size][-s | -d | -A next_path [-a next_node]
   [-n pgm] | -a next_node [-n pgm]]
```

auditmap

Create and write audit map files

```
auditmap [-m dirname]
```

auditoff

Disable auditing

```
auditoff
```

auditon

Enable auditing

```
auditon
```

auditrpt

Display recorded information from audit trail

```
auditrpt [-o] [-i] [-b | -w] [-x][-e[!]event[,...]]
   [-u user[,...]] [-f object_id[,...]]
   [-t object_type[,...]] [-s time] [-h time]
   [-a out come] [-m map] [-p all | priv[,...]]
   [-v subtype] [log [...]]
```

auditset

Select or display audit criteria

```
auditset [-d [-u user[,...] | -a]]
auditset [-s [operator]event[,...]]
   [-e[operator]event[,...] -u user[,...] |-a]
```

automount

Automatically mount NFS file systems

```
/usr/lib/nfs/automount [-mnTv] [-D name=value]
   [-M mount-directory] [-f master-file]
   [-t sub-options] [directory  map [-mount-options]] ...
```

autopush

Configure lists of automatically pushed STREAMS modules

```
autopush -f file
autopush -r -M major -m minor
autopush -g -M major -m minor
```

awk

Pattern scanning and processing language

```
awk  [-f progfile | 'prog']  [-Ffieldsep] [-v
  var=value] [file ...]
```

backup

(XENIX) perform backup functions

```
backup [-t] [-p | -c | -f files | -u "user1 [user2]"]
  -d device
backup -h
```

backup

Initiate or control a system backup session

```
backup  [-t table] [-o oname[:odevice]] [-m user]
  [-en] [-c week:day | demand]
backup  [-i] [-t table] [-o oname[:odevice]] [-m user]
  [-en] [-s | -v] [-c week:day | demand]
backup -S | -R | -C [-u user | -A | -j jobid]
backup [-p | -w | -f files |  -u "user1[user2]"]
  -d device
backup -h
```

banner

Make posters

```
banner strings
```

basename

Deliver portions of path names

```
basename string [suffix]
```

basename

(BSD) display portions of path names

```
/usr/ucb/basename string [suffix]
```

batch

Execute commands at a later time

```
batch
```

bc

Arbitrary-precision arithmetic language

```
bc [-c] [-l] [file ... ]
```

bcheckrc

System initialization procedures

```
/sbin/bcheckrc
```

bdiff

Big diff

```
bdiff file1 file2 [n] [-s]
```

bfs

Big file scanner

```
bfs [-] file
```

bfsdiskusg

Generate disk accounting data by user ID

```
/usr/lib/acct/bfsdiskusg [options] [files]
```

biff

(BSD) give notice of incoming mail messages

```
/usr/ucb/biff [ y | n ]
```

biod

NFS daemon

```
/usr/lib/nfs/biod
```

bkexcept

Change or display an exception list for incremental backups

```
bkexcept [-t file] [-d patterns]
bkexcept [-t file] -a|-r patterns
bkexcept -C [files]
```

bkhistory

Report on completed backup operations

```
bkhistory [-hl] [-f field_separator] [-d dates]
  [-o names] [-t tags]
bkhistory -p period
```

bkoper

Interact with backup operations to service media insertion prompts

```
bkoper [-u users]
```

bkreg

Change or display the contents of a backup register

```
bkreg -p period [-w cweek] [-t table]
bkreg -a tag -o orig -c weeks:days| demand -d ddev -m
   method|migration [-b moptions] [-t table] [-D de-
   pend] [-P prio]
bkreg -e tag [-o orig] [-c weeks:days| demand]
   [-m method|migration] [-d ddev] [-t table]
   [-b moptions] [-D depend] [-P prio]
bkreg -r tag [-t table]
bkreg [-A|-O|-R] [-hsv] [-t table] [-c weeks[:days]|
   demand]
bkreg -C fields [-hv] [-t table] [-c weeks[:days]|
   demand] [-f c]
```

bkstatus

Display the status of backup operations

```
bkstatus [-h] [-f field_separator] [-j jobids]
   [-s states | -a] [-u users]
bkstatus -p period
```

boot

UnixWare system boot program

bootp

Remote bootstrap configuration client

```
bootp [-a interface_name] [-c number_of_tries] [-d]
   device [hostname]
```

bootparamd
Boot parameter server

```
/usr/lib/nfs/bootparamd [-d]
```

bootpd
Internet Boot Protocol server

```
in.bootpd [-i -s -ttimeout -dlevel -cchdir-path]
   [bootptab [dumpfile]]
in.bootpgw [-i -s -ttimeout -dlevel] server
```

brc
System initialization procedures

```
/sbin/brc
```

c++filt
C++ name demangler

```
c++filt [-Vw] file ...
```

cal
Print calendar

```
cal [[month] year]
```

calendar
Reminder service

```
calendar
```

cancel

Cancel print requests

```
cancel [request-IDs] [printers]
cancel -u login-IDs [printers]
```

captoinfo

Convert a `termcap` description into a `terminfo` description

```
captoinfo [-v ... ] [-V] [-1] [-w width] file ...
```

cat

Concatenate and print files

```
cat [-suv [-et]] [file ... ]
```

catman

(BSD) create the `cat` files and `whatis` database for the manual

```
/usr/ucb/catman [-nptw] [-M directory] [-T mac_file]
    [sections]
```

cb

C program beautifier

```
cb [-s] [-j] [-l leng] [-V] [file ...]
```

cc

C compiler

```
cc [options] file ...
```

cc

(BSD) C compiler

```
/usr/ucb/cc [options] file ...
```

cd

Change working directory

```
cd [directory]
```

cdc

Change the `delta` comment of an SCCS `delta`

```
cdc -r SID [-m[mrlist]] [-y[comment]] file ...
```

cddevsuppl

Set or get major and minor numbers of a CD-ROM device file

```
cddevsuppl [-m mapfile | -u unmapfile] [-c]
```

cddrec

Read CD-ROM Directory Record

```
cddrec [-s number] [-b] file
```

cdmntsuppl

Set and get administrative CD-ROM features

```
cdmntsuppl [-D mode] [-F mode] [-g group] [-G gmfile]
    [-u owner] [-U umfile] [-c | [-l] [-m]] [-s | -x]
    mountpoint
```

cdptrec
Read CD-ROM Path Table Record

```
cdptrec [-b] directory
```

cdsuf
Read the System Use Fields from a System Use Area on CD-ROM

```
cdsuf [-s number] [-b] file
```

cdvd
Read the CD-ROM Primary Volume Descriptor

```
cdvd [-b] file
```

cdxar
Read CD-ROM Extended Attribute Record (XAR)

```
cdxar [-s number] [-b] file
```

cflow
Generate C flowgraph

```
cflow [-c] [-r] [-ix] [-i_] [-dnum] -V files
```

chargefee
Shell procedure for accounting

```
/usr/lib/acct/chargefee login-name number
```

checkeq
(BSD) typeset mathematics

```
/usr/ucb/checkeq [file] ...
```

checknr
(BSD) check nroff and troff input files; report possible errors

```
/usr/ucb/checknr [-fs] [-a.x1.y1.x2.y2....xn.yn]
   [-c.x1.x2.x3....xn] [file ...]
```

chgrp
Change the group ownership of a file

```
chgrp [-R] [-h] group file ...
```

chkey
Change user encryption key

```
chkey [-f]
```

chmod
Change file mode

```
chmod [-R] mode file ...
chmod [-R][ugoa]{ + | - | = }[rwxXlstugo] file ...
```

chown
Change file owner

```
chown [-h] [-R] owner[:group] file ...
```

chown

(BSD) change file owner

```
/usr/ucb/chown [-fhR] owner[.group] file ...
```

chroot

Change root directory for a command

```
/usr/sbin/chroot newroot command
```

chrtbl

Generate character classification and conversion tables

```
chrtbl [file]
```

ckbinarsys

Determine whether remote system can accept binary messages

```
ckbinarsys [-S] -s remote_system_name -t msg_type
```

ckdate

Prompt for and validate a date

```
ckdate [-Q] [-W width] [-f format] [-d default]
    [-h help] [-e error] [-p prompt] [-k pid [-s signal]]
```

ckgid

Prompt for and validate a group ID

```
ckgid [-Q] [-W width] [-m] [-d default] [-h help]
    [-e error] [-p prompt] [-k pid [-s signal]]
```

ckint

Display a prompt; verify and return an integer value

```
ckint [-Q] [-W width] [-b base] [-d default] [-h help]
   [-e error] [-p prompt] [-k pid [-s signal]]
errint [-W width] [-b base] [-e error]
helpint [-W width] [-b base] [-h help]
valint [-b base] input
```

ckitem

Build a menu; prompt for and return a menu item

```
ckitem [-Q] [-W width] [-uno] [-f file] [-l label]
   [[-i invis] ... ] [-m max] [-d default] [-h help]
   [-e error] [-p prompt] [-k pid [-s signal]]
   [choice1   choice2 ... ]
erritem [-W width] [-e error]    [choice1   choice2 ... ]
helpitem [-W width] [-h help]    [choice1   choice2 ... ]
```

ckkeywd

Prompt for and validate a keyword

```
ckkeywd [-Q] [-W width] [-d default] [-h help]
   [-e error] [-p prompt][-k pid [-s signal]]
   [keyword ... ]
```

ckpacct

Shell procedure for accounting

```
/usr/lib/acct/ckpacct [blocks]
```

ckpath

Display a prompt; verify and return a path name

```
ckpath [-Q] [-W width] [-a| l] [file_options] [-rtwx]
   [-d default][-h help] [-e error] [-p prompt]
   [-k pid [-s signal]]
```

```
errpath [-W width] [-a| l] [file_options] [-rtwx]
   [-e error]
helppath [-W width] [-a| l] [file_options] [-rtwx]
   [-h help]
valpath [-a | l] [file_options] [-rtwx] input
```

ckrange

Prompt for and validate an integer

```
ckrange [-Q] [-W width] [-l lower] [-u upper] [-b base]
   [-d default][-h help] [-e error] [-p prompt]
   [-k pid [-s signal]]
errange [-W width] [-l lower] [-u upper] [-e error]
   [-b base]
helprange [-W width] [-l lower] [-u upper] [-h help]
   [-b base]
valrange [-l lower] [-u upper] [-b base] input
```

ckroot (vxfs)

Set mount options for root file system

```
/etc/fs/vxfs/ckroot
```

ckstr

Display a prompt; verify and return a string answer

```
ckstr [-Q] [-W width] [[-r regexp] ...] [-l length]
   [-d default] [-h help] [-e error] [-p prompt] [-k pid
   [-s signal]]
errstr [-W width] [-e error] [[-r regexp] ...]
   [-l length]
helpstr [-W width] [-h help] [[-r regexp] ...]
   [-l length]
valstr input [[-r regexp] ...] [-l length]
```

cksum

Print checksum and byte count of a file

```
cksum [file ... ]
```

cktime

Display a prompt; verify and return a time of day

```
cktime [-Q] [-W width] [-f format] [-d default]
   [-h help] [-e error] [-p prompt] [-k pid [-s signal]]
errtime [-W width] [-e error] [-f format]
helptime [-W width] [-h help] [-f format]
valtime [-f format] input
```

ckuid

Prompt for and validate a user ID

```
ckuid [-Q] [-W width] [-m] [-d default] [-h help]
   [-e error] [-p prompt] [-k pid [-s signal]]
erruid [-W width] [-e error]
helpuid [-W width] [-m] [-h help]
valuid input
```

ckyorn

Prompt for and validate yes/no

```
ckyorn [-Q] [-W width] [-d default] [-h help] [-e error]
   [-p prompt] [-k pid [-s signal]]
erryorn [-W width] [-e error]
helpyorn [-W width] [-h help]
valyorn input
```

clear

Clear the terminal screen

```
clear
```

closewtmp

Overview of accounting and miscellaneous accounting commands

```
/usr/lib/acct/closewtmp
```

cmp

Compare two files

```
cmp [-l] [-s] file1 file2 [skip1 [skip2]]
```

cocreate

Communicate with a process

```
cocreate [-r rpath] [-w wpath] [-i id] [-R refname]
   [-s send_string] [-e expect_string] command
```

cocheck

Communicate with a process

```
cocheck proc_id
```

cof2elf

COFF to ELF object file translation

```
cof2elf [-iqV] [-Q{yn}] [-s directory] files
```

col

Filter reverse line-feeds

```
col [-b] [-f] [-x] [-p]
```

colltbl

Create collation database

```
colltbl [file | -]
```

comb

Combine SCCS deltas

```
comb [-o] [-s] [-pSID] [-clist] file ...
```

comm

Select or reject lines common to two sorted files

```
comm [-123] file file2
```

compress

Compress data for storage

```
compress [-dfFqcv] [-b bits] file...
```

comsat

`biff` server

```
in.comsat
```

configCheck

Autoconfigure mail

```
configCheck [-l on|off] [-s on|off]
```

configFiles

Autoconfigure mail

```
configFiles output_file prototype_file
```

configure

Map existing networking boards and protocols

```
/etc/confnet.d/configure [-i] [-p protocol -d device
  [-d device ... ]]
/etc/confnet.d/configure [-p protocol -d device]
  [-O "protocol specific opts"]
/etc/confnet.d/configure [-r -p protocol]
/etc/confnet.d/configure [-r -d device]
/etc/confnet.d/configure [-r -p protocol -d device]
```

configure_inet: configure

Internet-specific network boot parameters configuration

```
/etc/confnet.d/inet/configure -i -d device [-d device]
/etc/confnet.d/inet/configure -d device
  [-H ip_host -A ip_addr -I ifconfig_opt -S slink_opt]
/etc/confnet.d/inet/configure -r
/etc/confnet.d/inet/configure -r -d device [-d device]
```

convert

Convert archive files to common formats

```
convert [-x] infile outfile
```

copy

(XENIX) copy groups of files

```
copy [option] source ... dest
```

coreceive

Communicate with a process

```
coreceive proc_id
```

cosend

Communicate with a process

```
cosend [-n] proc_id string
```

cp

Copy files

```
cp [-r | -R] [-f] [-i] [-p] [-e extent_opt] file1
   [file2 ... ] target
```

cpio

Copy file archives in and out

```
cpio -i[bBcdfkmrsSTtuvV6] [-C bufsize] [-E file]
   [-G file] [-H hdr] [-e extent_opt] [-I file
   [-M message]] [-R ID]] [pattern ...]
cpio -o[aABcLvV] [-C bufsize] [-G file] [-H hdr]
   [-K mediasize] [-e extent_opt] [-O file [-M message]]
cpio -p directory |[adlLmuvV] [-R ID] [-e extent_opt]
```

cpqidamon

Compaq Intelligent Disk Array Monitoring Agent

```
cpqidamon start|stop [pollingtime]
```

cpqscsimon

Compaq Fast-SCSI-2 Monitor

```
cpqscsimon start [pollingtime]
cpqscsimon stop
```

cpqsmu
Compaq SCSI-2 Management Utility

```
cpqsmu [c] [-h] -ttype -nhanum -op
```

cpqsmuxd
Compaq Insight Manager SMUX peer

```
cpqsmuxd
```

cpqupsd
Compaq Insight Manager (CIM) UPS Agent

```
cpqupsd [-p time] -f file [-i] [-s OK | NOTOK]
  [-t OK | NOTOK]
```

crl
Bilateral IAF authentication scheme

```
cr1 [-r] [-u local_user] [-s local_service]
  [-U remote_user] [-M remote_machine]
  [-S remote_service]
```

crash
Examine system images

```
/usr/sbin/crash [-d dumpfile] [-n namelist]
  [-m moduledir] [-w outputfile]
```

createSurr
Autoconfigure mail

```
/usr/lib/mail/surrcmd/createSurr [-l on|off]
  [-s on|off]
```

creatiadb
Create `/etc/security/ia/index` and `/etc/security/ia/master` files

```
creatiadb
```

cron
Clock daemon

```
/usr/sbin/cron [nofork]
```

crontab
User `crontab` file

```
crontab [file]
crontab -e [username]
crontab -r [username]
crontab -l [username]
```

crypt
Encode/decode

```
crypt [password]
crypt [-k]
```

cryptkey
Add, delete, or modify a key in the `cr1 key` database

```
cryptkey [-a | -c | -d] [-s scheme] [local_principal]
    remote_principal
```

cs

Connection Server, a daemon that establishes connections for TLI/serial network services

```
/usr/sbin/cs [-d [-D debugsize]] [-L logsize]
/usr/sbin/cs [-x]
```

cscope

Interactively examine a C program

```
cscope [options] [file ... ]
```

csh

Shell command interpreter with a C-like syntax

```
csh [-bcefinstvVxX] [argument ... ]
```

csplit

Context split

```
csplit [-s] [-k] [-f prefix] [-n digits] file arg1
    [ ... argn]
```

ct

Spawn login to a remote terminal

```
ct [options] telno ...
```

ctags

Create a tags file for use with vi

```
ctags [-aBFtuvwx] [-f tagsfile] file ...
```

ctrace

C program debugger

```
ctrace [options] [file]
```

cu

Call another UNIX system

```
cu [options] [destination]
```

custom

(XENIX) install specific portions of SCO UNIX or XENIX packages

```
/sbin/custom
/sbin/custom -a [package ... ] [-m /dev/install |
  /dev/install1]
/sbin/custom -s existing_product [-ilr [package ... ]]
  [-f [file]] [-m /dev/install | /dev/install1]
```

cut

Cut out selected fields of each line of a file

```
cut -b list [-n] [file ... ]
cut -c list [file ... ]
cut -f list [-d char] [-s] [file ... ]
```

cvtomflib

Convert OMF (XENIX) libraries to ELF

```
cvtomflib [-v] [-o outfile] library [library ... ]
```

cxref

Generate C program cross-reference

```
cxref [options] files
```

date
Print and set the date

```
date [-u] [+format]
date [-u] [[mmdd]HHMM | mmddHHMM[[cc]yy]]
date [-a [-]sss.fff]
```

dc
Desk calculator

```
dc [file]
```

dcopy (generic)
Copy file systems for optimal access time

```
dcopy [-F FSType] [-V] [current_options]
   [-o specific_options] inputfs outputfs
```

dcopy (s5)
Copy s5 file systems for optimal access time

```
dcopy [-F s5] [generic_options] [-sX] [-an] [-d] [-v]
   [-ffsize[:isize]] inputfs outputfs
```

dcu
Device Configuration Utility

```
dcu [-C | -S]
```

dd
Convert and copy a file

```
dd [option=value] ...
```

ddbconv

Convert device table to Device Database format

```
ddbconv [-v]
```

debug

Source-level, interactive, object file debugger

```
debug [opts][[-f none|procs|all][-r][-l start_loc]
  cmd_line]
debug [opts][-f none|procs|all][-l object_file]
  live_object ...
debug [opts] -c core_file object_file
opts: [-V][-i c|x][-X opt][-d defaults][-s path]
  [-Yitem,dir]
```

defadm

Display/modify default values

```
defadm
defadm [filename [name[=value]] [name[=value]] [...]]
defadm [-d filename name [name] [...]]
```

delsysadm

sysadm interface menu or task removal tool

```
delsysadm task | [-r] menu
```

delta

Make a delta (change) to an SCCS file

```
delta [-rSID] [-s] [-n] [-glist] [-m[mrlist]]
  [-y[comment]] [-p] file ...
```

deluser
Remove a login from the system

```
deluser login_name Yes | No logdir
```

deroff
Remove nroff, troff, tbl, and eqn constructs

```
deroff [-w] [-mm | -ms | -ml] [-i] [file] ...
```

deroff
(BSD) remove nroff, troff, tbl and eqn constructs

```
/usr/ucb/deroff [-k] [-p] [-w] [-m(aelms)] file ...
```

desktop
Initialize the UnixWare Desktop

```
desktop [[client] options] [-- [server] [display]
    options]
```

devattr
List device attributes

```
devattr [-v] device [attribute [...]]
```

devflag
Driver flags

```
#include <sys/conf.h>
#include <sys/ddi.h>
int prefixdevflag = 0;
```

devfree

Release devices from exclusive use

```
devfree key [device ... ]
```

Arguments
```
key       Designates the unique key on which the device
          was reserved.
device    Defines device that this command will release
          from exclusive use. Can be the pathname of the
          device or the device alias.
```

devnm

Device name

```
/usr/sbin/devnm [name ... ]
```

devreserv

Reserve devices for exclusive use

```
devreserv [key [devicelist ... ]]
```

Arguments
```
key         Designates a unique key on which the device
            will be reserved. The key must be a positive
            integer.
devicelist  Defines a list of devices that devreserv
            will search to find an available device.
            (The list must be formatted as a single
            argument to the shell.)
```

df

(BSD) report free disk space on file systems

```
/usr/ucb/df  [-i] [-a] [-t type | file ... ]
```

df (generic), dfspace

Report number of free disk blocks and files/free disk space

```
df [-F FSType] [-begiklntVP] [current_options]
   [-o specific_options] [directory | special |
   resource...]
dfspace [-F FSType]
```

df (s5)

Report number of free disk blocks and inodes for s5 file systems

```
df [-F s5] [generic_options] [-f] [directory ... |
   special ...]
```

df (sfs)

Report free disk space on sfs file systems

```
df [-F sfs] [generic_options] [-o i] [directory |
   special]
```

df (ufs)

Report free disk space on ufs file systems

```
df [-F ufs] [generic_options] [-o i] [directory |
   special]
```

df (vxfs)

Report number of free disk blocks and inodes for vxfs file systems

```
df  [-F vxfs] [generic_options] [-o s] directory |
   special ...
```

dfmounts

Display mounted resource information

```
dfmounts [-F fstype] [-h] [-o specific_options]
   [restriction ... ]
```

dfmounts

Display mounted NFS resource information

```
dfmounts [-F nfs] [-h] [server ... ]
```

dfshares

List available resources from remote or local systems

```
dfshares [-F fstype] [-h] [-o specific_options]
   [server ... ]
```

dfshares

List available NFS resources from remote systems

```
dfshares [-F nfs] [-o] [-h] [server ... ]
```

diff

Differential file comparator

```
diff [-bitw] [-c | -e | -f | -h | -n] filename1 file-
   name2
diff [-bitw] [-C number] filename1 filename2
diff [-bitw] [-D string] filename1 filename2
diff [-bitw] [-c | -e | -f | -h | -n] [-l] [-r] [-s]
   [-S name] directory1 directory2
```

diff3

3-way differential file comparison

```
diff3 [-exEX3] file1 file2 file3
```

diffmk

(BSD) mark differences between versions of a `troff` input file

```
/usr/ucb/diffmk oldfile newfile markedfile
```

dig

Send domain name query packets to name servers

```
dig[@server]domain[query-type][query-class]
   [+query-option] [-dig-option] [%comment]
```

dinit

Run commands performed for multiuser environment after login processes

```
/sbin/dinit
```

dircmp

Directory comparison

```
dircmp [-d] [-s] [-wn] dir1 dir2
```

dirname

Deliver portions of path names

```
dirname string
```

dis

Object code disassembler

```
dis [-o] [-V] [-L] [-s] [-d sec] [-D sec] [-F function]
   [-t sec] [-l string] file ...
```

disable

Disable LP printers

```
disable [options] printers
```

disable_glogin

Disable the UnixWare Desktop graphical login

```
disable_glogin
```

diskadd

Disk setup utility

```
diskadd [-F dm_type] [disk_number]
diskrm [-F dm_type] [disk_number]
```

diskcfg

Update system files for PDI drivers

```
/etc/scsi/diskcfg [-S] [-R ROOT] [filename]
```

diskformat

Low-level format SCSI hard disk

```
diskformat /dev/rdsk/cCbBtTdDsO
```

disksetup

Disk setup utility

```
   Install Primary Disk
/usr/sbin/disksetup -I -B [-d defaults-file]
  -bbootfile raw-device [-s]

   Install Additional Disk
/usr/sbin/disksetup -I [-d defaults-file] raw-device
  [-s]
```

Write Boot Code to Disk
```
/usr/sbin/disksetup -b boot-file raw-device [-s]
```

diskusg

Generate disk accounting data by user ID

```
/usr/lib/acct/diskusg [options] [files]
```

dispadmin

Process scheduler administration

```
dispadmin -l
dispadmin -c class -g [-r res]
dispadmin -c class -s file
```

dispgid

Display a list of all valid group names

```
dispgid
```

displaypkg

Display all packages installed with installpkg

```
displaypkg
```

dispuid

Display a list of all valid user names

```
dispuid
```

dodisk

Shell procedure for accounting

```
/usr/lib/acct/dodisk [-o] [files ...]
```

domainname

Get/set name of current secure NIS domain

```
domainname [newname]
```

doscat

Access and manipulate DOS files

```
doscat [-r | -m] file ...
```

doscp

Access and manipulate DOS files

```
doscp [-R] [-r | -m] file1 file2
doscp [-r | -m] file ... directory
```

dosdir

Access and manipulate DOS files

```
dosdir directory
```

dosformat

Access and manipulate DOS files

```
dosformat [-fqv] drive
```

dosmkdir

Access and manipulate DOS files

```
dosmkdir directory ...
```

dosls

Access and manipulate DOS files

```
dosls directory ...
```

dosrm

Access and manipulate DOS files

```
dosrm [-R] file ...
```

dosrmdir

Access and manipulate DOS files

```
dosrmdir directory ...
```

dosslice

Set up UNIX nodes for accessing DOS partitions

```
dosslice [ 0 | 1 ]
```

download

Download host-resident PostScript Type 1 fonts

```
download [options] [files]
```

dpost
`troff` postprocessor for PostScript printers

```
/usr/lib/lp/postscript/dpost [options] [files]
```

drouter
List all networks recognized by the NetWare server router

```
drouter [-1 | -C | -h]
```

dsdm
Drop Site Database Manager - Motif/OPENLOOK drag-and-drop proxy agent

```
dsdm
```

dtadduser
Add a UnixWare Desktop user

```
dtadduser [-r remote] [user]
```

dtdeluser
Delete a UnixWare Desktop user

```
dtdeluser [user]
```

dtfilter
Add an entry to the UnixWare Desktop printer filter table

```
dtfilter -a [-o] file ...
dtfilter -d entry ...
```

dtm

UnixWare Desktop desktop manager

```
dtm [-display]
```

dtmodem

Add an entry to the modem table of the UnixWare Desktop

```
dtmodem -a [-o] file ...
dtmodem -d entry ...
```

dtprinter

Add an entry to the UnixWare Desktop printer table

```
dtprinter -a [-o] file ...
dtprinter -d entry ...
```

dtprivilege

Add an entry to the UnixWare Desktop privilege table

```
dtprivilege -a [entry]
dtprivilege -d entry ...
```

dtstatus

Update UnixWare Desktop system status parameters

```
dtstatus -a filename
dtstatus -d entry ...
dtstatus -f flag entry ...
```

dttypes

Add an entry to the document types table of UnixWare Desktop

```
dttypes -a [-o] file ...
dttypes -d entry ...
```

du
Summarize disk usage

```
du [-sarkx] [name ... ]
```

du
(BSD) display the number of disk blocks used per directory or file

```
/usr/ucb/du [-a] [-s] [filename ... ]
```

dump
Dump selected parts of an object file

```
dump options file ...
```

echo
Echo arguments

```
echo [ -n ] [arg] ...
```

echo
Put string on virtual output

```
echo [string ... ]
```

echo
(BSD) echo arguments

```
/usr/ucb/echo [-n] [arg] ...
```

ed

Text editor

```
ed [-s] [-p string] [-x] [-C] [file]
```

edit

Text editor (variant of **ex** for casual users)

```
edit [-r] [-x] [-C] [name ... ]
```

edquota

Edit user quotas for **ufs** file system

```
edquota [-p proto_user] username ...
edquota -t
```

edsysadm

sysadm interface editing tool

```
edsysadm
```

edvtoc

VTOC (Volume Table of Contents) editing utility

```
edvtoc -f vtoc-file raw-device
edvtoc -p raw-device
```

egrep

Search a file for a pattern

```
grep [-E|-F] [-c|-l|-q] [-bhinsvx] expression
   [file ... ]
grep [-E|-F] [-c|-l|-q] [-bhinsvx] -e expression ...
   [-f exprfile] ... [file ... ]
grep [-E|-F] [-c|-l|-q] [-bhinsvx] [-e expression] ...
   -f exprfile ... [file ... ]
```

emergency_disk
Create emergency recovery diskettes

```
emergency_disk [-d directory_name] disk_drive
```

emergency_rec
Create emergency recovery tape(s)

```
emergency_rec [-e] tape_drive
```

enable
Enable LP printers

```
enable printers
```

enable_glogin
Enable the UnixWare Desktop graphical login

```
disable_glogin
enable_glogin
start_glogin
```

env
Set environment for command execution

```
env [-] [name=value] ... [command args]
```

eqn
(BSD) typeset mathematics

```
/usr/ucb/eqn [-dxy] [-fn] [-pn] [-sn] [file] ...
```

errdate

Prompt for and validate a date

```
errdate [-W width] [-e error] [-f format]
```

errgid

Prompt for and validate a group ID

```
errgid [-W width] [-e error]
```

evgainit

Extended VGA keyboard/display driver initialization

```
evgainit card-type
```

ex

Text editor

```
ex [-s] [-v] [-t tag] [-r file] [-L] [-R] [-x] [-C]
[-c command] file ...
```

exportfs

Export and unexport directories to NFS clients

```
/usr/sbin/exportfs [-aiuv] [-o options] [pathname]
```

expr

Evaluate arguments as an expression

```
expr arguments
```

exstr

Extract strings from source files

```
exstr file ...
exstr -e file ...
exstr -r [-d] file ...
```

extcompose

Compose reference to external data for inclusion in a mail message

```
extcompose filename
```

factor

Obtain the prime factors of a number

```
factor [integer]
```

fastboot

(BSD) reboot the system without checking the disks

```
/usr/ucb/fastboot [boot-options]
```

fasthalt

(BSD) reboot/halt the system without checking the disks

```
/usr/ucb/fasthalt [halt-options]
```

fdetach

Detach a name from a STREAMS-based file descriptor

```
fdetach path
```

fdisk

Create or modify hard disk partition table

```
fdisk [argument]
```

ff (generic)

List file names and statistics for a file system

```
ff [-F FSType] [-V] [current_options]
   [-o specific_options] special ...
```

ff (s5)

Display i-list information

```
ff [-F s5] [generic_options] [-I] [-l] [-pprefix] [-s]
   [-u] [-an] [-mn] [-cn] [-nfile] [-ii-node-list]
   special ...
```

ff (ufs)

List file names and statistics for a ufs file system

```
ff [-F ufs] [generic_options] [-I] [-l] [-pprefix] [-s]
   [-u] [-an] [-mn] [-cn] [-nfile] [-ii-node-list]
   [-o a,m,s] special ...
```

ff (vxfs)

List file names and inode information for a vxfs file system

```
ff [-F vxfs] [generic_options] [-I] [-l] [-p prefix]
   [-s] [-u] [-a n] [-m n] [-c n] [-n file]
   [-i inode_list] [-o s] special ...
```

fgrep

Search a file for a character string

```
fgrep [options] string [file ... ]
```

file

Determine file type

```
file [-h] [-m mfile] [-f ffile] arg ...
file [-h] [-m mfile] -f ffile
file -c [-m mfile]
```

filepriv

Set, delete, or display privilege information associated with a file

```
filepriv [-f priv[, ...]] [-i priv[, ...]] file ...
filepriv -d file ...
```

find

Find files

```
find path-list [predicate-list]
```

finger

Display information about local and remote users

```
finger [-bfhilmpqsw] [username ... ]
finger username@hostname ...
```

fingerd

Remote user information server

```
in.fingerd
```

fixperm

(XENIX) correct or initialize XENIX file permissions and ownership

```
/usr/sbin/fixperm [-aCcDfgiLlnOpSsUvwX[-dpackage]
  [-u package]] specfile
```

fixshlib
(XENIX) alter executables to call SCO UNIX System V/386 Release 3.2-compatible `libnsl`

```
/usr/sbin/fixshlib file
```

fmlcut
Cut out selected fields of each line of a file

```
fmlcut -clist [file ... ]
fmlcut -flist [-dchar] [-s] [file ... ]
```

fmlexpr
Evaluate arguments as an expression

```
fmlexpr arguments
```

fmlgrep
Search a file for a pattern

```
fmlgrep [options] limited_regular_expression [file ... ]
```

fmli
Invoke FMLI

```
fmli [-a alias_file] [-c command_file]
  [-i initialization_file] file ...
```

fmlmax
Determine position or length of a field in a form

```
fmlmax [-c column] [-l] field1 ... fieldn
```

fmt
Simple text formatters

```
fmt [-cs] [-w width] [file ... ]
```

fmtmsg
Display a message on stderr or system console

```
fmtmsg [-c class] [-u subclass] [-l label]
    [-s severity] [-t tag] [-a action]  text
```

fold
Fold long lines

```
fold [-bs] [-w width | -width] [file ... ]
```

format
Format floppy disk tracks

```
/bin/format [-qvVE] [-f first] [-l last]
    [-i interleave] device[t]
```

fprof
Configure, start, control or analyze the results of a flow-profile experiment

```
fprof -C[Logging=on|off,][StartState=on|off,]
   [Accuracy=accurate|normal,][LogPrefix=pathname]
fprof -s [-C[Logging=on|off,][StartState=on|off,]
   [Accuracy=accurate|normal,]
   [LogPrefix=pathname]] command-line
fprof [-o|-O] [-m] log [log] ...
fprof [-i] [log] ...
```

fs

UnixWare X font server

```
fs [-config configuration_file] [-port tcp_port]
```

fsba

File system block analyzer

```
/usr/sbin/fsba [-b target_block_size] file-system1
   [file-system2 ... ]
```

fsck (generic)

Check and repair file systems

```
fsck [-F FSType] [-V] [-m] [special ... ]
fsck [-F FSType] [-V] [current_options]
 [-o specific_options] [special ... ]
fsck [-F FSType] [-V] [-PLbyw] [special ... ]
```

fsck (bfs)

Check and repair **bfs** file systems

```
fsck [-F bfs] [generic_options] [special ... ]
fsck [-F bfs] [generic_options] [-y | -n] [special ... ]
```

fsck (dosfs)

Check and repair **dosfs** file systems

```
fsck [-F dosfs] [generic_options] [-m] [-y | -n]
  special
```

fsck (s5)

Check and repair **s5** file systems

```
fsck [-F s5] [generic_options] [special ... ]
```

```
fsck -F s5 [generic_options] [-y] [-n] [-p] [-sX] [-SX]
   [-tfile] [-l] [-q] [-D] [-f] [special ... ]
```

fsck (sfs)

File system consistency check and interactive repair

```
fsck [-F sfs] [generic_options] [special ... ]
fsck [-F sfs] [generic_options] [(-y|-Y)|(-n|-N)]
   [-o p,b=#,w] > [-w] [special ... ]
```

fsck (ufs)

File system consistency check and interactive repair

```
fsck [-F ufs] [generic_options] [special ... ]
fsck [-F ufs] [generic_options] [(-y|-Y)|(-n|-N)]
   [-o p,b=blkno] [-w] [special ... ]
```

fsck (vxfs)

Check and repair **vxfs** file systems

```
fsck [-F vxfs] [generic_options] [-yY] [-nN] [-P]
   [ -o full,nolog ] special ...
```

fsck

(XENIX) check and repair XENIX file systems

```
fsck [options] [filesystem] ...
```

fsdb (generic)

File system debugger

```
fsdb [-F FSType] [-V] [current_options]
   [-o specific_options] special
```

fsdb (s5)
s5 file system debugger

```
fsdb [-F s5] [generic_options] [-z i-number]  special
     [-]
```

fsdb (sfs)
sfs file system debugger

```
fsdb [-F sfs] [generic_options] [-z i-number] special
```

fsdb (ufs)
ufs file system debugger

```
fsdb [-F ufs] [generic_options] [-z i-number] special
```

fsdb (vxfs)
vxfs file system debugger

```
fsdb [-F vxfs] [generic_options] [-z inumber] special
```

fsfpreset
Request font server to reread its catalog

```
fsfpreset port-number
```

fsirand
(BSD) install random inode generation numbers

```
/usr/ucb/fsirand [-p] special
```

fstyp (generic)

Determine file system type

```
fstyp [-v] special
```

ftp

File transfer program

```
ftp [-c | -C] [dgintv] [hostname]
```

ftpd

Internet file transfer protocol server

```
in.ftpd [-dlv] [-u mask] [-t timeout] [-T maxtimeout]
```

fur

Function relocator

```
fur -l functions relocatable-object
```

fuser

Identify processes using a file or file structure

```
/usr/sbin/fuser [-[c|f]ku] files | resources [[-]
     [-[c|f]ku] files | resources] ...
```

fwtmp, wtmpfix

Manipulate connect accounting records

```
/usr/lib/acct/fwtmp [-ic]
/usr/lib/acct/wtmpfix [files]
```

gated
Gateway routing daemon

```
in.gated [-cn] [-t [trace_options]] [-f config_file]
    [trace_file]
```

gcore
Get core images of running processes

```
gcore [-o file] [-p procdir] process-id ...
```

gencat
Generate a formatted message catalog

```
gencat [-mXlf format] catfile [msgfile ...]
```

get
Get a version of an SCCS file

```
get [-aseq-no.] [-ccutoff] [-ilist] [-rSID] [-wstring]
    [-xlist] [-l[p]] [-b] [-e] [-g] [-k] [-m] [-n] [-p]
    [-s] [-t] file ...
```

getacl
Display discretionary information for a file(s)

```
getacl [-ad] file ...
```

getconf
Get configuration values

```
getconf system_var
getconf path_var pathname
```

getdev

List devices defined in the Device Database based on criteria

```
getdev [-ae] [criteria [...]] [device [...]]
```

getdgrp

List device groups that contain devices that match criteria

```
getdgrp [-ael] [criteria [...]] [dgroup [...]]
```

getfilename

Ask the user to name a file in a given format

```
getfilename format filename
```

getfrm

Return the current frameID number

```
getfrm
```

getid

Retrieve system MIB variables from an SNMP entity

```
getid [-T timeout] entity_addr community_string
```

getitems

Return a list of currently marked menu items

```
getitems [delimiter_string]
```

getmany

Retrieve classes of objects from an SNMP entity

```
getmany [-T timeout] entity_addr community_string
    object_name...
```

getnext

Retrieve objects from an SNMP entity

```
getnext [-T timeout] entity_addr community_string
    object_name ...
```

getone

Retrieve objects from an SNMP entity

```
getone [-T timeout] entity_addr community_string
    object_name...
```

getopt

Parse command options

```
set-`getopt optstring $*`
```

getopts

Parse command options

```
getopts optstring name [arg ... ]
```

getoptcvt

Parse command options

```
/usr/lib/getoptcvt [-b] file
```

getroute

Extract routing information from an SNMP entity

```
getroute [-T timeout] entity_addr community_string
```

gettable

Get DoD Internet format host table from a host

```
gettable [-v] host [file]
```

gettxt

Retrieve a text string from a message database

```
gettxt msgfile:msgnum [dflt_msg]
```

getty

Set terminal type, modes, speed, and line discipline

```
getty [-h] [-t timeout] line [speed [terminal
  [linedisc]]]
getty -c file
```

getvol

Verify device accessibility

```
getvol -n [-l label] device
getvol [-f|-F] [-wo] [-l label | -x label] device
```

grep

Search a file for a pattern

```
grep [-E|-F] [-c|-l|-q] [-bhinsvx] expression
  [file ...]
grep [-E|-F] [-c|-l|-q] [-bhinsvx] -e expression ...
  [-f exprfile] ... [file ...]
```

```
grep [-E|-F] [-c|-l|-q] [-bhinsvx] [-e expression] ...
  -f exprfile ... [file ...]
```

groupadd
Add (create) a new group definition on the system

```
groupadd [-g gid [-o]] group
```

groupdel
Delete a group definition from the system

```
groupdel group
```

groupmod
Modify a group definition on the system

```
groupmod [-g gid [-o]] [-n name] group
```

groups
Print group membership of user

```
groups [user ...]
```

groups
(BSD) display a user's group memberships

```
/usr/ucb/groups [user ...]
```

grpck
(BSD) check group database entries

```
/usr/ucb/grpck [file]
```

gsetvideo
Set a high resolution video mode

```
gsetvideo
```

halt
(BSD) stop the processor

```
/usr/ucb/halt [-lnqy]
```

hashcheck
Find spelling errors

```
/usr/lib/spell/hashcheck
```

hashmake
Find spelling errors

```
/usr/lib/spell/hashmake
```

hd
(XENIX) display files in a specified format

```
hd [-[abwl][xdo][cA][t]] [-s offset] [-n count] [file]
```

head

Display first few lines of files

```
head [-n number] [file ... ]
head [-number] [file ... ]
```

help

Ask for help with message numbers or SCCS commands

```
help [args]
```

helpdate

Prompt for and validate a date

```
helpdate [-W width] [-h help] [-f format]
```

helpgid

Prompt for and validate a group ID

```
helpgid [-W width] [-m] [-h help]
```

hostid

Print the numeric identifier of the current host

```
/usr/ucb/hostid
```

hostname

(BSD) set or print name of current host system

```
/usr/ucb/hostname [name-of-host]
```

htable

Convert DoD Internet format host table

```
htable [-c connected-nets] [-l local-nets] [input-file]
```

iconv

Code set conversion utility

```
iconv -f fromcode -t tocode [file]
```

id

Print the user name and ID, and the group name and ID

```
id [user]
id -G [-n] [user]
id -g [-nr] [user]
id -u [-nr] [user]
id [-a]
```

ida_menu

Compaq Intelligent Disk Array Diagnostic Utility

```
/usr/bin/compaq/diags/ida/ida_menu
```

idadmin

ID map data base administration

```
idadmin [-S scheme [-l logname]]
idadmin -S scheme -a -r g_name -l logname
idadmin -S scheme -d [-r g_name] -l logname
idadmin -S scheme -I descr
idadmin -S scheme [-Duscf]
```

idbuild

Build new UNIX system base kernel and/or configure loadable modules

```
/etc/conf/bin/idbuild [-B] [-#] [-K] [-Q]
  [[-I include-path] ...] [-O output-file] [-S]
  [[-M module-name] ...] [-l symbol-list] [[-D symbol]
  ...] [[-U symbol] ...]
```

idcheck

Return selected information about the system configuration

```
/etc/conf/bin/idcheck -p module-name [-R dir]
/etc/conf/bin/idcheck -y module-name [-R dir]
/etc/conf/bin/idcheck -v vector [-R dir] [-r]
/etc/conf/bin/idcheck -d dma-channel [-R dir] [-r]
/etc/conf/bin/idcheck -a -l lower-address -u
  upper-address [-R dir] [-r]
/etc/conf/bin/idcheck -c -l lower-address -u
  upper-address [-R dir] [-r]
```

idconfupdate

Update system configuration files

```
idconfupdate [-f] [-o file] [-s] [-r confdir]
```

idinstall

Add, delete, update, or get kernel configuration data

```
/etc/conf/bin/idinstall -[adugGM] [-ek]
  [-msoptnirhACTbDFO] [-R rootdir] [-f major-list]
  module-name [-P pkg_name] dev_name
```

idmkinit

Construct `inittab` file from configuration data

```
/etc/conf/bin/idmkinit [-o directory] [-e directory]
  [[-M module-name] ...] [-#]
```

idmknod
Update device nodes to reflect kernel configuration

```
/etc/conf/bin/idmknod [-o device-dir] [-r config-dir]
  [[-M module-name] ...] [-s] [-d sdev] [-#]
```

idmodload
Load configured loadable kernel modules·

```
/etc/conf/bin/idmodload [-r root] [-f modlist] [-#]
```

idmodreg
Register loadable kernel modules with the running kernel

```
/etc/conf/bin/idmodreg [-r root] [-f modreglist]
  [[-M module-name] ...] [-#]
```

idresadd
Update Resource Manager database

```
idresadd [-r confdir] [-d] [-f] [-n] module_name
```

idspace
Determine if there is enough file system free space

```
/etc/conf/bin/idspace [-i inodes] [-r blocks | -u
  blocks | -t blocks]
```

idtune
Set or get the value of a tunable parameter

```
/etc/conf/bin/idtune [-f | -m] [-c] parm value
/etc/conf/bin/idtune -g [-c] parm
/etc/conf/bin/idtune -d [-c] parm
```

idtype

Set or get kernel build type

```
idtype [type]
```

ifconfig

Configure network interface parameters

```
ifconfig -a [parameters | protocol_family]
ifconfig interface [parameters | protocol_family]
```

indicator

Display application specific alarms and/or the "working" indicator

```
indicator [-b [n]] [-c column] [-l length] [-o] [-w]
   [string ... ]
```

indxbib

(BSD) create an inverted index to a bibliographic database

```
/usr/ucb/indxbib database-file ...
```

inetd

Internet services daemon

```
inetd [-d] [-s] [-t] [configuration-file]
```

info

STREAMS driver and module information

```
#include <sys/stream.h>
#include <sys/ddi.h>
struct streamtab prefixinfo = { ... };
```

infocmp
Compare or print out `terminfo` descriptions

```
infocmp [-d] [-c] [-n] [-I] [-L] [-C] [-r] [-u]
   [-s d|i|l|c] [-v] [-V] [-1] [-w width]
   [-A directory] [-B directory] [termname ... ]
```

init
Process control initialization

```
/sbin/init [0123456SsQqabc]
```

initprivs
Set the system privilege information

```
initprivs
```

inspect
Compaq hardware configuration inspect utility

```
/usr/bin/compaq/inspect
```

install
(BSD) install files

```
/usr/ucb/install [-cs] [-g group] [-m mode] [-o owner]
   file1 file2
/usr/ucb/install [-cs ] [-g group] [-m mode] [-o owner]
   file ... directory
/usr/ucb/install -d [-g group] [-m mode] [-o owner]
   directory
```

install
Install commands

```
/usr/sbin/install [-c dira] [-f dirb] [-i] [-n dirc]
   [-m mode] [-u user] [-g group] [-o] [-s] file [dirx ... ]
```

installf
Add a file to the software installation database

```
installf [-c class] pkginst pathname [ftype
   [major minor] [mode owner group]]
installf [-c class] pkginst -
installf -f [-c class] pkginst
installf [[-c class] pkginst path1=path2 [l|s]
```

installpkg
Install a software package

```
installpkg
```

installsrv
Configure a server to be a UnixWare Install Server

```
installsrv -q
installsrv -e|-u  [-n spx|tcp]
installsrv -l as|pe -d device -c spool|mount
   [-L locale]
installsrv -l as|pe -s server [-L locale]
```

intro
Introduction to driver data

```
#include <sys/types.h>
#include <sys/ddi.h>
```

ipcrm
Remove a message queue, semaphore set, or shared memory ID

```
ipcrm [options]
```

ipcs
Report interprocess communication facilities status

```
ipcs [options]
```

ipxinfo
Display the IPX socket and LAN statistics kept by the IPX driver

```
ipxinfo
```

ipxinfo
Display the IPX socket and LAN statistics kept by the IPX driver

```
ipxinfo
```

join
Relational database operator

```
join [-a file_no | -v file_no] [-e string] [-o list]
    [-t char] [-1 field] [-2 field] file1 file2
```

jsh
Shell, job control, command interpreter

```
jsh [-acefhiknprstuvx] [args]
```

kbdcomp

Compile code set and keyboard map tables

```
kbdcomp [-vrR] [-o outfile] [infile]
```

kbdload

Load or link kbd tables

```
kbdload [-p] filename
kbdload -u table
kbdload -l string
kbdload -L string
kbdload -e string
```

kbdpipe

Use the kbd module in a pipeline

```
kbdpipe -t table [-f tablefile] [-F] [-o outfile]
  [infile ... ]
```

kbdset

Attach to kbd mapping tables, set modes

```
kbdset [-o] [-a table] [-v string] [-k hotkey] [-m x]
  [-t ticks]
kbdset [-o] [-d table] [-v string] [-k hotkey] [-m x]
  [-t ticks]
kbdset [-q]
```

kdb

Kernel debugger

```
kdb
```

keyadm

Set and print resource limits

```
keyadm -a [-f  filename]
keyadm -g [resource ... ]
keyadm -s [-f filename]
keyadm -l
```

keylogin

Decrypt and store secret key

```
keylogin
```

keylogout

Unset a user's secret key on a local machine

```
keylogout [-f]
```

keymaster

Cr1 key database administration

```
keymaster [-k | -cn] [-s scheme]
```

keyserv

Server for storing public and private keys

```
keyserv [-dDn]
```

kill

Send a signal to a process

```
kill [-s signal] pid ...
kill -l [status]
kill [-signal] pid ...
```

killall

Kill all active processes

```
/usr/sbin/killall [signal]
```

ksh

Korn Shell, a standard command and programming language

```
ksh [_aefhikmnprstuvx] [_o option] ... [-c string]
    [arg ... ]
```

labelit (generic)

Provide labels for file systems

```
labelit [-F FSType] [-V] [current_options]
    [-o specific_options] special [operands]
```

labelit (s5)

Provide labels for s5 file systems

```
labelit [-F s5] [generic_options] [-n] special
    [fsname volume]
```

labelit (sfs)

Provide labels for sfs file systems

```
labelit [-F sfs] [generic_options] [-n] special
    [fsname volume]
```

labelit (ufs)

Provide labels for ufs file systems

```
labelit [-F ufs] [generic_options] [-n] special
    [fsname volume]
```

labelit (vxfs)
Provide labels for vxfs file systems

```
labelit [-F vxfs] [generic_options] [-n] special
[fsname volume ]
```

last
Indicate last user or terminal logins

```
last [-n number | -number] [-f file] [name | tty] ...
```

lastcomm
(BSD) show the last commands executed, in reverse order

```
/usr/ucb/lastcomm [command] ... [user] ... [terminal] ...
```

lastlogin
Shell procedure for accounting

```
/usr/lib/acct/lastlogin
```

lc
List contents of directory

```
lc [-abCcdeFfgiLlmnopqRrstux1] [name ... ]
```

ld
Link editor for object files

```
ld [options] file ...
```

ld

(BSD) link editor, dynamic link editor

```
/usr/ucb/ld [options]
```

ldd

List dynamic dependencies

```
ldd [-d | -r] file
```

ldsysdump

Load system dump from floppy diskettes or cartridge tape

```
/usr/sbin/ldsysdump destination_file
```

lex

Generate programs for simple lexical tasks

```
lex [-ctvn -V -Q[y|n]] [file]
```

lfmt

Display error message in standard format and pass to logging and monitoring services

```
lfmt [-c] [-f flags] [-l label][-s severity]
     [-g catalog:msgid] format [args]
```

line

Read one line

```
line
```

link

Link and unlink files and directories

```
/usr/sbin/link file1 file2
```

lint

C program checker

```
lint [options] file ...
```

listdgrp

List members of a device group

```
listdgrp dgroup
```

listen

Network listener port monitor

```
/usr/lib/saf/listen [-m devstem] net_spec
```

listusers

List user login information

```
listusers [-g groups] [-1 logins]
```

ln

Link files

```
ln -s [-f] [-n] file1 [file2 ...] target
```

ln

(BSD) make hard or symbolic links to files

```
/usr/ucb/ln [-fs] file [linkname]
/usr/ucb/ln [-fs] pathname ... directory
```

localmail

Look up local mail names

```
localmail [-p] [-P prefix] [-S suffix] user-name ...
```

lockd

Network lock daemon

```
/usr/lib/nfs/lockd [-t timeout] [-g graceperiod]
```

logger

Log messages

```
logger string ...
```

logger

(BSD) add entries to the system log

```
/usr/ucb/logger [-t tag] [-p priority] [-i] [-f file]
[message] ...
```

login

Sign on

```
login [-p] name [environ ... ]
```

logins
List user and system login information

```
logins [-dmopstuxab] [-g groups] [-l logins]
```

logname
Get login name

```
logname
```

longline
Get longest line

```
longline [file]
```

look
(BSD) find words in the system dictionary or lines in a sorted list

```
/usr/ucb/look [-d] [-f] [-tc] string [file]
```

lookbib
(BSD) find references in a bibliographic database

```
/usr/ucb/lookbib database
```

lorder
Find ordering relation for an object library

```
lorder file ...
```

lp

Send/cancel print requests

```
lp [print-options] [files]
lp -i request-ID print-options
```

lpadmin

Configure the LP print service

```
lpadmin -p printer -v device [options]
lpadmin -p printer -s server-name[!server-printer-name]
  [options]
lpadmin -p printer -U dial-info [options]
lpadmin -x dest
lpadmin -d [dest]
lpadmin -S print-wheel -A alert-type [-W minutes]
  [-Q requests]
```

lpc

(BSD) line printer control program

```
/usr/ucb/lpc [command [parameter ... ]]
```

lpfilter

Administer filters used with the LP print service

```
lpfilter -f filter-name -F pathname
lpfilter -f filter-name -
lpfilter -f filter-name -i
lpfilter -f filter-name -x
lpfilter -f filter-name -l
```

lpforms

Administer forms used with the LP print service

```
lpforms -f form-name options
lpforms -f form-name -A alert-type [-Q minutes]
  [-W requests]
```

lpmove

Move print requests

```
lpmove requests dest
lpmove dest1 dest2
```

lpq

(BSD) display the queue of printer jobs

```
/usr/ucb/lpq [-Pprinter] [-l] [+ [interval] ] [job# ... ]
  [username ... ]
```

lpr

(BSD) send a job to the printer

```
/usr/ucb/lpr [-P printer] [-# copies] [-C class]
  [-J job] [-T title] [-i [indent] ] [-w cols] [-B]
  [-r] [-m] [-h] [-s] [-filter_option] [file ... ]
```

lprm

(BSD) remove jobs from the printer queue

```
/usr/ucb/lprm [-Pprinter] [-] [job # ... ] [username ... ]
```

lprof

Display line-by-line execution count profile data

```
lprof [-p] [-P] [-s] [-x] [-I incdir] [-r srcfile]
  [-c cntfile] [-o prog] [-V] [-C]
lprof -m file1.cnt file2.cnt filen.cnt [-T] -d
  destfile.cnt
```

lpsched

Start the LP print service

```
/usr/lib/lp/lpsched
```

lpshut
Stop the LP print service

```
lpshut
```

lpstat
Print information about the status of the LP print service

```
lpstat [options] [request-ID-list]
```

lpsystem
Register remote systems with the print service

```
lpsystem [-t type] [-T timeout] [-R retry]
   [-y "comment"] system-name [system-name ... ]
lpsystem -l [system-name ... ]
lpsystem -r system-name [system-name ... ]
lpsystem -A
```

lptest
(BSD) generate line-printer ripple pattern

```
/usr/ucb/lptest [length [count]]
```

lpusers
Set print queue priorities

```
lpusers -d priority-level
lpusers -q priority-level -u login-ID-list
lpusers -u login-ID-list
lpusers -q priority-level
lpusers -l
```

lrt_scan

Analyze the results of a flow-profile experiment for locality of reference tuning

```
lrt_scan [-l] object log [log] ...
```

ls

List contents of directory

```
ls [-abCcdeFfgiLlmnopqRrstux1] [file ... ]
```

ls

(BSD) list the contents of a directory

```
/usr/ucb/ls [-aAcCdfFgilLqrRstu1] file ...
```

m4

Macro processor

```
m4 [options] [files]
```

mach

(BSD) display the processor type of the current host

```
/usr/ucb/mach
```

mail

Read mail or send mail to users

```
    Sending mail:
mail [-Mtw] [-m message_type] recipient ...

    Reading mail:
mail [-ehpPqr] [-f file]
```

```
     Forwarding mail:
mail -F recipient ...

     Debugging:
mail [-d] [-#] [-xdebug_level] [other_mail_options]
   [recipient ...]
mail -T mailsurr_file recipient ...
mail -R mailR_rewrite_file recipient ...
```

mail_pipe
Invoke recipient command for incoming mail

```
mail_pipe [-x debug_level] -r recipient -R
   path_to_sender -c content_type -S subject
```

mailalias
Translate mail alias names

```
mailalias [-s] [-p] [-r] [-v] [-P prefix]* [-S suffix]*
   name ...
```

mailcheck
Check for mail

```
mailcheck [-Z]
```

mailinfo
Extract mail configuration information

```
mailinfo -d | -n | -s | -u | configuration-parameter ...
```

maillog
Standard mail logger

```
maillog [-f date_format] [-m mode] [-O
   original_recipient] [-o output_file] return_path
   recipient [other_info ...] [-- ...]
```

mailproc
Mail file processor

```
mailproc -y
mailproc [-alnoprsvV] [-f filename] [-c command-file]
   [-d directory] [-e command-expression]
```

mailq
(BSD) display contents of mail queue

```
/usr/ucb/mailq
```

mailrevalias
Reverse translate mail alias names

```
mailrevalias [-s] [-p] name ...
```

mailstats
(BSD) print statistics collected by `sendmail`

```
/usr/ucb/mailstats [filename]
```

mailto
Simple multimedia mail sending program

```
mailto [-a] [-c] [-s] [recipient-name ... ]
```

mailx
Interactive message processing system

```
mailx [options] [name ... ]
```

make-owner

Add, remove, or change ID of a privileged user of the UnixWare Desktop

```
make-owner new-owner
make-owner new-owner old-owner
make-owner - old-owner
```

make

Maintain, update, and regenerate groups of programs

```
make [-f makefile] [-BeiknpPqrstuw] [names]
```

makedbm

Make a Network Information Service (NIS) **dbm** file

```
/usr/sbin/makedbm [-l] [-s] [-i yp_input_file]
  [-o yp_output_name] [-d yp_domain_name]
  [-m yp_master_name] infile outfile
makedbm [-u dbmfilename]
```

makekey

Generate encryption key

```
/usr/lib/makekey
```

man

Display reference manual pages; find reference pages by keyword

```
man [-] [-t] [-M path] [-T macro-package ]
  [[section] title ... ] title ...
man [-M path] -k keyword ...
man [-M path] -f file ...
```

mapchan
Configure `tty` device mapping

```
mapchan [-ans] [-f mapfile] [channels ...]
mapchan [-o] [-d] [channel]
```

mapkey
Configure monitor screen mapping

```
mapkey [-doxVSU] [datafile]
```

maplocale
(XENIX) convert Release 4 locale information to different format

```
maplocale -f new_format [-t territory ] [-c codeset ]
    SVR4_locale_name
```

mapscrn
Configure monitor screen mapping

```
mapscrn [-dg] [datafile]
```

mapstr
Configure monitor screen mapping

```
mapstr [-dg] [datafile]
```

mccntl
Medium changer control

```
mccntl [-E] [-l slot] [-e slot] [-x slot] [-d special]
    [-i] [-n] [-s] [-L] [-U] [-M]
```

mconnect
(BSD) connect to SMTP mail server socket

```
/usr/ucb/mconnect [-p port] [-r] [hostname]
```

mcs
Manipulate the comment section of an object file

```
mcs [-a string] [-c] [-d] [-n name] [-p] [-V] file ...
```

memsize
Report memory size in bytes

```
/sbin/memsize
```

menu
Menu/form interface generator

```
menu [-r] [-c] -f form-description-file -o output-file
```

menu_colors.sh
Menu tool environment variables

```
/etc/inst/locale/${LANG}/menus/menu_colors.sh
```

mesg
Permit or deny messages

```
mesg [-n] [-y]
```

message

Put arguments on FMLI message line

```
message [-t] [-b [num]] [-o] [-w] [string]
message [-f] [-b [num]] [-o] [-w] [string]
message [-p] [-b [num]] [-o] [-w] [string]
```

metamail

Infrastructure for mailcap-based multimedia mail handling

```
metamail [-b] [-B] [-c contenttype ...] [-d] [-e]
   [-E encoding] [-f from-name] [-h] [-m mailer-name]
   [-p] [-P] [-r] [-s subject] [-q] [-w] [-x] [-y] [-z]
   [filename]
```

metasend

Crude interface for sending nontext mail

```
metasend [-b] [-c cc] [-e encoding] [-f filename]
   [-m MIME-type] [-s subject] [-S splitsize] [-t to]
   [-z] [-n]
```

mimencode

Translate mail-oriented encoding formats

```
mimencode [-u] [-b] [-q] [-p] [filename]
```

mimeto7bit

Encode MIME message into 7-bit message

```
/usr/lib/mail/surrcmd/mimeto7bit < mime-message >
   encoded-mime-message
```

mkdir

Make directories

```
mkdir [-m mode] [-p] dirname ...
```

mkfifo

Make FIFO special file

```
mkfifo [-m mode] file ...
```

mkfontdir

Create `fonts.dir` file from directory of font files

```
mkfontdir [directory-names]
```

mkfontscale

Enable PostScript Type 1 outline font use for the UnixWare X server and `lp`

```
mkfontscale [directory] [...]
```

mkfs (generic)

Construct a file system

```
mkfs [-F FSType] [-V] [-m] [current_options]
   [-o specific_options] special  size [operands]
```

mkfs (bfs)

Construct a boot file system

```
mkfs [-F bfs] special size [inodes]
```

mkfs (dosfs)

Construct a dosfs file system

```
mkfs -F dosfs [-o specific options] special
```

mkfs (s5)

Construct an s5 file system

```
mkfs [-F s5] [generic_options] special
mkfs [-F s5] [generic_options] [-b block_size] special
  size[:i-nodes] [gap blocks/cyl]
mkfs [-F s5] [generic_options] [-b block_size] special
  proto [gap blocks/cyl]
```

mkfs (sfs)

Construct an sfs file system

```
mkfs [-F sfs] [generic_options] [-o specific_options]
  special [size]
```

mkfs (ufs)

Construct a ufs file system

```
mkfs [-F ufs]  [generic_options] special
mkfs [-F ufs] [generic_options] [-o specific_options]
  special size
```

mkfs (vxfs)

Construct a vxfs file system

```
mkfs [-F vxfs] [generic_options] [-o specific_options]
  special size
```

mkmsgs
Create message files for use by `gettxt`

```
mkmsgs [-o] [-i locale] inputstrings msgfile
```

mknetflop
Add a network interface card driver to a Network Installation Utilities diskette

```
mknetflop -s source-device -t target-device
```

mknod
Make a special file

```
mknod name b | c major minor
mknod name p
```

mknod
(XENIX) make a special file

```
mknod name b | c major minor
mknod name p
mknod name m
mknod name s
```

modadmin
Loadable kernel module administration

```
modadmin -l modname ... | pathname ...
modadmin -u modid ...
modadmin -U modname ...
modadmin -q modid ...
modadmin -Q modname ...
modadmin -s | S
modadmin -d dirname | D
```

monacct

Shell procedures for accounting

```
/usr/lib/acct/monacct number
```

montbl

Create monetary database

```
montbl [-o outfile] infile
```

more

Browse or page through a text file

```
more [-cdflrsuw] [-lines] [+linenumber] [+/pattern]
    [filename ... ]
```

mosy

Managed Object Syntax compiler (yacc-based)

```
mosy [-o  module.defs] -s  module.my
```

mount (generic)

Mount or unmount file systems and remote resources

```
mount [-v | -p]
mount [-F FSType] [-V] [current_options]
    [-o specific_options] {special | mount_point}
mount [-F FSType] [-V] [current_options]
    [-o specific_options] special mount_point
```

mount (bfs)

Mount bfs file systems

```
mount [-F bfs] [generic_options] [-r]
    [-o specific_options] {special | mount_point}
```

```
mount [-F bfs] [generic_options] [-r]
  [-o specific_options] special  mount_point
```

mount (cdfs)

Mount cdfs file systems

```
mount [-F cdfs] [generic_options] -r [-o cdfs_options]
  [special | mount_point]
mount [-F cdfs] [generic_options] -r [-o cdfs_options]
  special mount_point
```

mount (dosfs)

Mount dosfs file systems

```
mount [-F dosfs] special mount_point
```

mount (memfs)

Mount memfs file systems

```
mount [-F memfs] [generic_options] [-r]
  [-o specific_options] { special | mount_point }
mount [-F memfs] [generic_options] [-r]
  [-o specific_options] special mount_point
```

mount (nfs)

Mount or unmount remote NFS resources

```
mount [-F nfs] [-r] [-o specific_options] {server:path
  | mountpoint}
mount [-F nfs] [-r] [-o specific_options] server:path
  mountpoint
```

mount (nucam)

Mount nucam file systems

```
mount [-F nucam] special mount_point
```

mount (nucfs)

Mount NetWare UNIX Client File Systems (`nucfs`)

```
mount [-F nucfs] [generic_options] [-r]
  [-o specific_options] special mount_point
```

mount (profs)

Mount the processor file system

```
mount [-F profs] [generic_options] [-r]
  [-o specific_options] { processorfs|mount_point }
mount [-F profs] [generic_options] [-r]
  [-o specific_options] processorfs mount_point
```

mount (s5)

Mount `s5` file systems

```
mount [-F s5] [generic_options] [-r]
  [-o specific_options] {special | mount_point}
mount [-F s5] [generic_options] [-r]
  [-o specific_options] special  mount_point
```

mount (sfs)

Mount `sfs` file systems

```
mount [-F sfs] [generic_options] [-r]
  [-o specific_options] { special|mount_point }
mount [-F sfs] [generic_options] [-r]
  [-o specific_options] special mount_point
```

mount (ufs)

Mount `ufs` file systems

```
mount [-F ufs] [generic_options] [-r]
  [-o specific_options] { special|mount_point }
mount [-F ufs] [generic_options] [-r]
  [-o specific_options] special mount_point
```

mount (vxfs)

Mount vxfs file systems

```
mount [-F vxfs] [generic_options] [-r]
  [-o specific_options] {special | mount_point}
mount [-F vxfs] [generic_options] [-r]
  [-o specific_options] special mount_point
```

mountall

Mount multiple file systems

```
/sbin/mountall  [-F FSType] [-l | -r]
  [file_system_table]
```

mountd

NFS mount request server

```
/usr/lib/nfs/mountd
```

mouseadmin

Mouse administration

```
mouseadmin -l
mouseadmin [-nb] [-i interrupt] [-a terminal]  mouse
mouseadmin [-nb] [-d terminal]
mouseadmin -t
```

mt

Portable tape device control

```
mt [-f tape device] command [count]
```

mv

Move files

```
mv [ -f] [ -i] [ -e extent_opt] file1 [file2 ...] target
```

mvdir

Move a directory

```
/usr/sbin/mvdir dirname name
```

named

Internet domain name server

```
in.named [-d level] [-p port] [[-b] bootfile]
```

named-xfer

Internet domain name server zone-transfer utility

```
named-xfer [-P port] [-d debuglevel] [-f db_file ]
   [-l logfile] [-p port] [-q] [-s serial] [-t trace-
   file] [-z zone] internet-address...
```

ncheck (generic)

Generate a list of path names versus inumbers

```
/usr/sbin/ncheck [-F FSType] [-V] [current_options]
   [-o specific_options] [special ...]
```

ncheck (s5)

Generate path names versus inumbers for s5 file systems

```
ncheck [-F s5] [generic_options] [-i i-number ...] [-a]
   [-s] [special ...]
```

ncheck (sfs)

Generate path names versus inumbers for sfs file systems

```
ncheck [-F sfs] [generic_options] [-i i-list] [-a] [-s]
   [-o m] [special ...]
```

ncheck (ufs)

Generate path names versus inumbers for ufs file systems

```
ncheck [-F ufs] [generic_options] [-i i-list] [-a] [-s]
   [-o m] [special ... ]
```

ncheck (vxfs)

Generate path names versus inumbers for vxfs file systems

```
ncheck [-F vxfs] [generic_options] [-i ilist] [-a] [-s]
   [-o specific_options] [special ... ]
```

neqn

(BSD) typeset mathematics

```
/usr/ucb/neqn [file] ...
```

netdate

Notify time server that date has changed

```
netdate
```

netinfo

Interface to add/list/remove entries in netdrivers file

```
/usr/sbin/netinfo [-l dev] [-l proto] [-d device]
   [-p protocol]
/usr/sbin/netinfo [-u -l dev] [-u -l proto]
/usr/sbin/netinfo [-a -d device] [-a -d device -p
   protocol]
/usr/sbin/netinfo [-r -d device] [-r -p protocol]
   [-r -d device -p protocol]
```

netstat

Show network status

```
netstat [-Aan] [-f address_family] [-I interface]
   [-p protocol-name] [system] [core]
netstat [-n] [-s] [-i | -r] [-f address_family]
   [-I interface] [-p protocol-name] [system] [core]
netstat [-n] [-I interface] interval [system] [core]
```

newaliases

(BSD) rebuild the data base for the mail aliases file

```
/usr/ucb/newaliases
```

newform

Change the format of a text file

```
newform [-s] [-itabspec] [-otabspec] [-bn] [-en] [-pn]
   [-an] [-f] [-cchar] [-ln] [files]
```

newgrp

Log in to a new group

```
newgrp [ - ] [ group ]
```

newkey

Create a new key in the publickey database

```
newkey -h hostname
newkey -u username
```

news

Print news items

```
news [-a] [-n] [-s] [items]
```

newvt
Open virtual terminals

```
newvt [-e prog] [-n vt_number]
```

nfsd
NFS daemon

```
/usr/lib/nfs/nfsd [-a] [-p protocol] [-t transport]
```

nfsping
Check status of the NFS daemons

```
/usr/sbin/nfsping -a
/usr/sbin/nfsping -s
/usr/sbin/nfsping -c
/usr/sbin/nfsping -o name
```

nfsstat
Network File System statistics

```
nfsstat [-csnrz] [unix] [core]
```

nic_agent
Compaq Insight Manager (CIM) Network Interface Monitor

```
nic_agent [-p time] [-i] [-s OK | NOTOK]
   [-t OK | NOTOK]
```

nice
Run a command at low priority

```
nice [-increment] command [arguments]
```

nl
Number lines

```
nl [-btype] [-ftype] [-htype] [-vstart#] [-iincr] [-p]
   [-lnum] [-ssep] [-wwidth] [-nformat] [-ddelim] [file]
```

nlist
View a list of NetWare users, servers, or volumes

```
nlist [-abcn] [-o object_type] [-s server] [object]
```

nlsadmin
Network listener service administration

```
/usr/sbin/nlsadmin -x /usr/sbin/nlsadmin [options]
   net_spec
/usr/sbin/nlsadmin [options] -N port_monitor_tag
/usr/sbin/nlsadmin -V
/usr/sbin/nlsadmin -c cmd | -o pipename [-p modules]
   [-A address | -D] [-R prognum:versnum]
```

nm
Print name list of an object file

```
nm [-oxhvnurplCV] files
```

nohup
Run a command immune to hangups and quits

```
nohup command [arguments]
```

notify
Notify user of the arrival of new mail

```
notify -y
notify [-n]
```

nprinter
Control polling of configuration files for NetWare print queue requests

```
nprinter
```

npsd
NetWare protocol daemon

```
npsd [-v]
```

nrexecd
Remote execution server

```
nrexecd
```

nroff
(BSD) format documents for display or line-printer

```
/usr/ucb/nroff [-ehiqz] [-Fdir] [-mname] [-nN] [-olist]
   [-raN] [-sN] [-Tname] [-uN] [file ...]
```

ns_query
Domain name server test tools

```
ns_query [-d ] host [ server ]
```

nslookup
Query name servers interactively

```
nslookup [-option ... ] [host-to-find] | - [server]
```

nstest

Domain name server test tools

```
nstest [-d] [-i] [-p port] [-r] [-v ] [server]
   [log-file]
```

ntpdate

Set the date and time via NTP

```
ntpdate [-bdos] [-a keynum] [-e authdelay] [-k keyfile]
   [-p samples] [-t timeout] server ...
```

ntpq

Standard Network Time Protocol query program

```
ntpq [-dinp] [-c command] [host] [...]
```

nucd

NetWare UNIX Client daemon

```
nucd [-d]
```

nucsapd

NetWare service advertising protocol compatibility daemon

```
nucsapd server_type# ...
```

nulladm

Shell procedure for accounting

```
/usr/lib/acct/nulladm file
```

nullptr

Per-user NULL pointer reference checking

```
nullptr [enable | disable]
```

nwchecksums

Set client IPX checksum level

```
nwchecksums [0 | 1 | 2 | 3]
```

nwcloseconns

Remove all NetWare connections

```
nwcloseconns
```

nwcm

View and change NetWare configuration parameters

```
nwcm [-CcFqx -d parameter -D folder -h parameter -H
   folder -f folder -L folder-r parameter -R folder -s
   parameter=value -t parameter=value -v parameter -V
   folder]
```

nwdiscover

Discover and set IPX network configuration

```
nwdiscover [-auv] [-d pathname] [-e frame_type]
   [-fframe_type] [-r retry_count] [-t timeout]
```

nwlogin

Log in to a NetWare fileserver

```
nwlogin login
nwlogin server/login
```

nwlogout

Log out of a NetWare fileserver

```
nwlogout [-f] fileserver
nwlogout -a[f]
```

nwmp

Start/stop NetWare UNIX client package burst

```
nwmp [start | stop] [burst | noburst]
```

nwnetd

TLI application services daemon

```
nwnetd [-d] [configuration-file]
```

nwprimserver

Get or set the user's primary NetWare server

```
nwprimserver -g
nwprimserver -s server
nwprimserver -v
```

nwsapinfo

Display the Server Information tables

```
nwsapinfo [-adfFilLtxz] [-c num] [-C num] [-n num]
    [-s name] [-T num]
```

nwsaputil

Service Access Protocol utility

```
nwsaputil [-a | -d | -q] [-t type] [-s socket]
    [-n name]
```

nwsignatures

Set client NCP signature level

```
nwsignatures [0 | 1 | 2 | 3]
```

nwwhoami

View the NetWare fileserver to which you are attached by login

```
nwwhoami
```

od

Dump files in various formats

```
od [-v] [-A address_base] [-j skip] [-N count]
   [-t type_string] ... [file ... ]
od [-bcDdFfOoSsvXx] [file] [[+]offset][. | b | x]
```

os_agent

Compaq Insight Manager (CIM) Operating System Agent

```
os_agent [-p time] [-i] [-s OK | NOTOK] [-t OK | NOTOK]
```

otalk

Talk to another user

```
otalk username [ttyname]
```

otalkd

Remote user communication server

```
in.otalkd
```

pack
Compress and expand files

```
pack [-] [-f] name ...
```

page
Browse or page through a text file

```
page [-cdflrsuw] [-lines] [+linenumber] [+/pattern]
     [filename ... ]
```

pagesize
(BSD) display the size of a page of memory

```
/usr/ucb/pagesize
```

panel
User interface to the AST Manhatten front panel and special features

```
panel [-m] [-u|-t "text"] [-h|-s|-o] [-q]
      [-c configfile]
```

partsize
Return the size of the active UNIX system partition

```
partsize [-ds] raw-device
```

passwd
Change login password and password attributes

```
passwd [login_name]
```

```
passwd [-l | -d] [-f] [-x max] [-n min] [-w warn]
   login_name
passwd -s [-a]
passwd -s [login_name]
```

paste

Merge same lines of several files or subsequent lines of one file

```
paste file1 file2   ...
paste -dlist file1 file2   ...
paste -s [-dlist] file1 ...
```

patch

Apply patch changes to files

```
patch [-blNR] [-c| -e| -n] [-d dir] [-D define]
   [-i patchfile] [-o outfile] [-p num] [-r rejectfile]
   [file]
```

pathchk

Check the validity of a path name

```
pathchk [-p] path ...
```

pathconv

Search FMLI criteria for file name

```
pathconv [-f] [-v alias]
pathconv [-t] [-l] [-nnum] [-v string]
```

pathrouter

Path routing utility for UnixWare mailer

```
/usr/lib/mail/surrcmd/pathrouter [-p] [-d]
   [-T pathfile] address ...
```

pbind

Bind to a processor

```
pbind -b processor-id pid ...
pbind -u pid ...
pbind -q [pid ... ]
```

pcat

Compress and expand files

```
pcat name ...
```

pcfont

Modify character font on the 386 console

```
pcfont [config_file]
```

pchown

Change owner of mail files

```
pchown -m username
pchown -m :dirname
pchown -s username
pchown -T
pchown -S [dirname]
pchown -a alias.t
```

pcnfsd

NFS daemon for PC-NFS user authentication and remote printing

```
/usr/lib/nfs/pcnfsd
```

pdiadd
Add new disk, tape, or SCSI devices to the UNIX system kernel

```
/sbin/pdiadd [-O] [-I] [-d dma_channel] [-v vector]
  [-s sharing] [-i i/o_address] [-m memory_address]
  [-R ROOT] device
/sbin/pdiadd -h [-n] disk number
```

pdiconfig
Determine which PDI disk, tape, and SCSI controllers are present

```
/etc/scsi/pdiconfig [-R ROOT] [-f driver name,...]
  [filename]
```

pdimkdev
Generate device nodes for Portable Device Interface
(PDI) subsystem

```
/etc/scsi/pdimkdev [-fis] [-d filename]
```

pdimkdtab
Update the device table entries for the Portable Device Interface (PDI)
subsystem

```
/etc/scsi/pdimkdtab [-fi] [-d filename]
```

pdirm
Remove existing mass-storage devices from the UNIX system configuration

```
/sbin/pdirm -h [-n] disk number
```

pexbind
Exclusive processor bind operation

```
pexbind -b processor-id pid ...
```

```
pexbind -u pid ...
pexbind -q [pid ...]
```

pfb2pfa
Convert PostScript Type 1 outline fonts from binary to ASCII

```
pfb2pfa < pfb-file > pfa-file
```

pfmt
Display error message in standard format

```
pfmt [-l label][-s severity][-g catalog:msgid] format
  [args]
```

pg
File perusal filter for CRTs

```
pg [-number] [-p string] [-cefnrs] [+linenumber]
  [+/pattern/] [file ...]
```

pinfo
Get information about processors

```
pinfo [-v] [processor-id ...]
```

ping
Send ICMP ECHO_REQUEST packets to network hosts

```
/usr/sbin/ping host [timeout]
/usr/sbin/ping -s [-drvRlfnq] [-i wait] [-p pattern]
  host [data_size [npackets]]
```

pkgadd

Transfer software package or set to the system

```
pkgadd [-d device] [-r response] [-n] [-q] [-l]
   [-a admin] [-p] [pkginst1 [pkginst2[...]]]
pkgadd -s spool [-d device] [-q] [-l] [-p] [pkginst1
   [pkginst2[...]]]
```

pkgask

Store answers to a request script

```
pkgask [-d device] -r response [pkginst [pkginst [...]]
```

pkgcat

Copy software from a server to standard output

```
pkgcat [-v] [-n tcp|spx] -s source package
```

pkgchk

Check accuracy of installation

```
pkgchk [-l | -acfqv] [-nx] [-p path1[,path2 ... ]
   [-i file] [pkginst ... ]
pkgchk -d device [-l | v] [-p path1[,path2 ... ]
   [-i file] [pkginst ... ]
pkgchk -m pkgmap [-e envfile] [-l | -acfqv] [-nx]
   [-i file] [-p path1[,path2 ...   ]]
```

pkgcopy

Copy software from a server to a target host

```
pkgcopy [-v] [-n tcp|spx] -s source package
```

pkginfo

Display software package and/or set information

```
pkginfo [-q] [x|l] [-r] [-p|i] [-a arch] [-v version]
    [-c category1,[category2[, ...]]]
    [pkginst[,pkginst[, ...]]]
pkginfo [-d device [-q] [x|l] [-a arch] [-v version]
    [-c category1,[category2[, ...]]]
    [pkginst[,pkginst[, ...]]]
```

pkginstall

Install software from a server onto a target host

```
pkginstall [-v] [-N] [-n tcp|spx] -s source package
```

pkglist

List available software packages on a remote host

```
pkglist [-v] [-n tcp|spx] [-s source] package(s)
```

pkgmk

Produce an installable package

```
pkgmk [-o] [-c] [-d device] [-r rootpath] [-b basedir]
    [-l limit] [-B blocksize] [-a arch] [-v version]
    [-p pstamp] [-f prototype] [variable=value ...]
    [pkginst]
```

pkgparam

Displays package parameter values

```
pkgparam [-v] [-d device] pkginst [param ... ]
pkgparam -d device [-v] [param ... ]
pkgparam -f file [-v] [param ... ]
```

pkgproto

Generate a prototype file

```
pkgproto [-i] [-c class] [path1[=path2] ... ]
```

pkgrm

Remove a package or set from the system

```
pkgrm [-n] [-a admin] [pkginst1 [pkginst2[...]]]
pkgrm -s spool [pkginst]
```

pkgtrans

Translate package format

```
pkgtrans [-ions] [-z blocksize] device1 device2
    [pkginst1 [pkginst2 [...]]]
```

pmadm

Port monitor administration

```
pmadm -a [-p pmtag | -t type] -s svctag [-i id] -m
    "pmspecific" -v version [-f xu] [-S "scheme"]
    [-y "comment"] [-z script]
pmadm -r -p pmtag -s svctag
pmadm -e -p pmtag -s svctag
pmadm -d -p pmtag -s svctag
pmadm -l [-p pmtag | -t type] [-s svctag]
pmadm -L [-p pmtag | -t type] [-s svctag]
pmadm -g -p pmtag -s svctag [-z script]
pmadm -g -s svctag -t type -z script
pmadm -c -S "scheme" [-i id] -p pmtag -s svctag
pmadm -c -i id [-S "scheme"] -p pmtag -s svctag
```

postdaisy

PostScript translator for Diablo 630 files

```
/usr/lib/lp/postscript/postdaisy [options] [files]
```

postdmd

PostScript translator for DMD bitmap files

`/usr/lib/lp/postscript/postdmd [options] [files]`

postio

Serial interface for PostScript printers

`postio -l line [options] [files]`

postmd

Matrix display program for PostScript printers

`/usr/lib/lp/postscript/postmd [options] [files]`

postplot

PostScript translator for plot graphics files

`/usr/lib/lp/postscript/postplot [options] [files]`

postprint

PostScript translator for text files

`/usr/lib/lp/postscript/postprint [options] [files]`

postreverse

Reverse the page order in a PostScript file

`/usr/lib/lp/postscript/postreverse [options] [file]`

posttek

PostScript translator for tektronix 4014 files

```
/usr/lib/lp/postscript/posttek [options] [files]
```

PPP

Login shell for the Point-to-Point Protocol

```
/usr/lib/ppp/ppp
```

pppconf

Menu-driven interface for PPP configuration

```
pppconf
```

pppd

Point-to-Point Protocol Daemon

```
in.pppd [-d debug_level] [-w wait]
```

pppstat

Show PPP status

```
pppstat
```

pr

Print files

```
pr [-columns [-w width] [-a]] [-e[c][k]] [-i[c][k]]
   [-dFfprt] [+page] [-n[c][k]] [-o offset] [-l length]
   [-s[separator]] [-h header] [file ... ]
pr [-m [-w width]] [-e[c][k]] [-i[c][k]] [-dFfprt]
   [+page] [-n[c][k]] [-o offset] [-l length]
   [-s[separator]] [-h header] [file ... ]
```

prctmp

Shell procedure for accounting

```
/usr/lib/acct/prctmp
```

prdaily

Shell procedure for accounting

```
/usr/lib/acct/prdaily [-l] [-c] [mmdd]
```

prefix

Driver prefix

```
int prefixclose();
int prefixopen();
...
```

prfld

UNIX system profiler

```
/usr/sbin/prfld [system_namelist]
```

prfstat

UNIX system profiler

```
/usr/sbin/prfstat [off | on [system_namelist]]
```

prfdc

UNIX system profiler

```
/usr/sbin/prfdc file [period [off_hour
   [system_namelist]]]
```

prfsnap
UNIX system profiler

```
/usr/sbin/prfsnap file [system_namelist]
```

printenv
Set environment for command execution

```
env [-] [name=value] ... [command args]
```

printf
Print formatted output

```
printf format [arg ... ]
```

priocntl
Process scheduler control

```
priocntl -l
priocntl -d [-i idtype] [idlist]
priocntl -s [-c class] [class-specific options]
  [-i idtype] [idlist]
priocntl -e [-c class] [class-specific options] command
  [argument(s)]
priocntl -r size [-i idtype] [idlist]
priocntl -t interval [-i idtype] [idlist]
priocntl -q init min max [-i idtype] [idlist]
priocntl -g [-i idtype] [idlist]
```

prof
Display profile data

```
prof [-t | c | a | n] [-o | x] [-g | l] [-z] [-h]
  [-s] [-j] [-C] [-m mdata] -V [prog]
```

prfpr

UNIX system profiler

```
/usr/sbin/prfpr [-P processor_id[, ... ] | ALL] [-t]
   file [cutoff]
```

prs

Print an SCCS file

```
prs [-d[dataspec]] [-r[SID]] [-e] [-l] [-c[date-time]]
   [-a] file ...
```

prt

(BSD) display the delta and commentary history of an SCCS file

```
/usr/ucb/prt [-abdefistu] [-y[SID]] [-c[cutoff]
   [-r[rev-cutoff]] file ...
```

prtacct

Shell procedures for accounting

```
/usr/lib/acct/prtacct file ["heading"]
```

prtconf

Print system configuration

```
/usr/sbin/prtconf
```

prtvtoc

Disk information display utility

```
prtvtoc [-aep] [-f vtoc-file] raw-device
```

ps
Report process status

```
ps [options]
```

ps
(BSD) display the status of current processes

```
/usr/ucb/ps [-acglnrSuUvwx] [-tterm] [num]
```

pseudo
STREAMS interface for non-STREAMS devices

```
pseudo [-l] [-m line]
```

psradm
Processor administration

```
psradm -a -f|n [-v]
psradm -f|n [-v] processor_id [ ... ]
```

psrinfo
Processor administration information

```
psrinfo [-n]
psrinfo [-v] [processor_id [ ... ]]
psrinfo [-s] [processor_id]
```

putdev
Create and update the device database

```
putdev -a alias [attribute=value [...]]
putdev -m device attribute=value [attribute=value [...]]
putdev -d device [attribute [...]]
putdev -p device attribute=value[,value ...]
putdev -r device attribute=value[,value ...]
```

putdgrp
Edit device group table

```
putdgrp [-d] dgroup [device [...]]
```

pwck
Password file checkers

```
/usr/sbin/pwck [file]
```

pwck
(BSD) check password database entries

```
/usr/ucb/pwck [file]
```

pwconv
Install and update /etc/shadow with information from
/etc/passwd

```
pwconv
```

pwd
Working directory name

```
pwd
```

quot
Summarize ufs file system ownership

```
/usr/sbin/quot [-acfhnv] [filesystem ...]
```

quota

Display a user's disk quota and usage on `ufs` file system

```
/usr/sbin/quota [-v] [username]
```

quotacheck

`ufs` file system quota consistency checker

```
/usr/sbin/quotacheck [-v] [-p] filesystem ...
/usr/sbin/quotacheck -a [-p] [-v]
```

quotaoff

Turn `ufs` file system quotas off

```
/usr/sbin/quotaoff [-v] filesystem ...
/usr/sbin/quotaoff -a [-v] filesystem ...
```

quotaon

Turn `ufs` file system quotas on

```
/usr/sbin/quotaon [-v] filesystem ...
/usr/sbin/quotaon -a [-v] filesystem ...
```

random

(XENIX) generate a random number

```
random [-s] [scale]
```

rarpd

DARPA Reverse Address Resolution Protocol server

```
in.rarpd [-d] device [hostname]
in.rarpd -a [-d]
```

rc0
Run commands to stop the operating system

```
/sbin/rc0 [firmware | off | reboot]
```

rc1
Run commands to bring system to administrative state

```
/sbin/rc1
```

rc2
Run commands for multiuser environment

```
/sbin/rc2
```

rc3
Run commands to start distributed file sharing

```
/sbin/rc3
```

rc6
Run commands to stop the operating system

```
/sbin/rc6 [firmware | off | reboot]
```

rcp
Remote file copy

```
rcp [-p] filename1 filename2
rcp [-pr] filename ... directory
```

rdist

Remote file distribution program

```
rdist [-nqbRhivwyD] [-f distfile] [-d var=value]
   [-m host] [name ... ]
rdist [-nqbRhivwyD] -c name ... [login@]host[:dest]
```

read

Read standard input

```
read [-r] var1 ...
```

readfile

Read file

```
readfile file
```

reboot

(BSD) restart the operating system

```
/usr/ucb/reboot [-dlnq] [boot arguments]
```

red

Text editor

```
red [-s] [-p string] [-x] [-C] [file]
```

refer

(BSD) expand and insert references from a bibliographic database

```
/usr/ucb/refer [-b] [-e] [-n] [-ar] [-cstring] [-kx]
   [-lm,n] [-p filename] [-skeys] file ...
```

regcmp

Regular expression compile

```
regcmp [-] file ...
```

regex

Match patterns against a string

```
regex [-e] [-v "string"] [pattern template] ... pattern
[template]
```

reinit

Run an initialization file

```
reinit file
```

reject

Reject print requests

```
reject [-rreason] destinations
```

relogin

Rename login entry to show current layer

```
/usr/lib/layersys/relogin [-s] [line]
```

removef

Remove a file from software database

```
removef pkginst path1 [path2 ...]
removef pkginst -
removef -f pkginst
```

removepkg

Remove a software package

```
removepkg [pkg]
```

rename

Change the name of a file

```
rename old new
```

renice

Set system scheduling priorities of running processes

```
renice [-n increment] [-g | -p | -u] ID ...
```

renice

(BSD) alter priority of running processes

```
/usr/ucb/renice priority pid ...
/usr/ucb/renice priority [-p pid ...] [-g pgrp ...]
  [-u username ...]
```

reportscheme

Give authentication scheme information to client applications

```
/usr/sbin/reportscheme [-d]
```

repquota

Summarize quotas for a **ufs** file system

```
repquota [-v] filesystem ...
repquota -a [-v]
```

reset

Reset the current form field to its default values

```
reset
```

resmgr

Display and modify in-core Resource Manager Database

```
resmgr [-p "param1[ ... ]"]
resmgr -a -p "param1[ ... ]" -v "val1[ ... ]" [-d delim]
resmgr -f file
resmgr -k key [-p "param1[ ... ]"]
resmgr -k key -p "param1[ ... ]" -v "val1[ ... ]"
  [-d delim]
resmgr -m modname [-p "param1[ ... ]"] [-i brdinst]
resmgr -m modname -p "param1[ ... ]" -v "val1[ ... ]"
  [-d delim] [-i brdinst]
resmgr -r -k key
resmgr -r -m modname [-i brdinst]
```

restore

(XENIX) restore file to original directory

```
restore [-c] [-i] [-o] [-t] [-d device] | [pattern
  [pattern] ... ]
```

restore

Initiate restores of file systems, data partitions, or disks

```
restore -P  [-mn] [-s|v] [-o target] [-d date]
  partdev ...
restore -A  [-mn] [-s|v] [-o target] [-d date]
  diskdev ...
restore -S  [-mn] [-s|v] [-o target] [-d date] fsdev ...
restore [-w] [ i] [ O]  [-T]  [-W device |
  [pattern[pattern]] ...
```

rexec

Execute a service remotely through REXEC

```
rexec host service [parameters]
rx host command
rl host
rquery host
service host [parameters]
```

rexecd

Remote execution server

```
in.rexecd host.port
```

richtext

View a richtext document

```
richtext [-c] [-e] [-f] [-n] [-p] [-t] [-o] [filename]
```

ripinfo

Display router driver statistics from the protocol stack

```
ripinfo
```

ripquery

Query RIP gateways

```
ripquery [-n] [-p] [-r] [-v] [-w time] gateway ...
```

rksh

Korn Shell, a restricted command and programming language

```
ksh [_aefhikmnprstuvx] [_o option] ... [-c string]
  [arg ...]
rksh [_aefhikmnprstuvx] [_o option] ... [-c string]
  [arg ...]
```

rlogin
Remote login

```
rlogin [-L] [-7] [-8] [-ex] [-l username] hostname
```

rlogind
Remote login server

```
in.rlogind
```

rm
Remove files

```
rm [-firR] file ...
```

rmail
Send mail to users

```
rmail [-tw] [-m message_type] [-r originator]
    recipient ...
```

rmdel
Remove a `delta` from an SCCS file

```
rmdel -rSID file ...
```

rmdir
Remove directories

```
rmdir [-p] [-s] dirname
```

roffbib

(BSD) format and print a bibliographic database

```
/usr/ucb/roffbib [-e] [-h] [-Q] [-x] [-m name] [-np]
    [-olist] [-raN] [-sN] [-Tterm] [file] ...
```

route

Manually manipulate the routing tables

```
route [-fn] { add | delete } { destination | default }
    [host | net] [gateway [metric]]
```

routed

Network routing daemon

```
in.routed [-dgqst] [logfile]
```

rpcbind

Universal addresses to RPC program number mapper

```
rpcbind [-dq]
```

rpcgen

RPC protocol compiler

```
rpcgen infile
rpcgen [-Dname[=value]] [-T] [-K secs] infile
rpcgen -a|-b|-c|-C|-h|-I|-l|-L|-m|-N|-Sc|-Ss|-Sm|
    -t [-o outfile] infile
rpcgen -s nettype [-o outfile] infile
rpcgen -n netid [-o outfile] infile
rpcgen -i size
rpcgen -Y path
```

rpcinfo

Report RPC information

```
rpcinfo [-ms] [host]
rpcinfo -p [host]
rpcinfo -T transport host program [version]
rpcinfo -l host program version
rpcinfo [-n portnum] -u host program [version]
rpcinfo [-n portnum] -t host program [version]
rpcinfo -a serv_address -T transport program [version]
rpcinfo -b [-T transport] program version
rpcinfo -d [-T transport] program version
```

rrouter

Rebuild the router table

```
rrouter
```

rsh

Remote shell

```
rsh [-n] [-l username] hostname command
rsh hostname [-n] [-l username] command
hostname [-n] [-l username] command
```

rshd

Remote shell server

```
in.rshd  host.port
```

rsnotify

Display or modify the information identifying the individual in charge of restore requests

```
rsnotify [-u user]
```

rsoper

Service pending restore requests and service media insertion prompts

```
rsoper -d ddev [-j jobids] [-u user] [-m method] [-n]
   [-s|v] [-t] [-o oname[:odevice]]
rsoper -r jobid
rsoper -c jobid
```

rsstatus

Report the status of posted restore requests

```
rsstatus [-h] [-d ddev] [-f field_separator]
   [-j jobids] [-u users]
```

rtcpio

Restricted trusted import/export archiving

```
rtcpio -o[aLvVx] [-C bufsize] [-M message] -O
   output-file [-X low_level,high_level]
rtcpio -i[bdfkPrsStuvVx] [-C bufsize] [-E file] -I file
   [-M message] [-N level] [-nnum] [-R ID] [-T file]
   [-X low_level,high_level]   [pattern ... ]
```

rtpm

Real time performance monitor

```
rtpm [-h history_buffer_size][interval]
```

run

Run an executable

```
run [-s] [-e] [-n] program
```

runacct
Run daily accounting

`/usr/lib/acct/runacct [mmdd [state]]`

ruptime
Show host status of local machines

`ruptime [-alrtu]`

rusers
Show who's logged in on local machines

`rusers [-ahilu] [ host ... ]`

rusersd
Network username server

`/usr/lib/netsvc/rusers/rpc.rusersd`

rwall
Write to all users over a network

`/usr/sbin/rwall hostname ...`

rwalld
Network `rwall` server

`/usr/lib/netsvc/rwall/rpc.rwalld`

rwho

Show who's logged in on local machines

```
rwho [-a]
```

rwhod

System status server

```
in.rwhod
```

rxlist

List available REXEC services

```
/usr/lib/rexec/rxlist [-l] [-h]
```

rxservice

Add or remove an REXEC service

```
rxservice -a servicename [-d description] [-u]
   servicedef
rxservice -r servicename...
rxservice -l
```

rxservice

Add or remove an REXEC service

```
rxservice -a servicename [-d description] [-u]
   servicedef
rxservice -r servicename...
rxservice -l
```

sa1

System activity report package

```
/usr/lib/sa/sa1 [t n]
```

sa2

System activity report package

```
/usr/lib/sa/sa2 [-P processor_id[, ... ] | ALL]
    [-ubdycwaqvmpgrkAR] [-s time] [-e time] [-i sec]
```

sac

Service access controller

```
/usr/lib/saf/sac -t sanity_interval
```

sacadm

Service access controller administration

```
sacadm -a -p pmtag -t type -c cmd -v ver [-f dx]
    [-n count] [-y "comment"] [-z script]
sacadm -r -p pmtag
sacadm -s -p pmtag
sacadm -k -p pmtag
sacadm -e -p pmtag
sacadm -d -p pmtag
sacadm -l [-p pmtag | -t type]
sacadm -L [-p pmtag | -t type]
sacadm -g -p pmtag [-z script]
sacadm -G [-z script]
sacadm -x [-p pmtag]
```

sact

Print current SCCS file editing activity

```
sact file ...
```

sadc

System activity report package

```
/usr/lib/sa/sadc [t n] [ofile]
```

sapd

NetWare service advertising protocol daemon

```
sapd [-t]
```

sar

System activity reporter

```
sar [-P processor_id[, ... ] | ALL] [-ubdywaqvtmpgrkAR]
  [-o file] t [n]
sar [-P processor_id[, ... ] | ALL] [-ubdywaqvtmpgrkAR]
  [-s time] [-e time] [-i sec] [-f file]
```

sccs

(BSD) front end for the Source Code Control System (SCCS)

```
/usr/ucb/sccs [-r] [-dprefixpath] [-pfinalpath] command
  [SCCS-flags ... ] [file ... ]
```

sccsdiff

Compare two versions of an SCCS file

```
sccsdiff -rSID1 -rSID2 [-p] [-sn] file ...
```

scompat

(XENIX) set up XENIX system compatibility environment for console applications

```
scompat [-r interpretnumber] [command_line]
```

script

Make typescript of a terminal session

```
script [-a] [file]
```

sdiff

Print file differences side-by-side

```
sdiff [options] file1 file2
```

sed

Stream editor

```
sed [-n] [-e script] [-f sfile] [file ... ]
```

sendmail

(BSD) send mail over the Internet

```
/usr/ucblib/sendmail [options] [address ... ]
```

set

Set local or global environment variables

```
set [-l variable[=value]] ...
set [-e variable[=value ] ] ...
set [-ffile variable[=value ] ] ...
```

setacl

Modify the Access Control List (ACL) for a file(s)

```
setacl [-r] -s acl_entries file ...
setacl [-r] [-m acl_entries] -d acl_entries file ...
setacl [-r] -f acl_file file ...
```

setany

Retrieve and set objects in an SNMP entity

```
setany [-T timeout] entity_addr community_string
   [object_name-{i|o|d|a|c|g|t|s|n} value]...
```

setclk

Set system time from hardware clock

```
/sbin/setclk
```

setcolor

Set screen color

```
setcolor [-nbrgopc] argument [argument]
```

setcolor

Redefine or create a color

```
setcolor color red_level green_level blue_level
```

setcolour

Set screen color

```
setcolour [-nbrgopc] argument [argument]
```

setkey
Assign the function keys

```
setkey [-d] keynum string
```

setmnt
Establish mount table

```
/sbin/setmnt
```

setpass
Set or change your password on a NetWare fileserver

```
setpass fileserver/name
```

setsizecvt
Generates files in the space format for sets

```
setsizecvt
```

settime
(XENIX) change the access and modification dates of files

```
settime mmddhhmm[yy] [-f fname] name ...
```

setuname
Change system name or network node name

```
setuname [-s name] [-n node] [-t]
```

setvideomode

Set a high resolution video mode

```
setvideomode [options]
gsetvideo
```

sfsdiskusg

Generate disk accounting data by user ID

```
/usr/lib/acct/sfsdiskusg [options] [files]
```

sh

Shell, the standard command interpreter

```
sh [-acefhiknprstuvx] [args]
jsh [-acefhiknprstuvx] [args]
/usr/lib/rsh [-acefhiknprstuvx] [args]
```

share

Make local resource available for mounting by remote systems

```
share [-F fstype] [-o specific_options] [-d description]
   [pathname [resourcename]]
```

share

Make local NFS resource available for mounting by remote systems

```
share -F nfs [-o specific_options] [-d description]
   pathname [resource]
```

shareall

Share multiple resources

```
shareall [-F fstype[,fstype ... ]] [file]
```

shell

Run a command using shell

```
shell command [command] ...
```

showexternal

Display the body of a mail message included by reference

```
showexternal body-file access-type name [site
    [directory [mode [server]]]]
```

showmount

Show all remote mounts

```
/usr/sbin/showmount [-ade] [hostname]
```

shownonascii

View mail message in a non-ASCII font

```
shownonascii charset [-e command] filename ...
```

showpartial

Display the body of a mail message included by reference

```
showpartial filename id partnum totalnum
```

showpicture

View an image received in the mail

```
showpicture [-viewer program-name] filename ...
```

shserv

Provide the shell service as part of the login process

```
shserv
```

shutacct

Shell procedures for accounting

```
/usr/lib/acct/shutacct ["reason"]
```

shutdown

Shut down system, change system state

```
shutdown [-y] [-ggrace_period [-iinit_state]
```

shutdown

(BSD) close down the system at a given time

```
/usr/ucb/shutdown [-fhknr] time [warning-message ... ]
```

size

Print section sizes in bytes of object files

```
size [-F -f -n -o -V -x] files
```

slattach

Attach serial lines as network interfaces

```
slattach [{+|-}{c|e|f|i|m mtu|v} ...] tty_name
    source_address destination_address [baud_rate]
slattach [{+|-}{c|e|f|i|m mtu|v} ...] -d uucp_name
    source_address destination_address [baud_rate]
```

sleep

Suspend execution for an interval

```
sleep time
```

slink

STREAMS linker

```
slink [-v] [-f] [-p] [-u] [-c file] [func
    [arg1 arg2 ...]]
```

smf-in

Transfer a message from MHS to UnixWare mail

```
smf-in pathname ...
```

smf-out

Gateway an RFC822 message into the MHS system

```
smf-out [-h hop_count] -r sender_address destination+
```

smf-poll

Poll the MHS system for incoming messages

```
smf-poll
```

smfqueue

Queue mail for the MHS gateway

```
smfqueue [-d debug_level] [-h hop_count] -r
    sender_address recip ...
```

smfsched
Transfer messages in the `smfqueue` from UnixWare to NetWare

```
smfsched
```

smtp
Send mail to a remote host using Simple Mail Transfer Protocol

```
/usr/lib/mail/surrcmd/smtp [-d debug level]
```

smtpd
Receive incoming mail using Simple Mail Transfer Protocol

```
smtpd
```

smtpqer
Queue mail for delivery by SMTP

```
smtpqer [-d level] [-N] [-r] -f sender -s host recip ...
```

snftobdf
SNF to BDF font decompiler for X11

```
snftobdf [-p#] [-u#] [-m] [-l] [-M] [-L] [snf-file]
```

snmp
SNMP start/stop script

```
/etc/init.d/snmp start
/etc/init.d/snmp stop
```

snmpd
SNMP agent

```
in.snmpd [-v]
```

snmpstat
Show network status using SNMP

```
snmpstat [-a | -i | -r | -s | -S | -t] [-n]
  [-T timeout]
[entity_addr] [community_string]
```

soelim
(BSD) resolve and eliminate .so requests from nroff or troff input

```
/usr/ucb/soelim [file ... ]
```

sort
Sort and/or merge files

```
sort [-m] [-o output] [-bdfiMnru] [-t x] [-ykmem]
  [-zrecsz] [-k keydef] ... [file ... ]
sort -c [-bdfiMnru] [-t x] [-k keydef] [-ykmem]
  [-zrecsz] ... [file]
```

sortbib
(BSD) sort a bibliographic database

```
/usr/ucb/sortbib [-skey-letters] database ...
```

spell
Find spelling errors

```
spell [-b] [-i] [-l] [-v] [-x] [+local_file] [files]
```

spellin
Find spelling errors

```
/usr/lib/spell/spellin n
```

split
Split a file into pieces

```
split [-l line_count] [-a suf_length] [file [name]]
split -b n[k|m] [-a suf_length] [file [name]]
split [-line_count] [-a suf_length] [file [name]]
```

splitmail
Split a mail message into MIME-compliant partial messages

```
splitmail [-d] [-v] [-s splitsize] [-p prefix]
   [-i id-suffix] [filename]
```

spray
Spray packets

```
/usr/sbin/spray [-c count] [-d delay] [-l length]
   [-t nettype host]
```

sprayd
Spray server

```
/usr/lib/netsvc/spray/rpc.sprayd
```

spxinfo
Display statistics for the SPX driver

```
spxinfo [minor_number]
```

srchtxt
Display contents of, or search for a text string in, message data bases

```
srchtxt [-s] [-l locale] [-m msgfile, ... ] [text]
```

start_glogin
Start the UnixWare Desktop graphical login

```
start_glogin
```

startnps
Start the IPX protocol stack

```
startnps [-v]
```

startsapd
Start the Service Access Protocol daemon

```
startsapd
```

startup
Shell procedures for accounting

```
/usr/lib/acct/startup
```

statd

Network status monitor

`/usr/lib/nfs/statd`

statnps

Start the IPX protocol stack

`statnps [-v]`

stdeq_agent

Compaq Insight Manager (CIM) Standard Equipment Agent

```
stdeq_agent [-a] [-p time] [-i] [-r OK|NOTOK]
  [-s OK|NOTOK] [-t OK|NOTOK]
```

stopnp

Control polling of configuration files for NetWare print queue requests

`stopnp`

stopnps

Stop the IPX protocol stack

`stopnps`

stopsapd

Stop the Service Access Protocol (SAP) daemon

`stopsapd`

strace

Print STREAMS trace messages

```
strace [mid sid level] ...
```

strchg

Change or query stream configuration

```
strchg -h module1[,module2 ... ]
strchg -p [-a | -u module]
strchg -f file
```

strclean

STREAMS error logger cleanup program

```
strclean [-d logdir] [-a age]
```

strconf

Change or query stream configuration

```
strconf [-t | -m module]
```

strerr

STREAMS error logger daemon

```
strerr
```

strings

Find printable strings in an object file or binary

```
strings [-a] [-o] [-n number |-number] filename ...
```

strip
Strip symbol table, debugging and line number information from an object file

```
strip [-lVx] file ...
```

stty
Set the options for a terminal

```
stty [-a] [-g] [options]
```

stty
(BSD) set the options for a terminal

```
/usr/ucb/stty [-a] [-g] [-h] [options]
```

sttydefs
Maintain line settings and hunt sequences for `tty` ports

```
/usr/sbin/sttydefs -a ttylabel [-b] [-n nextlabel]
  [-i initial-flags] [-f final-flags]
/usr/sbin/sttydefs -l [ttylabel]
/usr/sbin/sttydefs -r ttylabel
```

su
Become another user

```
su [-] [name [arg ... ]
```

sulogin
Access single-user mode

```
sulogin
```

sum

Print checksum and block count of a file

```
sum [-r] file
```

sum

(BSD) calculate a checksum for a file

```
/usr/ucb/sum file
```

swap

Swap administrative interface

```
/usr/sbin/swap -a swapname swaplow swaplen
/usr/sbin/swap -c [filename]
/usr/sbin/swap -d swapname swaplow
/usr/sbin/swap -l [-s]
/usr/sbin/swap -s
```

sync

Update the super block

```
sync
```

sysadm

Visual interface for system administration

```
sysadm [menu name | task name]
```

sysdef

Output system definition

```
/usr/sbin/sysdef [-n namelist]
/usr/sbin/sysdef -i
```

syslogd

Log system messages

```
/usr/sbin/syslogd [-d] [-fconfigfile] [-m interval]
    [-p path]
```

tabs

Set tabs on a terminal

```
tabs [tabspec] [-Ttype] [+mn]
```

tail

Deliver the last part of a file

```
tail [-f][-c number | -n number] [file]
tail _[number][c|l|b][f|r] [file]
```

talk

Talk to another user

```
talk username [ttyname]
```

talkd

Remote user communication server

```
in.talkd
```

tape

Magnetic tape maintenance

```
tape [-type] command [device]
```

tapecntl

Tape control for tape device

```
tapecntl [-abelrtuvw] [-d arg] [-f arg] [-p arg]
   [special]
```

tar

File archiver

```
/usr/sbin/tar -c[vwfbLkFhienA[num]] [device] [block]
   [volsize] [incfile] [files]...
/usr/sbin/tar -c[vwfbLkXhienA[num]] [device] [block]
   [volsize] [excfile] [files]...
/usr/sbin/tar -r[vwfbLkFhienA[num]] [device] [block]
   [volsize] [incfile] [files]...
/usr/sbin/tar -r[vwfbLkXhienA[num]] [device] [block]
   [volsize] [excfile] [files]...
/usr/sbin/tar -t[vfLXien[num] device excfile [files ... ]
/usr/sbin/tar -u[vwfbLkXhienA[num]] [device] [block]
   [volsize] [excfile] [files]...
/usr/sbin/tar -u[vwfbLkFhienA[num]] [device] [block]
   [volsize] [incfile] [files]...
/usr/sbin/tar -x[lmovwfLXpienA[num]] device excfile
   [files ... ]
```

tbl

(BSD) format tables for nroff or troff

```
/usr/ucb/tbl [-me] [-ms] [-TX] [file] ...
```

tcpio

Trusted import/export archiving

```
tcpio -o[aLvVx] [-C bufsize] [-M message]] -O
   output-file [-X low_level,high_level]
tcpio -i[bdfkPrsStuvVx] [-C bufsize] [-E file] -I file
   [-M message] [-N level] [-nnum] [-R ID] [-T file]
   [-X low_level,high_level] [pattern ...]
```

tee
Pipe fitting

```
tee [-i] [-a] [file] ...
```

telinit
Process control initialization

```
/sbin/telinit [0123456SsQqabc]
```

telnet
User interface to a remote system using the TELNET protocol

```
telnet [-8][-E][-L][-a][-d][-e escape_char][-l user]
     [-n tracefile] [-r][host [port]]
```

telnetd
TELNET protocol server

```
in.telnetd [-debug [port]] [-h] [-D options]
```

test
Condition evaluation command

```
test expr
[expr]
```

test
(BSD) condition evaluation command

```
/usr/ucb/test expr
[expr]
```

tfadmin

Invoke a command, regulating privilege based on TFM database information

```
tfadmin [role:] cmd [args]
tfadmin -t [role:] cmd[:priv[:priv...]]
```

tftp

Trivial file transfer program

```
tftp [host]
```

tftpd

DARPA Trivial File Transfer Protocol server

```
in.tftpd [-s] [homedir]
```

tic

`terminfo` compiler

```
tic [-v[n]] [-c] file
```

time

Time a command

```
time command
```

timed

Time server daemon

```
in.timed [-t] [-M] [-n network] [-i network]
```

timedc
Timed control program

```
timedc [command [argument ... ]]
```

timex
Time a command, report process data and system activity

```
timex [options] command
```

tnamed
DARPA trivial name server

```
in.tnamed [-v]
```

touch
Update access and modification times of a file

```
touch [-amc] [-r ref_file | -t time] file ...
touch [-amc] [mmddhhmm[yy]] file ...
```

tput
Initialize a terminal or query `terminfo` database

```
tput [-Ttype] capname [parms ... ]
tput [-Ttype] init
tput [-Ttype] reset
tput [-Ttype] longname
tput -S  <<
```

tr
Translate characters

```
tr [-cds] [string1 [string2]]
```

tr

(BSD) translate characters

```
/usr/ucb/tr [-cds] [string1 [string2] ]
```

traceroute

Trace the route packets take in order to reach a network host

```
traceroute[-dnrv][-wwait][-mmax_ttl][-pport#]
    [-qnqueries][-ttos] [-ssrc_addr][-ggateway]
    host[packetsize]
```

track

Start and stop displaying incoming and outgoing SAP packets

```
track on
track off
track tables
```

trap_rece

Receive traps from a remote SNMP trap generating entity

```
trap_rece
```

trap_send

Send SNMP traps

```
trap_send entity_addr community_string trap_type
```

trchan

Translate character sets

```
trchan [-ciko] mapfile
```

troff

(BSD) typeset or format documents

```
/usr/ucb/troff [-afiz] [-Fdir] [-mname] [-nN] [-olist]
  [-raN] [-sN] [-Tdest] [-uN] [file] ...
```

trpt

Transliterate protocol trace

```
trpt [-afjst] [-p pcb_addr] [system [core]]
```

truss

Trace system calls and signals

```
truss [-p] [-f] [-c] [-a] [-e] [-i] [-[tvx] [!] syscall
  ...] [-s [!] signal ...] [-m [!] fault ...] [-[rw] [!]
  fd ...] [-o outfile] command
```

tsad

Daemon for Storage Management Services (SMS) Target Service Agent (TSA) for UnixWare

```
tsad [-f config_file] [-t register_timeout]
  [-c connect_timeout] [-p path_to_tsaunix]
```

tsaunix

Storage Management Services (SMS) Target Service Agent (TSA) for UnixWare

```
tsaunix
```

tset

Provide information to set terminal modes

```
tset [options] [type]
```

tset

(BSD) establish terminal characteristics

```
tset [-InQrs] [-ec] [-kc] [-m [port -ID [baudrate] :
   type] ... ] [type]
```

tset

(XENIX) provide information for setting terminal modes

```
tset [options] [type]
```

tsort

Topological sort

```
tsort [file]
```

tty

Get the name of the terminal

```
tty [-l] [-s]
```

ttyadm

Format and output port monitor-specific information

```
/usr/sbin/ttyadm [-b] [-c] [-r count] [-h] [-i msg]
   [-m modules] [-p prompt] [-t timeout] [-o] -d device
   -l ttylabel -s service
/usr/sbin/ttyadm -V
```

ttymap

Install and update /var/adm/ttymap.data based on /dev and
/etc/ttysrch

```
ttymap
```

ttymon

Port monitor for terminal ports

```
/usr/lib/saf/ttymon
/usr/lib/saf/ttymon -g [-h] [-d device] [-l ttylabel]
  [-t timeout] [-p prompt] [-m modules]
```

tunefs

Tune up an existing file system

```
tunefs [-a maxcontig] [-d rotdelay] [-e maxbpg]
  [-m minfree] [-o [s | space | t | time]] special |
  filesystem
```

tunefs (sfs)

Tune up an existing file system

```
tunefs [-a maxcontig] [-d rotdelay] [-e maxbpg]
  [-o [s | space | t | time]] special | filesystem
```

turnacct

Shell procedures for accounting

```
/usr/lib/acct/turnacct on | off | switch
```

uadmin

Administrative control

```
/sbin/uadmin cmd fcn
```

ufsdiskusg

Generate disk accounting data by user ID

```
/usr/lib/acct/ufsdiskusg [options] [files]
```

ufsdump

Incremental file system dump

```
/usr/sbin/ufsdump [options [arguments]] filesystem
```

ufsrestore

Incremental file system restore

```
/usr/sbin/ufsrestore options [arguments] [filename ...]
```

uidadmin

User-controlled ID map data base administration

```
uidadmin [-S scheme [-l logname]]
uidadmin -S scheme -a -r g_name  [-l logname]
uidadmin -S scheme -d [-r g_name] -l logname
uidadmin -S scheme [-cf]
```

ul

(BSD) underline

```
/usr/ucb/ul [-i] [-t terminal] [file ...]
```

umask

Set file-creation mode mask

```
umask [-S] [mask]
```

umount (generic)

Unmount file systems and remote resources

```
umount [-V] [-o specific_options] {special |
  mount_point}
```

umountall
Unmount multiple file systems

```
/sbin/umountall [-F FSType] [-k] [-l | -r]
```

uname
Print name of current UNIX system

```
uname [-amnprsv]
uname [-S system_name ]
```

uncompress
Uncompress and display compressed files

```
uncompress [-fqc] file...
```

unget
Undo a previous get of an SCCS file

```
unget [-rSID] [-s] [-n] file ...
```

unifdef
(BSD) resolve and remove ifdef lines from C program source

```
/usr/ucb/unifdef [-clt] [-Dname] [-Uname] [-iDname]
   [-iUname] ... [file]
```

uniq
Report repeated lines in a file

```
uniq [-ffields] [-schars] [-cdu] [input [output]]
uniq [+n] [-n] [-cdu] [input [output]]
```

units

Conversion program

```
units
```

unlink

Unlink files and directories

```
/usr/sbin/unlink file
```

unpack

Compress and expand files

```
unpack name ...
```

unset

Unset local or global environment variables

```
unset -l variable ...
unset -ffile variable ...
```

unshare

Make local resource unavailable for mounting by remote systems

```
unshare [-F fstype] [-o specific_options]
   {pathname | resourcename}
```

unshare

Make local NFS resource unavailable for mounting by remote systems

```
unshare {pathname | resource}
```

unshareall

Share, unshare multiple resources

```
unshareall [-F fstype[,fstype ... ]]
```

uptime

(BSD) show how long the system has been up

```
/usr/ucb/uptime
```

urestore

Request restore of files and directories

```
urestore -F [-mn] [-s|v] [-o target] [-d date] file ...
urestore -D [-mn] [-s|v] [-o target] [-d date] dir ...
urestore -c jobid
```

ursstatus

Report the status of posted user restore requests

```
ursstatus  [-h]  [-j jobids] [-f field_separator]
    [-d ddev] [-u users]
```

useradd

Administer a new user login on the system

```
useradd  [-u uid [-o] [-i]] [-g group]
    [-G group[[,group] ... ]] [-d dir] [-s shell]
    [-c comment] [-m [-k skel_dir]] [-f inactive]
    [-e expire] [-p passgen] [-a event[, ... ]] login
```

userdel

Delete a user's login from the system

```
userdel [-r] [-n months] login
```

usermod

Modify a user's login information on the system

```
usermod [-u uid [-U] [-o]] [-g group]
   [-G group[[,group] ... ]] [-d dir[-m]] [-s shell]
   [-c comment] [-l new_logname] [-f inactive]
   [-e expire] [-p passgen] [-a [operator1]event[, ... ]]
   login
```

users

(BSD) display a compact list of users logged in

```
/usr/ucb/users [file]
```

utmp2wtmp

Overview of accounting and miscellaneous accounting commands

```
/usr/lib/acct/utmp2wtmp
```

uucheck

Check the uucp directories and permissions file

```
/usr/lib/uucp/uucheck [options]
```

uucico

File transport program for the uucp system

```
/usr/lib/uucp/uucico [options]
```

uucleanup

uucp spool directory cleanup

```
/usr/lib/uucp/uucleanup [options]
```

uucollapse

Remove loops in uucp mail address

```
uucollapse address ...
```

uucp

UNIX-to-UNIX system copy

```
uucp [options] source-files destination-file
```

uudecode

Decode a file encoded with uuencode

```
uudecode [encoded-file]
```

uuencode

Encode a binary file

```
uuencode [source-file] file-label
```

uugetty

Set terminal type, modes, speed, and line discipline

```
/usr/lib/uucp/uugetty [-t timeout] [-r] line
  [speed [type [linedisc]]]
/usr/lib/uucp/uugetty -c file
```

uuglist

List service grades available on this UNIX system

```
uuglist [-u] [-x debug_level]
```

uulog

UNIX-to-UNIX system copy

```
uulog [options] system
```

uuname

UNIX-to-UNIX system copy

```
uuname [options]
```

uupick

Public UNIX-to-UNIX system file copy

```
uupick [-s system]
```

uusched

Scheduler for the uucp file transport program

```
/usr/lib/uucp/uusched [options]
```

uustat

uucp status inquiry and job control

```
uustat [-q]
uustat [-m]
uustat [-kjobid [-n]]
uustat [-rjobid [-n]]
uustat [-p]
uustat [-a [-j]] [-uuser] [-Sqric]
uustat [-ssystem [-j]] [-uuser] [-Sqric]
uustat -tsystem [-dnumber] [-c]
```

uuto

Public UNIX-to-UNIX system file copy

```
uuto [options] source-files destination
```

uux

UNIX-to-UNIX system command execution

```
uux [options] command-string
```

uuxqt

Execute remote command requests

```
/usr/lib/uucp/uuxqt [options]
```

uuxqt

Execute remote command requests

```
/usr/lib/uucp/uuxqt [options]
```

vacation

Automatically respond to incoming mail messages

```
vacation [-a alias] [-d] [-e exemption-file]
  [-f forward-id] [-i forward-id] [-j] [-l logfile]
  [-M canned_msg_file] [-m savefile]
vacation -n
```

vacation

(BSD) reply to mail automatically

```
/usr/ucb/vacation [-I]
/usr/ucb/vacation [-j] [-aalias] [-tN] username
```

val
Validate an SCCS file

```
val –
val [-s] [-rSID] [-mname] [-ytype] file ...
```

valdate
Prompt for and validate a date

```
valdate [-f format] input
```

valgid
Prompt for and validate a group ID

```
valgid input
```

vi
Screen-oriented (visual) display editor based on ex

```
vi [-t tag] [-r file] [-l] [-L] [-wn] [-R] [-x] [-C]
   [-c command] file ...
view [-t tag] [-r file] [-l] [-L] [-wn] [-R] [-x] [-C]
   [-c command] file ...
vedit [-t tag] [-r file] [-l] [-L] [-wn] [-R] [-x] [-C]
   [-c command] file ...
```

vidi
Set font and video mode for console

```
vidi [-d] [-f fontfile] font
vidi mode
```

volcopy (generic)
Make literal copy of file system

```
volcopy [-F FSType] [-V] [current_options]
   [-o specific_options] operands
```

volcopy (s5)
Make a literal copy of an s5 file system

```
volcopy [-F s5] [generic_options] [current_options]
   fsname srcdevice volname1 destdevice volname2
```

volcopy (sfs)
Make a literal copy of an sfs file system

```
volcopy [-F sfs] [generic_options] [current_options]
   fsname srcdevice volname1 destdevice volname2
```

volcopy (ufs)
Make a literal copy of a ufs file system

```
volcopy [-F ufs] [generic_options] [current_options]
   fsname srcdevice volname1 destdevice volname2
```

volcopy (vxfs)
Make a literal copy of a vxfs file system

```
volcopy [-F vxfs] [generic_options] [current_options]
   fsname srcdevice volname1 destdevice volname2
```

vsig
Synchronize a coprocess with the controlling FMLI application

```
vsig
```

vtgetty

Set terminal type, modes, speed, and line discipline

```
/etc/vtgetty [-h] [-ttimeout] line
   [[speed[type [linedisc]]]
```

vtlmgr

Monitor and open virtual terminals

```
vtlmgr [-k]
```

vxdiskusg

Generate disk accounting data by user ID

```
/usr/lib/acct/vxdiskusg [options] [files]
```

vxdump

Incremental file system dump

```
vxdump [options] filesystem
```

vxrestore

Incremental file system restore

```
vxrestore options [filename ... ]
```

vxupgrade (vxfs)

Upgrade a Version 1 vxfs file system to Version 2

```
vxupgrade [-r rawdev] mount_point
```

w
(BSD) show who is logged in and what are they doing

```
/usr/ucb/w [-hls] [user]
```

wait
Await completion of process

```
wait [pid ... ]
```

wall
Write to all users

```
/usr/sbin/wall [-g group] [file]
```

wc
Word count

```
wc [-lwc] [file ... ]
```

wchrtbl
Generate tables for ASCII and supplementary code sets

```
wchrtbl [file]
```

wellness_agent
Compaq Insight Manager (CIM) Wellness Agent

```
wellness_agent [-p time] [-i] [-s OK | NOTOK]
    [-t OK | NOTOK]
```

what

Print identification strings

```
what [-s] file ...
```

whatis

(BSD) display a one-line summary about a keyword

```
/usr/ucb/whatis command ...
```

which

(BSD) locate a command; display its path name or alias

```
/usr/ucb/which [file] ...
```

who

Show who is on the system

```
who [-uTlmHpdbrtas] [file]
who -q [-n x] [file]
who am i
who am I
```

whoami

Display the effective current username

```
/usr/ucb/whoami
```

whodo

Show who is doing what

```
/usr/sbin/whodo [-h] [-l] [user]
```

whois
Internet user name directory service

```
/usr/bin/whois [-h host] identifier
```

wksh
Windowing Korn Shell, graphical extensions to ksh

```
wksh [-mode] [_aefhikmnprstuvx] [_o option] ...
     [-c string] [arg ... ]
```

write
Write to another user

```
write user [line]
```

wtmpfix
Manipulate connect accounting records

```
/usr/lib/acct/wtmpfix [files]
```

x286emul
Emulate 80286 XENIX systems

```
x286emul [arg ... ] prog286
```

xargs
Construct argument list(s) and execute command

```
xargs [flags] [command [initial-arguments]]
```

xdm

X Display Manager

```
xdm [-config config_file] [-nodaemon]
  [-debug debug_level] [-error error_log_file]
  [-resources resource_file] [-server server_entry]
```

xhost

Server access control for X

```
xhost [+-] [hostname ... ]
```

xinstall

(XENIX) XENIX system installation shell script

```
/sbin/xinstall [device] [package]
```

xntpd

Network Time Protocol daemon

```
in.xntpd [-ab] [-c conffile] [-e authdelay]
  [-f driftfile] [-k keyfile] [-r broaddelay]
  [-t trustedkey]
```

xntpdc

Query/control program for the Network Time Protocol daemon

```
xntpdc [-dilnps] [-c command] [host] [...]
```

xpr

Print an X Window dump

```
xpr [-o output-name] [-a path-name [-n]] [-d name]
  [-h text] [-t text] [-W decimal-number]
```

```
[-H decimal-number] [-l] [-p] [-L decimal-number]
[-T decimal-number] [-s integer] [-S integer] [-r]
[path-name] [-C] [color-list] [input-name]
```

xrestor

Invoke XENIX incremental file system restorer

```
xrestor key [ arguments ]
```

xrestore

Invoke XENIX incremental file system restorer

```
xrestore key [ arguments ]
```

xset

User preference and font path-setting utility for X

```
xset [-display display] [[-]bc] [[-+]fp[-+=]
path[,path[,...]]] [fp default] [fp rehash] [m[ouse]
[accel_mult[/accel_div] [threshold]]] [m[ouse]
default] [p pixel color] [s [length [period]]]
[s blank/noblank] [s expose/noexpose] [s on/off]
[s default] [q]
```

xterm

Terminal emulator for X

```
xterm [-toolkitoption ...] [-option ...]
```

yacc

Yet another compiler-compiler

```
yacc [-vVdltw] [-p driver_file] [-Q[y|n]] file
```

yes

(XENIX) print string repeatedly

```
yes [string]
```

ypalias

Rebuild NIS database

```
cd /var/yp ; make  [map]
cd /var/yp ; ./ypbuild SHELL=/sbin/sh [map]
```

ypbind

NIS server and binder processes

```
/usr/lib/netsvc/yp/ypbind [-ypset |-ypsetme]
```

ypbuild

Rebuild NIS database

```
cd /var/yp ; make  [map]
cd /var/yp ; ./ypbuild SHELL=/sbin/sh [map]
```

ypcat

Print values in an NIS map

```
ypcat [-k] [-d ypdomain] mname
ypcat -x
```

ypinit

Build and install NIS database

```
/usr/sbin/ypinit -c
/usr/sbin/ypinit -m
/usr/sbin/ypinit -s master-name
```

ypmatch
Print the value of one or more keys from an NIS map

```
ypmatch [-d ypdomain] [-k] key... mname
ypmatch -x
```

yppasswd
Change your network password in the NIS database

```
yppasswd [username]
```

yppasswdd
Server for modifying NIS password file

```
/usr/lib/netsvc/yp/rpc.yppasswdd passwdfile shadowfile
   [-nogecos] [-noshell] [-nopw] [-m argument1
   argument2 ... ]
```

yppoll
Return current version of the map at the NIS server host

```
/usr/sbin/yppoll [-d ypdomain] [-h host] mapname
```

yppush
Force propagation of a changed NIS map

```
/usr/sbin/yppush [-v] [-d ypdomain] mapname
```

ypserv
NIS server and binder processes

```
/usr/lib/netsvc/yp/ypserv
```

ypset

Point `ypbind` at a particular NIS server

```
/usr/sbin/ypset [-d ypdomain] [-h host] server
```

ypupdated

Server for changing NIS information

```
/usr/lib/netsvc/yp/ypupdated [-i]
```

ypwhich

Return name of NIS server or map master

```
ypwhich [-d [ypdomain]] [hostname]
ypwhich [-d ypdomain] -m [mname]
ypwhich -x
```

ypxfr

Transfer NIS map from an NIS server to host

```
/usr/sbin/ypxfr [-c] [-f] [-d ypdomain] [-h host]
  [-s ypdomain] [-C tid prog server] mapname
```

zcat

Uncompress and display compressed files

```
zcat file...
```

zdump

Time zone dumper

```
/usr/sbin/zdump [-v] [-c cutoffyear] zonename ...
```

zic

Time zone compiler

```
zic [-v] [-d directory] [-l localtime] [filename ...]
```

I ndex

Boldfaced page numbers indicate primary discussions of a topic. *Italicized* page numbers

Boldfaced page numbers indicate primary discussions of a topic. *Italicized* page numbers
indicate illustrations.

Boldfaced page numbers indicate primary discussions of a topic. *Italicized* page numbers indicate illustrations.

Boldfaced page numbers indicate primary discussions of a topic. *Italicized* page numbers indicate illustrations.

Boldfaced page numbers indicate primary discussions of a topic. *Italicized* page numbers
indicate illustrations.

Boldfaced page numbers indicate primary discussions of a topic. *Italicized* page numbers indicate illustrations.

Boldfaced page numbers indicate primary discussions of a topic. *Italicized* page numbers indicate illustrations.

Boldfaced page numbers indicate primary discussions of a topic. *Italicized* page numbers
indicate illustrations.

Boldfaced page numbers indicate primary discussions of a topic. *Italicized* page numbers
indicate illustrations.

Boldfaced page numbers indicate primary discussions of a topic. *Italicized* page numbers
indicate illustrations.

Boldfaced page numbers indicate primary discussions of a topic. *Italicized* page numbers
indicate illustrations.

Boldfaced page numbers indicate primary discussions of a topic. *Italicized* page numbers indicate illustrations.

Boldfaced page numbers indicate primary discussions of a topic. *Italicized* page numbers indicate illustrations.

Boldfaced page numbers indicate primary discussions of a topic. *Italicized* page numbers indicate illustrations.

Boldfaced page numbers indicate primary discussions of a topic. *Italicized* page numbers indicate illustrations.

F

Boldfaced page numbers indicate primary discussions of a topic. *Italicized* page numbers
indicate illustrations.

Boldfaced page numbers indicate primary discussions of a topic. *Italicized* page numbers indicate illustrations.

Boldfaced page numbers indicate primary discussions of a topic. *Italicized* page numbers indicate illustrations.

Boldfaced page numbers indicate primary discussions of a topic. *Italicized* page numbers indicate illustrations.

Boldfaced page numbers indicate primary discussions of a topic. *Italicized* page numbers
indicate illustrations.

Boldfaced page numbers indicate primary discussions of a topic. *Italicized* page numbers indicate illustrations.

Boldfaced page numbers indicate primary discussions of a topic. *Italicized* page numbers indicate illustrations.

Boldfaced page numbers indicate primary discussions of a topic. *Italicized* page numbers indicate illustrations.

Boldfaced page numbers indicate primary discussions of a topic. *Italicized* page numbers indicate illustrations.

L

Boldfaced page numbers indicate primary discussions of a topic. *Italicized* page numbers
indicate illustrations.

Boldfaced page numbers indicate primary discussions of a topic. *Italicized* page numbers indicate illustrations.

Boldfaced page numbers indicate primary discussions of a topic. *Italicized* page numbers indicate illustrations.

Boldfaced page numbers indicate primary discussions of a topic. *Italicized* page numbers indicate illustrations.

Boldfaced page numbers indicate primary discussions of a topic. *Italicized* page numbers
indicate illustrations.

Boldfaced page numbers indicate primary discussions of a topic. *Italicized* page numbers indicate illustrations.

Boldfaced page numbers indicate primary discussions of a topic. *Italicized* page numbers indicate illustrations.

Boldfaced page numbers indicate primary discussions of a topic. *Italicized* page numbers indicate illustrations.

Boldfaced page numbers indicate primary discussions of a topic. *Italicized* page numbers indicate illustrations.

Boldfaced page numbers indicate primary discussions of a topic. *Italicized* page numbers indicate illustrations.

Boldfaced page numbers indicate primary discussions of a topic. *Italicized* page numbers indicate illustrations.

Boldfaced page numbers indicate primary discussions of a topic. *Italicized* page numbers indicate illustrations.

Boldfaced page numbers indicate primary dis-
cussions of a topic. *Italicized* page numbers indicate illustrations.

Boldfaced page numbers indicate primary discussions of a topic. *Italicized* page numbers indicate illustrations.

Boldfaced page numbers indicate primary discussions of a topic. *Italicized* page numbers
indicate illustrations.

removing, applications, **535–536**
Rename (Edit menu), 46
rename command, 837
renaming files, in NetWare mode name
    space, 159
REN command (DOS), 380
renice command, 837
reportscheme command, 837
repquota command, 837
reserved users, **24–26**
    user ID for, 29
    viewing available, 25–26
Reset button, 526
reset command, 838
resmgr command, 838
resolution, 22
    changing, **69–71**, **559–561**
    changing for Windows, **283**
    increasing, 670
    for laptop, 668
resources, 358
    listing use of, **457–462**
respawn field, in inittab entry, 14
restore command, 838
Restore window, *343*, 343–344, **543–544**,
    543
restoring
    backup data, **342–344**, **543–544**, 543
    from command line, **345–346**
    deleted files, 98, **642–643**
Reverse Video, as Terminal window
    property, 370
Reverse Wraparound, as Terminal
    window property, 370
rexec command, 198, 839
rexecd command, 839
RFCs (Request for Comment), 237
.rhosts file, 347, 587
richtext command, 839
ripinfo command, 839
RIP packets, report on, 445
ripquery command, 839

rksh command, 839
rlogin command, 229, **252**, 254, 255,
    506, 840
rlogind command, 840
rmail command, 840
rm (remove) command, **381**, 643, 840
rmdel command, 840
rmdir (remove directory) command, 643,
    382–383, 840
roffbib command, 841
root, 5
root directory (/)
    access in DOS session, 296
    sharing, 267
root folder (/), 89
root password, 24
root permissions, and number sign
    prompt, 5
root slice (/), 664
    space on, and install problems, 119
root user, 11, **23–24**, 635
    to change init states, 17
    to install applications, 120
    mail for, 524
    opening Text Editor as, 469
    permissions for, 23
    user ID for, 29
route command, 841
route.d daemon, 250
router, activating, **250**
routing
    in TCP/IP, **245–251**
    troubleshooting, **496**
Routing Setup, in Internet Setup window,
    235
routing table, checking, 251
rpcbind command, 841
rpcgen command, 841
rpcinfo command, 842
rpc script, 520
rrouter command, 842
rsh command, 253, **254–255**, 842

Boldfaced page numbers indicate primary discussions of a topic. *Italicized* page numbers indicate illustrations.

S

Boldfaced page numbers indicate primary discussions of a topic. *Italicized* page numbers
indicate illustrations.

Boldfaced page numbers indicate primary discussions of a topic. *Italicized* page numbers indicate illustrations.

Boldfaced page numbers indicate primary discussions of a topic. *Italicized* page numbers indicate illustrations.

Boldfaced page numbers indicate primary discussions of a topic. *Italicized* page numbers indicate illustrations.

Boldfaced page numbers indicate primary discussions of a topic. *Italicized* page numbers
indicate illustrations.

T

Boldfaced page numbers indicate primary discussions of a topic. *Italicized* page numbers
indicate illustrations.

Boldfaced page numbers indicate primary discussions of a topic. *Italicized* page numbers
indicate illustrations.

Boldfaced page numbers indicate primary discussions of a topic. *Italicized* page numbers
indicate illustrations.

Boldfaced page numbers indicate primary discussions of a topic. *Italicized* page numbers
indicate illustrations.

Boldfaced page numbers indicate primary discussions of a topic. *Italicized* page numbers indicate illustrations.

Boldfaced page numbers indicate primary discussions of a topic. *Italicized* page numbers indicate illustrations.

Boldfaced page numbers indicate primary discussions of a topic. *Italicized* page numbers indicate illustrations.

Boldfaced page numbers indicate primary discussions of a topic. *Italicized* page numbers
indicate illustrations.

Boldfaced page numbers indicate primary discussions of a topic. *Italicized* page numbers indicate illustrations.

Boldfaced page numbers indicate primary discussions of a topic. *Italicized* page numbers indicate illustrations.

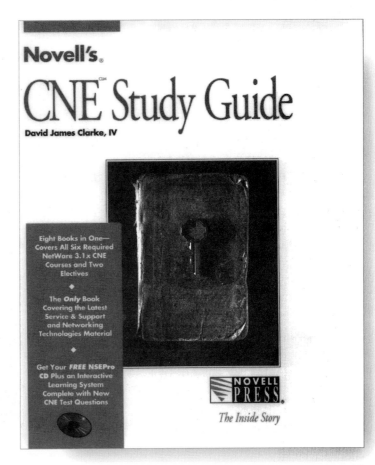

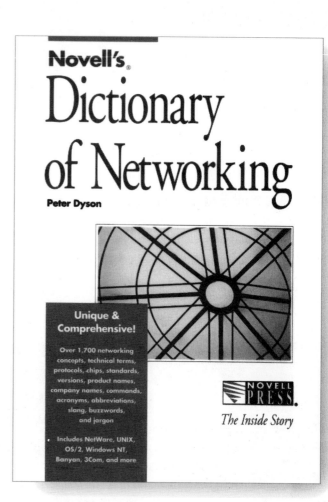

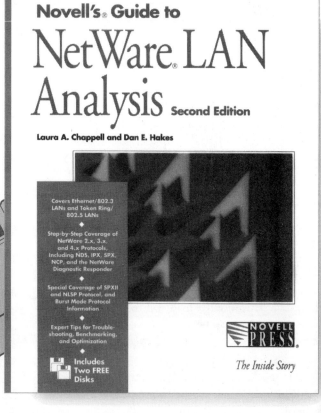

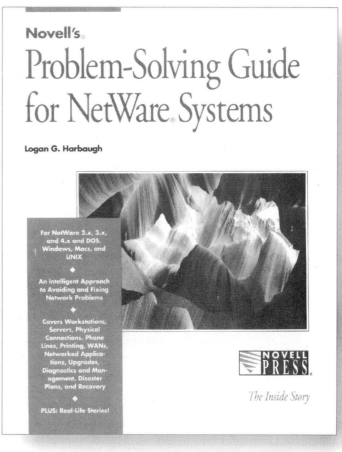

Novell Customer Resources Alliance

In its efforts to provide a wide range of accessible, high-quality resources for its customers, Novell Inc. has established a number of valuable partnerships over the years. The following pages contain essential information on the various Novell customer-resource partners—what they have to offer you and how you can reach them. Read on for useful information concerning:

- NetWire CompuServe
- Novell Application Notes
- Novell Authorized Education Centers
- Novell Buyer's Guide
- Novell Enterprise Solutions Programs
- Novell Press
- NPA (Network Professionals Association, formerly CNEPA)
- NUI (NetWare Users International)
- WordPerfect Magazine

CompuServe brings the world to your PC.

When you're online with CompuServe, you're a part of the world's premier personal computer network. It's where you'll find round-the-clock information and technical support to help you develop, sell, maintain, or simply use network services and products more effectively.

And you've got more than a wealth of technical databases working for you on CompuServe. In addition to Novell® experts, you can communicate with more than 750 other top manufacturers of computer hardware and software. Ask questions.

Receive tips. And benefit from their advice. The place to find this unparalleled support is CompuServe.

Take advantage of this FREE introductory membership to CompuServe now. As a bonus, you'll also receive a $15 usage credit toward extended and premium services. Call **1 800 524-3388** and ask for Representative 058. Outside the U.S. and Canada, call 614 529-1349.

The information service you won't outgrow.

Do you want to have the best shot at passing the CNE certification exams?

☐ Yes. (See below.)
☐ No. (See ya later.)

Novell Authorized Education Center

For the highest pass rate in the industry, look for this NAEC seal.

Congratulations! You're already well on your way. Now see how you do with some other important questions.

Would you guess that course material Novell engineers help develop just might be superior to ohh, say Cliff Notes?

Would you suppose that the Novell Authorized Education Centers (NAECs) might be the only place you could *get* these course materials? Not to mention training from Certified NetWare Instructors?

Would that explain why the Novell Authorized Education Centers have the highest pass rate in the industry?

If you've said "yes" to these questions, call the Novell Authorized Education Center near you.

yes NetWare Education

NOVELL. The Past, Present, and Future of Network Computing.

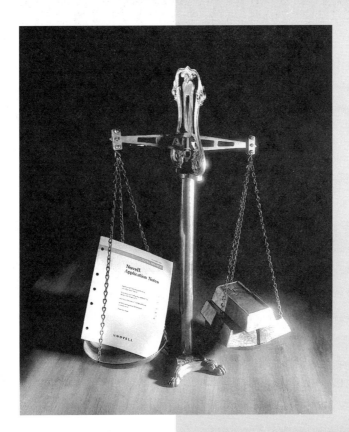

NOVELL

ENTERPRISE SOLUTIONS PROGRAMS

A Suite of Programs for Enterprise Solutions Providers

Whether you create or integrate network systems that are based on Novell's AppWare™, NetWare® or UnixWare™ platforms, you need more than superior products to deliver the complete solutions your users demand: you need top-notch support. *Novell's Enterprise Solutions Programs*, which encompass the *Novell Professional Developers' Program* and the *Novell Solution Providers Program,* provide the support, training and expertise you need to create powerful solutions by leveraging the strength of Novell's products and services.

Novell Professional Developers' Program

Designed for a broad spectrum of developers, including commercial, vertical and corporate developers, this program offers a wide array of services that facilitate the development and marketing of network applications for the AppWare, NetWare or UnixWare environments. Members of this program are automatically enrolled in Novell's popular YES Program. Plus, they get priority access to the Novell developer phone support, discount coupons for Novell 900 Series education classes and an annual subscription to the *Novell Developer Notes* technical publication.

Novell Solution Providers Program

This program targets system integrators, consultants and Value-Added Resellers who build distributed systems business opportunities with solutions based on Novell's products. Members of this program benefit from a variety of services, including marketing opportunities, participation in skill workshops and the Novell Compass program, and a subscription to Novell technical publications.

Join the program that best meets your needs by calling 1-800-NETWARE (1-800-638-9273) or 1-801-429-5588.

Profitable Networking Books Begin with Novell Press.

Novell's CNE™ Study Guide (1502-0); $89.99

Novell's Complete Encyclopedia of Networking (1290-0); $54.99

Novell's Guide to NetWare LAN Analysis (2nd Ed) (1362-1); $44.99

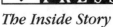

We're not here just to help **network professionals**

Stay Current

with

training labs,

a technical journal,

and technology give-aways,

Membership in the
**Network
Professional
Association**
is open to certified
networkcomputing
professionals, with
associate member-
ships availble to
those working toward
certification.
For more information
on the benefits of
membership and how
you can become
one of the many
helping to shape the
computer networking
profession —call
now:

801-429-7227

but also to help them

Define the Future

with

leadership opportunities,

conferences, and

networked communications.

Paper or plastic?

Hot off the presses, the new *Novell® Buyer's Guide* is your best resource for Novell networking solutions. Updated twice a year, it's chock full of everything you ever wanted to know about Novell's products, programs and services. Including the latest on NetWare® and UnixWare™networking software and the AppWare™ development platform.

What's more, it features a Corporate and Strategic Overview, with insights into Novell and the future of networking. And for technology heavyweights, there's a section covering Novell

Developer Tools that describes dozens of SDKs and provides ordering information.

So post one on the server or put one on the shelf. Any way you look at it, the *Novell Buyer's Guide* is made to order for you. To get your copy, call 800-346-6855 or 801-373-6779.

☰☰☰ NOVELL®

The Past, Present, and Future
of Network Computing.

NetWare Users International

1995 NetWare User Conferences

Sponsored by

::::NOVELL

1995 Schedule of Conferences

Houston	**Orlando**	**San Jose**
Jan. 17-18	April 19-20	Aug. 22-23
Toronto	**Vancouver**	**Minneapolis**
Jan. 31 - Feb. 2	May 16-17	Sept. 6-7
Baltimore	**Philadelphia**	**Atlanta**
March 1-2	May 31- June 1	Sept. 24-29
St. Louis	**Washington D.C.**	**Detroit**
March 21-22	July 5-6	October 10-11
Las Vegas	**Seattle**	**Phoenix**
March 27-31	July 20-21	Nov. 16-17
Boston	**Anaheim**	**Chicago**
April 4-5	Aug. 2-3	Nov. 28-29

Call 1-800-228-4684 *(menu option 2, then 1)*
to receive your free brochure describing the conference in your area.

NETWORK SOLUTIONS

Alright smarty-pants, answer 1 simple question, then 1 tough one.

(Answers found at the bottom of the page.)

1. What smart-looking, fun-to-read, inexpensive, delivered-to-your-door, productivity tools help you use WordPerfect easier, faster, and better?

A.

WordPerfect Magazine & WordPerfect for Windows Magazine

B.

WordPerfect Magazine & WordPerfect for Windows Magazine

2. How long was Paul Bunyan's blue ox "Babe"?

A. 42 ax handles   **B.** 43 ax handles

• practical application ideas • macros • tips and hints • questions and answers • desktop publishing • WordPerfect news

WordPerfect Magazines

call 1-800-228-9626

12 issues each, only $24 each per year*

Now available for your network printing.

Novell Authorized Education Center

Introducing Course 535: Printing with NetWare®.

Our newest course takes the work out of network printing. Developed in conjunction with Hewlett-Packard*, *Printing with NetWare* covers more than 100 network printing topics in three days, including print queues, print servers, printer customization and integration of different platforms.

When you're finished, you'll be able to troubleshoot common problems and configure your network for printing efficiency. That means you'll spend less time putting out fires, and more time putting out work. Your users will be happy. Your company will be happy. You'll be happy.

Call **1-800-233-EDUC** today for the location of your nearest Novell Authorized Education Center^{CLM}. We'll show you how to glide through your network printing.

yes Novell. Education

NOVELL® The Past, Present and Future of Network Computing.

GET A FREE CATALOG JUST FOR EXPRESSING YOUR OPINION.

Help us improve our books and get a *FREE* full-color catalog in the bargain. Please complete this form, pull out this page and send it in today. The address is on the reverse side.

Name _____   Company _____

Address _____   City _____ State ____ Zip _____

Phone (____) _____

1. How would you rate the overall quality of this book?

❑ Excellent
❑ Very Good
❑ Good
❑ Fair
❑ Below Average
❑ Poor

2. What were the things you liked most about the book? (Check all that apply)

❑ Pace
❑ Format
❑ Writing Style
❑ Examples
❑ Table of Contents
❑ Index
❑ Price
❑ Illustrations
❑ Type Style
❑ Cover
❑ Depth of Coverage
❑ Fast Track Notes

3. What were the things you liked *least* about the book? (Check all that apply)

❑ Pace
❑ Format
❑ Writing Style
❑ Examples
❑ Table of Contents
❑ Index
❑ Price
❑ Illustrations
❑ Type Style
❑ Cover
❑ Depth of Coverage
❑ Fast Track Notes

4. Where did you buy this book?

❑ Bookstore chain
❑ Small independent bookstore
❑ Computer store
❑ Wholesale club
❑ College bookstore
❑ Technical bookstore
❑ Other _____

5. How did you decide to buy this particular book?

❑ Recommended by friend
❑ Recommended by store personnel
❑ Author's reputation
❑ Sybex's reputation
❑ Read book review in _____
❑ Other _____

6. How did you pay for this book?

❑ Used own funds
❑ Reimbursed by company
❑ Received book as a gift

7. What is your level of experience with the subject covered in this book?

❑ Beginner
❑ Intermediate
❑ Advanced

8. How long have you been using a computer?

years _____
months _____

9. Where do you most often use your computer?

❑ Home
❑ Work

❑ Both
❑ Other _____

10. What kind of computer equipment do you have? (Check all that apply)

❑ PC Compatible Desktop Computer
❑ PC Compatible Laptop Computer
❑ Apple/Mac Computer
❑ Apple/Mac Laptop Computer
❑ CD ROM
❑ Fax Modem
❑ Data Modem
❑ Scanner
❑ Sound Card
❑ Other _____

11. What other kinds of software packages do you ordinarily use?

❑ Accounting
❑ Databases
❑ Networks
❑ Apple/Mac
❑ Desktop Publishing
❑ Spreadsheets
❑ CAD
❑ Games
❑ Word Processing
❑ Communications
❑ Money Management
❑ Other _____

12. What operating systems do you ordinarily use?

❑ DOS
❑ OS/2
❑ Windows
❑ Apple/Mac
❑ Windows NT
❑ Other _____

13. On what computer-related subject(s) would you like to see more books?

_____

_____

_____

14. Do you have any other comments about this book? (Please feel free to use a separate piece of paper if you need more room)

_____

_____

_____

- - - - - - - - - - PLEASE FOLD, SEAL, AND MAIL TO SYBEX - - - - - - - - - -

SYBEX INC.
Department M
2021 Challenger Drive
Alameda, CA
94501

A Sampling of UnixWare Desktop Windows

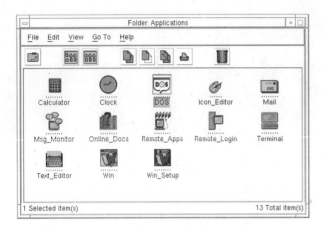

From the Folder: Applications window you can access:

- Calculator for math calculations

- Clock for viewing the time and setting alarms

- DOS for running DOS applications

- Icon_Editor for creating your own icons

- Mail for managing electronic mail

- Msg_Monitor for monitoring system messages

- Online_Docs for reading UnixWare documentation

- Remote_Apps for running applications located on remote systems

- Remote_Login for logging in to a remote system

- Terminal for opening a Terminal window for access to the UNIX shell

- Text_Editor for editing ASCII files

- Win for running Windows applications

- Win_Setup for installing Windows